W9-CUN-326

Lighthouses
of North America

Lighthouses of North America

Barry Pickthall

Associate contributors: Ed Boldero, Keith Taylor,

Victoria McElwee and Rich Roberts

CHARTWELL BOOKS, INC.

Published in 2005 by
Chartwell Books, Inc.
A division of Book Sales, Inc.
114 Northfield Avenue
Edison.
NJ 08837 USA

www.regencyhousepublishing.com

ISBN 0-7858-1821-9

Printed in China

Acknowledgements
This book could not have been produced without a great deal of effort from a team of writers and researchers, together with support from the U.S. Coast Guard, Canadian Coast Guard and the Lighthouse Digest. Particular thanks also goes to Ed Boldero, Stephanie Delamare, Clive Pickthall and Ann Winterbotham for their tireless efforts to gather all the information and material together.

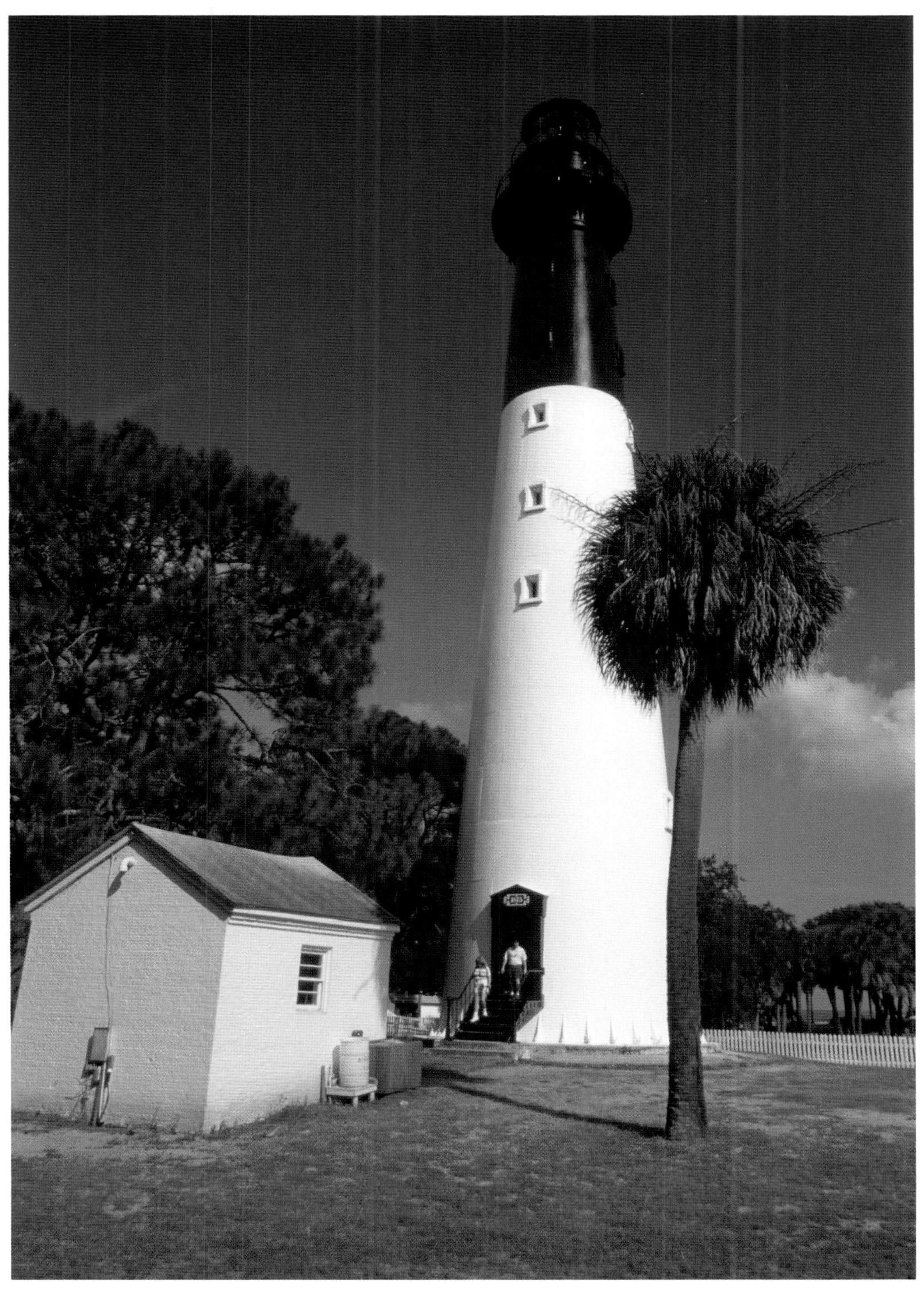

Chapter One
An Early History of Navigation Lights 8

Chapter Two
Lighthouse Keepers 15

Chapter Three
Lighthouse Construction 26

Chapter Four
Signalling Systems 34

Chapter Five
Lighthouses as Race Markers 37

Chapter Six
Lighthouses of the Great Lakes 50

Chapter Seven
Lighthouses of the North-East 108

Chapter Eight
Lighthouses of the South-East 248

Chapter Nine
Lighthouses of the West 304

Chapter Ten
Lighthouses of Canada 358

Index 443

Chapter One

The Early History of Navigation Lights

The use of lights as aids to navigation goes back as far as the 8th century BC, for references to beacons lit on hilltops to guide ships at sea occur in the *Iliad* and *Odyssey*, ascribed to the Greek poet Homer and the earliest works of European literature.

The first known man-made lighthouse, the Pharos of Alexandria in Egypt, was completed in 280 BC. Its architect, Sostratus of Cnidus, began the project during the reign of the Macedonian ruler Ptolemy I Soter (reigned 323–285 BC), and finished it under the watchful eye of Soter's son Ptolemy II (285–246 BC). It stood about 350ft (107m) high and was the highest man-made structure of ancient times after the pyramids of Giza. Taking its name from the island on which it was built in the harbour of Alexandria, it was regarded by the ancient Greeks as one of the Seven Wonders of the World. It was certainly a technological triumph.

The lighthouse was constructed in three stages: a square base of around 360ft (110m) supported a 100-ft (30.5-m) square tier that stood 236ft (72m) high and was topped by a 15-ft (5-m) octagonal storey. The latter supported an 85-ft (26-m) cylindrical tier with the fire at the top. It was not only an architectural wonder but an engineering one too, for metal was used to reinforce the huge blocks of stone. To keep the brazier burning at night, workers carried the wood up a spiral ramp within the building. The Pharos lasted longer than any of the other Seven Wonders, but when visited by the Arab traveller Ibn Battuta in the 14th century it was a ruin, some of the damage having been caused by a recent earthquake.

In 1994, the archaeologist Jean-Yves Empereur was commissioned by the Egyptian authorities to chart the area prior to the construction of a concrete breakwater over the site. He discovered hundreds of huge masonry blocks and statues from the Pharos, including a sculpture thought to depict Ptolemy II that dated back to the 3rd century BC. As a result, construction work was abandoned and the area has been turned into an underwater park, where scuba divers may explore the stone relics, statues and other remains of the lighthouse.

The Colossus of Rhodes, another of the Ancient Wonders of the World, is also believed to have been a lighthouse. A bronze statue of the sun god Helios, which stood 105ft (32m) above Mandrákion harbour on the Greek island of Rhodes, is thought to have had one hand shielding its eyes from the sun's rays through which a fire was visible to approaching ships. The statue, which was supported on an iron framework and ballasted with stone, was completed in 294 BC after it had taken 12 years to build. Destroyed in an earthquake around 226 BC, the broken bronze was left where it fell until AD 654, when the Arabs overran the island and carried the bronze – 900 camel-loads of it – away as scrap.

The Romans built as many as 30 light towers across their expanding empire. Probably the first was the tower at Ostia, the port of Rome, which was completed in AD 50. Others were erected as far afield as the Black Sea, Boulogne in France, and Dover in England. The remains of the Dover lighthouse can still be seen, but the oldest surviving tower is the Hercules Tower at La Coruña. Standing 185ft (56m) high, the Hercules Tower is believed to date from the reign of Trajan (AD 98–117). It may have stood on the site of an earlier Phoenician tower for, long before the Romans, the Phoenicians had developed trade routes throughout the Mediterranean and extending beyond it, perhaps as far as Britain. They marked many major headlands with towers lit with wood fires or torches, some of which, in particularly wet areas, were protected by roofs.

The Pharos of Alexandria, an illustration by Ann Winterbotham based on ancient records discovered by Hermann Thiersch in 1909.

MEDIEVAL LIGHTHOUSES

The fall of the Roman Empire in the 5th century was followed by a general decline in trade that lasted for several centuries, a period sometimes known as the Dark Ages, in which the attributes of Roman civilization, including the writing of history, disappeared. With the general collapse of social structures, naturally there were no lighthouses built, nor any demand for them, and it was not until about 1500 that references to them began to reappear in writings.

Other than torches, medieval lights generally burned coal. One of the most

St. George's Reef Light, California.

famous was the Lanterna of Genoa, which is thought to have been constructed outside the harbour of Genoa, the leading Mediterranean commercial power of the time, in 1139. The lighthouse keeper there in 1449 was Antonio Colombo, an uncle of Christopher Columbus. The Lanterna's 200-ft (61-m) tower was restored in 1544 and stands to this day, perhaps protected from lightning strikes, which have felled many a tower, by a statue of Columbus erected nearby. Other light towers were built near Livorno (Leghorn) in 1157 and 1304.

The Roman tower at Boulogne was restored in 800 by the Emperor Charlemagne and survived until 1644. But possibly the most famous medieval lighthouse was constructed in the 14th century by Edward the Black Prince (son of King Edward III of England), who ordered a light to be constructed on the isle of Cordouan in the Gironde estuary in Gascony. It must have been defunct by 1584, when Louis de Foix was commissioned to build a new light on the island, which in turn became one of the most significant buildings of its era. Standing 100ft (30m) high and 135ft (41m) in diameter, the tower was richly decorated with carved and gilded statuary and arched doorways and took 27 years to complete. The biggest problem De Foix had to overcome was subsidence. At the time his light was completed, in 1611, the island was covered by the sea at high tide, and the Cordouan light thus became the first lighthouse to be built on submerged foundations, the forerunner of present-day rock lighthouses such as St. George's Reef on the infamous Dragon's Rock, 14 miles (22.5km) off the Californian coast.

AMERICAN LIGHTS

As Spain, France and England gradually colonized America's eastern seaboard from the 16th century onwards, so European lighthouse technology was exported to the New World. The first to be built in the Americas was the Santo Antonio lighthouse guarding Salvador on All Saints Bay in Brazil in 1698. It was another 18 years before North America could boast a similar structure, built on Little Brewster Island in 1716 to mark the outer entrance of Boston harbour. Spurred on no doubt by the new trade this light helped to attract to the port, the French erected a 66-ft (20-m) tower to bring shipping to their own territory at Louisbourg on Cape Breton Island in 1734. It was lit by 16 whale-oil lamps but, after burning down three years later, it was replaced by the first concrete, fire-resistant tower.

A further light was built at Sambro, Halifax, and a wooden tower was erected at Brant Point in 1746 to mark the approach to Nantucket, Massachusetts. This proved too flimsy for the winter storms that regularly hit the north-east coast, and it was blown down several times, but was each time rebuilt by Nantucket's fishermen and whalers.

Beavertail Light, built on the eastern tip of Conanicut Island in 1749, brought Rhode Island's Narragansett Bay on to the trading route, and it was followed by Sandy Hook Light, to which New Yorkers contributed in 1764 in order to bring some of this shipping their way. The fact that they built it on land located within New Jersey did not concern them until the Garden State claimed it for its own during the War of Independence. A year later, another light was established at Cape Henlopen to mark the entrance to the Delaware River, and the Charleston Light came on line in 1767.

In 1768, the Plymouth Light marking the harbour founded by the Pilgrim Fathers was fitted with two lights to make it more easily recognizable, an idea followed at Cape Ann on another Massachusetts inlet, where two separate towers were built in 1771 to keep ships clear of Thatcher Island. Seven years later, the concept was further advanced by a range light at Newburyport, where one light was displayed on higher ground some distance behind the first. Mariners who saw the lights in alignment knew that they were sailing within the channel, but when the upper light appeared to veer to one side or the other, they knew that they were off course and in danger of running aground on the treacherous sand bars at the harbour mouth.

After the United States achieved independence, Congress took responsibility for navigation aids and lighthouse keepers were appointed by President George Washington in person. The first lighthouses built under the federal government were at Portland Head and Old Cape Henry, marking the southern side of the entrance to Chesapeake Bay, and construction thereafter continued at a rapid pace. The same year that the Chesapeake was marked, other towers sprang up at Tybee, Georgia; Seguin, Maine, completed in 1795; Bald Head Island, North Carolina, a year later, and Montauk Point, New York, in 1797. Bakers Island was lit in 1798 along with another light on Cape Cod, Massachusetts, while construction began at Cape Hatteras and Ocracoke in North Carolina. By the time of Washington's death two weeks short of the start of the 19th century, the building blocks he had laid, culminating in Gay Head, Massachusetts and Eatons Neck, New York, opened up the trading ports along the eastern seaboard that were to fuel the nation's rapid commercial expansion.

At that time the West had still to be settled, but the Russians had already explored the Bering Strait and Russian fur trappers and traders were active in Alaska, where they built the first light on top of Baronov Castle at Sitka (then New Archangel) in 1795.

It was not until after the U.S.-Mexican war had opened up California and the South-West that rapid U.S. westward expansion, augmented by the gold rush, began. In the 12 years up to 1855, U.S. shipyards launched 2,656 merchant ships, and it soon became obvious that many were destined for the rocks unless more guiding lights were constructed, not only along the East Coast, but also around the Great Lakes, the Gulf of Mexico and the Western seaboard.

Disasters occurred not only in remote

Beavertail Light, Newport, Rhode Island.

and distant areas of the Americas but within sight of the principal cities, such as New York and Boston. Danger spots included Minots Ledge, off Boston, where hundreds of mariners perished before the first light was built on this notorious hazard in 1850. The original structure lasted for less than a year and it was another decade before engineers managed to build a tower that would survive the rigours of wind and wave power for more than a few seasons. In New York harbour, Race Rock Reef was an infamous magnet for the unwary. Eight ships foundered there in as many years up to 1837 and the start of ferry services across Long Island Sound only increased the potential for disaster. It took two engineers, Francis Hopkinson Smith and Captain Thomas Albertson Scott, seven years simply to seat the foundations, but by 1879 the light was in service. Smith went on to lay the foundations for the Statue of Liberty, which also served as a lighthouse from 1886 to 1902.

On the other side of the continent, the entrance to the Columbia River was providing gold prospectors, who had survived the passage around Cape Horn, with an inhospitable welcome. At least 200 ships ended up on the unlit sandbars and rocks that extend many miles north and south of the estuary. When the state of Oregon was founded in 1848, the Congressional Act prompted the building of lighthouses at Cape Disappointment and New Dungeness, and they were followed by 16 more light towers between 1852 and 1858. These were designed by Ammi B. Young, a New England architect who modelled them on the Cape Cod house style. They were positioned at Alcatraz Island, Fort Bonita, Fort Point and the Farallon Islands around San Francisco, Cape Flattery, Crescent City, Humboldt Harbor, Smith Island, the entrance to the Umpqua River, and Willapa Bay, Washington.

During the Civil War, in which the Union controlled the navy, the Confederacy extinguished all the lights along the south-east and Gulf coasts. The naval war was secondary to the action on land, and the Union's battle fleet led by Commodore David G. Farragut was primarily employed to maintain a blockade to throttle the South's cotton trade with Europe. These operations highlighted the need for better charts and navigation aids around Southern coasts, and after the war the U.S. government moved quickly to increase the number of lights in that region. The tower at Bolivar Point, Galveston, built in 1873, saved 125 people who sought safety there from a hurricane in 1900 that razed much of the city, leaving up to 6,000 dead.

During the late 19th century, the U.S. government embarked on massive territorial acquisition by purchase, forceful adoption or by fostering convenient uprisings. Plantation owners led by Sanford P. Dole helped to organize a revolution in Hawaii in 1893 which led to U.S. dominance of the islands and, in 1898, annexation. Among its new responsibilities, the U.S. government acquired 35 lighthouses dotted around the archipelago. Two more were added at Makapuu Point on Oahu (1909) and Kauai (1913) to provide vital lights for U.S. shipping sailing to and from the Far East.

In 1867, the 586,412 square miles (1,518,807km^2) comprising the future state of Alaska were bought from Russia. The price paid was $7.2 million, around 12 cents an acre, and a considerable sum was allegedly expended in addition on bribes to persuade senators to ratify the treaty. No one then knew of the land's gold and oil deposits, and the modern economic development of Alaska dates from the stampede to the neighbouring Klondike gold fields in the 1890s. By that time the U.S. Lighthouse Board had restored the lighthouse first lit by the Russians at Baronov Castle, Sitka, a century before, but there was nothing else to guide the hundreds of ships carrying prospectors, and many were wrecked along this barren shoreline. The frequent disasters prompted the construction of nine more lighthouses between 1902 and 1905, including Scotch Cap and Cape Sarichev, which mark the passage through the Aleutian Islands.

After the one-sided Spanish-American War in 1898, the United States paid Spain $20 million for Puerto Rico, Guam and the Philippines, thus assuming responsibility for navigation in those regions. Puerto Rico already had 13 lighthouses, but the Americans built another on Mona Island to mark the passage between that island and

Makapuu Point, Hawaii.

the Dominican Republic. The British too were busy in this region, building or restoring similar lights in Bermuda, the Bahamas, Antigua and other islands of the Caribbean.

By 1910 the U.S. Lighthouse Board had been replaced by the Bureau of Lighthouses. It was responsible for a total of about 1,200 lighthouses and 54 lightships spread across U.S. waters. They were effectively under the control of one man, George Putnam, who, during the next 25 years, radically modernized the light system. Out went oil lamps, in came electricity, along with the latest reflector and lens systems. During Putnam's tenure, navigation aids of all kinds doubled to more than 25,000 towers, buoys, beacons and other indicators, while the number of people in the service which manned them actually fell by around 20 per cent.

By the time the lighthouse service was merged with the U.S. Coastguard in 1939 the writing was already on the wall for the traditional lighthouse keeper, and over the next three decades his role was gradually extinguished. At the end of the 20th century, the U.S. Coast Guard had an inventory of some 3,000 lighthouses, 6,000 minor lights and 4,000 lighted buoys, which it maintained at an annual cost of around $500 million.

Chapter Two

Lighthouse Keepers

During the early years of lighthouse construction around America's coastline, the appointment of lighthouse keepers was generally political, endorsed by the President. Whenever a new party came to power, it replaced the keepers with its own supporters. This system had obvious disadvantages, particularly in maintaining consistent service.

The role of the lighthouse keepers was a double one: as a first line of defence, to give warning of the arrival and movements of possibly hostile ships; secondly, as an aid to navigation, to advise commercial vessels of their position and the vicinity of hazards.

The job was never an honorary position, for lighthouse keeping was hard work. In the British model, which was also followed by some South American countries, three male lighthouse keepers were employed at each station, performing one eight-hour shift in each 24 hours. In the United States one person alone was responsible for keeping the light burning each night. It was for him to appoint assistants, whom he paid from his own stipend. To save money, married keepers invariably enrolled their whole family, with wives and children sharing the task of lighting up at dusk, trimming the wick every three or four hours and cleaning the lens to maintain the brightest possible light.

Cleaning the lens at the Langara Point Light, Prince Rupert, British Columbia.

The best keepers were usually old sailors accustomed to night watches who were more likely to turn out in bad weather to tend the lamp because they understood its importance in these conditions from their own experience. A landsman or political appointee, on the other hand, was more likely, in stormy conditions, to give way to the temptation to stay in bed, and in general it was not uncommon for lights to disappear in the early hours.

The Instructions to Light-Keepers clearly stated the keeper's duty to maintain a constant watch:

A light-house must never be left wholly unattended. Where there is a keeper and one or more assistants, either the keeper or one of the assistants must be present. If there is only one keeper, some competent member of his family, or other responsible person, must be at the station in his absence.

Keepers were often responsible for tending other minor lights in their area, and they were also allowed to take second jobs such as farming, fishing or acting as pilots for ships entering their harbour. When they were away, or fell ill, then it was their wives and children who took over the role of maintaining the lights. The job did not carry a pension, and whenever a keeper died families lost their livelihoods and were

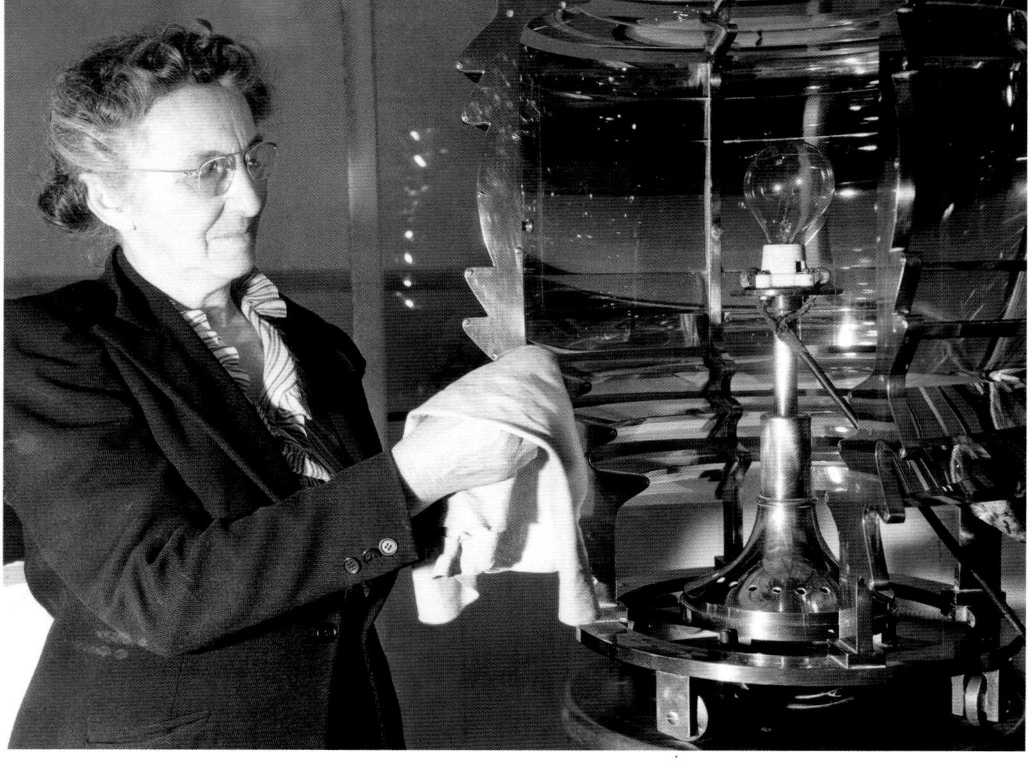

thrown out of their homes to make way for a fresh political appointee. It was only in the 1820s, after Stephen Pleasonton became Fifth Auditor of the Treasury Department, at that time the official responsible for administering the lighthouse system, that widows and offspring were permitted to inherit the role of lighthouse keeper. In a letter dated 7 June 1851 to Thomas Corwin, Secretary to the Treasury, Pleasonton voiced his frustrations at the incompetence and wasteful ways of inexperienced politically appointed keepers:

... I have had much inconvenience and difficulty to encounter from the frequent changes incidental to our form of government, in the light-house keepers, who for a time do not understand the management of their lamps, and consequently keep bad lights and waste much oil. So necessary is it that the lights should be in the hands of experienced keepers, that I have in order to effect that object as far as possible recommended, on the death of a keeper, that his widow, if steady and respectable, should be appointed to succeed him; and in this way some thirty widows have been appointed.

WOMEN KEEPERS

Hannah Thomas was the first recorded female lighthouse keeper in the United

INSTRUCTIONS TO THE KEEPERS OF LIGHT HOUSES WITHIN THE UNITED STATES

1. You are to light the lamps every evening at sun-setting, and keep them continually burning, bright and clear, till sun-rising.

2. You are to be careful that the lamps, reflectors, and lanterns, are constantly kept clean, and in order; and particularly to be careful that no lamps, wood, or candles, be left burning anywhere as to endanger fire.

3. In order to maintain the greatest degree of light during the night, the wicks are to be trimmed every four hours, taking care that they are exactly even on the top.

4. You are to keep an exact amount of the quantity of oil received from time to time; the number of gallons, quarts, gills, etc., consumed each night; and deliver a copy of the same to the Superintendent every three months, ending 31 March, 30 June, 30 September, and 31 December, in each year; with an account of the quantity on hand at any time.

5. You are not to sell, or permit to be sold, any spirituous liquors on the premises of the United States; but will treat with civility and attention, such strangers as may visit the Light House under your charge, and as may conduct themselves in an orderly manner.

6. You will receive no tube-glasses, wicks, or any other article which the contractors, Messrs Morgan & Co., at New Bedford, are bound to supply, which shall not be of suitable kind; and if the oil they supply, should, on trials, prove bad, you will immediately acquaint the Superintendent therewith, in order that he may exact from them a compliance with this contract.

7. Should the contractors omit to supply the quantity of oil, wicks, tube-glasses, or other articles necessary to keep the lights in continual operation, you will give the Superintendent timely notice thereof, that he may inform the contractors and direct them to forward the requisite supplies.

8. You will not be absent yourself from the Light House at any time, without first obtaining the consent of the Superintendent, unless the occasion be so sudden and urgent as not to admit of an application to that officer; in which case, by leaving a suitable substitute, you may be absent for twenty-four hours.

9. All your communications intended for this office, must be transmitted through the Superintendent, through whom the proper answer will be returned.

Fifth Auditor and Acting Commissioner of the Revenue
TREASURY DEPARTMENT
Fifth Auditor's Office
April 23rd 1835

States. She and her husband owned Gurnet Point, a narrow spit of land protecting the northern arm of Plymouth harbour, where a lighthouse with two lanterns was built in 1768. John Thomas, her husband, was paid five shillings a year rent for the land and £200 to act as the keeper. When he joined up to fight the British in 1776, his wife was left in charge of the lights. As war raged, she extinguished the lights whenever British frigates were in the area, which led to the lighthouse being attacked and a garrison stationed there to protect it. John Thomas failed to return from the war and, after Independence, Hannah employed a man to help her maintain the lights.

By the 1870s there were 49 official female keepers and several more unofficial. They were especially common in the hot, humid, coastal areas of the South where black women, who were deemed to be more suited to the conditions, were left to operate the lights while the official lighthouse keeper lived in more comfortable circumstances, often several miles away from the steamy coast.

OPPOSITE LEFT
Turkey Point Light, Maryland, with lighthouse keeper Fannie Salter.

OPPOSITE RIGHT
Fannie Salter, lighthouse keeper at Turkey Point from 1925–47.

BELOW LEFT
Ida Lewis, the keeper of the Lime Rock Light, Newport, Rhode Island, on the cover of Harper's Weekly *as the 'Heroine of Newport'.*

In other areas, the role of lighthouse keeper became a family tradition, passed on from one generation to the next, with families often intermarrying. At Turkey Point Light Station in Chesapeake Bay, for instance, where women manned the light for 86 years, three of the four lighthouse keepers became related through marriage. It was at Turkey Point that keeper Fannie Salter became something of a legend, manning the light for 42 years, from 1925 to 1947.

Keen to introduce more professional standards, Pleasonton laid down ground rules for being a lighthouse keeper. Typical

conditions of employment were issued to a keeper near New Bedford in 1835.
One of the most famous American female lighthouse keepers was Ida Lewis, who was born and bred in Newport, Rhode Island. Her father, Captain Hosea Lewis, was a coastal pilot who retired from the sea to become the first keeper of Lime Rock beacon, on a small island within Newport harbour, close to Fort Adams. Five years later he suffered a stroke, and Ida, then 15, took on the responsibility not only of tending to her disabled father and three younger brothers and sisters, but also the care of the light too. Each day she would row her siblings about 700 yds (600m) to and from school on the mainland. She acquired some reputation for handling a boat as well as for her strong swimming.

During her first year in charge, four youngsters would have drowned but for her seamanship. They were out sailing in the harbour when one of them shinned up the mast to rock the boat and frighten his friends. The boat capsized, and the four who could not swim clung to the upturned hull. Ida heard their cries and rowed out to the rescue. She was almost dragged overboard as the terror-stricken lads grabbed her instead of the boat, but she eventually pulled them in over the stern and got them safely ashore.

In 1866 three drunken soldiers, returning to Fort Adams, decided to take a

Ida Lewis Rock Light (formerly Lime Rock Light), Newport, Rhode Island.

RIGHT
Marcus Hanna, lighthouse keeper of the Cape Elizabeth Light, Maine.

short cut back to their barracks by 'borrowing' a small skiff on the beach. One of the men started to kick the planking and in his drunken state made a hole, so that the boat began to sink. His two friends swam for the shore, leaving the miscreant clinging to the swamped boat. Ida went out to rescue him, and after several vain attempts to get the drunk into her boat, tied a line around him and towed him back to the island, where she and her mother revived him.

The following January Ida was watching out of the window when a flock of panicky sheep fell over the edge of the wharf and plunged into the freezing waters of Newport harbour. Three shepherds took a boat and tried to round them up but finished up in the water themselves after a wave swamped the boat. Ida rushed to help the men but found them more concerned for the sheep than their own safety. However, she brought ashore not only the men but, within the next hour, the unhappy sheep as well.

Fort Adams was the all-too-frequent site of drunkenness and youthful excess on the part of the men, and they were lucky that Ida Lewis was on hand one cold February evening in 1881. Two soldiers, taking a short cut across the frozen harbour, fell through the ice. Ida heard their cries and went running across with a rope, undaunted, as the official report states, by '...the imminent danger of the soft brittle ice giving way beneath her, and also of being dragged into the hole by the men'. She hauled both out of the water, 'showing unquestionable nerve, presence of mind, and dashing courage'. For this she was awarded a silver medal by the Life Saving Benevolent Association of New York, together with a cheque for $100 – the equivalent of two months' pay.

During her 54 years on Lime Rock, Ida Lewis allegedly saved 18 lives, one of which incidents was immortalized in a painting commissioned by the U.S. Coast Guard (now in the National Archives), when she and her brother Rudolph went to the aid of a drowning man in 1869. The people of Newport organized a parade in her honour on Independence Day that year and presented her with a mahogany rowing boat dressed with red velvet cushions, gold braid and gold-plated rowlocks.

As her fame spread, thousands came to visit Lime Rock each year to catch a glimpse of this reluctant heroine, one of their number being President Ulysses S. Grant. One report suggests that when the president landed on the Lime Rock, he got his feet wet after stepping into the water and quotes him as saying, 'I have come to see Ida Lewis, and to see her I'd get wet up to my armpits if necessary.'

Her last known rescue took place in 1910 when Ida, now 63, launched her boat to go to the aid of a friend who had fallen in after unwisely standing up in a boat on the way to the lighthouse. Afterwards, Ida was asked where she found her strength and courage. 'I ain't particularly strong. The Lord Almighty gives it to me when I need it,

that's all,' she replied. Ida died a year later, still living in the lighthouse, shortly after being struck down by a paralyzing stroke. That night, bells on all vessels in Newport harbour were rung in her memory. In 1924, the Rhode Island state legislature changed the name of Lime Rock to Ida Lewis Rock and the lighthouse became the Ida Lewis Rock Light Station – the only time in U.S. history that a lighthouse has been named after its keeper.

In 1927 the lighthouse was automated and the last keeper left, but it continued in service until 1963 when the island was linked to the mainland and the house was converted into the Ida Lewis Yacht Club. The club's burgee carries 18 white stars, one for each person Ida Lewis rescued. Later, the New York Yacht Club, which now has its summer clubhouse on the mainland close by, obtained permission from the Coast Guard to reinstall a light and maintain it as a private aid to navigation. In 1995, the Coast Guard named the first of its 175-ft (53-m) Keeper Class coastal buoy tenders the *Ida Lewis*, in memory of that great heroine.

Another famous female lighthouse keeper was Julia Williams, who took over the Santa Barbara Light in California when her husband, Albert Johnson Williams, became disenchanted with the job in 1865. She continued to tend the light for the next 40 years, during which time, records confirm, she spent only two nights away from the station. She might have kept going even longer had she not fallen and broken her hip at the age of 81, for she died shortly afterwards.

LEFT
Scotch Cap Light, Alaska, before it was devastated by a tsunami.

OPPOSITE
Scotch Cap, c.1946, after its destruction.

HELPING HANDS

Lighthouse keepers were often forced to stand by as helpless witnesses while terrible tragedies unfolded within range of their lights, but many played significant roles in rescues. In 1933 the USS *George M. Cox* ran aground in a dense fog on the Rock of Ages in Lake Superior. The lighthouse keeper was able to lead the 125 passengers and crew to the safety of his tower, where they spent the night crowded on the spiral steps until rescue vessels could reach them the following morning.

During the 1860s, the captain and crew of a schooner lost their lives when wrecked during a terrible storm one night close to Hendricks Head Light off Boothbay harbour, Maine. Early the following morning, when the lighthouse keeper went to search through the wreckage thrown up on the rocks, he had little hope of finding any survivors, until he heard cries from an ice-encrusted mattress. There, tucked inside the padding, was a baby girl, together with a note from her father, the ship's captain, entrusting the child 'into God's hands'. The keeper and his wife later adopted her and brought her up as their own.

In 1839 another schooner, the SS *Deposit*, ran aground on rocks at Ipswich,

U.S. COAST GUARD
MEMORIAL
NEAR THIS SITE SCOTCH CAP LIGHT STATION WAS DESTROYED BY A SEISMIC SEA WAVE ON 1 APRIL 1946
THIS TABLET IS IN MEMORY OF:
ANTHONY LAURENCE PETIT
JACK COLVIN
PAUL JAMES NESS
DELEY DYKSTRA
LEONARD PICKERING
WHO LOST THEIR LIVES IN THIS DISASTER WHILE SERVING THEIR COUNTRY.

Massachusetts. T.S. Greenwood, the first keeper at Ipswich Range Lights, threw caution to the wind by rowing out through raging surf to save several members of the crew from drowning.

Some lighthouses are just too exposed for keepers to do anything more than monitor a situation. This was the case at Graves Ledge off Boston harbour during a January blizzard in 1941, when the *Mary O'Hara* ran onto the ledge. The keeper of the granite-built Graves Light, which had withstood the test of fierce winter storms since 1905, could only look on in horror as every member of the crew of 19 either drowned in the attempt to reach the rocks or froze to death after reaching them.

It is on harsh nights like this that sailors most appreciate the beacons that shine through storm and darkness, for there is tremendous reassurance in recognizing a light signal and thus being able to confirm the ship's exact position. There have been a few occasions, however, when the dangerous conditions extinguished the light, as they did to Whitefish Point Light off northern Michigan on 10 November 1975. The absence of the light that night disorientated the crew of the iron-ore freighter *Edmund Fitzgerald*, and she disappeared just a few miles north of the point with the loss of 29 lives.

At times, it was the keepers who were at greatest risk. Lighthouses are sited in some of the remotest parts of the coast, which makes them difficult to reach in bad weather. In 1716, two years after Boston Light, the first lighthouse to be commissioned in North America, became operational, the dangers were underlined when George Worthylake, the first lighthouse keeper, his wife, daughter and a friend, all drowned after a large wave swamped the rowboat carrying them out to the rock. The same fate befell Frederick Jordan, the keeper of Penfield Reef Light in Long Island Sound, near Fairfield, Connecticut. He was drowned on Christmas Day 1916 after his boat capsized while he was rowing ashore to have Christmas dinner with his family.

Apart from the ever-present threat of the sea itself, the inaccessibility of many lighthouses meant that food supply was often a cause for concern. Keepers generally kept a three-month supply of dried meat and ship's biscuit for times when the supply ship or wagon was unable to get through to them. During one lengthy storm off the New England coast, the hungry keeper at Boon Island grew so desperate that he tossed four bottled messages into the sea. A passing ship picked one up, but conditions were too bad to approach the island, so the crew, after calculating wind and tide, craftily employed the waves to float a barrel of food to the lighthouse.

On another occasion, Sam Burgess, the keeper of the Matinicus Rock Light off Maine, who had left his station to get food for his family and feed for the chickens, found himself stormbound, and unable to return for a month. During that time, Abby, his 14-year old daughter, kept the light burning and also took care of her ailing mother and three younger sisters. She even

OPPOSITE
Memorial plaque for those who died at the Scotch Cap Light.

RIGHT
Minots Ledge Light, Massachusetts.

managed to wade through the raging waters to save the hens. Somehow, she took care of everything until the storm finally abated, although suffering from acute hunger and exhaustion after the food reserves ran out during the fourth week.

A common graveyard for ships attempting to cross to the New World was Sable Island, about 80 miles (130km) east of Nova Scotia, where at least 100 vessels have foundered. A light was finally established there in 1856, but the notorious fog that regularly cloaks the Grand Banks often obliterated its beam. The groundings continued, the worst of them in 1864 when the passenger liner *Anglo-Saxon* ran up against the cliffs immediately below the tower. Casualties among passengers and crew numbered 290, but 130 others, who managed to reach the rocks, were led to safety by the lighthouse keepers.

In 1885, Marcus Hanna was the keeper at Cape Elizabeth Light, south of Portland, Maine, when the *Australia*, bound for Boston, ran aground on the stormy, snowy night of 28 January. Captain J.W. Lewis and a crew of two, Irving Pierce and William Keller, had set sail the previous day from Boothbay harbour. The full force of the storm hit them about 11 pm when the ship was off Halfway Rock Light, and they decided, first to run towards Portland, and then to stand off the mainland until morning light. The ship was heavily iced, and the crew set about jettisoning the deck cargo in an effort to keep her afloat.

At 8 am the following morning, they sighted Cape Elizabeth Light and hoisted the mainsail peak in an attempt to weather the headland, but the conditions drove the ship onto a ledge near the fog-signal station. Keeper Hanna had just gone to bed after working the fog signal all night, and it was his wife who, while putting out the lighthouse lamp at 9 am, first noticed the ship's masts about 440 yards (400m) offshore. By the time she reached the signal station and sounded the alarm, Captain Lewis had already been lost overboard, but the two crew members were seen clinging to the ship's rigging, half frozen by spray and fear. Hanna and his assistant, a man named Staples, rushed down with a good heaving line and hawser and, knee-deep in foam, tried to land the iron throwing weight on the ship, which by now was listing at 45°. Hanna made more than 20 attempts without success before he was forced to retire to the fog-signal station to warm his frozen limbs. He sent his assistant to get help but, as Staples left, a towering wave struck the vessel, lifting it bodily from the ledge and smashing it against the rocks immediately beneath the signal station. Hanna rushed down to the rocks and threw the line once more. This time it landed on the stricken vessel, but the two men, who had tied themselves to the rigging, remained frozen there, and the rope slid back into the sea.

The second attempt was more successful. This time Pierce managed to free himself and get hold of the rope, which he tied with some difficulty around his body. Shouting above the screaming winds, Hanna signalled him to jump into the sea and hauled him in over the rocks single-handedly. Blinded by salt and exposure, and with his jaws frozen rigid, Pierce was a shaking wreck, but there was no time to give first aid. The rope was hurled once more across to the fast-disintegrating ship where Keller was able to get a hand on it. As he too jumped into the ocean, Staples returned with two neighbours, and the four of them soon had the hapless sailor out of the surf.

The two men were carried up to the fog-signal station where their frozen clothing was cut away and cold water was rubbed on their limbs while stimulants were forced between their chattering teeth. The weather was too bad to carry them the few hundred yards back to the lighthouse until the following morning, and Hanna and his wife nursed them until the roads could be opened and they were transported to the marine hospital in Portland.

TSUNAMI

The greatest disaster to befall an American lighthouse occurred on April Fool's Day in 1946. At 1:30 am a section of the ocean floor 90 miles (145km) south-east of the Aleutian island of Unimak in the North Pacific suddenly shifted, triggering a massive undersea earthquake that measured 7.3 on the Richter Scale and set seismograph pens quivering right around the world. Members of the U.S. Coast Guard manning the Scotch Cap Light on Unimak island, where the Pacific meets the icy waters of the Bering Sea, were first to feel its effect. Earthquakes are common in this part of the world, so the men on duty in the radio shack on the cliffs 30ft (9m) above the lighthouse, were not unduly surprised. One checked by radiophone with the keeper on duty who reported no great damage.

Twenty-seven minutes later, the seabed heaved again with an even stronger tremor. The Signal Station log entry states: '01:57: Second severe quake felt. Shorter in duration but harder than at 01:30....Again, no apparent damage, although building shook severely'.

It was enough to rock the confidence of the five men on Scotch Cap, but even then they could not have foreseen the devastating force of nature that would envelop them 21 minutes later. The earthquakes raised the ocean floor, and the sudden rush of water that filled the chasm generated a huge counter-surging wave known as a tsunami. The island of Unimak and the men at Scotch Cap were its first victims.

The wave, estimated to be 115ft (35m) high and travelling at 72mph (116km/h), came rushing out of the pitch darkness with a huge roar to explode against the lighthouse and cliff face.

The signalman's log read as follows: *02:18: Heard terrific roaring of the sea followed by huge sea immediately. Top of wave rose above the cliff back of Scotch Cap light station and struck D/F station, causing considerable damage. Crew ordered to high ground. Can't make radio contact, so broadcast following message:*
....TIDAL WAVE X MAY HAVE TO ABANDON THIS PLACE X BELIEVE LIGHTHOUSE LOST...

Repeated calls to the lighthouse failed to raise an answer, and with the beacon no longer shining, the survivors from the flooded radio shack feared the worst. But it was not until first light the following day, when the waves had subsided, that anyone dared to go down to gather emergency stores and to look for their five missing lighthouse colleagues.

What they found was utter devastation. Nothing recognizable was left from the lighthouse building and nothing of the men, save a small piece of human intestine found on the hillside. A few days later, parts of two bodies were located, but the sea had swallowed up everything else.

At Unimak Island, where the tsunami first struck, a new Scotch Cap lighthouse was built in 1950, in concrete and higher up the cliff. Being so isolated, the post was never considered suitable for family occupation, and the Coast Guard keepers posted there earned a year's leave for every four that they served in that bleak outpost. The lighthouse was automated in 1971.

In 1927 and 1928 Alaskan earthquakes also caused severe damage to Cape Hinchinbrook Light, standing on cliffs overlooking Prince William Sound, and although there was no loss of life, the station had to be completely rebuilt from the foundations up.

The Santa Barbara Light, where Julia

Williams had served as keeper for 40 years, was destroyed in a similar manner in 1925. It was replaced the following year with a simpler 'quake-proof' building designed to withstand further shifts in the San Andreas Fault line that runs north-south through California.

FORCES OF NATURE

Hurricane-force winds and the gigantic seas that they whip up have all too often led to the loss of keepers as well as serious damage and destruction to their lighthouses. In 1906, the lighthouse keeper at Horn Island, south of Pascagoula, Mississippi, together with his wife and daughter, were killed when violent winds demolished the lighthouse and much of whatever else was on the island. The same hurricane also cost the lives of the keeper and the wives of two assistants stationed on Sand Island Light, which marked the west side of the entrance to Mobile Bay, Alabama.

Another area prone to hurricanes, which sweep in from the Caribbean, is the Florida Keys; in 1845 the island of Sand Key and the original brick-built light tower were swept away, along with the keeper and several members of his family who were visiting him at the time. After that experience, future towers constructed on these reefs were made of iron.

The power of seas constantly breaking around a lighthouse is of a magnitude that few people can comprehend. Even buildings designed to withstand hurricane-force winds and seas require considerable maintenance if they are to remain intact. The seas will exploit the smallest crack in stone or mortar, and rip the building's fabric to shreds within a very short time. That is what happened at Whale Rock lighthouse guarding the entrance to Rhode Island's Narragansett Bay in September 1938, when a hurricane ravaged much of the New England coastline. Built in 1871, it was a typical open-water caisson lighthouse with a central cast-iron cylinder, yet when the winds came they tore into the foundations and, overnight, completely destroyed the building, killing the assistant keeper who was on duty. In the same Narragansett waters, the wooden, six-room accommodation block built next to the octagonal granite tower of Prudence Island Light, which had withstood the wind and sea for 80 years, was washed away in the 1938 hurricane, and although the keeper survived, his wife and family died.

Lurking just beneath the waves off Cohasset, Massachusetts, is a formidable menace to navigation known as Minots Ledge, mentioned above. This vicious obstacle had wrecked dozens of ships and snuffed out many lives, but no attempt was made to erect a lighthouse on the submerged ledge until the middle of the 19th century because the project was considered all but impossible. However, during the late 1840s a tall iron-skeleton tower was constructed on lengthy iron pilings and by early 1850 the station was ready for service. Although designed to withstand the fiercest Atlantic storm, the tower toppled in a mighty gale less than a year after it was completed, taking the lives of two assistant keepers in the process.

In the days before electricity, with oil being carried up the tower daily to fuel the lantern, fire was always a risk. Yet there are not many records of loss of life through fire, as keepers, well aware of the dangers, were both extremely cautious and no doubt usually able to get away from the building in the event of fire. One tragedy did occur in 1878 when the Sand Point lighthouse at Baraga, Michigan, caught fire, killing Mary Terry, its keeper. (The square brick tower and house has since been restored and now houses a museum.)

Collisions were an occupational hazard for men serving on lightships. Lightships were built to withstand a great deal of abuse, so the many glancing blows they received from passing shipping usually did little more than scrape their red paint.

One lightship that suffered two such incidents during its short life was No. 117 *Nantucket*, commissioned in 1931 to warn shipping of fog-shrouded shoals off the New England coast. In her first year her crew had to raise anchor to go to the rescue of the eight-man crew of a fishing vessel that got into difficulties and sank five miles from the light.

The *Nantucket*'s crew had ample reason to be thankful that its lightship had its own propulsion system (many lightships did not) when, during a fierce storm in June 1933, her anchors dragged and she drifted 32 miles (51km) off station before the crew was able to regain control.

A year later the lightship survived a glancing blow from the SS *Washington*, but four months after that the British White Star liner *Olympic* rammed her amidships in dense fog and she sank within minutes. Four of the *Nantucket*'s crew went down with the ship, and of the seven survivors picked up by the *Olympic*'s lifeboats, three later died of their injuries.

One can see why lighthouse keepers were less troubled by ships ramming their premises, though an exception was the keeper of the Newport harbour lighthouse on Goat Island in 1921, when a submarine ran up on the rocks and destroyed his house.

Another incident during the 1980s that might have had a similar outcome was circumvented by advances in technology since 1921. The officer of the watch on a U.S. aircraft carrier, peering from the bridge into the pitch-black night, suddenly noticed a light on a collision course with his ship. Grabbing the radio mike, he barked out an order to those in charge of the offending light to 'change your course ten degrees east'. The signal back was equally emphatic. 'Change your course, sir, ten degrees east.'

Angrily, the watch officer barked back 'I am an American naval officer. Change your course, sir!'

'I'm a Canadian seaman 2nd Class', came the reply. 'Change *your* course, sir.'

Furious, the navigating officer shouted back across the air waves: 'This is an American aircraft carrier, one of the largest, most potent vessels in the world. I strongly suggest that you change your course. Now!'

The Canadian seaman replied: 'And I'm a lighthouse sitting atop one of the biggest cliffs in this region. I strongly suggest that you change *your* course, sir!'

Chapter Three
Lighthouse Construction

Lighthouses give the impression of being able to withstand all weathers. They are certainly designed that way, and some have stood the test of time for several centuries, despite their often-precarious positions. But not all have managed to withstand nature's cruellest blows.

One who believed he had designed an indestructible lighthouse was Henry Winstanley, who died being proved wrong in one of the greatest storms ever to hit the British Isles. The lessons learned from that tragic night caused lighthouse architects to rethink the construction process and had a direct bearing on the building of lighthouses across the New World later on.

THE EDDYSTONE LIGHTHOUSE

It was November 1703 and Atlantic gales had been ravaging England and Wales for two weeks, bottling up shipping in harbours and estuaries throughout the south-west. On Thursday 25 November, there was a welcome calm. Many captains took the opportunity to weigh anchor, including Winstanley, who gathered a work party to sail the 14 miles (22km) to the Eddystone Rocks, situated in the Western Approaches south-west of Plymouth, to carry out routine maintenance on the lighthouse that he had completed four years earlier.

The favourable conditions continued on Friday, and no one could have foreseen that one of the most awesome storms ever recorded in Britain was to follow that night.

The winds struck without the warning of rain, thunder or lightning shortly before midnight and swept across the southern counties of England. Ships dragged their anchors and smashed against rocks and harbour walls or into one another. Ships caught out at sea attempted to run before the storm up the English Channel and out into the North Sea, while many were dismasted and blown as far as Scandinavia. In London, there was wholesale carnage both on land and on the River Thames, where the chains strung across the river to provide moorings for ships waiting to dock all snapped under the huge strain, leaving the vessels helpless. Casualties were unparalleled. All told, some 8,000 sailors died, 1,500 of them serving in the Royal Navy, which also lost 15 warships.

Henry Winstanley had undoubtedly been rubbing his hands together with the onset of the first winds. He had often stated that he wanted nothing more than to be inside his 'indestructible' lighthouse 'during the greatest storm that ever was'. He got his wish. The wooden Eddystone Lighthouse was right in the path of what meteorologists now suggest must have been a hurricane originating in the Caribbean that, instead of dying out in the Atlantic, gained fresh strength as it crossed the ocean. Unrestricted by land for nearly 3,000 miles (5000km), it had generated a huge tidal wave. Part of it swept up the Severn estuary that divides south-west England from Wales, to flood the city of Bristol and hundreds of miles of countryside. This, or a similar wave, it is thought, hit Winstanley's polygonal tower, an ornamental stone and timber structure,

LEFT
Henry Winstanley's Eddystone Lighthouse, Plymouth, England. Built in 1699, it was destroyed in a storm in 1703.

OPPOSITE LEFT
Smeaton's Tower, Plymouth.

OPPOSITE RIGHT
The Eddystone Lighthouse today. The stump of Smeaton's Tower can still be seen.

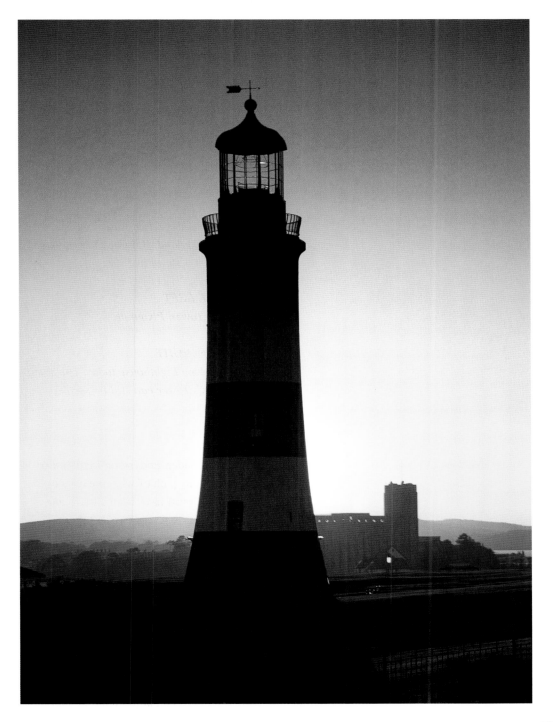

which disappeared from the Eddystone Rock without trace, taking its designer, the lighthouse crew and Winstanley's work party with it.

A second tower, largely of oak with the lower part filled with stone, was completed by John Rudyerd in 1709. It survived for 46 years until destroyed by fire in 1755.

It was followed by John Smeaton's famous, revolutionary stone lighthouse of 1759. An engineer, Smeaton had the idea of pre-cutting the masonry blocks at the quarry so that they would dovetail together with the utmost precision. This interlocking pattern gave the tower great integral strength, but his design also relied on its own mass to withstand the power of the sea, being wider at the base than at the top. His final touch of brilliance was to lay the stonework in a curved vertical taper, to encourage the waves to sweep up the wall and dissipate their energy over a wide area.

Smeaton's innovative design survives to this day, though in a different location. In 1882, 123 years after it was built, movement in the rock itself led to the tower being dismantled and a new, taller lighthouse built adjacent to it. The top section of Smeaton's original tower was then rebuilt as a memorial to him on Plymouth Hoe. The stump remains clearly visible on the Eddystone Rock. Smeaton's design was followed in other sea-swept towers, such as those at The Smalls in Wales, Bell Rock in Scotland, South Rock in Ireland and Minots Ledge off Boston, Massachusetts.

FAR LEFT
Abbot's Harbour Light, West Pubnico, Nova Scotia.

LEFT
The Lorain Light, Ohio, a screwpile tower.

OPPOSITE LEFT
Libby Island Light, Maine, a masonry tower.

OPPOSITE RIGHT
Point Loma Light (New), California, a skeletal tower.

WOODEN TOWERS

Lighthouses continued to be built largely of wood into the early 20th century, despite their vulnerability to fire and hurricane damage. In many cases, wood was the best local resource and early pioneers persevered with the material despite its drawbacks. Disasters, of course, may have been due to imperfect methods of construction as well as to the fabric of the structure.

The Brant Point Light on Nantucket Island is one example of the apparent failure of wood. The original building stood for 12 years but burned down in 1758. Its wooden replacement fared no better, being demolished by a hurricane in 1774. The third tower succumbed to fire nine years later and the fourth fell during a storm in 1788. Perhaps it was the difficulty of employing a keeper for this unlucky site that led eventually to the construction of a brick tower in 1856. This is still standing, but it was replaced in 1901 by another wooden tower, which was built because the channel had shifted. This too remains intact and operational, thanks in part to the advent of electricity, which largely negated the hazard of fire.

Among other survivors built during the mid to late 19th century are three on Prince Edward Island, while others have been moved to new sites as tourist attractions or museums. They include the lighthouse that once stood at Point Farming, guarding San Pedro harbour in California, which now graces a park in Los Angeles, and a timber dwelling-style beacon built in 1874 to mark Hereford Inlet, New Jersey, which is now a museum in North Wildwood.

MASONRY TOWERS

Stone and brick-built lighthouses proved more enduring, and many early examples remain across the Americas. Early stone lighthouses, like the 34-ft (10-m) tower at Castle Hill, Newport, Rhode Island, were built of locally quarried rough stone, otherwise known as 'rubblestone'. This was followed by dressed stone, often pre-cut to interlock with adjacent blocks cut from granite, and much later by brick towers. Where possible, the stone foundations were laid directly on underlying bedrock, but where the ground was less firm, wood or iron piles were driven down to support a 'crib' (cribbage) – a supportive framework of strong beams – on which the stone foundations were laid.

The British went to great lengths – literally – to obtain granite, shipping it 16,000 miles (25750km) around Cape Horn in the mid-19th century for lighthouses built on Canada's west coast, such as that on Fisgard Island. More often, builders had to rely on what was available locally. Some lighthouses were built of sandstone; others, including St. David's lighthouse, Bermuda, and Point Amour, above Forteau Bay in Canada, of limestone.

Bricks were used to line stone towers to improve insulation and provide greater stability in the event of earthquakes, and bricks became the favoured material during the late 19th century when the U.S.

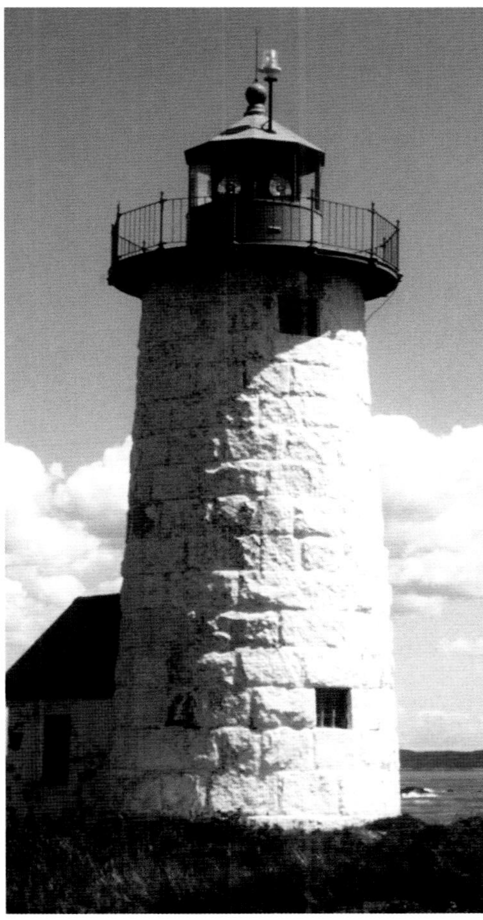

Lighthouse Board began upgrading existing lights and building new towers.

The most significant of these new towers was the Cape Hatteras lighthouse in North Carolina. The 193-ft (59-m) black-and-white 'barber-pole' tower is the tallest in the United States. It replaced an earlier 95-ft (29-m) tower of 1803, which a naval inspector slammed 'as the worst light in the world'. The original tower did little to lessen the danger of shipwreck because it was not tall enough to be seen by vessels approaching the treacherous Diamond Shoals that lie to the south-west.

The promontory of Cape Hatteras is notorious for fickle weather and dangerous shoals. The warm Gulf Stream flowing up from the Caribbean meets the cold Labrador Current coming down from the Arctic, and they meet with such force that their power can not only alter the coastline but also influence the weather locally. Over the centuries, some 2,300 ships have come to grief in the shoals.

The existing brick tower was designed and built by Dexter Stetson in 1870 on a granite base supported by iron pilings and a crib of cross timbers. It survived gales and hurricanes for 130 years until the seas eroded the surrounding beaches to such an extent that the tower had to be moved bodily about 1,800ft (550m) inland in 1999, in a slow, heart-stopping $12-million operation.

CAST-IRON TOWERS

Cylindrical or conical iron towers were a product of Britain's Industrial Revolution during the early 19th century, when British engineering firms exported cast-iron lighthouses in prefabricated form to the four corners of the globe.

Cast-iron towers have several significant advantages over their masonry counterparts. Not only are they relatively cheap to manufacture and quick to erect but, as the past century has witnessed, they are also extremely hardwearing. The twin drawbacks of being lighter than masonry towers (and thus less stable in hurricane-force winds), and cold to the touch, were overcome by lining the inside with bricks. Bolivar Point lighthouse at Galveston proved the effectiveness of this form of construction: successive hurricanes have devastated the area but left the tower intact, protecting many people who sought refuge within when hurricanes approached.

The curved or conical plates were cast, complete with flanges, then numbered, ready to be bolted together once they had been shipped to the construction site. They were then erected on foundations similar to those of a masonry tower.

SKELETAL TOWERS

These steel structures were a direct development from cast-iron towers, and

were built from the late 19th century to provide a lightweight solution for sites offering relatively weak natural foundations, such as sand, swamp or coral. The prefabricated towers generally consisted of an openwork cylinder about 10ft (3m) in diameter, with a spiral stairway inside, and were manufactured in a variety of heights up to 190ft (58m). The tower consisted of a latticework of open steel tubing, similar to oil derricks, which presented far less resistance to wind and waves than a solid surface. Initially, skeletal towers were used to replace older masonry lighthouses that were threatened by erosion, such as the 191-ft Cape Charles Light at Smith Island in Virginia. This was erected in 1895 to replace a brick-built tower which was threatening to collapse after 30 years of service.

SCREWPILE TOWERS

The first screwpile lighthouse was the brainchild of a brilliant, blind Irish marine engineer, Alexander Mitchell. The feasibility of his idea to build a permanent structure on shifting sands by drilling piles deep into the seabed was confirmed by the construction of a test platform on Maplin Sands in the Thames estuary in 1838. He moved on to build the first screwpile lighthouse at Fleetwood in Lancashire. Here, he utilized iron augurs attached to the bottom of the piles, which were then drilled into the ground by a large windlass at the top. This was rotated by a team of men standing on a floating barge with a hole in the centre, through which the pile was screwed downwards. It took a day to drill each pile 15ft (4.5m) down, the shape of the augur holding it firm in the soft substrate. A prefabricated, octagonal skeletal tower was finally constructed on top of the piles and the lighthouse was completed in June 1840. It subsequently survived gales and even collisions with ships attempting to reach the port. One vessel, the *Elizabeth Jane*, when her anchor dragged, drifted into the piles with such force that the keeper's house was lifted off the platform and onto the ship's foredeck!

The success of Mitchell's design, which he patented, encouraged other builders to adopt his idea to solve similar problems elsewhere in the world. The first screwpile lighthouse built in the United States was at Brandywine shoal in Delaware Bay, where the previous light tower, set on straight piles driven into the seabed, had been wrecked by moving ice during its first winter of operation. To protect the new structure from the same fate, it was surrounded by a second, and later a third row of screwpiles to break up the ice.

In fact, vulnerability to ice was the Achilles heel of screwpile designs, but similar foundations fitted with base plates to seat down on sand and coral, provided an inexpensive solution for towers around the Florida Keys and among the shoals off Louisiana.

LEFT
Thomas Point Shoal Light, Maryland – an example of a caisson tower.

OPPOSITE
St. David's Light, Bermuda, a masonry tower.

CAISSON TOWERS

Caisson construction allows workers to operate below the surface in a dry environment. In its simplest form, a caisson is an open-ended cylinder of large diameter which can be lowered until one end rests on the seabed and, filled with rubble, forces the water out. Open caissons of that type were exploited in China 500 years ago and today, constructed of steel with a cutting bottom edge, may still be used where the seabed is soft and receptive.

A more significant development was the pneumatic caisson, which became viable when the versatile British admiral and inventor, Thomas Cochrane (Lord Dundonald), invented the air lock, in about 1830. Another British inventor, Lawrence Potts, demonstrated how the concept would help in building underwater foundations, and for bridges in particular, in 1842.

In a pneumatic caisson, the working chamber at the bottom is sealed off and

filled with compressed air to keep the water out, the workers entering and leaving it through an air lock. As the caisson sinks further into the substrate, extra sections are added at the top to keep it always above the surface of the water. From the mid 19th century, the system, pioneered by British engineers, was widely used for river bridges. The St. Louis Bridge (begun 1867) was an early example of its use at considerable depth.

The first lighthouse tower to be built in this way was the Roter Sand Lighthouse marking the mouth of the Weser River in Germany, where the bottom was shifting sand about 20ft (6m) below water level at low tide. Construction proved extremely difficult, and the first attempt, in 1881, failed when the caisson tilted; but a second effort finally succeeded, the caisson being sunk 72ft (22m) below the surface and the interior filled with concrete. It was completed in 1885.

The first use of the caisson method for lighthouse construction in the United States was in the Fourteen Foot Bank Light in Delaware Bay, where winter ice had demolished earlier screwpile designs. In this and other towers that shortly followed in Chesapeake Bay, the steel caissons were up to 40ft (12m) in diameter. As they descended into the seabed, extra sections were added to the top. Once the bottom had penetrated 50ft (15m) into the seabed, the cylinders were filled with concrete to form the foundation on which the lighthouse was built. This is an extremely strong method of construction and was therefore particularly favoured in sites subject to drifting ice.

The crib and cofferdam foundation systems favoured in the Great Lakes are variations on the caisson concept suitable for shallow waters. An early example was Spectacle Reef, a limestone shoal in Lake Huron, Michigan, where two sailing ships had been recently wrecked. The lighthouse was completed in 1874. A wooden framework, or crib, 32ft (10m) in diameter, was constructed on shore before being lowered into position on the soft reef and the water pumped out. Once dry, stone was lowered into the crib to anchor it, and concrete was built up on top to form a platform above the surface where the high conical lighthouse rose for 86ft (26m).

TEXAS TOWERS

Texas towers were so named for their similarity to the offshore oil rigs that sprang up off the Gulf coast during the 1960s. Using modern drilling techniques, the steel piles were driven as deep as 150ft (45m) into the seabed. The platform they supported housed a light tower, navigation beacon, and a helicopter pad. Fifteen of these towers were erected in the United States, the first at Buzzards Bay, Massachusetts, in 1961, but their high cost of construction and maintenance have led to most being replaced by large buoys.

CONCRETE TOWERS

While concrete has been used in the construction of light towers since the 1830s, it was not until the advent of prestressed and reinforced concrete a century later that this material came into its own. Reinforced concrete is not only hardwearing and low in maintenance, but has enormous tensile strength, making it ideal for construction in areas that are prone to earthquakes. The first U.S. lighthouse to be constructed of this material has stood at Point Arena, California, directly on the San Andreas Fault, since 1908. The success of this 115-ft (35-m) tower led to more being built in other parts of California, as well as in Hawaii and Alaska, regions also prone to seismic activity. Canada too has its share of concrete towers, most notably at Estevan Point and Point Atkinson, both on Vancouver Island, which have rocket-like profiles and were constructed about the same time as the Point Arena Light.

OPPOSITE
Gibb's Hill, Bermuda, a cast-iron lighthouse.

BELOW RIGHT
The America's Cup Jubilee race at Cowes, Isle of Wight, England, alongside the NAB lightship.

LIGHTSHIPS

Lightships have been utilized since 1732 to mark dangerous areas where it was impossible to build a permanent tower, or where the shifting sands dictated the need for a movable light. The first lightship was the *Nore*, a converted single-masted sailing ship equipped with two candle-powered lanterns, which was stationed in the Thames estuary to mark the Nore Sands.

The first U.S. lightship was commissioned in 1820 to mark Willoughby Spit in Chesapeake Bay, before being moved to calmer waters off the mouth of the Elizabeth River in Hampton Roads at the south end of the bay. The economics of converting redundant vessels into lightships found favour with the U.S. Treasury, and within 30 years there were 42 lightships guarding hazards in U.S. coastal waters. The first Canadian lightship was hurriedly acquired to mark South Sands Head, where the River Fraser flows into the Strait of Georgia south of Vancouver, when the gold rush brought hundreds of ships to British Columbia in 1858.

For the crew of each lightship, usually 15–20 men, the experience was largely one of boredom, interspersed with periods of peril due to storms, dense fog or other maritime hazards. When the weather was bad, lightships were liable to drag their anchors or, worse, the anchor chains would break, with the result that the vessel, which was usually without means of propulsion, was at the mercy of the very dangers it had been positioned to guard against. During bad visibility, moreover, the vessels' horns and canon did not always guard them against collision from other ships navigating blindly in and out of port. As related in the previous chapter, the *Nantucket* lightship guarding the fog-shrouded banks off Massachusetts was rammed twice, the second time with fatal results.

When lightships started to be purpose-built, costs escalated, and by the end of the 19th century many were being replaced by screwpile and caisson light towers, more recently by lightbuoys. Those that remained were automated. The *Ambrose* lightship, marking the Ambrose Channel into New York harbour, was one of the last lightships to be stationed in U.S. waters, in 1907; it was replaced by a platform light in 1967. Like many other examples, she is now a museum piece, on view at South Street Seaport Museum in New York City.

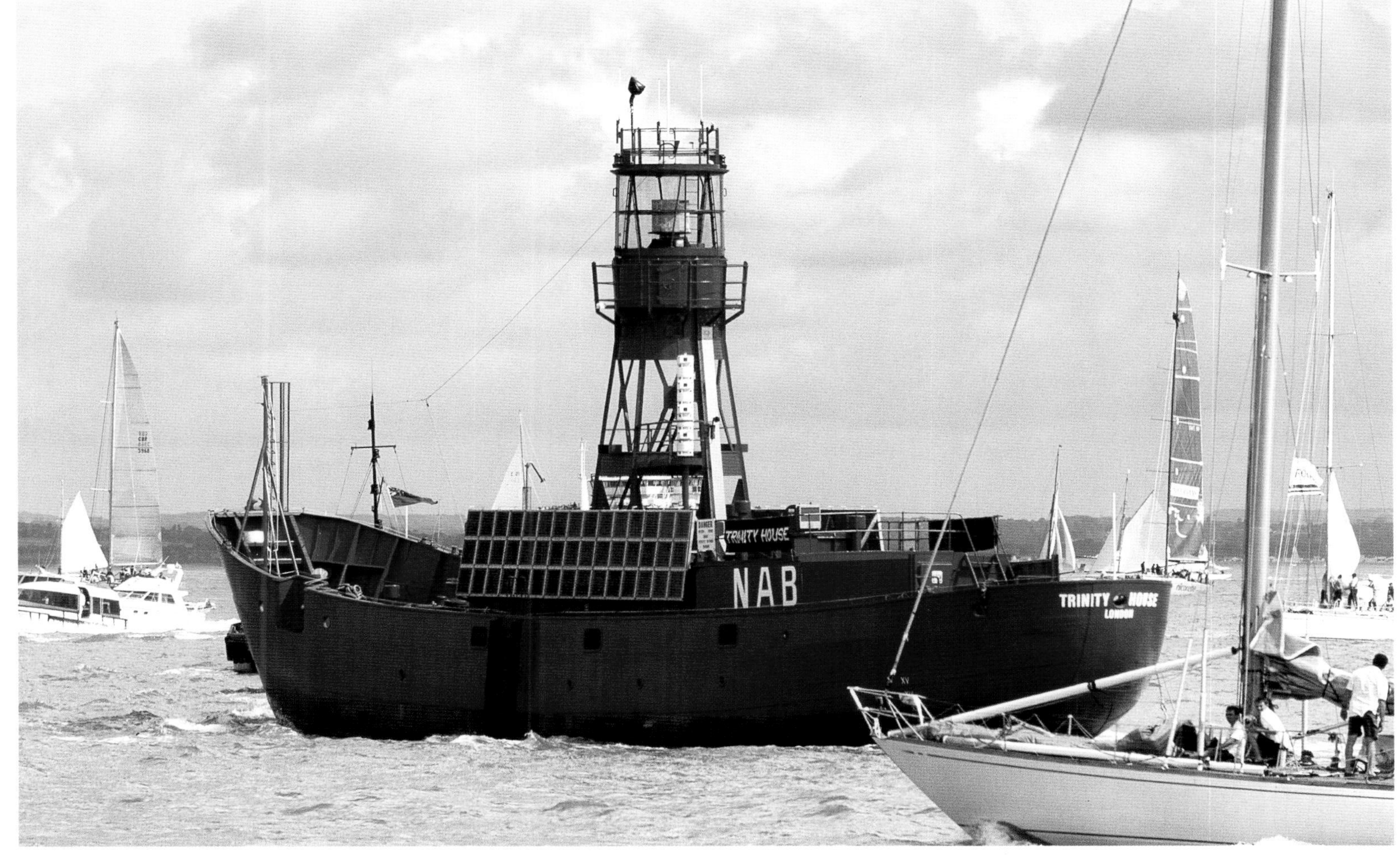

Chapter Four
Signalling Systems

The wood-burning navigational beacons developed by the Egyptians and Greeks from as early as 8000 BC continued until coal began to take over as the favoured fuel across northern Europe in early modern times. This black fossil rock provides a far more incandescent light than any other form of fuel and was much preferred by sailors to candles or oil, though all three were a plague to lighthouse keepers, who had to deal with the acrid black smoke that continually blackened the lantern glass. This was not solved until Aimé Argand's Swiss smokeless oil lamp was invented in 1782, which was soon accepted within the lighthouse world.

The Argand lamp has a circular wick and a glass chimney shaped to allow an adequate draft of air up the centre to ensure proper combustion. These lamps burned fish, vegetable and, later, mineral oil, and had as many as ten wicks. They remained the principal light source for navigation towers into the 1880s.

In 1901 Britain's Arthur Kitson invented the vaporized oil burner. This utilizes kerosene, vaporized under pressure, which, when mixed with air is burned to heat an incandescent mantle in the same way that camp stoves and pressure lamps operate today. It provides as much as six times the light power that Argand lamps produce. At the same time, Sweden's Gustaf Dalén was busy perfecting his acetylene gas lamp, which produced a light equal to an oil lamp but with the advantage that it could be turned on and off automatically. This had a major effect on lighthouse developments, and by 1910 the first automated lighthouses using the Dalén lamp began operation in remote areas of the globe.

Electric carbon arc lights were experimented with as early as 1862, the first being used at the Dungeness Light in England, but they were later converted back to oil because of their cost and complexity. It was not until 1913 that the system was advanced enough to give out 38 million candlepower of light at Germany's Heligoland lighthouse in the North Sea.

Edison's electric filament lamp won acceptance as the standard light source in the 1920s, and brought an end first to the three-hourly climbs each night to check or trim wicks and mantles, and eventually the end of the lighthouse keeper's job entirely.

OPTICAL EQUIPMENT

While the ancient Egyptian Pharos is believed to have been equipped with a crudely beaten copper reflector, it was the British inventor William Hutchinson who developed the first practical lighthouse mirrors in 1777. His paraboloidal, silvered, glass reflectors focused the light into a narrow beam which, once fully developed, increased light intensity 400 times. The problem with a narrow beam is that it cannot be seen from other angles, so designers came up with the revolving beam concept in 1781, which created the well-known flashing pattern. The first of these was installed in the Swedish lighthouse at Carlsten, Marstrand.

Inspired by developments in Britain, the American Captain Winslow Lewis developed a similar reflective system to the one he had seen at South Stack lighthouse in Wales, and sold the concept to Congress in 1810 for a reputed $60,000. He was then commissioned to convert all 49 lighthouses in operation across the United States and doubtless died a very rich man.

Robert Stephenson also experimented with rotating mechanisms for his Bell Rock lighthouse, built on a famously difficult site off the Firth of Forth in Scotland in 1811. He added red glass on opposing sides to provide his tower with a unique identifying pattern of alternate red and white flashes.

A major breakthrough came during the mid 1820s when the French physicist Augustin-Jean Fresnel installed the first example of what became known as the Fresnel lens in the Cordouan Light at Bordeaux, France. He had been working to reduce the weight of existing lenses, and discovered that the efficiency of a lens depends much more on the contours than the thickness of the glass. By removing the excess glass from the outer prism shapes, he reduced the weight by a factor of ten, improved light capture to a level of 70 per cent and increased the reflectiveness from around 20,000 candlepower, offered by the earlier Argand lamp mirror system, to 80,000 candlepower – equivalent to a modern car headlight. This was later improved to 100,000 candlepower when used with a pressurized oil lamp.

Fresnel harnessed the refracting properties of glass by developing a series of concentric prisms that are moulded, then

The lantern of the Cape Horn Lighthouse, showing a close-up of the lens.

ground and polished individually to capture the light and reflect it outwards in a narrow, horizontal beam. The vertical panels directly in front of the light are bull's-eye lenses surrounded by concentric prismatic rings. The panels directly above and below are curved prisms, which are topped by a beehive-shaped lens to redirect the light at a more acute angle. To refocus light that would otherwise be lost up into the sky or down towards the ground, Fresnel added angled mirrors at the top and bottom of the lens, together with a series of triangular prisms on the floor and ceiling to collect the light shining up and down and redirect it out through the lens. The additional advantage of this design was that the individual components, which together added up to many hundreds of pieces of glass, were much easier to transport than earlier mirrors, and the individual prisms could always be replaced relatively easily.

Fresnel later developed a modified version of his lens system to produce a cylindrical drum lens that provided an all-round light. These eliminated the need for any form of rotating mechanism and are still in wide use today to project the flashing lights on buoys and beacons.

Fresnel's original rotating lens system weighed more than 11,000lb (5000kg), half of which would have been in the four glass lenses, each 12ft (3.5m) high. The turntable rotated in a cast-iron trough of mercury, which minimized friction. It was driven by a weighted clockwork motor, though later models fitted with acetylene gas lights were turned using the same pressurized gas.

Fresnel lenses were made in several different sizes, called 'orders'. The largest, first-order lenses were about 6ft (2m) in diameter and up to 12ft (3.5m) in height. Fourth- and fifth-order lenses were about 10in (25cm) in diameter and 3ft (1m) high.

Fresnel's principles remain valid today, but the latest lenses are moulded in plastic, they stand no taller than 2ft 6in (76cm) high, and they rely on electricity to power a 250-watt lamp as well as the rotating platform, which now runs on ball bearings.

RANGE

Range depends on geographical factors as well as luminosity. Because of the curved surface of the Earth, the higher the light, the farther it can be seen. In good weather, a light 100ft (30m) high has a range of 16 nautical miles. A light only 30ft high can be seen at a distance of eight nautical miles.

Barbados Light.

Atmospheric conditions can have a marked effect on visibility. This is defined in terms of a percentage of a set transmission factor which can be around 80 per cent in northern and southern latitudes, and as much as 90 per cent in the tropics, increasing the luminous range of a 10,000 candlepower light by as much as 50 per cent, or from 18 to 27 miles (29 to 43km). In these conditions, the beam will show its presence well beyond the horizon because some light is diffused upwards by water vapour within the atmosphere, a phenomenon known as a loom. Conversely, this range will be reduced significantly in misty conditions or fog, when sailors may not spot the light until they are almost upon it.

Because clear-weather conditions vary from one region to another, the luminous range of lighthouses is measured against a standard clear-weather condition that corresponds to a daytime meteorological visibility of ten nautical miles or 74 per cent transmission. This is termed the nominal range of a light, and conversion tables are required to determine the actual luminous range in the prevailing visibility for a given lighthouse.

IDENTIFICATION SIGNALS

Each light can be identified by its unique pattern of flashes, which are regulated by the International Association of Lighthouse Authorities, based in Paris. These are defined as group-flashing lights. Fixed lights are designed to provide navigators with an accurate approach path to harbours and estuaries. These are displayed either with red (for danger) and green sectors, or as two fixed lights of different height positioned a fixed distance apart, with which the navigator keeps his vessel aligned.

Lighthouses also act as day marks and are therefore painted to stand out against their surroundings. Onshore lighthouses are painted white, while those positioned offshore, or against neutral background, are given wide bands of red or black.

SOUND SIGNALS

Poor visibility was always a nightmare for lighthouse keepers, who in the early days would have had to sound a bell or fire a cannon at regular intervals day and night. Generally these could be heard up to 4 miles (6.5km) away, but the development of compressed-air fog signals early in the 20th century doubled the range. Although they could operate automatically, the lighthouse keeper got little sleep while the signal was blasting out. Automated lighthouses are now equipped with electric sound-signalling equipment triggered by a change in the atmospheric conditions.

RADIO AIDS

The development of radio beacons, which were first introduced in the early 1920s, was another step towards the redundancy of the lighthouse keeper. By sending out an identifying signal at regular intervals, a vessel's direction-finding receivers give navigators an accurate bearing, day or night, whatever the weather.

The radar responder, or racon as it is called in maritime circles, transmits a coded pulse whenever it receives a signal from a vessel's rotating radar scanner. These devices have been in use on ships since 1966 and have become a valuable navigation aid for fixing range and identifying such points as buoys or offshore gas and oil platforms in otherwise featureless areas.

AUTOMATION

Lighthouse automation began in the 1920s following the development of the acetylene-gas illumination system. The role of the lighthouse keeper finally ended with the advent of electricity and the development of back-up generators that come on-line automatically whenever there was a failure in equipment or supply. Lighthouses are now monitored by remote control and maintenance visits are generally limited to once a year. Today, many lights utilize solar power linked to back-up batteries that store excess capacity and keep the lights running through the night hours. Such have been the advances in this technology that Canada and Norway now operate solar-powered lights in their Arctic regions, where the night hours are considerably longer than the daylight hours during the winter months.

Chapter Five

Lighthouses as Race Markers

Lighthouses have long marked the official start and finish of ocean voyages and races. It is a tradition that began with the clipper ships, those great greyhounds of the sea that brought to Europe tea and other luxuries from the Far East, as well as gold from Australia, and carried prospectors and their equipment on the immense voyage from New York around Cape Horn and up the Pacific coast to San Francisco during the gold rush.

THE CLIPPERS

The demand for the first tea shipment of the season, coupled with a change in the way ships were measured and taxed, led to the development of the speedy clipper ships ('clipper' is a generic term for fast-sailing, square-rigged ships, first applied to speedy Baltimore 'clippers', which were actually fore-and-aft-rigged schooners, not clippers at all). They were the fastest method of intercontinental transport from the 1830s until about the end of the 19th century.

The first of the tea crop, picked in the middle of April when the leaves were still sparse but most fragrant, would fetch as much as 18 shillings per pound in London's tea market, three times or more than the price tea would fetch later in the season. The problem for merchants keen to capitalize on this premium crop was that the picking coincided with the south-west monsoon in the South China Sea – wind conditions that the traditional bluff-bowed, flat-bottomed ships could not easily sail against. Instead, the old merchantmen waited for the favourable monsoon that blows between November and May to carry them out into the Indian Ocean. They would not be sighted off Dover until six months later, and some of their cargo might lie in store for a year as insurance against a poor crop, or calamities at sea or some other disaster creating a shortfall the following season. If ships could beat against the monsoon, those prime leaves could be brought to market much earlier – a thought that no doubt passed through the minds of more than one ship owner.

It was the change in the rules governing the measurement of ships' tonnage in 1835, as much as the idea of quicker profits, that brought the clipper concept into being. Since 1773, tonnage, on which tax is based, had been reckoned according to a formula that was suitable for the typical ships of the period – bluff-bowed, full-bodied, generally squarish – but unsuitable for longer, slimmer hulls. Under the new regulations of 1835, this disadvantage was overcome. First, the capacity of the hull below the deck was calculated in cubic feet and divided by 100 (100 cubic feet was taken as one ton). This gave the gross tonnage. But it included space, such as quarters for the crew, that was not used for cargo. Therefore a second calculation was made of this non-cargo space; that figure was deducted from the gross tonnage to give net tonnage on which tax was based. Shipbuilders now had greater scope to design sleeker ships than their apple-bowed forebears – ships that could make good progress in unfavourable conditions – without being penalized by the method of tax assessment.

In those days, communications were no faster than the ships themselves, so there would be no news of the clippers until they were first sighted in the English Channel – usually by the lighthouse keeper at Lizard Point in Cornwall. Their names would then be carried by horseback or carriage to London where the news would cause a great deal of excitement. One tea broker had a wind indicator mounted on the roof of his sale room, which was eagerly watched for any sign of a change that might effect the time taken on the final run from the lighthouse at Dover to arrival in the Thames.

Some of the first clippers that were designed with these new rules in mind were built in Aberdeen. Displacing around 450 tons, they had sharply raked bows, overhung sterns and much finer lines. They were the first to get home with the new season's tea during the 1840s, proving that the monsoon was no fatal obstacle, and the trend they set was to be followed and extended by shipyards in the Old and New Worlds for the next three decades.

The crews of the clippers would count the time from passing abeam the sentinels at Foochow (Fuchau), Hong Kong and in particular Anyar, which marks the Sunda Strait between Java and Sumatra, the marine gateway to the Far East. Here, the original stone lighthouse, built by the Portuguese, was destroyed by the eruption of Mount Krakatoa in 1883 and replaced with a prefabricated iron structure in 1885. Although the ships sailed from several,

widely separated Chinese ports, they all passed the lighthouse at Anyar which therefore became the best point from which individual sailing times to London or Amsterdam could be measured.

The race to bring back the season's first tea captured the European public's imagination. The expectancy of a fast passage, the close competition between rival captains and the final chase up the English Channel to be first to off-load their tea, gave these voyages special interest.

U.S.-registered ships built towards the end of the clipper era gained some advantage in speed because they had passenger accommodation between decks, which made them relatively lighter-loaded and thus faster than their smaller, cargo-laden counterparts from Europe. As far as records show, the fastest one-day run through the Southern Ocean was achieved by the *Champion of the Seas*, a U.S.-registered ship of 1,947 tons, with accommodation for 780 passengers, built in Boston by the most famous of the clipper builders, Donald McKay, for the Liverpool Black Ball Line. During her maiden voyage from Liverpool to Melbourne, she covered 404 miles (650km) during the 23 hours 17 minutes between sights on 11–12 December 1854 – an average speed of just under 17 knots!

Another of McKay's rather over-canvassed American clippers was the 230-ft (70-m) *Flying Cloud*, built in 1850, with a displacement of 1,139 tons. She was designed to compete on the Gold Rush run from New York to San Francisco against the *Challenge*, designed by William Webb of New York and the most extreme clipper ship ever built. She measured 230ft and displaced 2,006 tons and held the record for the New York–San Francisco run for many years. The two ships sailed from New York in June 1851 and took as their starting point the Ambrose Light. Both had the ablest captains at sea, with Josiah Cressy master on *Flying Cloud* and the brutal Robert 'Bully' Waterman in charge of *Challenge*. The most significant difference between them was their crews. The *Flying Cloud* had a good team, but Waterman's crew was all but mutinous, whose main interest was panning for gold in the digging fields.

Flying Cloud set sail on 2 June and was spotted by the lighthouse keeper in San Francisco Bay on 21 August, having taken 89 days 21 hours to complete 14,000 miles (22530km) around the Horn. Her logbook records a frequent loss of spars and their replacement, and the tearing and repairing of sails as her crew pushed the ship to speeds of 18 knots or more. A maximum day's run of 373 miles (600km) was also recorded, the fastest 24-hour run so far. By contrast,

ABOVE
Flying Cloud.

FAR LEFT
Anyar Lighthouse, Indonesia. It was erected by the Dutch but manufactured in Britain.

Challenge had a poor voyage. Starting later, she was slowed by light winds and this, combined with the antagonism between captain and crew, extended her passage time to 108 days. By the time she arrived off San Francisco, five sailors had died of disease, four had drowned after falling from the rigging, and two had been killed by their captain!

Another famous McKay-built clipper, the celebrated *Sovereign of the Seas*, made several record runs. This 2,240-ton vessel, 258ft (79m) long, was captained by Lauchlan McKay, the builder's brother, and logged incredible distances when conditions were favourable. During one voyage she averaged 378 land miles (608km) over four consecutive days, and on another sailed 3,630 miles (5842km) in 11 days. Her fastest noon-to-noon distance was 411 miles (661km) on 18 March 1853 – a day when the log recorded a speed of 19 knots for three successive hours. Her record for the London–Melbourne run (65 days) was not beaten for 30 years.

AFTER THE CLIPPERS

The clipper ships are now long gone, but their records are still regarded as benchmarks by adventurous sailors in their high-tech multihulls and monohulls. The first man to sail solo, non-stop, westward around the world, the British pioneer of long-distance sailing Chay Blyth, thought of challenging the clipper-ship times from New York to San Francisco in a trimaran, but his first vessel sank during the delivery trip across the Atlantic. In a second trimaran, Blyth and his one-man crew made good speed south through the Atlantic, but at Cape Horn were confronted by the sort of weather that clipper-ship men had dreaded. Their 53-ft (16-m) trimaran was capsized by ferocious waves and they were left wallowing in their upturned craft for 19 hours, with Blyth nursing a broken shoulder until rescued by a passing ship. In the days of the clippers, life expectancy for anyone falling overboard in these near-freezing waters was measured in minutes, and only their modern survival suits saved Blyth and his companion from death.

This daunting experience, far from acting as a deterrent, encouraged many enterprising people to take up the challenge to build a boat that could not only compete with the high speeds of the clipper ships but also weather the storms for which Cape Horn in particular is so notorious. In February 1994 a record of 63 days 5 hours 55 minutes was set by French yachtswoman Isabelle Autissier in her monohull *Ecureuil Poitou Charentes*.

Long before the days of the lone long-distance yachtsmen and women, the age of steam had finally put all sailing ships, including the clippers, out of business. But steamships too aimed to set records, especially on the highly competitive Atlantic run, where liners such as the *Queen Mary* and the *United States* vied for the Blue Riband, awarded to the ship that made the fastest crossing between New York's *Sandy Hook* lightship and Bishop Rock lighthouse off the Scilly Isles in the Western Approaches to the English Channel. As these great ships were in turn overtaken by air transport, it seemed that the final record of 3 days 10 hours set by the *United States* on her maiden voyage in 1952 might never be broken.

The Bishop Rock lighthouse marks some of the most dangerous waters in the North Atlantic, where waves, pushed by the prevailing winds across over 2,500 miles (4000km) of ocean, are suddenly funnelled into the English Channel. The first lighthouse on Bishop Rock was swept away by heavy seas in 1847, midway through its construction. The present tower, made of interlocking granite blocks, was erected in 1858 but later extended to 146ft (44.5m) as well as further reinforced against the elements. The harsh weather also made it impossible for keepers to know for certain when they would be relieved. Conditions that make it impossible to bring a boat alongside the rock can last for weeks. A radio reporter and his engineer, who planned a pre-Christmas broadcast from the lighthouse in 1946, found themselves marooned there with the lighthouse keeper for 28 days before the weather cleared sufficiently for the Scilly Isles lifeboat to pick them up.

A generation after the great liners used to sound their sirens to mark the completion of their timed transatlantic run as the Bishop Rock lighthouse came abeam, engine design and propulsion units for large pleasure craft had advanced to the point where powerboats could challenge outright records across oceans.

Richard Branson, an adventurous British businessman, was one who took up the challenge. He was particularly interested in reviving the Hales Trophy, a gaudily gilded prize first awarded in 1838 to the current holder of the Blue Riband, which had been gathering dust in the American Merchant Marine Museum for four decades. He had the 64-ft (19.5-m) catamaran *Virgin Atlantic Challenger* built, and after waiting in New York for the right weather conditions, set out in 1985 with a team of acknowledged endurance specialists that included the round-the-world yachtsman Chay Blyth and powerboat champion Ted Toleman to beat the time set by the *United States*.

After a fuel leak forced them to seek fresh supplies from a passing ship in mid-Atlantic, the boat hit a submerged object (probably a ship's container) and was wrecked 138 miles (222km) from Bishop

Ambrose Light Tower, New York.

Rock. Branson and his crew survived unscathed and tried again a year later with *Virgin Atlantic Challenger II*, a 72-ft (22-m) monohull powered by twin 2,000-hp diesel engines which gave a top speed of 55mph (89km/h). She passed the Ambrose light tower on 27 June 1986 and covered the first 526 miles (846km) at 53mph (85km/h). The team had set up a rendezvous with refuelling ships at three points along the course, and it was at the second of these, 1,236 miles (1989km) across the Atlantic when *Virgin Atlantic II* was two hours inside the record, that things began to unravel. Mysteriously, a third of the 2,500 gallons of fuel transferred from the bowser turned out to be water. The crew lost valuable time clearing the tanks and refilling them with clean diesel. The tanks, however, were filled with an anti-surge material which kept releasing water every time the hull hit a large wave. This water then caused the paper filters in the system to swell and restrict the supply of fuel to the engines, necessitating frequent stops to change the cartridges. Soon, they ran out of filters, but the Royal Air Force saved the day by air-dropping a fresh supply to the boat. These delays cost them dearly, for a depression, sweeping across the Atlantic, eventually caught up with the boat, turning the last stage into something of a bruising nightmare. At the finish, Branson and his crew took the record with just 2 hours 8 minutes to spare, after averaging 41mph (66km/h) over the 3,000-mile (4828-km) distance.

The trustees of the American Merchant Marine Museum were not impressed. The thought of surrendering the trophy to a speedboat appalled them. Citing the 147-year-old deed of gift, they claimed that only commercial passenger-carrying vessels could claim the Hales Trophy. Branson's suggestion that Chay Blyth had been their paying passenger on board *Virgin Atlantic Challenger II*, understandably cut little ice.

The irrepressible Branson accordingly commissioned his own trophy – a silver model of the Bishop Rock lighthouse. The first to make a challenge for it was a Hawaiian property tycoon and powerboat enthusiast, Tom Gentry. In 1989 he launched the 112-ft (34-m) 11,500-hp *Gentry Eagle*, which shattered the transatlantic record with a time of 2 days 14 hours 7 minutes.

The Blue Riband might now have been back in American hands, but the trustees at the American Merchant Marine Museum refused to entertain the idea of handing the Hales Trophy to Gentry's powerboat. They took the same line even when a genuine commercial passenger vessel completed the course in 1990.

The *SeaCat*, a surface-piercing catamaran, built as a car ferry by Incat in Tasmania, claimed the trophy after making the Atlantic crossing in 3 days 7 hours. The trustees maintained that a catamaran, though large, was not a steam-powered ocean liner. *SeaCat*'s owners, Hoverspeed Great Britain, took them to court, claiming that the original deed allowed for the trophy to be awarded to the fastest vessel making a surface transatlantic crossing, whether it was powered by steam or oil, and had one hull or two. They won the case, and the Hales Trophy was grudgingly handed over.

SeaCat's commercial record lasted until 1998, when it was broken twice, again by Incat-built catamarans. The current holder, *Cat-Link V*, is a 183-ft (56-m) Spanish car and passenger ferry. Her attempt was eventful: a few hours after leaving New York she was diverted to a search mission off the coast of Canada, which delayed her by two hours. Even so, she crossed the Atlantic in 2 days 20 hours, the first transatlantic voyage by a commercial vessel in under three days, and the first to attain an average speed of over 40 knots (46mph/74 km/h).

The current outright power record stands at 2 days 10 hours 34 minutes, set in 1992 by the Aga Khan's gas-turbine-powered 223-ft (68-m) *Destriero* at an average of 52.55mph (84.57km/h).

THE KAISER'S CUP

Interest in sailing across the Atlantic has grown ever stronger. For sailing ships, the traditional start and finish marks have been the Ambrose Light (later a lightship) off New York and the Lizard lighthouse on England's southernmost tip.

As the age of commercial sail came to an end, it it was succeeded by sailing for sport, and this tradition has continued to this day. Rivalry has sometimes been fierce, beginning with the Emperor Wilhelm II of Germany.

Wilhelm was jealous of his more

ABOVE
In 1989, the 112-ft 11,500-hp Gentry Eagle *made a record transatlantic crossing of 62hrs 7mins, with a top speed of 73mph.*

popular uncle, King Edward VII of England, and caused offence in some circles of Anglo-American society by his criticisms of the king. The comment that finally got him blackballed from both the Royal Yacht Squadron in England and the New York Yacht Club was characteristically graceless: after hearing that a falling rope block had almost killed the British monarch while he was sailing on the yacht *Shamrock* of his friend, the tea tycoon Sir Thomas Lipton, Wilhelm remarked, 'Serves him right for going yachting with his grocer.' The two premier yacht clubs let it be known that the Kaiser and his friends would no longer be welcome on their premises.

Not to be outdone, Kaiser Wilhelm replied by putting up a $5,000 gold cup – the Kaiser's Cup – for a yacht race of his own, run entirely in international waters. The proposed course was, of course, from the Ambrose Light to the Lizard.

The event caught the attention of Wilson Marshall, an otherwise undistinguished American millionaire, whose chief distinction, according to his obituarist, was to serve as vice commodore of the Larchmont Yacht Club. Marshall owned a 187-ft (57-m) yacht, *Atlantic*, one of many schooner-rigged private vessels of the period designed to make the most of the reaching trade winds between the eastern seaboard of the United States and the Caribbean. Designed by

LEFT
The Aga Khan's yacht, Destriero.

ABOVE
The SeaCat catamaran car ferry off New York at the start of a transatlantic record-breaking attempt. The vessel broke the record for commercial shipping to win the Hales Trophy and Blue Riband.

William Gardner, the yacht was fitted with a large, cast-iron daggerboard (a type of keel or centreboard), which could be hoisted into a watertight casing within the hull to reduce drag when running downwind. Early trials had shown her to be a poor performer in any wind, and Gardner was persuaded to replace the daggerboard with a hefty lead shoe bolted on under the hull. The modification not only transformed *Atlantic*'s performance but also her looks, for apart from providing extra stability, this massive lump of lead sank the yacht well below her designed waterline, thus imparting an unwonted sleekness of line – though also making her extremely wet!

The Kaiser's Cup challenge was just what Marshall needed to prove his new toy and he ordered her to be repainted a lustrous black to set off her gleaming brasswork and 18,514sq ft (1720m^2) of sail. Said to have been 'a man who could not tie a knot to save his life', Marshall was not rash enough to assume command of *Atlantic* himself. Instead, he hired Captain Charles Barr, a three-time defender of the famous America's Cup, to skipper the yacht for the race.

Barr was one of the best and most sought-after skippers of his day. A former greengrocer's assistant from Gourock near Glasgow, he learned his sailing skills on the Clyde estuary. He and his brother gained Atlantic experience delivering Scottish-built yachts to their new owners, having first sailed to America in 1885. Just five feet tall, the diminutive Barr made up for his small stature with a massive black moustache and a strong Clydeside accent in which he barked out orders that outsiders found hard to understand. He would take no nonsense from crew or owners, but Barr's skill on the race course made him a favourite of the Bristol, Rhode Island, designer Nat Herreshoff, who brought him on board to command *Columbia*, built for the banker J.P. Morgan. She defeated Thomas Lipton's first America's Cup challenger, *Shamrock*, in 1899. Barr repeated the victory three years later against *Shamrock II*, and also captained the 143-ft (43.5-m) *Reliance* to win the cup for the third time in succession against *Shamrock III* in 1903. This led to questions in Congress about the propriety of relying on a 'foreign mercenary' to uphold American pride on the race course, which forced Barr grudgingly to take out U.S. citizenship before he took the wheel of *Atlantic* two years later.

Altogether, 11 yachts took up the Kaiser's challenge for this 1905 transatlantic race. Among them was the German flagship *Hamburg*, a two-master which had originally been named *Rainbow* when launched in Glasgow seven years earlier. The Earl of Crawford entered his 245-ft (75-m) square-rigger *Valhalla*, and Lord Brassey brought his 159-ft (49-m) barquentine *Sunbeam* to the Ambrose Light start line. One of the favourites was *Endymion*, owned by banker George Lauder, a 137-ft (42-m) schooner that held the record for the transatlantic crossing with a time of 13 days 20 hours 36 minutes. *Thistle*, at 150ft (46m) overall, was another fancied entrant, but was perhaps handicapped because her owner, stockbroker Robert E. Todd, opted to take command himself. The smallest entrant was *Fleur de Lys*, only 105ft (32m) long; she was also the only one with a woman on board – Candace Stimson – a doctor's daughter from Gloucester, Massachusetts.

Atlantic carried the shortest odds. She had the best skipper in Charlie Barr, and having already won two other lighthouse races, the Brenton Reef and Cape May events, was acknowledged as the fastest American yacht on the eastern seaboard.

The starting cannon was fired at 12:15 on 17 May 1905 by Captain Count Hebbenhaus, the German naval attaché in Washington. It was a misty day with winds blowing fitfully from the east – hardly record-breaking weather! *Hamburg* was the early leader, followed by *Fleur de Lys*, as the fleet headed out in search of the Gulf Stream, that warm body of water flowing two or three knots north-east across the North Atlantic.

There is a choice of three sailing routes to the Western Approaches to the English Channel. The Trade-Wind route along the 40th parallel provides reaching winds and sunny skies as far as the Azores, leaving vessels with uncertain conditions only while heading north across the Bay of Biscay. The Great Circle route has the advantage of being the shortest, but takes vessels directly across the fog-shrouded Grand Banks. The final alternative is a slightly longer, composite course to a point just south of the banks where vessels join the Great Circle track to the English Channel. This was the course that Charlie Barr selected; according to the yachting historian Alfred F. Loomis, 'Barr seems never to have made an error, never to have wasted so much as half an hour'.

By contrast, *Apache*, 198-ft (60-m) barque, chose the Trade-Wind route, but in spite of an easy passage, sighted the Lizard Light a week behind the winner, while *Fleur de Lys*, which stuck to the Great Circle, sailed straight into calms on the Grand Banks and reached the finish well behind.

During the first 24 hours, *Atlantic* endured the same light, easterly winds and glassy seas as the rest of the fleet. The following day, however, the breeze backed round to the south-west and slowly filled. By midnight, *Atlantic*'s log showed that she was creaming along at ten knots. On the third day, the wind swung to the west, and members of *Atlantic*'s crew – made up of Grand Banks fishermen – had to climb the mainmast to replace a split topsail. The fourth day presented much the same conditions, but the fifth almost saw an end to any prospects of a record. It produced *Atlantic*'s worst day's run – just 112 miles (180km), and without the advantage of modern weather faxes, satellite pictures and radio reports to forecast what lay ahead, their slow progress must have had a dispiriting effect on Barr and his crew. Things were made worse by the sighting of icebergs just south of the fog-shrouded Grand Banks, which forced Barr to change course to avoid the potential danger.

Conditions did not pick up until 48 hours later, when the winds finally shifted to south-south-east and began to build. In the 24 hours between noon on 24 and 25 May, her seventh day at sea, *Atlantic* covered 341 miles (549km) to beat the noon-to-noon record set by the yacht *Dauntless* in 1887 by 13 miles. Barr was jubilant and ordered a double issue of rum.

By the eighth day, *Atlantic* was running before a full storm and carrying nothing more than a single square sail and storm trysail. As darkness closed in, her decks were awash with water, oil bags had been set up along her weather rail in an effort to calm the immediate seas, and two men were lashed to the wheel for exhausting half-hour stints in an effort to keep the boat on a straight course. As the winds increased during the night, Barr ordered the on-watch to take off the square sail – a perilous task at the best of times – and made far more dangerous by the angry seas.

At the forefront of owner Wilson Marshall's mind would have been the tale of six men lost overboard in similar conditions from the schooner *Fleetwind* during the first transatlantic race back in 1866. Terrified, he pleaded with Barr to heave-to before it was too late, but *Atlantic*'s skipper would have none of it. 'We're here tae race, Mister Marshall. I'm keeping her going,' Barr retorted, and locked Wilson in his stateroom along with his six guests. They allegedly spent the rest of the night in prayer.

Mercifully, there were no serious mishaps, and Barr's dogged determination was rewarded with a day's run of 279 miles (449km). *Atlantic* maintained this rate for the next three days and was timed passing Bishop Rock lighthouse by the pilots from nearby St. Mary's on 29 May, 11 days 16 hours and 21 minutes after starting from New York. But then the winds died, and it took a further 12 nail-biting hours to complete the final 49 miles before *Atlantic* was timed across the Lizard Light finish by the German cruiser *Pfeil* after 12 days 4 hours 1 minute and 17 seconds, equivalent to an average speed of 10.32 knots. It was a record that would stand for the next 75 years and beat the time of second-placed *Hamburg*, whose skipper had chosen to heave-to during the worst of the storm, by almost a day.

Atlantic's record withstood many assaults from all manner of vessels until 1 August 1980, when the legendary French yachtsman Eric Tabarly and his radical foil-assisted trimaran *Paul Ricard* clipped almost two days off her time. Ironically, this breakthrough came just six weeks after the *Sunday Times* in London had put up a £10,000 purse for the first yacht to break the record. The paper's shocked editors had banked on *Atlantic*'s record enduring for another two decades at least!

Since then, the margin has been paired down by successive record-breakers, both multihull and monohull, multi-crewed and single-handed. Steve Fossett's 125-ft (38-m) American catamaran *Playstation 2* set an outright record of 4 days 17 hours 28 minutes and 6 seconds on 1 October 2001. *Mari Cha IV*, a 140-ft (43-m) two-master owned by Britain's Robert Miller, reduced the monohull record to 6 days 17 hours 52 minutes and 39 seconds on 9 October 2003, and Frenchman Laurent Bourgnon set a solo record for the same 2,925-miles (4707-km) distance in June 1994 in his 60-ft (18-m) trimaran *Primagaz*, with a time of 7 days 2 hours 34 minutes and 42 seconds.

Primagaz – *holder of the OSTAR transatlantic speed record.*

THE BERMUDA RACE

The concept of racing yachts across oceans and beating the sailing-ship times from one lighthouse to another first caught on at the beginning of the 20th century. One of its champions was Thomas Fleming Day, the controversial editor of the yachting magazine *Rudder*, who used his pages as a forum to encourage others to join him. Day began by organizing a race from Brooklyn, New York, to Marblehead, north-east of Boston, a daring 330-mile (531-km) chase between two lighthouses that attracted six entries – and columns of criticism in the New York and Boston papers! Unperturbed, he organized a second event a year later from Brooklyn to Hampton Roads, Virginia, and blasted back at his critics from the pages of his magazine:

Newspaper men ought to know better than consult a lot of gray-bearded rum soaked piazza scows. What do these miserable old hulks who spend their days swigging booze on the front stoop of a clubhouse know about the dangers of the deep? If they make a voyage from Larchmont to Cow Bay in a 10 knot breeze, it is the event of their lives, an experience they never forget and never want to repeat.

This printed banter did wonders for promoting the concept of racing beyond the horizon – and doubtless for the readership figures of *Rudder* magazine.

After the Hampton Roads race, which had attracted nine yachts, owners turned to Day for something more ambitious, 'a real ocean race, one that would take them well offshore and into blue water'. The *Rudder* editor needed little encouragement, and with help from Sir Thomas Lipton, who provided a £100 cup for the winner, the race to Bermuda was born, with the finish line off St. David's Light.

The criticism within the press was vociferous and the public campaign led some to send memorial wreaths and undertakers' cards to those planning to enter the race. Despite this, three yachts, *Lila, Gauntlet* and *Tamerlane*, appeared for the start at 3 pm on Saturday 26 May 1906. *Lila* suffered rigging damage soon after the start and was forced to return, accompanied by *Tamerlane*, though she set out again for Bermuda the following Tuesday. This 38-ft (12-m) yawl owned by Commodore Frank Maier of the Eastern Yacht Club also carried Day on board. He reported in the July issue of *Rudder* an uneventful passage that took 5 days 6 hours and 9 minutes – an average of 5.22 knots.

RIGHT
Carina *in the 2000 Newport–Bermuda Race.*

OPPOSITE LEFT
The St. David's Light Trophy.

OPPOSITE RIGHT
Start of the 2000 Newport–Bermuda Race.

Over on the West Coast, Clarence MacFarlane, a yachtsman from Hawaii, was busy promoting the idea of a transpacific race, and invited several sailors in San Francisco and Los Angeles to race to the islands. The event was scheduled for the early summer of 1906, but when MacFarlane sailed his 48-ft (14.5-m) schooner into San Francisco Bay it was not the opposition of the press but an earthquake that forced him to change his plans. The city lay in ruins following the infamous quake 27 days earlier, but MacFarlane was not easily discouraged. He simply changed the starting point to Los Angeles, and except for one nostalgic return to San Francisco for the start in 1939, the event has started from the Los Angeles area ever since. The line is set from the lighthouse at Point Fermin near San Pedro on the Palos Verdes peninsula, and the finish is a line drawn from Diamond Head lighthouse just east of Honolulu, a distance of 2,225 nautical miles.

In New York, a second Bermuda race was planned for 1907, this time with a $1,000 purse, which brought 13 yachts to the line. The 85-ft (26-m) schooner *Dervish* won in a time of 90 hours 20 minutes, which was so much faster than the 1906 benchmark that the St. David's lighthouse finish line had not even been set up when she arrived off Bermuda.

So many big yachts were laid up during the Depression years that only two, Harold S. Vanderbilt's 62-ft (19-m) schooner *Vagrant*, and Demarest Lloyds's 50-ft (15-m) *Shiyessa*, made it to the start of the 1910 Bermuda race and the event almost died. The same

happened to the Transpac (transpacific) race on the West Coast where only two yachts answered the starting cannon for the 1932 race. Yet the two events survived and are now run in alternate years, with the longer Transpac attracting as many as 80 entries and the 635-mile (1022-km) Bermuda Race, whose start was moved to Newport, Rhode Island, in 1946, with more than 180 yachts coming to the line. One reason for this, perhaps, is that the winner of the latter keeps a silver model of the St. David lighthouse worth more than $20,000!

While crews in the Bermuda race have the formidable Gulf Stream to confront, the Transpac is an out-and-out downwind race, thanks to the north-east trade winds that carry the yachts directly to Honolulu.

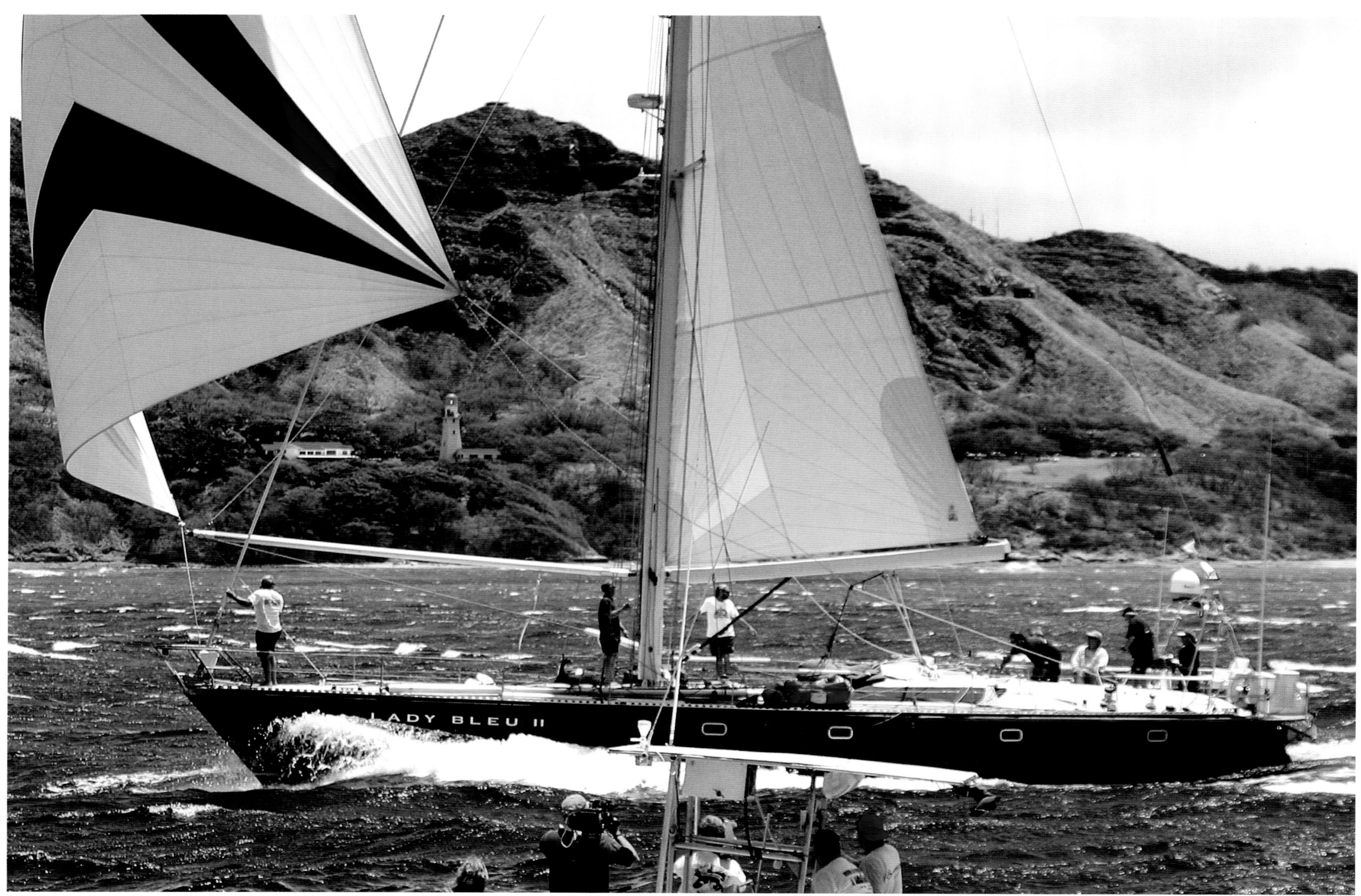
LADY BLEU II

OPPOSITE
Lady Bleu II *finishing the Transpac 2003 in Hawaii, with the Diamond Head lighthouse in the background.*

BELOW RIGHT
Francis Chichester on Gipsy Moth III *at the end of the first* Observer *Single-Handed Transatlantic Race (OSTAR), as the cruise liner* Queen Elizabeth *passes into New York harbour. Chichester won the race, taking 40 days to complete the 3,000-mile crossing.*

The records for both races are held by *Pewaukee*, a 73-ft (22-m) Reichel/Pugh-designed, ultralight maxi yacht, owned by Roy E. Disney. After setting a time of just under 7 days 12 hours in the 1999 Transpac race, she took the record for the Bermuda three years later. These records are likely to be quickly superseded, however, for Disney and his immediate rivals have invested in a new breed of faster maxi yachts, the MaxZ86 class, due to participate in the Bermuda classic in 2004 and the Transpac race in 2005.

Like the transatlantic, the Newport–Bermuda and Transpac courses have also attracted the attention of multihull record-chasers. In 1995 Steve Fossett's 60-ft (18-m) trimaran *Lakota* reached the Diamond Head lighthouse in 6 days 16 hours 7 minutes 16 seconds and held the outright record for two years until Frenchman Bruno Peyron and his 86-ft (26-m) catamaran *Explorer* bettered this with a time of 5 days 9 hours 18 minutes 26 seconds. Fossett, whose life ambition, it seems, is to break as many air and sea records as possible, also holds the Newport–Bermuda record of 1 day 14 hours 36 minutes 53 seconds, sailing his 125-ft (38-m) catamaran *Playstation 2* in January 2000, as well as the solo record set with his earlier trimaran *Lokota* that is only 2 hours 15 minutes longer!

THE OSTAR

The idea of racing across the Atlantic against the prevailing winds held little appeal for some time, especially when Lt. Col. H.G. 'Blondie' Hasler, who had conceived and led the famous 'Cockleshell Heroes' canoe raid on German ships in the French port of Bordeaux, proposed doing it single-handedly! His yellowing proposal languished as an item pinned to the notice board of the Royal Ocean Racing Club headquarters in London for three years, until Francis Chichester, who lived around the corner from the club, challenged Hasler with a wager – half a crown (12.5p or about 35 cents). Eventually, the Royal Western Yacht Club agreed to organize the start from the lighthouse marking the breakwater at Plymouth and the *Observer* newspaper decided to sponsor what was to become the first *Observer* Single-handed Transatlantic Race, or OSTAR, as it became better known, in 1960. The 'one man, one boat and the ocean' race, which attracted only five starters, finished off the *Ambrose* lightship in New York.

Most people thought the 'Famous Five' who took part were mad, especially Chichester, who had recently recovered from lung cancer and had no experience of sailing alone in a boat bigger than 12ft (3.6m). At 39ft (12m) overall, his *Gipsy Moth III* was the largest in the race, causing the sages to suck on their pipes and murmur that she was far too big for one man to handle. Then, when he won, they said well, of course, because he had the biggest boat! Chichester reached the Ambrose Light in 40 days. Hasler, sailing his 25-ft (7.6-m) junk-rigged folkboat *Jester* arrived eight days later.

For the second OSTAR in 1964, the fleet had grown to 15 boats, including a catamaran and two trimarans. The race committee only admitted the multihulls after much soul-searching about the ability of these seemingly 'cranky' boats to punch to windward across a stormy open ocean. The first five competitors from 1960 were back, including Jean Lacombe, who had finished fifth. The other French entrant in a mostly British field was a 32-year-old naval lieutenant named Eric Tabarly. After sailing, testing and training aboard a new light-displacement 32-ft (10-m) boat, Tabarly opted for something bigger and faster, and commissioned a purpose-built 44-ft (13-m) hard-chine ketch (in which the angle between the bottom and the sides is sharper than normal) which he named *Pen Duick II*. Her size called for a crew of eight for conventional racing but Tabarly, a superb and strong seaman, had been working on systems to drive it hard without additional help. The British pundits shook their heads but Tabarly forged ahead, overcoming a late start on construction. He led the fleet from the starting gun, despite the fact that on the morning of the race he was still caulking his radical perspex navigation dome, which he had salvaged from an old flying boat.

The race finish had been moved, and now ended at Newport harbour lighthouse, shortening the course by about 100 miles (160km). Tabarly and Chichester took over the early running, sailing parallel courses for the first 14 days but out of sight of each other. While Chichester regularly radioed in his position, Tabarly was silent. His boat's self-steering vane had broken after the first week and the Frenchman was pushed beyond normal human limits, coaxing *Pen Duick II* to self-steer whenever possible and taking

OPPOSITE
*Plymouth Sound: the start of the 1976 OSTAR (*Observer *Single-Handed Transatlantic Race).*

RIGHT
Fujicolor *rounding the Eddystone Lighthouse at the start of the 1996 OSTAR.*

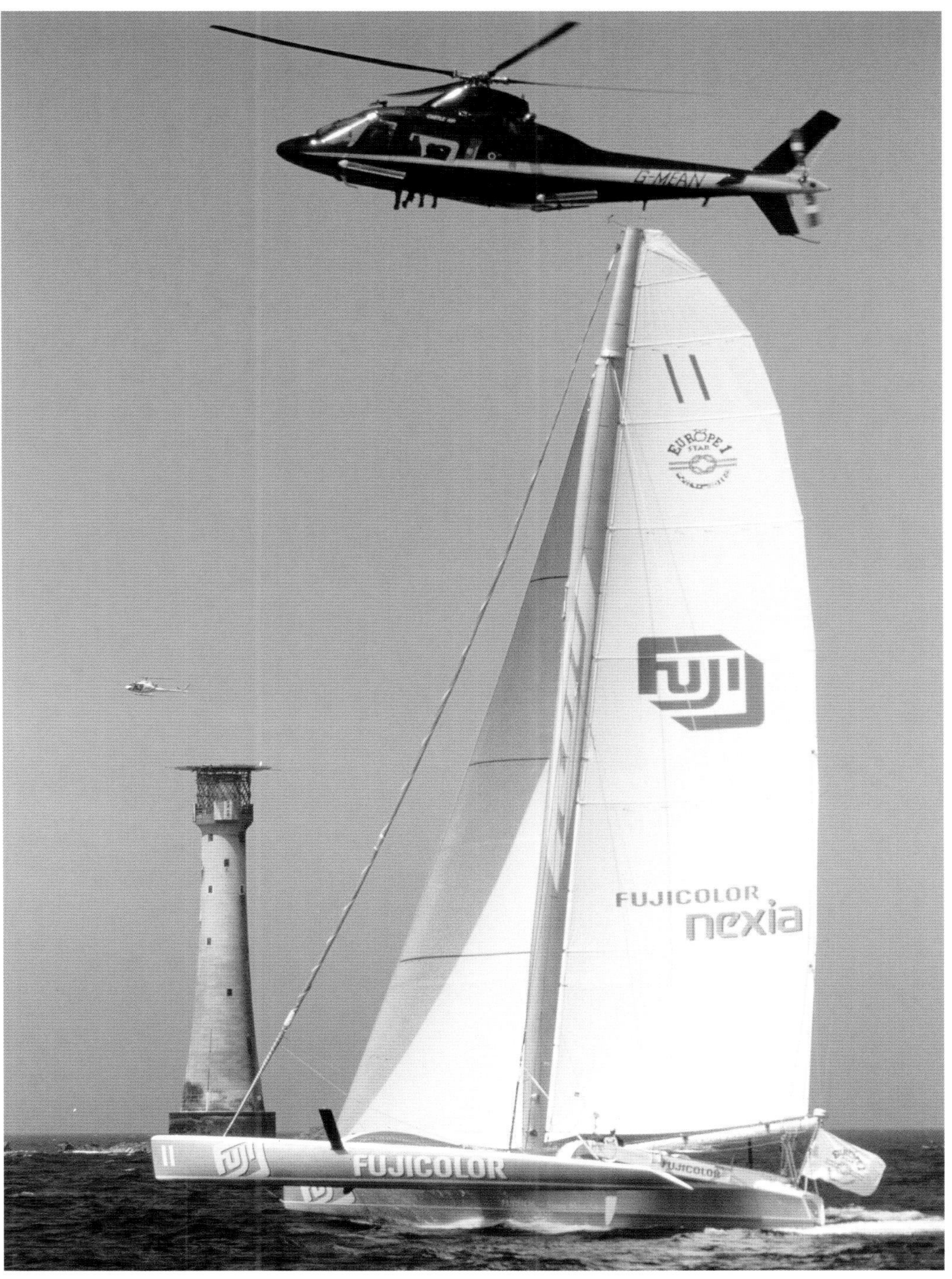

the helm himself when she refused. He won in 27 days, finishing nearly three days ahead of Chichester and five and a half days ahead of third-placed Val Howells, sailing the 35-ft (11-m) *Akka*. Remarkably, apart from one boat that retired and returned to Plymouth, the whole fleet made it to the finish.

The OSTAR has been held every four years ever since. The greatest number of entrants – 125 – congregated at Plymouth for the 1976 race. Such was the enthusiasm for the event that the race committee had received over 600 inquiries about rules and conditions. The starters ranged in size and power from Alain Colas's gigantic 236-ft (72-m) four-masted schooner *Club Mediterranée*, only accepted after the Frenchman's battle with the committee, to a handful of little 25-ft (8-m) boats, including Blondie Hasler's original *Jester*, now sailed by Mike Richey. It proved to be the toughest OSTAR ever sailed with numerous gales, including two depressions, reaching Storm Force 10, battering the fleet. Seventy-three boats finished inside the time limit, but the rest either sank, broke up or retired. For the first and only time there was loss of life. Briton Mike McMullen, whose wife Lizzie had been killed in an accident two days before the start, simply vanished in his trimaran, *Three Cheers* (some wreckage was found in Iceland three years later). Mike Flanagan, an Irishman living in America, was lost overboard from his monohull *Galloping Gael*. The boat was later found sailing with no one on board off the coast of Newfoundland. *Jester*, which would go on to compile a total of eight OSTAR starts, failed for the first time to finish a race. Richey withdrew, signalling the committee: 'Decided to abandon in favour of Irish cruise. No damage. No incident.'

With a superhuman effort, Tabarly finished first in his powerful 73-ft (22-m) ocean-racing monohull, *Pen Duick VI*, which was originally built for racing around the world with a crew of 15. Colas finished seven hours later but was penalized 10 per cent of his time for accepting outside assistance in Halifax, Newfoundland, where he replaced sails and halyards. The third boat to finish, just a day after Tabarly, was the little 31-ft (9.5-m) trimaran *Third Turtle*, designed by Dick Newick and sailed by Mike Birch, a quiet and unassuming Canadian yacht-delivery skipper. It was a stunning performance and the beginning of Birch's outstanding career in short-handed and marathon sailing.

The record for this 2,800-mile (4500-km) race currently stands at 9 days 23 hours, set in 2000 by Francis Joyon in his 60-ft (18-m) trimaran *Eure et Loire*. The 2004 event has been renamed the Transat, with the finishing line at Boston, Massachusetts.

Chapter Six
Lighthouses of the Great Lakes

Illinois

Chicago Harbor Guide Wall Lights

Chicago Harbor, Lake Michigan, IL
Built: 1938
Style: Partially enclosed skeletal towers
No: 20010 and 20012
Focal plane: 30ft (9m)
Range: 9 miles (14.5km)

These two 30-ft lighthouses were built to mark the sea wall guarding Chicago's Navy Pier. Their structure is unusual in that the top section of the tower is enclosed. The open legs offer less resistance to waves breaking over the wall.

Chicago Harbor Light

Chicago, IL
Built: 1832 and 1893
Style: Rubblestone conical tower, floodlit
No: 19960
Position: 41 53 22 N. 87 35 26 W
Focal plane: 82ft (25m)
Range: 24 miles (39km)

This was one of the first stations to be built on the Great Lakes. The original lighthouse was constructed in 1832 to mark the mouth of the Chicago River and was replaced in 1893 by a 48-ft (15-m) rubblestone tower complete with boathouse, keeper's quarters and fog signal. Its third-order Fresnel lens was originally made for a lighthouse in Southern California. The station was automated in 1979.

Grosse Point Light

Evanston, IL
Built: 1873
Style: Conical brick tower

The 113-ft (34.5m) Grosse Point lighthouse is one of the highest towers on the Great Lakes. Built in 1873, the brick lighthouse, with its extensive keeper's dwelling, fog-signal house and outbuildings, was given a second-order Fresnel lens – the most powerful light on the Great Lakes. Grosse Point was decommissioned in 1935 but has since been fully restored.

Indiana

Buffington Breakwater Light

Buffington Harbor, IN
Built: 1926
Style: Conical tower
No: 19630
Position: 41 38 48 N. 87 24 36 W
Focal plane: 48ft (15m)
Range: 15 miles (24km)

The Buffington Breakwater lighthouse stands above the end of the harbour wall, but is now difficult to site in daylight because of the tall buildings that have appeared behind the steel tower since it was built in 1926.

Gary Breakwater Light

Lake Michigan, Gary, IN
Built: 1911
Style: On cylindrical tower
No: 19610
Position: 41 37 48 N. 87 19 12 W
Focal plane: 40ft (12m)
Range: 12 miles (19km)

The 40-ft Gary Breakwater lighthouse was built on the harbour wall in 1911. Painted red, it stands out well against the background of the port.

Indiana East Breakwater Light

East Chicago Harbor, IN
Style: Square tower
No: 19675
Position: 41 40 51 N. 87 26 28 W
Focal plane: 78ft/ 24m, 24ft/7m
Range: 20 miles (32km)
Height: 75ft (23m)

The square steel-constructed Indiana East Breakwater lighthouse stands 75ft above the sea wall and acts as a leading light into East Chicago Harbor.

Michigan City Light

Michigan City, IN
Built: 1837 and 1858
Style: Tower and dwelling

The first lighthouse at Michigan City was a simple brick and stone tower built in 1837. This was replaced in 1858 by the present keeper's dwelling and squat tower mounted on the roof, which held a fifth-order Fresnel lens with a 52-ft (16-m) focal plane. In 1861, Harriet E. Colfax took over the duties of lighthouse keeper and remained at her post until 1904, when she reluctantly retired

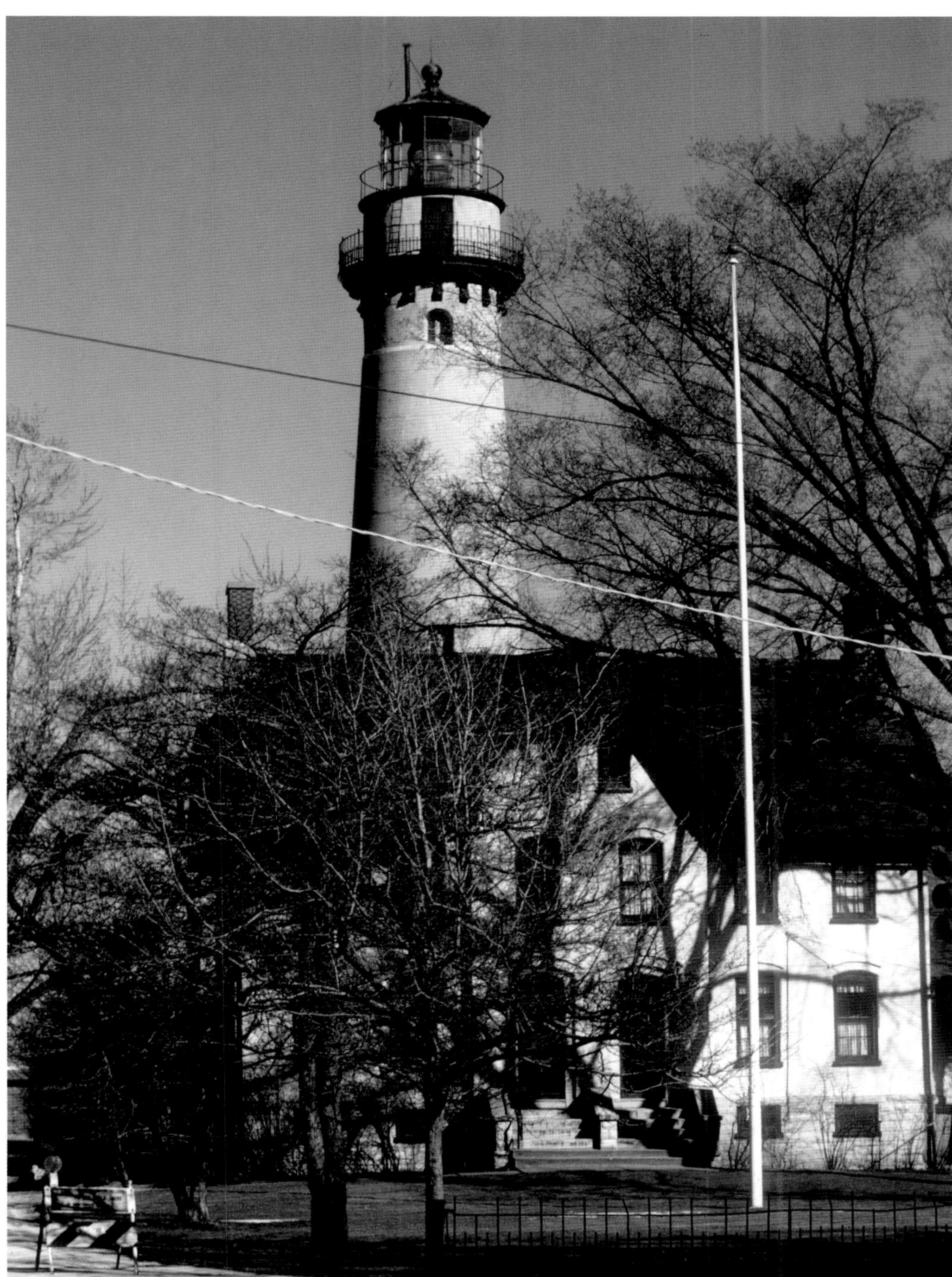

Grosse Point Light, Illinois.

at the age of 80. That same year the lighthouse was deactivated, and the building is now managed by the Michigan City Historical Society and serves as a museum.

Michigan City East Pier Light

Michigan City, IN
Built: 1904
Style: Octagonal tower attached to building
No: 19545
Position: 41 43 42 N. 86 54 42 W
Focal plane: 55ft (17m)
Range: 12 miles (19km)
Height: 49ft (15m)

The lighthouse was built in 1904 to guide vessels into the city harbour. Constructed on a square concrete platform, the octagonal tower has a pyramid-shaped roof above the lantern and is sheathed in steel to protect it from storms. The station houses a fog signal and a rotating 2130c optic lens, which replaced its fifth-order Fresnel lens when the tower was automated in 1960.

Old Michigan City Light

Michigan City Harbor, IN
Built: 1853 and 1858
Style: Square tower on top of keeper's house

There have been at least two Old Michigan City lighthouses. The first proper tower, built in 1853, was a 40-ft (12-m) structure which was later superseded by a light tower built on the roof of the house built for the keeper on land deeded to the city by Isaac and Maria Elston. This housed a fifth-order Fresnel lens in the roof top tower to give the light a focal plane of 52ft (16m). In 1904, the light was transferred to a new tower built on the pier but the house was retained for the keeper. The building is now managed by the Michigan City Historical Society, which has transformed it into a museum.

Michigan

Alpena Light

Alpena, MI
Built: 1875, 1914
Style: Square pyramidal
No: 11370
Position: 45 03 36 N. 83 25 24 W
Focal plane: 44ft (13m)
Range: 13 miles (21km)
Height: 14ft (4m)

The present Alpena Light, marking the entrance to Thunder Bay, is known locally as the Sputnik for its resemblance to an early space vehicle. It was built in 1914 to replace an earlier tower dating back to 1875 and is fitted with a fourth-order Fresnel lens.

Beaver Island Harbor Light (St. James)

Beaver Island, MI
Built: 1856 and 1870
Style: Cylindrical

The present 41-ft (12.5-m) lighthouse marks the entry to the port. It replaced an earlier lighthouse built in 1856, which proved too small to provide a clear light.

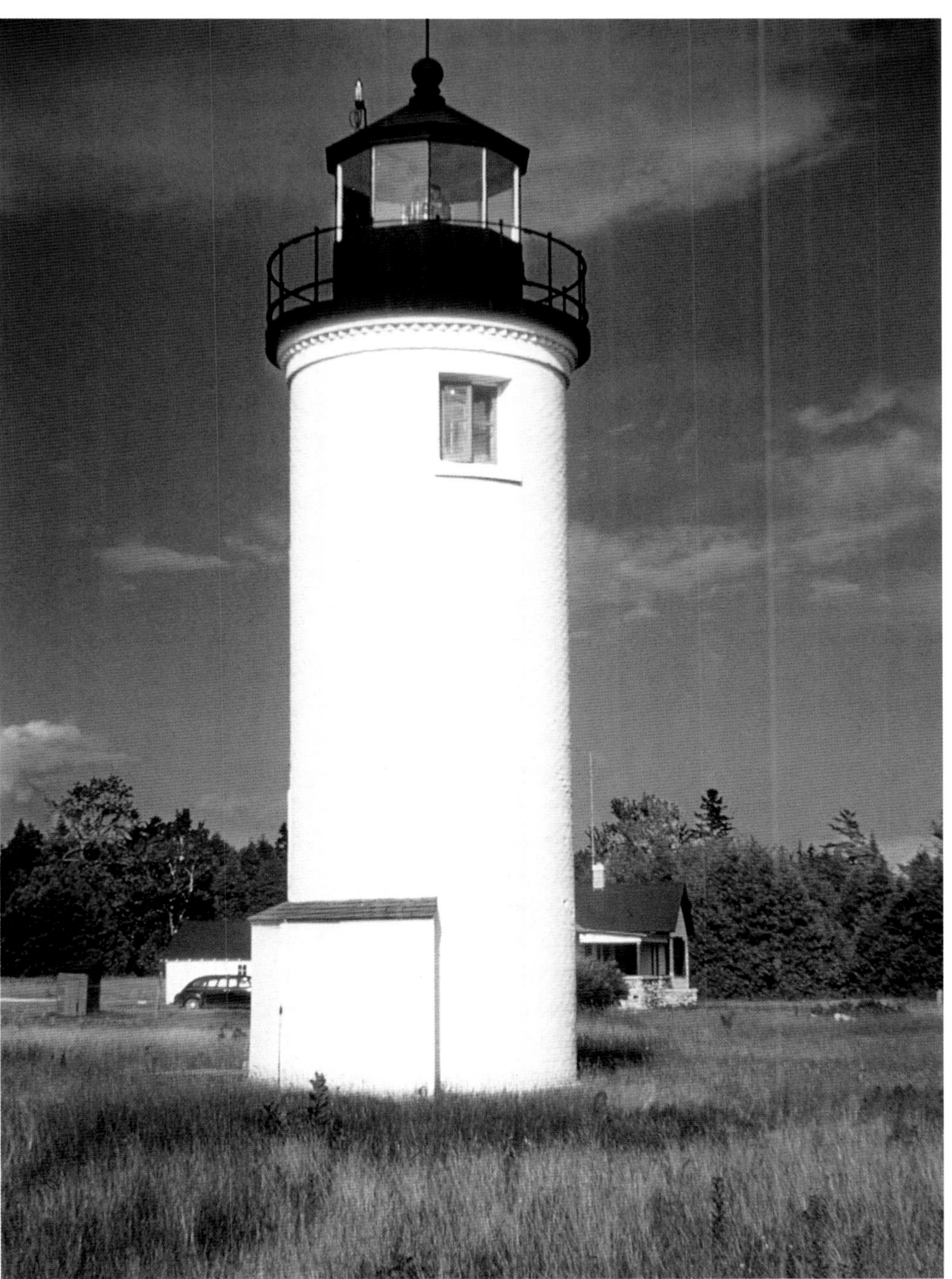

OPPOSITE
Michigan City Light, Indiana.

LEFT
Beaver Island Harbor Light (St. James), Michigan.

Beaver Island Light

Beaver Island, MI
Built: 1851 and 1858.
Style: Cylindrical tower
No: 16570
Position: 47 16 48 N. 91 15 30 W
Focal plane: 20ft (6m)
Range: 6 miles (10km)

The first lighthouse on Beaver Island was built in 1851 to guide vessels through the western approaches to the Mackinac Straits. The building lasted less than 7 years and a second 46-ft (14-m) brick tower was built in its place in 1858. This was fitted with a fourth-order Fresnel lens, which remained in use until the lighthouse was deactivated in 1970. The building is now an environmental education centre for Charlevoix County schools.

Big Bay Point Light

Big Bay, MI
Built: 1896
Style: Square tower and attached dwelling

The brick-built lighthouse and its attached keeper's house was built in 1896 to guide vessels across an otherwise darkened stretch of water to the north of the Huron Mountain range. The station, which was equipped with a third-order Fresnel lens, continued to operate until 1941 when the light was moved to a skeletal tower erected nearby. The house has since been restored and is now a bed and breakfast inn.

Big Sable Point Light

Ludington, MI
Built: 1876
Style: Conical
No: 18525
Position: 44 03 30 N. 86 30 54 W
Focal Plane: 106ft (32m)
Range: 15 miles (24km)
Height: 107ft (33m)

The lighthouse was built in 1876 to warn vessels to keep clear of the west Michigan shore. By 1920 the lighthouse was in danger of collapsing and the tower was encased in iron plating and painted with distinctive black and white stripes. The lighthouse, which was fitted with a third-order Fresnel lens, remains active, and is now managed by the Ludington State Park.

Bois Blanc Island Light

Cheboygan, MI
Built: 1829
Style: Square tower

The 38-ft (11.5-m) brick lighthouse was built in 1829 to illuminate the Straits of Mackinac. The station was decommissioned in 1924 and the light transferred to a skeletal tower. The original house is now a private dwelling.

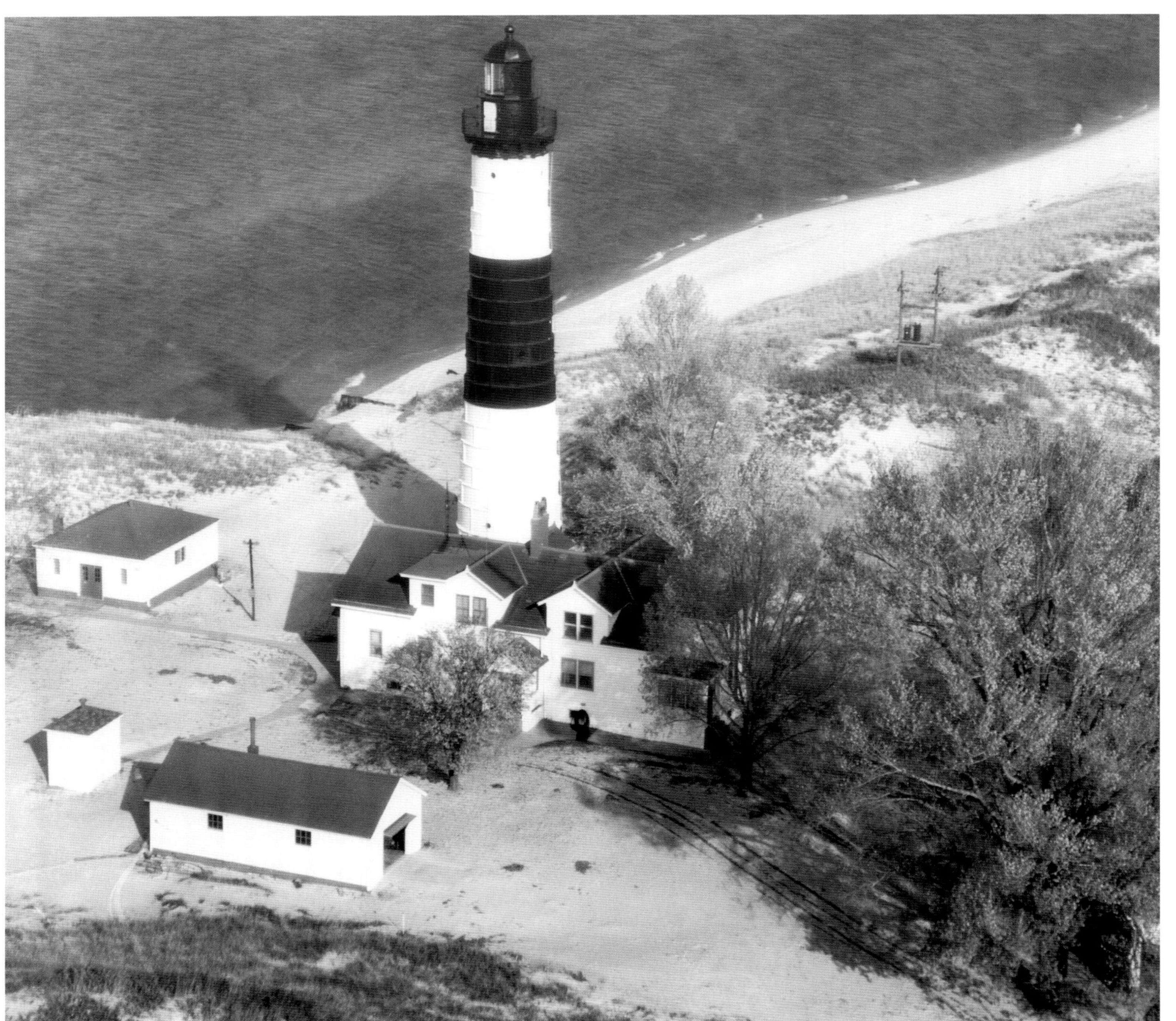

LEFT
Big Sable Point Light, Michigan.

OPPOSITE
Big Bay Point Light, Michigan.

Charlevoix South Pierhead Light

Charlevoix, MI
Built: 1885 and 1948
Style: Square tower
No: 17925
Position: 45 19 13 N. 85 15 53 W
Focal Plane: 41ft (12.5m)
Range: 12 miles (19km)

The first Charlevoix South Pierhead lighthouse was built in 1885 to mark the channel between the little Lake Charlevoix and Lake Michigan. The original wooden tower was replaced in 1948 with a square steel tower and was subsequently automated and fitted with a solar-powered optic lens.

Cheboygan Crib Light

Cheboygan, MI
Built: 1910 and 1988
Style: Octagonal

The 25-ft (8-m) Cheboygan Crib began life as an offshore lighthouse. Fitted with a fourth-order Fresnel lens, the cast-iron tower was salvaged in 1988 after the concrete and stone crib it stood on began to sink into the lake. The lighthouse was then re-erected at the end of a small pier in Gordon Turner Park, Cheboygan.

LEFT
Bois Blanc Island Light, Michigan.

OPPOSITE
Cheboygan Crib Light, Michigan.

Cheboygan River Range Light

Cheboygan, MI
Built: 1880
Style: Square tower

The wooden Cheboygan River Range Light, with its two-storey keeper's dwelling, was built in 1880 to guide vessels into Cheboygan harbour and was fitted with a sixth-order Fresnel lens. The light was decommissioned many years ago and the building is now maintained as a government office.

Copper Harbor Light

Copper Harbor, MI
Built: 1849 and 1869
Style: White skeleton tower near dwelling
No: 15175
Position: 47 28 30 N. 87 51 36 W
Focal plane: 90ft/27m, 27ft/8m
Range: 21 miles (34km)
Height: 62ft (19m)

The first Copper Harbor lighthouse was built in 1849, five years after a mineral find gave this town its name, to guide an increasing level of shipping into the port. In 1856 the stone tower was updated with a fourth-order

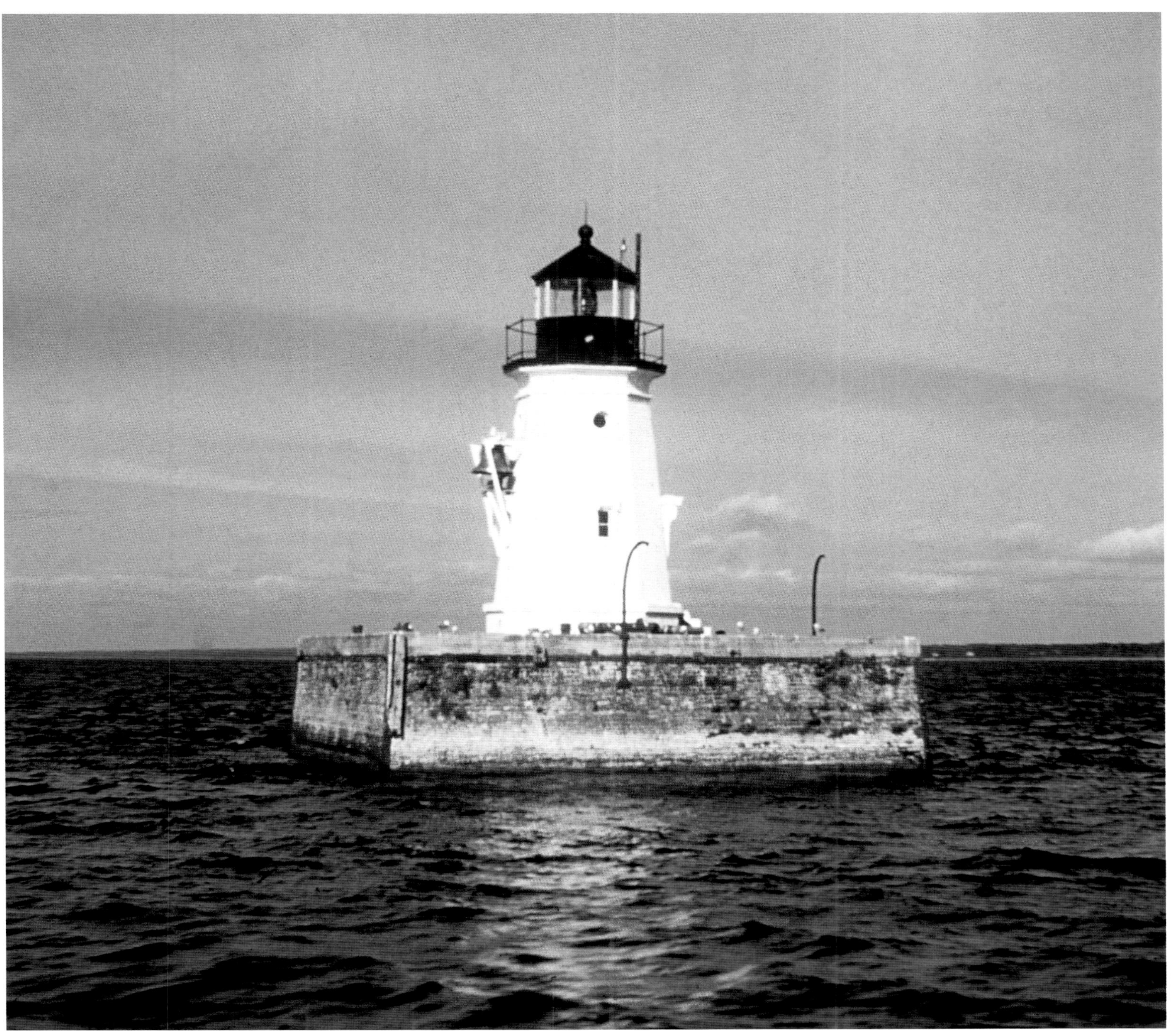

Fresnel lens, which was then transferred to the present tower built on the water's edge in 1869.

Copper Harbor Rear Range Light

Copper Harbor, MI
Built: 1849, 1869 and 1933
Style: Skeletal tower
No: 15190
Focal plane: W 41ft/12.5m, R 12ft/4m
Range: 32 miles (51.5km)

The first lighthouse was built in 1849 as part of an updating navigation programme for the harbour. The 42-ft (13-m) square tower was attached to Fort Wilkins and was equipped with a parabolic reflector. This beam was replaced by a sixth-order Fresnel lens in 1856 and a fourth-order lens in 1859. In 1933, the light was transferred to an 60-ft (18-m) steel tower erected at the water's edge.

Crisp Point Light

Paradise, MI
Built: 1904
Style: Conical

Crisp Point lighthouse was built in 1904 to illuminate the remote Whitefish Point on Lake Superior. The 58-ft (18-m) conical brick tower was equipped with a fourth-order Fresnel lens. The station's buildings were all torn down when the tower was automated in 1965 and the light continued in service until 1993. The building is now managed by the Crisp Point Lighthouse Society.

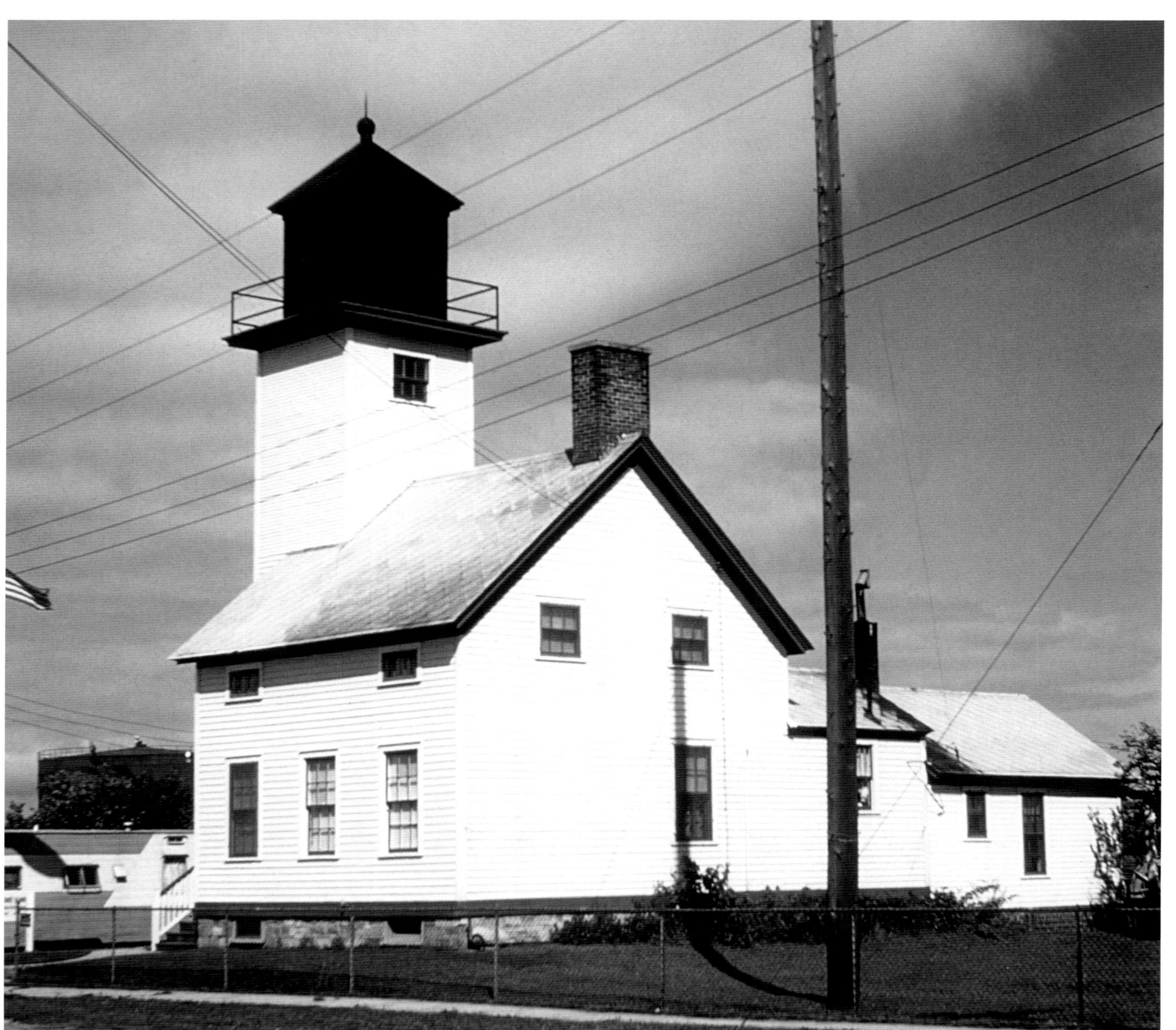

LEFT
Cheboygan River Range Light, Michigan.

OPPOSITE LEFT
De Tour Reef Light, Michigan.

OPPOSITE RIGHT
Detroit River Light, Michigan.

De Tour Reef Light

De Tour, MI
Built: 1847 and 1931
Style: Square superstructure on concrete crib
No: 12770
Position: 46 56 54 N. 83 54 12 W
Focal plane: 74ft (22.5m)
Range: R 15 miles/24km, W 18 miles/29km
Height: 23ft (7m)

The first lighthouse was built in 1847 to guide vessels into the mouth of the St. Mary's River on Lake Huron. The present tower was built in 1931 and still has its original three-and-a-half-order Fresnel lens.

Detroit River Light

South Rockwood, MI
Built: 1885
Style: Conical tower with hexagonal upper section
No: 6885
Position: 42 00 00 N. 83 08 30 W
Focal plane: 55ft/17m,17ft/5m
Range: 10 miles (16km)
Height: 49ft (15m)

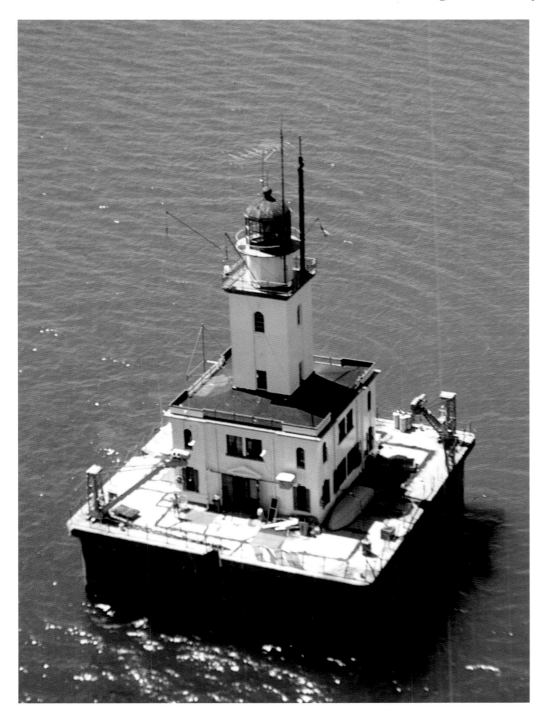

The Detroit River lighthouse was built in 1885 to mark the dangerous Bar Point Shoal extending out from the Canadian shore. The lighthouse was built on a prefabricated crib and still utilizes its original fourth-order Fresnel lens.

Eagle Harbor Light

Keweenaw Peninsula, MI
Built: 1851 and 1871
Style: Octagonal tower on red dwelling
No: 15195
Position: 47 27 36 N 88 09 30 W
Focal plane: 60ft/18m, 18ft/5.5m
Range: W 29 miles/47km, R 22 miles/35km
Height: 44ft (13.5m)

The Keweenaw Peninsula was a prime mining area for copper during the mid-19th century. Eagle Harbor Light was built in 1851 to guide the ships into the harbor to load ore. The light was first equipped with Argand lamps and parabolic reflectors, but these were replaced with a fourth-order Fresnel lens in 1857. Twenty winters spent on the edge of Lake Superior took their toll on the tower and in 1871 the present brick tower was built in its place. The original Fresnel lens continued to serve in the new lighthouse until it was replaced by an aero-beacon in 1968. The tower was finally automated in 1980.

LEFT
Eagle Harbor Light, Michigan.

OPPOSITE
Fort Gratiot Light, Michigan.

Eagle River Light

Eagle River, MI
Built: 1854
Style: Cylindrical on square base

The Eagle River is another lighthouse on the Keweenaw Peninsula to date back to the copper-mining era in the mid-19th century. The station served from 1854 to 1908 and is now a private residence.

Escanaba Harbor Light

Escanaba, MI
Built: 1938
Style: Square crib tower

The Escanaba Harbor lighthouse was built in 1938 on a round, concrete crib to mark a shoal at the entrance to this Lake Michigan port. The light was automated in 1976.

Fort Gratiot Light

Port Huron, MI
Built: 1825, 1829 and 1861
Style: Conical
No: 9990
Position: 42 59 36 N. 82 25 36 W
Range: 11 miles (18km)
Height: 81ft (25m)

Established in 1825, the first lighthouse at

Fort Gratiot was built to guide the growing number of immigrant ships into Port Huron, but its construction was so shoddy that the wooden tower collapsed within four years. The present stone and brick tower was erected in 1829, and is the oldest lighthouse in Michigan. The tower was extended to 81ft in 1861 and was fitted with a fifth-order Fresnel lens in 1861. It was automated in 1933.

Forty Mile Point Light

Rogers City, MI
Built: 1897
Style: Square tower
No: 11715
Position: 45 29 12 N. 83 54 48 W
Focal Plane: 66ft (20m)
Range: 20 miles (32m)
Height: 53ft (16m)

The lighthouse was built in 1897 to guide shipping between the last dark stretch of water on the Great Lakes between Cheboygan and Presque Isle. The square tower is equipped with a fourth-order Fresnel lens and is attached to a quaint keeper's dwelling that features two gables. The station, which is surrounded by beautiful grounds and a long stretch of beach, also includes a brick oil house and fog-signal building.

Fourteen Foot Shoal Light

Cheboygan, MI
Built: 1930
Style: Conical tower on concrete crib

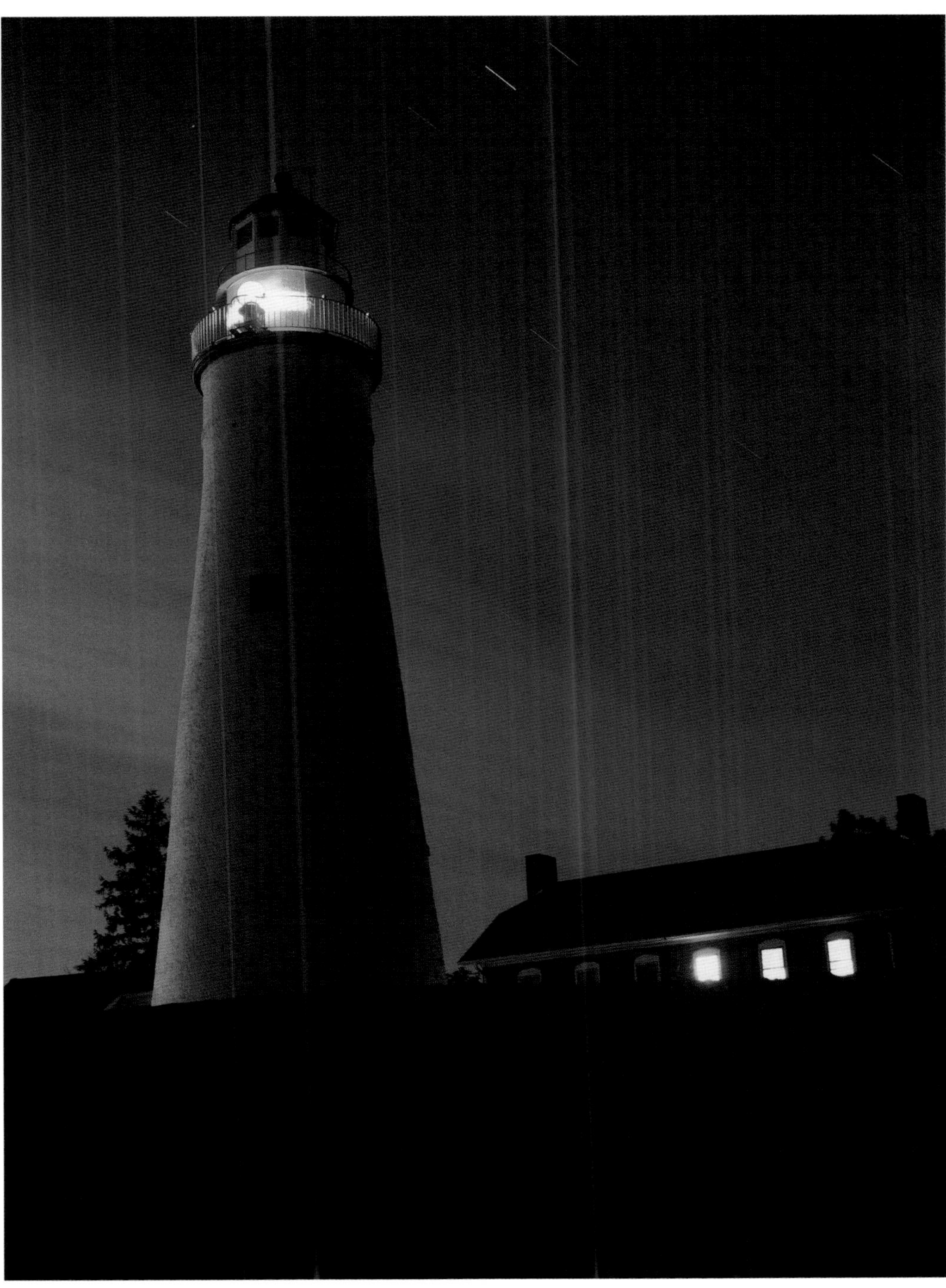

No: 11765
Position: 45 40 48 N. 84 26 06 W
Focal plane: 16ft (5m)
Range: 10 miles (16km)

The lighthouse was built in 1930 to guide vessels into Cheboygan Harbor and was operated remotely from Poe Lighthouse. The lighthouse, which stands on the roof of a fog-signal building, was equipped with a fourth-order lens which has since been replaced with a modern 250mm optic.

Fourteen Mile Point Light

Rogers City, MI
Built: 1897
Style: Brick tower

The 55-ft (17-m) lighthouse was built in 1897 in one of the most remote areas of the Great Lakes. The brick-built tower was automated in 1934 and its acetylene gas light continued to brighten the night sky until a fire gutted the station in 1984. The lighthouse is now in private hands and is undergoing full restoration.

Frankfort North Breakwater Light

Frankfort, MI
Built: 1873 and 1932
Style: Square pyramidal tower
No: 18375
Position: 44 37 54 N. 86 15 06 W
Focal plane: 22ft (7m)
Range: 16 miles (26km)
Height: 67ft (20m)

Frankfort North Breakwater Light, Michigan.

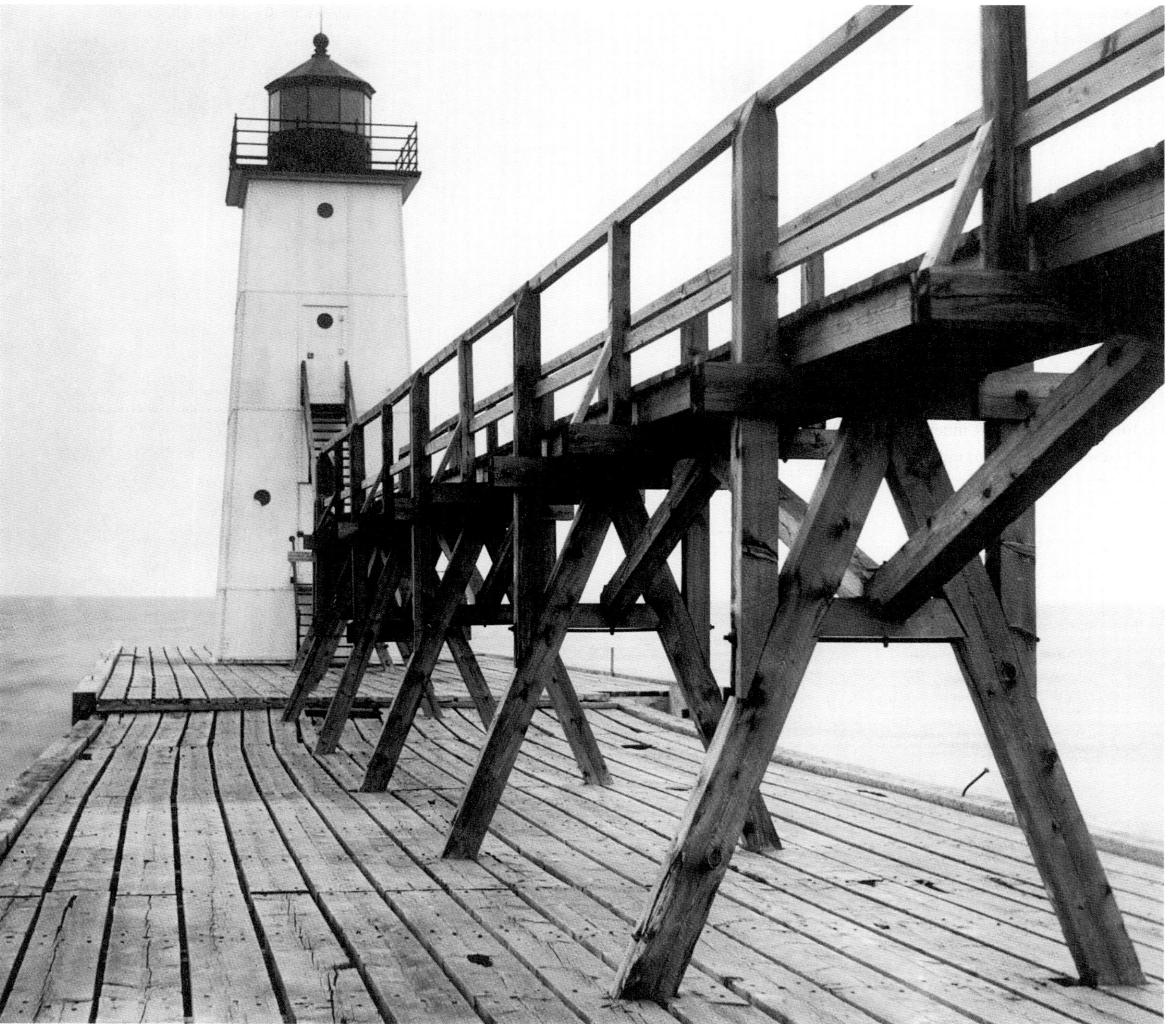

The lighthouse was built in 1932 to replace an earlier tower overlooking the eastern shores of Lake Michigan, built in 1873. It still retains its original fifth-order Fresnel lens.

Grand Haven Pier Lights

Grand Haven, MI
Built: 1895 and 1905
Style: Cylindrical tower and square building
No: 18965
Position: 43 03 25 N. 86 15 22 W
Focal plane: 42ft (13m)
Range: 13 miles (21km)

South Pierhead Inner Light

No: 18975
Focal plane: 52ft (16m)
Range: 16 miles (26km)
Height: 51ft (15.5m)

These striking lighthouses stand at the entrance to Grand Haven River, one of Michigan's deepest harbours. The inner light is a red-painted steel tower equipped with a sixth-order Fresnel lens. The wooden Pier Light was once a foghorn tower; it was moved to its present location and encased in iron plates when the pier was extended in 1905.

Grand Marais Harbor Range Lights

Grand Marais, MI
Built: 1895 and 1898

Style: Skeletal towers
No: 14550 (Harbor of Refuge Outer Light)
Position: 46 41 00 N. 85 58 18 W
Focal plane: 40ft (12m)
Range: 12 miles (19km)
Height: 34ft (10m)

No: 14560 (Harbor of Refuge Inner Light)
Focal pane: 54ft (16.5m)
Range: 16 miles (26km)
Height: 47ft (14m)

The two skeletal range lights guiding vessels into Grand Marais harbour were built in the 1890s. The outer lighthouse was first to be lit, followed by its 47-ft inner tandem light. Both have a watch room built beneath their lanterns.

Grand Traverse Light

Northport, MI
Built: 1853
Style: Square tower and integrated dwelling

Built in 1853 on Cat Head Point, the Grand Traverse lighthouse, with its imposing brick-built two-storey keeper's house, guided vessels into Grand Traverse. Fitted with a fourth-order Fresnel lens, the lighthouse served mariners for 119 years until it was decommissioned in 1972. The station is now a lighthouse museum.

Granite Island Light

Granite Island, MI
Built: 1869
Style: Square tower, attached building

The 40-ft (12-m) Granite Island lighthouse and its two-storey limestone keeper's cottage was built in 1869. The tower was fitted with a fourth-order Fresnel lens and was automated in 1939, but following its decommission, has fallen into disrepair. The station is now in private hands.

Gravelly Shoal Light

Standish, MI
Built: 1839
Style: Square tower on cylindrical base
No: 10540
Positiion: 44 01 12 N. 83 32 18 W
Focal plane: 75ft (23m)
Range: 23 miles (37km)
Height: 11ft (3m)

The lighthouse, built on a pier off Standish in 1839, replaced Charity Island Lighthouse. The art-deco steel tower was automated from the outset.

Grays Reef Light

Lake Michigan East Straight Passage, MI
Built: 1891 and 1936
Style: Octagonal
No: 17775
Positiion: 45 46 00 N. 85 09 12 W
Focal plane: 82ft (25m)
Range: 25 miles (40km)
Height: 15ft (4.5m)

The Grays Reef Light was built in 1936 and is manned each year during the annual Bayview–Mackinac yacht race. A light was first established on the reef close to the Mackinac Straits in 1891, but the role of warning vessels was then taken over by a lightship until the present crib-based tower was completed. The lighthouse was automated in 1976.

Grosse Île Channel Light

Grosse Îsle, MI
Built: 1894
Style: Octagonal

The 50-ft (15-m) Grosse Île North Channel Front Lighthouse was erected on the lower Detroit River in 1984. The station was decommissioned in 1963 and is now managed by the Grosse Île Historical Society.

Gull Rock Light

Copper Harbor, MI
Built: 1867
Style: Square tower on dwelling
No: 15165
Position: 47 25 00 N. 87 39 48 W
Focal plane: 50ft (15m)
Range: 9 miles/14.5km, 46 miles/74km
Height: 15ft (4.5m)

The lighthouse was built in 1867 to stand guard over a rock outside Copper Harbor that threatened the ships carrying ore from the port. The brick tower was equipped with a fourth-order lens, which was replaced with a 250-mm solar-powered optic when the station was automated.

Harbor Beach Light

Harbor Beach, MI
Built: 1885
Style: Conical tower
No: 10130
Position: 43 50 42 N. 82 37 54 W
Focal plane: 16ft (5m)
Range: W 19 miles/30km, R 16 miles/26km

The 45-ft (14-m) cast-iron lighthouse was constructed in 1885. This 'spark-plug' tower was fitted with a fourth-order Fresnel lens, which was replaced with a 190-mm optic when the station was automated in 1968. The Fresnel lens is now on display at the Grice Museum.

Holland Harbor Light

Holland, MI
Built: 1872 and 1936
Style: Square tower

The first Holland Harbor lighthouse to shine out over Black Lake was built in 1872 but eventually succumbed to the harsh winter storms and ice. Its 1936 replacement was sheathed in steel to provide additional protection. The tower rises from the substantial keeper's dwelling, the whole structure being painted red – hence its nickname, 'Big Red'. It held a sixth-order Fresnel lens until the station was decommissioned in 1970.

Huron Island Light

Skanee, MI
Built:1868
Style: Granite tower on dwelling
No: 14730
Focal plane: 197ft/60m, 60ft/18m

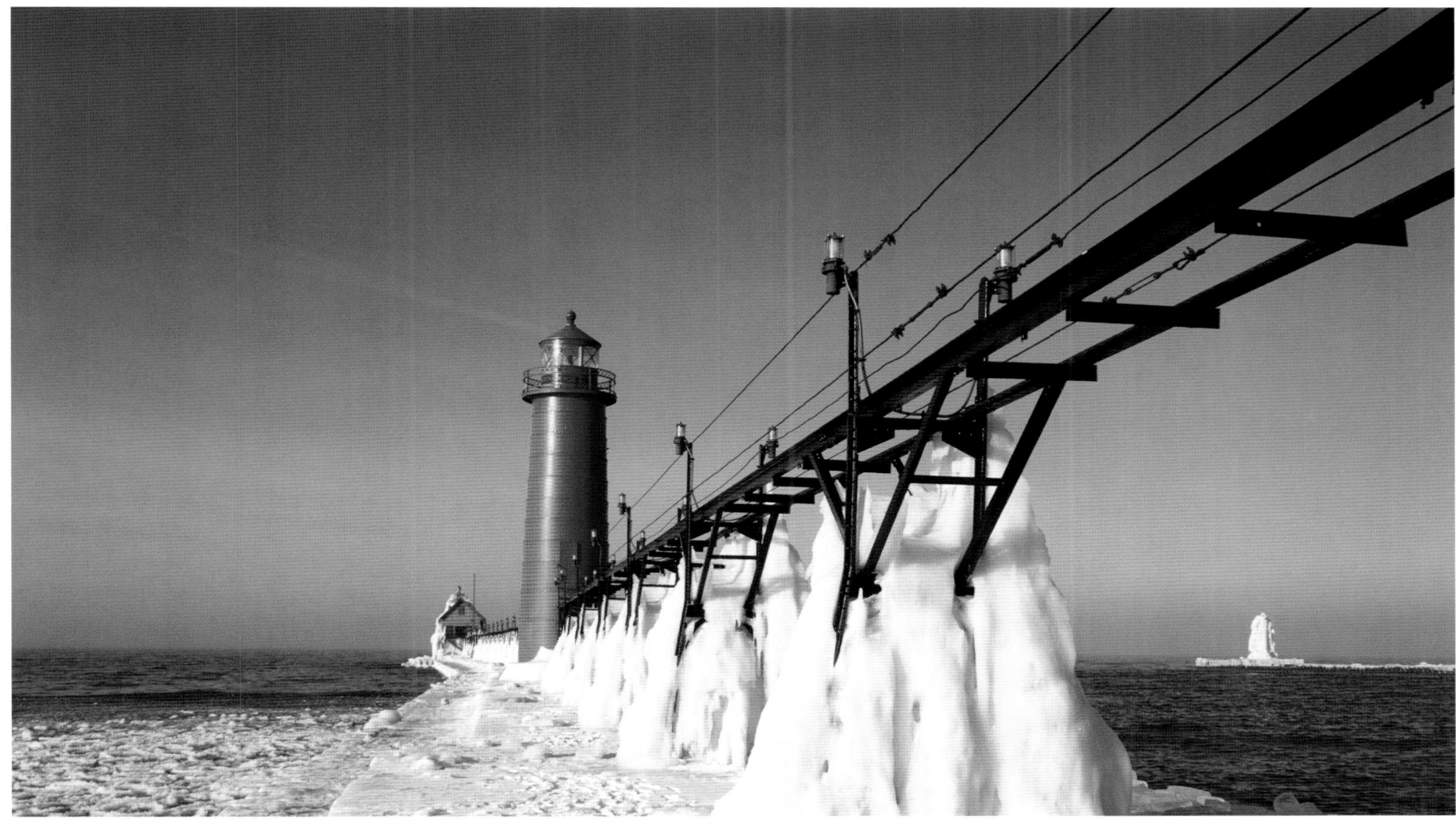

OPPOSITE and LEFT
Grand Traverse Light, Michigan.

Range: 15 miles (24km)
Height: 39ft (12m)

The lighthouse was built high on West Huron Island to improve navigation around this and Granite Island. The brick-built tower and its attached two-storey keeper's dwelling stands above the lake waters, and holds a three-and-a-half-order Fresnel lens. The station was automated in 1972.

Huron Lightship

Port Huron, MI
Built: 1920
Builder: Consolidated Shipbuilding Co., NY
No: 103
Length overall: 96ft 05in (29m)
Beam: 24ft (7m)
Draft: 9ft 06in (3m)
Displacement: 310 tons
Propulsion: Steam/Diesel
Illuminating Apparatus: One 300-mm acetylene lens lantern

Station Assignments:
1921–23: Relief
1924–26: Grays Reef (MI)
1927–28: Relief (Twelfth District)
1929: Grays Reef (MI)
1929–33: Relief (Twelfth District)
1934–35: North Manitou Shoal (MI)
1935: Relief (Eleventh District)
1936–70: Lake Huron (MI)

The *Huron* is the last surviving lightship on the Great Lakes. The relief vessel was the only black-painted lightship in service and operated right around Lake Michigan for much of its active life. She was equipped originally with a steam engine but this was replaced with a diesel engine in 1949. The ship was finally decommissioned in 1970 and is now the centrepiece of the Port Huron Marine Museum.

Isle Royale Light

Isle Royale, MI
Built: 1875
Style: Octagonal tower with attached house
No: 16710
Position: 47 56 54 N. 88 45 42 W
Focal plane: 72ft/22m, 22ft/7m
Range: 16 miles (26km)
Height: 61ft (18.5m)

This lighthouse stands on a rock overlooking Siskiwit Bay. The lantern room houses a fourth-order Fresnel lens, which was automated in 1913.

Keweenaw Waterway Lower Entrance Light

Jacobsville, MI
Built: 1868 and 1920
Style: Octagonal

The 31-ft (9.5-m) lighthouse, which is known locally as the Portage Lake Light, replaced an earlier tower that dated back to 1868. The station is equipped with a fourth-order Fresnel lens and automated in 1973.

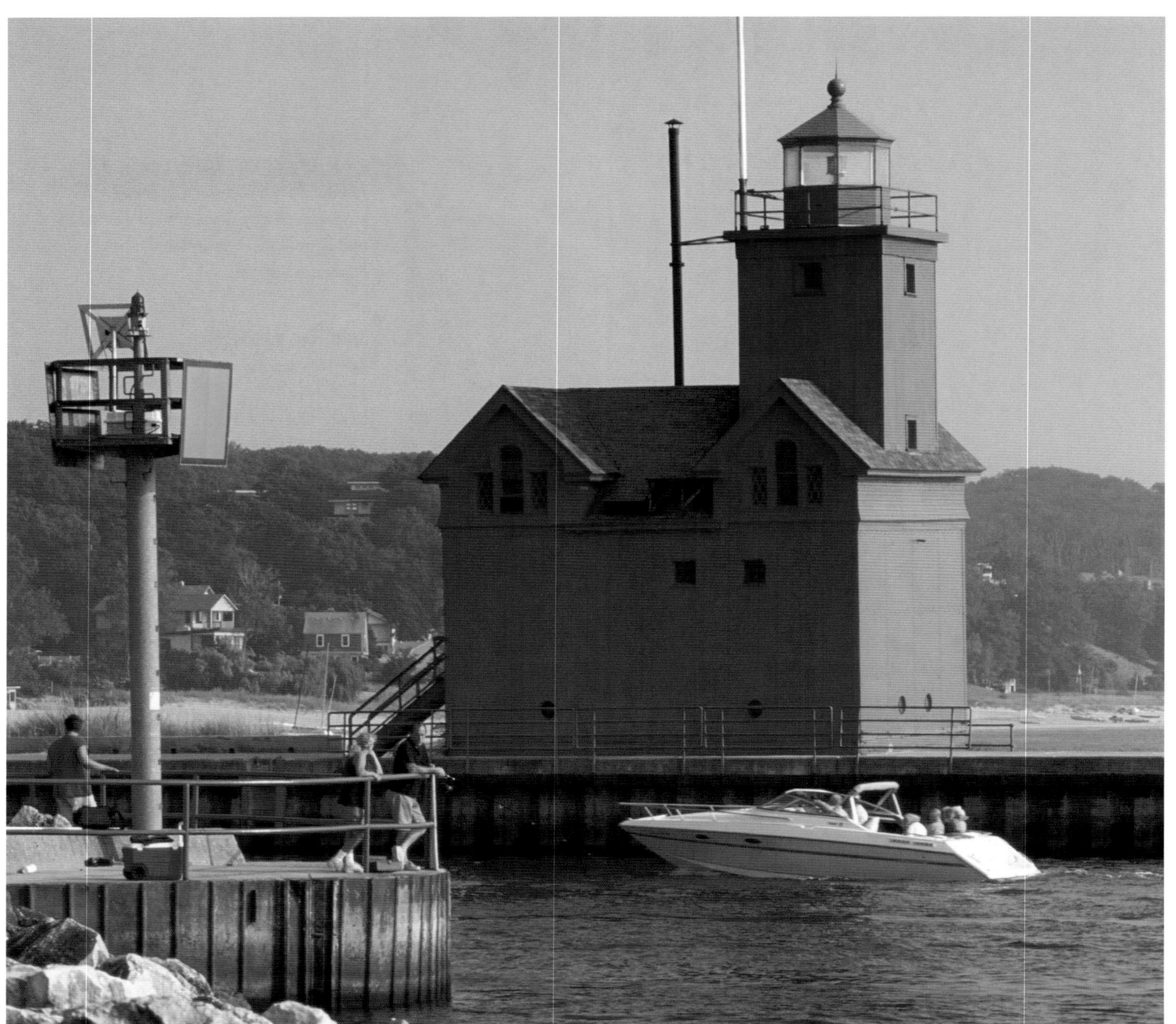

LEFT
Holland Harbor Light, Michigan.

OPPOSITE
Keweenaw Pierhead Light, Michigan.

Keweenaw Pierhead Light
Houghton, MI
Built: 1874 and 1950
Style: Square tower on fog-signal building
No: 20955
Position: 44 27 30 N. 87 29 48 W
Focal plane: 45ft (14m)
Range: 14 miles (22.5km)

The present art deco-style lighthouse tower, standing at the end of the harbour's breakwater, was built in 1950 to replace a 30-ft (9-m) tower and attached dwelling that dated back to 1874.

Lake St. Clair Light
Lake St. Clair, MI
Built: 1941
Style: Square tower on cylindrical base
No: 8525
Position: 42 27 54 N. 82 45 18 W
Focal plane: 52ft (16m)
Range: 16 miles (26km)

The Lake St. Clair lighthouse stands on a concrete crib between the Detroit and St. Clair Rivers.

Lansing Shoal Light
Naubinway, MI

Built: 1900
Style: Square tower on concrete crib
No: 21535
Position: 45 54 12 N. 85 33 42 W
Focal plane: 69ft/21m, 21ft/6.5m
Range: 15 miles (24km)
Height: 59ft (18m)

The concrete lighthouse was built in 1900 to mark this Lake Michigan hazard. The tower was equipped with a third-order Fresnel lens, but this was replaced with a 190-mm solar-powered optic when the station was automated in 1976.

Little Sable Point Light

Mears, MI
Built: 1874
Style: Conical brick tower
No: 18645
Position: 43 39 09 N. 86 32 24 W
Focal plane: 108ft (33m)
Range: 17 miles (27km)
Height: 107ft (33m)

This was the model for its nearby sister tower completed two years later on Big Sable Point. The two towers are both 107 ft high, built of brick, and were each fitted with a third-order Fresnel lens. The difference between them now is that while Little Sable remains very much as it was built, its sister tower has had to be encased in ironwork to stop it from falling down. Little Sable was automated in 1954 when the keeper's dwelling and outhouses were demolished.

Little Traverse Light

Harbor Springs, MI
Built: 1884
Style: Square tower, integrated dwelling

The 40-ft (12-m) lighthouse was built in 1884 to provide a navigation bearing across Little Traverse Bay. The square brick tower and its attached dwelling held a fourth-order Fresnel lens until the station was decommissioned in 1963. The lighthouse is now a private home.

Ludington North Breakwater Light

Ludington, MI
Built: 1924
Style: Square pyramidal tower
No: 18530
Position: 43 57 12 N. 86 28 12 W
Focal plane: 55ft (17m)
Range: 17 miles (27km)

The lighthouse's white steel tower, which has now developed a distinct list, was equipped with a fourth-order Fresnel lens, but this has been on display at the White Pine Village Maritime Museum since the station was automated and the lens replaced with a modern optic.

Mackinac (Old) Point Light

Mackinaw City, MI
Built: 1892
Style: Cylindrical with attached dwelling

Built in 1892, the 40-ft (12-m) Mackinac Point lighthouse and its castle-like dwelling, continued in service until 1957, when the station was made obsolete by a bridge built over the Mackinac Strait. The building is now used as an information centre and maritime museum within an historic park.

Manistee North Pierhead Light

Manistee, MI
Built: 1927
Style: Cylindrical
No: 18450
Position: 44 15 07 N. 86 20 49 W
Focal plane: 55ft/17m, 17ft/5m

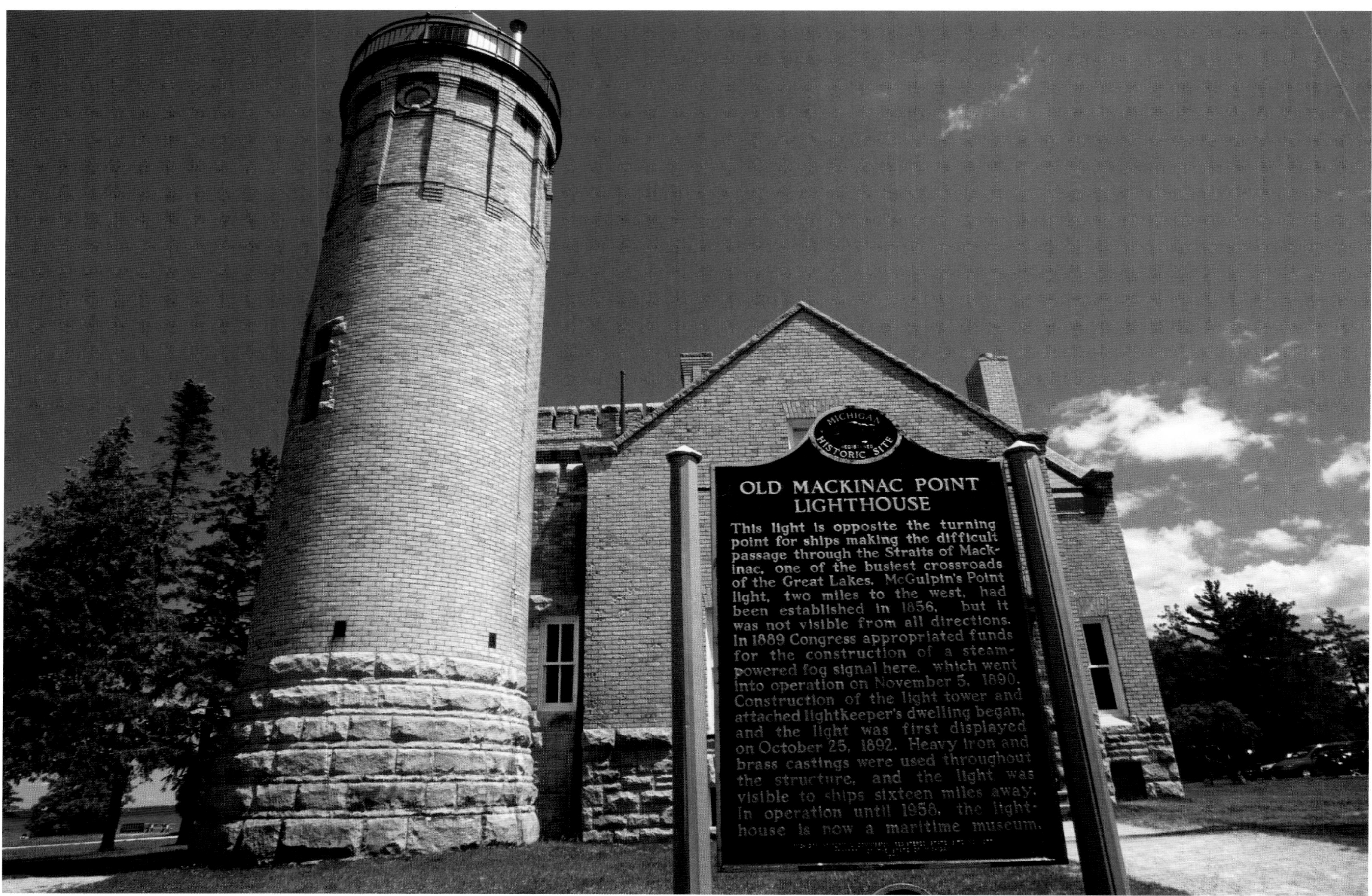
MICHIGAN
HISTORIC SITE
OLD MACKINAC POINT
LIGHTHOUSE
This light is opposite the turning point for ships making the difficult passage through the Straits of Mackinac, one of the busiest crossroads of the Great Lakes. McGulpin's Point light, two miles to the west, had been established in 1856, but it was not visible from all directions. In 1889 Congress appropriated funds for the construction of a steam-powered fog signal here, which went into operation on November 5, 1890. Construction of the light tower and attached lightkeeper's dwelling began, and the light was first displayed on October 25, 1892. Heavy iron and brass castings were used throughout the structure, and the light was visible to ships sixteen miles away. In operation until 1958, the lighthouse is now a maritime museum.

OPPOSITE
Mackinac Point Light, Michigan.

RIGHT
Manistee North Pierhead Light, Michigan.

Range: 15 miles (24km)
Height: 39ft (12m)

The lighthouse was built in 1927 at the entrance to the Manistee River. The steel tower was equipped with a fifth-order Fresnel lens but this was replaced with a modern 300-mm optic when the station was automated.

Manistique Light, Manistique

Manistique, MI
Built: 1915
Style: Short tower
No: 21475
Position: 45 56 42 N. 86 14 48 W
Focal plane: 50ft (15m)
Range: 15 miles (24km)
Height: 11ft (3.5m)

The lighthouse's cast-iron tower was equipped with a fourth-order Fresnel lens, but this was replaced with a 300-mm optic when the station was automated in 1969.

Manitou Island Light

Calumet, MI
Built: 1850 and 1861
Style: Skeletal tower

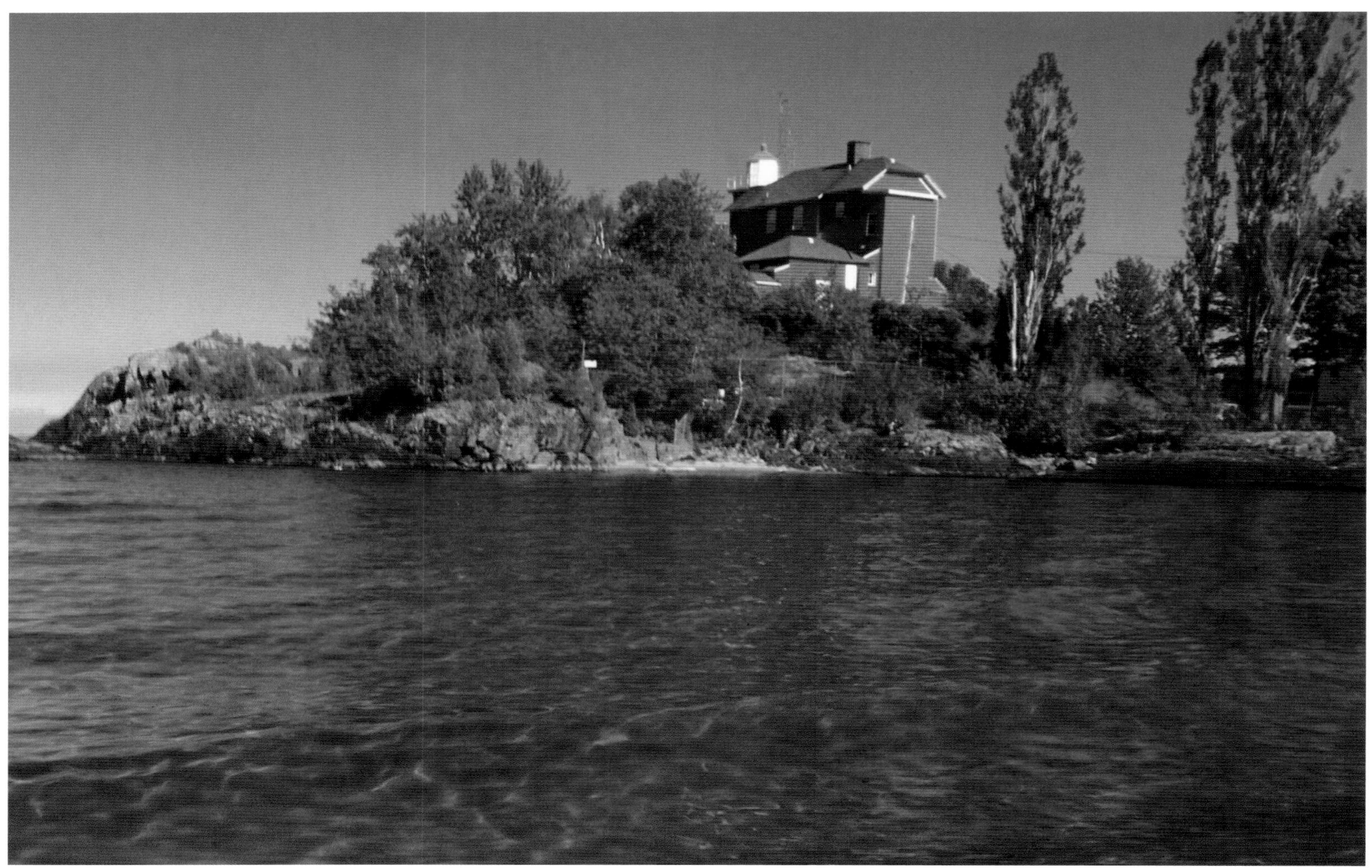

LEFT
Marquette Harbor Light, Michigan.

OPPOSITE
Menominee Pierhead Light, Michigan.

No: 15170
Position: 47 25 12 N. 87 35 12 W
Focal plane: 81ft (25m)
Range: 25 miles (40km)
Height: 80ft (24m)

The 80-ft Manitou Island skeletal lighthouse was erected near Keweenaw Point in 1861 after the first tower, built 11 years earlier, had been toppled by erosion. The station's original third-order Fresnel lens was replaced with a 190-mm optic when the tower was automated.

Marquette Harbor Light

Marquette, MI
Built: 1853 and 1866
Style: Square tower on dwelling
No: 14630
Position: 46 32 48 N. 87 22 36 W
Focal plane: 77ft (23.5m)
Range: 23 miles (37km)
Height: 40ft (12m)

The first Marquette Harbor lighthouse was built in 1853 to guide the ore carriers in and out of this rich mining area. The red tower lasted only 13 years and was replaced by the present 40-ft square masonry tower equipped with a fourth-order Fresnel lens. This was replaced with an aero-marine beacon when the tower was automated. The lighthouse and its attached red-painted keeper's dwelling is now a Coast Guard base.

Martin Reef Light

Cedarville, MI
Built: 1927
Style: Square tower on concrete crib
No: 12205
Position: 45 54 48 N. 84 08 54 W
Focal plane: 65ft (21m)
Range: 20 miles (32km)
Height: 52ft (16m)

The lighthouse was built in 1927 to mark this Lake Huron hazard. The white concrete tower, extending from the roof of the keeper's dwelling, stands above the lake and still has its original fourth-order Fresnel lens.

Mendota Light

Bête Grise, MI
Built: 1870 and 1895
Style: Square brick tower
No: 15151
Position: 47 22 24 N. 87 58 00 W
Focal plane: 44ft (13m)

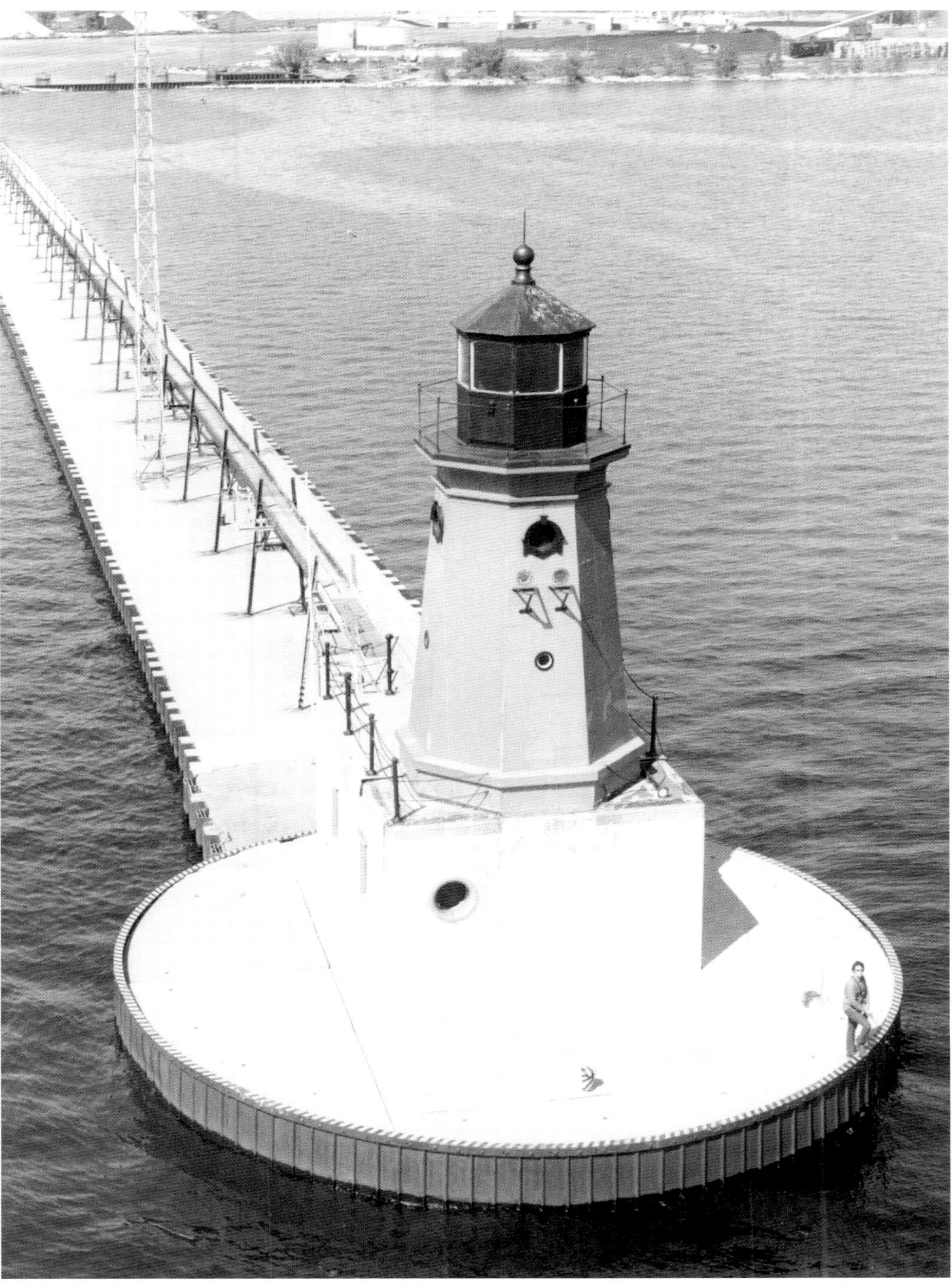

Range: 13 miles (21km)
Height: 37ft (11m)

The present lighthouse marking the entrance channel connecting Bête Grise Bay on Lake Superior with Lac La Belle in the Keweenaw peninsula, was built in 1895 to replace an earlier light that dated back to about 1870. The white tower, and its attached keeper's cottage, still has its original fourth-order Fresnel lens. The station was automated in 1933 and decommissioned in 1960, but the tower, which is now privately owned, was relit as a private aid to navigation in 1998.

Menominee Pierhead Light

Menominee, MI
Built: 1877 and 1927
Style: Octagonal tower on concrete base
No: 21935
Position: 45 05 48 N. 87 35 12 W
Focal plane: 46ft (14m)
Range: 9 miles (14.5km)

The present lighthouse was built in 1927 to replace a previous tower that marked the entrance to Lake Michigan's Menominee River from 1877. The red cast-iron tower still has its original fourth-order Fresnel lens which was automated in 1972.

Michigan Reef Lights

Lake Huron, MI
Built: 1874
Style: Crib

The Michigan Reef Lights were completed in 1874 as part of a chain of beacons to guide a growing amount of shipping passing through the narrow Straits of Mackinac connecting Lake Huron with Lake Michigan. Ships had to run the gauntlet between a number of treacherous reefs and hazardous shallows and these lighthouses pinpointed the most dangerous ones.

Middle Island Light

Alpena, MI
Built: 1905
Style: Conical
No: 11515
Position: 45 11 36 N. 83 19 18 W
Focal plane: 78ft (24m)
Range: 17 miles (27km)
Height: 71ft (22m)

The lighthouse was built in 1905 on the shore of Lake Huron between Thunder Bay and Presque Island. The tower was fitted with a fourth-order Fresnel lens and painted with an unusual orange band, and although automated at one time, has been abandoned for many years. The tower is now managed by the Middle Island Light Keepers Association, which has plans to convert the lighthouse into a bed-and-breakfast inn.

Minneapolis Shoal Light

Escanaba, MI
Built: 1935
Style: Square tower
No: 21610
Position: 45 34 54 N. 86 59 54 W
Focal plane: 82ft (25m)

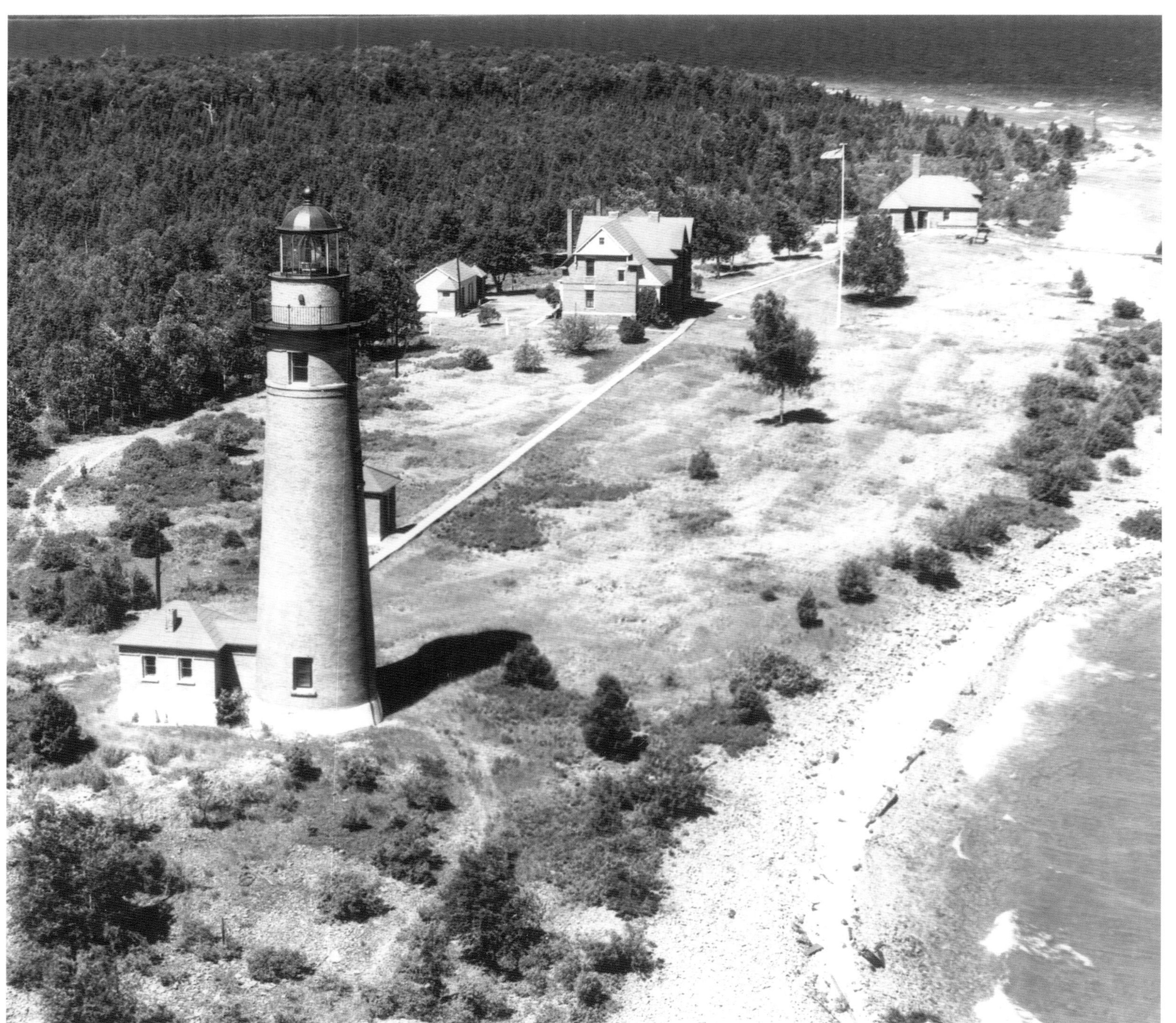

LEFT
Middle Island Light, Michigan.

OPPOSITE LEFT
Minneapolis Shoal Light, Michigan.

OPPOSITE RIGHT
North Manitou Shoal Light, Michigan.

Range: 25 miles (40km)
Height: 16ft (5m)

The red-sriped concrete Minneapolis Shoal lighthouse was built in Green Bay, Lake Michigan, in 1935 and still retains its original fourth-order Fresnel lens.

Munising Range Lights

Munising, MI
Built: 1908
Style: Conical towers
No: 14575 (Range Front Light)
Position: 46 24 54 N. 86 39 42 W
Focal plane: 79ft (24m)
Height: 58ft (18m)

The conical 58-ft steel front tower and a 38-ft (11.5-m) rear tower were built in 1908. It is unusual for the front tower to be bigger than its partner, but standing in what is now the Picture Rocks National Lakeshore, the Munising Front Range lighthouse with its locomotive-type lamp, is far more impressive than the rear tower, which stands well back on the hillside.

Muskegon South Pier Light

Muskegon, MI
Built: 1903
Style: Conical
No: 18710
Position: 43 13 36 N. 86 20 29 W
Focal plane: 50ft (15m)
Range: 15 miles (24km)
Height: 48ft (15m)

The lighthouse was built in 1903 during a period when a number of similar conical towers were erected at the end of breakwaters or piers along the eastern shores of Lake Michigan. The tower houses a fourth-order Fresnel lens and continues to guide ships across the passage between Muskegon Lake and Lake Michigan.

New Presque Isle Light

Presque Isle, MI
Built: 1840 and 1871
Style: Conical

Presque Isle boasts no less than four lighthouses within a 100-acre (40-hectare) park. The first light was Old Presque Isle lighthouse, a 30-ft (9-m) white, conical tower dating back to 1840. During the Civil War, the port was equipped with front and rear range lights to mark the channel into Presque Isle harbour, and a year later Old Presque Isle lighthouse was decommissioned. This was replaced by the present 113-ft (34.5-m) New Presque Isle Light, which remains one of the tallest on the Great Lakes. This was fitted with a third-order Fresnel lens, giving the light a range of 25 miles (40km). It was

automated in 1970 and is now managed by the Presque Isle Historical Society.

North Manitou Shoal Light

Glen Arbor, MI
Built: 1910 and 1935
Style: Square structure on concrete base
No: 18340
Focal plane: 79ft (24m)
Range: 24 miles (39km)
Height: 23 ft (7m)

The lighthouse was built on a crib off Glen Arbor in 1935 to guide vessels through the Manitou Passage and replace a lightship that had marked the shoal since 1910. The station

OPPOSITE
Old Presque Isle Light, Michigan.

RIGHT
Poe Reef Light, Michigan.

was equipped originally with a fourth-order Fresnel lens but this was replaced with a modern optic when the tower was automated in 1980.

Old Mission Point Light

Near Traverse City, MI
Built: 1879
Style: Square tower on dwelling

Old Mission Point lighthouse was built in 1879 on the 45th Parallel, exactly halfway between the Equator and the North Pole. Marking the end of a peninsula that divides Traverse Bay, the station continued in service until 1933. The wooden tower served as a vital point for mariners to navigate the dangerous peninsula that divides Traverse bay. The lighthouse, with its clapperboard dwelling, is now a central tourist attraction within Lighthouse Park.

Old Presque Isle Light

Presque Isle, Michigan.
Built: 1840
Style: Conical

The 30-ft (9-m) Old Presque Isle lighthouse was built in 1840 to guide vessels into one of

Point Iroquois Light, Michigan.

Lake Huron's best natural harbour refuges. The tower, decommissioned in 1871 and replaced by another lighthouse built a mile away, is now privately owned.

Ontonagon Light

Ontonagon, MI
Built: 1852
Style: Square

The 34-ft (10-m) lighthouse was one of the first such lights on Lake Superior. The station's fifth-order Fresnel lens was replaced with a modern optic in 1964 and the light was decommissioned a year later. The tower and it attached keeper's dwelling are now utilized by the Coast Guard Auxiliary.

Passage Island Light

Isle Royale, MI
Built: 1882
Style: Octagonal tower
No: 16835
Position: 48 13 24 N. 88 22 00 W
Focal plane: 24ft (7m)
Range: 17 miles (27km)
Height: 44ft (13m)

The lighthouse was built in 1882 to mark the channel between Passage Island and Isle Royale. The rubblestone tower still has its original fourth-order Fresnel lens and was automated in 1978. It sits on the south-western point of the island.

Pipe Island Light

De Tour Village, MI
Built: 1888
Style: Octagonal tower with black skeleton superstructure
No: 12875
Position: 46 01 00 N. 83 54 00 W
Focal plane: 52ft (16m)
Range: 16 miles (26km)
Height: 44ft (13m)

The original brick-built lighthouse marking the St. Mary's River on Lake Superior dates back to 1888, but was decommissioned in 1937 and replaced by a steel skeletal tower built nearby.

Poe Reef Light

Cheboygan, MI
Built: 1929
Style: Square tower on concrete crib
No: 11750
Position: 45 41 42 N. 84 21 42 W
Focal plane: 71ft (22m)
Range: 22 miles (35km)

The lighthouse was built in 1929 to replace a lightship that had been stationed here since 1893. The 60-ft (18-m) square, concrete tower and keeper's house stand on a crib base to guide vessels through the narrow passage between Bois Blanc Island and the mainland. The concrete tower, containing the light, extends from the roof of the keeper's dwelling. The lighthouse was originally equipped with a third-order Fresnel lens, but this was replaced with a 375-mm optic when the station was automated in 1974.

Pointe aux Barques Light

Port Austin, MI
Built: 1848 and 1857
Style: Conical

The French origin of Pointe aux Barques, the 'Point of Little Boats' dates from the time when many traders gathered here in canoes each year for the fur-trading season. The town grew into a prime shipping port, which prompted the Federal government to commission the first lighthouse in 1848. The $5,000 allocated for its construction was barely enough and the tower had to be replaced nine years later by the present 89-ft (27-m) brick tower. The lighthouse was fitted with a third-order Fresnel lens giving it a range of 18 miles (29km). This was replaced with a modern optic when the station was automated in 1958; the original lens is on display at the Grice Museum in Port Austin.

Point Betsie Light

Frankfort, MI
Built: 1858
Style: Cylindrical tower attached to dwelling
No: 18370
Position: 44 41 29 N. 86 15 19 W
Focal plane: 52ft (16m)
Range: 19 miles (30.5km)
Height: 37ft (11m)

The lighthouse was built in 1858 to guide vessels in and out of the Manitou Passage, and it remains one of the most important navigational aids on the Great Lakes. Fitted with a fourth-order Fresnel lens, the tower was one of the last in the area to be automated, with resident keepers maintaining a watchful eye on shipping movements until 1983. The house is now a private residence.

Point Iroquois Light

Brimley, MI
Built: 1855 and 1871
Style: Conical tower

The 65-ft (20-m) conical brick lighthouse was built in 1871 to replace the previous wooden tower dating back to 1855. The light, which was automated in 1962 and decommissioned nine years later, guided vessels through the hazardous reefs at Gross Cap and on into the St. Mary's River. The station is now owned by the Bay Mills-Brimley Historical Research Society, and houses a museum.

Portage River Light

Jacobsville, MI
Built: 1856
Style: Conical

The 45-ft (14-m) conical, brick lighthouse was decommissioned in 1900 when it was replaced by the Keweenaw Pier Lights. The original tower and attached keeper's dwelling is now a private residence.

Port Austin Reef Light

Port Austin, MI
Built: 1878
Style: Square tower with house attached
No: 10275
Position: 44 04 54 N. 82 58 54 W
Focal plane: 76ft (23m)
Range: 23 miles (37km)
Height: 8ft (2.5m)

The lighthouse is set 2 miles (3km) out into Lake Huron. The station was automated in 1953 and the Port Austin Reef Light Association was established in 1984 to renovate the tower.

Presque Isle Harbor Range Lights

Presque Isle, MI
Built:1870
Style: Conical

The Presque Isle Harbor Rear Range and Front Range Lights were built in 1870 to guide vessels towards the harbour entrance. The Rear Range Light stands above a dwelling that is now privately owned and the Front Range has been moved to the road leading to the Old Presque Isle lighthouse. Both lights were decommissioned in 1941 when they were replaced by the Presque Isle Harbor West Breakwater Light.

Presque Isle Harbor West Breakwater Light

Marquette, MI
Built: 1941
Style: Square pyramidal tower
No: 3705
Position: 41 58 48 N. 80 33 30 W
Focal plane: 80ft (24m)
Range: W 18 miles/29km, R 15 miles/24km

The concrete lighthouse was built in 1941 to mark the end of the 2,600-ft (790-m) harbour breakwater and replace the Presque Isle Harbor Range Lights.

Port Sanilac Light

Port Sanilac, MI
Built: 1886
Style: Octagonal tower
No: 10115
Position: 43 25 48 N. 82 32 24 W
Focal Plane: 69ft (21m)
Range: 16 miles (26km)
Height: 59ft (18m)

The lighthouse, positioned at the mouth of the St. Clair River, was built in 1886 as part of a 300-mile (480-km) chain of beacons to guide vessels along Michigan's eastern shoreline. The tower holds a fourth-order Fresnel lens, which continues to give the light a range of 16 miles. The keeper's cottage is now a private residence.

Rock Harbor Light

Isle Royale, MI
Built: 1855
Style: Conical

The 50-ft (15-m) lighthouse has had something of a chequered history. Built in 1855 to guide the copper and iron-ore carriers past a hazardous shoal near the harbour entrance, the light was deactivated when mining ceased four years later. Then, in 1874, a fresh seam was discovered and the ships were summoned once more to the port, necessitating the light to be recommissioned. The mining boom was short-lived and the lighthouse, with its fourth-order Fresnel lens, was decommissioned for good in 1878. The lighthouse is now managed by Isle Royale National Park.

Rock of Ages Light

Lake Superior, MI
Built: 1910
Style: Conical tower on cylindrical base
No: 16655
Position: 47 52 01 N. 89 18 49 W
Focal plane: 130ft (40m)
Range: 17 miles (27km)
Height: 117ft (36m)

The Rock of Ages lighthouse was built on a concrete-filled steel caisson in 1910 to guide vessels through the lee side of Isle Royale. The tower was fitted with a second-order Fresnel lens, which was replaced with a modern optic rated at 700,000 candlepower when the light was automated in 1978, making this the most powerful lighthouse on the Great Lakes. In 1933, the USS *George M. Cox* ran aground during dense fog on the Rock of Ages, as related earlier, and the keeper led the 125 passengers and crew to the safety of the tower, where they spent the night until rescue vessels could reach them the following morning.

Rock of Ages Light, Michigan.

Round Island Light

Round Island, MI
Built: 1895
Style: Square tower and attached dwelling
No: 12580
Position: 45 50 36 N. 84 36 54 W
Focal plane: 71ft (22m)
Range: 14 miles (22.5km)

Strategically positioned between Mackinac and Bois Blanc Island, Round Island lighthouse guides mariners through a difficult stretch of the Straits of Mackinac. Built in 1895, the brick tower extends above one corner of a two-storey keeper's dwelling. The lighthouse was automated in 1924, but fell into disrepair after being decommissioned in 1947. The station has since been taken over by the Hiawatha National Forest Service, which has restored the lighthouse to its former glory.

Saginaw River Rear Range Lights

Bay City, MI
Built: 1841
Style: Square pyramidal

The lighthouses were built in 1841 and are claimed to be the first erected in the United States. The 55-ft (17-m) pyramidal brick tower with two-storey attached keeper's

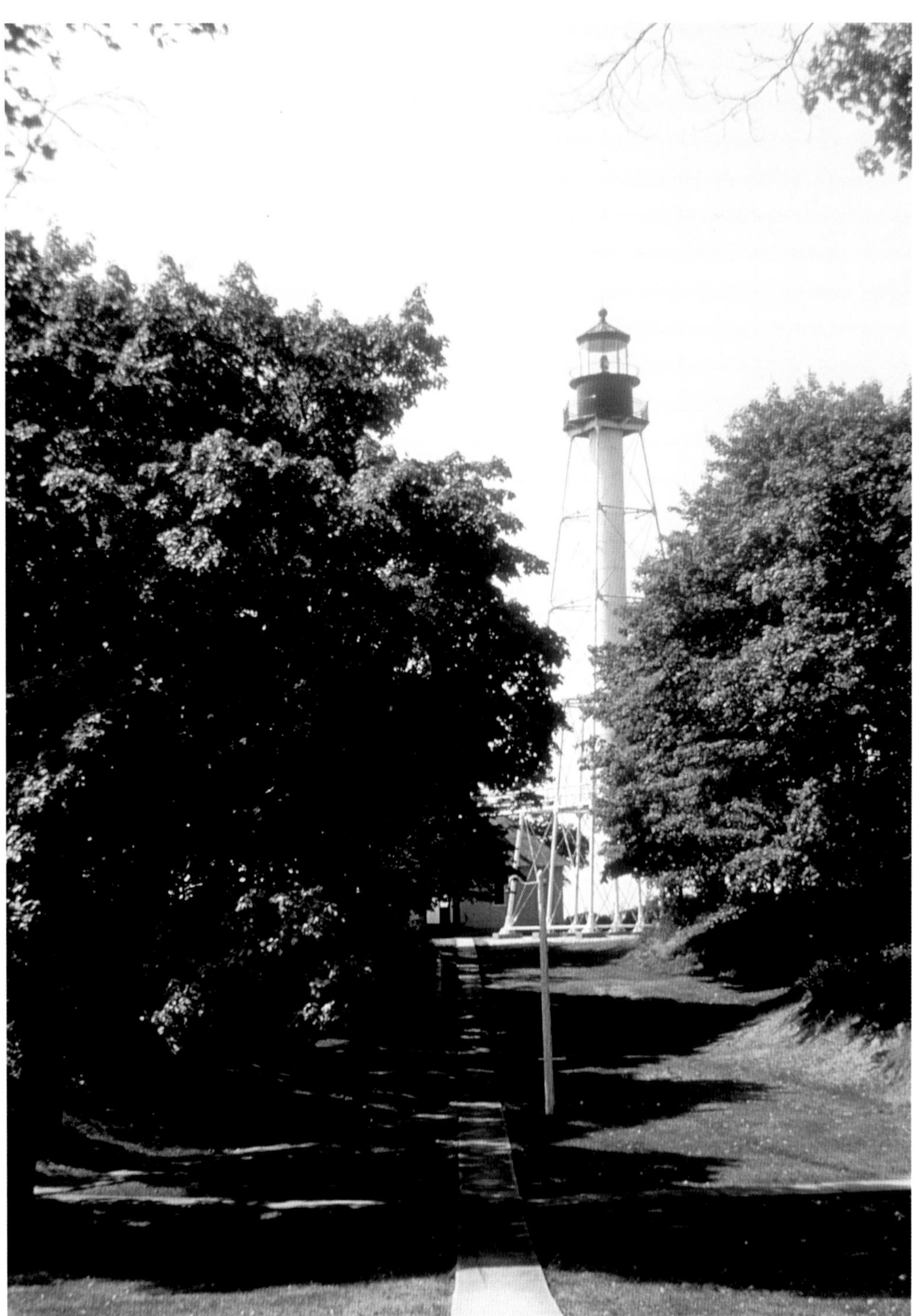

house was decommissioned in 1967, and the buildings are now destined to become a museum managed by the Saginaw River Maritime Historical Society.

Sand Hills Light

Eagle River, MI
Built: 1917
Style: Square tower and integrated building
The 91-ft (28m) lighthouse was built in 1917 to mark the entrance to the Eagle River. The tower, which has a large keeper's house attached, was equipped with a fourth-order Fresnel lens, which was transferred to the Dossin Great Lakes Museum in Detroit when the station was automated in 1939. The site then became a Coast Guard training centre until the station was decommissioned in 1954. The lighthouse and its keeper's dwelling is now a bed and breakfast inn.

Seul Choix Pointe Light

Gulliver, MI
Built: 1895
Style: Conical tower connected to dwelling.
No: 21490
Position: 45 55 18 N. 85 54 42 W
Focal plane: 80ft (24m)
Range: 24 miles (39km)
Height: 26ft (8m)

The lighthouse was built to mark one of the few refuge harbours on the north shore of Lake Michigan. The tower's cast-iron lantern housed a third-order Fresnel lens until automation came in 1972, when it was replaced with an aero-marine beacon.

Skillagalee Light (Île aux Galets)

Cross Village, MI
Built: 1850
Style: Octagonal tower
No: 17795
Position: 45 40 36 N. 85 10 18 W
Focal plane: 58ft (18m)
Range:18 miles (29km)

The Skillagalee Lighthouse, which is also known as the Île aux Galets Light, was built in 1850 on the south-western end of Waugoshance Island in Lake Michigan. The brick-built white tower was equipped with a fourth-order Fresnel lens, which was replaced with a 300-mm optic when the station was automated in 1969.

South Fox Island Light

Traverse City, MI
Built: 1868 and 1934
Style: Skeletal tower

The 60-ft (18-m) skeletal South Fox Island lighthouse was transferred in 1934 from Sapelo Island, Georgia, where it had stood since 1905. The tower was brought across the country to replace the original 38-ft (11.5-m) South Fox Island lighthouse that also stands on the site. Both have been decommissioned.

South Haven South Pierhead Light

South Haven, MI
Built: 1872 and 1903
Style: Conical tower
No: 19505
Position: 42 24 06 N. 86 17 18 W

OPPOSITE
South Fox Island Light, Michigan.

RIGHT
South Manitou Island Light, Michigan.

Focal plane: 37ft (11m)
Range: 12 miles (19km)
Height: 35ft (11m)

The cast-iron lighthouse was erected at the far end of Harbor Pier to replace an earlier light guiding vessels in and out of the Black River. The red-painted tower is still equipped with its original fifth-order Fresnel lens and is fully automated.

South Manitou Island Light

South Manitou Island, Leland, MI
Built: 1839, 1858 and 1871
Style: Conical

Three lighthouses have stood at this important point along the Manitou Passage. The present 104-ft (32-m) lighthouse has withstood the elements since 1871, but the previous two, built in 1839 and 1858, both had to be demolished. The tower was equipped with a third-order Fresnel lens until the station was deactivated in 1958. It is now a tourist attraction within the Sleeping Bear Dunes National Lakeshore.

Spectacle Reef Light

Lake Huron, MI
Built: 1874
Style: Conical tower on concrete pier
No: 11730
Position: 45 46 24 N. 84 08 12 W
Focal plane: 86ft (26m)
Range: 17 miles (27km)

Two schooners wrecked on Spectacle Reef led Congress to agree to a lighthouse being built to mark this Lake Huron danger spot. Work commenced in 1870, but because of the severe winters, the $406,000 programme took 200 men four years to complete. During the particularly severe winter of 1873–74, the builders returned to the lighthouse to find it encased in a 30ft (9m) high iceberg and had to tunnel their way in. The 86-ft tower was designed and constructed by General Sherman's chief engineer, Major O.M. Poe, and is solid stone for the first 34ft (10m). Equipped with two second-order Fresnel lenses, the light has a range of 17 miles.

Squaw Island Light

Gladstone, MI
Built: 1892
Style: Octagonal

The brick-constructed Squaw Island lighthouse was built in 1892 to the north of the Beaver Island archipelago and was decommissioned in 1928. The tower and its keeper's dwelling are now privately owned.

Spectacle Reef Light, Michigan.

St. Clair Flats Old Canal Range Lights

Harsens Island, MI
Built: 1859 and 1875
Style: Skeletal and pyramidal towers
No: 8535 (Range Front Light)
Position: 42 33 00 N. 82 39 06 W
Focal plane: 44ft (13.5m)
Height: 36ft (11m)

No: 8540 (Rear Light)
Focal plane: 108ft (33m)

The original St. Clair Flats Old Channel Front and Rear Range Lights were erected in 1859. The Rear Range tower, which is listed in the National Register of Historic Places, was rebuilt in 1875 when it was equipped with a fourth-order Fresnel lens.

St. Joseph North Pier Lights

St. Joseph, MI
Built: 1832 and 1906
Style: Cylindrical and octagonal towers
No: 19515
Position: 42 07 00 N. 86 29 42 W
Focal plane: 31ft (9.5m)
Range: 15 miles (24km)
Height: 30ft (9m)

No: 19520 (North Pier Inner Light)
Focal plane: 53 ft (16m)
Range: 16 miles (26km)
Height: 53ft (16m)

A lighthouse built on the mainland in 1832 once served St. Joseph's harbour. This was superseded in 1907 by the St. Joseph North Pier Lights, to which mariners must keep in perpendicular alignment to keep in the safe channel when approaching the harbour entrance. The outer range light is a cylindrical white tower housing a fifth-order Fresnel lens, while the inner light is a white octagonal tower equipped with a fourth-order lens.

St. Helena Light

St. Helena Island, MI
Built: 1873
Style: Conical tower connected to house
No: 17720
Positiion: 45 51 18 N. 84 51 48 W
Focal plane: 71ft (22m)
Range: 6 miles (10km)
Height: 71ft (22m)

The lighthouse was equipped with a three-and-a-half-order Fresnel lens, which was replaced with a modern plastic optic when the station was automated in 1922. The tower then suffered from decades of neglect and vandalism and would have fallen into total disrepair had the Great Lakes Lighthouse Keepers Association not decided to restore it and its keeper's cottage.

St. Martin Island Light

Fairport, MI
Built: 1905
Style: Hexagonal tower
No: 21450
Position: 43 30 19 N. 86 45 30 W
Focal plane: 84ft (26m)
Range: W 18 miles/29km, R 15 miles/24km
Height: 75ft (23m)

The lighthouse was built in 1905 in the north-west of Lake Michigan and is one of the first concrete light towers to be built in the United States. It was equipped with a fourth-order Fresnel lens, which was replaced with a 190-mm optic when the station was automated.

Stannard Rock Light

Marquette, MI
Built: 1868 and 1882
Style: Conical tower on cylindrical crib
No: 14725
Position: 47 11 00 N. 87 13 30 W
Focal plane: 102ft (31m)
Range: 31 miles (50km)
Height: 10ft (3m)

The caisson-based lighthouse was built in 1882 to mark a dangerous hazard lying 23 miles (37km) to the south-east of Manitou Island on Lake Superior. Before this, Stannard Rock had been marked by a simple day beacon. Work began to prepare the reef in 1877 with equipment that had been used to construct the similar lighthouse on Spectacle Reef. Construction was finally completed at a cost of $320,000 five years later. The tower was equipped with a second-order Fresnel lens, which gives it a range of 31 miles.

Sturgeon Point Light

Alcona, MI
Built: 1870
Style: Conical tower attached to dwelling
No: 11345
Position: 44 42 42 N. 83 16 18 W
Focal plane: 69ft (21m)
Range: 14 miles (22.5km)
Height: 68ft (21m)

Sturgeon Point marks a treacherous reef on Lake Huron where several ships have been wrecked, including the wooden steamer *Marine City*, which burned out in 1880, the 233-ton schooner *Venus*, which ran on the rocks in 1887 and the *Ispeming*, which followed in 1903. The tower, built in 1870, houses a three-and-a-half-order Fresnel lens, which was automated in 1939. The station is now managed by the Alcona County Historical Society, which has converted the keeper's residence into a museum.

Tawas Point Light

Tawas City, MI
Built: 1853 and 1876
Style: Cylindrical

The lighthouse marks the northern side of Saginaw Bay. The first tower, built in 1853, was rendered useless by the rapidly shifting shoreline, which resulted in the lighthouse being over a mile from the shore within 20 years. The present 67-ft (20-m) white tower was erected in 1876 and equipped with a rotating fourth-order Fresnel lens, since automated. The keeper's house is now a private residence for a high-ranking Coast Guard officer.

LEFT
Tawas Point Light, Michigan.

OPPOSITE
Whitefish Point Light, Michigan.

Thunder Bay Island Light
Alpena, MI
Built: 1832
Style: Conical tower with dwelling attached
No: 11495
Position: 45 02 12 N. 83 11 42 W
Focal plane: 63ft (19m)
Range: 19 miles (30.5km)
Height: 17ft (5m)

The original Thunder Bay Island lighthouse dates back to 1832 when the brick-built tower was built to warn vessels away from the reef on the south-east corner of the island. The tower was equipped with a fourth-order lens until automation in 1980 led to its replacement with a solar-powered 190-mm optic.

Waugoshance Light
Mackinaw City, MI
Built: 1851
Style: Conical crib

The 76-ft (23-m) lighthouse was built over the Waugoshance Shoals, a dangerous hazard in the Straits of Mackinac. The lighthouse, which had a fifth-order Fresnel lens, was decommissioned in 1912 when it

WHITEFISH POINT
LIGHT STATION
1849

LEFT
White River Light, Michigan.

OPPOSITE
Ashtabula Light, Ohio.

was replaced by the White Shoal Light. The conical brick tower standing on its crib has lain abandoned ever since, perhaps because it is said to be haunted by the ghost of John Herman, a keeper who fell to his death from the parapet in 1894. The Waugoshance Lighthouse Preservation Society has since been established to renovate the lighthouse.

Whitefish Point Light

Paradise, MI
Built: 1848 and 1861
Style: Skeletal tower
No: 14530
Position: 46 46 18 N. 84 57 24 W
Focal plane: 80ft (24m)
Range: 24 miles (39km)
Height: 26ft (8m)

The present lighthouse was built in 1861 to replace an earlier masonry tower dating back to 1848. The skeletal tower, with its third-order Fresnel lens, was automated in 1970 and now houses the Great Lakes Shipwreck Museum. One of the tragedies featured concerns the iron-ore freighter *Edmund Fitzgerald*, which sank close to the lighthouse with the loss of 29 crew members on the night of 10 November 1975. The same storm that led to this loss also knocked out the power to the lighthouse, which probably disoriented the watch officers.

White River Light

Whitehall, MI
Built: 1875
Style: Octagonal

The White River lighthouse was built in 1875 and fitted with a third-order Fresnel lens. The station was decommissioned in 1966 and now houses the Great Lakes Marine Museum.

White Shoal Light

Mackinaw City, MI
Built: 1910
Style: Conical tower on conical crib
No: 17750
Position: 45 50 30 N. 85 08 06 W
Focal plane: 125ft (38m)
Range: 17 miles (27km)

The lighthouse was built in 1910 to mark the western approaches to the Straits of Mackinac on Lake Michigan. The steel tower, which is painted with spiralling red and white stripes, originally held a second-order Fresnel lens. This was replaced with a 190-mm optic when the tower was automated.

William Livingston Memorial Light

Belle Isle, MI
Built: 1929
Style: Fluted marble tower
No: 8240
Position: 42 20 48 N. 82 57 18 W
Focal plane: 58ft (18m)
Range: 18 miles (29km)
Height: 15ft (4.5m)

This is the only marble light tower in the U.S., and probably the world. It was built in 1929 in honour of William Livingston, a former president of the Lake Carriers Association, to mark Belle Island in the Detroit River.

Windmill Point Light

Detroit, MI
Built: 1933

The present 42-ft (13-m) Windmill Point lighthouse was built in 1933 to mark the entrance to the Detroit River and is fitted with a sixth-order Fresnel lens.

Ohio

Ashtabula Light

Ashtabula Harbor, OH
Built: 1916
Style: Cylindrical tower on square house
No: 3745
Position: 41 55 06 N. 80 47 48 W
Focal Plane: 51ft (15.5m)
Range: 9 miles (14.5km)

The squat lighthouse, set on the roof of the keeper's house, was built on a concrete foundation at the end of a long breakwater. The tower was equipped with a fourth-order Fresnel lens and was automated in 1973. The dwelling now houses the Great Lakes Marine and the U.S. Coast Guard Memorial Museum, which traces the navigation aids at this location that date back as far as 1835.

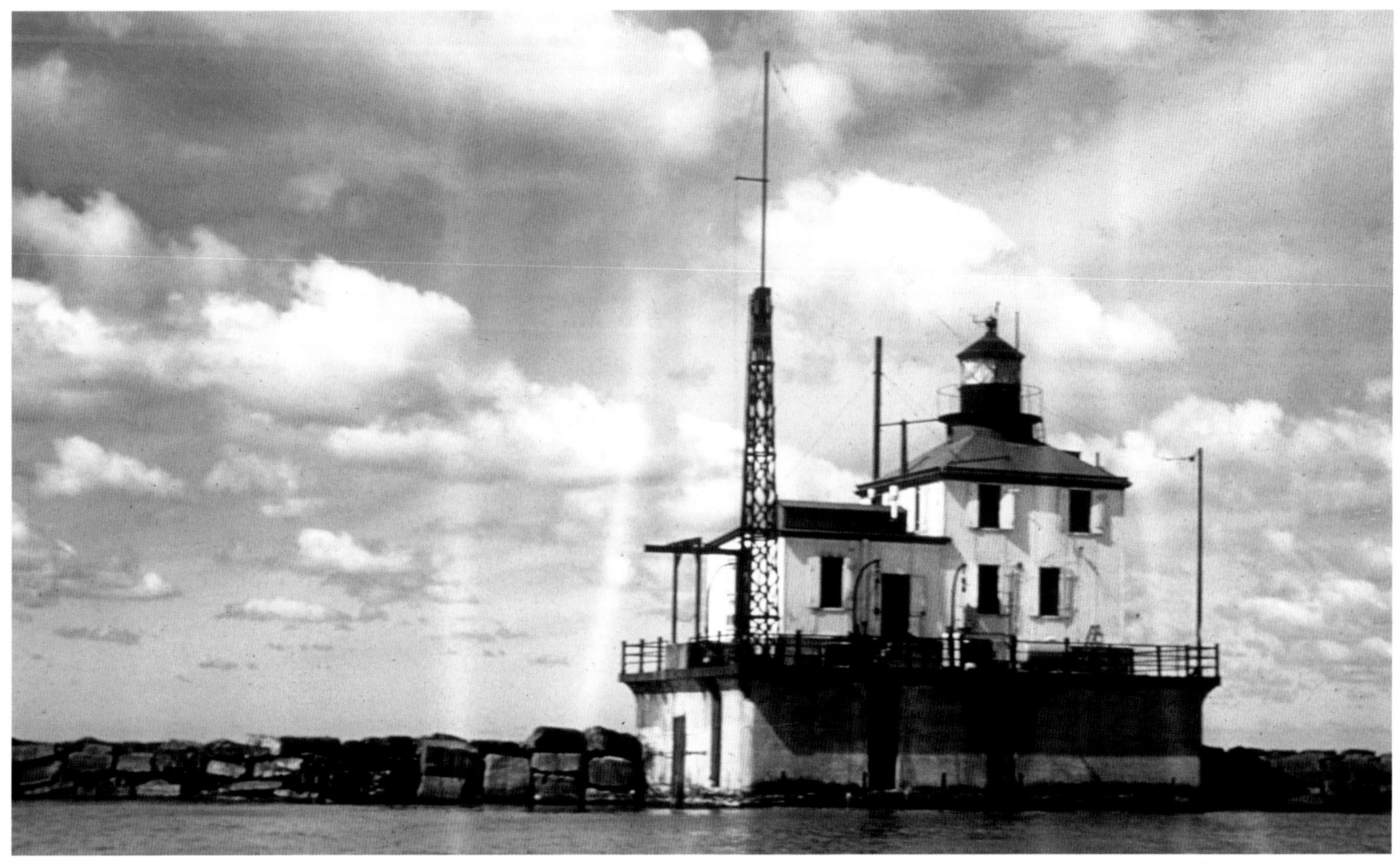

Old Conneaut West Breakwater Light, Ohio.

Cedar Point Light
Sandusky, OH
Built: 1839
Style: Skeletal tower

Built in 1839, the original lighthouse stood over Sandusky Bay at the end of a rough breakwater before being replaced by its current skeletal steel tower in 1935. A square steel lantern stands atop the tower, but it is no longer operational.

Cleveland East Pierhead Light
Cleveland, OH
Built: 1831, 1869, 1910 and 1911
Style: Conical

The Cleveland Pierhead Light is a 25-ft (8-m) cast-iron conical tower standing on a concrete crib on the tip of the breakwater. Originally housing a fifth-order Fresnel lens, the light was automated in 1959 and now holds a solar-powered modern optic. Paired with the Cleveland West Breakwater Light (see below), the East Pierhead Light defines one end of Cleveland's inner harbour.

Cleveland West Breakwater Light

Cleveland, OH
Built: 1910
Style: Conical

The 67-ft (20-m) white conical brick tower of the West Breakwater Light marks the entrance to the Cuyahoga River and Cleveland's inner harbour. It originally held a red-and-black lantern with a fourth-order Fresnel lens (now on display at the Great Lakes Science Center in Cleveland) but is now fitted with a modern optic. The lighthouse originally had a steam foghorn, which was affectionately known as 'the cow', because of its particular warning signal, but this has since been replaced by a steel foghorn building connected to the tower by a covered passageway. The high winds and low temperatures at this site in winter mean that the buildings are often enshrouded in ice. Automated in 1965 the tower is now no longer operational.

Conneaut West Breakwater Light

Conneaut, OH
Built: 1835, 1936
Style: Pyramidal

Standing on its concrete crib on the Conneaut River at the entrance to Lake Erie, the lighthouse is an imposing three-storey structure, made to endure rough winds. The tower has a pyramidal structure and is painted white with a black band in a style known as streamlined modern. The 375-mm lens was automated in 1972. Pictured here is the original 1835 square tower with attached quarters.

Fairport Harbor Light

Fairport, OH
Built: 1825, 1871 and 1876
Style: Conical

The first Fairport Harbor lighthouse, located at the entrance to the Great River on Lake Erie, was built in 1825, the same year the Erie Canal was opened. This became an important refuelling stop for steamers carrying immigrants and freight from Buffalo out to the American Midwest. The 30-ft (9-m) Berea sandstone tower had 3-ft thick walls and was upgraded with a third-order Fresnel lens in 1871. However, the tower was in need of considerable maintenance and Congress eventually voted to spend $30,000 to replace it with the present sandstone tower, which was erected 5 years later. The lighthouse was decommissioned in 1925 and replaced with a combination light and foghorn station. The tower and its keeper's dwelling now house a maritime museum maintained by the Fairport Harbor Historical Society.

Fairport Harbor West Breakwater Light

Fairport Harbor, OH
Built: 1925
Style: Square Tower with quarters in crib
No: 3870
Focal plane: 56ft (17m)
Range: 17 miles (27km)
Height: 10ft (3m)

Overlooking the entrance to the Grand River on Lake Erie, the white brick tower stands squarely on its concrete pierhead. With its red roof and period windows with shutters marking its flanks, the tower, now automated, still holds its original fourth-order Fresnel lens.

Huron Harbor Light

Huron, OH
Built: 1835, 1936
Style: Square pyramidal tower
No: 4475
Position: 41 24 17 N. 82 32 38 W
Focal plane: 80ft (24m)
Range: 24 miles (39km)
Height: 72ft (22m)

Originally established in 1835, the steel conical tower of Huron Harbor Light, standing on its concrete breakwater on Lake Erie, was previously known as the West Pierhead Light. Built in 1936, the current structure is white, in an art deco moderne style. Automated in 1972, the site has a 375-mm lens.

Lorain Light

Lorain, OH
Built: 1837 and 1917
Style: Caisson

The Lorain Light began life as a simple lantern hung on the end of a pole to mark the Lorain shoreline of Lake Erie. In 1837 the first wooden lighthouse was constructed on the end of a pier, but it burned too much soot. In 1917 the Army Corps of Engineers was given the task of constructing the present stone lighthouse and two-storey dwelling on a giant concrete-filled caisson to withstand the worst of the storms and ice that badly effect Lake Erie during the winter. This was equipped with a rotating fourth-order Fresnel lens to give the station a range of 15 miles (24km). The Lorain Light was finally decommissioned in 1965 and locals spent five years raising $850,000 to save the landmark from demolition.

Manhattan Range Lights

Toledo, OH
Built: 1918
Style: Skeletal towers

The two towers that made up the Manhattan Range Lights were steel skeletons with focal planes at 40 and 86ft (12 and 26m). They were used to guide ships on the Maumee River near Toledo and had square steel lantern rooms. The rear light housed a fifth-order lens, but is now privately owned and inactive.

Marblehead Light

Bay Point, OH
Built: 1821
Style: Conical tower
No: 5250
Position: 41 32 12 N. 82 42 42 W
Focal Plane: 67ft (20.5m)
Range: 11miles (18km)
Height: 65ft (20m)

This is the oldest lighthouse on the Great Lakes. The conical stone tower has changed

LEFT
Huron Harbor Light, Ohio.

OPPOSITE
Lorain Light, Ohio.

little over the years except for its light. Originally, this was powered by 13 oil lamps which were replaced first by a fourth-order Fresnel lens, and in 1903 by the present third-order system. The station is now automated and the keeper's cottage houses a museum managed by the Ottawa County Historical Society.

Old Port Clinton Light

Port Clinton, OH
Built: 1833
Style: Square pyramidal

The lighthouse stands on the Portage River where it joins Lake Erie. With its white wooden tower and square pyramidal design, the light served the area for 131 years until it was decommissioned in 1964. The top portion of the light now serves as an attraction at Brands Marina in Port Clinton.

Perry Memorial Light

South Bass Island, OH
Built: 1913
Style: Monumental
No: 5670
Position: 41 39 12 N. 82 48 36 W

Focal plane: 335ft (102m)
Range: 102 miles (164km)
Height: 15ft (4.5m)

Located at Put-In Bay this light is a monument to Oliver Hazard Perry for the victory over the British fleet in the War of 1812.

South Bass Island

Put-in-Bay, OH
Built: 1897
Style: Square tower

The South Bass Island Light consists of a square red brick tower with a red octagonal lantern attached to its three-storey Queen Anne-style dwelling. The fourth-order Fresnel lens, that was once held by the lantern, is now at the Lake Erie Island Historical Museum on South Bass Island. Deactivated in 1962 and sold to Ohio State University in 1967, the site is now owned by the F.T. Stone Laboratory.

Toledo Harbor Light

Toledo, OH
Built: 1904
Style: Square dwelling with tower
No: 6030
Position: 41 45 42 N. 83 19 42 W
Focal plane: 72ft (22m)
Range: 10 miles (16km)
Height: 70ft (21m)

Built in 1904, the Toledo Harbor lighthouse captivates visitors with its unusual architecture. Its Romanesque arches, the

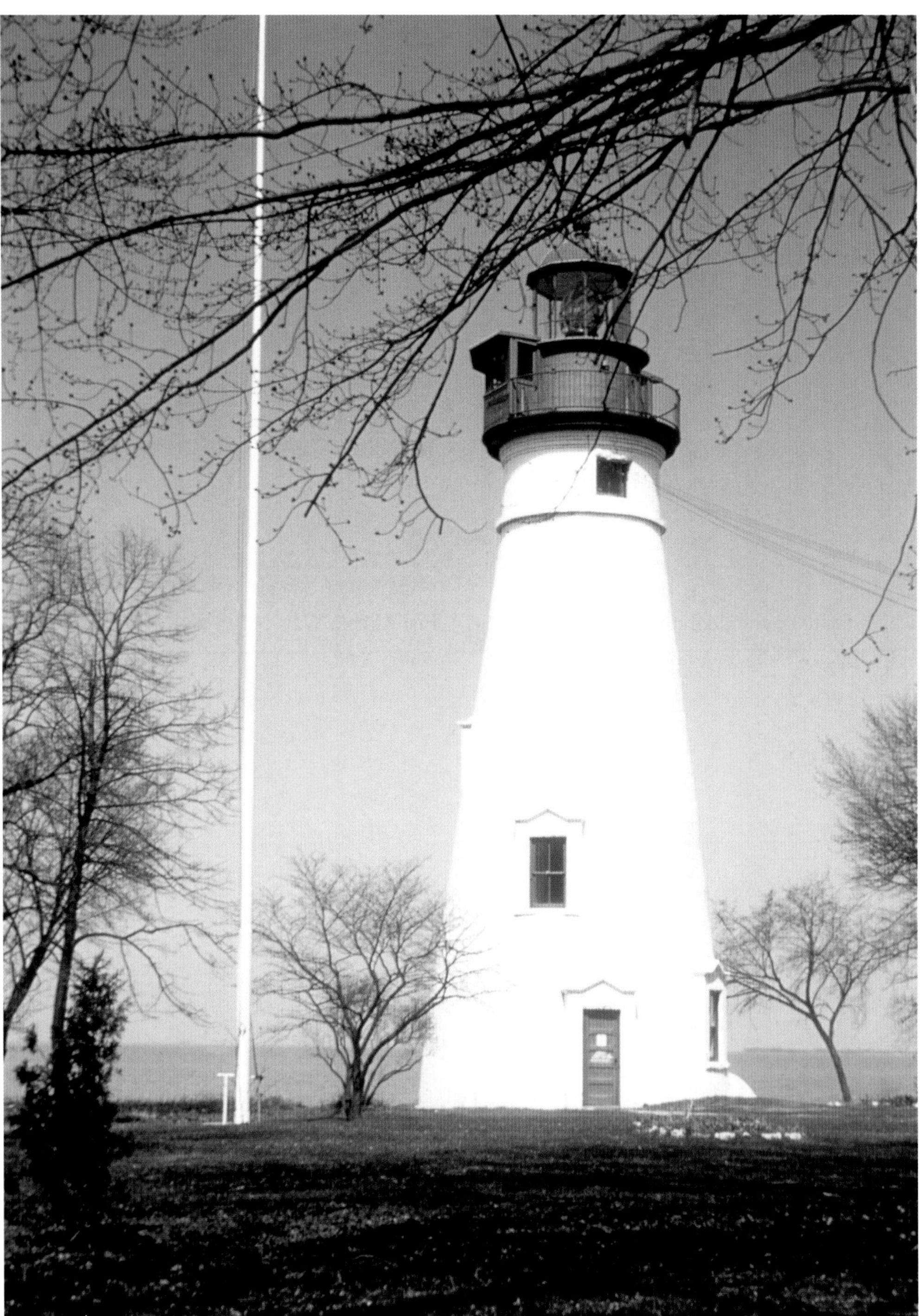

church-like tower, and the ghostly tales that surround the building – invented, some say, to deter vandalism – all add to its interest. The station, which is made up of a three-storey dwelling with a black conical tower sitting on the roof, stands on a 20-ft (6-m) high stone and concrete crib. There is also a one-storey wing to house the fog signal. Situated to the north-east of Toledo Bay at a point where the Army Corps of Engineers dredged a deep channel between Lake Erie and the Maumee River, this lighthouse and its artery helped to put Toledo City on the map as a major freight harbour. The station was automated in 1965.

Vermilion Light

Vermilion, OH
Built: 1877 and 1991
Style: Octagonal

The lighthouse now standing at Vermilion on the shores of Lake Erie has never shone its light out into the lake. It is, however, an exact replica of the first Vermilion lighthouse built in 1877, which had to be demolished after decades of storms had damaged the structure beyond repair.

West Sister Island Light

Oak Harbor, OH
Built: 1821 and 1848
Style: Conical tower
No: 5550
Position: 41 44 12 N.83 06 36 W
Focal plane: 17ft (5m)
Range: 8 miles (13km)
Height: 55ft (17m)

LEFT
Marblehead Light (Formally Sandusky Light), Ohio.

OPPOSITE
Ashland Breakwater Light, Wisconsin.

The limestone and brick conical tower of the West Sister Island Light was built in 1821 and was connected to a dwelling by a covered passageway. Receiving a fourth-order Fresnel lens in 1848, the lighthouse emitted a fixed, white light. The year 1868 saw further renovations, with the addition of an iron staircase and new lantern. Automated in 1937, the lighthouse is now a wildlife refuge, and although it endured shelling, as the island was used for target practice during WWII, it is still active today with a 300-mm plastic lens.

Wisconsin

Algoma Pierhead Light

Algoma, WI
Built: 1893
Style: Square tower on fog signal building
No: 20955
Position: 44 27 30 N. 87 29 48 W
Focal plane: 45ft (14m)
Range: 14 miles (22.5km)
Height: 15ft (4.5m)

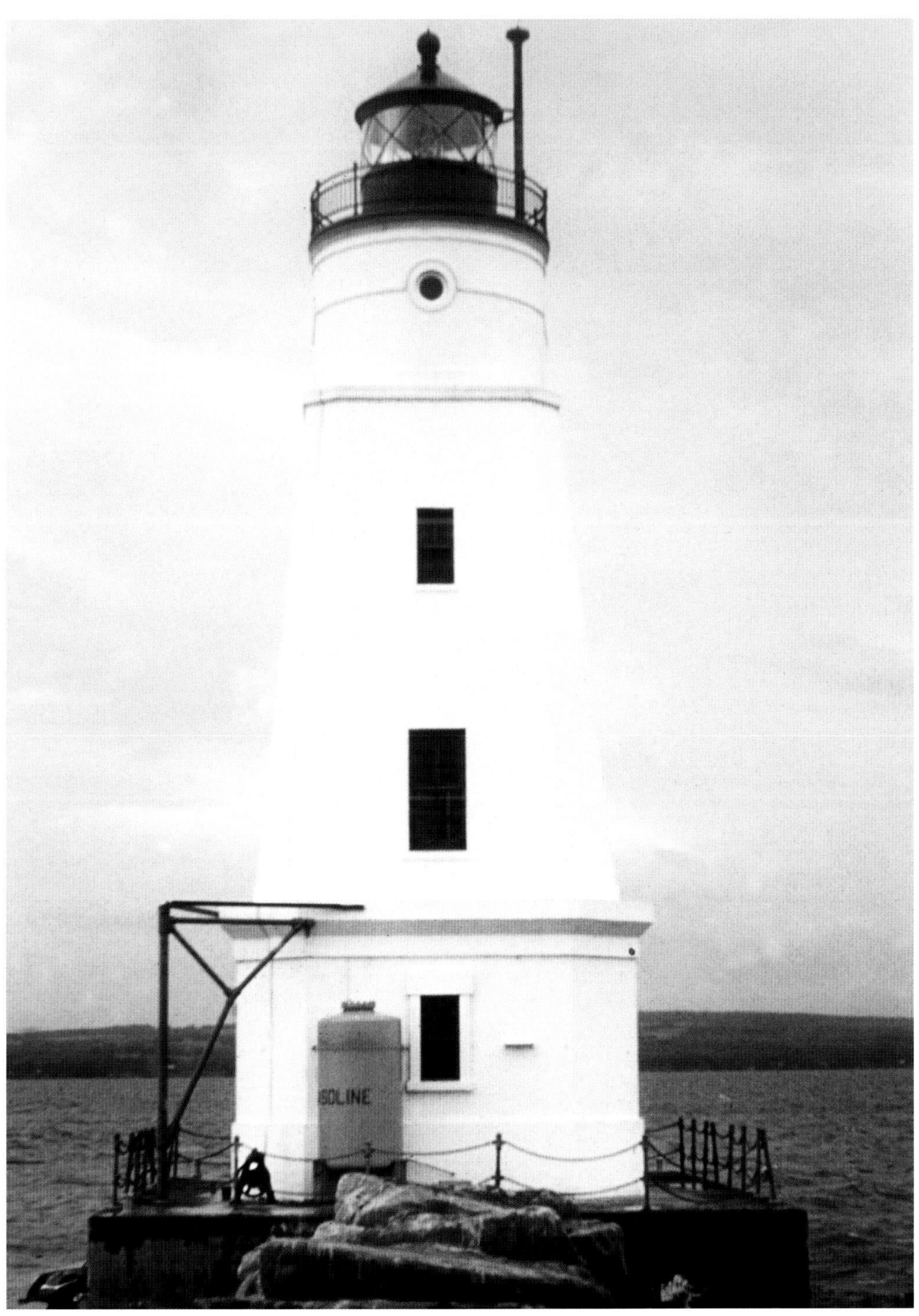

The lighthouse was built in 1893 to guide vessels into the Ahnapee River. The tower is equipped with a fifth-order Fresnel lens and was automated in 1973.

Ashland Breakwater Light

Ashland, WI
Built: 1911
Style: White octagonal pyramidal tower
No: 15310
Position: 46 37 42 N. 90 52 12 W
Focal plane: 60ft (18m)
Range: 18 miles (29km)
Height: 9ft (3m)

The concrete lighthouse is built on a crib set in Chequamegon Bay, Lake Superior. The white painted pyramidal tower has a cylindrical watch room holding a fourth-order Fresnel lens set above a hexagonal base.

Bailey's Harbor & Range Lights

Door County, WI
Built: 1853
Style: Wooden cupola and irregular tower

These were built in 1853 on the Door County peninsula. The Rear Range light is mounted on the roof of the keeper's 2-storey quarters, while the Front light is a 21-ft (6.5-m) wooden tower. The lights were decommissioned in 1930 and now form part of the Ridges Wildlife Sanctuary.

Cana Island Light

Bailey's Harbor, WI
Built: 1870
Style: Conical tower connected to dwelling
No: 21255
Position: 45 05 18 N. 87 02 48 W
Focal plane: 83ft (25m)
Range: 25 miles (40km)
Height: 86ft (26m)

The lighthouse guides ships along the northern approaches to Bailey's Harbor. When the yellow brickwork began to erode in 1902, engineers encased the tower and its keeper's dwelling in steel, which continues to protect the structure. The station still has its third-order Fresnel lens, which is now automated. The keeper's house is now a private residence.

Chamber's Island Light

Fish Creek, WI
Built: 1868
Style: Octagonal

The yellow brick tower was originally built in 1868. The light through its fourth-order Fresnel lens guided ships along Green Bay's west passage, from the north-west end of Chambers Island. The tower was attached to a one-and-a-half-storey gable-roofed dwelling, which is now used as a summer residence. In 1961 the U.S. Coast Guard moved the light to a steel skeleton tower.

Chequamegon Point Light

Apostle Islands, Bayfield, WI
Built: 1898
Style: White cylindrical tower
No: 15295
Position: 46 43 42 N. 90 48 36 W
Focal plane: 33ft (10m)

Range: 10 miles (16km)
Height: 29ft (9m)

The lighthouse was built as a part of the Apostle Islands Lights on Long Island. It is partnered on the island by the La Pointe Light, and was attended by the same keeper until both stations were automated in 1964. The Chequamegon Light has retained its original fourth-order Fresnel lens.

Devil's Island Light

Apostle Islands, Bayfield, WI
Built: 1891 and 1901
Style: Cylindrical tower
No: 15565
Position: 47 04 48 N. 90 43 42 W
Focal plane: 100ft (30.5m)
Range: 30 miles (48km)
Height: 71ft (22m)

The cylindrical lighthouse was built in 1901 to replace a temporary wooden tower constructed ten years earlier. This was the final light to be built in the Apostle Islands and, though automated in 1978, has retained its third-order Fresnel lens.

Eagle Bluff Light

Ephraim, WI
Built: 1868
Style: Square tower attached to dwelling
No: 21825
Position: 45 10 06 N. 87 14 12 W
Focal plane: 75ft (23m)
Range: 23 miles (37km)
Height: 43ft (13m)

OPPOSITE
Cana Island Light, Wisconsin.

RIGHT
Chamber's Island Light, Wisconsin.

The lighthouse has a unique design that gives a keeper easy access to its tower. It is therefore ironic that it was automated in 1909, making it one of the first lighthouses able to dispense with a keeper. The keeper's dwelling is a yellow one-and-a-half-storey red-roofed building, on the corner of which sits the tower itself. Standing a total of 76ft (23m) above the lake, the light shone through a three-and-a-half-order Fresnel lens. The light has been a museum since the 1960s.

Green Bay Harbor Entrance Light

Green Bay, WI
Built: 1935
Style: Conical tower on cylindrical base
No: 22130
Position: 44 39 12 N. 87 54 06 W
Focal plane: 72ft (22m)
Range: 22 miles (35km)
Height: 12ft (4m)

The lighthouse stands on a steel caisson marking the west side of the channel into Green Bay Harbor. Built in 1935 the light is still in operation, shining forth from its cylindrical steel art-deco tower.

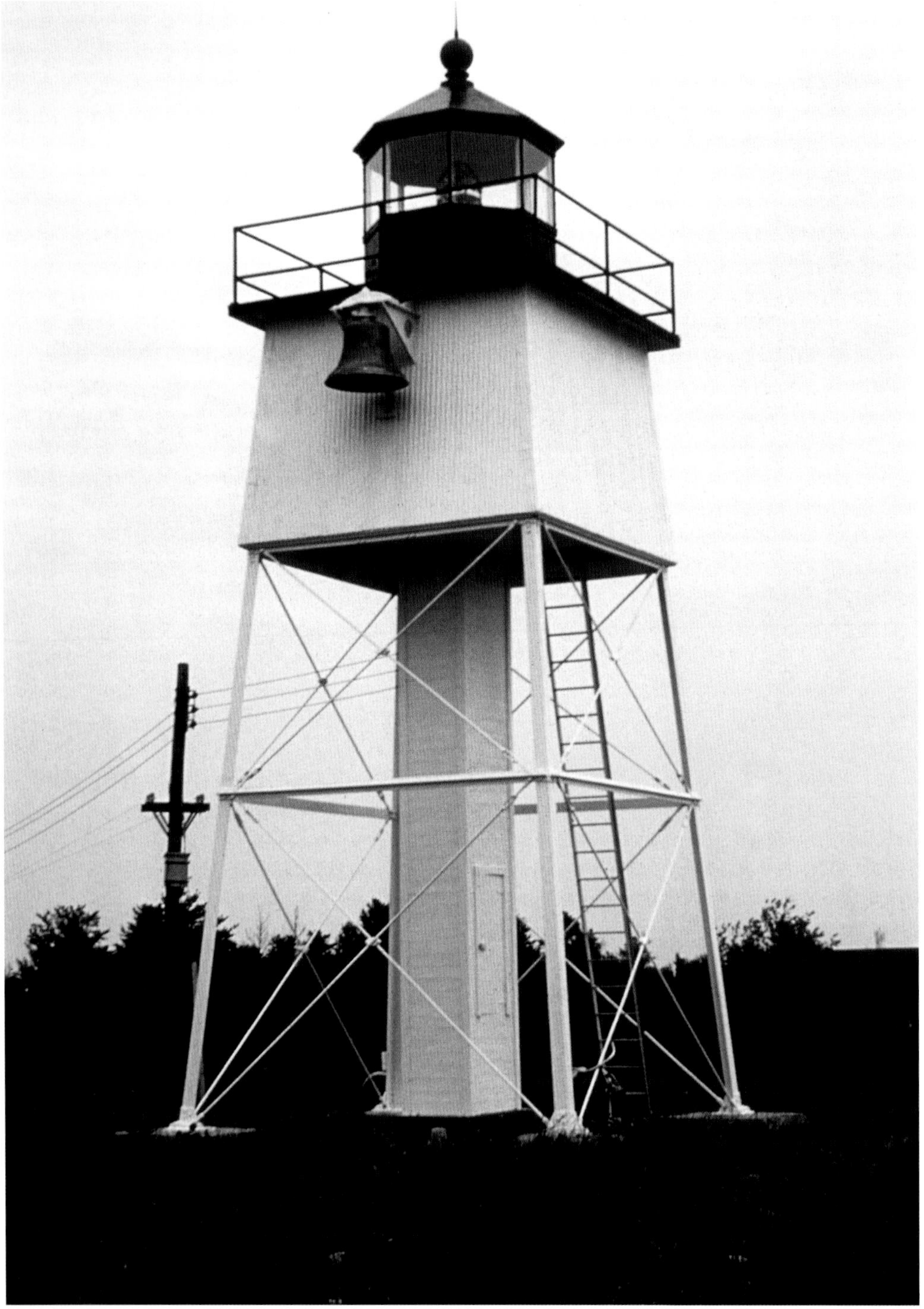

OPPOSITE LEFT
Chequamegon Point Light, Wisconsin.

OPPOSITE RIGHT
Devil's Island Light, Wisconsin.

RIGHT
Eagle Bluff Light, Wisconsin.

Kenosha Pierhead Light

Kenosha, WI
Built: 1906
Style: Conical tower
No: 20415
Position: 42 35 20 N. 87 48 31 W
Focal plane: 50ft (15m)
Range: 15 miles (24km)
Height: 50ft (15m)

The lighthouse was built in 1906 to replace the Old Southport Lighthouse, a 55-ft (17-m) brick tower that still stands and has marked Kenosha harbour entrance since 1866. The newer red-painted cast-iron conical tower, which is now part of a range-light system, is fitted with a fourth-order Fresnel lens.

La Pointe Light

Long Island, Bayfield, WI
Built: 1858 and 1895
Style: White cylindrical tower
No: 15280
Position: 46 43 42 N. 90 47 06 W
Focal plane: 70ft (21m)
Range: 21 miles (34km)
Height: 51ft (15.5m)

The lighthouse was built in 1895 and stands on the opposite side of Long Island to Devil's Island Light. It replaced an earlier wooden lighthouse that dated back to 1858 and is similar in design to Michigan Island, another in the Apostle Islands chain of lights. When first built, La Pointe shared the same keeper as the Chequamegon Point Light until its automation in 1964, when its fourth-order Fresnel lens was replaced by an aero-marine beacon.

Manitowoc Light

Manitowoc, WI
Built: 1840 and 1895
Style: Cylindrical tower on house

The Manitowoc North Breakwater lighthouse was built in 1895 to guide vessels into Green Bay, replacing an earlier tower dating back to 1840. The white cylindrical tower holds a fourth-order Fresnel lens and was automated in 1971.

Michigan Island Light

Apostle Islands, Bayfield, WI
Built: 1857, 1869 and 1930
Style: White cylindrical tower
No: 15275

FAR LEFT
Green Bay Harbor Entrance Light, Wisconsin.

BELOW
Kenosha Pierhead Light, Wisconsin.

OPPOSITE
Manitowoc Light, Wisconsin.

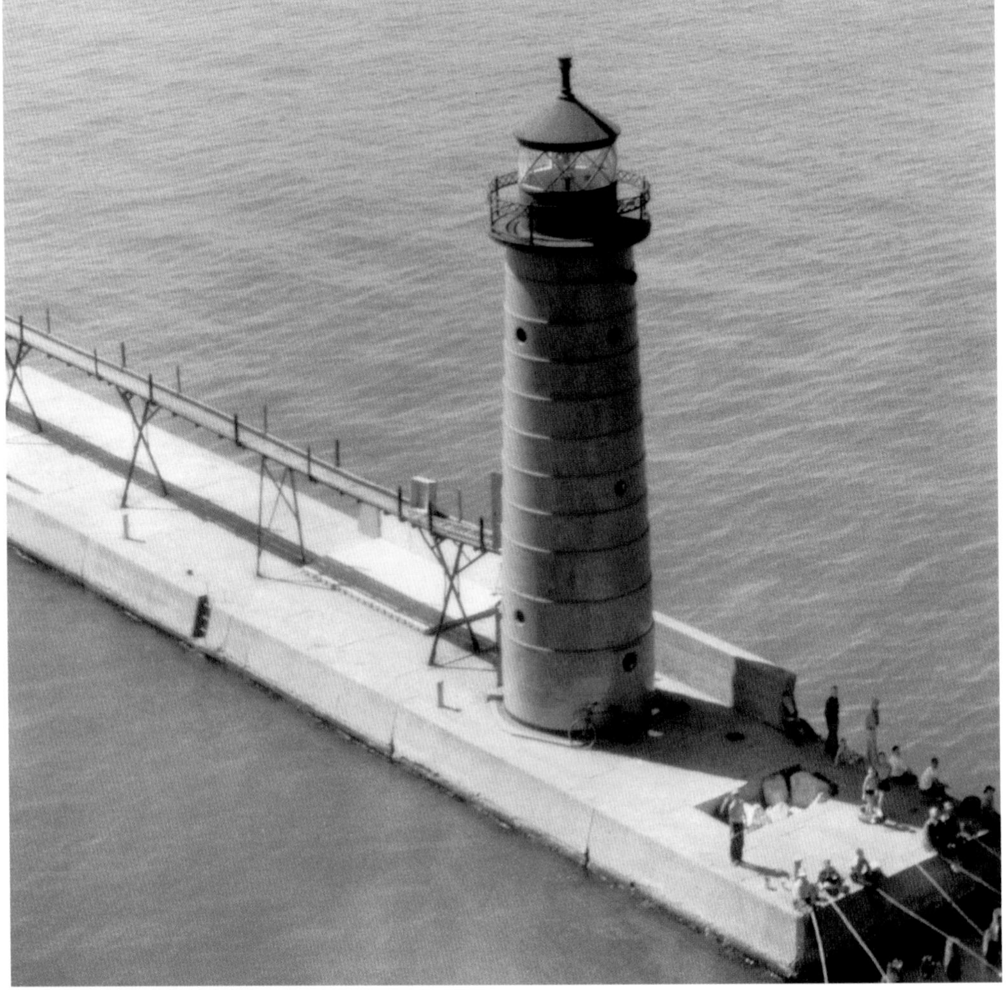

Position: 46 52 18 N. 90 29 48 W
Focal plane: 170ft (52m)
Range: 52 miles (84km)
Height: 102ft (31m)

This is the oldest station within the Apostle Islands chain. The original masonry tower, dating back to 1857, was built on the island by mistake. It should have been erected at La Pointe on nearby Long Island, and another lighthouse had to be commissioned a year later. The Michigan light was then decommissioned until it was fitted with a three-and-a-half-order Fresnel lens in 1869. It continued to operate until 1930, when the present 102-ft skeletal tower was erected.

Milwaukee Breakwater Light

Milwaukee, WI
Built: 1926
Style: Black lantern on square structure
No: 20635
Position: 43 01 37 N. 87 52 55 W
Focal plane: 61ft (19m)
Range: 19 miles (31km)
Height: 53ft (16m)

The lighthouse was built in 1926 to guide vessels into the port. Fitted with a fourth-order Fresnel lens, the station was automated in 1966.

Milwaukee Pierhead Light

Milwaukee, WI
Built: 1872 and 1906
Style: Conical

The red-painted lighthouse was built in 1906 to replace an earlier tower dating back

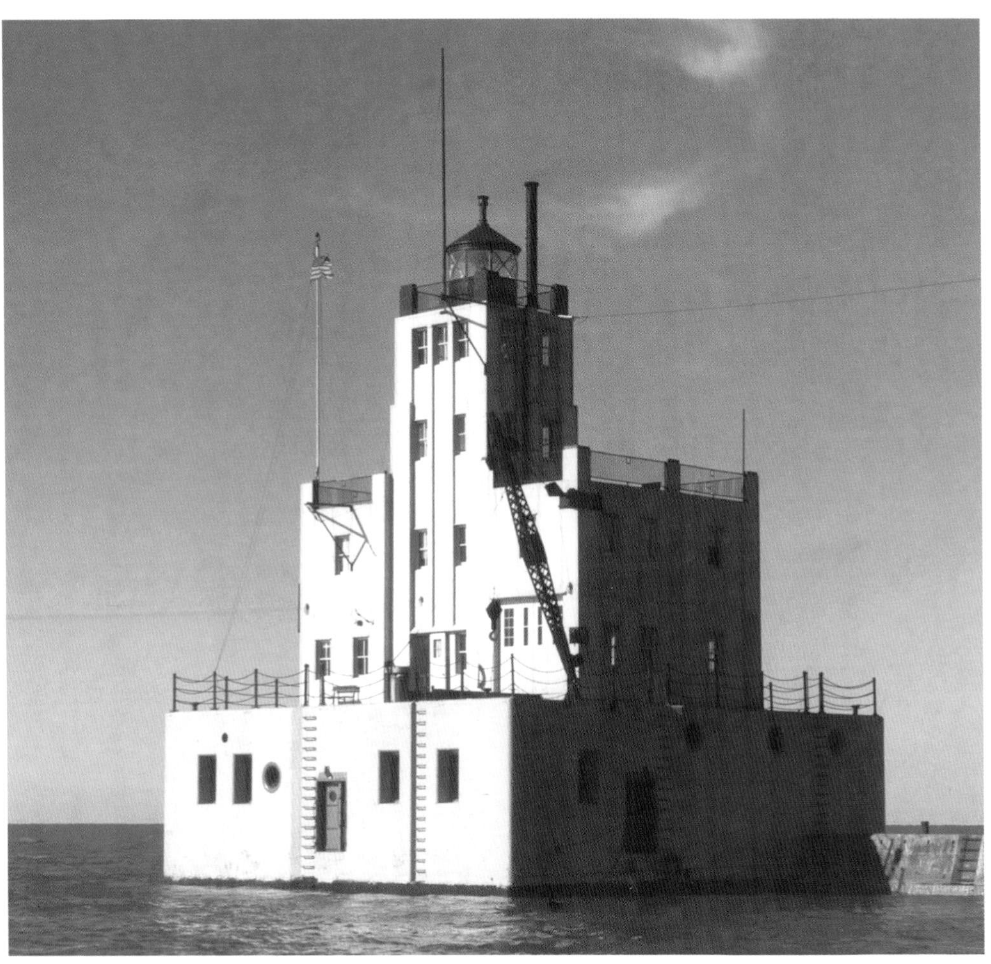

to 1872. The station, which is now decommissioned, once held a fourth-order Fresnel lens.

North Point Light

Milwaukee, WI
Built: 1855, 1888 and 1912
Style: Octagonal pyramid

The 74-ft (22.5-m) North Point lighthouse marking the entrance to the Milwaukee River, has something of a chequered history. The first tower, built in 1855, was undercut by erosion. A second 30-ft (9-m) cast-iron tower was erected in 1888, but this became overshadowed by trees. Rather than cutting them down, the lighthouse engineers decided to build a third 40-ft (12-m) tower and bolt the 1888 model on top. This and its fourth-order Fresnel lens has stood the test of time ever since.

Old Southport (Kenosha) Light

Kenosha, WI
Built: 1866
Style: Red conical tower
No: 20415
Position: 42 35 20 N. 87 48 31 W
Focal plane: 50ft (15m)
Range: 15 miles (24km)
Height: 50ft (15m)

This is the original tower marking Kenosha harbour. Built in 1866, its fourth-order Fresnel lens was deactivated in 1906 when the Kenosha Pierhead Light was completed a short way along the beach. The tower, which stands in Simmon's Island Park, is now managed by the Kenosha County Historical Society, which uses the light as a private aid to navigation.

LEFT
Milwaukee Breakwater Light, Wisconsin.

BELOW
Milwaukee Pierhead Light, Wisconsin.

OPPOSITE
Outer Island Light, Wisconsin.

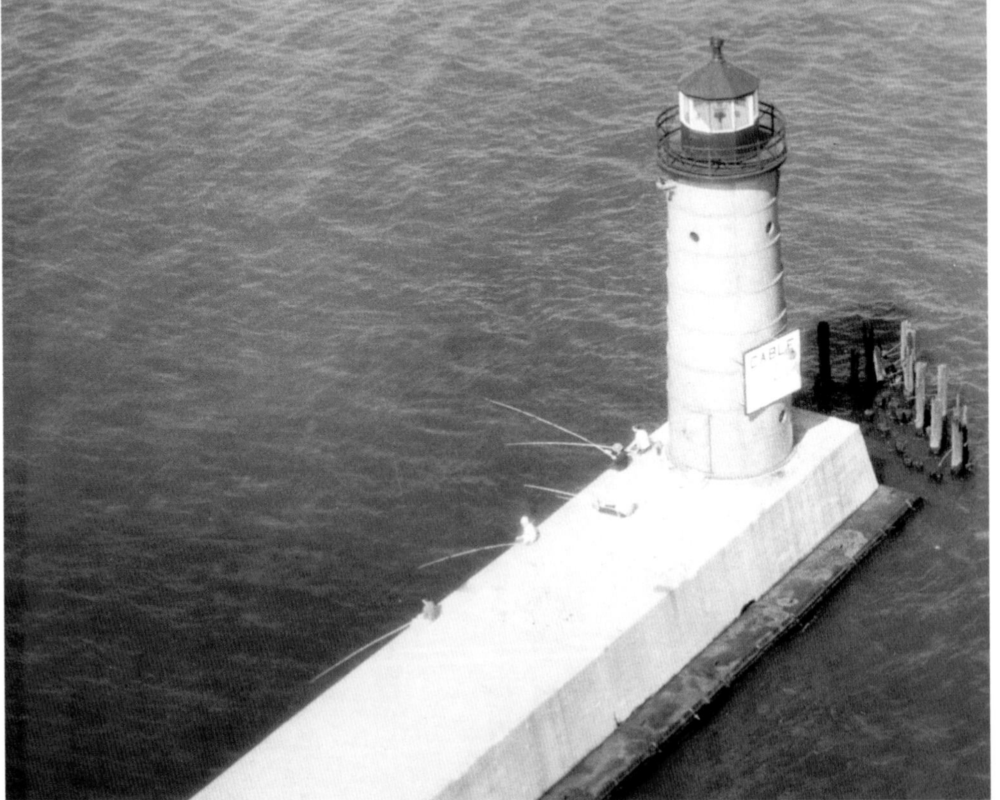

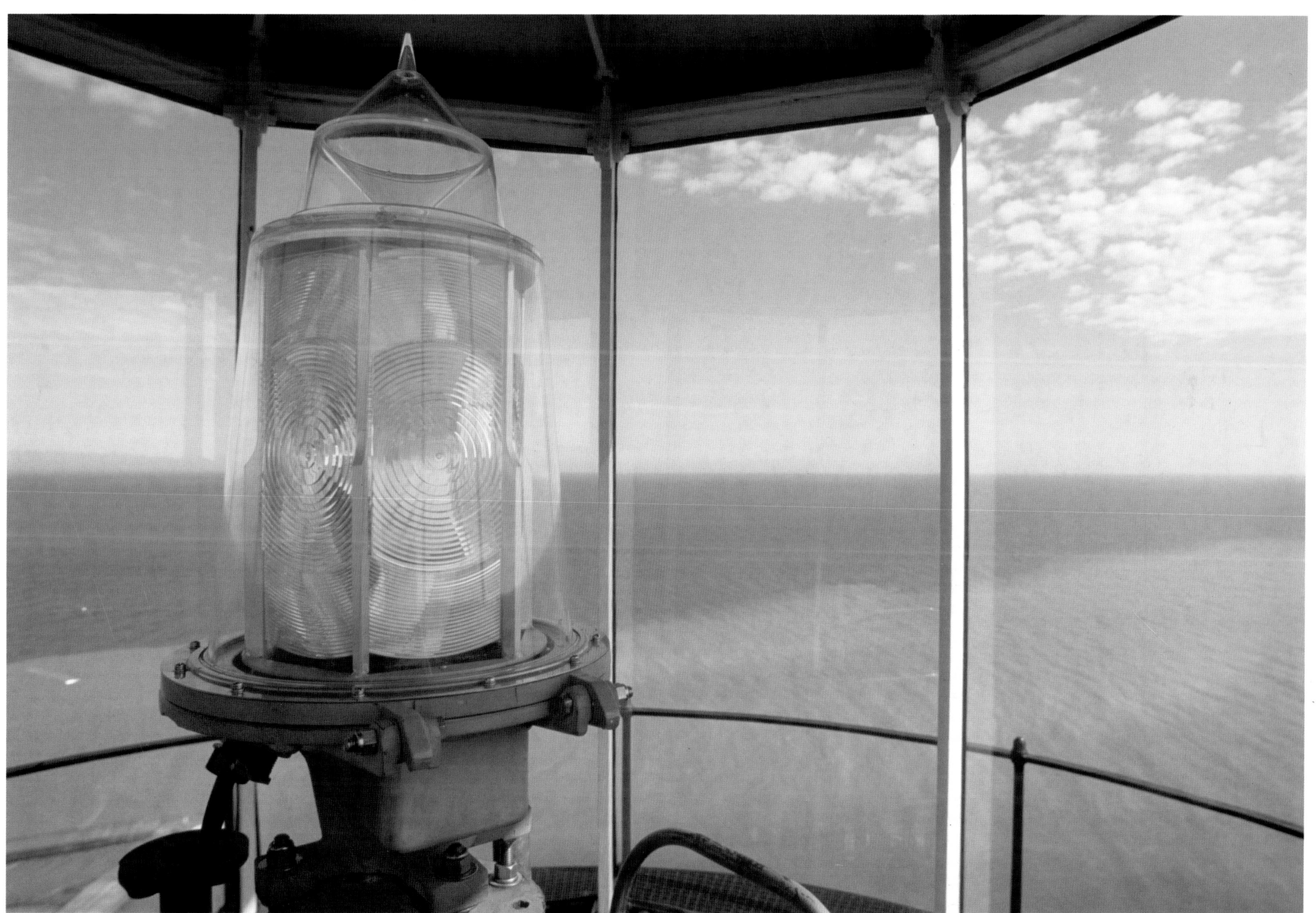

Outer Island Light

Apostle Islands, Bayfield, WI
Built: 1874
Style: White conical tower with dwelling
No: 15255
Position: 47 04 36 N. 90 25 00 W
Focal plane: 130ft (40m)
Range: 40 miles (64km)
Height: 80ft (24m)

The lighthouse was built on the north-east tip of the Apostle Islands. It is one of six lighthouses built along this chain of islands after the completion of the Soo Locks had opened Lake Superior to shipping from the other Great Lakes. The other towers are the Michigan Island (1857), the Chequamegon Point and the La Pointe on Long Island (1858), the Raspberry Island (1863), Sand Island (1881) and Devil's Island (1891). Outer Island was fitted with a third-order Fresnel lens, replaced by a solar-powered modern optic when the station was automated in 1961.

Peshtigo Reef Light

Peshtigo, WI
Built: 1934
Style: White column with red band.
No: 21990
Position: 44 57 24 N. 87 34 48 W
Focal plane: 72ft (22m)
Range: 22 miles (35km)

Still active today, the conical steel tower of the Peshtigo Reef lighthouse, built on a concrete crib three miles off Peshtigo Point, marks the south-eastern side of the shoal. It stands in open water across the bay from the Sherwood Point Light.

Pilot Island Light

Pilot Island, WI
Built: 1850
Style: Square tower attached to dwelling
No: 21325
Position: 45 17 06 N. 86 55 12 W
Focal plane: 48ft (15m)
Range: 15 miles (24km)
Height: 46ft (14m)

The lighthouse was built in 1850 to mark the hazardous passage to Green Bay. Originally, the tower was 37-ft high and the lantern room was raised a further 9ft in 1858. The station's fourth-order Fresnel lens was replaced with a modern plastic optic when the tower was automated.

Plum Island Range Lights

Lake Michigan, WI
Built: 1897
Style: Skeletal and cylindrical towers
No: 21305
Position: 45 18 12 N. 86 57 12 W
Focal plane: 41ft (12.5m)
Range: 12 miles (19km)

The skeletal Rear Range lighthouse and its partnering Front Range cylindrical tower were built in 1897 and continue to keep vessels within a narrow channel on Lake Michigan. The Rear Range tower still has its original fourth-order Fresnel lens.

Port Washington Light

Port Washington, WI
Built: 1860 and 1935
Style: Square tower on open-leg base
No: 20770
Position: 43 23 10 N. 87 51 35 W
Focal plane: 78ft (24m)
Range: 24 miles (39km)

The original lighthouse was built in 1860 on a bluff overlooking Lake Michigan to guide vessels towards the harbour. The tower, which now houses a museum, was decommissioned in 1935 when the light was transferred to a new arched concrete lighthouse built on the end of the harbour pier. This too lost its lantern when the station was automated in 1975.

Pottawatamie Light

Gills Rock, WI
Built: 1836 and 1856
Style: Square tower

The masonry Pottawatamie Light, known locally as the Rock Island Light, was built to replace an earlier tower dating 20 years earlier that fell in the hurricane of 1856. The light warned vessels of the hazardous rocks extending out from the Door Peninsula. The station was decommissioned during the 1920s and is now the subject of a restoration programme led by the Wisconsin Historical Society.

Racine North Breakwater Light

Racine, WI
Built: 1903
Style: Square pyramidal

Racine's North Breakwater Light, and its more recent South Breakwater Light, welcome vessels entering Racine harbour from Lake Michigan. The square, pyramidal North Breakwater tower dates to 1903 and originally stood on a crib in open water until the wall was extended to join the tower's foundations.

Rasberry Island Light, Wisconsin.

Raspberry Island Light

Apostle Islands, Bayfield, WI
Built: 1863 and 1959
Style: Column with box base
No: 15555
Position: 46 58 18 N. 90 48 18 W
Focal plane: 58ft (18m)
Range: 18 miles (29km)

The original Raspberry Island Light was built in 1863 as part of a chain of lighthouses covering the Apostle Islands. Mounted on the roof of the keeper's residence, which was extended later to house three families, the station's fifth-order Fresnel lens was transferred in 1959 to a mast set on a bluff that offers a clearer view of the light.

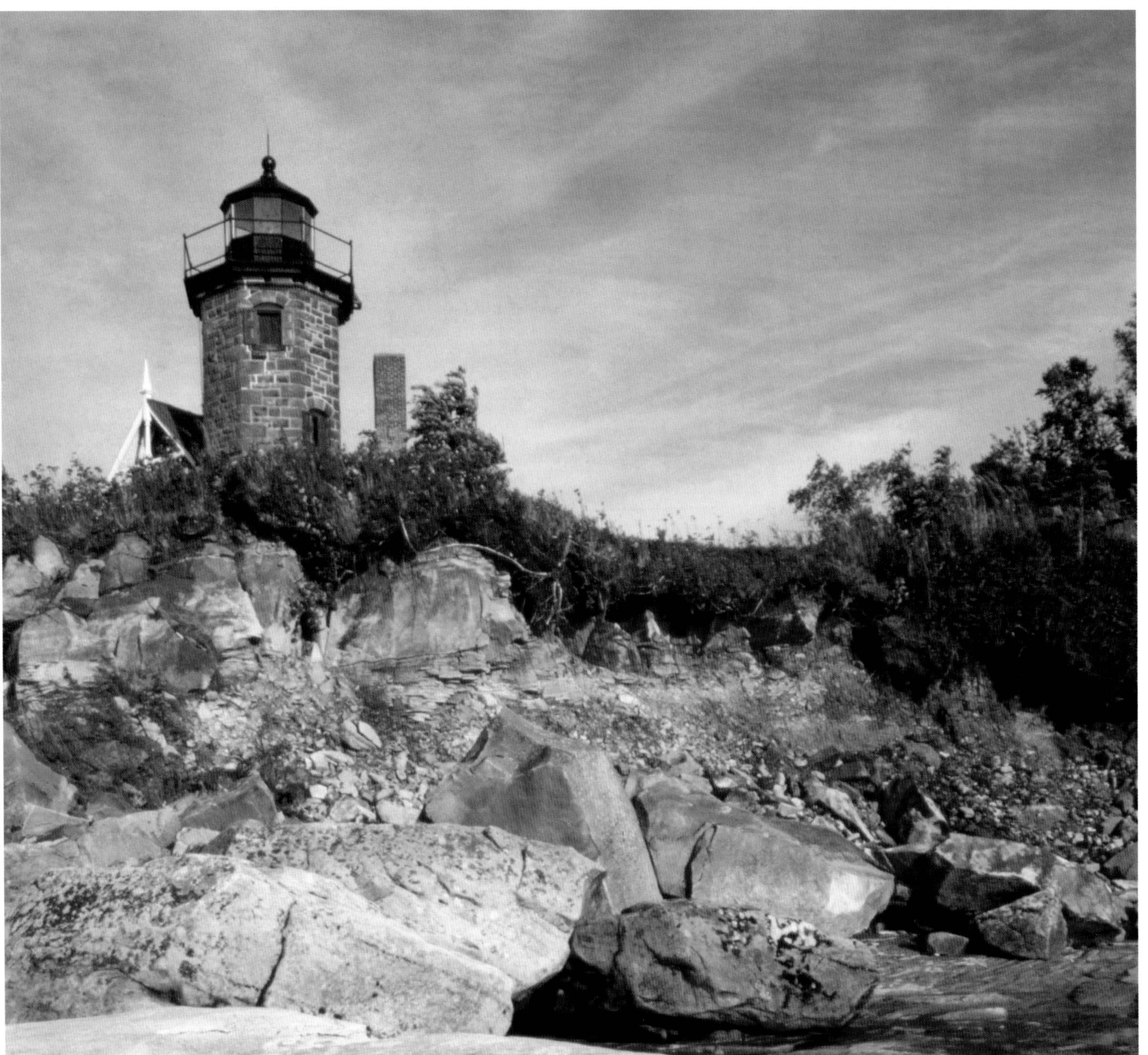

Sand Island Light, Wisconsin.

Rawley Point Light
Two Rivers, WI
Built: 1853, 1874 and 1894
Style: Skeletal tower
No: 20935
Position: 44 12 42 N. 87 30 30 W
Focal plane: 113ft (34m)
Range: 34 miles (55km)
Height: 111ft (34m)

The first Rawley Point station was established in 1853 to warn vessels away from a hazardous shoal. This was replaced by a square brick tower and two-storey keeper's dwelling in 1874. This in turn was superseded in 1894 by the present 111-ft skeletal tower, which is known locally as the Twin River Point Light. This cast-iron structure, with its eight bracing legs, was fitted with a third-order Fresnel lens, which was replaced with an aeromarine beacon when the tower was automated in 1979.

Sand Island Light
Apostle Islands, Bayfield, WI
Built: 1881
Style: Octagonal tower

The attractive brownstone Sand Island lighthouse was built in 1881 as part of the chain of lights erected across the Apostle

Islands after the Soo Locks had opened up Lake Superior to shipping from the other Great Lakes. The octagonal tower, with its attached keeper's dwelling, is sited on the north-west corner of the island and was equipped with a fourth-order Fresnel lens. This was updated with an acetylene light in 1921 before the station was decommissioned in 1933, when the light was transferred to a skeleton tower.

Sturgeon Bay Canal Light

Sturgeon Bay, WI
Built: 1899 and 1903
Style: Skeletal tower
No: 20995
Position: 44 47 42 N. 87 18 48 W
Focal plane: 107ft (33m)
Range: 33 miles (53km)
Height: 98ft (30m)

The skeletal lighthouse was built in 1903 to replace an earlier experimental steel latticed tower constructed four years earlier that had failed to withstand the test of winter storms. This second tower, with its third-order Fresnel lens, has stood for more than a century and now marks a Coast Guard base.

Superior South Breakwater Light

Wisconsin Point, WI
Built: 1913
Style: Cylindrical

The lighthouse was built in 1913 to mark the entrance to this harbour. The white concrete tower still retains its original fourth-order Fresnel lens.

Wind Point Light

Racine, Wisconsin.
Built: 1866 and 1880
Style: Conical tower connected to dwelling
No: 20605
Position: 42 46 52 N. 87 45 30 W
Focal plane: 111ft (34m)
Range: 34 miles (55km)
Height: 108ft (33m)

The lighthouse was built in 1866 to mark the shoal and guide vessels towards Racine harbor. The tower was extended in 1880 to its present height and was fitted with two lights to provide a clear beam for ships sailing in from the north. The station's third-order Fresnel lens provided the principal light, while the smaller fifth-order Fresnel lens sent a red warning signal out over the hazardous Racine shoal. The tower was automated in 1964 when the Fresnel lenses were replaced with an aero-marine beacon.

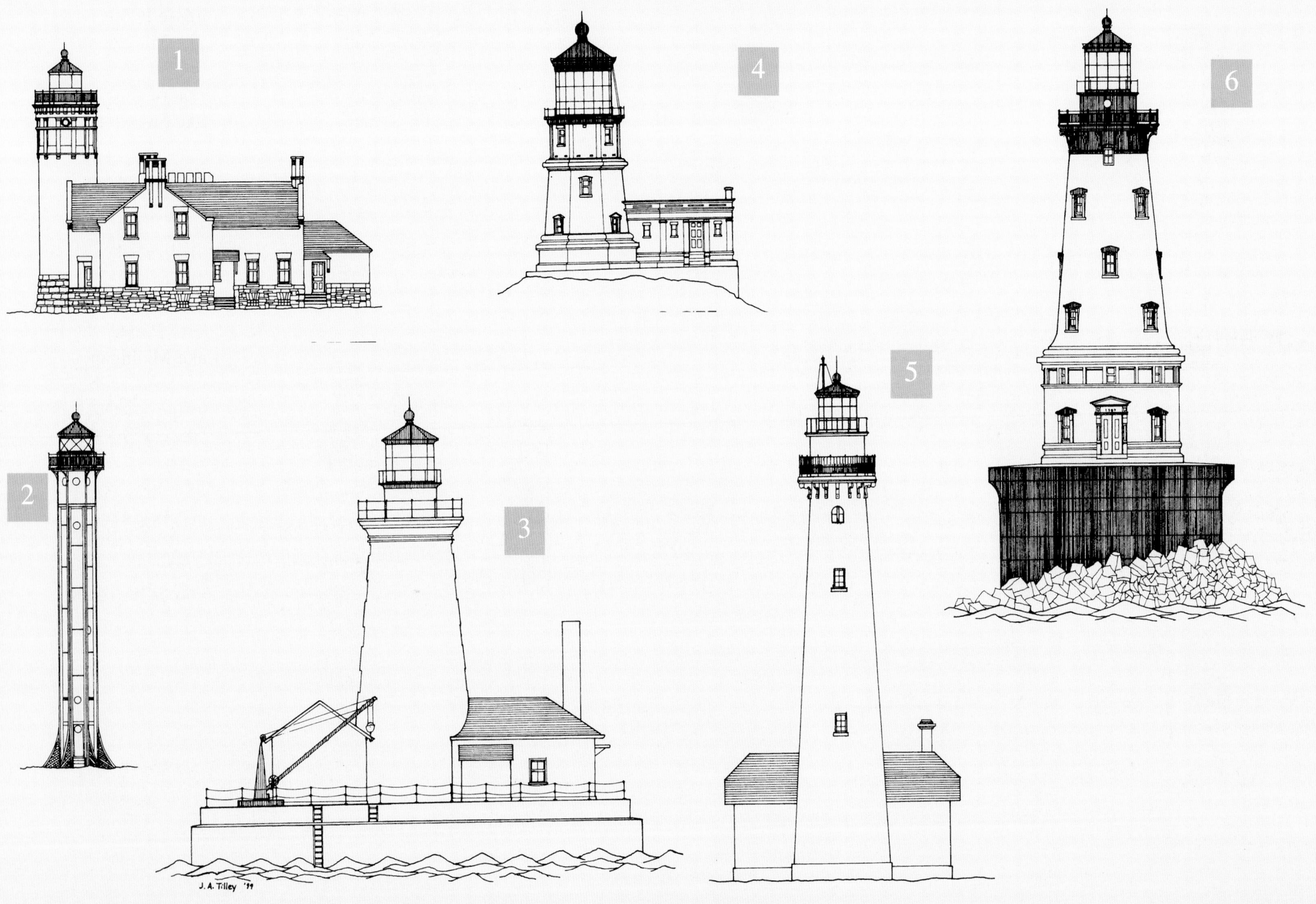
1
4
6
5
2
3
J. A. Tilley '99

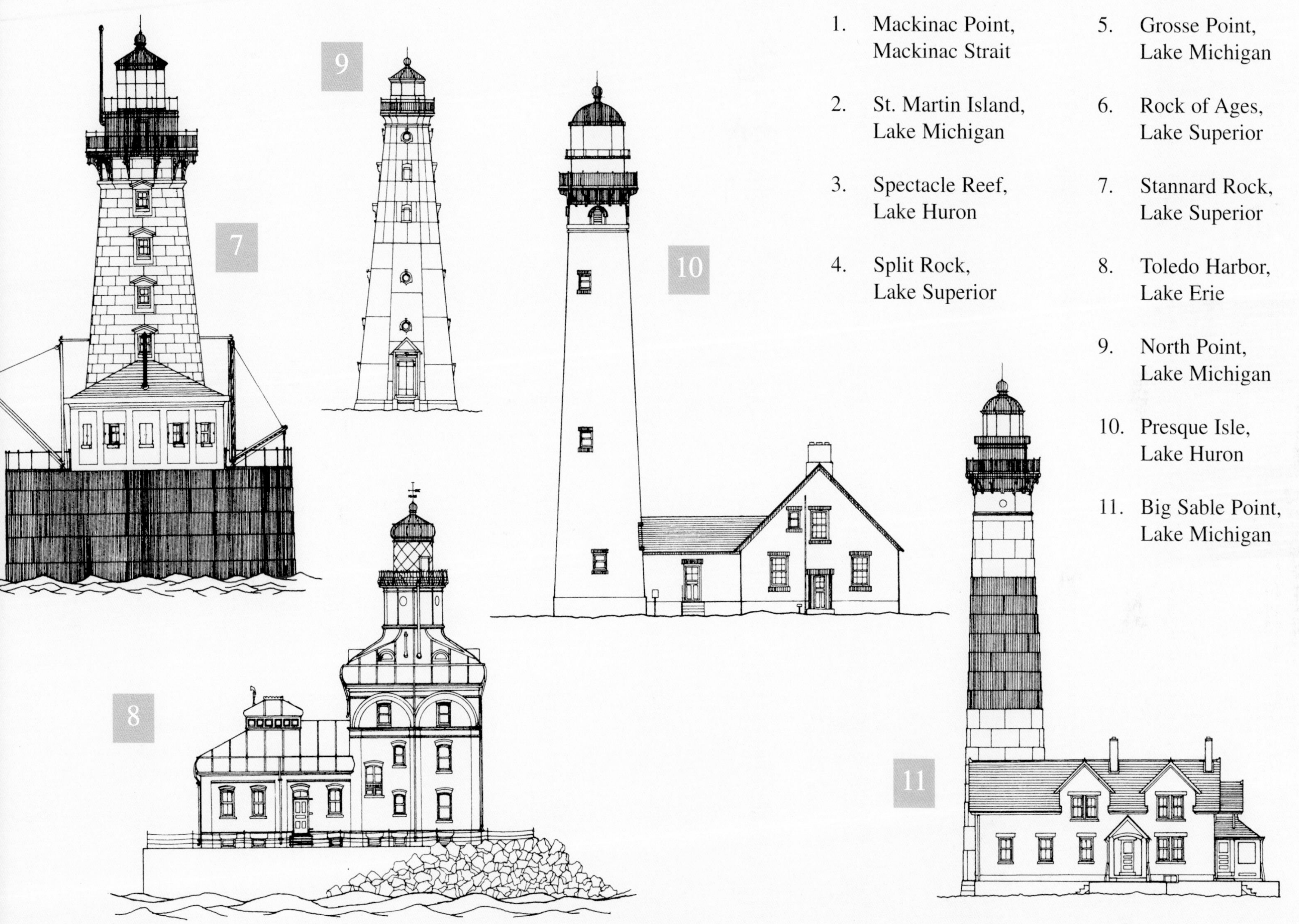

1. Mackinac Point, Mackinac Strait
2. St. Martin Island, Lake Michigan
3. Spectacle Reef, Lake Huron
4. Split Rock, Lake Superior
5. Grosse Point, Lake Michigan
6. Rock of Ages, Lake Superior
7. Stannard Rock, Lake Superior
8. Toledo Harbor, Lake Erie
9. North Point, Lake Michigan
10. Presque Isle, Lake Huron
11. Big Sable Point, Lake Michigan

Chapter Seven

Lighthouses of the North-East

Connecticut

Avery Point Light

Groton, CT
Built: 1944
Style: Octagonal

Avery Point was built up as a private estate by the yachtsman Morton Plant. When he died, the property was taken over by the U.S. Coast Guard, which built the 55-ft (17-m) Avery Point lighthouse as part of its training centre. The light was deactivated in 1967 when the Groton training centre became a university campus.

Black Rock Harbor Light

Fayerweather Island, Bridgeport, CT
Built: 1808 and 1823
Style: Octagonal

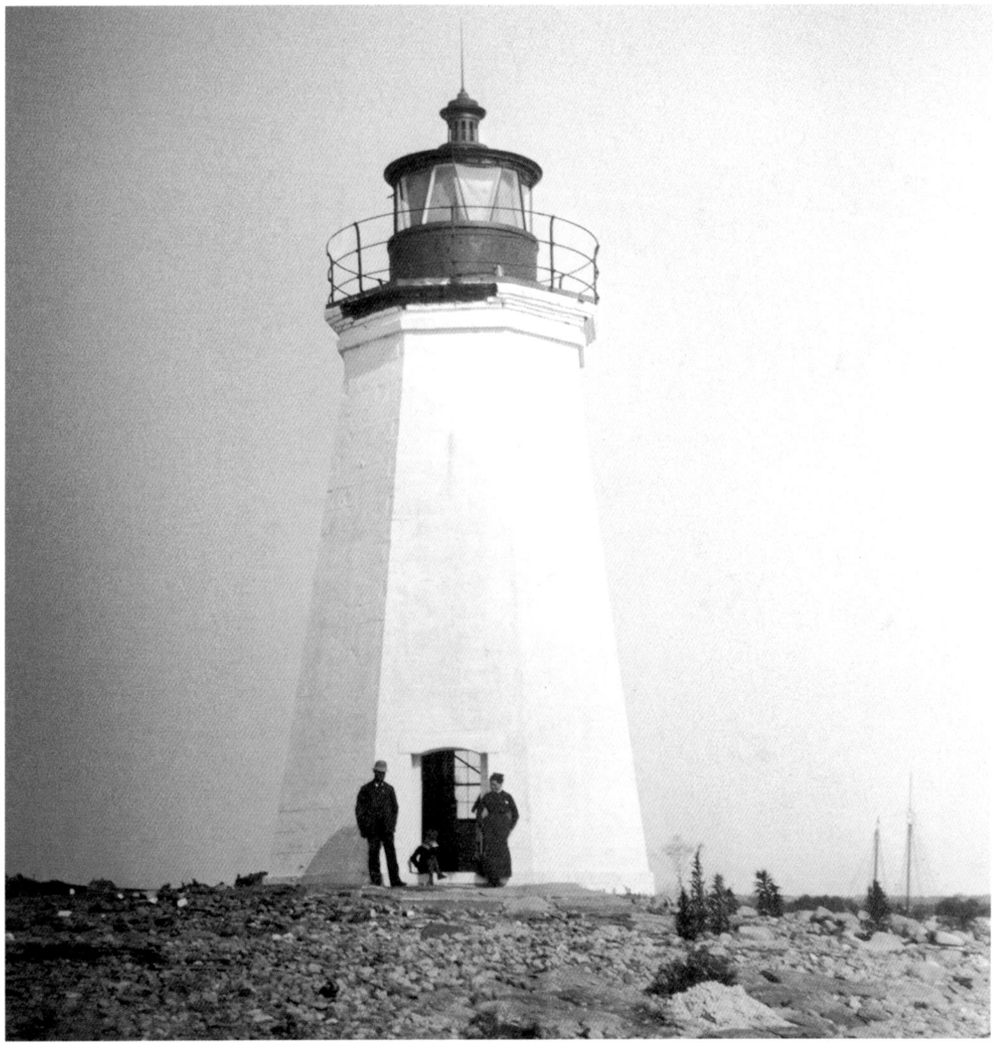

RIGHT
Black Rock Harbor Light, Connecticut.

OPPOSITE
Bridgeport Breakwater Light, Connecticut.

Black Rock lighthouse was built on Fayerweather Island to mark the harbour entrance. The first tower was destroyed by a hurricane in 1821 and its 47-ft (14-m) replacement, completed in 1823 and constructed of stone and wood, has survived ever since. It was equipped with a fifth-order Fresnel lens until deactivated in 1933. The tower, which is also known as Seaside Light, is lit at night by preservationists but is no longer an official navigation aid.

Bridgeport Breakwater Light (Tongue Point Light)

Bridgeport, CT
Built: 1895
Style: Conical tower

Bridgeport Breakwater lighthouse stands beside Bridgeport's harbour. The 21-ft (6-m) black tower, which has the look of a teapot, remains an active navigation aid, but the main light was moved in 1921 to Tongue Point on the other side of the harbour. Locals resisted plans by the Coast Guard to remove the lighthouse in 1967, and the light's original sixth-order Fresnel lens was replaced by a modern reflector in 1988.

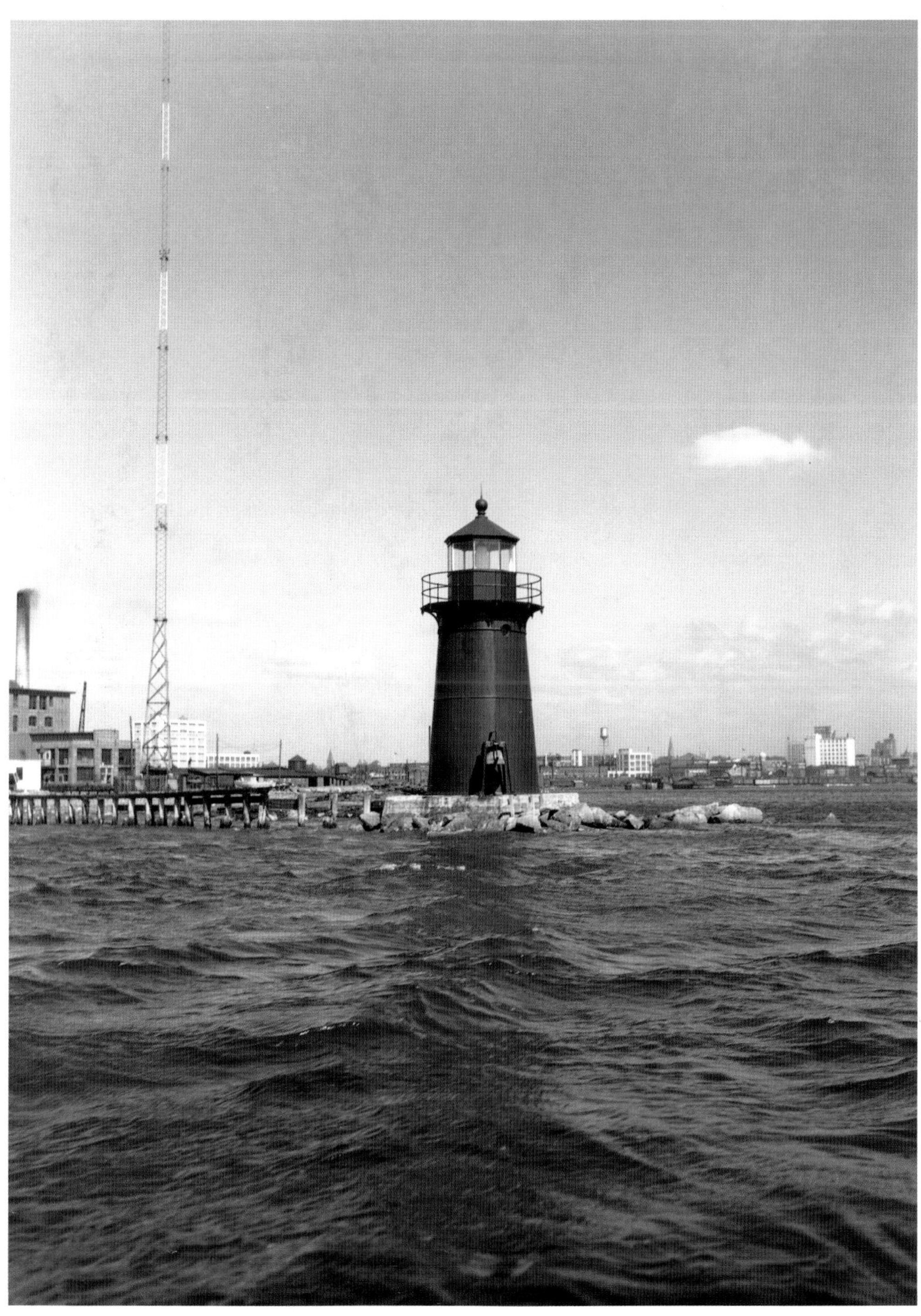

Faulkner's Island Lighthouse

Guilford, CT
Built: 1802
Style: Octagonal

The Faulkner's Island station is Connecticut's second oldest lighthouse. In 1976 it was almost destroyed by fire, and local preservationists are struggling to save what remains from the eroding effects of burrowing rabbits as much as wind and sea. The fieldstone structure was built (in what is now a bird sanctuary) to warn vessels away from the notorious rocks that line this section of the Connecticut coast.

Five Mile Point Light

New Haven, CT
Built: 1805 and 1847
Style: Octagonal

A lighthouse was first established on Five Mile Point in 1805, but the original 30-ft (9-m) wooden tower was an inadequate navigation aid for vessels entering New Haven. However, it was not replaced until 1847 by the present 65-ft (20-m) sandstone and brick octagonal tower, which was equipped with a fourth-order Fresnel lens in 1855. The construction of a new lighthouse on Southwest Ledge outside the harbour mouth in 1877 rendered the Five Mile Point light redundant and it was deactivated.

Great Captain Island Light

Long Island Sound, Greenwich, CT
Built: 1830 and 1860
Style: Stone tower

The purpose of the lighthouse on Great Captain Island was to guide vessels up the western reaches of Long Island Sound. The current schoolhouse-style stone tower of 1860 was fitted with a fourth-order Fresnel lens until decommissioned in 1970, when a featureless steel tower was erected to replace it.

Greens Ledge Light

Norwalk, CT
Built: 1902
Style: Conical iron tower on cylindrical pier
No: 21340
Position: 41 02 30 N. 73 26 38 W

The lighthouse was one of the first concrete caisson structures. The 52-ft (16-m) cast-iron tower built on it was equipped with a fourth-order Fresnel lens until it was replaced with a modern optic, which can be seen across Long Island Sound for up to 17 miles (27km).

Lynde Point Light

Old Saybrook, CT
Built: 1803 and 1835
Style: Octagonal
No: 22520
Position: 41 16 17 N. 72 30 35 W
Height: 65ft (20m)

The original lighthouse in Old Saybrook was an octagonal wooden tower equipped with whale-oil lamps. It was replaced with the current octagonal stone tower in 1835 and houses a fifth-order Fresnel lens with a range of 14 miles (22.5km).

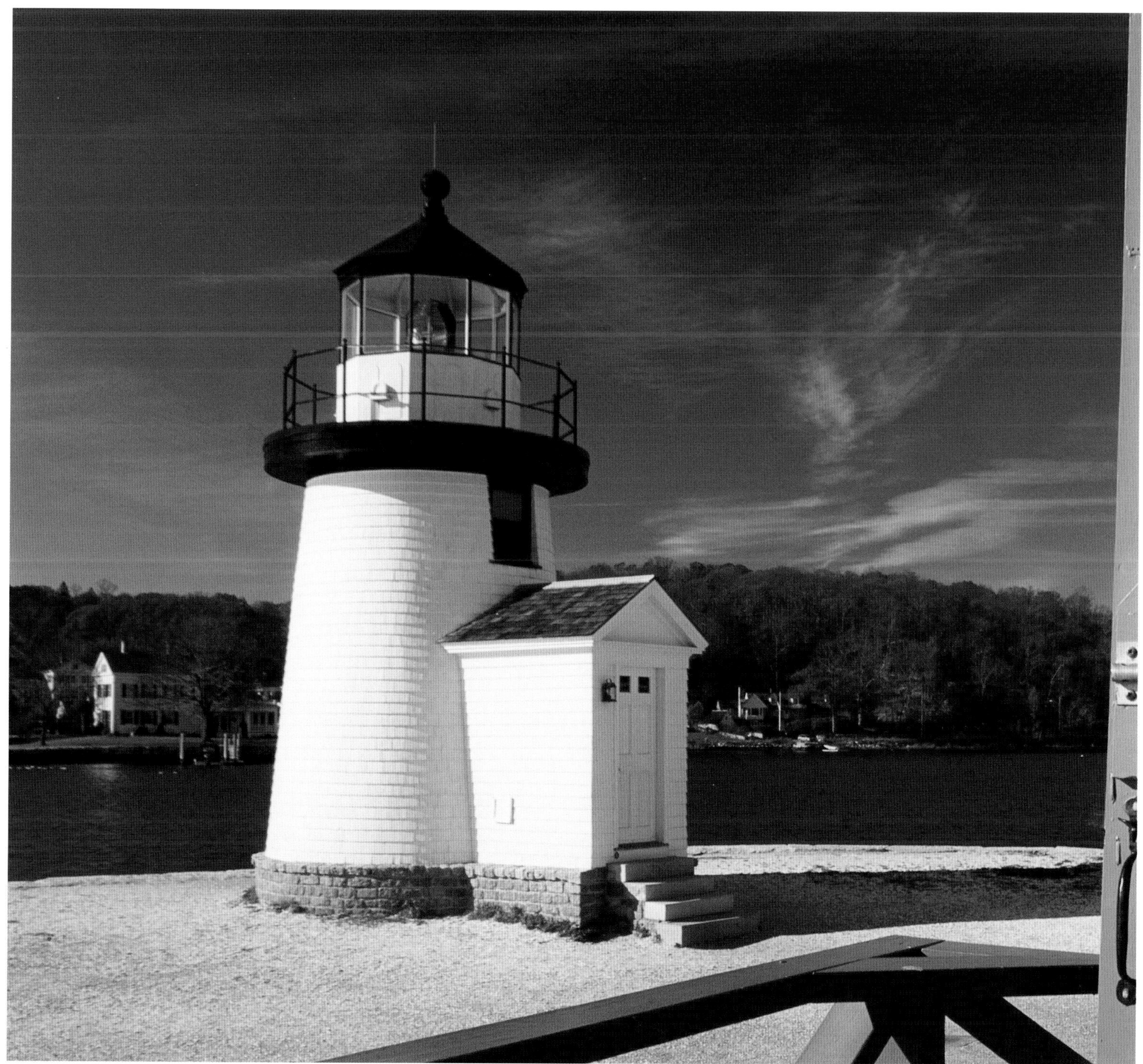

OPPOSITE LEFT
New London Harbor Light, Connecticut.

OPPOSITE RIGHT
Great Captain Island Light, Connecticut.

LEFT
Mystic Seaport Light, Connecticut.

Morgan Point Light

Noank, CT
Built: 1831 and 1868
Style: Octagonal

The original Morgan Point lighthouse was a 25-ft (8-m) granite tower built to guide vessels into the Mystic River. It proved less than adequate, so in 1868 it was replaced by a two-storey granite building supporting a 60-ft (18-m) cast-iron tower equipped with a sixth-order Fresnel lens. The lighthouse was decommissioned in 1919 and was replaced by an automated beacon to the east. The building is now a private residence.

Mystic Seaport Light

Mystic, CT
Built: 1901
Style: Conical

This is a replica of the Brant Point lighthouse on Nantucket Island and stands on a bend in the Mystic River. It is part of Connecticut's living-history museum town of Mystic Seaport.

New London Harbor Light

New London, CT
Built: 1760 and 1801
Style: Octagonal
No: 21845
Position: 41 19 00 N. 72 05 24 W
Range: W 17 miles/27km, R 14 miles/23km
Height: 80ft (24m)

The first stone lighthouse at New London harbour was built in 1760, funded by a public lottery. It was the fourth to be built in colonial America. The current 80-ft stone tower of 1801 still uses the same fourth-order Fresnel lens that was fitted in 1857.

New London Ledge Light

New London, CT
Built: 1910
Style: Cylindrical tower on brick building
No: 21825
Position: 41 18 18 N. 72 04 42 W
Focal plane: 58ft (18m)
Range: W 17 miles/27km, R 14 miles/23km

This is one of the most architecturally striking buildings of its kind in the United States. Modelled on the French Empire style, the three-storey building, which marks a dangerous ledge at the entrance to the Connecticut River, has a small cylindrical tower on the roof. It was equipped originally with a fourth-order Fresnel lens, but this was replaced in 1984 by a modern optic.

Peck Ledge Light

Norwalk, CT
Built: 1906
Style: Conical tower on cylindrical pier
No: 24930
Position: 41 04 39 N. 73 22 11 W
Focal plane: 61ft (18.5m)
Range: 7 miles (11km)
Height: 54ft (16.5m)

The Peck Ledge lighthouse, marking the shoals to the east of Norwalk Island on Long Island Sound, has a brick-lined tower based on a concrete caisson similar to Greens Ledge lighthouse. It was equipped with a fourth-order Fresnel lens, but the lighthouse was automated at an early stage and now has a modern plastic lens with a range of 7 miles.

Penfield Reef Light

Fairfield, CT
Built: 1874
Style: Tower on dwelling on cylindrical pier
No: 21290
Position: 41 07 00 N. 73 13 18 W
Focal plane: 51ft (15.5m)
Range: 15 miles (24km)
Height: 35ft (11m)

Penfield Reef is one of the most dangerous shoals in Long Island Sound. About a mile south of Fairfield, it has torn the bottom out of many a vessel. The present stone-built lighthouse has a tower rising from the roof of the keeper's residence. It once had a fourth-order Fresnel lens but is now equipped with a modern automated optic. In 1916, Frederick Jordon, the keeper of the Penfield Light, was tragically drowned when his boat capsized as he rowed ashore to have Christmas dinner with his family.

Saybrook Breakwater Light

Old Saybrook, CT
Built: 1886
Style: Conical tower on cylindrical pier
No: 22495
Position: 41 15 48 N. 72 20 34 W
Focal plane: 58ft (18m)
Range: 11 miles (18km)
Height: 50ft (15m)

The cast-iron tower was erected in 1886 and stands at the end of a stone jetty to mark a sandbar at the mouth of the Connecticut River. It was once equipped with a fifth-order Fresnel lens but this has since been replaced by an automated plastic lens.

Sheffield Island Light

Norwalk, CT
Built: 1828 and 1868
Style: Octagonal, integrated schoolhouse

A lighthouse was first commissioned at Sheffield Island in 1828, The current two-storey keeper's home and steeple light was operational from 1868 until 1902. It has been restored by the Norwalk Seaport Association.

Southwest Ledge Light

New Haven, CT
Built: 1877
Style: Octagonal on cylindrical pier
No: 24060
Position: 41 14 04 N. 72 54 44 W
Focal plane: 57ft (17m)
Range: 13 miles (21km)

This was one of the first U.S. caisson-built light towers. It was displayed at the 1876 Philadelphia Centennial Exposition before being sunk directly on this dangerous ledge outside New Haven the following year. The design has survived the winter ice for more than 120 years. In 1988 its fourth-order Fresnel lens was replaced by a modern optic.

Stamford Harbor Light

Stamford, CT
Built: 1882
Style: Caisson

This 60-ft (18-m) cast-iron tower sits on a large concrete caisson which was sunk on Chatham Rock to mark the entrance to Stamford harbour in 1882. The light was decommissioned in 1953, and although now privately owned, is maintained as a working navigation light.

Stonington Harbor Light

Stonington, CT
Built: 1823 and 1840
Style: Stone

The museum lighthouse at Stonington was built in 1823 on the west side of the harbour entrance. Sea erosion began to threaten the tower during the 1830s and it was dismantled and moved to its present site in 1840. The station was first equipped with a Lewis lamp, a lamp-and-reflector system, but this was upgraded with a sixth-order Fresnel lens in 1855. The lighthouse was decommissioned in 1899 when a cast-iron lighthouse was erected on the breakwater. This too is no longer in use.

Stratford Point Light

Stratford, CT
Built: 1822 and 1881
Style: Conical

The first lighthouse at Stratford Point, a wooden tower, was replaced by the present 35-ft (11-m) brick-lined, cast-iron tower in 1822. It was equipped with a third-order Fresnel lens, which was replaced by a modern optic in 1990.

Stratford Shoal Middle Ground Light

Bridgeport, CT
Built: 1877
Style: Octagonal granite tower on house
No: 21230
Position: 41 03 35 N. 73 06 05 W
Focal plane: 60ft (18m)
Range: 13 miles (21km)
Height: 35ft (11m)

Stratford Shoal, midway between Bridgeport and Long Island, was originally guarded by a lightship, first stationed there in 1837. The present granite tower and keeper's house replaced her in 1877. The station, which is also known as Middle Ground Light, was equipped with a fourth-order Fresnel lens, replaced by a modern optic in 1988. Never a popular posting, the isolation of the lighthouse drove an assistant keeper mad in 1905 and he tried to wreck the lantern. It was finally automated in 1970.

Delaware

Bellevue Rear Range Light

Wilmington, DE
Built: 1909
Style: Steel skeletal tower
No: 3085
Focal plane: 90ft (27m)

This typical steel skeletal light tower, positioned close to the Christina River entrance to Wilmington, is one of several stations along Delaware Bay and River. The 104-ft (32-m) black tower was erected in 1909 and displays a fixed, green light which was emitted via a Fresnel lens until replaced by a plastic optic.

Brandywine Shoal Light

Delaware Bay, DE
Built: 1850 and 1914
Style: Cylindrical concrete tower
No: 1555
Position: 38 59 10 N. 75 06 47 W
Focal plane: 60ft (18m)
Range: W 19 miles/31km, R 13 miles/21km

New London Ledge Light, Connecticut.

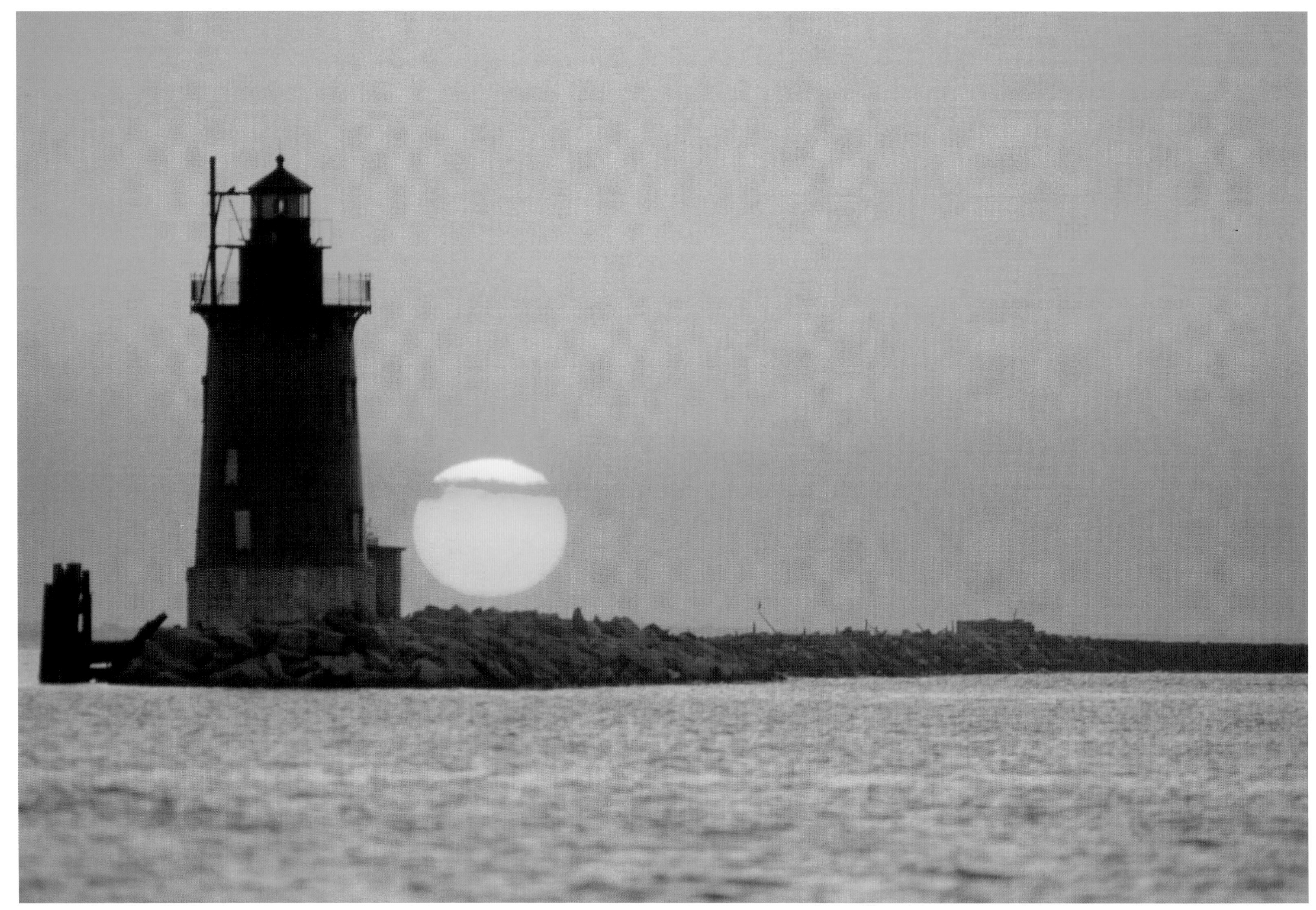

OPPOSITE
Delaware Breakwater East Light, Delaware.

RIGHT
Fenwick Island Light, Delaware.

The Brandywine Shoal in Delaware Bay was first marked by a lightship in 1823. Initial attempts to build a permanent structure failed until the screwpile-platform design was tried in 1850. An outer ring of piles protected the platform from the crushing effects of the ice floes and it remained in place for 64 years before being replaced by the present caisson tower in 1914.

Delaware Breakwater East Light

Lewes, DE
Built: 1885
Style: Conical

This is a 49-ft (15-m) conical 'sparkplug'-type tower erected in 1885 at the end of a stone breakwater off Lewes. It was decommissioned in 1996 but has since been renovated and now acts as a day mark.

Fenwick Island Light

Fenwick Island, DE
Built: 1858
Style: Conical tower
No: 205
Position: 38 27 06 N. 75 03 18 W
Focal plane: 83ft (25m)
Range: 8 miles (13km)
Height: 87ft (26.5m)

The Fenwick Island lighthouse marks both the outer Delaware coast and the eastern end of the Mason-Dixon Line. The brick-built tower still has its original third-order Fresnel lens, but the keeper's house is now a museum.

Fourteen Foot Bank Light

Bowers Beach, DE
Built: 1876 and 1888
Style: Tower and house on cylindrical pier
No: 1575
Position: 39 02 54 N. 75 10 56 W
Focal plane: 59ft (18m)
Range: W 13 miles/21km, R 10 miles/16km

The dangerous Fourteen Foot Bank, midway between Wilmington and the open sea, originally had a lightship stationed there. This was replaced in 1888 by a concrete caisson and cast-iron tower which has been in continuous operation ever since, though its original fourth-order Fresnel lens has now been replaced by a solar-powered optic.

Harbor of Refuge Light

Lewes, DE
Built: 1896 and 1926
Style: Conical on cylindrical substructure
No: 1530
Position: 38 48 52 N. 75 05 33 W
Focal plane: 72ft (22m)
Range: W 19 miles/31km, R 16 miles/26km
Height: 66ft (20m)

The Delaware Bay area is notorious in heavy weather and over the centuries many vessels have foundered on its lee shore. In

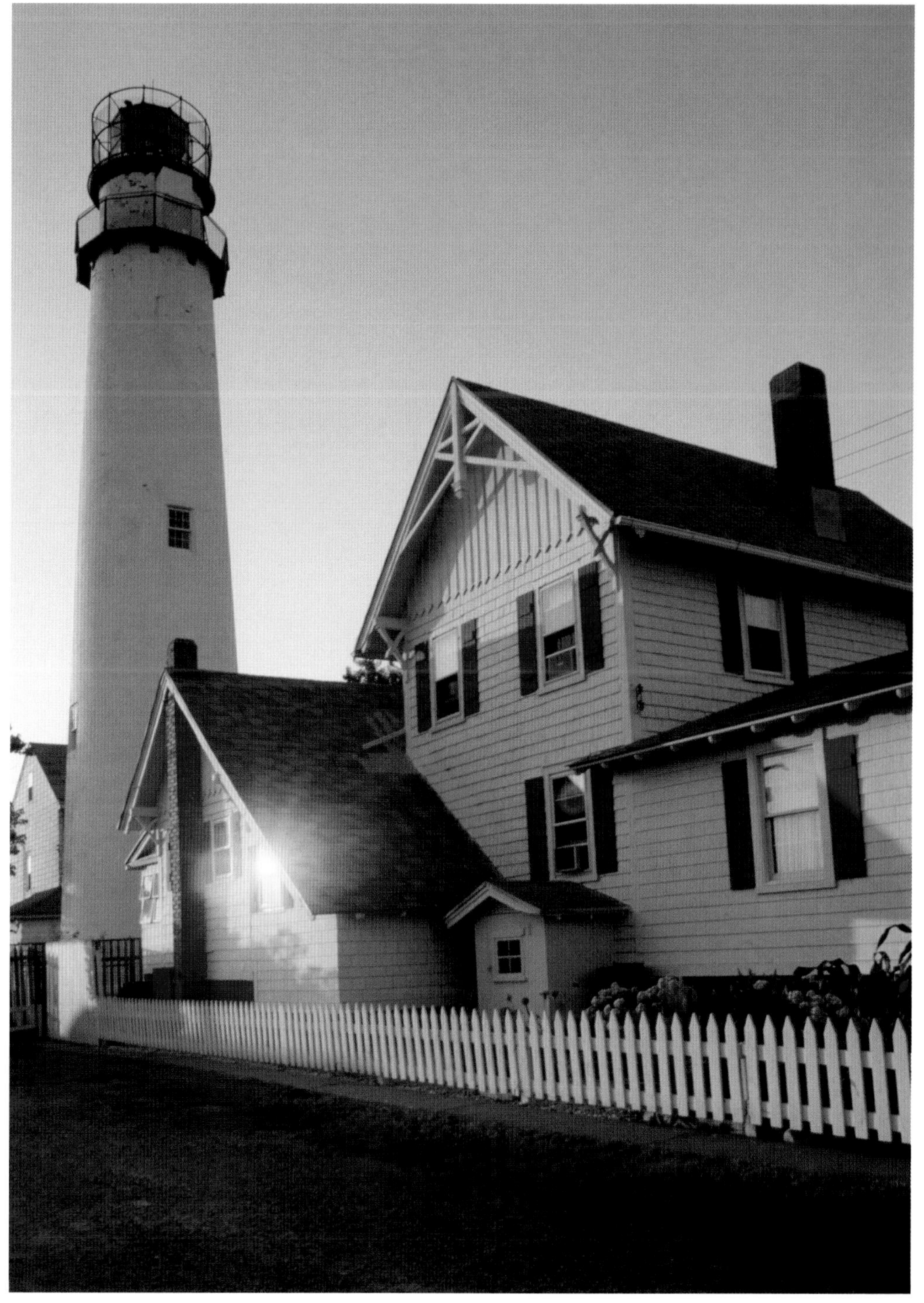

RIGHT and OPPOSITE
Harbor of Refuge Light, Delaware.

the mid-19th century a harbour of refuge was established at the mouth of Delaware Bay, east of Cape Henlopen, to provide shelter from the worst of the Atlantic storms. The harbour still serves battered mariners and their ships. The entrance is marked by this cast-iron 'sparkplug'-type tower which was erected in 1926 to replace an earlier tower built in 1896. The existing tower was originally equipped with a fourth-order Fresnel lens, but was automated in 1973 and now has a solar-powered optic.

Liston Front and Rear Range Lights

Fort Penn, DE
Built: 1877 and 1906
Style: Skeletal tower with house
No: 2445 (Front Light)
Position: 39 28 57 N. 75 35 30 W
Focal plane: 45ft (14m)

The Liston Front Range tower stands 45ft above sea level on top of the keeper's wooden house, and is partnered by a 120-ft (37-m) black steel skeletal tower which was equipped originally with a second-order Fresnel lens. The station was automated in 1976 and this rear light was replaced by an aero-marine beacon.

DELAWARE
DRBA

Marcus Hook Range Lights

Bellefonte, DE
Built: 1918
Style: Skeleton tower
No: 3135 (Front Light)

No: 3140 (Rear Light)
Style: Concrete square tower

The 85-ft (26-m) high concrete tower and its 100-ft (30.5-m) steel skeletal front range partnering tower were built at Marcus Hook in 1918 to guide vessels up the Delaware River. They have since been automated.

Mispillion Creek Light

Milford, DE
Built: 1875 and 1929
Style: Wooden tower and house

The Mispillion Light was designed and built by local people in 1875, and the two-storey house with its 48-ft (15-m) tower has been added to and renovated several times, mixing styles and construction methods. It was equipped with a sixth-order Fresnel lens, but the station was replaced by an automated steel light tower in 1929.

Reedy Island Rear Range Light

Taylor's Bridge, DE
Built: 1839 and 1910
Style: Skeleton tower
No: 2510
Focal plane: 110ft (33.5m)
Height: 57ft (17m)

The original Reedy Island Rear Range Light stood for 61 years until superseded by the present 110-ft pyramidal, slatted-steel skeletal tower in 1910. The keeper's house and outbuildings remain, but the tower's fifth-order Fresnel lens has long been replaced by a modern optic.

Ship John Shoal Light

Fortesque, Delaware Bay, DE
Built: 1874
Style: Octagonal structure on cylindrical pier
No: 1640
Focal plane: 50ft (15m)
Range: W 16 miles/26km, R 12 miles/19km
Height: 50ft (15m)

The red-painted cast-iron tower and concrete-filled caisson that forms the Ship John Shoal lighthouse, is sited at the mouth of the Delaware River. It was originally equipped with a fourth-order Fresnel lens until it was replaced by a modern optic lens during automation.

LEFT
Marcus Hook Rear Range Lights, Delaware.

OPPOSITE
Ship John Shoal Light, Delaware.

LEFT
Liston Range Lights, Delaware.

OPPOSITE
Bass Harbor Head Light, Maine.

Maine

Baker Island Light

Baker Island, ME
Built: 1828 and 1855
Style: Cylindrical stone tower
No: 2045
Position: 44 14 30 N. 68 11 54 W
Focal plane: 105ft (32km)
Range: 10 miles (16km)
Height: 43ft (13km)

Baker Island and its lighthouse was the subject of a 40-year dispute between the Gilley family, who manned the light for 21 years and the Lighthouse Board. The 43-ft brick tower and keeper's house were built in 1855 to replace an earlier wooden structure dating back to 1828. William Gilley, the first keeper of the new tower, lost his job in 1849 and subsequent keepers were harassed by Gilley's sons into paying landing fees whenever they came and went, as well as pasture rights for their cattle. When this was reported to the Lighthouse Board, the Inspectorate brought a lawsuit against the Gilley family, charging them with squatting. The Gilleys won the case after proving title to the land, and a compromise was reached allowing the Board to retain 19 acres of land around the lighthouse. The feud continued to rumble on, however, and 40 years later the two parties faced each other in court once

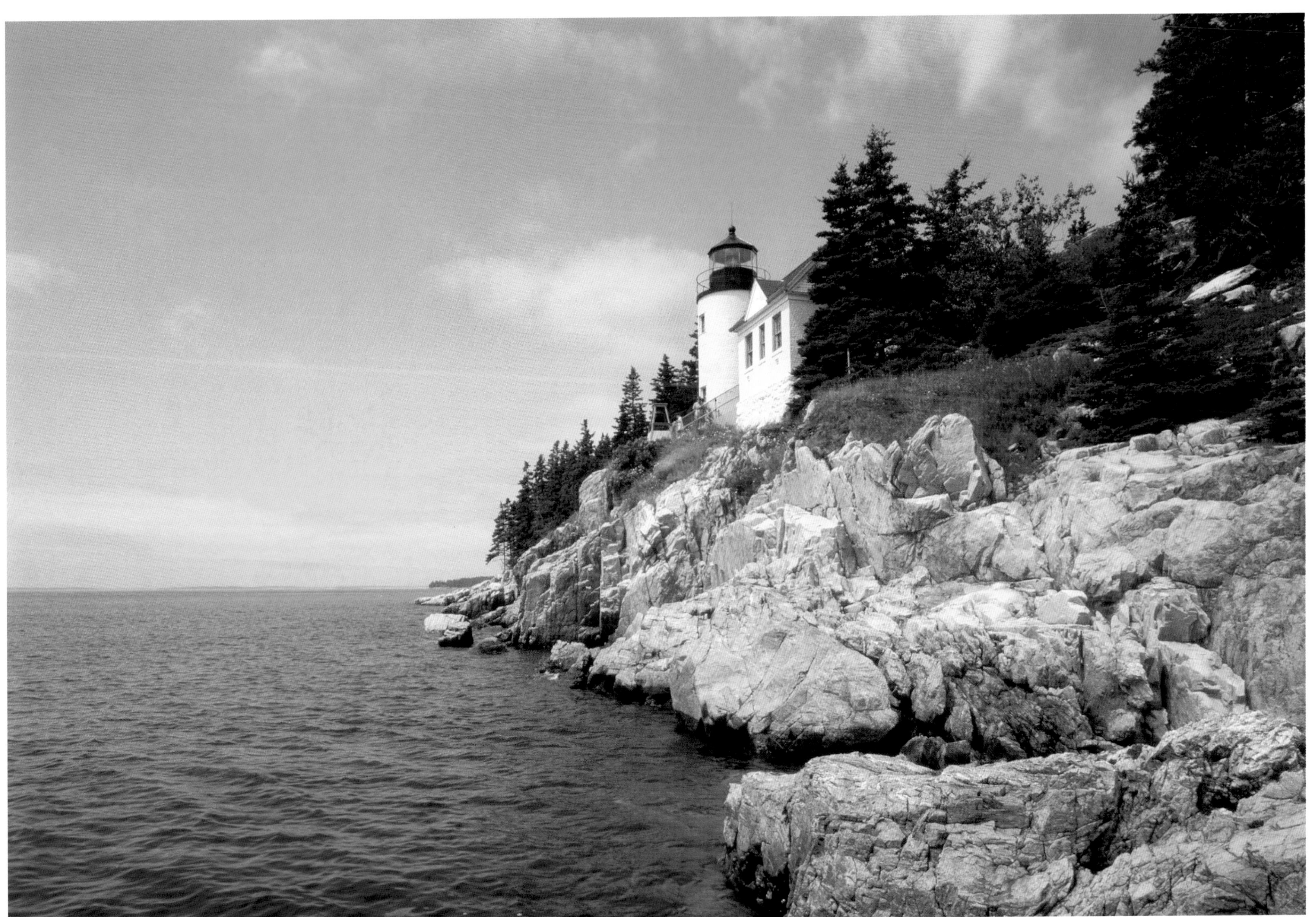

Bear Island Light, Maine.

more. This time the judge sided with the Lighthouse Board and the Baker Island Light has continued to burn ever since. It was automated in 1966, when the original fourth-order Fresnel lens was replaced by a battery-powered plastic optic.

Bass Harbor Head Light

Bass Harbor, Mount Desert Island, ME
Built: 1858
Style: Tower connected to dwelling
No: 2335
Position: 44 13 19 N. 68 20 14 W
Focal plane: 56ft (17m)
Range: 13 miles (21km)

This is one of the most picturesque lighthouses in the United States. Situated on cliffs on the west side of Mount Desert Island, the tower with its attached dwelling has been guiding vessels into Bass Harbor since 1858. The lighthouse is equipped with a fourth-order Fresnel lens.

Bear Island Light

Bear Island, ME
Built: 1839, 1853 and 1889
Style: Brick tower

Three light towers have been built to mark Bear Island. The first was a rustic stone building, and the last, built on the site of the second tower 50 years later, was of brick construction. This has a 33-ft (10-m) tower with a focal plane 100ft (30.5m) above the water. It was fitted with a fifth-order Fresnel lens. The station was decommissioned in 1982 when a buoy took over the role of guiding vessels into the harbour.

Blue Hill Bay Light

Green Island, ME
Built: 1857
Style: Cylindrical tower

The Blue Hill Bay lighthouse and its Cape Cod-style house on Green Island guided vessels towards Eggemoggin Reach from 1857 until a tower was erected nearby in 1935. The original station is now a private home.

Boon Island Light Station

York Beach, ME
Built: 1800, 1804, 1811 and 1855
Style: Conical tower connected to dwelling
No: 155
Position: 43 07 18 N. 70 28 36 W
Focal plane: 137ft (42m)
Range: 19 miles (30.5km)
Height: 133ft (40.5m)

The seas breaking on Boon Island a few miles south-east of York Beach have provided lighthouse designers with one of their most serious tests. Early attempts in 1800, 1804 and 1811 were simply swept away by the winter storms. In 1855 the money was eventually found to built a granite lighthouse fitted with a second-order Fresnel lens, which has survived the test of time, although the tower is now equipped with a solar-powered Vega light.

Browns Head Light

Vinalhaven, ME
Built: 1832
Style: Cylindrical tower attached to dwelling
No: 3965
Positiion: 44 06 42 N. 68 54 36 W
Focal plane: 39ft (12m)
Range: W 14 miles/23m, R 11 miles/18km
Height: 20ft (6m)

This stone tower and keeper's house marks the western approaches to Vinalhaven Island and was built in 1832 at a reputed cost of $4,000. It was originally equipped with a fifth-order Fresnel lens, but this was replaced by a more powerful fourth-order lens in 1902. The station was automated in 1987 and is now a private residence.

Burnt Coat Harbor Light

Swan Island, ME
Built: 1872
Style: Square tower connected to dwelling
No: 2700
Position: 44 08 03 N. 68 26 50 W
Focal plane: 75ft (23m)
Range: 9 miles (14.5km)
Height: 47ft (14m)

The attractive square tower and its connecting keeper's house date back to 1872. The station derived its name from a renegade British soldier who burned his coat to prove his defection and fled to Swan Island in 1776. Burnt Coat was one of a pair of range lights built on Hockamock Head to guide fishermen into harbour, but their combined signals proved so confusing that they led to several boats being wrecked on the rocks they were designed to warn against. These disasters led to the smaller of the two towers being pulled down in 1885 and left Burnt Coat Harbor Light to provide a single signal.

Burnt Island Light

Boothbay Harbor, ME
Built: 1821
Style: Conical tower connected to dwelling
No: 5520
Position: 43 49 30 N. 69 38 24 W
Focal plane: 61ft (18.5m)
Height: 30ft (9m)

The brick and stone tower marking the entrance to Boothbay Harbor and its wood-framed keeper's cottage were built in 1821. The tower was originally equipped with a Winslow Lewis oil lamp and reflector, but this was replaced by a fourth-order Fresnel lens when the lighthouse was enlarged in 1957. It is now automated and fitted with a plastic lens.

Cape Elizabeth Light

Cape Elizabeth, ME
Built: 1828 and 1874
Style: Conical tower
No: 7520
Position: 43 34 00 N. 70 12 00 W
Focal plane: 129ft (39m)
Range: 15 miles (24km)
Height: 67ft (20m)

Cape Elizabeth was given two lighthouses, one flashing, the other fixed, so that navigators could plot their position on a chart

LEFT
Cape Elizabeth Light (East Tower), Maine.

OPPOSITE
Browns Head Light, Maine.

from any approach. The original stone towers, standing 900ft (274m) apart, were later replaced with the present cast-iron towers. They continued to operate in tandem until 1924, when the Coast Guard ceased to use twin lights. The keeper's house, from which Marcus Hanna went out in 1885 to rescue two seamen, is now in private ownership, as is the west tower. The 67-ft east lighthouse continues to operate.

Cape Neddick Light

York, ME
Built: 1879
Style: Conical tower connected to dwelling
No:125
Position: 43 09 54 N. 70 35 30 W
Focal plane: 88ft (27m)
Range: 13 miles (21km)
Height: 41ft (12.5m)

The cast-iron Cape Neddick lighthouse has been warning mariners of the dangers posed by Nubble Island, a barren outcrop of rocks off Nubble Point, since 1879. The brick-lined tower has an attractive wooden-framed keeper's cottage reached via a covered walkway.

Cuckolds Light

Cape Newagen, ME
Built: 1892

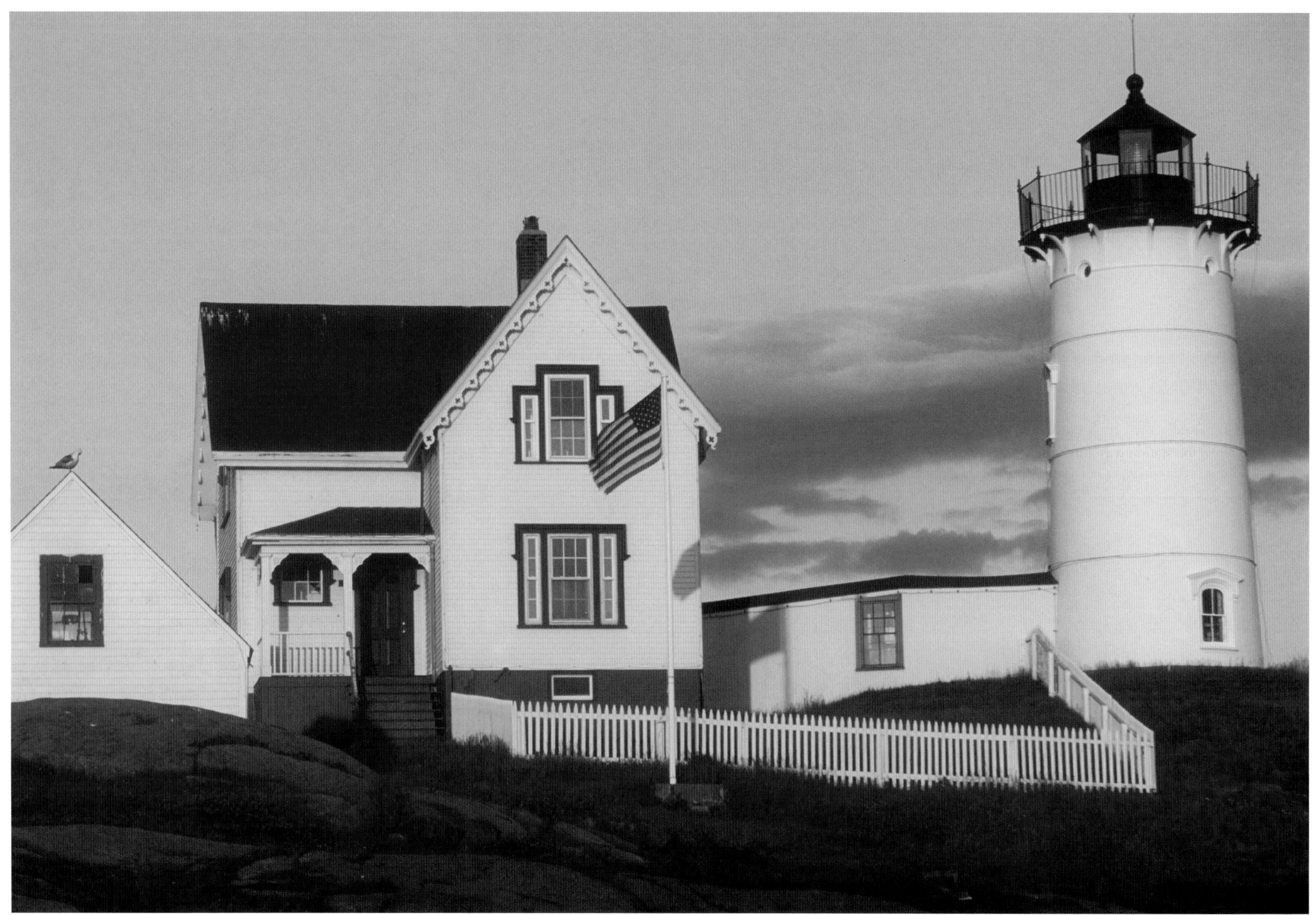

OPPOSITE
Cape Neddick Light ('The Nubble'), Maine.

RIGHT
Curtis Island Light, Maine.

Style: Octagonal tower on dwelling
No: 5485
Position: 43 46 48 N. 69 39 00 W
Focal plane: 59ft (18m)
Range: 12 miles (19km)
Height: 48ft (15m)

The wood and stone lighthouse was built as part of the navigation system to guide vessels towards Boothbay Harbor. It was equipped originally with a fourth-order Fresnel lens, but this was replaced some years ago with a Vega optic when the station was automated. The old Fresnel lens is now displayed at the Shore Village Museum in Rockland.

Curtis Island Light

Camden, ME
Built: 1836 and 1896
Style: Cylindrical tower
No: 4310
Position: 44 12 06 N. 69 02 54 W
Focal plane: 52ft (16m)
Range: 8 miles (13km)
Height: 25ft (8m)

The present brick tower and clapboard keeper's house on Curtis Island were built in 1896 to replace an earlier tower that had stood there for 60 years. The lighthouse is still equipped with its original fourth-order Fresnel lens.

Deer Island Thoroughfare Light

Stonington, Mark Island, ME
Built: 1857
Style: Square tower
No: 3095
Position: 44 08 06 N. 68 42 12 W
Focal plane: 52ft (16m)
Range: 8 miles (13km)
Height: 25ft (8m)

The square brick tower is all that remains on Mark Island of the pre-Civil War station. It was built in 1857 to guide vessels into the thoroughfare between the small fishing port of Stonington and the open Atlantic. The tower was equipped originally with a fourth-order Fresnel lens, but this has been replaced by an automated plastic optic.

Dice Head Light

Castine, ME
Built: 1829 and 1956
Style: Conical skeletal tower
No: 3530
Position: 44 22 54 N. 68 49 12 W
Focal plane: 27ft (8m)
Range: 11 miles (18km)

Castine is one of the oldest towns in the United States, beginning as a French fur-trading station. A rubblestone and brick lighthouse was established on the cliffs above Dice Head in 1829 and the colonial-style keeper's house was added in 1858, when the lighthouse was upgraded to a fourth-order Fresnel lens. It was decommissioned in 1956 and replaced by a skeletal tower built at the bottom of the

OPPOSITE
Cuckolds Light, Maine.

RIGHT
Deer Island Thoroughfare Light, Maine.

cliffs. The house was badly damaged by fire in 1999.

Doubling Point Light

Arrowsic Island, Bath, ME
Built: 1899
Style: Octagonal tower on pier
No: 6145
Position: 43 53 00 N. 69 48 24 W
Focal plane: 23ft (7m)
Range: 9 miles (14.5km)

The wooden lighthouse was one of a number of similar towers constructed along the Kennebec River during the late 1890s to guide shipping upriver into Bath harbour. It was equipped originally with a fourth-order Fresnel lens, which was replaced by a modern optic when automated in 1988.

Doubling Point Range Lights

Arrowsic Island, Bath, ME
Built: 1898
Style: Octagonal tower
No: 6135 (Front Light): 6140 (Rear Light)
Position: 43 53 00 N. 69 47 42 W
Focal plane: 18ft (5.5m)

The two wooden Doubling Point Range towers standing 21ft (6.5m) and 13ft (4m) on Arrowsic Island are the only examples of

LEFT
Dice Head Light (Old), Maine.

OPPOSITE
Doubling Point Range Lights, Maine.

their type still operating in Maine. They help shipping pilots to stay in the safe but narrow channel towards Bath harbour. Navigators keep one light directly above the other. If one appears to slip to the left or right, they know immediately to steer in the opposite way. Both towers were equipped with fifth-order Fresnel lenses, but these were replaced with modern optics when the lights were automated in 1979.

Eagle Island Light

Eagle Island, ME
Built: 1839
Style: Conical granite tower
No: 3455
Position: 44 13 04 N. 68 46 04 W
Focal plane:106ft (32m)
Range: 9 miles (14.5m)

The whitewashed rubblestone tower stands 100ft (30.5m) above sea level on the cliffs of Eagle Island. Its original fourth-order Fresnel lens was replaced by an automated plastic optic in 1963.

Egg Rock Light

Bar Harbor, ME
Built: 1875
Style: Square tower attached to house
No: 1865
Position: 44 21 12 N. 68 08 18 W

LEFT
Egg Rock Light, Maine.

OPPOSITE
Fort Point Light, Maine.

Focal plane: 64ft (19.5m)
Range: 18 miles (29km)
Height: 40ft (12m)

Named after the seabirds that nest here, the tower is built above the house. It was equipped with a fourth-order Fresnel lens, but this was replaced with an aero-marine beacon when the station was automated in 1976.

Fort Point Light

Stockton Springs, ME
Built: 1836
Style: Square tower on dwelling
No: 3585
Position: 44 28 00 N. 68 48 42 W
Focal plane: 88ft (27m)
Range: 15 miles (24km)
Height: 31ft (9.5m)

The wooden tower was built on cliffs to guide lumber ships heading towards the Penobscot River and Bangor, once the world's largest lumber port, away from the dangerous Hardhead Shoals. The station was the last U.S. lighthouse to be automated, in 1988, and is still equipped with its fourth-order Fresnel lens.

Franklin Island Light

Friendship, ME
Built: 1805

Style: Cylindrical
No: 4980
Position: 43 53 32 N. 69 22 29 W
Focal plane: 57ft (17m)
Range: 8 miles/13km, but obscured by trees
Height: 45ft (14m)

The brick and sandstone lighthouse on Franklin Island, west of Port Clyde, is one of the oldest working lighthouses in America. Equipped originally with a whale-oil lamp, it was later upgraded with a fifth-order Fresnel lens.

Goat Island Light

Kennebunkport, ME
Built: 1835 and 1859
Style: Cylindrical tower
No: 8100
Position: 43 21 30 N. 70 25 30 W
Focal plane 38ft (11.5m)
Range 12 miles (19km)

Goat Island lighthouse was the last station in Maine to retain a keeper, thanks to its proximity to President George Bush's family home on Walker Point. The present brick tower and Cape Cod-style keeper's cottage, dating from 1859, made an ideal security post. The station was finally automated in 1990 when the original fourth-order Fresnel lens was replaced by a plastic optic.

Goose Rock Light

Vinalhaven, ME
Built: 1890
Style: Conical tower

OPPOSITE
Goat Island Light, Maine.

RIGHT
Franklin Island Light, Maine.

No: 3885
Position: 44 08 08 N. 68 49 50 W
Focal plane: 51ft
Range:W 12 miles/19km, R 11 miles/18km
Height: 50ft (15.5m)

The cast-iron tower was erected on a concrete caisson sunk over the dangerous Goose Rock Ledge lurking just beneath the waves in Fox Island Thoroughfare, a favourite shortcut between Vinalhaven and North Haven islands for shipping heading towards the Penobscot Bay channels. It was manned until 1963 when the light was automated, and is now equipped with a solar-powered beacon.

Great Duck Island Light

Duck Island, ME
Built: 1890
Style: Cylindrical tower
No: 2295
Position: 44 08 30 N. 68 14 42 W
Focal plane: 67ft (20m)
Range: 19 miles (30.5km)
Height: 42ft (13m)

The keepers of the lighthouse once shared this isolated spot with petrels and eider ducks until the station was automated in 1986. The brick-built tower was equipped with a fifth-order Fresnel lens, replaced

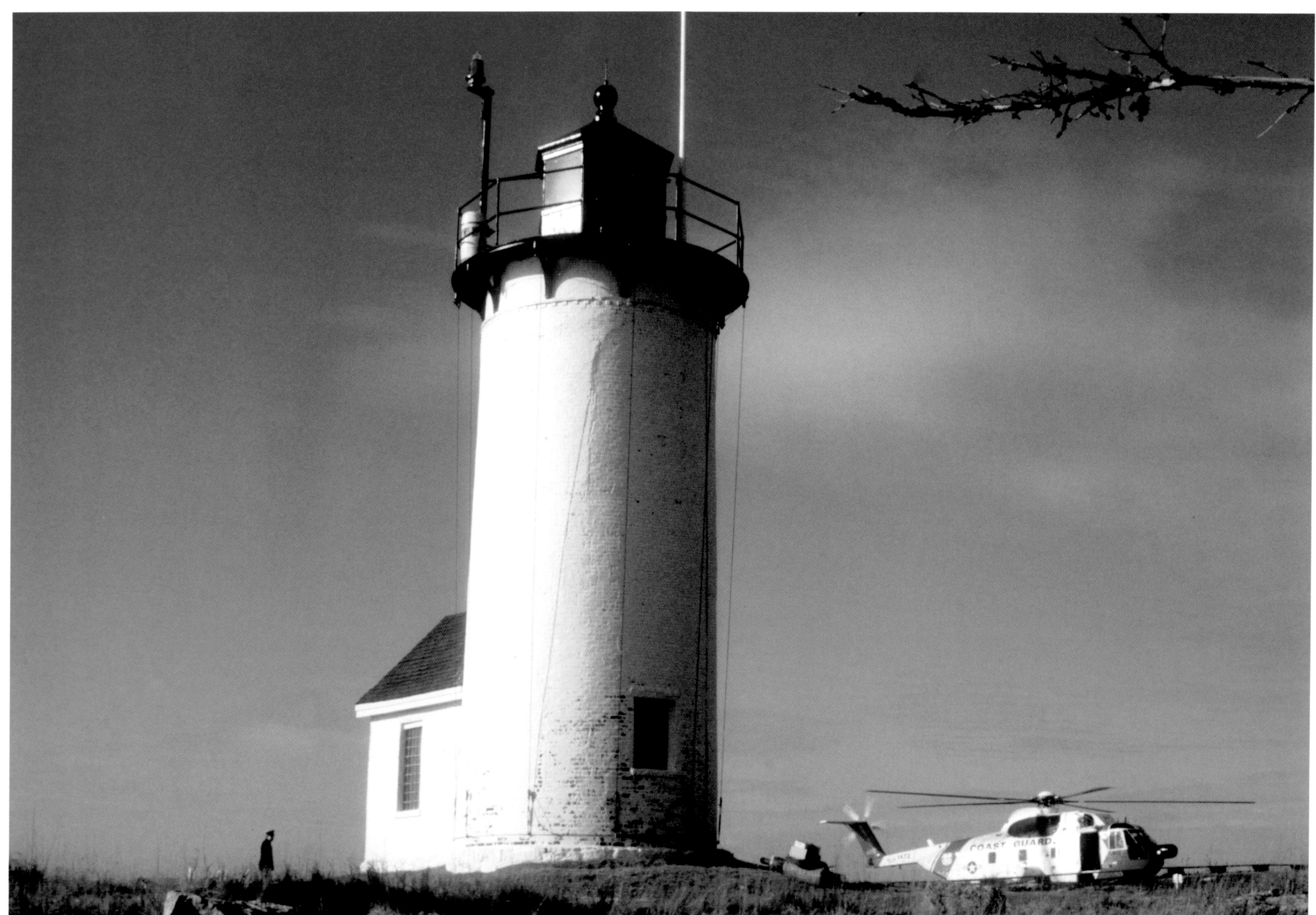
COAST GUARD

OPPOSITE
Great Duck Island Light, Maine.

RIGHT
Grindle Point Light, Maine.

during automation with a plastic lens. The building is now a bird sanctuary.

Grindle Point Light

Islesboro, ME
Built: 1850 and 1874
Style: Square

The 39-ft (12-m) lighthouse, situated beside the ferry dock, was built in 1874 to replace an earlier wooden tower. The light was decommissioned in 1934, but pressure from the local population led the Coast Guard to reinstate its flashing green light in 1987.

Halfway Rock Light

Bailey Island, ME
Built: 1871
Style: Conical tower attached to building
No: 6675
Position: 43 39 21 N. 70 02 12 W
Focal plane: 77ft (23.5m)
Range: 19 miles (30.5km)
Height: 76ft (23m)

The granite lighthouse marking the wave-swept Halfway Rock in Casco Bay, 10 miles from Portland, is similar in construction to the interlocking blocks of Minots Ledge lighthouse in Massachusetts. It took two years to construct and was fitted with a

third-order Fresnel lens until 1970, when a solar-powered beacon was installed.

Hendricks Head Light

Boothbay Harbor, ME
Built: 1829 and 1875
Style: Square tower connected to house
No: 5665
Position: 43 49 24 N. 69 41 24 W
Focal plane: 43ft (13m)
Range: W 9 miles/14m, R 7 miles/11m
Height: 39ft (12m)

Hendricks Head off Boothbay Harbor claimed the lives of the captain and crew of a schooner wrecked here during a terrible storm in the 1860s. When the lighthouse keeper searched through the wreckage the following morning, he found a baby girl, whom he and his wife adopted. The first tower was burned down in 1875 when the present tower and its attractive keeper's house was built to replace it.

Heron Neck Light

Green Island, ME
Built: 1853
Style: Cylindrical tower attached to dwelling
No: 3760
Position: 44 01 30 N. 68 51 44 W
Focal plane: 92ft (28m)
Range: W 13 miles/21km, R 10 miles/16km
Height: 20ft (6m)

Heron Neck's distinctive red and white beacon was built on Green Island in 1853 to guide fishing boats into Carver's Harbor. Its fifth-order Fresnel lens was replaced by a plastic optic in 1982 and the lighthouse is now managed by the Island Institute.

LEFT
Halfway Rock Light, Maine.

OPPOSITE
Hendricks Head Light, Maine.

Indian Island Light

Rockport, ME
Built: 1850
Style: Square, brick-built

The lighthouse was decommissioned in 1934 when its fourth-order Fresnel lens was removed. It is now privately owned.

Isle au Haut Light

Isle au Haut, ME
Built: 1907
Style: Conical
No: 3360
Position: 44 03 54 N. 68 39 06 W
Focal plane: 48ft (15m)
Range: W 8 miles/13km, R 6 miles/10km

This granite and brick tower with a bridge connecting it to land at Isle au Haut stands on a rocky ledge. The light was automated in 1934 and the keeper's house is now a hotel.

Lady's Delight Light

Lake Cobbosseecontee, Winthrop, ME
Built: 1908
Style: Square

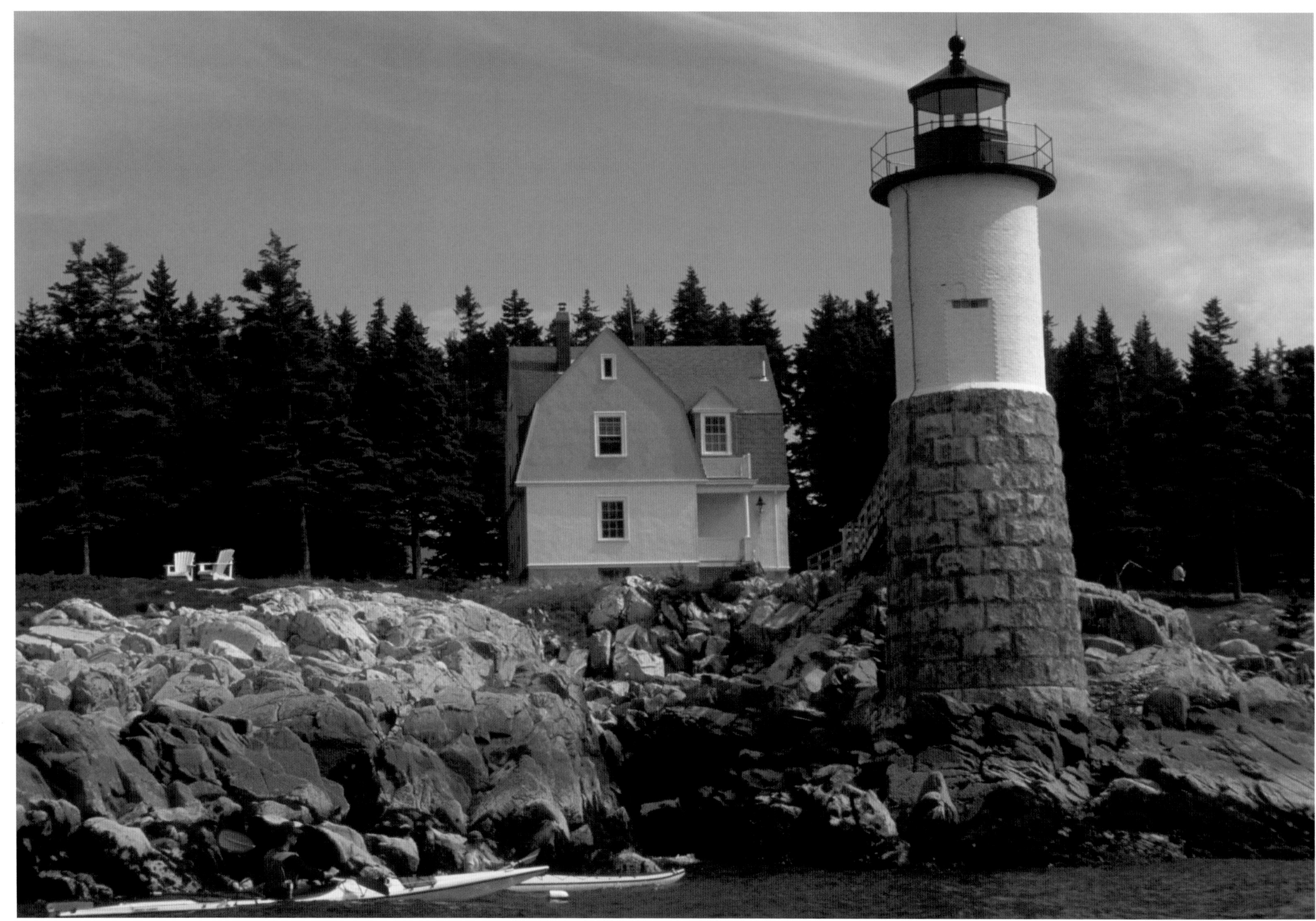

OPPOSITE
Isle au Haut Light, Maine.

RIGHT
Lubec Channel Light, Maine.

The lighthouse was built to mark a reef extending from Lady's Delight Island in Lake Cobboseecontee. The 25-ft (8-m) tower cost just $500 to build and holds a 75-watt electric bulb lighting a lens that originated as a ship's anchor light. It is now maintained by the local yacht club.

Libby Island Light

Machias, ME
Built: 1817 and 1822
Style: Conical granite tower
No: 1120
Position: 44 34 06 N. 67 22 00 W
Focal plane: 91ft (28m)
Range: 25 miles (40km)
Height: 42ft (13m)

A lighthouse was first built on Libby Island in 1817 to warn vessels of a dangerous bar near the entrance to Machias Bay. Four years later the wooden tower was blown down during a gale, and it was replaced by the present granite tower. This was equipped with a fourth-order Fresnel lens, which was replaced with modern plastic optic when the station was automated in 1974.

Little River Light

Cutler, ME
Built: 1847 and 1876
Style: Cylindrical

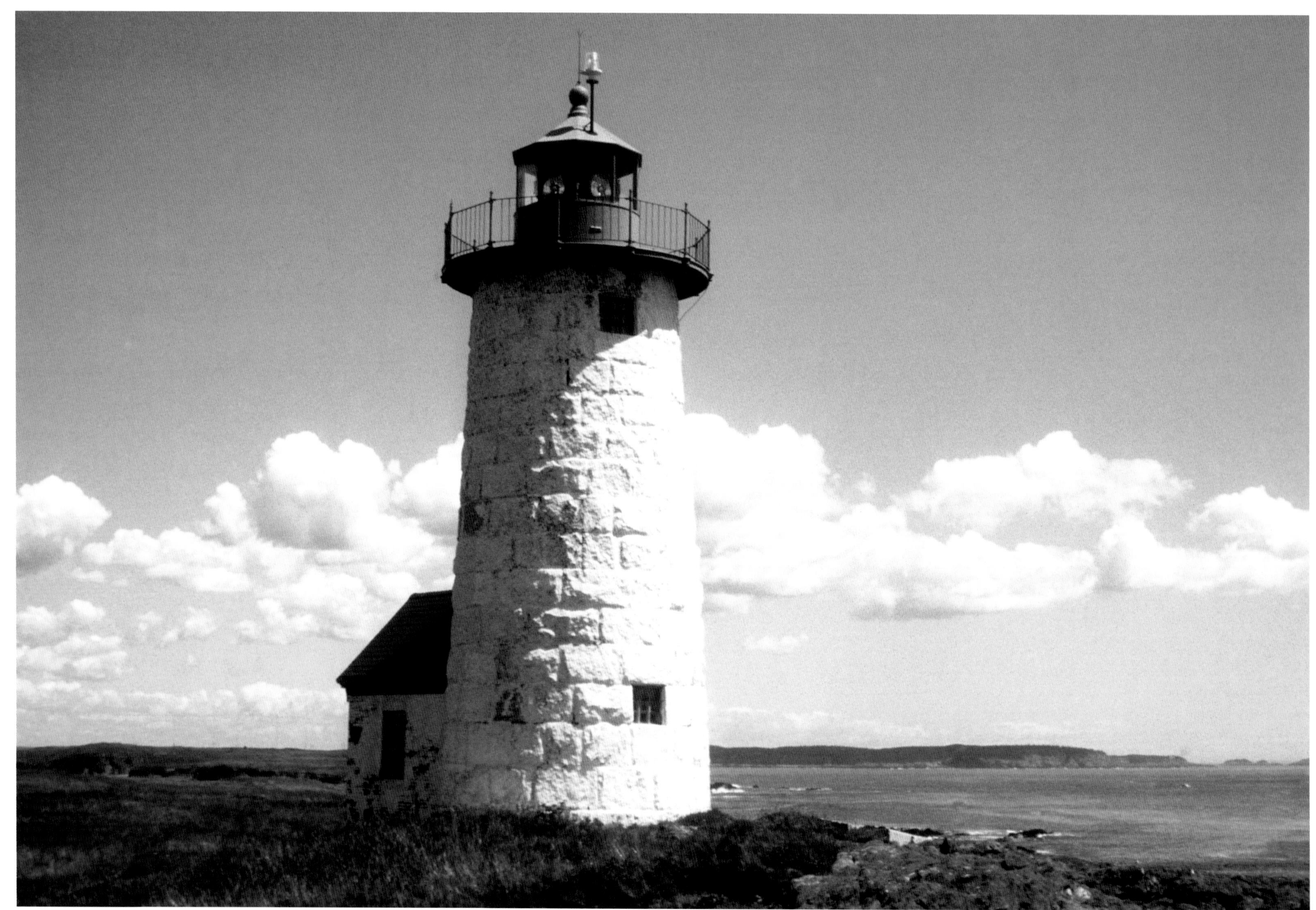

OPPOSITE
Libby Island Light, Maine.

RIGHT
Matinicus Rock Light (Twin Towers), Maine.

The first Little River lighthouse was built on the island near Cutler in 1847. It was replaced by the present 35-ft (11-m) cast-iron tower and keeper's house in 1876. The station was decommissioned in 1975 and was left empty until the American Lighthouse Foundation acquired the property in 2000 and set out to restore it to its former glory.

Lubec Channel Light

Lubec, ME
Built: 1890
Style: Caisson tower on cylindrical pier
No: 860
Positiion: 44 50 30 N. 66 58 36 W
Focal plane: 53ft (16m)
Range: 6 miles (10km)

This was set in the Lubec Channel dividing Maine from Canada's Campobello Island in 1890 to guide vessels heading for Lubec, Eastport and Calais on the St. Croix River. It was fitted with a fifth-order Fresnel lens rotated by a weight-driven clockwork mechanism, which remained in place until replaced by a modern plastic lens in 1969. The keeper and his assistant lived year round in the spartan quarters below the lamp until an oil fire took hold in 1939. The station was automated during the renovation.

Machias Seal Islands Light

Cutler, ME
Built: 1832
Style: Octagonal
No: 1090
Position: 44 30 06 N. 67 06 06 W
Focal plane: 82ft (25m)
Range: 17 miles (27km)
Height: 60ft (18m)

The lighthouse has marked these wind-swept rocks 10 miles south-east of Cutler since 1832. The United States and Canada have disputed possession of the islands but share responsibility for the navigation aids. The U.S. Coast Guard operates the Machias Light, and the Canadian Coast Guard another lighthouse elsewhere on this chain of rocks. These required a keeper to operate them, who reported to the head keeper on Mohegan Island. The signal station is now automated.

Marshall Point Light

Point Clyde, ME
Built: 1832 and 1858
Style: Cylindrical
No: 4780

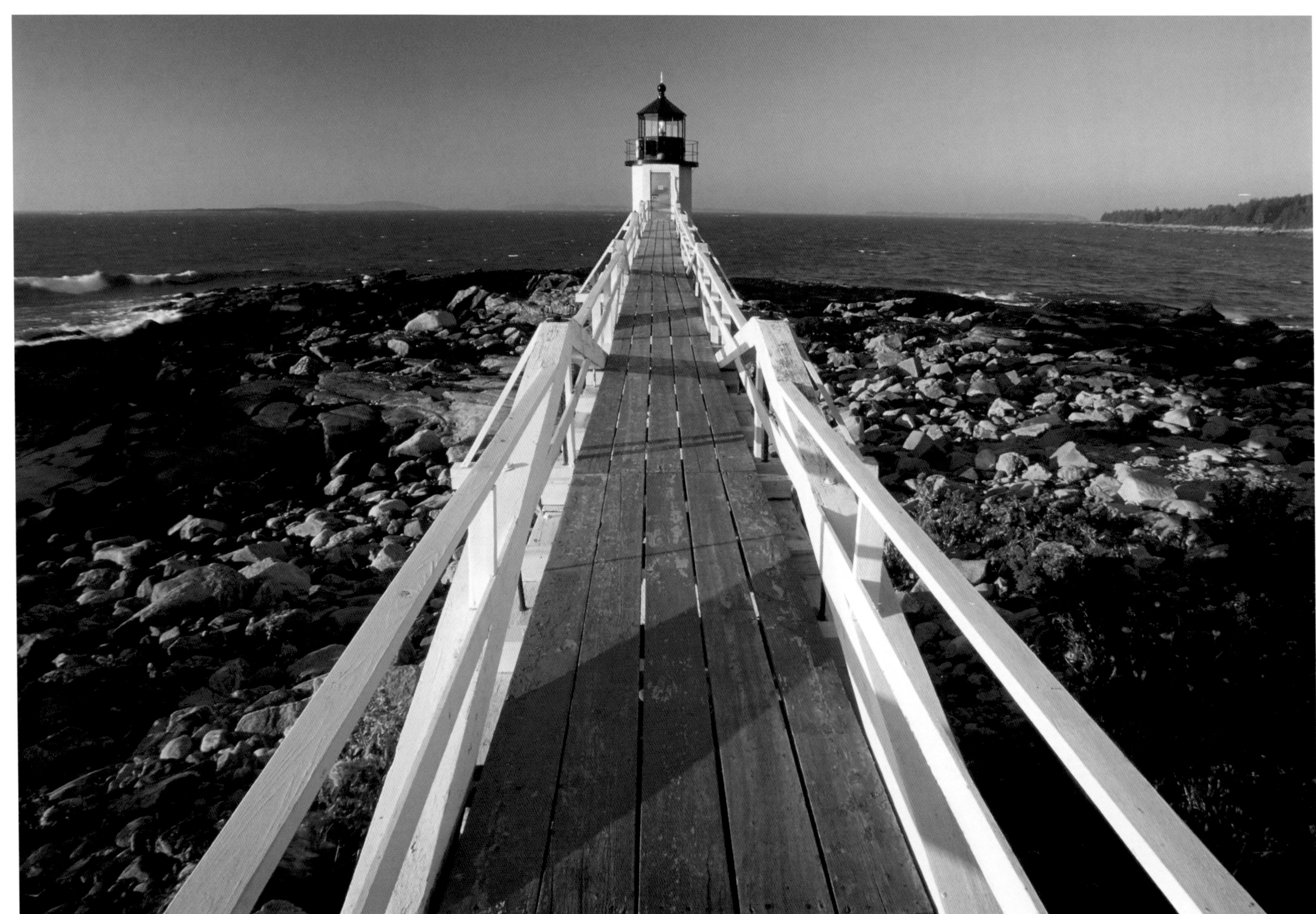

Marshall Point Light, Maine.

Position: 43 55 00 N. 69 15 42 W
Focal plane: 30ft (9m)
Range: 12 miles (19km)

The original lighthouse was replaced by the present stone tower in 1858, which is accessed by a wooden walkway. Its fifth-order Fresnel lens was replaced by a plastic optic in 1980. The keeper's house is now a museum managed by the St. George Historical Society.

Matinicus Rock Light

Rockland, Matinicus Island, ME
Built: 1827 and 1846
Style: Cylindrical granite
No: 3195
Position: 43 47 00 N. 68 51 18 W
Focal plane: 90ft (27m)
Range: 20 miles (32km)
Height: 48ft (15m)

Matinicus Rock used to be marked by a pair of towers to help identify this dangerous coastline. The first were of wooden construction and were replaced with granite lighthouses in 1846. Eleven years later, both were refurbished and equipped with third-order Fresnel lenses which gave them a range of 20 miles. Today, only the northern lighthouse is operational, and the Fresnel lens from the defunct south tower is displayed at the Shore Village Museum in Rockland.

Mohegan Island Light & Manana Island Fog Signal Station

Mohegan Island, ME
Built: 1822 and 1851
Style: Conical
No: 4925 (Mohegan Island Light)
Position: 43 45 54 N. 69 18 54 W
Focal plane: 178ft (54m)
Range: 20 miles (32km)
Height: 47ft (14m)

No: 4930 (Manana Island Station)
Position: 43 45 48 N. 69 19 36 W

The coastline around Maine is notorious for its fog banks, which often enshroud Mohegan, Manana and other rocky outcrops in this dangerous archipelago 20 miles off the coast. Monhegan first had a lighthouse in 1822. Its replacement, built in 1851 to a design by Alexander Parris, is a concrete tower that stands 178ft above sea level and was equipped with a second-order Fresnel lens until 1959, when the station was automated and a plastic lens was installed. The keeper's house is now a museum.

In 1854, the nearby Manana Island was equipped with a fog. This was replaced by a louder steam-powered trumpet in 1877. These required a keeper to operate them, who reported to the head keeper on Mohegan Island. The signal station is now automated.

Moose Peak Light

Jonesport, ME
Built: 1827
Style: Conical
No: 1390
Position: 44 28 30 N. 67 31 54 W
Focal plane: 72ft (22m)
Range: 25 miles (40km)
Height: 57ft (17m)

The brick-built lighthouse at the eastern end of Mistake Island, often shrouded in fog, has been operational since it was built. The light was renovated in 1857, when it was fitted with a second-order Fresnel lens, but this was replaced by a plastic optic in 1972. The keeper's house was demolished ten years later. Mistake Island and the lighthouse station are now owned by Nature Conservancy.

Mount Desert Light

Mount Desert Rock, ME
Built: 1830, 1857 and 1893
Style: Pyramidal
No: 2290
Position: 43 58 06 N. 68 07 42 W
Focal plane: 75ft (23m)
Range: 20 miles (32km)
Height: 58ft (18m)

Mount Desert Rock is one of the America's most barren outposts. Lashed by the Atlantic, the island, 20 miles off the Maine coast, is 900-ft (275-m) long and has always presented a significant hazard to shipping. The first lighthouse was mounted on the roof of the keeper's house and was not very effective. It was replaced in 1857 by a conical stone tower designed by Alexander Parris, which remained in place until the present stone lighthouse was built, elevating the light 75ft above sea level. It was equipped with a third-order Fresnel lens which was only replaced with a modern optic in 1977, when the station was finally automated. Before that, the lighthouse keepers and their families, who were stationed here year-round, relied on lobstermen to bring them supplies, including fresh topsoil each spring to make a vegetable garden among the rocks. In 1902 the keeper and his wife managed to rescue all but one of the crew of the *Astral*, an ocean-going tug that smashed into the fog-shrouded rocks, not having seen the light.

Narraguagus Light

Milbridge, ME
Built: 1853
Style: Conical

Marking a ledge just off Pond Island in Narraguagus Bay, this 31-ft (9.5-m) stone and brick tower served as a lighthouse from 1853 until its decommission in 1934. It is now a day mark.

Nash Island Light

Addison, ME
Built: 1838 and 1874
Style: Square

Nash Island Light used to guide vessels towards the busy entrance to Pleasant Bay, south of Addison. Built in 1838 and

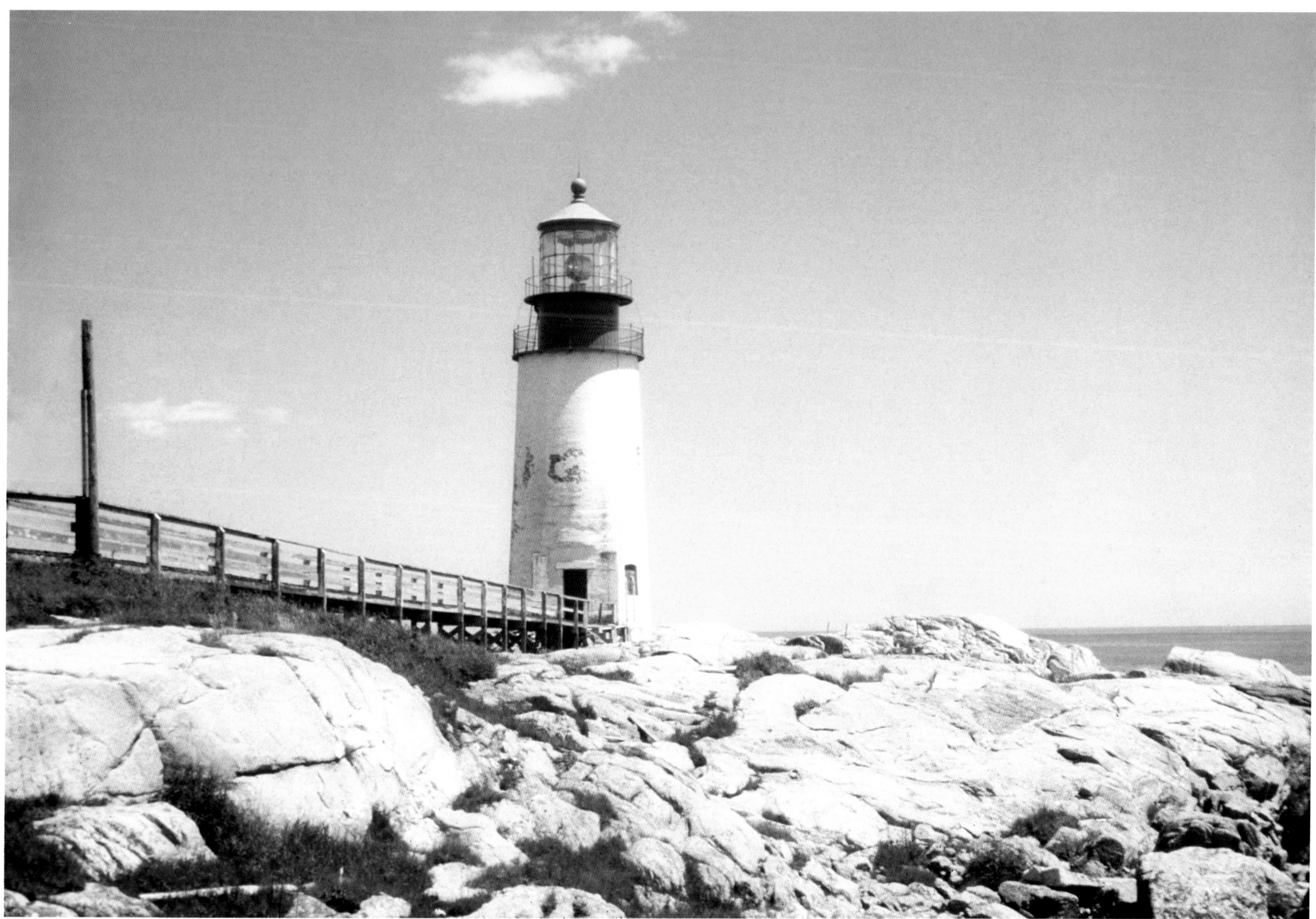

PAGE 146
Mohegan Island Light, Maine.

PAGE 147
Moose Peak Light, Maine.

OPPOSITE
Pemaquid Point Light, Maine.

RIGHT
Nash Island Light, Maine.

renovated in 1874, the station included housing for three families plus a one-room schoolhouse. It was closed down in 1981 and all that remains now is the 51-ft (15.5-m) tower, which has fallen into disrepair.

Pemaquid Point Light

New Harbor, ME
Built: 1822, 1851 and 1857
Style: Conical
No: 5145
Position: 43 50 12 N. 69 30 21 W
Focal plane: 79ft (24m)
Range: 15 miles (24km)
Height: 38ft (11.5m)

The present stone tower and wood-framed keeper's house, standing more than 40ft (12m) above sea level, date back nearly 150 years, though the first light station was established at Pemaquid Point in 1822. The construction of light towers was in its infancy then, and it took three efforts to build a lighthouse strong enough to withstand the harsh Atlantic storms. The tower still has its original fourth-order Fresnel lens. The keeper's dwelling now houses a museum.

Perkins Island Light

Georgetown and Bath, ME
Built: 1898
Style: Octagonal
No: 6070
Position: 43 47 12 N. 69 47 06 W
Focal plane: 41ft (12.5m)
Range: W 6 miles/10km, R 5 miles/8km
Height: 23ft (7m)

The brick and wood Perkins Island Light is one of several inland lighthouses built along the Kennebec River in 1898–99 to guide shipping inland towards Bath. The original fifth-order Fresnel lens has been replaced by a modern optic, but the keeper's cottage and outbuildings remain.

Petit Manan Light

Petit Manan Island, ME
Built: 1817 and 1855
Style: Conical granite tower
No: 1735
Position: 44 22 03 N. 67 51 52 W
Focal plane: 123ft (37.5m)
Range: 19 miles (30.5km)
Height: 119ft (36m)

After a number of ships were wrecked on Petit Manan Island during the early 19th century, a 53-ft (16-m) lighthouse was erected here in 1817. Its Winslow Lewis oil lamps were too dim to provide an effective warning and continued shipping losses prompted the construction of a second 119-ft granite and brick lighthouse in 1855.

This still stands today, despite strong winds visibly rocking the tower on occasions. Its original second-order Fresnel lens gave the light a range of 25 miles (40km), but this was replaced by a modern optic when the station was automated in 1972.

Pond Island Light

Popham Beach, ME
Built: 1821
Style: Cylindrical
No: 6025
Position: 43 44 24 N. 69 46 12 W
Focal plane: 52ft (16m)
Range: 10 miles (16km)

The lighthouse has marked the entrance to the Kennebec River and the port of Bath since 1821. The keeper's house and outbuildings were torn down when the station was automated in 1979, leaving just the 20-ft (6-m) tower. Its fifth-order Fresnel lens has since been replaced by a modern optic. The lighthouse is situated within a bird sanctuary.

Portland Breakwater Light/Petroleum Docks Light

South Portland, ME
Built: 1855 and 1875
Style: Conical

Nicknamed the 'Bug Light', the Portland Breakwater lighthouse was built in Victorian times when architects were encouraged to design public buildings as works of art. It replaced an earlier tower marking what was then a long breakwater defending the entrance to Portland Harbor. A land-reclamation project has led to the coastline engulfing all but the lighthouse, which was decommissioned in 1942.

LEFT
Petit Manan Light, Maine.

OPPOSITE
Pond Island Light, Maine.

Portland Head Light

Portland, ME
Built: 1791
Style: Conical tower connected to dwelling
No: 7565
Position: 43 37 24 N. 70 12 30 W
Focal plane: 101ft (31m)
Range: 24 miles (39km)
Height: 80ft (24m)

The lighthouse is one of the oldest structures in the United States. The stone tower and its keeper's house, built on a rocky headland in what is now Fort Williams Park, caught the interest of President George Washington and marked the beginning of the process of political nominations of lighthouse keepers. A guiding light for vessels entering Portland harbour, the station's fourth-order Fresnel lens was replaced in 1989 with a modern beacon, and the house is now a museum where visitors can view the second-order bivalve lens that was at one time here.

Prospect Harbor Point Light
Prospect Harbor, ME
Built: 1850 and 1891
Style: Conical
No: 1785
Position: 44 24 12 N. 68 00 48 W
Focal plane: 42ft (13m)
Range: W 9 miles/14.5km, R 7 miles/11km
Height: 38ft (11.5m)

The lighthouse looks like a typical wood-framed fisherman's cottage, but with a tower extending upwards from its seaward wall. It was built in 1891 to replace an earlier stone lighthouse that had survived for 40 years, and provides a welcoming light for the local fishing fleet. It is now automated, and the keeper's accommodation is a guest house for those visiting the naval base nearby.

Pumpkin Island Light
Sargentville, ME
Built: 1854

The cylindrical lighthouse was constructed in 1854 to guard the western end of Eggemoggin Reach, which lies between Deer Island and Little Deer Island. The 28-ft (8.5-m) brick tower was decommissioned in 1933 and is now a private home.

Ram Island Ledge Light
Cape Elizabeth, ME
Built: 1873 and 1905
Style: Conical
No: 7575
Position: 43 37 54 N. 70 11 12 W
Focal plane: 77ft (23.5m)
Range: 8 miles (13km)

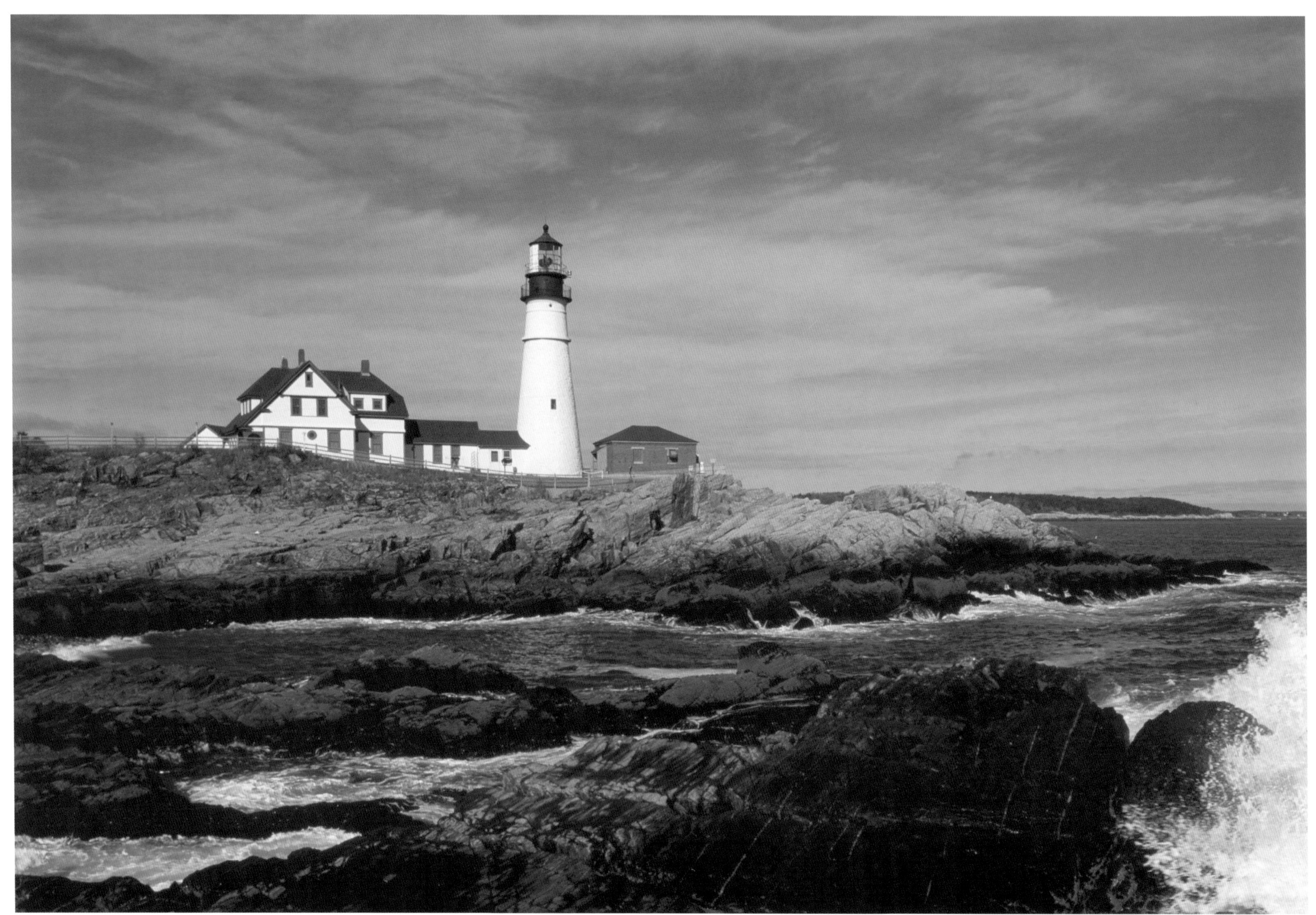

OPPOSITE
Portland Head Light, Maine.

RIGHT
Ram Island Ledge Light, Maine.

The lighthouse marks the dangerous Portland Ledge off Portland Head lighthouse. The original beacon of 1873 was a wooden tripod tower, which was replaced by a granite tower in 1905. This was equipped with a third-order Fresnel lens until replaced by an aero-marine beacon when the station was automated in 1959.

Ram Island Light

Ocean Point, ME
Built: 1883
Style: Cylindrical
No: 5420
Position: 43 38 14 N. 69 35 57 W
Focal plane: 36ft (11m)
Range: W 11 miles/18m), R 9 miles/14.5km

The 35-ft granite and brick Ram Island lighthouse was built to mark the passage leading to Boothbay Harbor. It was equipped with a fourth-order Fresnel lens which has since been replaced by a modern optic. The keeper lives in an L-shaped house a short distance away from the lighthouse, which was built at the same time.

Rockland Breakwater Light

Rockland, ME
Built: 1888 and 1902
Style: Square tower on fog-signal house

There has been a lighthouse at Rockland ever since the breakwater was built there in 1888. The first tower was replaced in 1902 by a 25-ft (8-m) tower set on the roof of the keeper's two-storey house. The original fourth-order Fresnel lens has been replaced by a modern plastic lens.

Saddleback Ledge Light

Isle au Haut, ME
Built: 1839
Style: Conical
No: 3325
Position: 44 00 54 N. 68 43 36 W
Focal plane: 54ft (16.5m)
Range: 9 miles (14.5km)
Height: 42ft (13m)

The granite tower, designed by Alexander Parris, has marked the Saddleback Ledge since 1839. It still has its original fourth-order Fresnel lens, which was automated in 1954. This must have been a welcome relief to the keeper, for this lighthouse is one of the most remote outposts in the north-east. Storms kept one lighthouse keeper away for 21 days and it was left to his 15-year-old son to tend the light, which he did, despite running out of food.

Seguin Island Light

Georgetown, ME
Built: 1795, 1820 and 1857
Style: Conical tower on cylindrical pier

In 1795, President George Washington ordered the first lighthouse to be built on Seguin Island, to mark the mouth of the

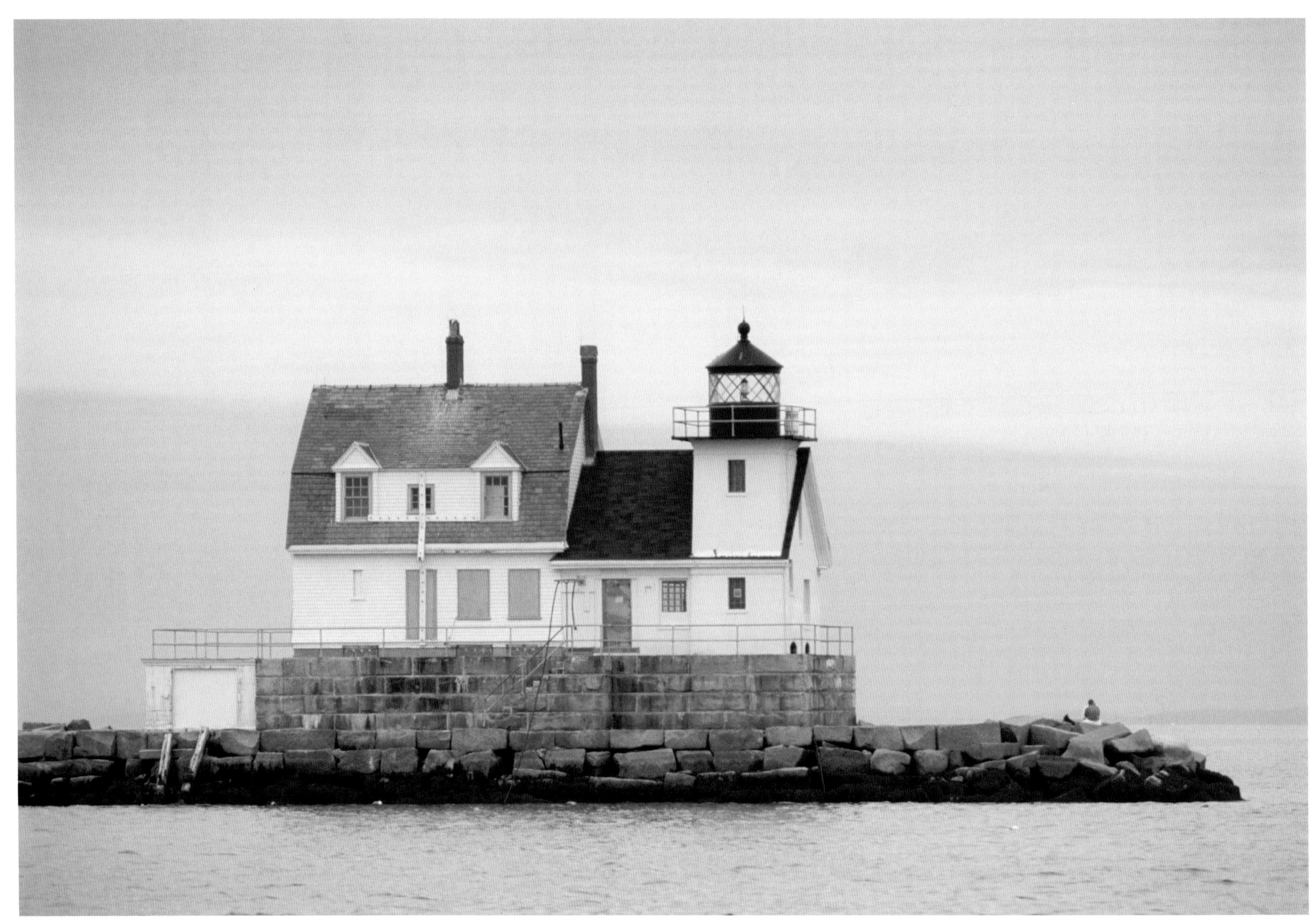

OPPOSITE
Rockland Breakwater Light, Maine.

RIGHT
Prospect Harbor Point Light, Maine.

Kennebec River, and nominated John Polersky, a Revolutionary War soldier, as the station's first keeper. That tower was toppled during a storm in 1820, and a second sentinel survived until 1857, when the present 53-ft (16-m) granite tower was built. This is equipped with a first-order Fresnel lens and has a range of 18 miles (29km).

Spring Point Ledge Light

Portland, ME
Built: 1895
Style: Conical tower on cylindrical pier
No: 7610
Position: 43 39 06 N. 70 13 24 W
Focal plane: 54ft (16.5m)
Range:11 miles (18km)

The lighthouse stands above a caisson sunk on dangerous rocks that extend out into the shipping channel between Portland harbour and the open sea. These rocks caught many mariners unaware before the lighthouse was built, including the lime freighter *Nancy*, which hit the ledge and sank in 1832. The light's original fifth-order Fresnel lens was replaced by a modern optic when the station was automated in 1934.

ABOVE
Saddleback Ledge Light, Maine.

OPPOSITE
Seguin Island Light, Maine.

Squirrel Point Light

Phippsburg and Bath, ME
Built: 1898
Style: Octagonal
No: 6100
Position: 43 49 00 N. 69 48 06 W
Focal plane: 25ft (8m)
Range: W 9 miles/14.5km,
R 7 miles/11km

The Squirrel Point lighthouse, like its twin on Perkins Island, is a wooden tower built to mark the navigation channel up the Kennebec River towards Bath Harbor.

Tenants Harbor Light

Tenants Harbor, ME
Built: 1857
Style: Cylindrical

The 27-ft (8-m) brick-built Tenants Harbor lighthouse operated from 1857 to 1933. The station was then sold to the famous artist, Andrew Wyeth. It is now owned by his son Jamie, also an artist, who maintains the lighthouse building and has his studio there.

Two Bush Island Light

Rockland, ME
Built: 1897
Style: Square tower
No: 4540
Position: 43 57 51 N. 69 04 26 W
Focal plane: 65ft (20m)
Range: W 17 miles/27km, R 15 miles/24km
Height: 42ft (13m)

The name of this lighthouse stems from two trees that once guided mariners towards the western entrance to Penobscot Bay. In 1897, a tower was built and equipped with a fifth-order Fresnel lens, which was replaced by a modern optic when the station was automated in 1963

West Quoddy Head Light

Lubec, ME
Built: 1808 and 1858
Style: Conical
No: 1040
Position: 44 48 54 N. 66 57 00 W
Focal plane: 83ft (25m)
Range: 18 miles (29km)
Height: 49ft (15m)

This is one of Maine's oldest stations, and marks the easternmost point of the United States. The original rubblestone tower was demolished in 1858, rebuilt in brick, and

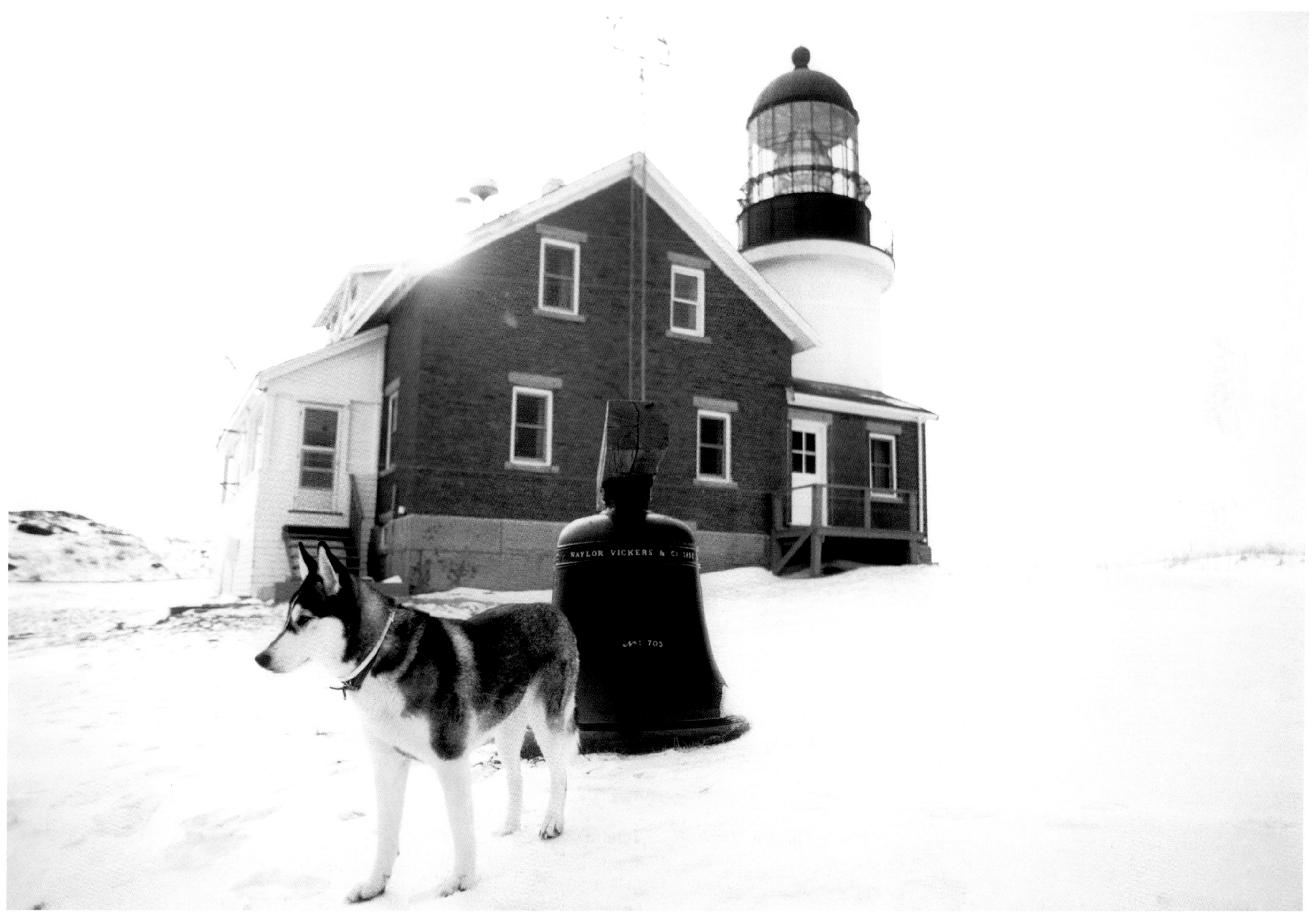
NAYLOR VICKERS & Co
No: 705

OPPOSITE
Spring Point Ledge Light, Maine.

RIGHT
Whitlock's Mill Light, Maine.

equipped with a third-order Fresnel lens. The candy-striped tower guides vessels into Lubec, while a separate building houses the station's automated foghorn. Earlier fog signals included a cannon, a 1,500-lb (680-kg) bell and a steam whistle. The station was finally automated in 1988 despite a vigorous campaign by its last lighthouse keepers.

Whitehead Light

Thornaston, Sprucehead Island, ME
Built: 1807 and 1857
Style: Conical tower attached to building
No: 4580
Position: 43 58 43 N. 69 07 27 W
Focal plane: 75ft (23m)
Range: 6 miles (10km)
Height: 41ft (12.5m)

This was one of the first lighthouses to be built in Maine, though the present granite tower is 50 years younger. The station was once equipped with a 2,000-lb (900-kg) sea-powered fog bell that rang whenever waves struck the shore. Ellis Dolph, one of Whitehead's early keepers, lost his job when it was found that he had been selling the lighting oil for personal gain. In later years, Abbie Burgess Grant and her husband served as keepers from 1875 until their retirement in 1889. The station was finally automated in 1982.

Whitlock's Mill Light

St. Croix, ME
Built: 1892 and 1909
Style: Conical
No: 985
Focal plane: 32ft (10m)
Range: 5 miles (8km)
Height: 25ft (8m)

The first lighthouse was a simple lantern strapped to a tree. This was replaced by a stone tower in 1892 to service the growing lumber trade along the St. Croix River. The current lighthouse was built in 1909 and was fitted with a fourth-order Fresnel lens, which operated until the station was automated in 1969 when a modern optic replaced it. The light remains active, but the other buildings are now privately owned.

Winter Harbor Light

Mark Island, ME
Built: 1856
Style: Tower attached to house

Located on Mark Island, west of the Schoodic peninsula, the Winter Harbor lighthouse was operated until 1934. It is now privately owned and maintained.

Wood Island Light

Biddeford Pool, York County, ME
Built: 1858
Style: Conical tower connected to house
No: 95
Position: 43 27 24 N. 70 19 42 W
Focal plane: 71ft (22m)
Range: W 18 miles/29km, G 16 miles/26km
Height: 47ft (14m)

OPPOSITE
West Quoddy Head Light, Maine

BELOW RIGHT
Postcard showing Bakers Island, Massachusetts, when there were two lights.

The lighthouse was originally fitted with a fourth-order Fresnel lens. This was replaced with a modern optic when the station was automated, and the old fog bell is now displayed in the local church. The lighthouse, which stands in a bird sanctuary, once had a boathouse and ramp, but these were destroyed by fire in 1991.

Massachusetts

Annisquam Harbor Light

Annisquam, MA
Built: 1801 and 1897
Style: Cylindrical
No: 9615
Position: 42 39 42 N. 70 40 54 W
Focal plane: 45ft (14m)
Range: W 14 miles/22km, R 11 miles/18km
Height: 41ft (12.5m)

The light station on Wigwam Point is one of the oldest in the U.S. There have been several wooden towers on this site, all of them failing the test of time, and only the keeper's house is original. The present brick tower was built in 1897 with walls that are up to 4ft (1.2m) thick in places. It was equipped with a fifth-order Fresnel lens until automation led to its replacement by a modern optic.

Bakers Island Light

Manchester-by-the-Sea, MA
Built: 1798 and 1821
Style: Conical
No: 9975
Position: 42 32 11 N. 70 47 09 W
Focal plane: 111ft (34m)
Range: W 16 miles/26km, R 14 miles/22km
Height: 59ft (18m)

The existing granite tower, built in 1821, was one of a pair. One of the towers was pulled down after it was decommissioned as part of an economy measure in 1870, but the two keepers' cottages remain, along with a foghorn.

Bass River Light

West Dennis, MA
Built: 1855
Style: Cylindrical tower on dwelling

The lighthouse was built to replace a lantern a West Dennis householder once kept lit in his window as an aid to vessels navigating Nantucket Sound. The old Victorian house, with its lighthouse mounted on the roof, is located at the entrance to the Bass River. The station was decommissioned in 1914 and is now a restaurant, but the light was reinstated in 1989 to serve as a private navigation aid.

Bird Island Light

Marion, MA
Built: 1819
Style: Conical

Bird Island lighthouse served the port of Rochester from 1819 until the great hurricane of 1938 knocked down all but the 30-ft (9-m) stone tower. The problems of rebuilding the station led to the lighthouse being decommissioned the following year, but during the 1990s it was restored and is now maintained as a private aid to navigation.

Borden Flats Light

Fall River, MA
Built: 1881
Style: Conical tower on cylindrical pier
No: 18925
Position: 41 42 18 N. 71 10 30 W
Focal plane: 47ft (14m)

The cast-iron lighthouse, built on an open caisson on the Fall River, is reputed to have received its name from Lizzie Borden, who killed her parents with an axe. It was fitted with a fourth-order Fresnel lens and has a range of 11 miles (18km), but after damage sustained during the great hurricane of 1938 the lens was replaced by a modern optic.

Boston Light

Little Brewster Island, MA
Built: 1716 and 1783
Style: Conical
No: 425
Position: 42 19 42 N. 70 53 24 W
Focal plane: 102ft (31m)
Range: 27 miles (43.5km)

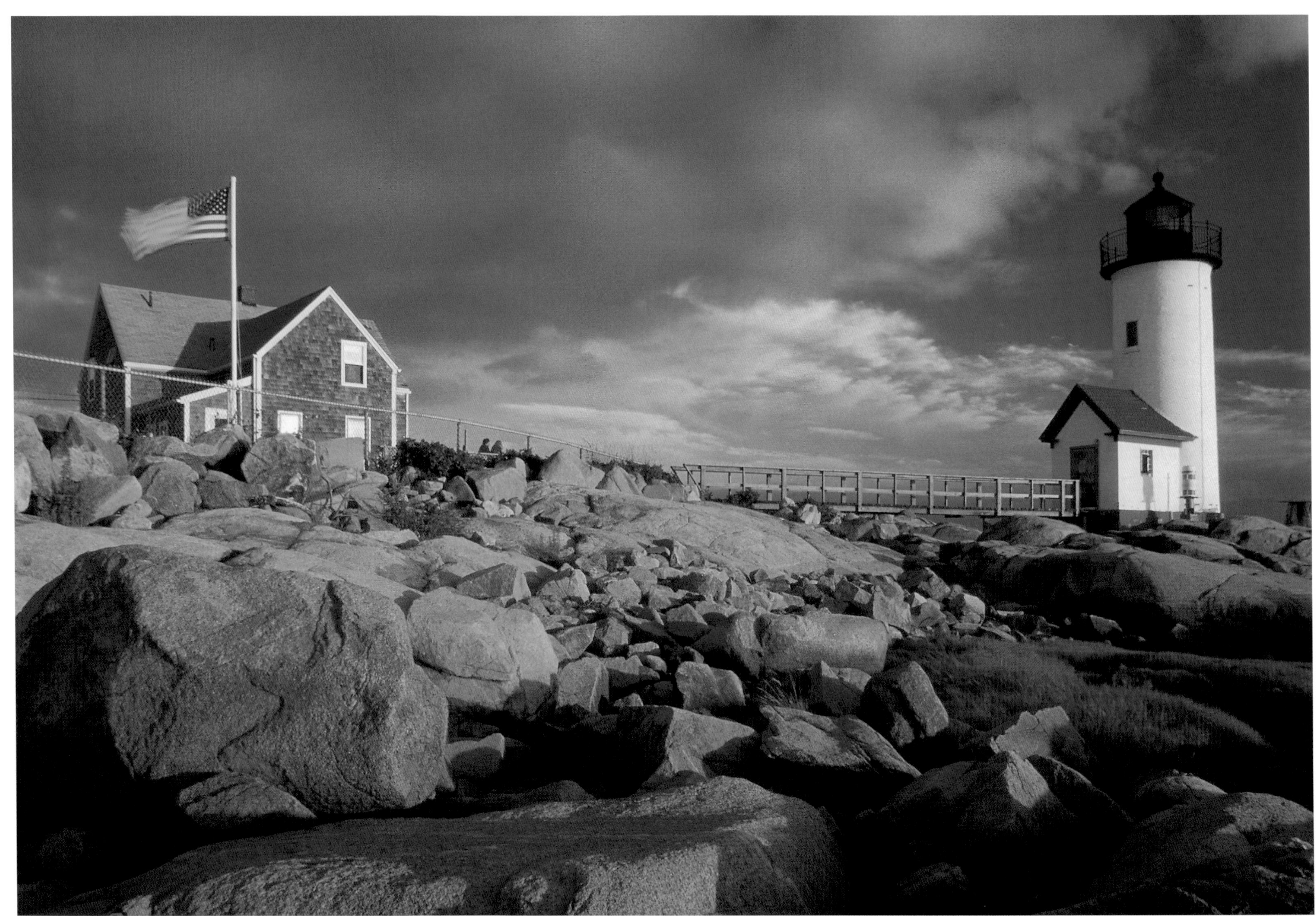

OPPOSITE and RIGHT
Annisquam Harbor Light, Massachusetts.

This was the first station to be built in North America and helped to make Boston the leading trading port. It was first lit in 1716, and a fog cannon was carried across to the Brewster Island base three years later. George Worthylake, a local pilot, was the first paid keeper, but he and his family were lost at sea when making their way back from the island. The tower was the scene of several skirmishes during the War of Independence and the British destroyed it completely before they left. A new granite tower was built in 1783 with walls 7ft (2m) thick to withstand not only the Atlantic weather but also further attacks from artillery. In 1853 the tower was raised by 15ft (5m) to 89ft (27m) and its inner walls were lined with brick. Apart from the reinforcing steel hoops which were added in 1983, the tower remains unchanged since then. The second-order Fresnel lens installed in 1859 is still in service, and has a range of 27 miles. The station was the last to be automated, in 1998, and the Coast Guard continues to maintain a presence on the island.

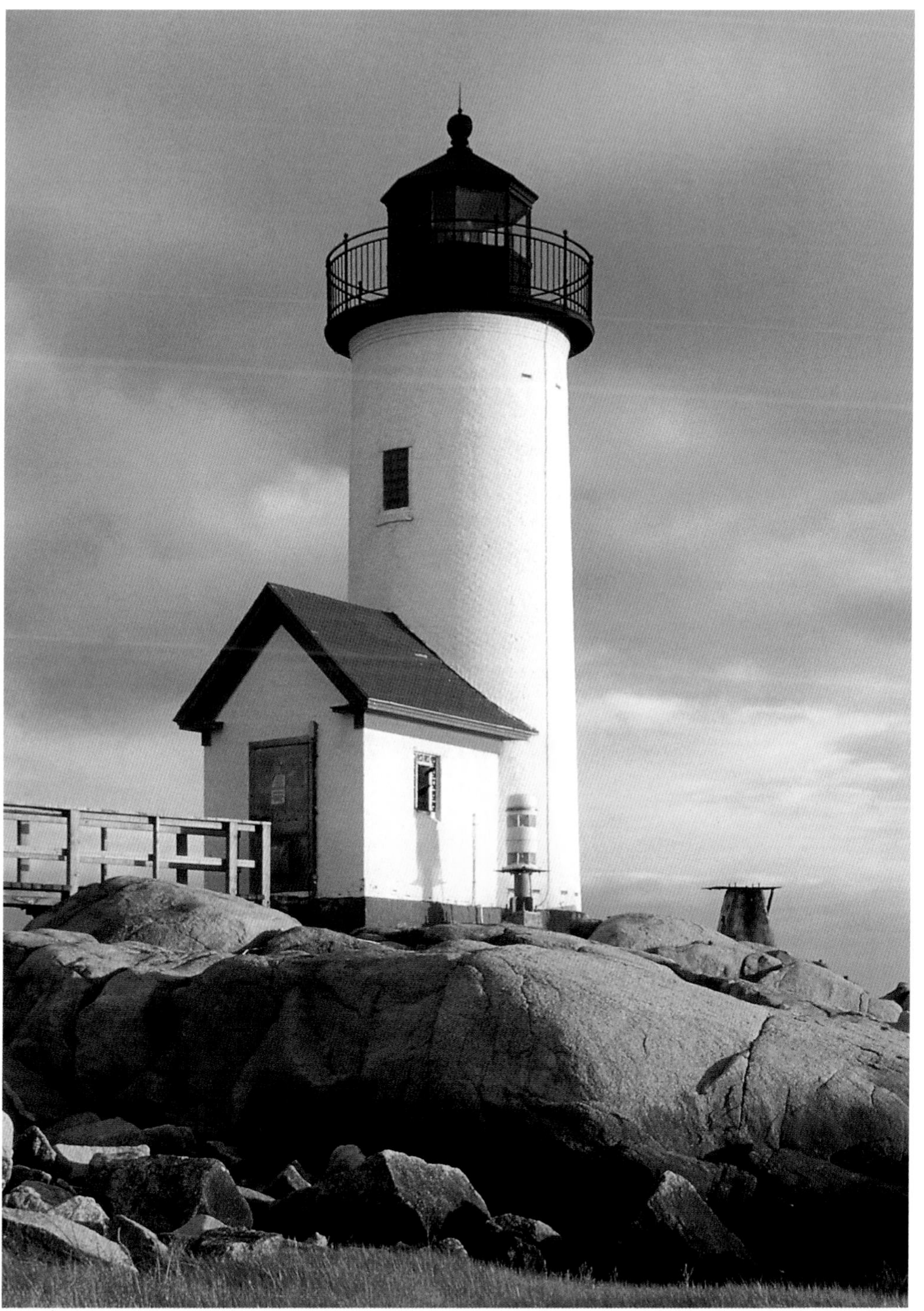

Brant Point Light

Nantucket, MA
Built: 1746, 1759 and 1901
Style: Cylindrical tower
No: 15205
Position: 41 17 24 N. 70 05 25 W
Focal plane: 26ft (8m)
Range: 10 miles (16km)

Brant Point Light is the third oldest light station in the United States. The wooden tower, that currently marks the approach to Nantucket, is the third such light, erected in 1901. It was equipped with a fifth-order Fresnel lens until it was fitted with a modern optic with a range of 10 miles. The first tower was destroyed by fire. The second, built in 1759, also caught fire several times and was repaired by the Nantucket fishermen, who relied on its light to see them safely home.

Butler Flats Light

New Bedford, MA
Built: 1898
Style: Conical tower on cylindrical base
No: 16853
Position: 41 36 12 N. 70 53 42 W
Focal plane: 53ft (16m)
Range: 4 miles (6.5km)

The brick-built tower of Butler Flats caisson lighthouse has been marking the main channel into New Bedford since 1898, and still has its original Fresnel lens with a range of 4 miles. It is now a private aid to navigation.

LEFT
Bass River LIght, Massachusetts.

OPPOSITE
Bird Island Light, Massachusetts.

Buzzards Bay Light

Buzzards Bay, MA
Built: 1961
Style: Texas tower
No: 15985
Position: 41 23 48 N. 71 02 01 W
Focal plane: 67ft (20m)
Range: 17 miles (27km)

The Buzzards Bay lighthouse is one of the few open-water Texas towers that remains in operation. Built in 1961, the platform stands on concrete-filled steel piles and marks the channel to Buzzards Bay and the town of New Bedford.

Cape Ann Light

Thatcher Island, MA
Built: 1771 and 1861
Style: Conical
No: 295
Position: 42 38 12 N. 70 34 30 W
Focal plane: 166ft (50.5m)
Range: 17 miles (27km)
Height: 124ft (38m)

Twin Cape Ann lighthouses have stood on Thatcher Island since 1771. The first 45-ft (14-m) colonial towers were replaced by the present 124-ft granite towers in 1861, but today only the southern tower is active. It was fitted with a first-order Fresnel lens until

automation in 1932. In 1919, the foghorn operated at Cape Ann saved the ship carrying President Woodrow Wilson home from Europe after signing the Treaty of Versailles. With the lights shrouded in fog, the captain of the SS *America* heard the horn at the last moment and was able to alter course in time to avoid crashing into the rocks.

Cape Cod Highland Light

Truro, MA
Built: 1798 and 1857
Style: Conical

The Highland lighthouse station is the oldest on the Cape Cod peninsula. The original 30-ft (9-m) brick tower was built in 1798 which, standing on a bluff 120ft (36.5m) high, gave the light a 20-mile (32-km) range. Within half a century, the seas had eroded much of this ground, and in 1857 a new 66-ft (20-m) brick tower was built about 500ft (150m) back from the cliff edge. Another century on and the waters were threatening the foundations again, prompting local preservationists to begin a $1.5 million fund-raising campaign to save this historic sentinel. In 1997, the tricky engineering feat of moving the tower several hundred feet back was finally completed. The light was equipped with a mighty first-order Fresnel lens, which was replaced in 1945 by an aero-marine beacon with a range of 23 miles (37km).

Cape Poge Light

Martha's Vineyard, MA
Built: 1801 and 1844
Style: Conical
No: 13715
Position: 41 25 10 N. 70 27 08 W
Focal plane: 65ft (20m)
Range: 9 miles (14.5km)

The light station on Chappaquiddick Island off Martha's Vineyard has been in existence since 1801, although the original structure was replaced by the existing wood-shingled lighthouse in 1844. The latter was moved to its present location in 1893. It was originally equipped with a fourth-order Fresnel lens, but is now served by a solar-powered optic.

Chatham Light

Chatham, MA
Built: 1808, 1836 and 1877
Style: Conical
No: 525
Position: 41 40 17 N. 69 57 01 W
Focal plane: 80ft (24m)
Range: 30 miles (48km)
Height: 48ft (15m)

OPPOSITE
Brant Point Light, Massachusetts.

RIGHT
Chatham Light, Massachusetts.

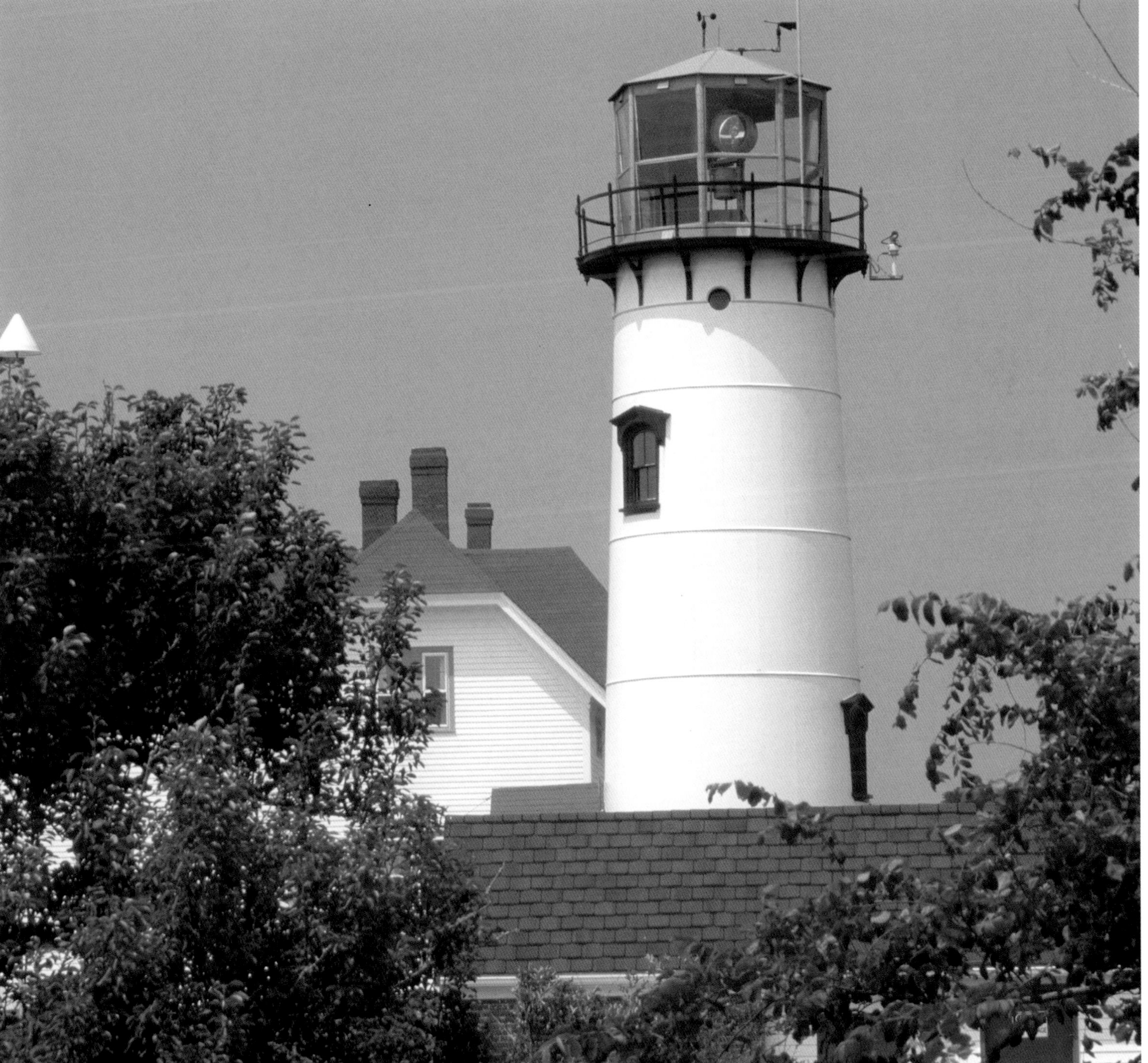

The waters surrounding Cape Cod have a preponderance of warning beacons – so many in fact that in the early 19th century mariners had difficulty identifying them. In 1808 officials conceived the idea of marking the busy channel leading to Chatham harbour with a double light. The original wooden towers were built on a sandy ridge where erosion necessitated reconstruction in 1836. In 1877 the lights were replaced altogether by two 48-ft cast-iron towers fitted with fourth-order Fresnel lenses on the opposite side of the harbour. In 1923, one of these was dismantled and re-erected at Nauset Beach to replace the even rarer triple beacon known as the Three Sisters light. The Chatham beacon is now illuminated through a modern optic.

Clark's Point Light

New Bedford, MA
Built: 1804 and 1869
Style: Square

Clark's Point light station was originally a 42-ft (13-m) stone tower, constructed as an aid to vessels heading for New Bedford. It was lost from sight during the Civil War when a fort was built in front of it, and in 1869 the light was repositioned on the ramparts of the fort. It remained in use until

OPPOSITE
Cape Cod Highland Light, Massachusetts.

RIGHT
Derby Wharf Light, Massachusetts.

1898 and has now been restored as an historical monument.

Cleveland East Ledge Light
Pocasset, MA
Built: 1943
Style: Cylindrical tower and dwelling
No: 16080
Position: 41 37 51 N. 70 41 39 W
Focal plane: 74ft (22.5m)
Range: 15 miles (24km)

The concrete lighthouse sits on a stone caisson built in 1943 to mark the passage through Buzzards Bay west of Cape Cod. It was originally fitted with a fourth-order Fresnel lens, which was replaced by a modern optic when the station was automated in 1978.

Deer Island Light
Boston, MA
Built: 1890 and 1984
Style: Caisson

The caisson marking the channel through Presidents Roads once supported a 51-ft (15.5-m) cast-iron lighthouse, but this was replaced in 1984 by an automated fibreglass structure.

Derby Wharf Light

Salem, MA
Built: 1871
Style: Square tower
No: 10140
Position: 42 30 59 N. 70 53 01 W
Focal plane: 25ft (8m)

Derby Wharf light tower was built in Salem in 1871 for Elias Derby, an early millionaire. The tower first housed a whale-oil lamp, which was replaced first by a fifth-order and, later, by a sixth-order Fresnel lens. Since automation, the tower has been lit by a solar-powered optic lens.

Duxbury Pier Light

Plymouth, MA
Built: 1871
Style: Conical tower
No: 12580
Position: 41 59 12 N. 70 38 54 W
Focal plane: 35ft (11m)
Range: 6 miles (10km)
Height: 47ft (14m)

The lighthouse marks the channel into Plymouth's inner harbour. It is one of the oldest 'coffee-pot' towers and was built on a concrete-filled iron caisson. It was originally equipped with a fourth-order Fresnel lens, but is now fitted with a modern optic giving a flashing red signal.

East Chop Light

Oak Bluffs, Martha's Vineyard, MA
Built: 1877
Style: Conical

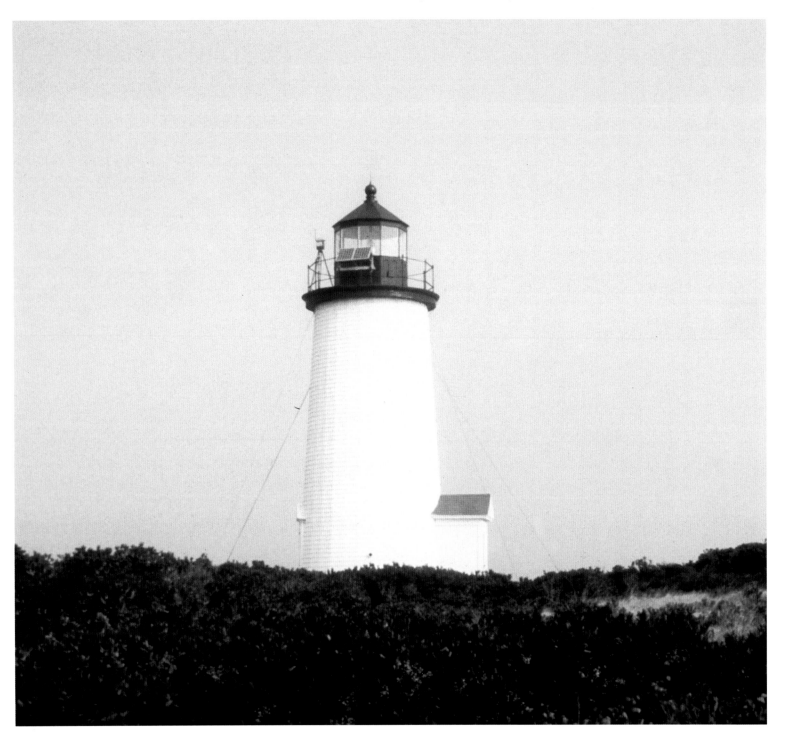

LEFT
Cape Poge Light, Massachusetts.

OPPOSITE
East Chop Light, Massachusetts.

No: 13745
Position: 41 28 13 N. 70 34 03 W
Focal plane: 79ft (24m)
Range: 9 miles (14.5km)
Height: 40ft (12m)

The cast-iron East Chop lighthouse was built to guide vessels into Vineyard Haven. It is one of several historic light towers still in operation on Martha's Vineyard.

Eastern Point Light

Gloucester, MA
Built: 1832, 1848 and 1890
Style: Conical tower
No: 330
Position: 42 34 49 N. 70 39 52 W
Focal plane: 57ft (17m)
Range: 20 miles (32km)
Height: 36ft (11m)

The first tower was constructed at Eastern Point to guide fishing boats into Gloucester harbour. It was renovated in 1848 before the present brick tower was constructed in 1890, together with the keeper's dwelling and fog-signal house.

Edgartown Harbor Light

Edgartown, MA
Built: 1828 and 1875

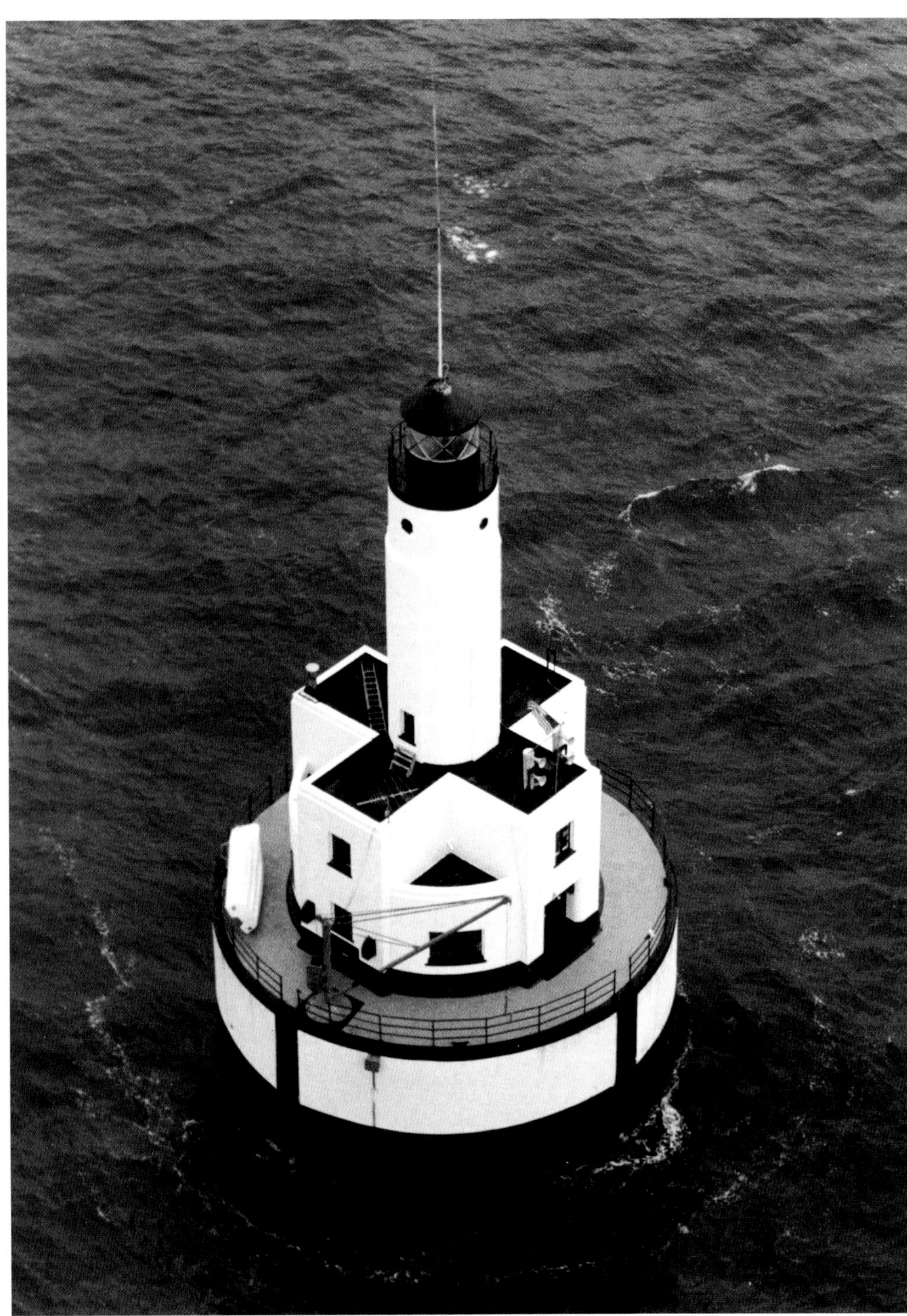

Style: Conical
No: 15420
Position: 41 23 27 N. 70 30 11 W
Focal plane: 45ft (14m)
Range: 5 miles (8km)

The cast-iron lighthouse, sited on a sandy spit outside Edgartown's harbour on Martha's Vineyard, first served the port of Ipswich, north of Boston. The tower was moved to Edgartown in 1939 to replace the port's 1828 Cape Cod-style lighthouse, which had been destroyed by the hurricane of 1938. The lighthouse was equipped with a fourth-order Fresnel lens until it was replaced by a modern optic in 1988.

Fort Pickering Light

Winter Island, Salem, MA
Built: 1872
Style: Conical tower on concrete base
No: 10090
Position: 42 31 36 N. 70 52 00 W
Focal plane: 28ft (8.5m)

Fort Pickering lighthouse guided the whaling ships and freighters towards Salem's once bustling Derby Wharf after it was completed in 1872. The 20-ft (6-m) conical brick tower, which is positioned on Winter Island, dates back to 1872 and is now a private aid to navigation.

Gay Head Light

Martha's Vineyard, MA
Built: 1799 and 1856
Style: Cylindrical brick tower
No: 15610
Position: 41 20 54 N. 70 50 06 W

LEFT
Cleveland East Ledge Light, Massachusetts.

OPPOSITE LEFT
Derby Wharf Light, Massachusetts.

OPPOSITE RIGHT
Duxbury Pier Light, Massachusetts.

Focal plane: 170ft (52m)
Range: W 24 miles/39km, R 20 miles/32km
Height: 51ft (15.5m)

The first lighthouse on Gay Head was an octagonal wooden tower. The present brick tower was originally fitted with a first-order Fresnel lens, which has since been replaced by a modern aero-marine optic with a range of 24 miles.

Gloucester Breakwater Light

Gloucester, MA
Built: 1894
Style: House and tower on skeletal frame

This 37-ft (11-m) skeletal platform lighthouse is part of the breakwater marking the entrance to Gloucester harbour.

Graves Light

Boston, MA
Built: 1905
Style: Conical
No: 390
Position: 42 21 54 N. 70 52 09 W
Focal plane: 98ft (30m)

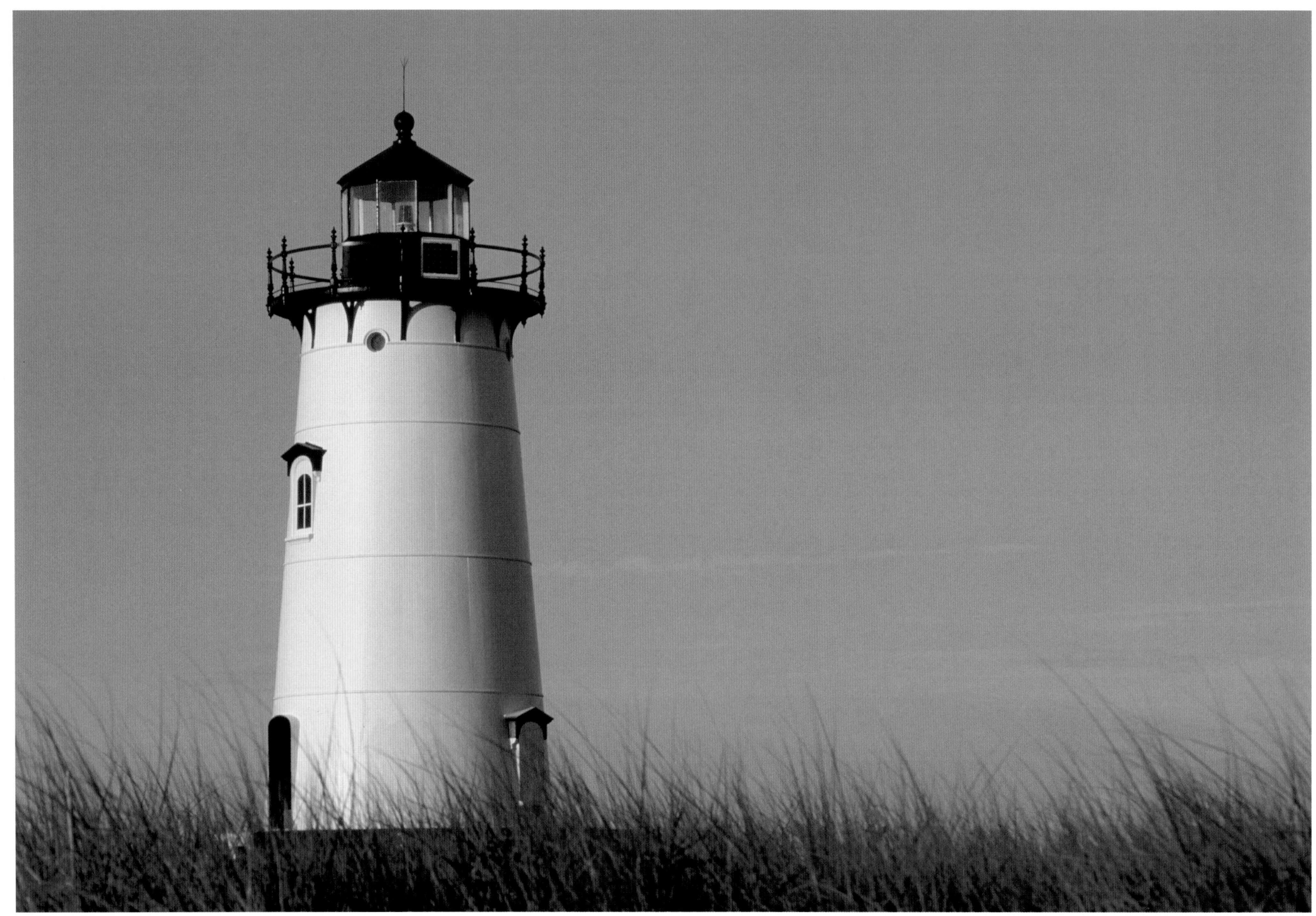

OPPOSITE
Edgartown Harbor Light, Massachusetts.

RIGHT
Eastern Point Light, Massachusetts.

Range: 25 miles (40km)
Height: 113ft (34m)

The stone-built Graves lighthouse near the mouth of Boston harbour marks Graves Ledge, named after Thomas Graves, a leading Massachusetts merchant in colonial times, and not (as one might assume) the last resting places of the many seamen who lost their lives near this spot. One of the many tragedies to occur here was the sinking of the schooner *Mary O'Hara*, which ran onto the ledge during a blizzard in January 1941. Nineteen men died, either drowned or frozen to death, after making it to the rocks. The lighthouse was never a popular posting for keepers and it was eventually automated in 1976. It was originally equipped with a first-order Fresnel lens but this has since been replaced by a plastic optic.

Hospital Point Range Lights

Beverly, MA
Built: 1872 and 1927
Style: Pyramidal tower
No: 10000 (Front Light)
Position: 42 32 48 N. 70 51 24 W
Focal plane: 70ft (21m)
No: 10005 (Rear Light)
Focal plane: 183ft (56m)

LEFT
Gay Head Light, Massachusetts.

OPPOSITE
Graves Light, Massachusetts.

PAGE 178
Hospital Point (Range Front Light), Massachusetts.

PAGE 179
Long Island Head Light, Massachusetts.

The 45-ft (14-m) brick-built Hospital Point Front Range lighthouse is twinned with a second light set on the spire of a church in Beverly to keep vessels safely lined up through the narrow channel towards Salem. The Front Range tower was fitted originally with the uncommon three-and-a-half-order Fresnel lens, used more often on the Great Lakes, until it was replaced by a standard third-order lens.

Hyannis Harbor Light
Hyannis, MA
Built: 1849
Style: Conical

The brick-built lighthouse at Hyannis Harbor replaced a ship's lantern hung in the window of a fisherman's shack in 1849. It acted as a rear range light until decommissioned in 1929. The tower is now in private ownership.

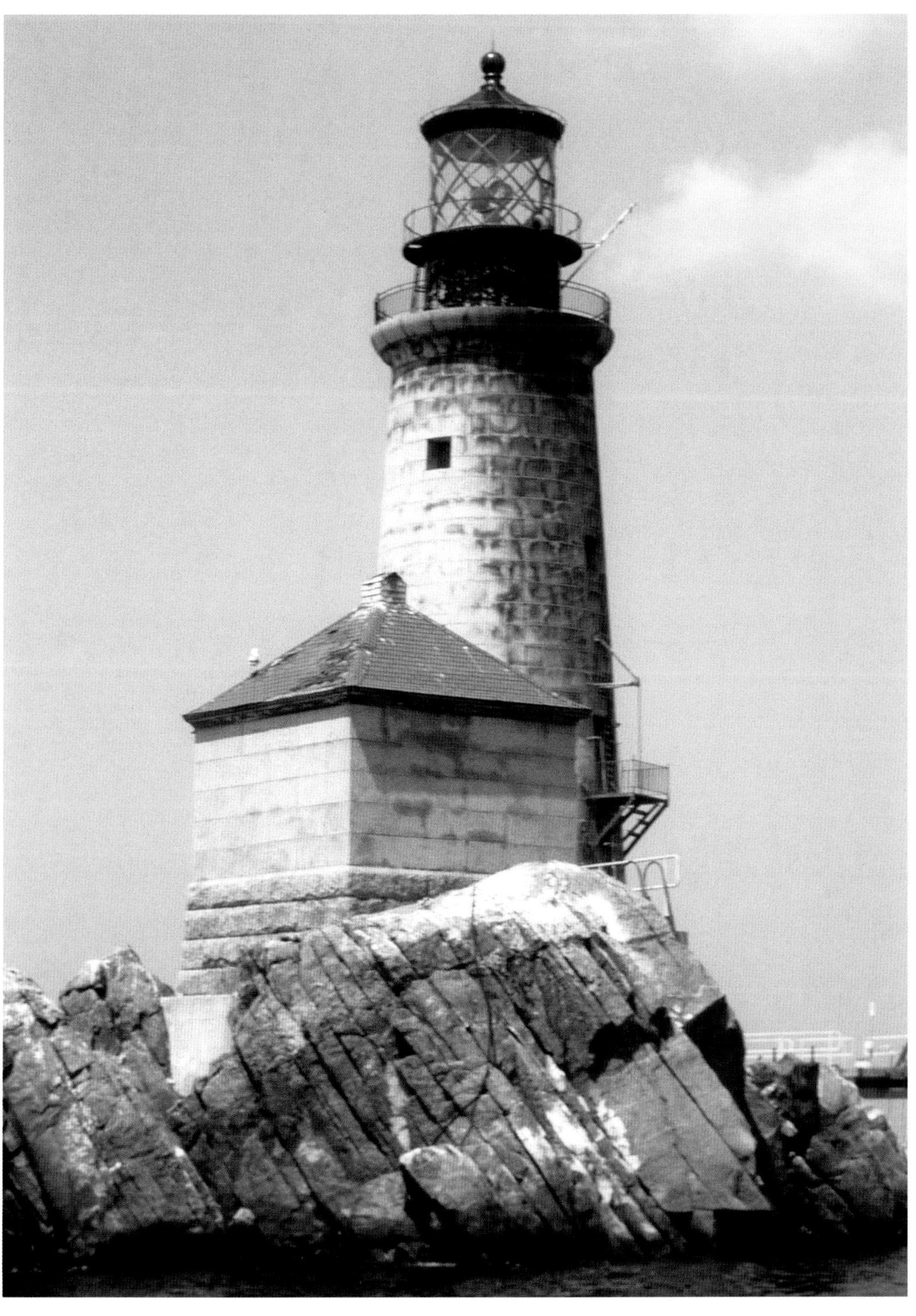

Long Island Head Light

Boston, MA
Built: 1820, 1844 and 1919
Style: Cylindrical
No: 10800
Position: 42 19 48 N. 70 57 30 W
Focal plane: 120ft (36.5m)
Range: 6 miles (10km)

The Long Island Head light station was first established in 1820 to guide vessels navigating Presidents Roads, leading to Boston harbour. The original lighthouse, a 23-ft (7-m) stone tower, was replaced in 1844 by the first cast-iron tower in the United States. The existing brick tower was fitted with a three-and-a-half-order Fresnel lens, which has since been replaced by a modern plastic lens.

Long Point Light

Provincetown, MA
Built: 1826 and 1875
Style: Square tower
No: 13275
Focal plane: 36ft (11m)
Range: 8 miles (13km)

The lighthouse station first established at Long Point, Provincetown, guarding the tip of Cape Cod, was replaced by the present brick tower in 1875. The station was automated in 1980, when the keeper's house and outbuildings were pulled down and the tower's fourth-order Fresnel lens was replaced by a modern optic.

Marblehead Light

Salem, MA
Built: 1836 and 1895
Style: Skeletal tower

The present 105-ft (32-m) steel skeletal tower erected in 1895 replaced a much smaller tower of 1836. The station was automated in 1960, when it was fitted with a modern optic.

Minots Ledge Light

Cohasset, MA
Built: 1850 and 1860
Style: Conical
No: 440
Position: 42 16 12 N. 70 45 30 W
Focal plane: 85ft (26m)
Range: 10 miles (16km)
Height: 114ft (35m)

Minots Ledge, hidden beneath the waves off Cohasset, is one of the most formidable threats to navigation on the East Coast and has been responsible for dozens of shipwrecks. The technology to build a structure capable of withstanding the open-sea environment was not available until the mid-19th century, and the first effort, a cast-iron skeletal tower lit in 1850, lasted less than a year and cost the lives of its two keepers. Engineers then turned to England for answers and copied the interlocking granite-block construction used to build the Bell Rock lighthouse. The resulting Minots Ledge lighthouse of 1860, which required 2,300 tons of granite, has withstood the

OPPOSITE
Long Point Light, Massachusetts.

RIGHT
Minots Ledge Light, Massachusetts.

Atlantic gales ever since. Its original second-order Fresnel lens was replaced by a modern optic when automated in 1947.

Monomoy Point Light

Chatham, MA
Built: 1849
Style: Skeletal tower

The cast-iron cylinder tower on Monomoy Point is the oldest surviving skeletal lighthouse in the country. Records confirm that it was built in 1849, predating the similar tower on Minots Ledge by a year. The latter was short-lived, but the Monomoy lighthouse had a less exacting site. Decommissioned in 1923, it was restored in 1989 under the auspices of the Cape Cod Museum of Natural History and is now within the Monomoy National Wildlife Refuge.

Nantucket Great Point Light

Nantucket Island, MA
Built: 1749, 1818 and 1986
Style: Conical tower
No: 13650
Focal plane: 71ft (22m)
Range: W 14 miles/22km, R 12 miles/19km
Height: 70ft (21m)

The first lighthouse at Great Point was a wooden tower built in 1749, which burned down in 1817. This was replaced the following year by a rubblestone tower, which survived for 166 years until blown down during a fierce winter storm in 1984. Its replacement is a concrete and plastic replica funded by a $2-million federal grant gained with the support of Massachusetts Senator Ted Kennedy, which was completed in 1986. The second lighthouse was equipped with a third-order Fresnel lens, which was replaced with a modern plastic lens long before the tower was destroyed. The new tower has a solar powered optic.

Nauset Beach Light

Eastham, MA
Built: 1838, 1877, 1923 and 1996
Style: Conical
No: 510
Position: 41 51 36 N. 69 57 12 W
Focal plane: 114ft (35m)
Range: W 24 miles/39km, R 20 miles/32km
Height: 48ft (15m)

The lighthouse station at Nauset Beach, built in 1838, had three separate light towers to distinguish it from the many others around Cape Cod, and consequently became known as the Three Sisters of Nauset. When it was threatened by erosion in 1923, one of the twin cast-iron towers at Chatham harbour was dismantled and re-erected here. In time, this too was threatened by the changing coastline, and in 1996, the 90-ton brick-lined, red-and-white tower was moved a second time, to a safer location farther from the cliffs. The station is now managed by the National Park Service.

OPPOSITE
Nantucket Great Point Light, Massachusetts.

RIGHT
Nauset Beach Light, Massachusetts.

Ned Point Light

Mattapoisett, MA
Built: 1837 and 1888
Style: Conical
No: 17095
Position: 41 39 03 N. 70 47 44 W
Focal plane: 41ft (12.5m)
Range: 12 miles (19km)

The light station at Ned Point, guiding vessels into Mattapoisett, was a rubblestone tower, originally 35ft (11m) high. It was raised by a little over 4ft (1.2m) in 1888 when a fifth-order Fresnel lens was installed, giving the lighthouse a range of 12 miles. This remained in place until automation in 1952.

Newburyport Harbor Front Range Light

Newburyport, MA
Built: 1873
Style: Cylindrical

This 15-ft (4.5-m) cast-iron Front Range tower at Newburyport, and its tandem light built next to Water Street, served to guide vessels up the deep-water channel in the Merrimac River from 1873 until both were decommissioned in 1961. A group of local historians now hopes to restore the towers.

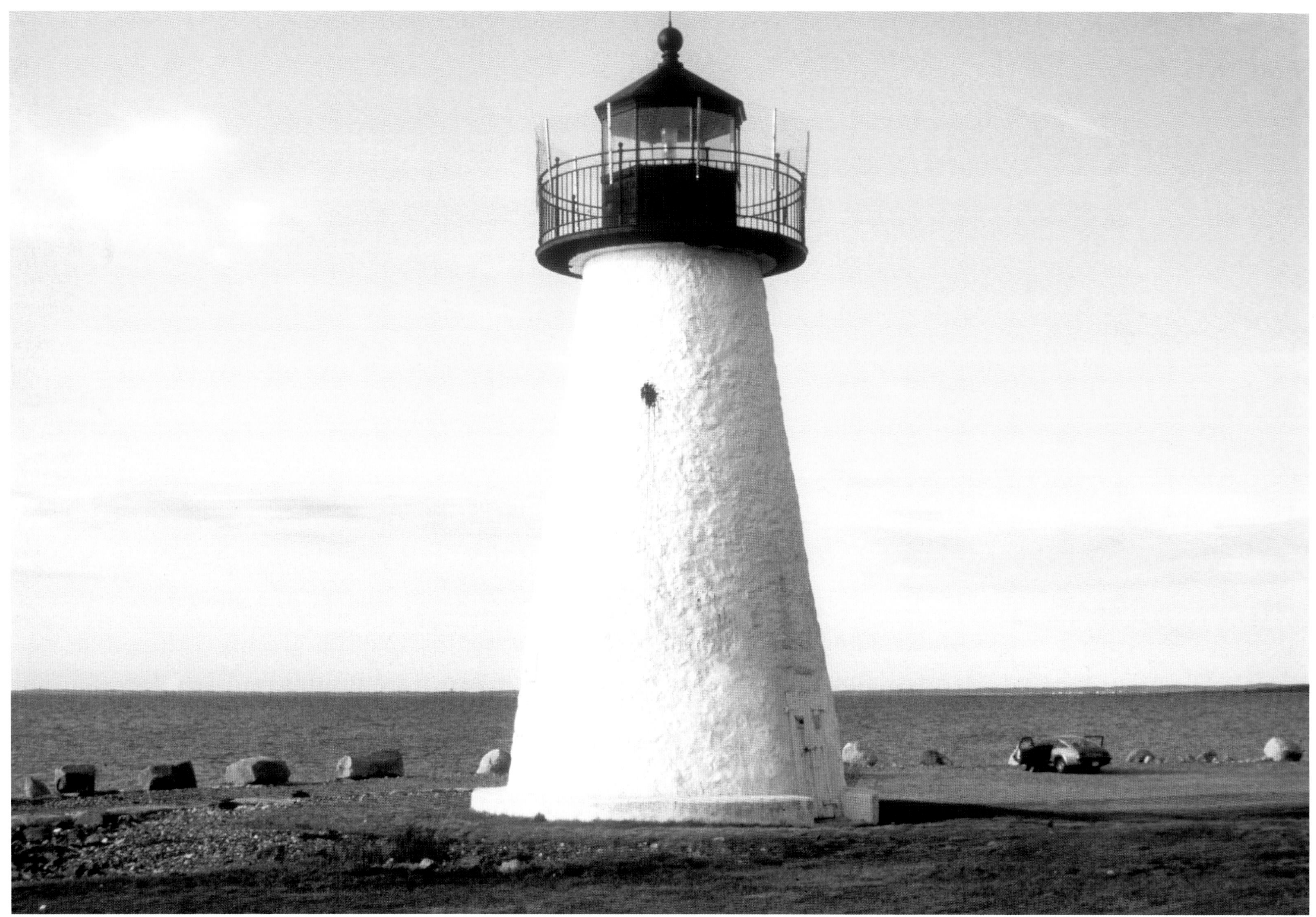

OPPOSITE
Ned Point Light, Massachusetts.

RIGHT
Newburyport Harbor Light, Massachusetts.

Newburyport Harbor Light

Newburyport, MA
Built: 1788 and 1898
Style: Conical
No: 260
Position: 42 48 54 N. 70 49 06 W
Focal plane: 50ft (15m)
Range: 10 miles (16km)

Newburyport can boast of having one of the first lighthouse stations in the country. First established in 1788, the two towers were in fact the eleventh station in the newly founded United States. They served as range lights guiding vessels up the Merrimac River. Now, only the rear range tower, built in 1898, remains; its fourth-order Fresnel lens was replaced with a plastic optic when the light was automated in 1981.

Nobska Point Light

Woods Hole, MA
Built: 1828 and 1876
Style: Cylindrical
No: 15560
Position: 41 30 57 N. 70 39 18 W
Focal plane: 87ft (26.5m)
Range: W 13 miles/21km, R 11 miles/18km

The light station on Nobska Point has warned shipping away from the Cape Cod shoals known as Hedge Fence and L'Hommedieu since 1828. The original lighthouse, a stone cottage with a small lantern on its roof, was replaced by the present 40-ft (12-m) brick-lined cast-iron tower in 1876. The tower still has its original fourth-order Fresnel lens. It displays a red sector to those in danger of running onto the shoals, and a white sector to those in safe waters.

Palmers Island Light

New Bedford, MA
Built: 1849
Style: Conical tower on stone pier
No: 16898
Position: 41 37 36 N. 70 54 36 W
Focal plane: 42ft (13m)
Range: 5 miles (8km)

The rough fieldstone Palmer Island lighthouse of 1849 was built strong enough to survive a fire in 1866 and a century-and-a-half of winter storms. The tower was first fitted with a fifth-order Fresnel lens, but this was later replaced by a fourth-order lens and that in turn by a modern plastic optic.

Plymouth Light

Plymouth, MA
Built: 1769, 1803 and 1843
Style: Octagonal
No: 12545
Position: 42 00 12 N. 70 36 00 W
Focal plane: 102ft (31m)
Range: W 17 miles/27km, R 15 miles/24km
Height: 39ft (12m)

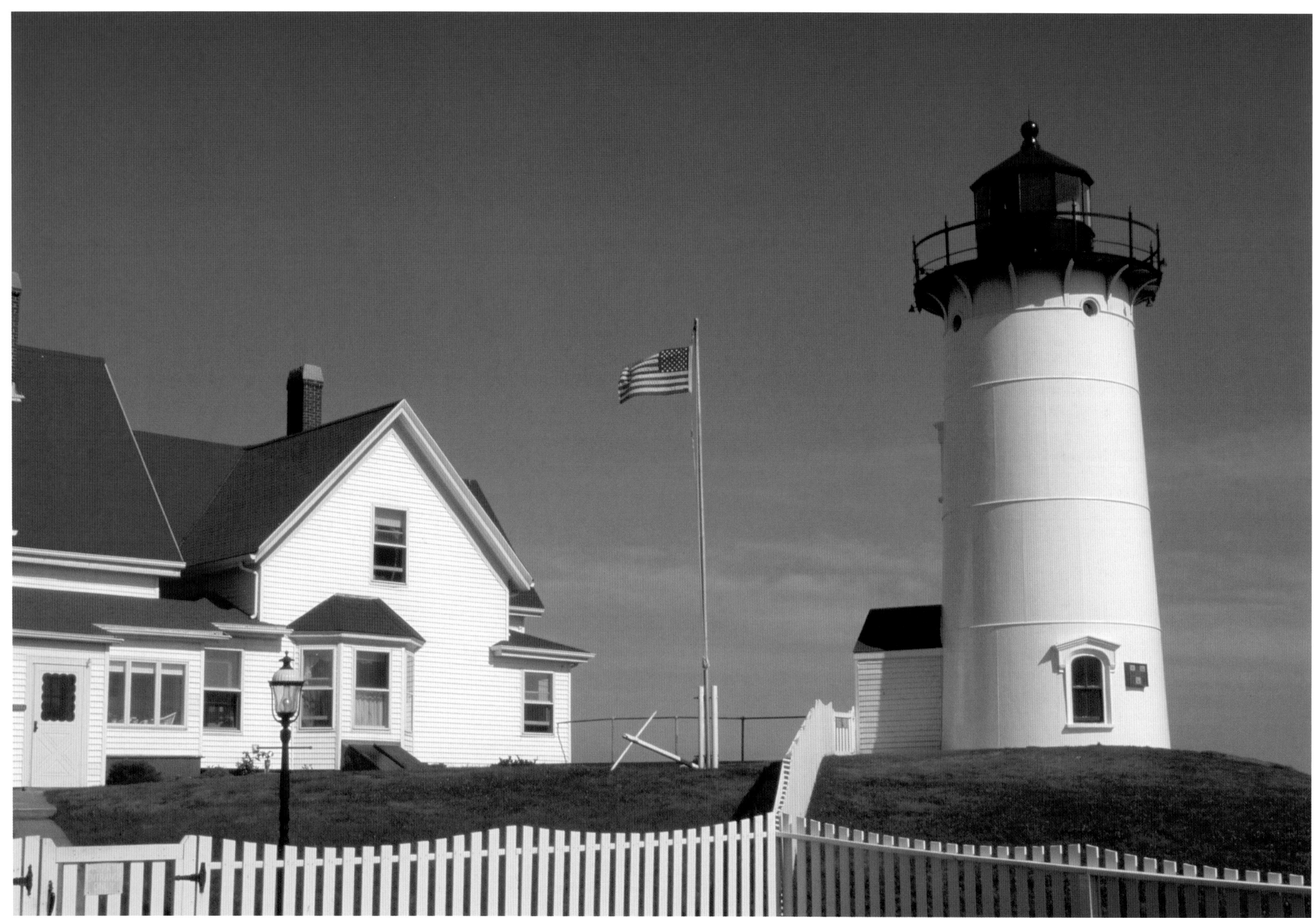

OPPOSITE
Nobska Point Light, Massachusetts.

RIGHT
Plymouth Light, Massachusetts.

The Plymouth light station is one of America's earliest lighthouses and stands close to the point where the Pilgrim Fathers landed in 1620. Established in 1769, the point was marked by a pair of wooden towers built only a few feet apart. After a fire in 1801 they were replaced; these towers, in turn, were replaced 40 years later by two 39-ft octagonal lighthouses, each equipped with a fourth-order Fresnel lens. One of the pair, fitted with a modern optic lens with a range of 17 miles, remains today, but its twin was pulled down in 1924.

Point Gammon Light

Hyannis, MA
Built: 1816

All that now remains are the ruins of a conical stone tower. The light was deactivated in 1858 and stands as a memorial to the Peak family, who manned it throughout its 42 years of service.

Race Point Light

Provincetown, MA
Built: 1816 and 1876
Style: Cylindrical
No: 485
Position: 42 03 45 N. 70 14 35 W
Focal plane: 41ft (12.5m)
Range: 16 miles (26km)

The present cast-iron lighthouse at Race Point was built in 1876 to replace the original rubblestone tower. The station, which is a 45-minute walk across sand dunes from Provincetown, was automated in 1978, but subsequently fell into disrepair. The station is now managed by the American Lighthouse Foundation, which has renovated the buildings and converted the keeper's dwelling into a guest house.

Sandy Neck Light

Barnstable, MA
Built: 1826 and 1857
Style: Cylindrical

The lighthouse marks the tip of a 7-mile (11-m) peninsula to the west of Barnstable harbour. The first Cape Cod-style lighthouse was replaced by the current brick tower in 1857. The station was decommissioned in 1952 and is now in private hands.

Sankaty Head Light

Nantucket Island, MA
Built: 1850
Style: Conical
No: 555
Position: 41 17 01 N. 69 57 54 W
Focal plane: 158ft (48m)
Range: 24 miles (39km)
Height: 70ft (21m)

The brick-built Sankaty Head lighthouse, with its central red band, marks the 100-ft (30-m) cliffs on Nantucket's ocean shoreline. Erected in 1850, it was the first lighthouse in Massachusetts to be equipped with a Fresnel lens. This second-order optic, with its clockwork rotating mechanism, remained in place until the station was automated in 1950.

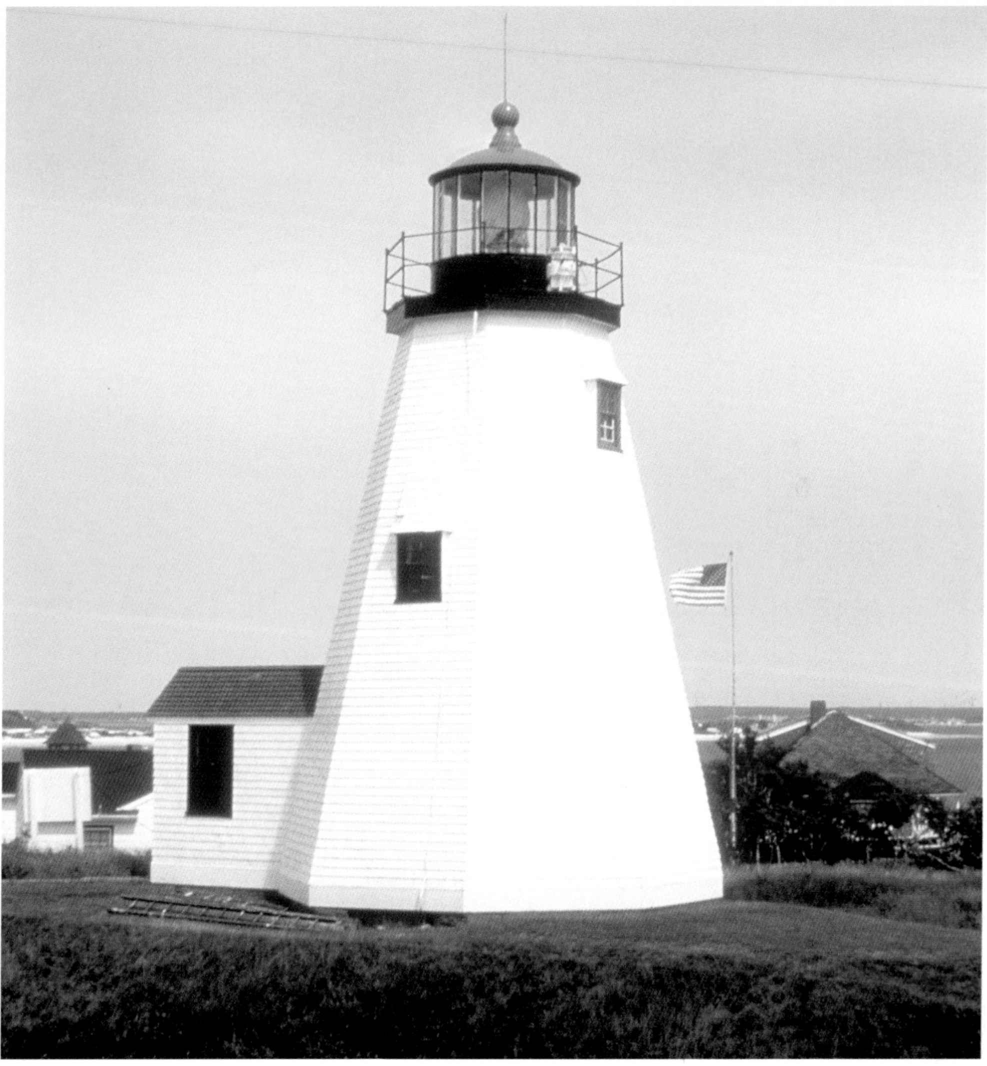

Scituate Light

Scituate, MA
Built: 1810

The 50-ft (15-m) octagonal stone lighthouse provided mariners with a vital bearing when navigating near the dangerous Minots Ledge. The station was decommissioned when the second Minots Ledge lighthouse was completed in 1860. Restored to working order in 1990, it now shines its light inland.

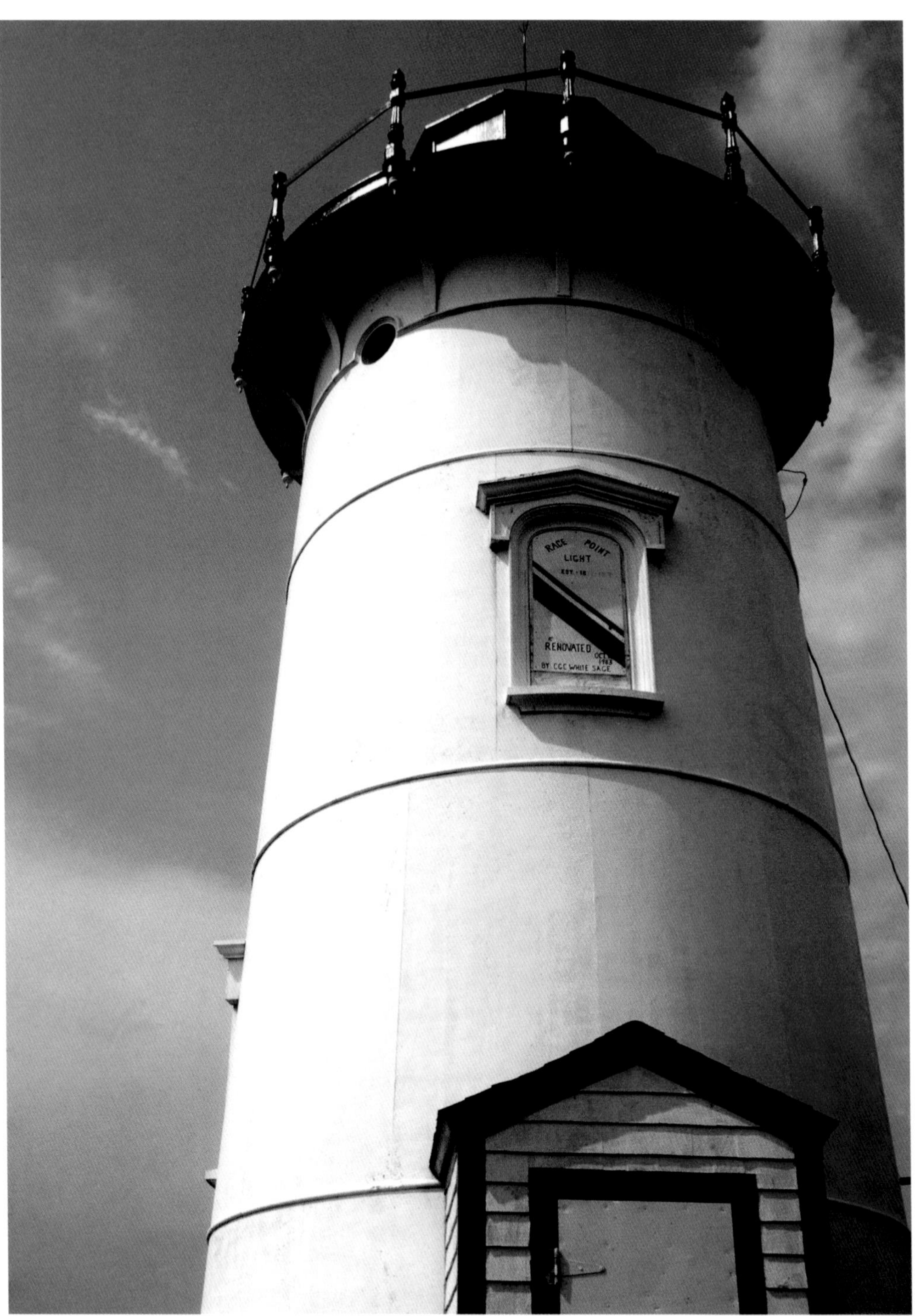

Stage Harbor Light

Chatham, MA
Built: 1890
Style: Conical

Chatham's cast-iron Stage Harbor lighthouse was erected in 1890 and its kerosene-powered fourth-order Fresnel lens continued in operation until the light was decommissioned in 1933. The tower and keeper's dwelling are now privately owned.

Straitsmouth Light

Rockport, MA
Built: 1835 and 1896
Style: Cylindrical

The first Straitsmouth Harbor lighthouse was a small octagonal brick tower built in 1835. This was replaced by the present 29-ft (9-m) brick tower constructed in 1896 and with a range of 6 miles (10km). The station is now maintained by the Massachusetts Audubon Society.

Tarpaulin Cove Light

Naushon Island, Gosnold, MA
Built: 1817 and 1856
Style: Conical tower with attached building
No: 15580
Position: 41 28 08 N. 70 45 27 W
Focal plane: 78ft (24m)
Range: 9 miles (14.5km)
Height: 76ft (23m)

Tarpaulin Cove, on Naushon within the Elizabeth Islands, south-west of Cape Cod, was once a favourite haunt of pirates. A 39-ft rubblestone lighthouse was built to mark the cove in 1817 and was replaced in 1856 by the present brick tower. The keeper's house was demolished in 1962 when the station was automated and its fifth-order Fresnel lens was replaced by a modern optic.

LEFT
Race Point Light, Massachusetts.

OPPOSITE
Sankaty Head Light, Massachusetts.

PAGE 190
Stage Harbor Light, Massachusetts.

PAGE 191
Wood End Light, Massachusetts.

Ten Pound Island Light

Gloucester, MA
Built: 1821 and 1881
Style: Cylindrical

Ten Pound Island outside Gloucester harbour derived its name from the alleged price paid to the local people for the island by early settlers. The first lighthouse, a 40-ft (12-m) stone tower and wood-framed keeper's house, were built here in 1821. The present 30-ft (9-m) brick-lined, cast-iron tower, which replaced it in 1881, was fitted with a fifth-order Fresnel lens, replaced by a modern optic when the station was automated.

West Chop Light
Tilsbury, Martha's Vineyard, MA
Built: 1818
Style: Conical
No: 13775
Positiion: 41 28 51 N. 70 35 59 W
Focal plane: 84ft (26m)
Range: W 14 miles/22km, R 10 miles/16km
Height: 52ft (16m)

The concrete lighthouse marks the western approaches to Martha's Vineyard and Vineyard Haven. The station's fourth-order Fresnel lens has operated since 1857.

Wing's Neck Light
Pocasset, MA
Built: 1848 and 1890
Style: Conical tower

The first lighthouse on Wing's Neck peninsula was a hexagonal wooden tower completed in 1848. A second tower, together with a large keeper's house, was built on the site in 1890 and remained in use until the station was decommissioned in 1945. The tower and dwelling are now privately owned.

Wood End Light
Provincetown, MA
Built: 1864 and 1872
Style: Square
No: 13270
42 01 16 N. 70 11 37 W
Focal plane: 45ft (14m)
Range: 13 miles (21km)
Height: 39ft (12m)

The first Wood End lighthouse was a wooden pyramid tower, which burned down less than a decade after it was constructed. The present 39-ft brick-built tower was equipped with a fifth-order Fresnel lens until it was automated in 1961, when a modern optic was fitted..

New Hampshire

Burkhaven Light
Burkhaven Harbor, Lake Sunapee, NH
Built: 1893 and 1936.
Style: Octagonal platform

Burkhaven Light is one of three stations built around Lake Sunapee during the 1890s to guide the steamboats on this resort lake, which is 10-miles (16-km) long. The first lighthouse marking the entrance to the harbour was destroyed by ice floes, but the second, an octagonal platform, has successfully withstood winter's threat since 1936. The light is maintained today by the New Hampshire Department of Marine Control.

Herrick Cove Light
Lake Sunapee, NH
Built: 1893
Style: Octagonal platform

The platform and small white lighthouse marking Herrick Cove on Lake Sunapee, like Burkhaven Light, is maintained by the New Hampshire Department of Marine Control.

Isle of Shoals Light, New Hampshire.

Isle of Shoals Light
Portsmouth, NH
Built: 1821 and 1859

The first light station dates back to 1821 and lasted for 38 years. It was replaced in 1859 by the present 58-ft (18-m) tower equipped with a second-order Fresnel lens. The light was upgraded to a modern optic when the station was automated in 1987.

Loon Island Light
Lake Sunapee, NH
Built: 1893 and 1960
Style: Octagonal tower

Loon Island Light marks a dangerous reef in Lake Sunapee. The white octagonal tower was built at the same time as the neighbouring towers at Herrick Cove and Burkhaven. The exposed rock was a particular danger to the early steam ferries that plied the lake at night or in fog. At least one of them, the *Edmund Burke*, struck the rock in 1891. The first light cost $400 to erect but later burned down. The present tower was erected in 1960.

Portsmouth Harbor (New Castle) Light
Fort Constitution, New Castle Island, NH
Built: 1771, 1784, 1804 and 1877
Style: Conical tower with building attached
No: 8330
Position: 43 04 18 N. 70 42 30 W
Focal plane: 52ft (16m)
Range: 12 miles (19km)

Portsmouth Harbor Light is one of America's oldest stations, dating back to 1771 when a lantern swung from a pole on Fort Constitution. This was replaced by an 80-ft (24-m) wooden tower in 1784, which was rebuilt 20 years later. The present 48-ft (15-m) cast-iron tower dates from 1877. The fort and its lighthouse have had a number of notable visitors, the most distinguished being George Washington, the 'father' of the U.S. Lighthouse Service, who took a tour of the lighthouse in 1789 and was so appalled by its condition that he fired the keeper!

Whaleback Light
Portsmouth, NH
Built: 1820, 1831 and 1872
Style: Conical
No: 200
Position: 43 03 30 N. 70 41 48 W
Focal plane: 59ft (18m)
Range: 18 miles (29km)
Height: 75ft (23m)

Whaleback Ledge is one of a number of killer rocks that obstruct the approaches to the Piscataqua River and Portsmouth's harbour. The first lighthouse was built here in 1820 but was toppled in a storm ten years later. A second tower succumbed to similar weather in the late 1860s, and the present granite tower was completed in 1872. Its fourth-order Fresnel lens was replaced by a modern optic when the station was automated in 1963.

NEW JERSEY

Absecon Light
Atlantic City, NJ
Built: 1857
Style: Conical

Absecon Light, named after the native American people who lived along the New Jersey coast, was established in 1857. The 170-ft (52-m) brick tower was designed and built by George Meade, an army engineer, who later led the Union forces to victory at the Battle of Gettysburg. The light was focused by a first-order Fresnel lens that had a range of 20 miles (32km), but it was not strong enough to compete with the bright lights of Atlantic City and the station was decommissioned in 1933. The station's historic value was finally recognized in 1997 when the lighthouse was relit to become the centrepiece of a museum.

Ambrose Light
Sandy Hook, NJ
Style: Skeletal tower
No. 720
Position: 40 27 00 N. 73 48 00 W
Focal plane: 76ft (23m)
Range: 18 miles (29km)

The Ambrose Lightship that marked the approaches to New York was finally retired from service in 1967 and replaced by a Texas tower fitted with a 10-million-candlepower beacon. This in turn was replaced by a steel skeletal tower which stands above the water on three legs.

Barnegat Light
Long Beach Island, NJ
Built: 1835 and 1859
Style: Conical

The original 50-ft (15-m) stone Barnegat lighthouse was designed and built by Winslow Lewis in 1835, but succumbed to a storm 24 years later. It was replaced by the present 172-ft (52-m) tower designed by the future General George Meade. It was fitted with a first-order Fresnel lens costing $15,000 – almost a third as much as the lighthouse! It had a range of 30 miles (48km) but was decommissioned in 1944 and is now a museum.

Cape May Light
Cape May, NJ
Built: 1824, 1847 and 1859
Style: Conical, red-topped tower
No: 155
Position: 38 55 59 N. 75 57 37 W
Focal plane: 165ft (50m)
Range: 24 miles (39km)
Height: 157ft (48m)

The first lighthouse that guided ships around Cape May towards Delaware was an 88-ft (27-m) stone tower, which was replaced by a 68-ft (21-m) brick-built lighthouse in 1847. The present lighthouse dates back to 1859 and has become one of the country's best-known landmarks. The plastic lens that replaced the original first-order Fresnel lens has a range of 24 miles. The station is now maintained by the Mid-Atlantic Center for the Arts, which has spent $2 million restoring the tower and turning it into an active museum.

Chapel Hill Light

Leonardo, NJ
Built: 1856
Style: Square

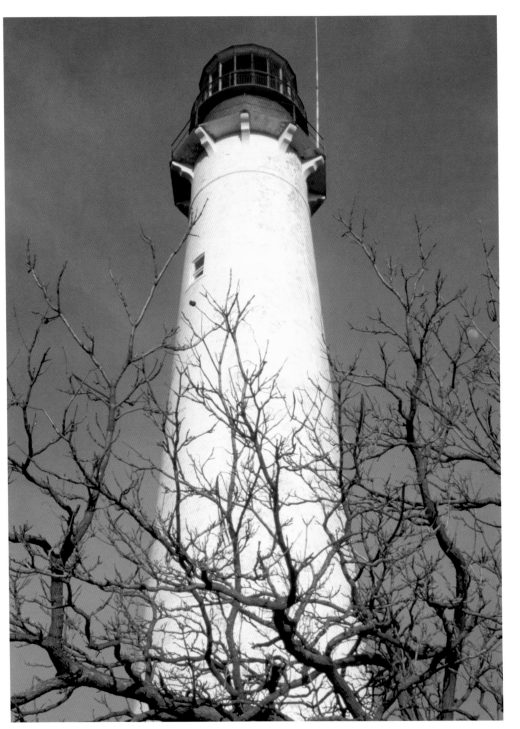

The shipping channel into Lower New York Bay was once marked by several sets of range lights. One of these was the Chapel Hill lighthouse, which partnered a light on Conover Beach. Built in 1856, the wood and brick Chapel Hill lighthouse is now a private home, and its second-order Fresnel lens is displayed at the Twin Lights Museum at Navesink, New Jersey.

FAR LEFT
Absecon Light, New Jersey.

LEFT
Cape May Light, New Jersey.

OPPOSITE
Barnegat Light, New Jersey.

Conover Beach Light

Chapel Hill, NJ
Built: 1852 and 1941
Style: Skeleton

The original Conover Beach range beacon, which partnered the Chapel Hill lighthouse, was a six-sided wooden structure commissioned in 1852. It was replaced in 1941 by a skeletal tower and aero-marine beacon. The tower still stands, though the light has long since been decommissioned.

East Point Light

Maurice River, NJ
Built: 1849
Style: Lantern on dwelling

The distinctive East Point lighthouse, perched on the roof of the two-storey brick keeper's house, has been guiding shipping in and out of the Maurice River since 1849. The light was equipped with a sixth-order Fresnel lens but is now fitted with a modern optic. In 1971 the building was damaged by fire, but the light continues and the building has been restored to its former glory by the Maurice River Historical Society.

Elbow of Cross Ledge Light

Downe, NJ
Built: 1910 and 1952
Style: Skeletal tower
No: 1600
Position: 39 10 56 N. 75 16 06 W
Focal plane: 61ft (18.5m)
Range: W 15 miles/24km, R 11 miles/18km

The Elbow of Cross Ledge lighthouse began life in 1910 as a caisson-based tower marking a dangerous ledge in Delaware Bay. The tower suffered serious damage during a storm in 1951, and no sooner had the unlucky structure been repaired than it was demolished by a freighter in 1952. The lighthouse was then replaced by the present skeletal tower.

Finns Point Rear Range Light

Pennsville, NJ
Built: 1877
Style: Skeletal

The 115-ft (35-m) iron tower that marks the rear range light at Finns Point guided ships up the narrow Delaware River channel from

LEFT
Chapel Hill Light, New Jersey.

OPPOSITE LEFT
Great Beds Light, New Jersey

OPPOSITE RIGHT
Miah Maull Shoal Light, New Jersey.

1877 until it was decommissioned, along with its front range light, in 1950. The rear light has since been restored by local conservationists.

Fort Mifflin Light

Billingsport, NJ
Built: 1880 and 1887
Style: Skeletal

The skeletal tower now standing at Fort Mifflin to mark the shipping channel near Billingsport is the modern replacement for two earlier wooden towers of the 1880s.

Great Beds Light

Tottenville, NJ
Built: 1880
Style: Conical tower on pier
No: 36430
Focal plane: 61ft (18.5m)
Range: 6 miles (10km)
Height: 60ft (18m)

The cast-iron Great Beds lighthouse stands on a caisson in the Raritan River between Staten Island and New Jersey. Painted white

OPPOSITE and LEFT
Navsink Twin Lights, New Jersey.

and black, the tower was fitted with a fourth-order Fresnel lens in 1880. This was replaced with a modern optic when the station was automated in 1945.

Hereford Inlet Light

North Wildwood, NJ
Built: 1874
Style: Square tower with cupola on dwelling
No: 90
Position: 39 00 24 N. 74 47 28 W
Focal plane: 57ft (17m)
Range: 24 miles (39km)

Built in 1874, the Hereford Inlet lighthouse is one of the best examples of Victorian architecture. The building has a long porch, balusters and a pitched roof, all typical of its stick-style design. Fortunately for those who love lighthouses and lovely buildings, the residence and tower survived the 1889 hurricane and continued in operation until decommissioned in 1964. The station, with its fourth-order Fresnel lens, is now maintained as a private aid to navigation.

Miah Maull Shoal Light

Delaware Bay, Downe, NJ
Built: 1913
Style: Conical tower on pier
No: 1585
Focal plane: 59ft
Position: 39 07 36 N. 75 12 36 W
Focal plane: 59ft (18m)
Range: W 15 miles/24km, R 12 miles/19km

The red-painted 45-ft (14-m) cast-iron lighthouse, founded on a massive caisson, marks a dangerous shoal in the middle of Delaware Bay. It was originally equipped with a fourth-order Fresnel lens, which was replaced by a plastic optic when the light was automated.

Navsink Twin Lights

Highlands, NJ
Built: 1828 and 1862
Style: Square tower and octagonal 'fortress'

The twin lights at Navesink were the first in U.S. waters to be equipped with Fresnel lenses. The original stone towers were built 330ft (100m) apart in 1828. The north tower was given a first-order lens in 1838 and a revolving, bull's-eye-type second-order lens was fitted in the south tower. In 1862 the station was completely rebuilt to look like a fortress, with a stone wall linking a new square tower to the north and an octagonal structure to the south. The north tower was deactivated in 1898, when the south tower was fitted with a massive first-order lens giving it a range of 25 miles (40km). The south tower was decommissioned in 1953, but nine years later the north tower was relit as a private aid to navigation and fitted with a sixth-order Fresnel lens. It is now the centrepiece of a museum.

Sandy Hook Island Light

Sandy Hook, NJ
Built: 1764
Style: Octagonal

Sandy Hook is the oldest standing lighthouse tower in the United States. The 85-ft (26-m) octagonal stone and brick tower dating from 1764 has withstood not only two-and-a-half centuries of storms but, in colonial times, an attempt to blow it up to foil the British. The cost of the tower was raised by a lottery organized by a group of merchants in New York City. Later, ownership of the lighthouse was the subject of a court battle between the states of New Jersey and New York. The station was lit by a 48-wick open-panned oil lamp until 1857, when it was fitted with a third-order Fresnel lens that continues to project the light for 20 miles (32km).

Sea Girt Light

Sea Girt, NJ
Built: 1896
Style: Tower and dwelling

The 40-ft (12-m) brick-built lighthouse and its adjoining keeper's dwelling, which was the first in the United States to have a radio beacon installed (in 1921), remained in continuous operation until 1945. The station has since been restored by local historians, who equipped it with a copy of the tower's original fourth-order Fresnel lens. It is now maintained as a private aid to navigation.

Ship John Shoal Light

Fortescue, Delaware Bay, NJ
Built: 1874
Style: Octagonal on cylindrical pier
No: 1640

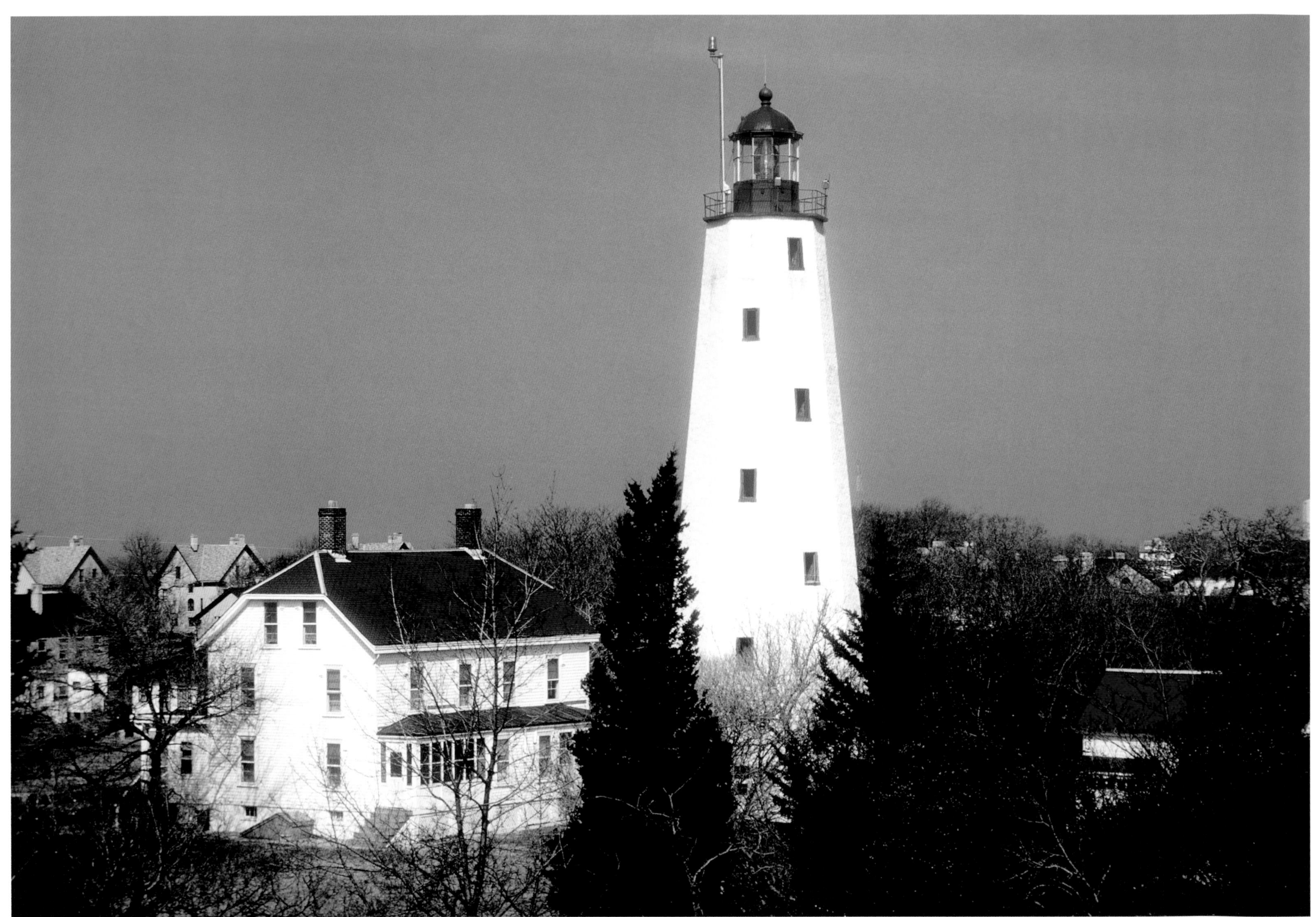

Sandy Hook Island Light, New Jersey.

Position: 39 18 19 N. 75 22 36 W
Focal plane: 50ft (15m)
Range: W 16 miles/26km, R 12 miles/19km
Height: 50ft (15m)

The red-painted cast-iron tower and concrete-filled caisson has been sited at the mouth of the Delaware River since 1874. It had a fourth-order Fresnel lens until it was automated and given a modern optic.

Tinicum Range Lights

Paulsboro, NJ
Built: 1880
Style: Skeletal tower
No: 3285 (Front Light)
Position: 39 50 52 N. 75 15 10 W
Focal plane: 38ft (11.5m)

No: 3290 (Rear Light)
Style: Galleried pyramidal skeleton structure
Focal plane: 112ft (34m)

The 80-ft (24-m) Rear Range light tower, together with its partner, closer to the water, were erected to mark a safe channel up the Delaware River. The two lights were automated in 1967.

New York

Ambrose Lightship

South Street Seaport Museum, NY
Built: 1908
No: 87
Length overall: 135ft 5in (41m)
Beam: 29ft (9m)
Draft: 12ft 9in (4m)
Displacement: 683 tons
Illuminating apparatus: Cluster of three oil lanterns raised to each masthead
Fog signal: 12-in (30-cm) steam chime whistle plus hand-operated bell

Station Assignments:
1908–32: Ambrose Channel (NY)
1932–36: Relief (NY)
1936–42: Scotland (NJ)
1942–44: Examination Vessel (wartime)
1944–47: Vineyard Sound (MA)
1947–62: Scotland (NJ)

The *Ambrose* lightship was built in 1908 and remained on station marking the outer channel into New York Harbor until 1932. The vessel, which was the first U.S. lightship to be equipped with a vacuum-tube radio beacon, continued in service at various stations until 1962. She was then decommissioned and became a floating exhibit in New York's maritime museum.

Barbers Point Light

Westport, NY
Built: 1873 and 1935
Style: Skeletal

The original Barbers Point Light featured a white, octagonal tower atop the roof of a two-storey blue limestone and wood keeper's house. The tower's fifth-order Fresnel lens was deactivated in 1935 when an automated skeleton tower replaced it.

Barcelona Light

Barcelona, NY
Built:1829
Style: Conical

The 40-ft (12-m) conical fieldstone-built lighthouse is famous for being the first public building in the U.S. to be lit by natural gas. Early settlers discovered a pool of water that would catch fire, and named it 'burning spring'. The gas was later piped directly to the lighthouse which gave the light much greater brightness. However, in 1838 the gas ran out and the lighthouse was converted back to its original oil lamps. The station was deactivated in 1859 when it was discovered that the lighthouse had been built to lead ships into a harbour that Barcelona never had. The tower is now a private residence.

Bluff Point Light

Near Plattsburgh, NY
Built: 1874
Style: Octagonal

The 35-ft (11-m) red-and-white tower of Bluff Point Light was established in 1874 and sits atop its square, one-and-a-half-storey keeper's house. The lighthouse used a fifth-order Fresnel lens before it was automated and deactivated in 1930.

Braddock Point Light

Hilton, NY
Built: 1876
Style: Octagonal

The 97-ft (29.5-m) red brick tower was originally built to guide ships along the western approach to Rochester. The two-and-a-half-storey brick Victorian keeper's house and the third-and-one-half-order Fresnel lens were added later, in 1896. The site was deactivated in 1954 and sold as a private residence, while the top two-thirds of the tower was dismantled because of storm damage and vandalism. The private owners have since added a faux lantern to the tower to make it look more authentic.

Buffalo Main Light

Buffalo, NY
Built:1818 and 1833
Style: Octagonal

The original station was the first on the Great Lakes, rising from the ruins of the town after it had been burned down by the British. The opening of the Erie Canal in 1825 helped to transform the city into an important commercial centre, which resulted in a new tower being built in 1833. Made from limestone, the 68-ft (21-m) tower stood at the end of a 1,400-ft pier. In 1872 a second breakwater station was erected with a fourth-order fixed red light, and the Buffalo Main Light was decommissioned. In 1985 the Buffalo Lighthouse Association raised money to restore the old lighthouse which was re-lit in 1987 to celebrate the first International Friendship Festival.

Cape Vincent Breakwater Light

Cape Vincent, NY
Built: 1900

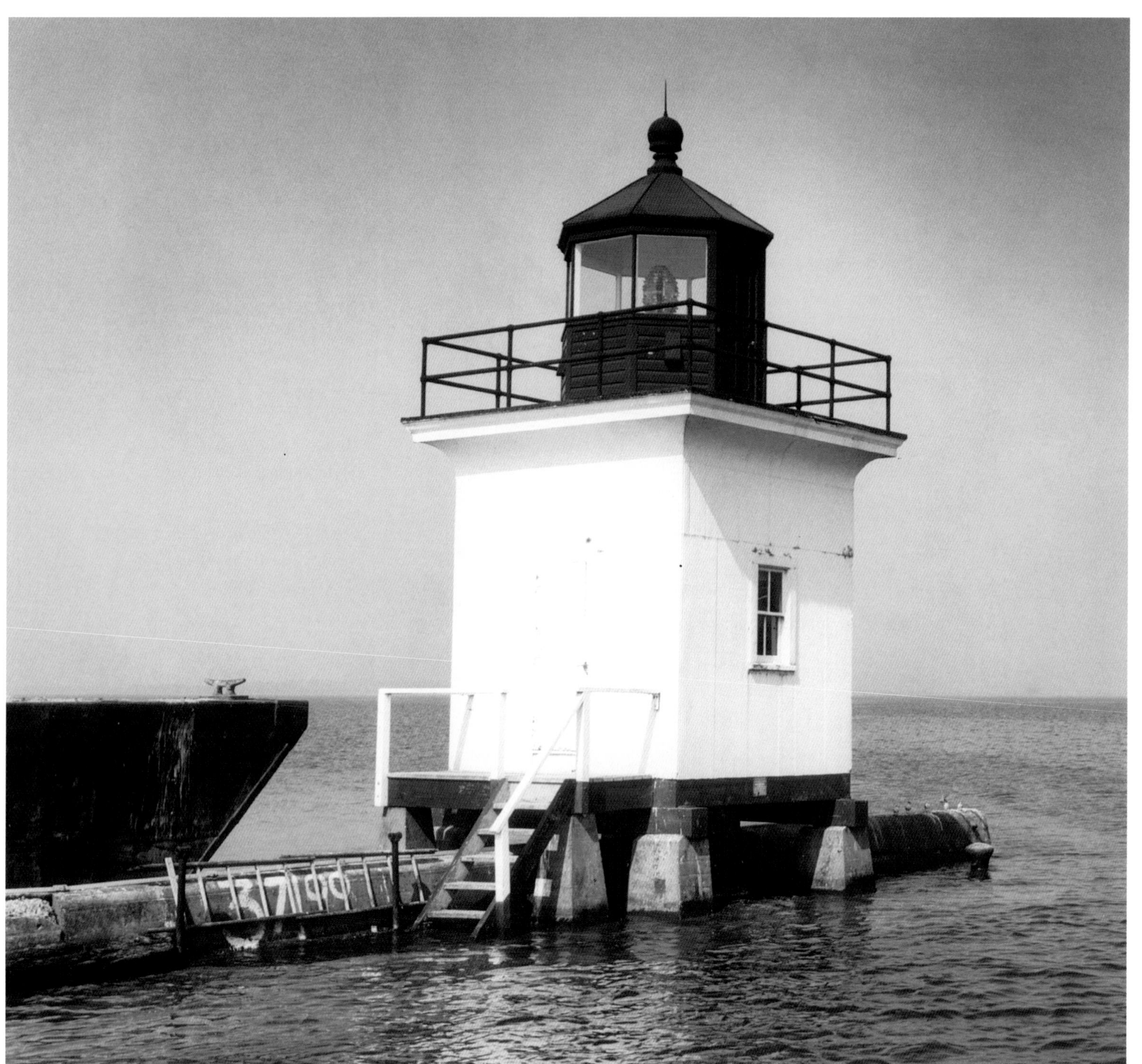

LEFT
Cape Vincent Breakwater Light, New York.

OPPOSITE
Braddock Point Light, New York.

Originally part of a pair of lights built in 1900 to stand at the end of a breakwater on Lake Ontario, the lighthouse featured a short, square white tower with a black lantern. It was decommissioned in 1934 and in 1951 the decision was made to move it into town, where it now stands in the grounds of the town offices.

Cedar Island Light

Sag Harbor, Long Island, NY
Built: 1855
Style: Square stone tower

The 44-ft (13-m) square granite lighthouse on Sag Harbor was equipped with a sixth-order Fresnel lens when the station was opened in 1855. The keeper's cottage was added 13 years later. The station was abandoned in 1934 when the Cedar light was replaced by a skeletal tower erected on the breakwater.

Charlotte-Genessee Light

Rochester, NY
Built: 1822
Style: Octagonal

The 40-ft (12-m) limestone tower is the second oldest lighthouse on the Great Lakes and stands over the intersection of the

Genesee River and Lake Ontario. Originally consisting of ten Argand lamps and a set of reflectors, the system was upgraded in 1853 to a fourth-order Fresnel lens. The tower has a limestone dwelling nearby, which is connected to it by a passageway. The lighthouse fell into disuse around 1882 when a small pierhead light was built close by. The tower was saved from demolition through petitioning by Charlotte High School students and it was later restored by the Charlotte-Genesee Historical Society.

Coney Island Light

New York, NY
Built: 1890
Style: Square skeletal tower
No: 34910
Focal plane: 75ft (23m)
Range: 16 miles (26km)
Height: 68ft (21m)

The lighthouse was erected in 1890 along with a partnering range light to guide vessels in and out of New York Harbor. The second light was decommissioned more than a century ago, while the Coney Island tower was fitted with a fourth-order Fresnel lens with a range of 16 miles. It still operates, and the original lens is displayed at the South Street Seaport Museum in Manhattan.

Crossover Island Light

Crossover Island, NY
Built: 1848
Style: Conical

Standing on an island in the St. Lawrence River near the U.S. border with Canada, the

OPPOSITE
Coney Island Light, New York.

RIGHT
Dunkirk Light, New York.

lighthouse is now privately owned. It has a white conical tower, constructed from cast iron and brick, with a sixth-order Fresnel lens, which it gained in 1882. In 1941 it was deemed to be no longer essential for navigation and was deactivated.

Crown Point Light

Crown Point, NY
Built:1857 and 1912
Style: Cylindrical, neo-Classical

The original lighthouse was 57ft (17m) tall, the fifth-order Fresnel lens emitting a fixed white light, and stood near the historic Grenadier Battery, which held French and English fortifications. A steamboat wharf was added in 1888. This tower was replaced in 1912 with a neo-Classical, ornamental tower, featuring eight Doric columns and a bronze sculpture presented by the Republic of France. It was made as a memorial to Samuel de Champlain, and is also known as the Crown Point Memorial Lighthouse. It was deactivated in 1929.

Cumberland Head Light

Plattsburgh, NY
Built: 1838
Style: Conical

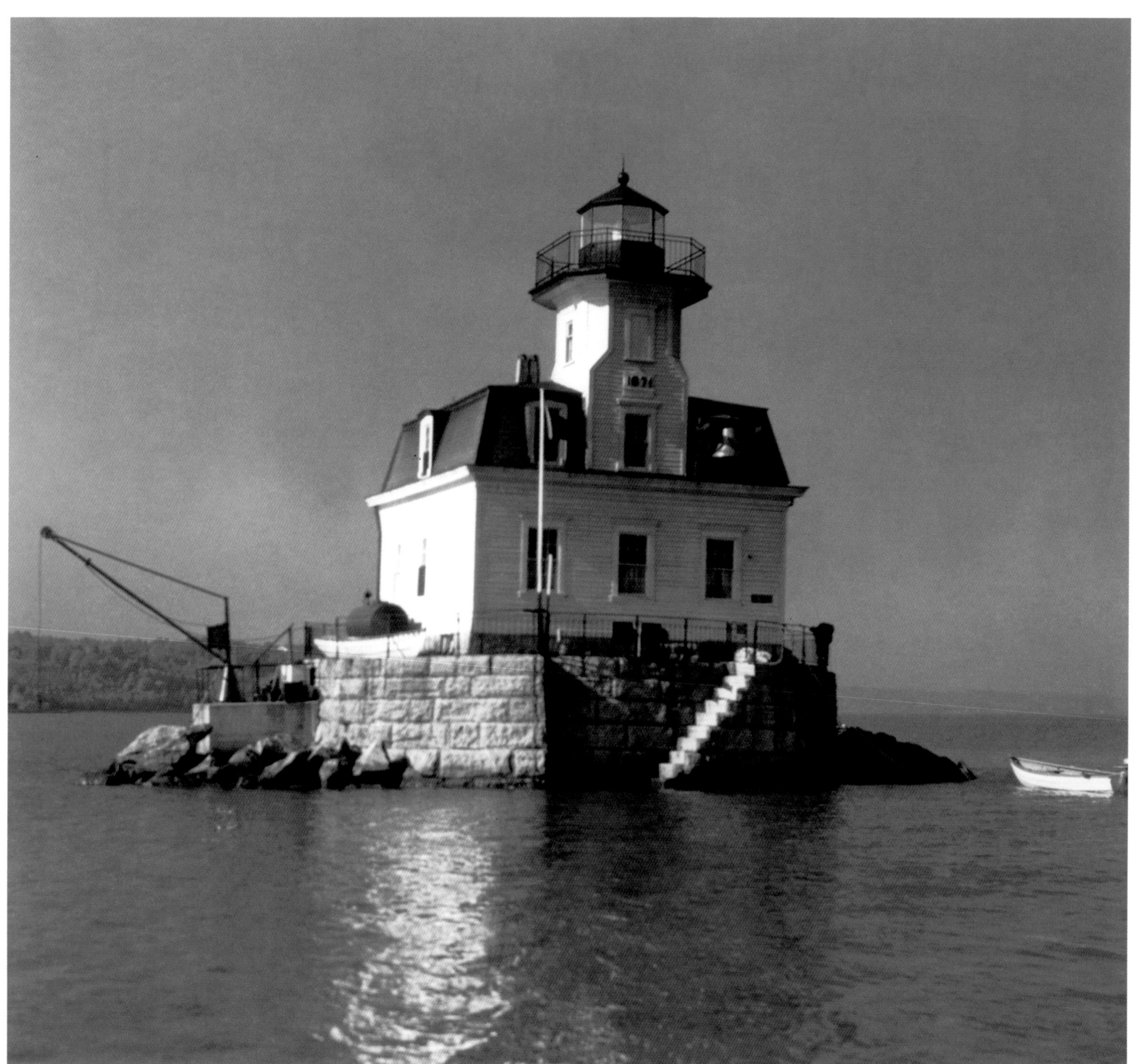

LEFT
Esopus Meadows Light, New York.

OPPOSITE
Fire Island Light, New York.

The original lighthouse, built in 1838 and dominating Cumberland Head on Lake Champlain, was a limestone tower with 11 lamps and reflectors, replaced in 1852 by a fourth-order Fresnel lens. It assumed its current incarnation in the form of a 50-ft (15-m) conical limestone tower and keepers' dwelling in 1867. Though deactivated in 1934 the Cumberland Head lighthouse still features on the seal of the city of Plattsburgh.

Dunkirk Light

Point Gratiot, NY
Built: 1829 and 1875
Style: Square tower with attached dwelling
No: 3410
Position: 42 29 36 N. 79 21 12 W
Focal plane 82ft (25m)
Range: 16 miles (26km)
Height: 61ft (18.5m)

The original Dunkirk Light, built in 1829 by Jesse Peck, had the distinction of being the first to be powered by whale oil. After several unsuccessful attempts at converting the tower to natural gas, a third-order Fresnel lens was installed when the tower was moved and re-built on a 20-ft (6-m) high bluff to give the light a range of 16 miles. The present lighthouse was built in 1875 with a beautiful Victorian Gothic dwelling attached. Unfortunately the lighthouse did not always stop disasters from occurring. In 1893 the cargo ship, *Dean Richmond*, was wrecked nearby, as was the *Idaho* in 1895. The lighthouse was automated in 1960 and now doubles as a museum.

East Charity Shoal Light

Brownville, NY
Built: 1935
Style: Octagonal

The lighthouse was established off Cape Vincent on Lake Ontario in 1935. The tower, however, had been erected in 1877 in Vermilion, Ohio. It was moved to New York after a severe ice storm in 1929. Still operational today, the 52-ft (16-m) octagonal cast-iron tower is situated on a concrete and cast iron caisson. The white tower has a black lantern, which at one time held a fourth-order Fresnel lens. In 1922, the light received a modern optic.

Eatons Neck Light

Huntington Bay, Long Island Sound, NY
Built: 1799
Style: Octagonal
No: 21325
Focal plane: 144ft (44m)
Range: 18 miles (29km)
Height: 73ft (22m)

The fieldstone light tower marking Huntington Bay is one of six remaining U.S. towers that date back to the 18th century. The station's third-order Fresnel lens, installed in 1858, remains in use.

Esopus Meadows Light

Esopus, NY
Built: 1872
Style: Octagonal tower on dwelling

This is one of several imposing mid-river stations built during the 19th century to guide shipping on the Hudson River. It consists of a two-storey wooden keeper's house with a short octagonal tower on its roof. It was decommissioned in 1965 and is now the subject of a restoration programme.

Execution Rocks Light

Long Island, NY
Built: 1850
Style: Conical
No: 21440
Focal plane: 62ft (19m)
Range: 15 miles (24km)
Height: 60ft (18m)

The lighthouse is said to have been given its sinister name after an incident in the War of Independence when the British chained prisoners to the reef and left them to drown under the rising tide. The tower, designed by Alexander Parris, continues to guide vessels making for New York City.

Fire Island Light

West Islip, NY
Built: 1826 and 1858
Style: Conical
No: 695
Position: 40 37 57 N, 73 13 07 W
Focal plane: 167ft (51m)
Range: 24 miles (39km)

The first 74-ft (22.5-m) brick-built lighthouse was erected in 1826, but the weak beam from its light did little to warn vessels away from the shoals it was guarding. Nothing was done to improve matters until a disaster happened in1850, when the cargo ship *Elizabeth* hit the shoal and sank a short distance from the dimly-lit tower. The loss of lives led maritime officials to order a new tower twice the height of the original. The present 180-ft (55-m) tower, completed in 1858, was fitted with a first-order Fresnel lens, replaced by a modern optic when the station was automated.

Fort Niagara Light

Youngstown, NY
Built: 1781, 1823 and 1872
Style: Conical

The lighthouse marks the mouth of the Niagara River as it flows into Lake Ontario, once the only artery between Lake Ontario and Lake Erie. Built by the British in 1781, the first lighthouse was constructed out of stone, but was then dismantled following the American Revolution. In 1823 a new light was built above a mess house at the fort. However, new canals cut through to link the two lakes reduced Fort Niagara to a minor trading port and the wooden lighthouse soon fell into disrepair. The present 50-ft (15-m) limestone lighthouse, with a small attached workroom, was built just south of the fort in 1872 and was installed with a fourth-order Fresnel lens. The tower was heightened by 11ft (3m) in 1900 to give the beacon a range of 25 miles (40km) and continued to operate until 1993 when the station was decommissioned. The site and its tower now form part of a museum run by the Old Fort Niagara Association.

LEFT
Fort Niagara Light, New York.

OPPOSITE
Galloo Island Light, New York.

Fort Wadsworth Light

Staten Island, New York, NY
Built: 1903
Style: Square

The lighthouse at Fort Wadsworth was built into the defensive walls in 1903 to mark the Verazzano Narrows, but the construction of the bridge here rendered the light station obsolete and, though still standing, it was decommissioned in 1963.

Galloo Island Light

Galloo Island, New York.
Built: 1820 and 1867
Style: Conical

The 55-ft (17-m) limestone tower of the current lighthouse was built in 1867. Its site, at the south-western end of the island, was established in 1820 when the original tower was built. Next to the lighthouse is a two-storey limestone keeper's dwelling, as well as a fog-signal building and iron oil house, which was added in 1897. It was automated in 1963 and has since been deactivated.

Great Beds Light

Tottenville, NY
Built: 1880
Style: Conical on conical pier
No: 36430
Position: 40 29 12 N. 74 15 12 W
Focal plane: 61ft (18.5m)
Range: 6 miles (10km)
Height: 60ft (18m)

The cast-iron lighthouse sits on a caisson in the Raritan River between Staten Island and New Jersey. It originally had a fourth-order Fresnel lens, replaced by a modern optic when the station was automated in 1945.

Horse Island Light

Horse Island, NY
Built: 1870
Style: Square

There has been a lighthouse here since 1831, but the existing tower, along with its barn, privy and oil house were not built until 1870. The lighthouse has an attached Queen Anne-style dwelling and provided illumination from a black lantern, which held a fifth-order Fresnel lens. In 1957 the light was deactivated and replaced by a steel skeleton tower.

Horton Point Light

Southold, Long Island Sound, NY
Built: 1857
Style: Square tower
No: 21150
Position: 41 05 06 N. 72 26 44 W
Focal plane: 103ft (31m)
Range: 14 miles (22.5km)

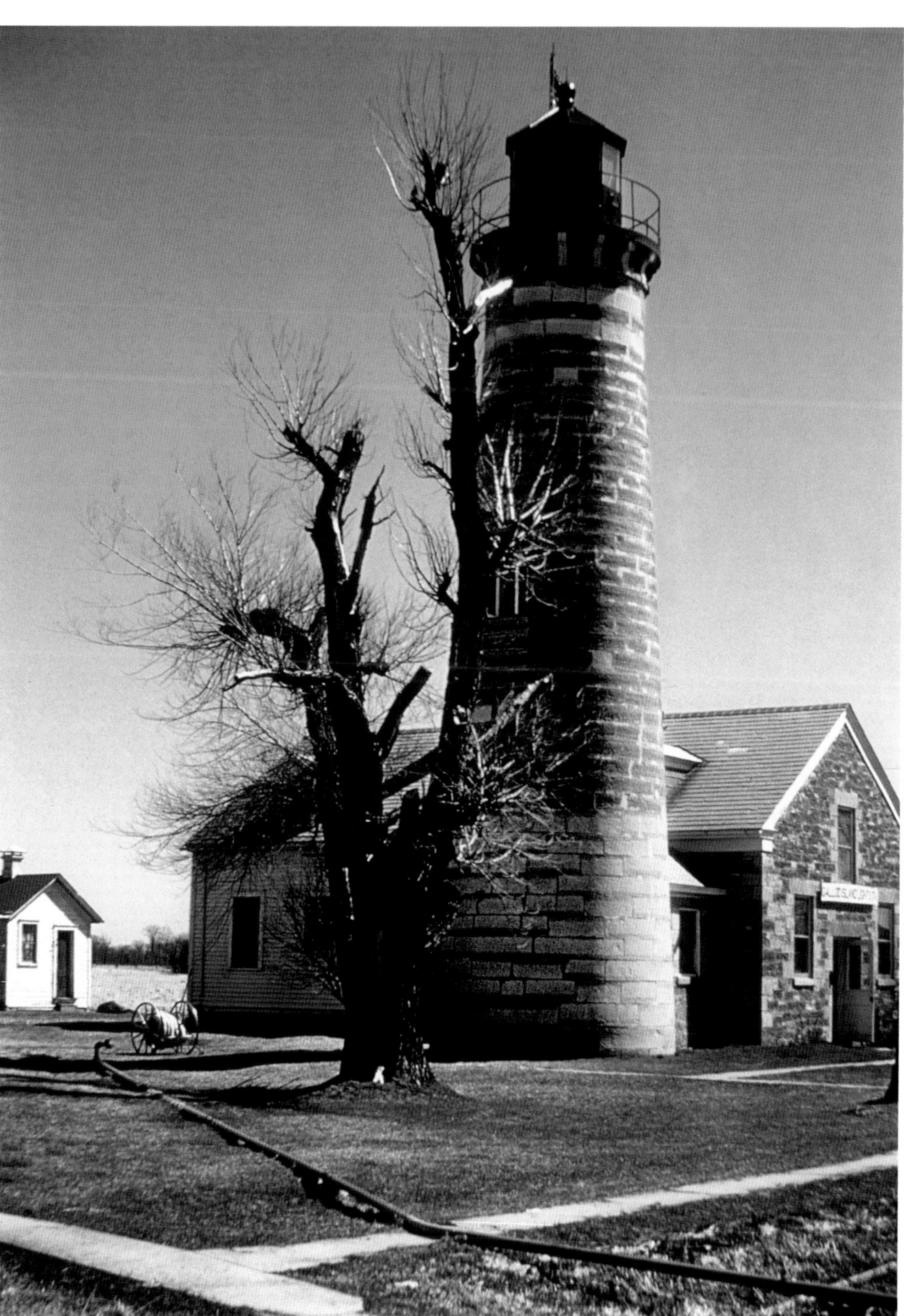

The 58-ft (18-m) lighthouse and its connecting keeper's house at Southold was originally equipped with a third-order Fresnel lens, which was replaced by a modern optic when the station was automated. The buildings are managed by the Southold Historical Society and now house a museum.

Hudson-Athens Light

Hudson City, NY
Built: 1874
Style: Square

The lighthouse was built in 1874 to mark the Middle Ground Flats in the Hudson River. The brick and stone tower was equipped with a fifth-order Fresnel lens, but this was replaced by a modern optic when the station was automated. The lighthouse is still in service, but the building is now managed by a local preservation society.

Jeffrey's Hook Light

New York, NY
Built: 1920
Style: Conical

The lighthouse was built to replace two stake lights that once marked the narrows between Manhattan Island and New Jersey. It served its purpose for only 11 years, for it was made obsolete by the construction of the George Washington Bridge, which now spans the river directly above what became known as the 'Little Red Lighthouse'.

Latimer Reef Light

Fishers Island Sound, NY
Built: 1804 and 1884
Style: Conical tower on cylinder base
No: 20085
Position: 41 18 18 N. 71 56 00 W
Focal plane: 55ft (17m)
Range: 9 miles (14.5km)
Height: 49ft (15m)

The light station dates back to 1804, but the present caisson and its cast-iron tower was completed 80 years later. It was once fitted with a fifth-order Fresnel lens, but this was replaced with a modern optic when the station was automated in 1983.

Little Gull Island Light

Orient Point, NY
Built: 1806 and 1867
Style: Conical tower with attached dwelling
No: 19830
Position: 41 12 23 N. 72 06 25 W
Focal plane: 91ft (28m)
Range: 18 miles (29km)

The station dates back to 1806, but the present granite lighthouse was constructed in 1867 and, though badly damaged in a hurricane in 1938, the tower remained standing. It was equipped with a second-order Fresnel lens, but this was replaced with a modern optic when the station was automated in 1978. The original lens is now on display at the East End Seaport Maritime Museum in Greenport.

Lloyd Harbor Light

Huntington Bay, NY

LEFT
Horton Point Light, New York.

OPPOSITE
Hudson-Athens Light, New York.

Built: 1857
Style: Square tower on crib

The 42-ft (13-m) Lloyd Harbor lighthouse, sometimes referred to as the Huntington Harbor Light, had a fifth-order Fresnel lens installed in 1912, replaced by a modern optic when the station was automated in 1967. The original wooden-framed keeper's dwelling was destroyed by fire in 1947 and its replacement is destined to become a museum.

Long Beach Bar Light

Gardiners Bay, Greenport, NY
Built: 1870 and 1990
Style: Lantern on dwelling

The original lighthouse of 1870 was destroyed by fire in 1963. The wooden dwelling and its roof-top light was replicated in 1990 by the East End Seaport and Marine Foundation. The light is automated.

Montauk Point Light

Montauk, Long Island, NY
Built: 1797
Style: Octagonal, pyramidal tower
No: 660
Position: 41 04 15 N. 71 51 26 W
Focal plane: 168ft (51m)
Range: 20 miles (32km)
Height: 110ft (33.5m)

Montauk Point, at the eastern end of Long Island, was one of the first lighthouses commissioned by President George Washington. It is the first sight of America that most immigrants see on their way into New York Harbor. The original 110-ft sandstone tower cost $22,300 to construct – a sizeable amount two centuries ago. Standing 168ft (50m) above sea level, the lighthouse is now equipped with an aero-marine beacon.

New Dorp Light

New York, NY
Built: 1856
Style: Lantern on square dwelling

The lighthouse was built on Staten Island in 1856 above the wood-framed keeper's cottage as one of a pair of range-light beacons to guide vessels across New York Bay. Decommissioned in 1964, the building is now a private dwelling.

North Dumpling Light

Fishers Island, NY
Built: 1871
Style: Octagonal tower on dwelling
No: 20145
Position: 41 17 18 N. 72 01 12 W
Focal plane: 94ft (29m)
Range: W 9 miles/15km, R 7 miles/11km
Height: 60ft (18m)

The lighthouse, built on the roof of the keeper's house, was decommissioned and sold in 1959, and replaced by a skeletal tower. The house, now in private hands, was

LEFT
Jeffrey's Hook Light, New York.

OPPOSITE
Latimer Reef Light, New York.

restored in 1980. The light in the 31-ft (9.5-m) tower was relit, though not with its original fifth-order Fresnel lens, which has been replaced with a modern optic.

Ogdensburg Harbor Light

Ogdensburg, NY
Built: 1834
Style: Square

Standing guard at the mouth of the Oswegatchie River on Lake Ontario, the 65-ft (20-m) Ogdensburg lighthouse features a square stone tower in white and grey with a red lantern. The lighthouse and its attached one-and-a-half-storey keeper's dwelling are now used as a private residence.

Old Field Point Light

Port Jefferson, NY
Built: 1823 and 1868
Style: Octagonal tower on dwelling

The original Old Field Point Light was a 30-ft (9-m) octagonal tower which survived for 45 years. It was replaced in 1868 by the present dwelling with a 35-ft (115-m) cast-iron tower extending from the roof. In 1933 the station was decommissioned and replaced by an automated skeletal tower, but in 1991 the house and its light were

LEFT
Little Gull Island Light, New York.

OPPOSITE
Montauk Point Light, New York.

reactivated, and it continues to guide vessels between Bridgeport and Port Jefferson.

Old Front Range Light
Grand Island, NY
Built: 1917
Style: Octagonal

The 36-ft (11-m) lighthouse was built to guide ships on the Tonawanda Channel of the Niagara River. The octagonal wooden tower is now part of the Buffalo Launch Club's marina. It is no longer operational.

Old Orchard Shoal Light
New York, NY
Built: 1893
Style: Conical tower on cylindrical pier
No: 35395
Position: 40 30 44 N. 74 05 55 W
Focal length: 51ft (15.5m)
Range: W 7 miles/11km, R 5 miles/8km
Height: 51ft (15.5m)

The cast-iron Old Orchard Shoal lighthouse of 1893 is one of a number of similar 'spark-plug' towers erected during this period to mark the approaches to New York City. It was equipped originally with a fourth-order Fresnel lens, but this was replaced by a modern optic when the station was automated.

LEFT
New Dorp Light, New York.

OPPOSITE LEFT
Old Field Point Light, New York.

OPPOSITE RIGHT
Ogdensburg Harbor Light, New York.

Orient Point Light

Oyster Pond Reef, Long Island, NY
Built: 1899
Style: Conical tower
No: 21095
Position: 41 09 48 N. 72 13 24 W
Focal plane: 64ft (19.5m)
Range: 17 miles (27km)
Height: 45ft (14m)

Better known as the 'Old Coffee Pot', the brown and white-painted cast-iron tower stands 45ft above its caisson base to mark Oyster Pond Reef. The original station was equipped with a fifth-order Fresnel lens, but this was replaced with a modern optic when the station was automated in 1988.

Oswego West Pierhead Light

Oswego Lake, NY
Built:1822, 1836 and 1934
Style: Square tower on corner of building
No: 2080
Position: 43 28 24 N. 76 31 00 W
Focal plane: 57ft (17m)
Range: 17 miles (27km)
Height: 12ft (4m)

The lighthouse stands at a crucial navigational point at the mouth of the Oswego River. The first light was built by the strategic Fort Ontario in 1822, but further development of the port of Oswego led to a new tower being built at the end of a stone breakwater in 1836. Holding a third-order Fresnel lens, this octagonal, grey tower emitted a fixed, white light that could be seen up to 15 miles (24km) away. This second lighthouse served for almost a century until a 57-ft tower replaced it in 1934. This light is still in operation today and holds a fourth-order rotating lens which produces a red light through the lens' red-coloured panels. The lighthouse was automated in 1942, partly due to a boat accident which occurred during a change of duty between lighthouse keepers. A radio beacon is provided by two large antennae at the site.

LEFT
North Dumpling Light, New York.

OPPOSITE
Orient Point Light, New York.

Plum Island Light

Gardiners Bay, Long Island Sound, NY
Built: 1827
Style: Square tower above dwelling

Plum Island Light dates back to 1827 when a 30-ft (9-m) tower was first erected on the island. The present two-storey house with its rooftop tower was built in 1870 and was staffed by a team of keepers until automated in 1978. The station was decommissioned in 1981 and the building would have been ripe for restoration but for the fact that Plum Island is off limits to the public.

Prince's Bay Light

New York, NY
Built: 1826 and 1864
Style: Conical

The 106-ft (32-m) Prince's Bay lighthouse stands adjacent to the Mount Loreto Mission on Staten Island. It was built in 1864 to replace the earlier tower of 1826. The brownstone tower, which was fitted with a fourth-order Fresnel lens, was deactivated in 1922.

Point au Roche Light

Beekmantown, New York.
Built: 1858
Style: Octagonal

LEFT
Oswego West Pierhead Light, New York.

OPPOSITE
Old Orchard Shoal Light, New York.

Point au Roche Light (known also as Point aux Roches), marks the La Roche Reef near Beekmantown on Lake Champlain. It was built in 1858 and had a 50-ft (15-m) octagonal granite tower attached to a one-and-a-half-storey keeper's dwelling and held a sixth-order Fresnel lens. This was later upgraded to a modern 250-mm optic, but was deactivated in 1989.

Race Rock Light

Fishers Island, NY
Built: 1879
Style: Stone tower attached to dwelling
No: 19815
Position: 41 14 37 N. 72 02 49 W
Focal plane: 67ft (20m)
Range: 16 miles (26km)
Height: 45ft (14m)

The caisson-based tower, perched on a dangerous outcrop close to Fishers Island, was designed and built by F. Hopkinson Smith, the same engineer who laid the foundations for the Statue of Liberty. It was equipped originally with a fourth-order Fresnel lens, which was replaced with a modern optic when the station was automated.

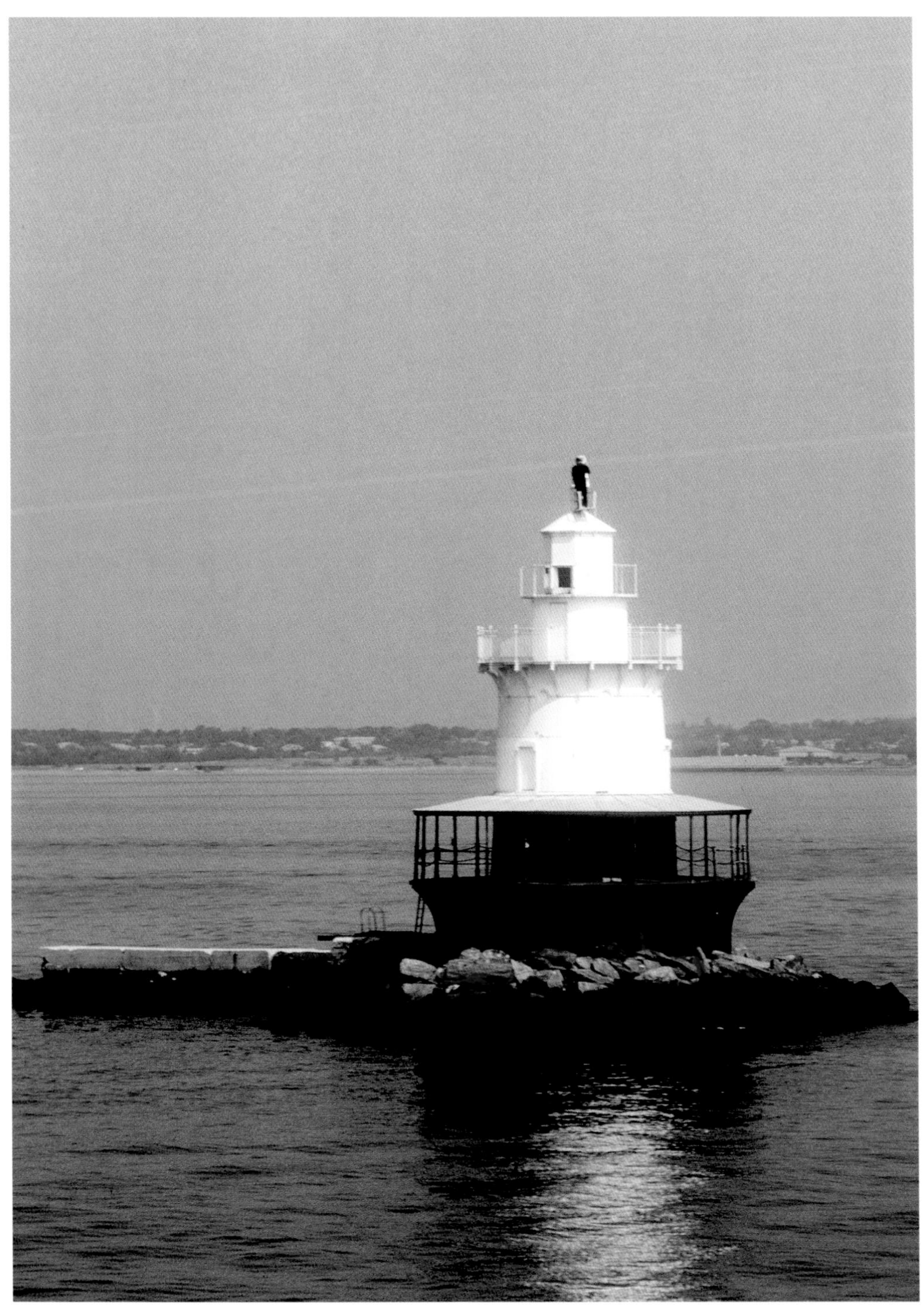

Robbins Reef Light

Staten Island, NY
Built: 1839 and 1883
Style: Conical
No: 34975
Position: 40 39 24 N. 74 04 00 W
Focal plane: 56ft (17m)
Range: 7 miles (11km)

The present lighthouse, which stands on a stone pier to mark the main channel to Upper New York Bay, was built in 1883 to replace an earlier stone tower of 1839. The station's original fourth-order Fresnel lens was replaced by a modern optic when the lighthouse was automated in 1966. The lighthouse was manned for 34 years by Kate Walker, who took over as keeper when her husband died in 1885 and served until 1919, during which time she saved 75 lives.

Rochester Harbor Light

Rochester, NY
Built: 1822 and 1995
Style: White cylindrical tower with red band
No: 2320
Position: 43 15 48 N. 77 36 00 W
Focal plane: 40ft (12m)
Range: 12 miles/19km, 14 miles/23km
Height: 35ft (11m)

The Rochester Harbor Light (also called the Rochester Pierhead Light) is sited at the mouth of the Genesee River. Originally established on the site in 1822, alterations to the pier have led to the light being relocated a number of times. Built in 1995, the current 35-ft cylindrical steel tower is still in operation today, and is painted white with red central band for daytime visibility.

Rock Island Light

Near Clayton, NY
Built: 1847
Style: Conical

The best preserved of the six lighthouses on the St. Lawrence River, the 40-ft (12-m) conical limestone tower of Rock Island Light stands just offshore on a stone walkway with a concrete foundation. In the 1800s the white tower's black lantern was upgraded to a sixth-order Fresnel lens, and in 1882 a number of buildings, including a two-storey Shingle-style dwelling, a clapboard boathouse, a carpenter's shop, a generator shop and an oil house, were added to the site. The station was decommissioned and the lens removed in 1958.

Romer Shoal Light

Staten Island, NY
Built: 1838 and 1898
Style: Conical tower on cylindrical pier
No: 35070
Position: 40 30 48 N. 74 00 48 W
Focal plane: 54ft (16.5m)
Range: 16 miles (26km)

A lighthouse was first built over the Romer Shoal in Lower New York Bay in 1838 and was replaced in 1898 by the present cast-iron caisson-based tower, which was fitted with a fourth-order Fresnel lens until the station was automated in 1924.

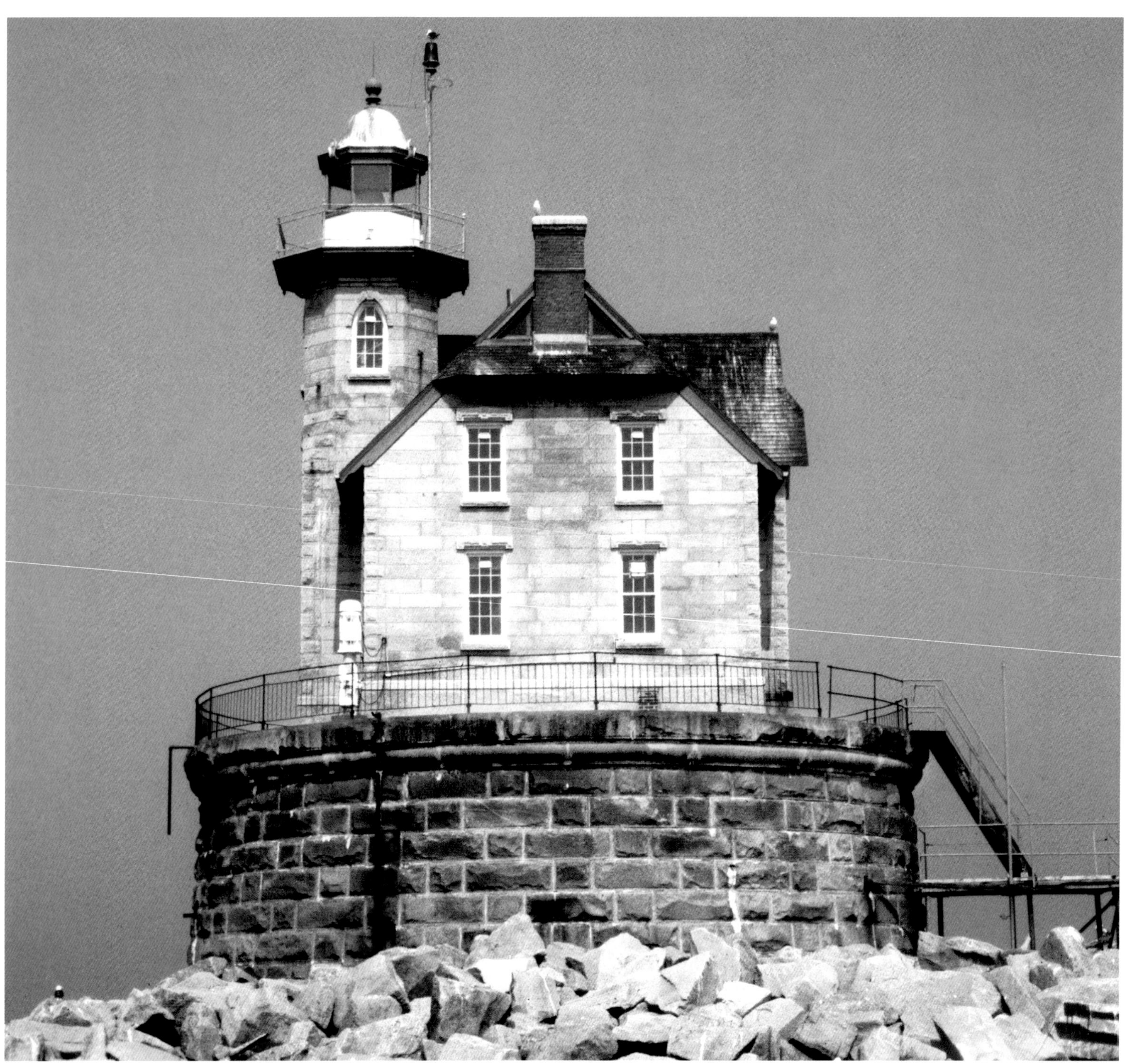

Rondout Creek Light

Kingston, NY
Built: 1880 and 1915
Style: Square tower and attached house

The Rondout Creek light station guides vessels into the inland port of Kingston. The present 52-ft (16-m) brick-built lighthouse and its attached keeper's house, built in 1915, stand on a concrete platform in the middle of the Hudson River. The building is now a museum.

Roosevelt Island Light

New York, NY
Built: 1874
Style: Stone tower

Roosevelt Island and its lighthouse have had several names, including Blackwells and Welfare Island. The 46-ft (14-m) stone lighthouse was designed by James Renwick Jr. and was built – with convict labour – on the northern end of the island. The building was fully restored in 1979.

Sand's Point Light

Long Island Sound, Port Washington, NY
Built: 1809 and 1868
Style: Octagonal

The octagonal brownstone tower dates from 1809, and the two-storey brick keeper's house was added in 1868. The station operated until it was decommissioned in 1922. Five years later, the site was bought by the newspaper tycoon, William Randolph Hearst, who built a mansion in the grounds.

OPPOSITE
Race Rock Light, New York.

RIGHT
Robbins Reef Light, New York.

The original tower and house remain in private ownership.

Saugerties Light

Saugerties, NY
Built: 1836 and 1869
Style: Square caisson

The first lighthouse at Saugerties, built in 1836, survived the winter ice floes for 30 years. The present imposing, two-storey, square building with its attached tower was built over a large concrete caisson in 1869 and remained in commission until 1954. The building has been fully restored and is managed by Saugerties Lighthouse Conservancy.

Selkirk Light

Selkirk (Pulaski), NY
Built: 1838
Style: Octagonal

Built in 1838, the Selkirk Light, consisting of an octagonal red wooden tower atop a two-and-a-half-storey gabled-roof fieldstone house, is also known as the Point Ontario and Salmon River Light. Although the site was deactivated from 1859 it is once again in operation after the owner activated a Coast Guard-approved 190-mm lens in 1989. This lens replaced the original silver birdcage-style lantern, which held a lens with eight lamps and 14-in (35-cm) reflectors, as well as its later sixth-order Fresnel. Used previously as a hotel, the keeper's residence is now rented to vacationers.

Sisters Island Light

Three Sisters Island, NY
Built: 1870
Style: Tower on dwelling

Standing on an island in the Thousand Island chain in the St. Lawrence River, the 60-ft (18-m) Sisters Island Light (also called the Three Sisters Island Light) was built on a limestone block on a rock reef in 1870. The tower is perched atop its one-and-a-half-storey keeper's dwelling and provided a signal for boats sailing north-east of Alexandria Bay until its deactivation in the 1950s.

Sodus Point (Sodus Outer) Light

Sodus Bay, NY
Built: 1825, 1871, 1938 and 1901
Style: Square, pyramidal tower
No: 2170
Focal plane: 51ft (15.5m)
Range: 16 miles (26km)
Height: 49ft (15m)

A number of lighthouses have stood on the sites overlooking Sodus Bay on Lake Ontario since the first rough, splitstone tower and dwelling were built in 1825. When they fell into disrepair, a 45-ft square limestone tower, attached to a two-and-a-

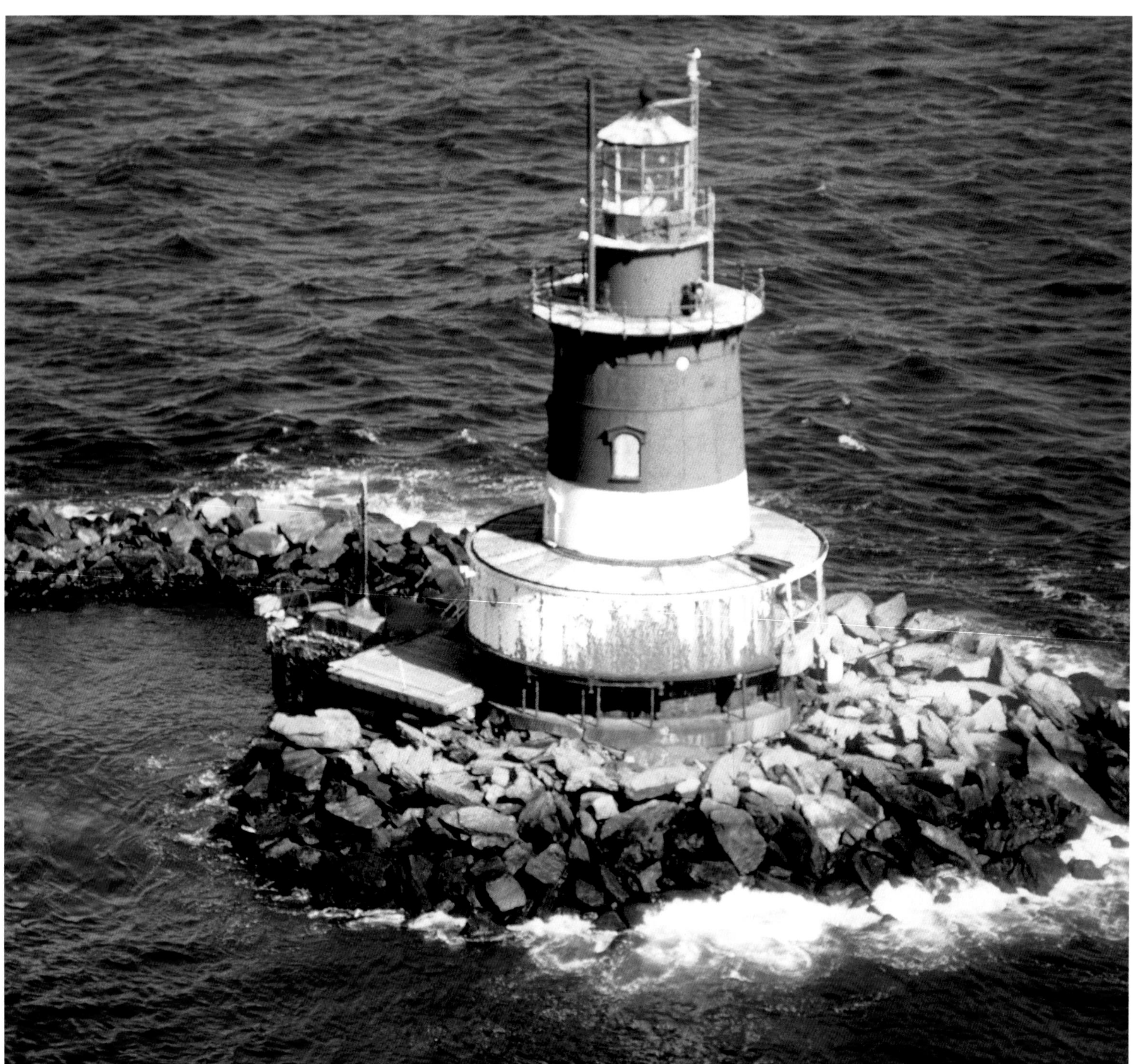

Romer Shoal Light, New York.

half-storey keeper's dwelling, was built to replace the light in 1871. It had a black cast-iron lantern housing a sixth-order Fresnel lens. Deactivated in 1901, when the Sodus Bay West Pier Light was built at the end of a nearby pier, lighthouse personnel still used the keeper's dwelling until 1984.

The Sodus Point and Sodus Outer Light are also referred to as the Sodus Bay West Pier Light, built on the end of a breakwater in 1901 to guide ships into Sodus Bay. The previous tower was replaced in 1938 by a 49-ft square cast-iron pyramidal tower, with a white lantern and a red roof. Still in operation today, the light received a three-and-one-half-order Fresnel lens in 1985.

South Buffalo South Side Light

Buffalo, NY
Built: 1903
Style: Conical

Built in 1903, the 27-ft (8-m) cast-iron lighthouse presides over Buffalo Harbor. Conical in shape, the tower is white, topped with a black lantern, which originally held a fourth-order Fresnel lens. Automated in 1935 and maintained by the U.S. Coast Guard, the light is still an active navigation aid, with its 300-mm lens and fog signal.

Split Rock Light

Whallon Bay, NY.
Built: 1838
Style: Octagonal

The octagonal limestone tower of the Split Rock Light stood overlooking Whallon Bay on Lake Champlain. The tower, and its attached keeper's dwelling, were built in natural rock with white trim. The lighthouse received a fourth-order Fresnel lens in 1857, but was decommissioned in 1928.

Staten Island Rear Range Light

New York, NY
Built: 1912
Style: Octagonal brick tower on stone base
No: 34795
Focal plane: 231ft (70m)
Range: 18 miles/29km. Visible only on range line
Height: 90ft (27m)

The octagonal brick-built Staten Island lighthouse was built on high ground to dominate the skyscrapers around New York Bay. It was fitted with a second-order bivalve lens imported from Great Britain, which is still in use. With its focal plane 231ft above sea level, the tower acts as a rear range light in partnership with the cast-iron, caisson-built West Bank lighthouse 5 miles (8km) away. The keeper's residence is now in private hands.

Statue of Liberty

New York, NY
Built: 1886

The Statue of Liberty was given to the people of the United States in 1886 by the French, and its function as a lighthouse was incidental. The 115-ft (35-m) copper-clad statue was the first lighthouse to be converted to electricity in 1916. It helped to guide ships in and out of New York Harbor until 1932, when the U.S. Army fort on Bedlow Island, where it stands, was decommissioned. The island was renamed Liberty Island and the 225-ton statue was opened to the public.

Stepping Stones Light

Kings Point, Long Island Sound, NY
Built: 1877
Style: Square tower on stone pier
No: 21505
Position: 40 49 28 N. 73 46 29 W
Focal plane: 46ft (14m)
Range: 8 miles (13km)
Height: 38ft (11.5m)

The brick-built lighthouse at Kings Point was built in 1877 and fitted with a fifth-order Fresnel lens, replaced by a modern optic when the station was automated in 1967.

Stony Point Light

Stony Point, Henderson, NY
Built: 1826
Style: Square tower

The Stony Point or Henderson lighthouse, built to stand over Henderson Bay on Lake Ontario, had a square brick tower attached to a keeper's dwelling. Its black lantern held a fourth-order Fresnel lens before it was deactivated in 1945, when it was replaced by a steel tower.

Sunken Rock Light

Bush Island, NY
Built: 1847 and 1884
Style: Tower on concrete base
No: 1340
Focal plane: 28ft (8.5m)
Range: 9 miles (14.5km)

As its name suggests, Sunken Rock Light sits on a submerged rock on the artificially created Bush Island. Built originally in 1847 and rebuilt in its present form in 1884, the tower is identifiable by day by its white conical cast-iron tower and green lantern, and by night by the light emitted by its sixth-order Fresnel lens, now automated and solar-powered. The light marks the south-west side of Sunken Rock Shoal, about 70ft (21m) outside channel limits.

Tarrytown Light

Hudson River, NY
Built: 1882
Style: Conical

The Tarrytown lighthouse served for 83 years, from 1882 to 1965, as one of eight guiding lights along the eastern bank of the Hudson River. The tower is now preserved by the County of Westchester.

Thirty Mile Point Light

Somerset, NY
Built: 1876
Style: Square tower

Located 30 miles (48km) east of the Niagara River, the lighthouse overlooks Lake Ontario from atop Golden Hill. Built in 1876, the 54-ft (16.5-m) tower, built from squared stone from Chaumont Bay, is attached on its north side to a two-storey grey stone dwelling. It had a third-order Fresnel lens, while active, which emitted a flashing white light. In 1885, the site received electricity, but 1959 saw the tower both automated and then later deactivated. It was replaced by a steel tower with an automated beam.

Tibbetts Point Light

Cape Vincent, NY
Built: 1827 and 1854
Style: White conical tower
No: 1735
Position: 44 06 00 N. 76 22 12 W
Focal plane: 69ft (21m)
Range: 21 miles/34km, 16 miles/26km
Height: 59ft (18m)

First built in 1827, the original lighthouse was constructed of brick and white-painted stucco with a black cast-iron lantern. The light was produced by a whale-oil lamp and reflector beacon, which was upgraded to a fourth-order Fresnel lens that emitted a flashing white light in 1854, when the tower's height was also increased by 10ft (3m). 1880 saw the addition of a two-and-a-half-storey keeper's dwelling, and a duplex-style keeper's residence was added in 1907. Automated in 1981 and still operational today, the tower marks the spot where the St. Lawrence River joins Lake Ontario, and is also a museum and youth hostel.

West Bank Front Range Light

New York, NY
Built: 1901
Style: Conical tower on cylindrical base
No: 34790
Position: 40 32 18 N. 74 02 36 W
Focal plane: 69ft (21m)
Range: W 23 miles/37km, R 12 miles/19km

The 55-ft (17-m) caisson-based lighthouse of 1901 was adopted as the front range beacon to partner Staten Island Light when it was erected in 1912. This is one of the few lighthouses that is still equipped with its original fourth-order Fresnel lens.

PENNSYLVANIA

Erie Land Light

Presque Isle Peninsula, Lake Erie, PA
Built: 1818, 1858 and 1867
Style: Conical sandstone tower

Now part of Lake Erie's Dunn Park, the 49-ft (15-m) sandstone tower has a focal plane of 128ft (39m). Built in 1818, the original 20-ft (6-m) tower was one of the first lighthouses to be built on the Great Lakes. This was replaced by a 56-ft (17-m) brick tower in 1858 and by the current one in 1867, when it received a third-order Fresnel lens. It was deactivated in 1899 and

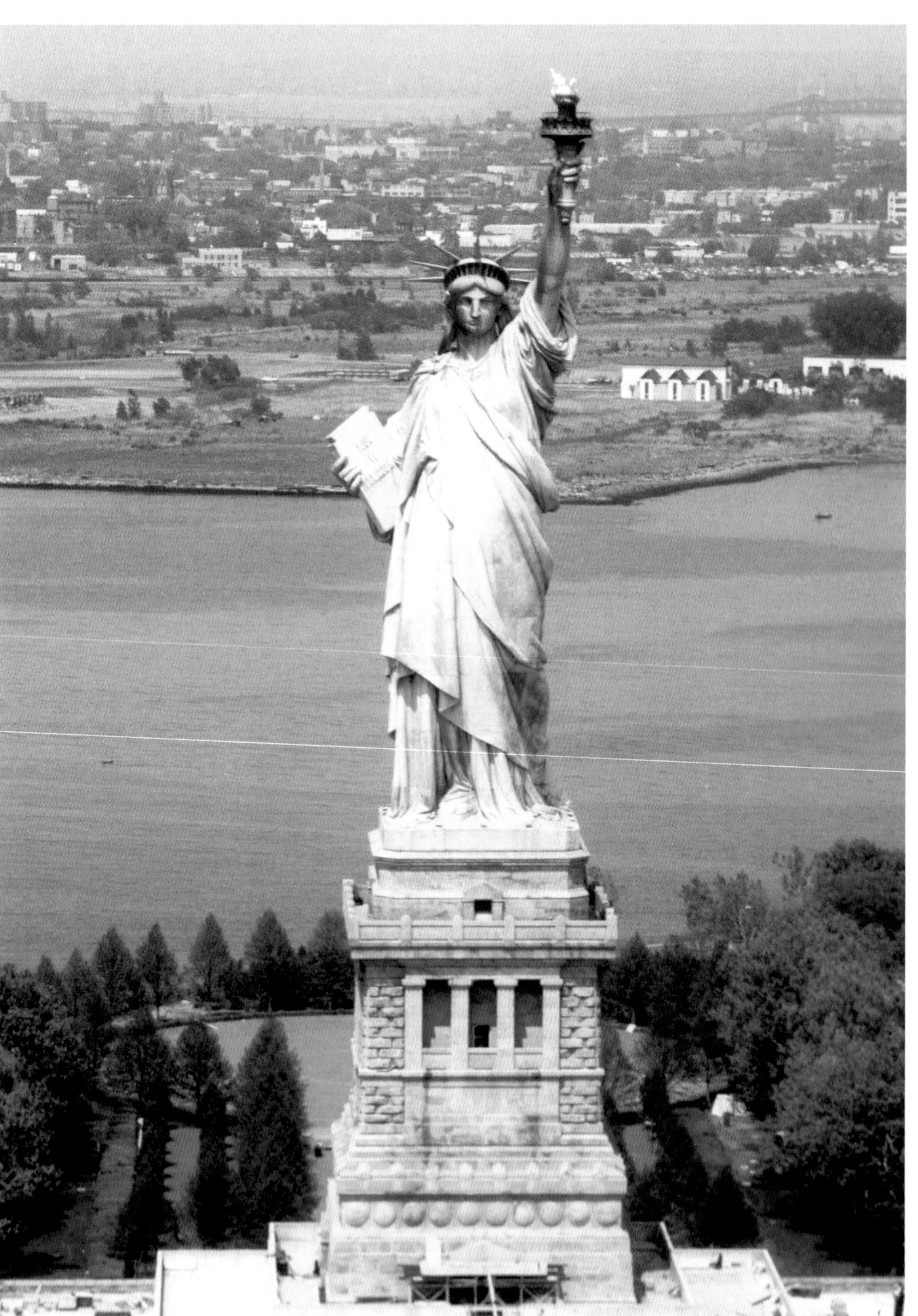

LEFT
Statue of Liberty, New York.

OPPOSITE
Stepping Stones Light, New York.

in 1989 a replica lantern was installed to complete the tower so that it is now a tourist attraction again.

Erie Pierhead Light

Erie Harbor, Lake Erie, PA
Built: 1830 and 1858
Style: Square iron tower banded in black

The 34-ft (10-m) square tower of the Erie North Pierhead Light (also known as Presque Isle North Pier Light) was built of iron in 1858, replacing a destroyed wooden tower that was on the site around 1830. The current tower, once housing a fourth-order lens, has been moved several times, and was automated in 1940. It is still an active aid to navigation today.

Presque Isle Light

Lake Erie, Pennsylvania.
Built: 1873
Style: Square tower
No: 3690
Position: 42 09 48 N. 80 06 54 W
Focal Plane: 73ft (22m)
Range: 15 miles (24km)
Height: 68ft (21m)

The lighthouse was built in 1873 to mark a

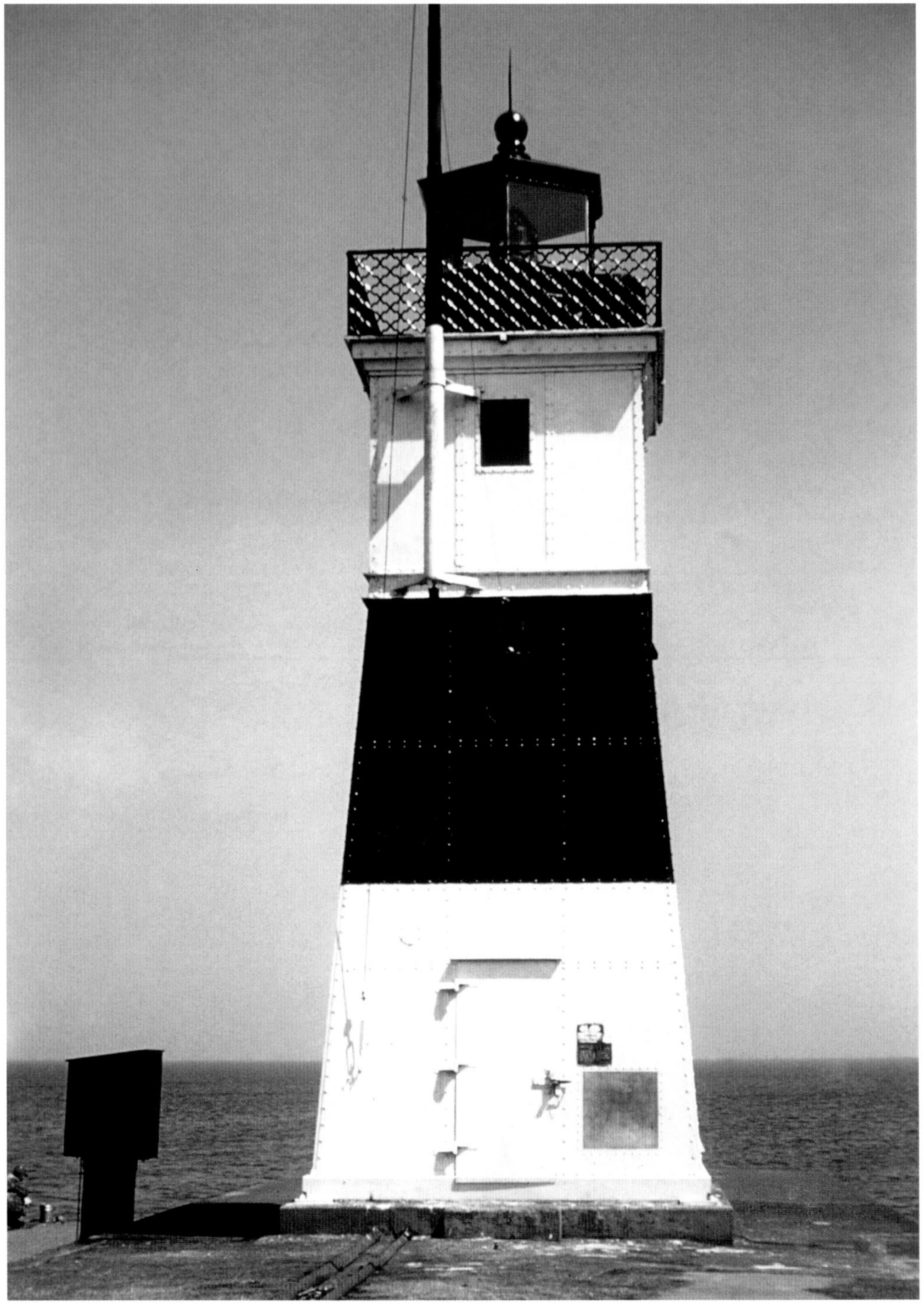

OPPOSITE LEFT
Tibbetts Point Light, New York.

OPPOSITE RIGHT
Erie Pierhead Light, Pennsylvania.

BELOW
Beavertail Light, Rhode Island..

finger of sand that stretches 7 miles (11km) out into Lake Erie. It first held a fourth-order Fresnel lens but this was changed for a 300-mm lens when the station was automated. The two-storey keeper's house attached to the tower is now home to the manager of the Presque Isle State Park.

Turtle Rock Light

Philadelphia, PA
Built: 1887
Style: Cylindrical, integrated with quarters

Completed in 1887 using the sponsorship of the Fairmont Park Commission, the Turtle Rock Light was established to improve the maritime safety of growing commerce on the Schuylkill River at Philadelphia. It cost less than $3,000. The light is currently cared for by the Sedgeley Club and is only lit for special events.

RHODE ISLAND

Beavertail Light

Jamestown, RI
Built: 1749 and 1856
Style: Square tower with attached dwelling
No: 17780
Position: 41 26 58 N. 71 23 59 W
Focal plane: 64ft (19.5m)
Range: 15 miles (24km)

Beavertail Light, established in 1749, is the fourth oldest U.S. light station – only Boston Harbor, Tybee Island and Brant Point stations are older. The first tower, built to guide ships into Narragansett Bay, was burned down by the British during the War of Independence. It was rebuilt and continued in service until the present square building and tower replaced it in 1856. It was equipped with a third-order Fresnel lens, which was replaced by a modern optic when the station was automated in 1991. The keeper's house is now a museum.

Block Island North Light

Block Island, RI
Built: 1828 and 1867
Style: Square tower on dwelling
No : 19480
Position: 41 13 42 N. 71 34 36 W
Focal plane: 58ft (18m)
Range: 13 miles (21km)
Height: 52ft (16m)

There have been several light towers marking Sandy Point on Block Island's north-west shore dating back to 1828. The present granite Block Island North lighthouse was built in 1867 and served until 1973, when it was superseded by a skeletal tower erected nearby. The building was then utilized as an information centre for a wildlife refuge until its light was restored. It now acts as a lighthouse museum.

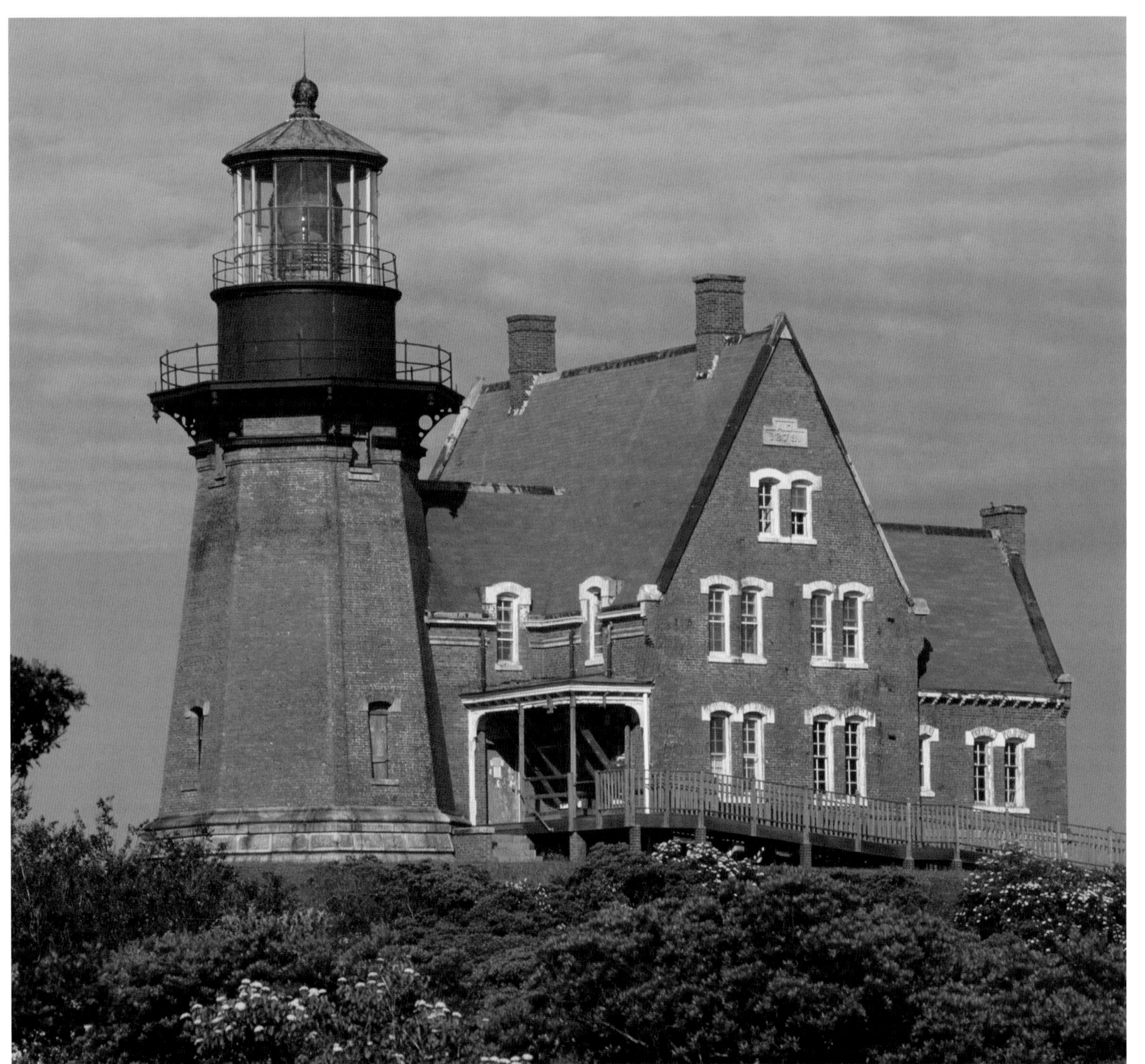

LEFT
Block Island Southeast Light, Rhode Island.

OPPOSITE
Bristol Ferry Light, Rhode Island.

Block Island Southeast Light
Block Island, RI
Built: 1875
Style: Octagonal tower and house
No: 640
Position: 41 09 10 N. 71 33 04 W
Focal plane: 261ft (79.5m)
Range: 20 miles (32km)
Height: 67ft (20m)

The Gothic-style lighthouse, situated on Mohegan Bluff, was built in 1875 to help mariners thread their way through the rocks and shoals that extend out from the south-eastern end of Block Island. The light's red-brick octagonal tower and magnificent keeper's house were in danger themselves after sea erosion brought the 200-ft (60-m) cliffs within a few feet of the front door. To keep the historic treasure from falling down, preservationists raised $2 million to have the 2,000-ton building jacked up and rolled back on railway tracks to a safe distance from the cliff edge. The station's first-order Fresnel lens previously served in Cape Lookout lighthouse in North Carolina.

Bristol Ferry Light

Bristol Ferry, RI
Built: 1848, 1857 and 1902
Style: Square tower

The dangers posed by two shoals on either side of the entrance into the Mount Hope River from Narragansett Bay led local fishermen to built a private light at Bristol Ferry in 1848. This was replaced nine years later by a 28-ft (8.5-m) official lighthouse with attached keeper's dwelling. It was equipped with a sixth-order Fresnel lens to give the light a range of 11 miles (18km). In 1902 it was decided that a more powerful light was required: the brick tower was raised by 6ft (2m) and the lantern room was fitted with a fifth-order lens. The construction of Mount Hope Bridge directly above the tower in 1927 made the lighthouse obsolete and it was decommissioned.

Castle Hill Light

Newport, RI
Built: 1890
Style: Conical
No: 17795
Position: 41 27 44 N. 71 21 47 W
Focal plane: 40 ft (12m)
Range: 12 miles (19km)
Height: 34ft (10m)

The lighthouse has marked Narragansett's East Bay passage since 1890. While the rubblestone tower withstood the worst of the Atlantic weather, the keeper's cottage did not, falling to the 1938 hurricane that damaged so many of New England's

buildings. The tower was fitted with a fifth-order Fresnel lens until the station was automated in 1957.

Conanicut Island Light

Jamestown, RI
Built: 1886
Style: Square tower with attached house

The wooden-framed lighthouse and its attached keeper's residence served to guide mariners around the northern tip of the island from 1886 until 1934, when its fifth-order Fresnel lens was removed. The station is now a private house.

Conimicut Light

Warwick, RI
Built: 1868 and 1883
Style: Conical tower on cylindrical pier
No: 18305
Position: 41 43 01 N. 71 20 42 W
Focal plane: 15ft (4.5m)
Range: 13 miles (21km)

The inadequacies of the Nyatt Point lighthouse, built on the mainland in 1828 to warn vessels away from the dangers of the Conimicut Shoal, west of Barrington, were overcome only with the advances in lighthouse technology that allowed engineers to build towers in exposed open-water sites. The granite tower that first stood directly over the Conimicut Shoal, completed in 1868, borrowed much from the construction of the Minots Ledge lighthouse, built eight years earlier. However, while the tower on Minots Ledge still stands, this one failed to withstand the pressures of the ice and had to be demolished within 15 years. It was replaced by a 55-ft (17-m) caisson-based cast-iron tower with a fourth-order Fresnel lens. This was lit by acetylene until it was automated in 1960.

Dutch Island Lighthouse

Jamestown, RI
Built: 1826 and 1857
Style: Square

Dutch Island lighthouse, close to Jamestown in Narragansett Bay, derived its name from the Dutch traders who used it as a base to barter with local tribes. A 30-ft (9-m) stone lighthouse was built on the island in 1826 and was maintained by William Dennis, a war veteran who stayed at his post until well into his 90s. The present 42-ft (13-m) brick-built lighthouse was constructed in 1857 and was fitted with a fourth-order Fresnel lens. It remained in commission until 1977, when the station was left to decay. Only the tower remains now.

Hog Island Shoal Light

Hog Island, Bristol, RI
Built: 1886 and 1901
Style: Caisson-based iron tower

The dangerous shoals off Hog Island, near the entrance to Bristol harbour, were marked by a lightship from 1886 to 1901. She was replaced by the present 60-ft (18-m) cast-iron caisson-based lighthouse fitted with a fifth-order Fresnel lens, which was exchanged for a modern optic when the station was automated in 1964. The light has a range of 12 miles (19km).

Castle Hill Light, Rhode Island.

Ida Lewis Rock Light

Newport, RI
Built: 1854
Style: Rectangular, integral stone building
No: 17850
Position: 41 29 36 N. 71 19 36 W
Focal plane: 33ft (10m)
Range: 11 miles (18km)

This is the only station in the United States to be named after its keeper. Ida Lewis took over the running of the modest Lime Rock lighthouse in Newport harbour at the age of 15 when her sea-captain father had a stroke. As related earlier, she saved 18 lives from the icy waters off Narragansett Island during her 54 years manning the light.

The Lime Rock lighthouse was little more than a house built on the rock, with a sixth-order Fresnel light displayed from a top window. The station was automated in 1927 and remained in commission until 1963, when the building was converted to house the Ida Lewis Yacht Club. The light is still maintained as a private aid to navigation by the New York Yacht Club, which has its summer quarters on the harbour close to Lime Rock.

OPPOSITE
Ida Lewis Rock (Formerly Lime Rock), Rhode Island.

Newport Harbor Light

Goat Island, Newport, RI
Built: 1824, 1838 and 1865
Style: Conical stone tower
No: 17850
Position: 41 29 36 N. 71 19 36 W
Focal plane: 33ft (10m)
Range: 11 miles (18km)

A light has guided vessels passing Goat Island into Newport harbour since 1824. The present 35-ft (11-m) granite lighthouse is the third tower on the site, built in 1865. It was equipped with a fifth-order Fresnel lens, which did not deter an elderly submarine from slamming into the station and destroying the keeper's cottage in 1921. The Fresnel lens was replaced with a modern optic when the station was automated.

Nyatt Point Light

Barrington, RI
Built: 1828 and 1856
Style: Square

The Nyatt Point lighthouse was built at the mouth of the Providence River to warn vessels of the dangerous Conimicut Shoal offshore. The light proved inadequate, and even when the tower was rebuilt in 1856 and equipped with a fourth-order Fresnel lens, its beam, 30ft (9m) high, was often not seen until it was too late. The tower, which still stands, was replaced in 1868 by the caisson-based Conimicut Light constructed directly over the shoal.

Plum Beach Light

Jamestown, RI
Built: 1899
Style: Caisson

The 53-ft (16-m) cast-iron caisson-based Plum Beach Light is another of Rhode Island's lighthouses to have been overtaken by events. Built in 1899 on the west side of Conanicut Island to guide vessels moving up and down the west channel of Narragansett Bay, the tower's fourth-order Fresnel lens was lit originally by kerosene lamps. The station was made redundant by the construction of the vast Jamestown Bridge and the light was decommissioned in 1941.

Point Judith Light

Point Judith, RI
Built: 1810 and 1816
Style: Octagonal
No: 19450
Position: 41 21 42 N. 71 28 54 W
Focal plane: 65ft (20m)
Range: 16 miles (26km)
Height: 51ft (15.5m)

The first wooden tower built at Point Judith in 1810 was blown down by a gale within five years. The existing octagonal brownstone tower was completed in 1816 and was one of the first to be equipped with a rotating clockwork mechanism to provide a flashing light. A fourth-order Fresnel lens was installed in 1857 and remains in service.

Pomham Rocks Light

Providence, RI
Built: 1871
Style: Square with integrated dwelling

This was built on an outcrop just off the east side of the the Providence River, and was named for a Narragansett Native American chief. The two-storey keeper's residence and its 40-ft (12-m) rooftop tower date back to 1871. It was equipped with a fourth-order Fresnel lens until the station was decommissioned in 1974. The house and its tower are now owned by an oil refinery.

Poplar Point Light

Wickford, RI
Built: 1831
Style: Octagonal with attached dwelling

This is another lighthouse that is now a private house, though it once guided vessels in and out of Wickford harbour. Fitted with a fifth-order Fresnel lens, it served until 1882, when a tower was erected about 600ft (180m) offshore.

Prudence Island Light

Portsmouth, RI
Built: 1852
Style: Octagonal
No: 18125
Position: 41 36 21 N. 71 18 13 W
Focal plane: 28ft (8.5m)
Range: 6 miles (10km)

The octagonal granite lighthouse on Prudence Island first served on Goat Island for 30 years before being relocated in 1852 to guide vessels through the narrow reach that divides the island from the mainland. A wooden six-roomed keeper's cottage, built on the water's edge, was blown down in the 1938 hurricane. The tower's fifth-order Fresnel lens was replaced by a modern optic when the station was automated in 1961.

Rose Island Light

Newport, RI
Built: 1870
Style: Octagonal tower on dwelling.
No: 17857
Position: 41 29 42 N. 71 20 36 W
Height: 48ft (15m)

Rose Island is another of Narragansett's historic lighthouses to have been rendered redundant by the building of Newport Bridge. Constructed in 1870, the tower rises from the roof of the keeper's house, which is in the then-popular style of the French Second Empire, and once held a sixth-order Fresnel lens. The station was decommissioned once the bridge had been opened, but the building has since been restored by the Rose Island Lighthouse Foundation to become a museum and guest-house. Its light has also been relit and is now maintained as a private aid to navigation.

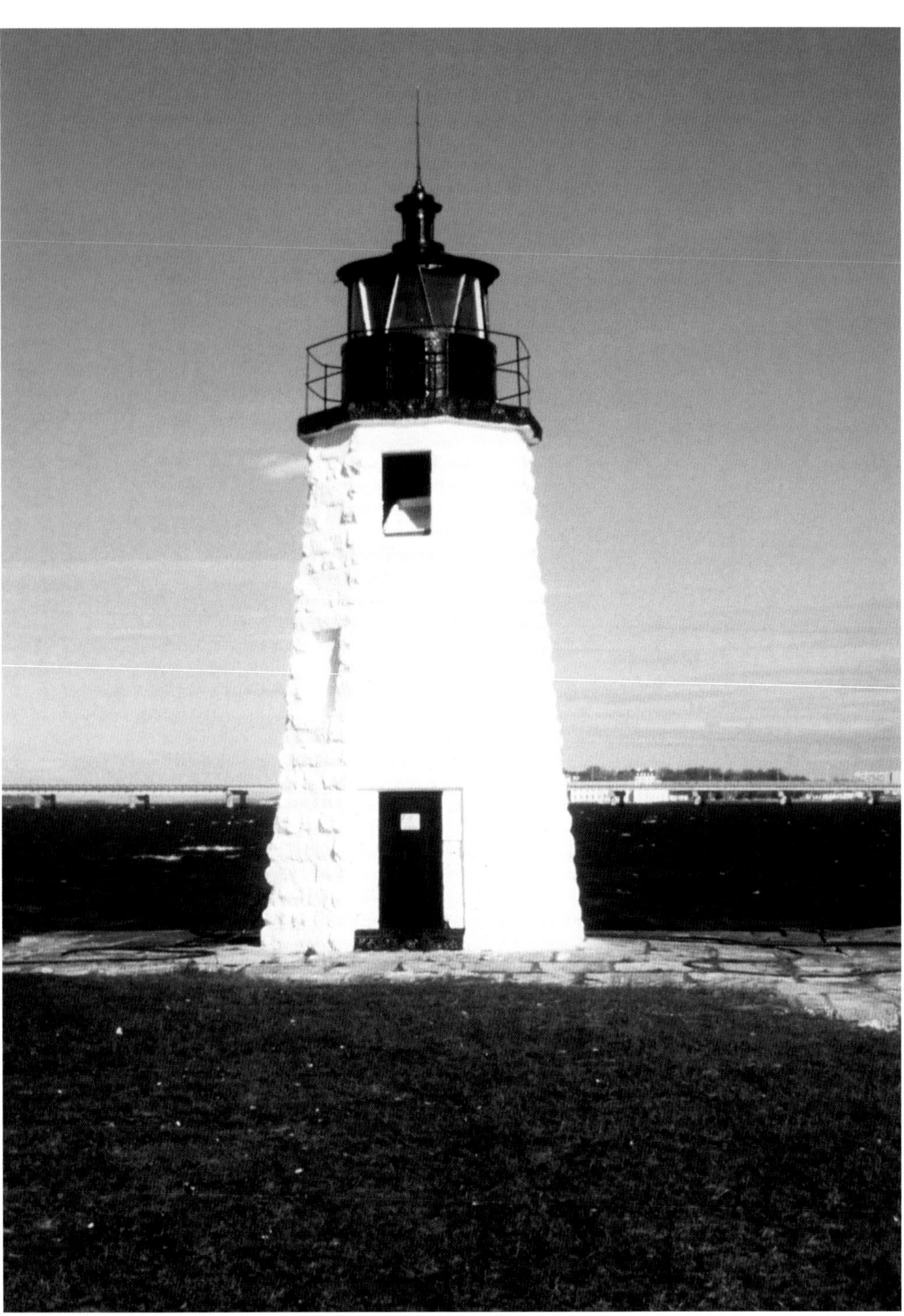

Sakonnet Point Light

Little Compton, RI
Built: 1884
Style: Conical tower on cylindrical base

Although the lighthouse was deactivated by the Coast Guard in 1957, it was relit in 1997 and is now operated as a private aid to navigation by the Friends of Sakonnet Point Lighthouse. Built in 1884, the 66-ft (20-m) cast-iron tower stands on a large rock in the Sakonnet River. The station's original fourth-order Fresnel lens was removed in 1957 and is now on display at the Shore Village Museum in Rockland, Maine. The lighthouse is best seen from the beach in the village of Sakonnet.

Warwick Light

Warwick, RI
Built: 1826, 1889 and 1932
Style: Conical
No: 19345
Position: 41 40 00 N. 71 22 42 W
Focal plane: 66ft (20m)
Range: 12 miles (19km)
Height: 51ft (15.5m)

Constructed in 1826, the original lighthouse was tiny, consisting of a simple two-roomed stone cottage attached to a 30-ft (9-m) wooden tower. Over the years the cramped dwelling was enlarged considerably, and in 1889 a handsome Victorian residence finally replaced it. Afterwards, the original dwelling was used as a barn. A fourth-order Fresnel lens served the station from 1856 until it was replaced by a modern optic in 1985.

LEFT
Newport Harbor Light, Rhode Island.

OPPOSITE
Rose Island Light, Rhode Island.

With erosion threatening to swallow up the old lighthouse, a new, more durable steel tower was erected. Eventually, the 51-ft conical structure had to be moved inland away from the rapidly eroding cliffs. The station remains in operation, displaying a green light with a range of about 12 miles.

Watch Hill Light

Watch Hill, RI
Built: 1808 and 1857
Style: Square tower with attached house
No: 19795
Position: 41 18 12 N. 71 51 30 W
Focal plane: 61ft (18.5m)
Range: W 16 miles/26km, R 14 miles/23km
Height: 51ft (15.5m)

The town of Watch Hill was probably named after a tower built as a lookout to warn local militiamen of approaching French ships in the mid-18th century. More than half a century later a lighthouse was built at Watch Hill. The round wooden tower, hammered together by local carpenters, was fitted with whale-oil lamps. The square 51-ft granite tower and attached dwelling that stands here today was completed in 1857, when a sparkling fourth-order Fresnel lens replaced the station's old lamps and reflectors. An automated modern lens serves the station

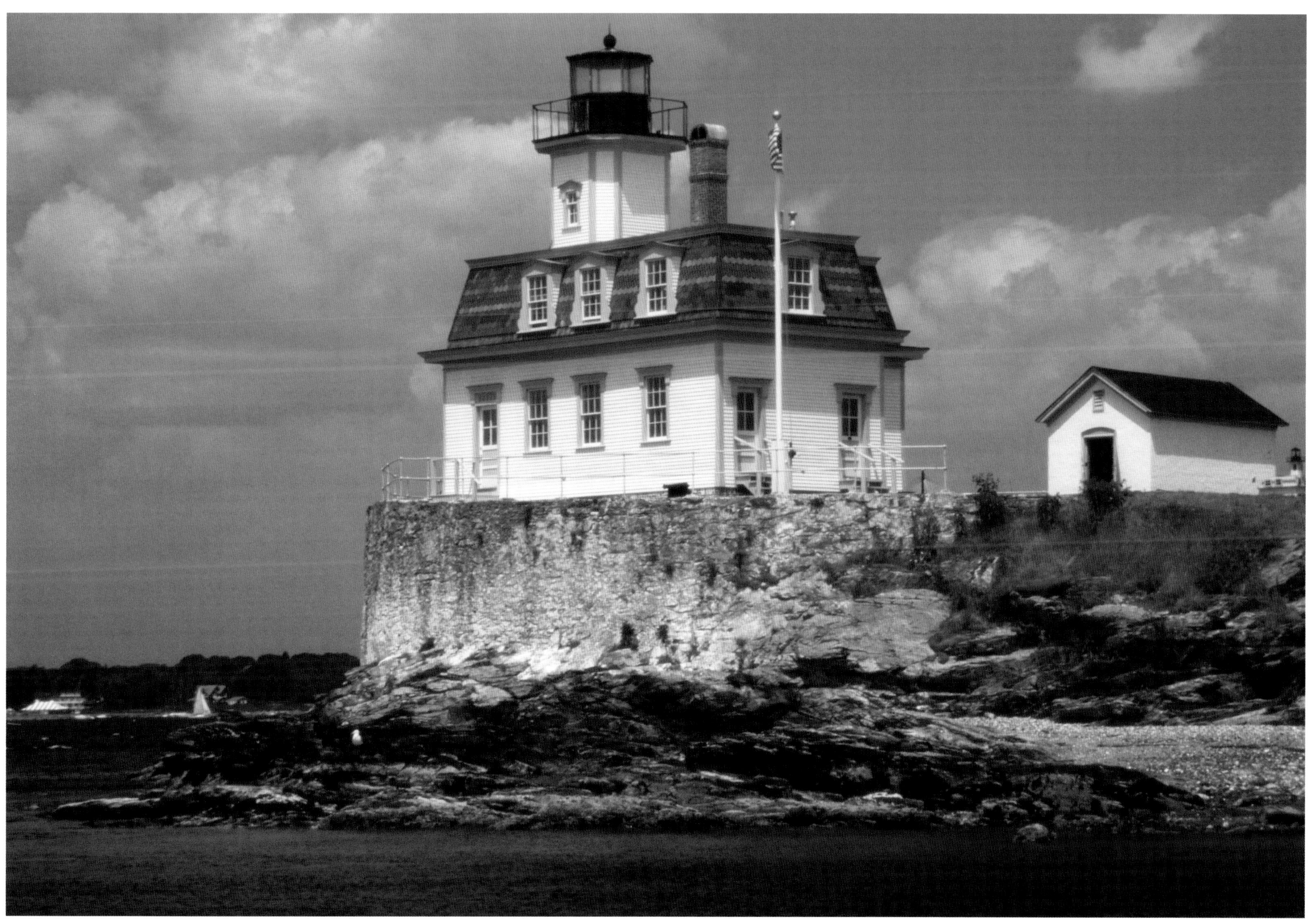

today, and the keeper's house is a small museum featuring the station's original Fresnel lens.

Whale Rock Light

Narragansett Bay, RI
Built: 1871
Style: Caisson-based

The Whale Rock lighthouse, which no longer exists, rose far above the waves on a massive concrete foundation located near the entrance of Narragansett Bay. It was a typical open-water caisson lighthouse with a central cast-iron cylinder, but it was destroyed by the 1938 hurricane and the assistant keeper on duty was killed.

Wickford Harbor

North Kingstown, RI
Built: 1882
Style: Square with attached house

Established in 1882 to guide vessels into Wickford's busy harbour, the lighthouse served mariners for more than 50 years. It consisted of a square wooden tower attached to a keeper's dwelling, and was equipped with a fifth-order Fresnel lens and fog bell. Unfortunately, the lovely old building has gone, having been demolished shortly after the station was deactivated in 1930.

VERMONT

Isle La Motte Light

Isle La Motte, VT
Built: 1829 and 1881
Style: Conical cast-iron tower

Once an important beacon on Lake Champlain, the lighthouse, with its 25-ft (8-m) tower, focal plane of 46ft (14m) and keeper's quarters, now stands unlit. In 1829 it consisted of a privately operated lantern, but gained a stone pyramid in 1857 and in 1880 a keeper's house, fog signal and oil house. 1881 saw the addition of a cast-iron tower with a sixth-order Fresnel lens. The tower was decommissioned in 1933 when it was replaced by a solar-powered automated light on a skeleton tower.

Juniper Island Light

Burlington, Lake Champlain, VT
Built: 1826 and 1846
Style: Cylindrical cast iron tower

The Juniper Island Light has the distinction of being the site of Vermont's first lighthouse and is also one of America's earliest cast-iron lighthouses. The first 30-ft (9-m) tower was built in 1826, while the second 25-ft (8-m) tower was built in its place in 1846. It was decommissioned in 1954, when it was replaced by an automatic skeleton tower. The tower has been in private hands since 1956.

Windmill Point Light

Alburg, Lake Champlain, VT
Built: 1858
Style: Granite conical tower

The 40-ft (12-m) granite tower of Windmill Point, with its rustic-looking keeper's quarters, is situated very close to the Canadian border. Originally established in 1830 and rebuilt in 1858, the light used a sixth-order Fresnel lens, with a focal plane at 52ft (16m), before it was deactivated and replaced by a skeleton tower in 1931.

Warwick Light, Rhode Island.

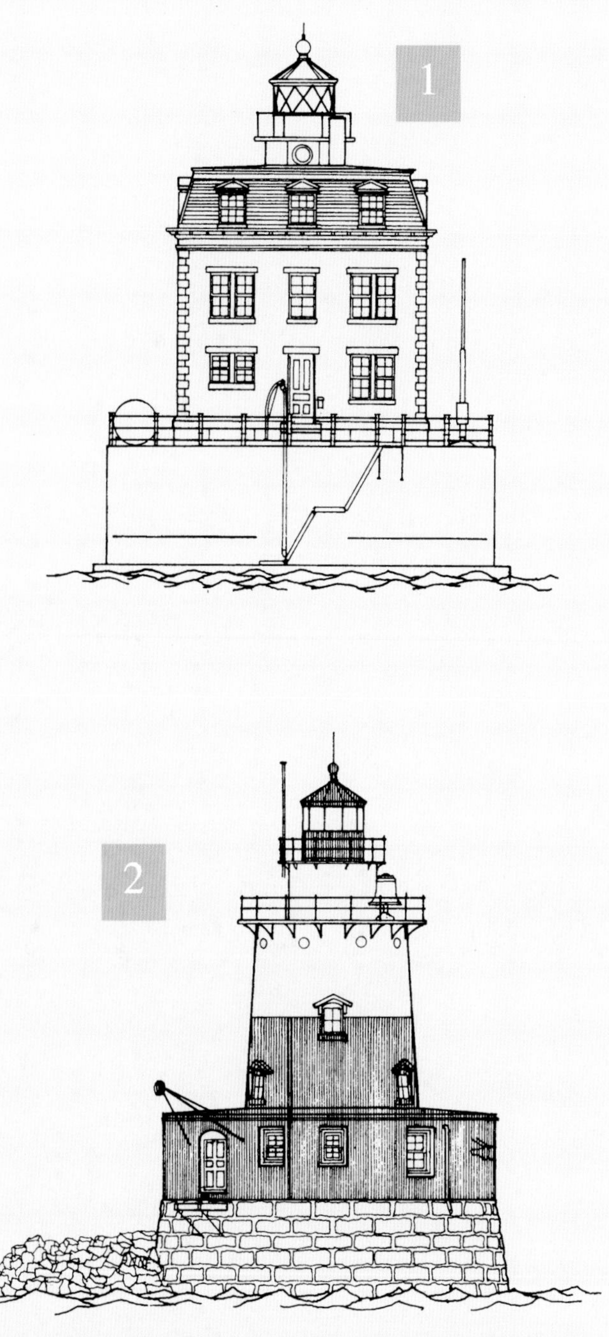
1
2

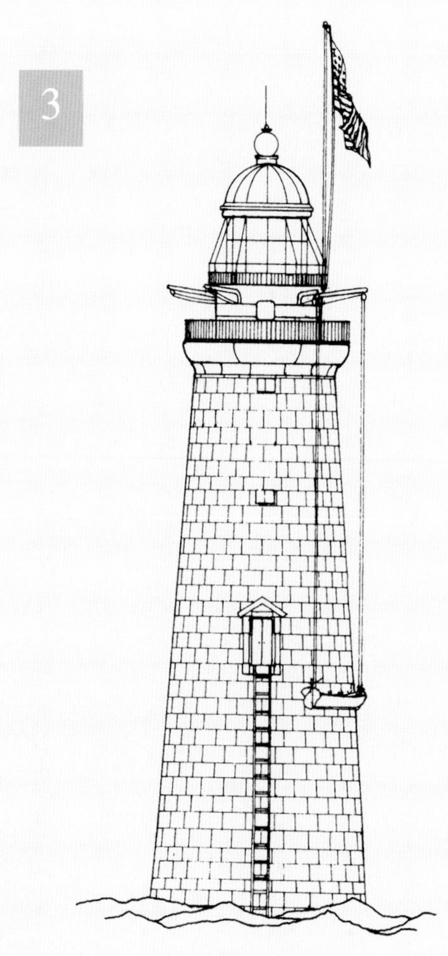
3

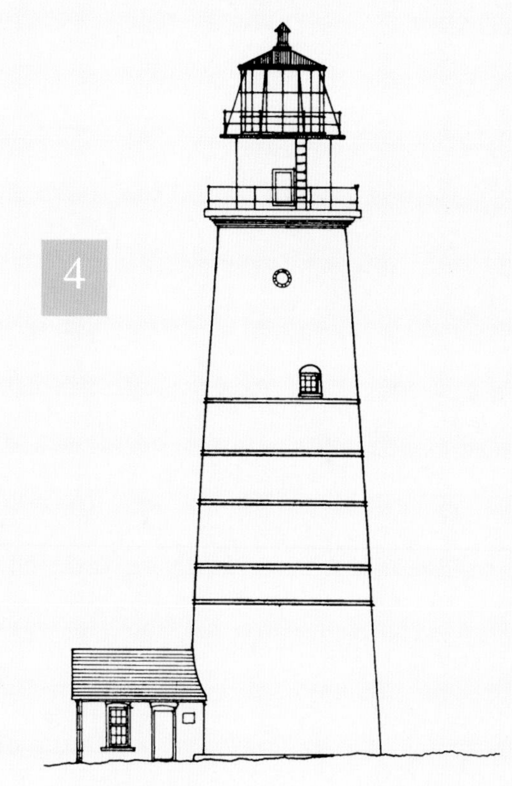
4

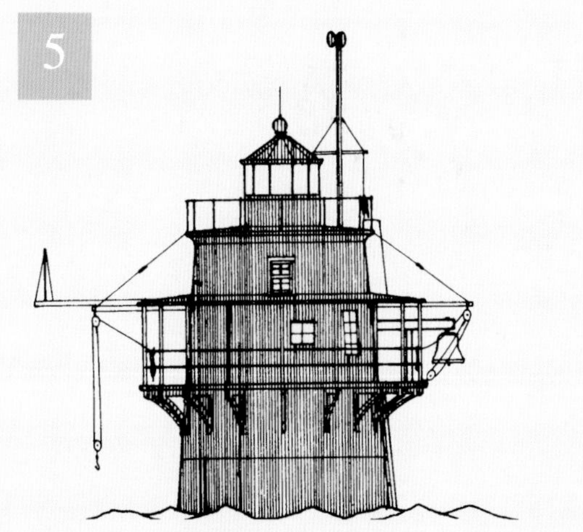
5

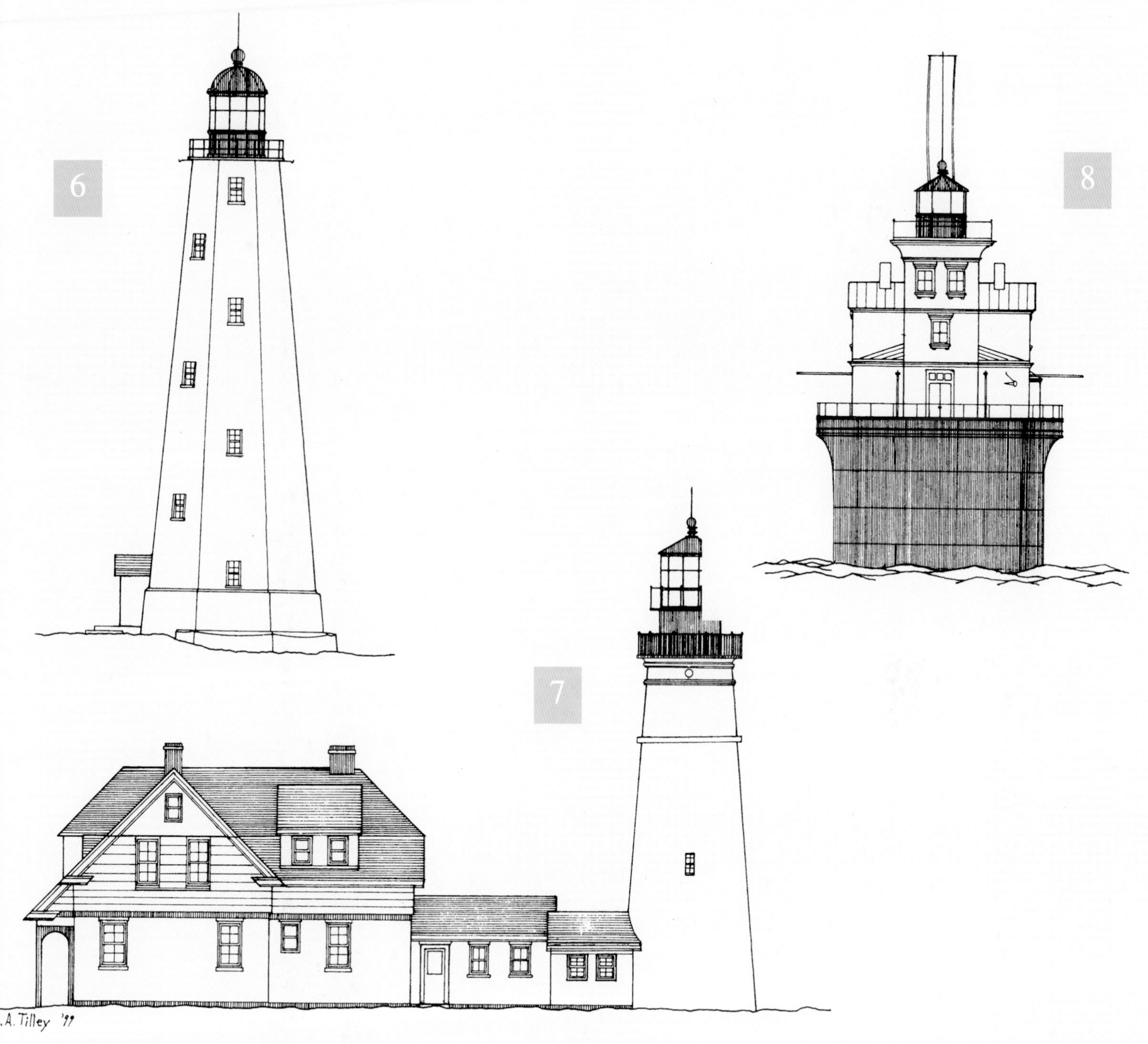

1. New London Ledge, Connecticut
2. Robbins Reef, New York
3. Minots Ledge, Massachusetts
4. Boston Light, Massachusetts
5. Duxbury Pier, Massachusetts
6. Sandy Hook Island, New Jersey
7. Portland Head, Maine
8. Fourteen Foot Bank, Delaware

Cape Horn Light, Isla Hornos, Chile

Style: White tower with red horizontal band
No: G1336
Focal plane: 128ft (39m)
Range: 7 miles (11km)
Height: 13ft (4m)
Chile: Canal Brecknock, also known as Cabo de Hornos

Cape Horn is one of the most notorious corners of the globe. It is a place that has gale-force winds most days, increasing to hurricane strength for at least one or two days every month.

It was a turning point in more ways than one for the many panhandlers seeking their fortunes during the Gold Rush. During the mid-19th century, Cape Horn aside, the fastest and safest route from the east to the west coast of America was to sail aboard one of the clipper ships from New York bound for San Francisco or British Columbia and gamble on good weather at the cape. The alternative was to cross the Wild West by wagon and run an even greater risk of being scalped!

For ships, the greatest danger comes, not from the winds, but from the huge seas that develop here. Driven by the Roaring Forty and Furious Fifty storms that run unhindered for 5,000 miles across the Southern Ocean, these waves are compressed down through the narrow 500-mile (800-km) Drake's Passage, which forms a ventua *between Cape Horn and Antarctica. The year 1905 was one of the worst years on record, when more than 400 square-riggers made, or attempted to make voyages around this infamous cape. Six ships disappeared without trace, and many more were wrecked, driven aground on the tooth-like rocks surrounding Cabo de Hornos. Others suffered so much damage at the hand of wind and sea that the vessels were deemed total losses when they eventually limped into port. At least 40 were forced to turn and run in distress for the Falklands, Montevideo or Rio de Janeiro. A dozen more gave up the battle altogether, and simply ran off east before the Roaring Forty gales to reach their destination from the other side of the globe.*

It was these high risks that led Cape Horners to wear a golden earring in their left ear lobes, not so much to mark a successful rounding, but to provide the means for a decent burial should their bodies be found in the sea. As a mark of respect to the thousands who have lost their lives in these waters, the Chileans have erected a memorial to the Unknown Sailor on Cape Horn. This 20-ft (6-m) multi-layered steel sculpture, which stands close to Cape Horn Lighthouse on the north-west corner of the island, was erected in 1992 and depicts an albatros on the wing, gliding over the Southern Ocean.

Cape Horn Lighthouse is also a modern, and perhaps an unduly modest structure to stand on such an evocative headland. The fibreglass tower stands just 13-ft tall and has a range of only 7 miles, probably because most vessels give the cape a very wide berth indeed, rounding the 100 miles (160km) or more off this southern tip of South America to avoid the short, sharp seas that can run here. It is only round-the-world race yachts that take the shorter inshore course, together with the few who decide to cruise down en route to Antarctica and stop off at the island to have their passports stamped by the lighthouse keepers.

In many ways, yachts have an easier passage than the clipper ships did a century or more ago. A yacht will ride the waves like a cork and when necessary have the speed and agility to run ahead of the worst wave formations. A heavy sailing ship, on the other hand, was always in danger of being pooped by the huge breaking crests that can build up within just a few hours. In those days, a man at the helm – and often there had to be two or more to turn the wheel – was protected by strong iron shelters designed as much as to stop the helmsmen from seeing the huge rolling crests as to protect him from being washed away. There is one celebrated case where a sailor was washed clean off the foredeck of his ship when the bows dipped into these fearsomely steep seas, and was then dumped, half drowned, back on the poop deck by the next wave! His was a miraculous escape, for most who have fallen overboard in these waters are rarely seen again. Yet, this

LEFT
Cape Horn Memorial.

OPPOSITE
The southernmost church in the world alongside Cape Horn Lighthouse, Chile.

LEFT
The Beagle coins, Cape Horn.

BELOW LEFT
The cairn where the coins were found.

OPPOSITE
A yacht rounding the perilous Cape Horn.

old salt lived to tell the tale to anyone who would listen for another half a century.

Cape Horn Lighthouse is manned by three Chilean Naval ratings, who maintain a 24-hour watch on the waters as well as guarding Chilean sovereignty against claims from neighbouring Argentina. Back in 1982, Argentina, which has long laid claim to Cape Horn, had plans to invade these southern islands to detract attention away from the country's declining economy. In the end, General Galtieri and his Argentine military junta decided to invade the Falkland Islands instead; by then, however, the Chilean defenders had not only mined the surrounding waters around Cape Horn, but had also seeded the islands with land mines in readiness for an attack. The mines are still there because the albatros and penguin that inhabit the beaches and moorlands here are too light-footed to set them off. As a result, all the land south of the Beagle Channel and surrounding waters of Cape Horn are banned to all private and commercial vessels. Only at the north-western tip of Cape Horn, where a mooring has been laid in a sheltered cove, are sailors welcomed to visit the lighthouse keepers and the most southerly Catholic church in the world.

It was the British warship HMS Beagle, *which carried Charles Darwin on his famous Voyage of Discovery, that first charted these waters. It was not an easy voyage. Less than a third of the crew sent out to serve here completed their tour of duty, for accidents and death took a heavy toll. Discipline too was strict, and Darwin, who sailed aboard the* Beagle *from 1930 during the last five years of her commission, wrote that her captain meted out no less than 600 lashes of the whip on the backs of his crew during this period. While today's round-the-world yachtsmen pride themselves on 'shooting the Horn' these early sailors were less than enamoured with the prospect. Captain Pringle Stokes, the first master of the 235-ton* Beagle, *became so depressed when he received orders to stay at his post, having already served one two-year commission, that he went out and shot himself. This unhappy end led others within* Beagle*'s crew to realize their own plight, as much as to honour their captain with a remarkable grave site overlooking the Beagle Channel, now carefully maintained by the Chilean Navy. The inscription on the gravestone reads:*

Commander Pringle Stokes RN, HMS *Beagle*, who died from the effects of the anxieties and hardships while surveying the waters and shores of Tierra del Fuego.

He was replaced by Lt. Robert Fitzroy, a high-flying naval officer and a grandson of the Duke of Grafton, who won the captainship of Beagle *at the young age of 23. Fitzroy had proved a brilliant student: he had been sent to the Royal Naval College at*

RHÔNE-POULENC

OPPOSITE
Cape Horn Lighthouse.

RIGHT
The all-important generators that power the lighthouse at keeper's house.

Portsmouth, England, at the age of 12, won the mathematics prize and first place in his year, and first sailed to South America as a school volunteer at the age of 14. Promoted to midshipman a year later, he had won his stripes as a lieutenant by the time he was 19. He so impressed Admiral Ottway, then Commander-in-Chief of Britain's South American station at Rio de Janeiro, that Ottway chose him as his aide-de-camp. Fitzroy had one quality that distinguished him from other older, more experienced officers – enthusiasm. It was this that led Ottway to give him the captaincy of the Beagle *and the care of its demoralized crew.*

Fitzroy may have favoured the whip to lash his crew into shape, but he also knew the value to morale of sending parties ashore to work with Darwin to record animal and plant life in the region, and to bury time capsules at strategic points. The first of these was found in 1981 on the Isle of Skyring by a helicopter crew serving in the Chilean Navy. These naval artefacts so intrigued its captain, Christian de Bonnafos Gandara, that he set about searching other possible sites, including ones on Cape Horn.

Darwin has not written much concerning these matters, so there was no ready record of where these capsules might be found. Cape Horn, however, was the most obvious spot. Captain Gandara began by researching early naval documents. He read Darwin's extraordinary tale of wildlife found in the area, and dug up Fitzroy's biography. Gandara had to put himself in Fitzroy's shoes as well as rely on his own Chilean naval training, which is based on British traditions, to second-guess where any testimonies to Beagle*'s explorations might have been placed. The final piece of this historic jigsaw –* Beagle*'s log – was not unearthed until three months after Gandara made his 'find' on Cape Horn.*

His opportunity came when the captain and I attended the blessing of the 20-ft (6-m) monument to the Unknown Sailor in 1992. He had taken the opportunity to fly over the cape to look for any markers such as a cairn of stones, but had seen nothing. It was only after the ceremony that he realized where he had gone wrong. 'It was only when taking a cup of coffee outside the lighthouse that I put myself in Fitzroy's shoes and wondered where I would leave something for a future generation to find. It had to be a unique place, and at Cape Horn there is only one – at the top of the cliff.' With the help of engineering officer Eduardo Troncoso Unwin, they took a second flight to the top of Cape Horn's famous rock, only this time they landed to make a closer inspection. There was no obvious cairn, but what did catch their eye was a group of rocks that were different from those surrounding them.

'We started to move these stones, some of which were over 400lb, and dug down to the peat. Then we started to unearth little pieces of yellow-coloured ceramic, very similar in composition to the pot found at Skyring.' Gardara added, 'We continued to dig with our hands, careful not to destroy anything, pulling out more pieces of ceramic before finding a bronze tablet with the words 'Beagle 1830' *inscribed on it.*

The delighted Gandara continued his dig, and within three hours had unearthed 41 bronze and silver coins from Britain, Spain, Germany and Brazil, dating between 1784 and 1828. There were medals, a mug, the rotted remains of a Union Jack flag, a Royal Marine's bronze belt buckle, 15 bronze buttons, a wooden insignia stamp, carey stones (similar to opals), a knife, an iron object to make holes which matched the markings on the Beagle *plate, and a small box inscribed with the name James Bennett – Fitzroy's servant aboard HMS* Beagle.

This 'find' is now on display at the Chilean Naval Museum at Valparaiso, and Captain Gandara now hopes to locate other capsules on South Georgia or in the South Sandwich Islands. Ironically, just as this testimony was found on Cape Horn, the Chilean Navy buried its own time capsule beneath the memorial to the Unknown Sailor and filled it with sailing memorabilia from the 1990s.

It would be interesting to know what future sailors visiting this last outpost think of this second cache in another 150 years. One thing is for sure – the weather conditions will be as notorious as ever!

Chapter Eight

Lighthouses of the South-East

ALABAMA

Middle Bay Light

Mobile Harbor, AL
Built: 1885 and 1905
Style: Hexagonal screwpile

The present Middle Bay lighthouse was built in 1905 to replace an earlier one of 1885 that marked the entrance channel to Mobile harbour. Standing 54-ft (16.5-m) high, the six-sided keeper's house has the lantern on its roof and was modelled on a similar lighthouse at Hooper Strait, Maryland. The Middle Bay lighthouse suffered serious damage in the 1916 hurricane, which left the station out of service. The screwpile tower, which once held a fourth-order Fresnel lens, has since been restored by the Middle Bay Light Centennial Committee and now houses a marker beacon.

RIGHT
Sand Island Light, Alabama.

OPPOSITE
Gibb's Hill Light, Bermuda.

Sand Island Light

Mobile Bay, AL
Built: 1838, 1859 and 1873
Style: Conical brownstone tower

The 131-ft (40-m) Sand Island lighthouse was built in 1873 to mark the west side of Mobile Bay at a spot that has seen two previous towers. The first, designed and built by Winslow Lewis, designer of the oil lamps that bear his name, survived for little more than two decades. Its replacement was a 150-ft (46-m) tower built in 1859, but this was destroyed by Confederate troops during the Civil War. In 1906, a hurricane swept away not only the keeper's dwelling, and those who were in it, but Sand Island too, although the tower remained upright. Its first-order Fresnel lens, which gave the tower a range of 20 miles (32km), was finally put out of commission in 1971. The tower is now in danger from sea erosion.

CARIBBEAN

BERMUDA

Gibb's Hill Light

Southampton Parish, Bermuda
Built: 1846
Style: Conical cast-iron tower

LEFT
Cape San Juan Light, Puerto Rico.

OPPOSITE
St. David's Light, Bermuda.

The 117-ft (36-m) Gibb's Hill lighthouse was built in 1846 to provide vessels navigating around the reefs on the southern side of Bermuda with a strong reference point. The light was sorely needed for, in the decade before, a total of 39 vessels had been wrecked on the western end of the island where the reefs extend some 16 miles (26km) out to sea. The prefabricated tower, which was cast in England and shipped out to Bermuda in sections, is one of the oldest in the world. Standing on a hill 245ft (75m) above sea level, the tower has a 1,000-watt electric bulb, which gives the light a range of 40 miles (64km). Back in 1846, a concentrated burner with four circular wicks produced the light. This was replaced by a five-wick burner and glass chimney in 1904, and by a kerosene burner in 1923. Electricity was installed in 1952 when the tower was automated, but the station still has two keepers, who spend much of their day leading visitors up and down the 185 steps.

St. David's Light

St. David's Island, St. George's Parish, Bermuda

Built: 1879
Style: Octagonal limestone tower
No: J4472
Focal plane: 196ft (60m)
Range: 23 miles (37km)
Height: 55ft (17m)

The lighthouse was built in 1879 to mark the easternmost point of Bermuda. Built from local limestone, the tower stands on Lighthouse Hill, some 280ft (85m) above the Atlantic. It is powered by a 1,500-watt electric light bulb and has a range of 23 miles. The famous red-and-white-painted tower is the finishing point for the biennial Newport–Bermuda yacht race.

Puerto Rico

Arecibo Light

Arecibo, Puerto Rico
Built: 1898
Style: Hexagonal
No: J5492
Position: 18 29 00 N. 66 41 54 W
Focal plane: 120ft (36.5m)
Range: 14 miles (22.5km)

Arecibo Light is also known as Punta Morillos. White with a black lantern, the hexagonal tower, with its attached square, flat-roofed keeper's dwelling, was equipped with a third-order Fresnel lens, but this was

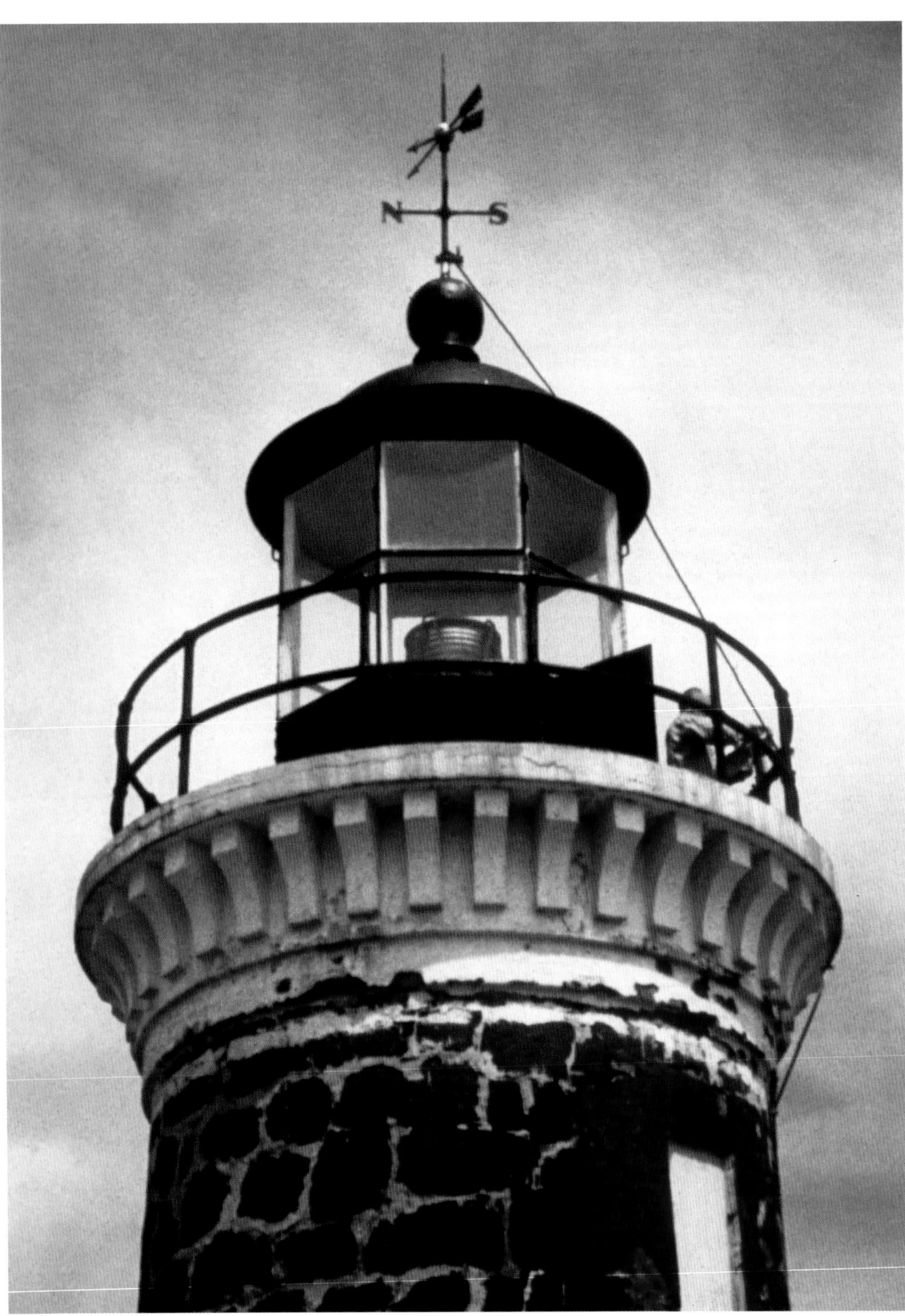

LEFT
Culebrita Island Light, Puerto Rico.

OPPOSITE
Cardona Island Light, Puerto Rico.

replaced with a 190-mm lens when the station was automated. The city of Arecibo now plans to restore the lantern and use the residential quarters as offices.

Cape San Juan Light

Fajardo, San Juan, Puerto Rico
Built: 1880
Style: Cylindrical, attached to building.
No: J5528, 31155
Position: 18 22 54 N. 65 37 06 W
Focal plane: 260ft (79m)
Range: 24 miles (39km)

Cape San Juan Light was built in 1880 and equipped with a third-order Fresnel lens. Also known as the Cabezas de San Juan lighthouse, the cylindrical tower has a black-and-white band around its base and a black lantern. The tower is also utilized as a marine-science interpretative centre.

Cardona Island Light

Ponce, Puerto Rico.
Built: 1889
Style: White cylindrical tower on dwelling
No: 31950
Position: 17 57 24 N. 66 38 06 W
Focal plane: 46ft (14m)
Range: 8 miles (13km)

The lighthouse was built in 1889 and equipped with a sixth-order Fresnel lens. The white tower with its black lantern is also known as Cayo Cardona lighthouse. The tower also contains a marine centre.

Culebrita Island Light

Culebrita Island, Culebra, Puerto Rico
Built: 1889
Style: Cylindrical tower on dwelling
No: J5608, 31685
Position: 18 18 48 N. 65 13 42 W
Focal plane: 305ft (93m)
Range: 13 miles (21km)

The stone-coloured tower of Culebrita Light, with its red trim, is attached to a flat-roofed dwelling. It remains active although it now houses an information centre.

Mona Island Light

Mona Island, Mayaguez, Puerto Rico
Built: 1900
Style: Skeletal tower with central cylinder
No: 32295
Position: 18 06 36 N. 67 54 30 W
Focal plane: 323ft (98m)
Range: 14 miles (22.5km)

Mona Island lighthouse was the first of two light stations built on Puerto Rico by the U.S. Government. The light, which remains active, was relocated to its present position in 1977.

Point Tuna Light

Guayama, Maunabo, Puerto Rico
Built: 1892
Style: Octagonal tower on dwelling

OPPOSITE
Point Tuna Light, Puerto Rico.

RIGHT
Port San Juan Light, Puerto Rico.

BELOW
Mona Island Light, Puerto Rico.

No: 31800
Focal plane: 181ft (55m)
Position: 17 59 24 N. 65 53 06 W
Focal plane: 111ft (34m)
Range: 16 miles (26km)

Punta Tuna Light, known locally as Puerto Maunabo lighthouse, was built in 1892 and once held a third-order Fresnel lens, replaced with a 190-mm optic when the station was automated.

Port San Juan Light

San Juan, Puerto Rico
Built: 1908
Style: Square tower, octagonal base
No: 30735
Position: 18 28 24 N. 66 07 24 W
Focal plane: 181ft (55m)
Range: 24 miles (39km)

Port San Juan lighthouse boasts a Moorish-style tower and has a third-order Fresnel lens. The tower was restored in 1991 and is now managed by the National Parks Service.

OPPOSITE
Klein Curaçao Lighthouse, Netherlands Antilles.

RIGHT
Alligator Reef Light, Florida.

Netherlands Antilles

Klein Curaçao Light

Klein Curaçao, Curaçao
Built: 1879
Style: Cylindrical
No. J6400
Focal plane: 75ft (23m)
Range: 14 miles (22.5km)
Height: 75ft (23m)

The lighthouse was built in 1879 to warn vessels of this featureless, almost flat island three miles south-east of Curaçao. The lighthouse is the only permanent structure on the island, which is uninhabited other than by fishermen who use it as a temporary base. The white, cylindrical, coral-brick tower has an attached two-storey keeper's dwelling. The light is now automated but there was an interim period when the lighthouse was lit and extinguished each day by a keeper, who would travel to the island by boat. The beacon now runs on solar power, but the buildings are in need of repair.

Florida

Alligator Reef Light

Matecumbe Key, FL
Built: 1873

LEFT
American Shoal Light, Florida.

OPPOSITE
Amelia Island Light, Florida.

Style: Octagonal pyramid skeleton tower
No: 980
Position: 24 51 06 N. 80 37 06 W
Focal plane: 136ft (41.5m)
Range: W 16 miles/26km, R 13 miles/21km
Height: 103ft/31m)

The skeletal Alligator Reef lighthouse was erected in 1873 to mark the hazardous shoals off Matecumbe Key, where the U.S. Navy schooner *Alligator* was lost in 1822. The cast-iron tower is similar in design to Carysfort Reef Light and is anchored to the coral reef by steel piles 10ft (3m) long. The lighthouse is equipped with a fourth-order Fresnel lens that is solar powered since the station was automated.

Amelia Island Light

Old Fernandina Beach, FL
Built: 1839
Style: Conical tower
No: 565
Position: 30 40 24 N. 81 26 30 W
Focal plane: 107ft (33m)
Range: W 23 miles/37km, R 19 miles/31km
Height: 64ft (19.5m)

The Amelia Island Light stood for 18 years on Little Cumberland Island, Georgia, before it was dismantled and transported to the mouth of St. Marys River in 1839. The tower was extensively renovated in 1885, when it was equipped with its third-order Fresnel lens. The lighthouse station remains an active U.S. Coast Guard base.

American Shoal Light

Sugarloaf Key, FL
Built:1880
Style: Octagonal pyramidal skeleton tower
No: 1015
Position: 24 31 30 N. 81 31 12 W
Focal plane: 109ft (33m)
Range: 10 miles (16km)
Height: 109ft (33m)

The purpose of the skeletal American Shoal Light was to warn vessels away from the hazardous American Shoals north-east of Key West. It was built in a shipyard in New Jersey in 1880, much as an offshore oil rig might be built today. The tower was then transported by ship about 1,500 miles (2500km) to the Florida Keys, where it was erected above prepared foundations pile-driven into the coral seabed. The tower carried a first-order bivalve Fresnel lens, but this was replaced with a solar-powered plastic optic when the station was automated in 1963.

Anclote Key Light

Anclote Island, FL
Built: 1887
Style: Skeletal

The 102-ft (31-m) Anclote Key lighthouse was erected in 1887 to provide a reference point along Florida's Gulf Coast and mark the entrance to the Anclote River. The lighthouse was decommissioned in 1984 and plans are now at hand to restore it.

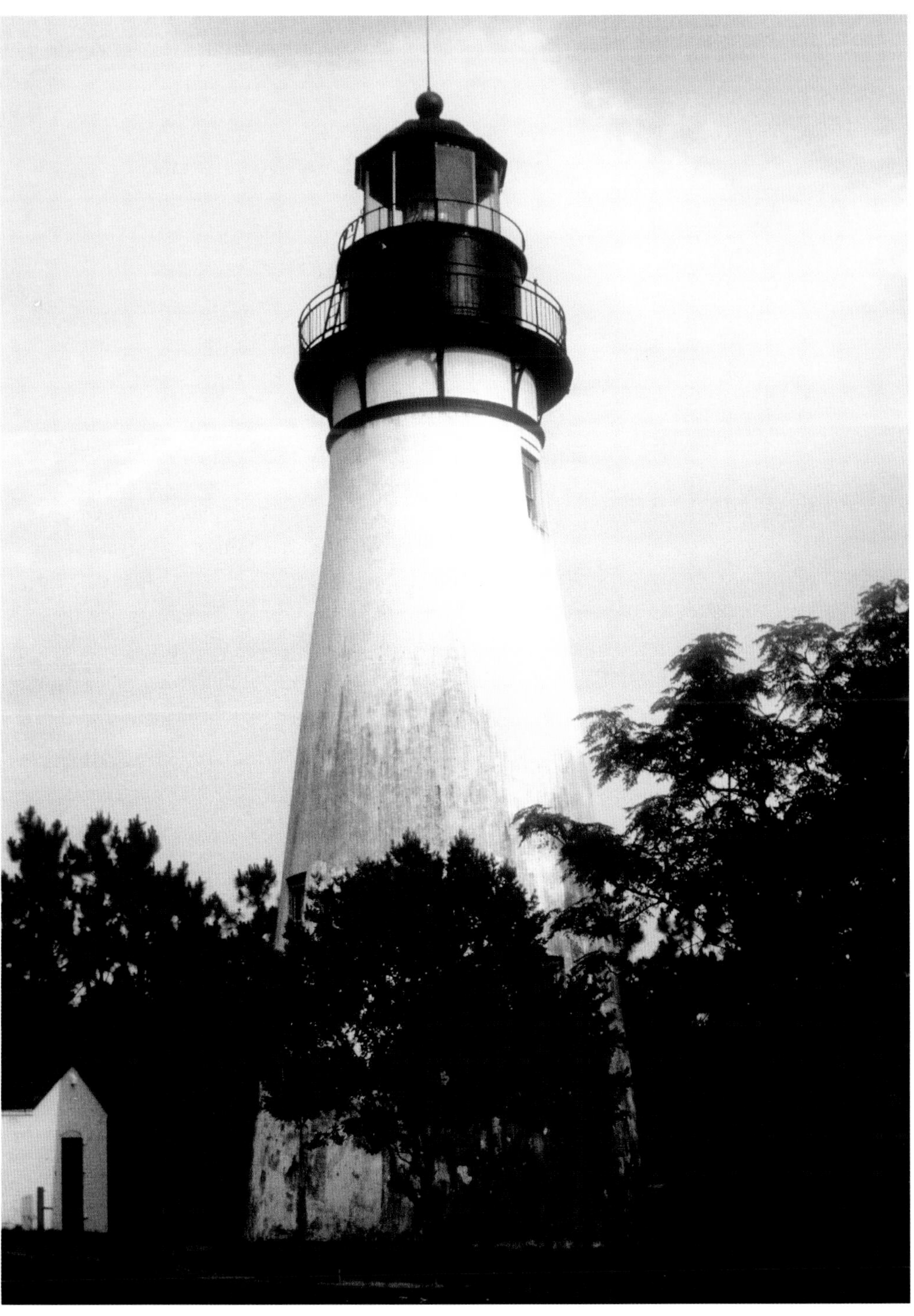

Boca Grande Rear Range Light

Boca Grande, FL
Built: 1932
Style: Skeletal
No: 19965
Position: 26 43 02 N. 82 18 00 W
Focal plane: 41ft (12.5m)
Range: 12 miles (19km)
Height 105ft (32m)

The Boca Grande Rear Range Light was built on Gasparilla Island in 1932 and was partnered by the Gasparilla Island lighthouse positioned a mile away at Port Boca Grande. The station is equipped with an aero-marine beacon.

Cape Canaveral Light

Cape Canaveral, FL
Built: 1848 and 1868
No: 625
Position: 28 27 37 N. 80 32 36 W
Focal plane: 137ft (42m)
Range: 24 miles (39km)
Height: 145ft (44m)

Cape Canaveral, as it was formerly known, is now best known for the Kennedy Space Center, but in the 19th century it was the treacherous shoals surrounding the cape that marked it out for special attention. A 65-ft (20-m) brick lighthouse was erected in 1848 to counter the problem, but its feeble light caused more harm than good, for crews often ran their ships aground looking for the signal. After the Civil War, the tower was replaced with the current 145-ft brick-lined, cast-iron lighthouse. Finished in 1868, it had a giant 'clamshell' first-order Fresnel lens and a range of 18 miles (29km). In 1893, sea erosion led to the lighthouse being moved a mile inland. The tower's Fresnel lens was replaced with an aero-marine beacon when the station was automated in 1993, and the original lantern is now on display at the Ponce Inlet Museum.

Cape Florida Light

Key Biscayne, FL
Built:1825
Style: Conical

The original 65-ft (20-m) Cape Florida lighthouse faced an unusual threat when it was attacked by a Seminole war party in 1836. Unable to flush out the keeper and his assistant, the warriors set fire to the tower. The assistant keeper was killed, but John Thompson, the keeper, who was badly burned, survived the attack by clinging to a ledge at the top of the tower until the arrival of a naval warship saved him. The tower survived, but because of the threat of further attacks, it stood empty for ten years. When the tower was brought back into operation in 1846, its height was raised to 95ft (29m). The station was decommissioned in 1878 and replaced by the Fowey Rocks lighthouse, but the old tower has remained standing and, after being refurbished, was relit during the 1996 Miami Centennial celebrations.

Cape San Blas Light

Apalachicola, FL
Built: 1847, 1856, 1859 and 1885
Style: Skeletal tower

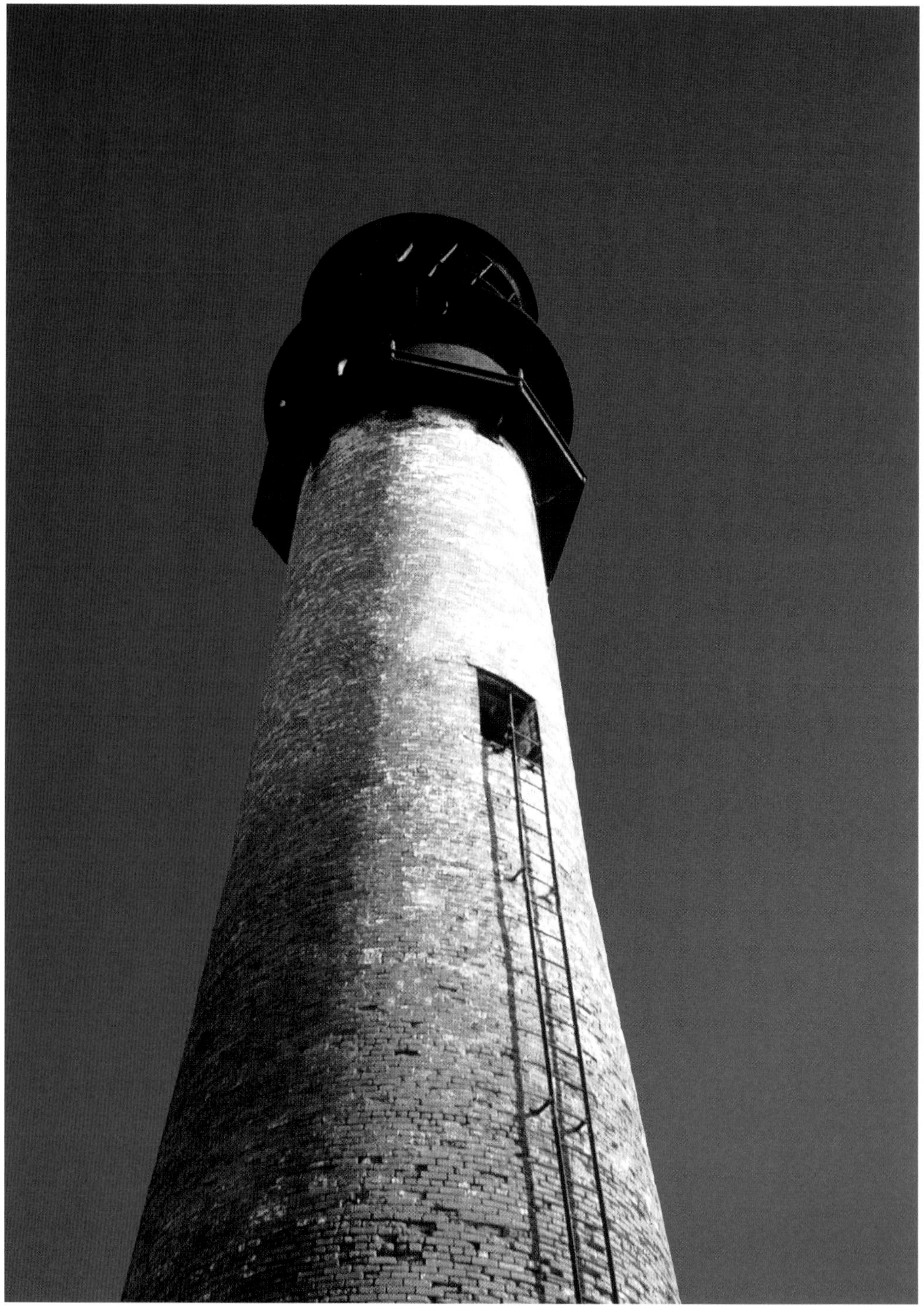

OPPOSITE
Cape St. George Light, Florida.

RIGHT
Egmont Key Light, Florida.

in 1852, represented a new approach to solving the problems of setting up towers on the sandy, wave-swept islands and submerged reefs around Florida. Standing on eight iron legs, each supported by a heavily secured screwpile, the tower was designed by I.W.P. Lewis, a nephew of Winslow Lewis. Built under the supervision of George Meade, the U.S. Army engineer and future victor of Gettysburg, the tower has successfully stood the test of time. The light's third-order Fresnel lens was replaced with a modern solar-powered optic when the station was automated in 1960.

Cedar Key Light

Seahorse Key, FL
Built: 1854
Style: Square, integrated tower

Cedar Key was built, like the towering Carysfort Reef Light two years earlier, by George Meade. This one, however, is only 28ft (8.5m) tall but, standing on a hill 75ft (23m) above the channel used by lumber ships collecting Cedar Key hardwood for making pencils, the tower's fourth-order Fresnel lens had a range of 15 miles (24km). Cedar Key's economy declined towards the end of the 19th century and in 1915 the station was decommissioned. Today the lighthouse serves as a marine laboratory managed by the University of Florida.

Dry Tortugas Light

Loggerhead Key, Dry Tortugas, FL
Built: 1858
Style: Conical tower
No: 1095
Position: 24 38 00 N. 82 55 12 W
Focal plane: 151ft (46m)
Range: 20 miles (32km)
Height: 151ft (46m)

The lower half of the lighthouse is white, the upper half black. It was built to supplement the weak light at Garden Key. Built for $35,000, its height, coupled with a second-order Fresnel lens, gave the beacon a range of 20 miles, which was more than enough to keep ships away from the shoals. The tower was severely damaged in 1873 by the same hurricane that destroyed Garden Key Light, but the repair work was so effective that the tower still stands today. The station was automated in 1925, and its original 'clamshell' Fresnel lens was replaced by a modern optic in 1986.

Egmont Key Light

St. Petersburg, FL
Built: 1848 and 1858
Style: White tower
No: 1370
Position: 27 36 03 N. 82 45 38 W
Focal plane: 85ft (26m)
Range: 24 miles (39km)
Height 87ft (26.5m)

The Egmont Key lighthouse on the Gulf Coast was the first of several towers built by Francis Gibbons to serve the Tampa Bay region. The original tower was built in 1848 but destroyed ten years later by a hurricane. The present 87-ft white masonry tower that replaced it has walls 3ft (1m) thick to prevent this from happening again. The original first-order Fresnel lens was replaced by an aero-marine beacon when the station was automated.

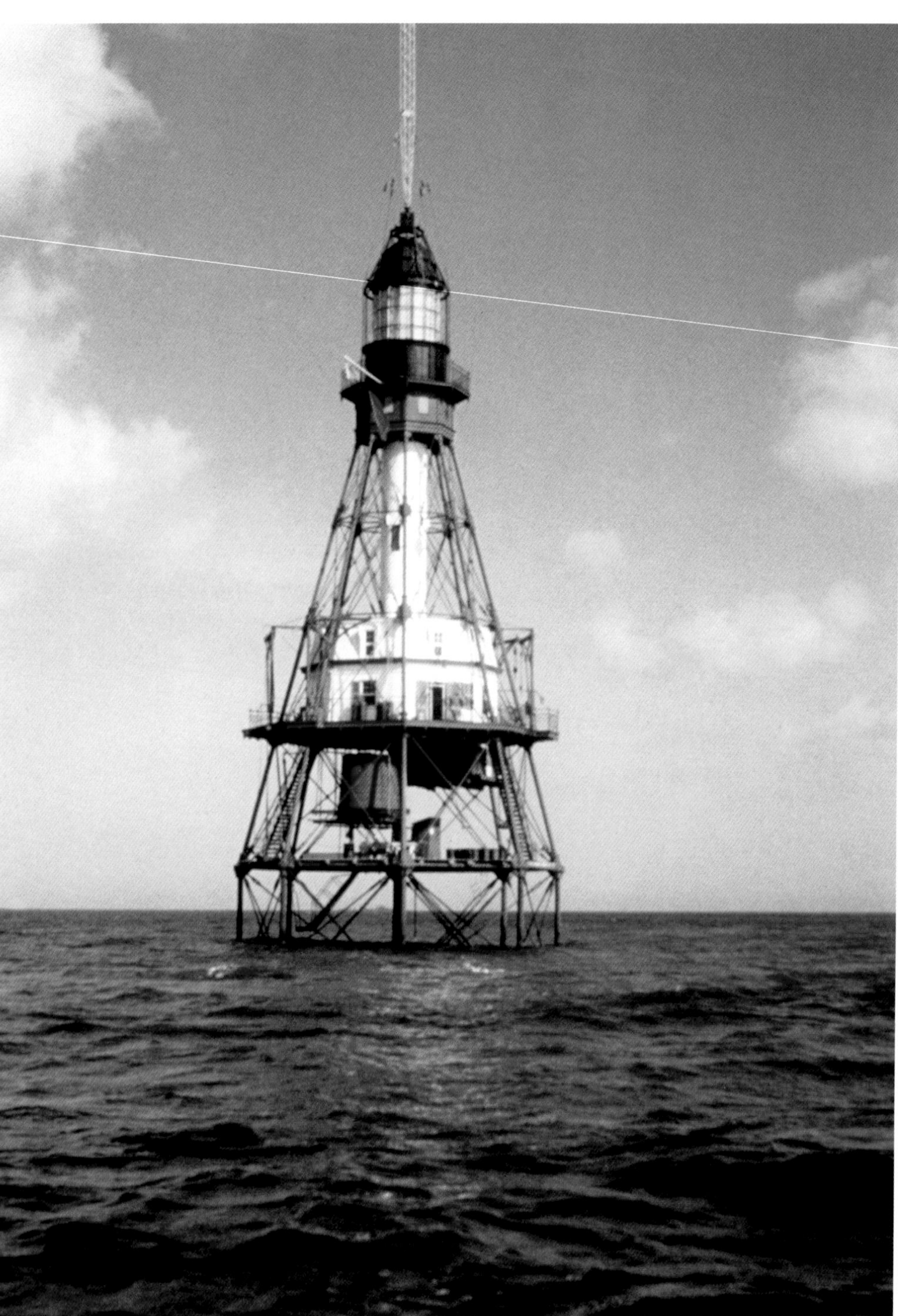

Fowey Rocks Light, Florida.

Fowey Rocks Light

Cape Florida, FL
Built:1878
Style: Octagonal pyramidal skeleton tower
No: 920
Position: 25 35 24 N. 80 05 48 W
Focal plane: 110ft (33.5m)
Range: W 15 miles/24km, R 10 miles/16km
Height 110ft (33.5m)

Established in 1878, the cast-iron lighthouse was built in 1878 to mark a shoal named after the British naval frigate HMS *Fowey*, which sank here in 1748. The skeletal construction allows the storms and hurricanes to pass through the structure without causing serious damage. The tower was automated in 1974, when its first-order Fresnel lens was replaced with an aero-marine beacon.

Garden Key Light

Fort Jefferson, Dry Tortugas, FL
Built: 1826 and 1876
Style: Conical

The original 70-ft (21-m) brick lighthouse at Garden Key was one of Florida's earliest light stations. Built in 1826, the lighthouse warned mariners of the reefs and low-lying islands that make up the Dry Tortugas archipelago. The need for a light here was reinforced when the ship carrying the building materials was wrecked on the very shoals the lighthouse was intended to guard. A few years after its construction, the tower gained a new neighbour in the form of Fort Jefferson, which was built to protect the vital sea lanes linking the Caribbean and the Atlantic with the Gulf of Mexico. By 1846 the fort had grown so large that the Garden Key Light was barely visible above the ramparts, so when the tower was severely damaged by a hurricane in 1873, its 37-ft (11-m) cast-iron replacement was built on top of the fort. The lighthouse was equipped with a fourth-order Fresnel lens giving the light a range of 16 miles (26km). The tower remains, but the light was decommissioned in 1912.

Gasparilla Rear Range Light

Gasparilla Island, FL
Built: 1932
Style: Hexagonal pyramidal skeleton tower
No: 1310
Position: 26 44 31 N. 82 15 48 W
Focal plane: 105ft (32m)
Range: W 12 miles/19km, R 10 miles/16km
Height 105ft (32m)

The steel-skeleton Gasparilla Rear Range Light was built in 1932. It partnered the Gasparilla Island lighthouse at Port Boca Grande to guide chemical freighters serving Florida's phosphate plants. It remains in service and is now equipped with an aero-marine beacon.

Hillsboro Inlet Light

Pompano Beach, FL
Built: 1907
Style: Octagonal iron skeleton tower
No: 775
Position: 26 15 33 N. 80 04 51 W
Focal plane: 136ft (41.5m)
Range: 28 miles (45km)
Height: 136ft (41.5m)

The cast-iron lighthouse, which stands over a navigable inlet near Pompano Beach, was erected in 1907. The tower was built in a Chicago foundry and first appeared at the St. Louis Exposition in 1904. The tower was then bought by the U.S. Government, dismantled, and moved to Florida, where its original first-order Fresnel lens continues to flash its signal 28 miles out to sea.

Jupiter Inlet Light

Jupiter, FL
Built: 1860
Style: Red brick tower
No: 725
Position: 26 56 55 N. 80 04 55 W
Focal plane: 146ft (44.5m)
Range: 25 miles (40km)
Height 125ft (38m)

The construction of the Jupiter Inlet lighthouse in 1860 was overseen by two army engineers who later met on opposing sides at Gettysburg. The site was surveyed by Robert E. Lee, while George Meade was responsible for its construction. The Civil War also affected the tower, for a year after its completion the light was extinguished by Confederate raiders. The tower remained dark until keeper James Armour found the tower's first-order Fresnel lens hidden in a creek a year later. This lens remains in use today. The tower has also taken its share of battering from the weather. In 1928, a hurricane knocked out both the primary and emergency electric power, which forced Charles Seabrook, the keeper, to resurrect the station's old mineral lamps. When the keeper became exhausted, his 16-year-old son took over the job of rotating the giant lens by hand and keeping the light burning.

Key West Light

Key West, FL
Built: 1825 and 1847
Style: Conical

Built in 1825 on Whitehead Point, the original 65-ft (20-m) lighthouse guided vessels in and out of Key West harbour. In 1846, the brick tower was toppled by the same storm that destroyed Sand Key Light. The tower was rebuilt a year later and has undergone a number of renovations since, including the addition of a third-order Fresnel lens in 1872 and the raising of the light by 20ft (6m) in 1892. The tower was decommissioned in 1969 but restored to service in 1972 as a private aid to navigation. The buildings now house a museum.

Mayport/St. Johns Light

Mayport, FL
Built: 1954
Style: Square tower on building
No 575
Position: 30 23 06 N. 81 23 54 W
Focal plane: 83ft (25m)
Range: 19 miles (30.5km)
Height: 64ft (19.5m)

Built in reinforced concrete in 1954, the St. Johns Light lacks the old-fashioned elegance of the nearby St. Johns River lighthouse. Instead of a traditional lantern room, the tower has a revolving aero-marine optic positioned on the tower's flat roof.

Pacific Reef Light

Florida Keys, FL
Built: 1921
Style: Skeleton tower on piles
No: 935
Position: 25 22 12 N. 80 08 30 W
Focal plane: 44ft (13.5m)
Range: 9 miles (14.5km)

Built in 1921, the black-painted Pacific Reef lighthouse is a skeletal tower designed to survive hurricanes in open water. The light was originally equipped with a fourth-order Fresnel lens but now holds a 300-mm optic.

Pensacola Light

Pensacola, FL
Built: 1824 and 1858
Style: Conical brick tower
No: 180
Position: 30 20 48 N. 87 18 30 W

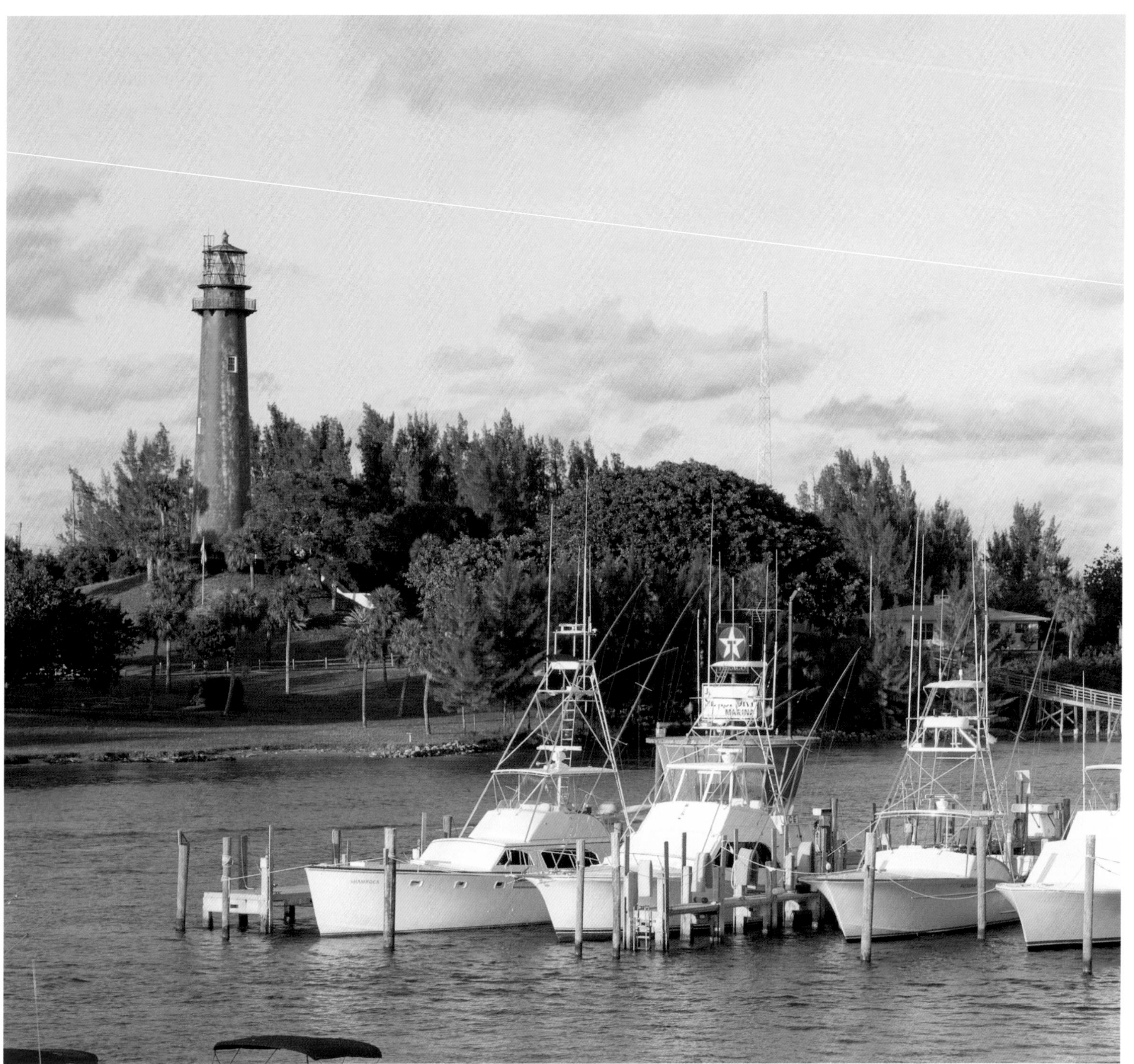

LEFT
Jupiter Inlet Light, Florida.

OPPOSITE
Pensacola Light, Florida.

Focal plane: 191ft (58m)
Range: 27 miles (43.5km)
Height: 171ft (52m)

The original 45-ft (14-m) Winslow Lewis-designed lighthouse was built in 1824 to guide warships in and out of the Pensacola naval base. When the United States acquired Florida from Spain in 1819, President James Monroe ordered the navy to flush out pirates operating in the Gulf of Mexico, and Pensacola proved to be the perfect place for a permanent base. The original lighthouse did not last long. Like so many other Winslow Lewis lighthouses, it was never considered adequate and was replaced in 1858 by the present 171-ft brick tower. Now automated, the tower's original first-order Fresnel lens still sheds its light 27 miles out to sea.

Ponce de Leon Inlet Light

Ponce Inlet, FL
Built: 1835 and 1887
Style: Red brick conical tower
No: 610
Position: 29 04 48 N. 80 55 42 W
Focal plane: 159ft (48.5m)
Range: 17 miles (27km)
Height: 159ft (48.5m)

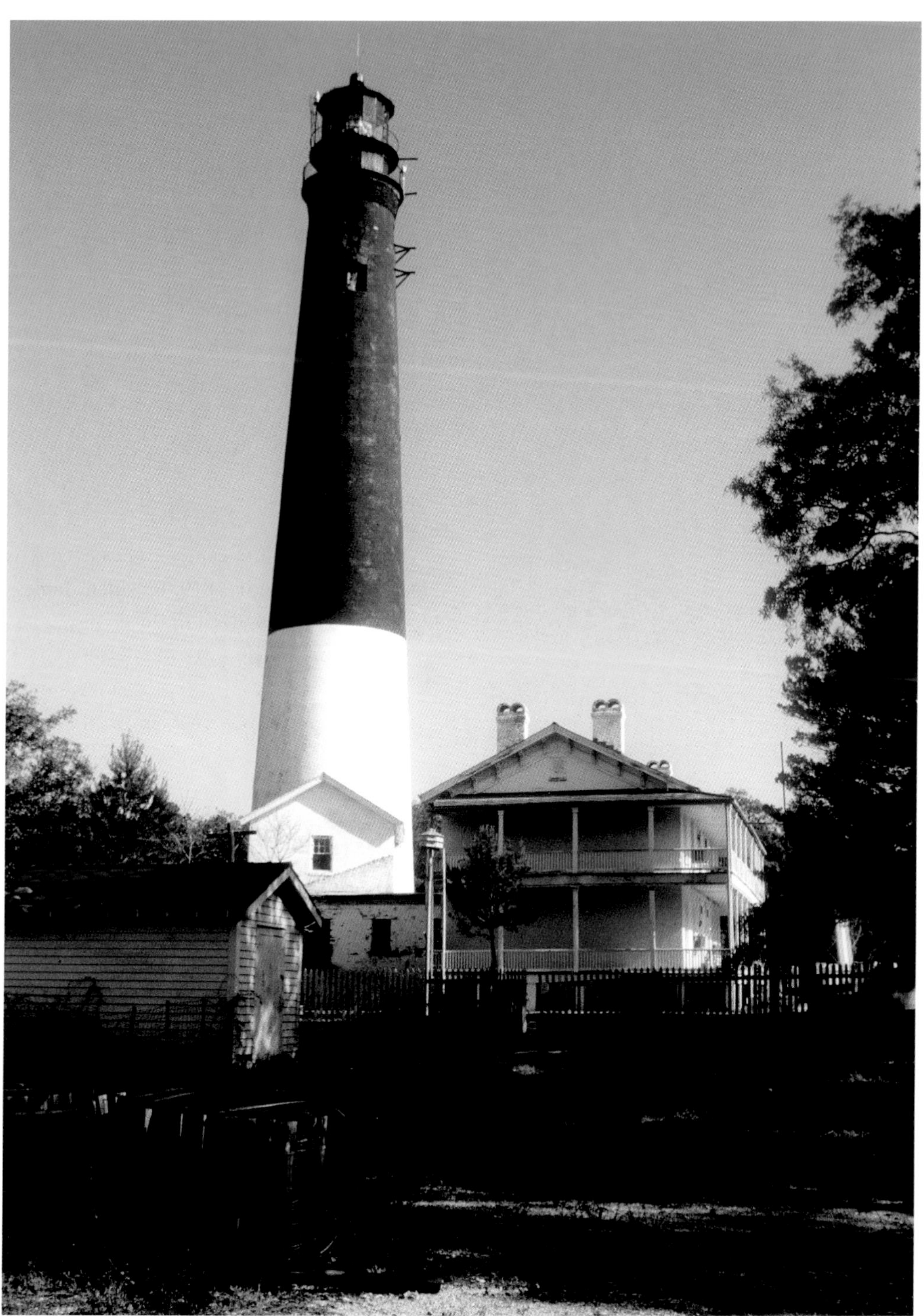

The first attempt to build a lighthouse at Ponce de Leon Inlet was made in 1835, but the tower collapsed during a storm before the light was even lit. Half a century passed before another attempt was made. The present 159-ft tower was built in 1887, with bricks shipped from Baltimore, and fitted with a first-order Fresnel lens. (The station's original five-wick kerosene lamp was designed by George Meade.) The Coast Guard decommissioned the light on economic grounds in 1970, replacing it with a simple steel tower erected at the Smyrna Dunes Coast Guard station, but neighbouring high-rise developments soon rendered this light ineffective. This led to Ponce de Leon lighthouse being recommissioned in 1983. The tower is now equipped with an aero-marine beacon and the station buildings are home to a lighthouse museum.

Port Boca Grande Light

Gasparilla Island, FL
Built: 1890
Style: Wooden tower on dwelling
No: 19965
Position: 26 43 02 N. 82 18 00 W
Focal plane: 41ft (12.5m)
Range: 12 miles (19km)

Port Boca Grande Light was built on Florida's Gulf Coast to guide vessels into Charlotte Harbor. The wooden tower and square keeper's house are set on screwpile foundations, and the tower was equipped with a three-and-a-half-order Fresnel lens. The station was decommissioned in 1967 and erosion later threatened to overwhelm the site. However, with assistance from the Gasparilla Island Conservation Association, the lighthouse is now linked by a jetty 265ft (81m) long, and was recommissioned in 1986.

Pulaski Shoal Light

NW of Key West, FL
Built: Between 1921 and 1935
Style: Hexagonal skeleton tower on piles
No: 1185
Position: 24 41 36 N. 82 46 24 W
Focal plane: 56ft (17m)
Range: 9 miles (14.5km)
Height: 50ft (15m)

The Pulaski Shoal Light, on the east side of the shoal, is one of several unmanned lights along the Keys. The sturdy skeleton tower is designed to survive hurricanes in open water by providing minimal resistance to wind and waves.

Sand Key Light

Key West, FL
Built: 1827 and 1853
Style: Square pyramidal skeleton tower
No: 1055
Position: 24 27 14 N. 81 52 39 W
Focal plane: 109ft (33m)
Range: 14 miles (22.5km)
Height: 11ft (3.5m)

The original Sand Key lighthouse was a brick-built tower dating back to 1827, and one of the first to light the Florida Keys. Its construction was no match for the fierce weather, and on 9 October 1846 a hurricane washed both the lighthouse and the island

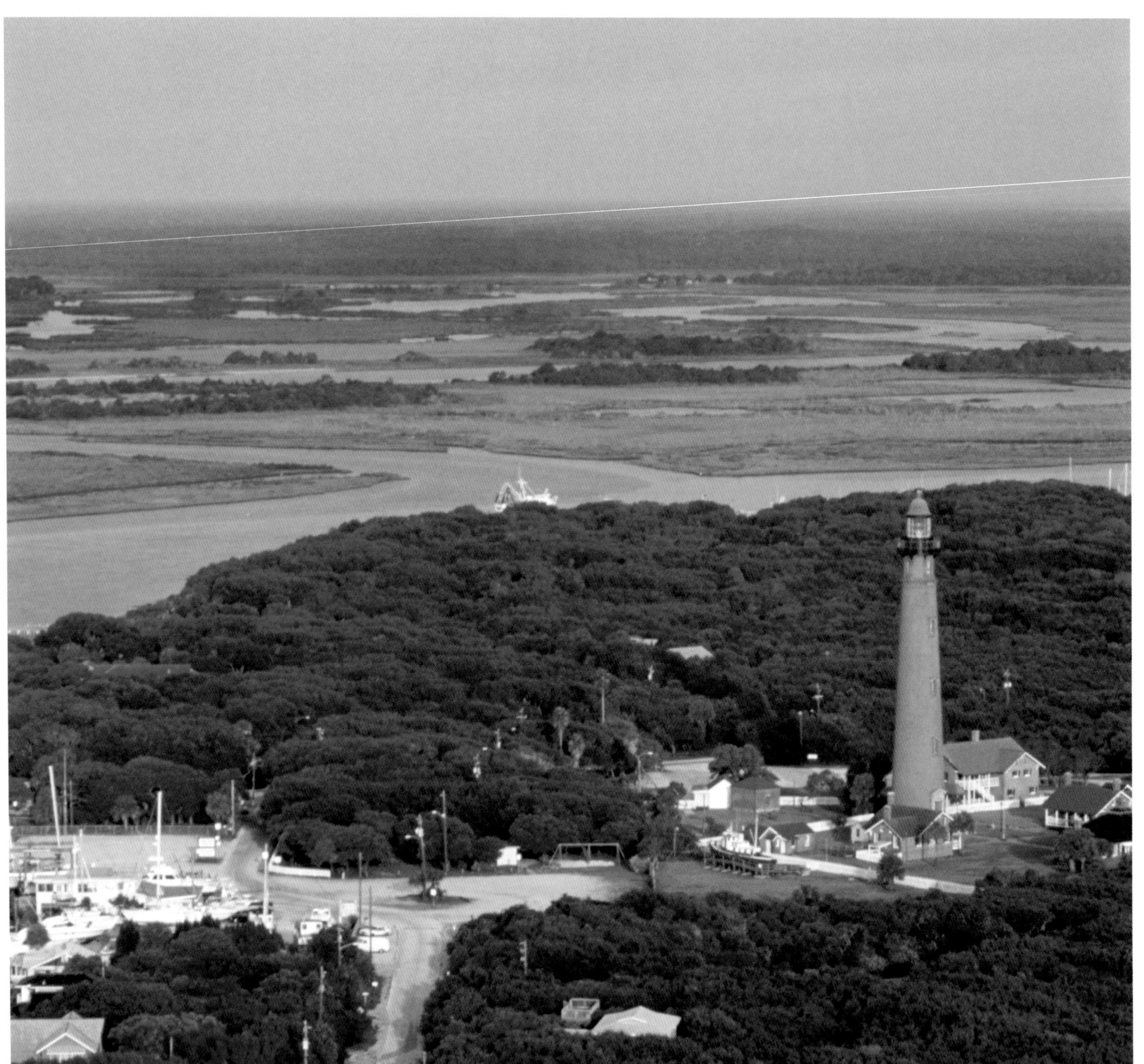

LEFT
Ponce de Leon Inlet Light, Florida.

OPPOSITE
Sand Key Light, Florida.

away, killing the keeper and visiting members of his family. A lightship took its place until a replacement tower was built in 1853. This was a more suitable iron-skeleton structure, standing 109ft high in open water. It was built by George Meade, who anchored the tower to steel pilings driven deep into the coral. The lantern room used to hold a first-order Fresnel lens, but this was removed when the station was automated in 1941. The tower was badly damaged by fire in 1989, but has since undergone a $500,000 restoration programme.

Sanibel Island Light

Sanibel Island, FL
Built: 1884
Style: Square pyramidal skeleton tower
No: 1245
Position: 26 27 11 N. 82 00 51 W
Focal plane: 98ft (30m)
Range: 13 miles (21km)
Height: 100ft (30.5m)

The Sanibel Island Light was built in 1884 to guide ships past the dangerous shoals at the entrance to the port of Punta Rassa. Its iron-skeleton design allows storm-driven winds to pass harmlessly straight through. In 1883 the ship carrying the prefabricated tower struck these shoals and sank. Fortunately, most of the materials were salvaged and the lighthouse was completed a year later. The skeletal design supports a central cylinder with 127 steps to the lantern room, which once housed a third-order Fresnel lens. The light is now produced by a modern plastic optic. The tower is accompanied by keepers' cottages, which are built on piles to keep them above the flood tides brought by gales and hurricanes.

Sombrero Key Light

Marathon, FL
Built: 1858
Style: Octagonal pyramidal skeleton tower
No: 1000
Position: 24 37 36 N. 81 06 36 W
Focal plane: 142ft (43m)
Range: W 15 miles/24km, R 12 miles/19km
Height: 160ft (49m)

The skeletal Sombrero Key lighthouse stands on an island halfway between Key Largo and Key West and took four years to erect. Designed and built by George Meade, it was one of the first to utilize galvanized-steel construction. The tower, completed in 1858, cost $150,000, and the fact that it is still standing almost 150 years later shows it was well worth the cost. The tower was fitted originally with a first-order Fresnel lens, but this was replaced with a solar-powered optic when the station was automated in 1984.

St. Augustine Light

St. Augustine, FL
Built: 1824 and 1874
Style: Conical tower
No: 590
Position: 29 53 08 N. 81 17 19 W
Focal plane: 161ft (49m)
Range: F 19 miles/31km, Fl 24 miles/39km
Height: 165ft (50m)

The present 165-ft St. Augustine lighthouse was built in 1874 and towers over Anastasia Island. The brick tower, with its distinctive black-and-white barber's-pole stripes, was built to replace the previous lighthouse, which had collapsed into the sea earlier that year. This was the 73-ft (22-m) brick tower of 1824 which, though it suffered during the Civil War, had stood for almost 50 years. That in turn had replaced a Spanish stone watchtower, which first guided ships into St. Augustine. The present tower still has its original first-order Fresnel lens, despite damage to some of the prisms caused by rifle fire in 1986. Replacements were no longer available, so an industrial digitizing process was used to scan the elements that had not been damaged in order to create exact duplicates. The lighthouse is now maintained as a private aid to navigation and houses a museum.

St. Johns River Light

Mayport, FL
Built: 1830, 1835 and 1859
Style: Conical

The St. Johns River has been marked by navigational lights since the first lighthouse was built in 1830. This lasted for just five years before sea erosion led to its downfall. Its replacement suffered the opposite problem as sand dunes piled up to a point where they blocked the signal. The third, a 66-ft (20-m) brick-built tower, was raised in 1859 and its third-order Fresnel lens shone until 1864, when Confederate forces shot out the light. The tower was relit after the Civil War and an extra 15ft (4.5m) was added to its height in 1887. It remained active until 1929, when a lightship was brought in to replace the light at the mouth of the river. A naval air station has since been built up around the tower, the first 20ft (6m) of which has been encased in a runway extension.

St. Marks Light

St. Marks, FL
Built: 1831, 1831, 1840 and 1867
Style: White conical tower
No: 10
Position: 30 04 18 N. 84 10 48 W
Focal plane: 82ft (25m)
Range: 8 miles (13km)
Height: 73ft (22m)
The first lighthouse at St. Marks on the Gulf Coast was established in 1831 but was so

RIGHT
St. Augustine Light, Florida.

OPPOSITE
Sombrero Key Light, Florida.

badly constructed that it had to be demolished almost immediately. Its replacement lasted only until 1840, and the third tower was destroyed by gunpowder charges set off by Confederate troops. The present 73-ft lighthouse dates from 1867 and stands on foundations 12ft (3.5m) deep. Although automated, the tower still retains its original fifth-order Fresnel lens.

Tennessee Reef Light

Long Key, FL
Built: 1933
Style: Hexagonal skeleton tower on piles
No: 990
Position: 24 44 48 N. 80 46 54 W
Focal plane: 49ft (15m)
Range: 8 miles (13km)

Tennessee Reef lighthouse, on the west side of the shoal, is one of several unmanned lights established around the Keys during the 1930s. The skeletal tower held a fourth-order Fresnel lens but is now equipped with a 300-mm optic.

GEORGIA

Cockspur Island Light

Savannah, GA
Built: 1849
Style: Conical

The 36-ft (11-m) Cockspur Island lighthouse is the sole survivor of a pair of lights built in 1849 to mark the north and south channels of the Savannah River. The tower survived the crossfire that destroyed its twin during the Civil War, but is now threatened by

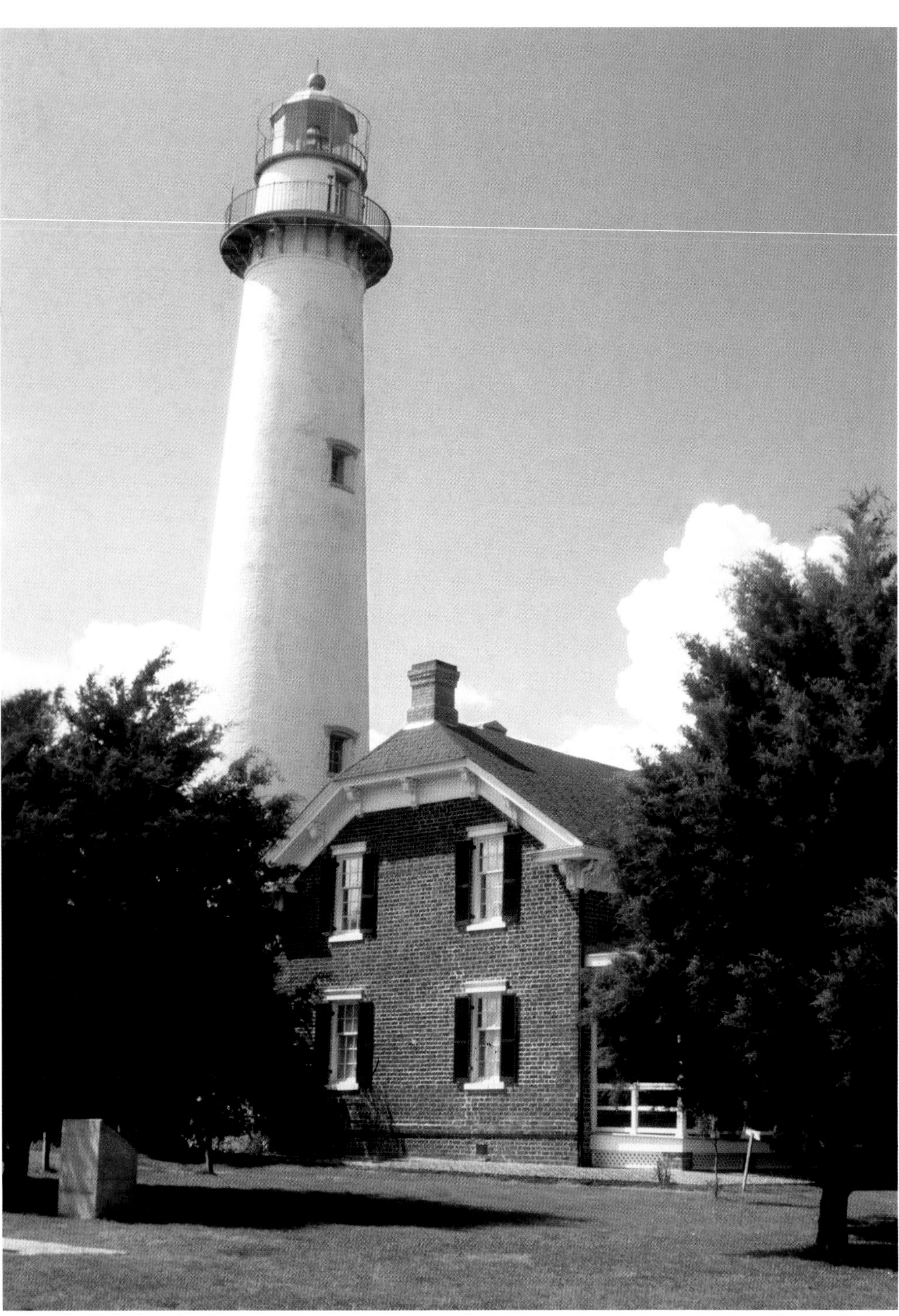

rising waters. The tower, which held a fourth-order Fresnel lens, was decommissioned in 1949 but has since been restored by the National Park Service.

Little Cumberland Island Light

Brunswick, GA
Built: 1820 and 1838
Style: Conical brick tower, cast-iron lantern

The present 60-ft (18-m) Little Cumberland Island lighthouse was built in 1838. It replaced an earlier 50-ft (15-m) tower built by Winslow Lewis, which was dismantled brick by brick and transported to Amelia Island in Florida, where it still stands. The present tower had a third-order Fresnel lens to guide vessels round a narrow spit that extends north of Little Cumberland Island, but was decommissioned in 1915 and is now the subject of a restoration programme.

Sapelo Island Light

Darien, GA
Built: 1820
Style: Conical

The red-and-white banded 70-ft (21-m) brick tower has been standing on what is now the Sapelo Island Estuarine Reserve since 1820. The tower was given a fourth-order Fresnel lens in 1853 but was decommissioned in 1899. The tower has since been restored and now serves as a private aid to navigation.

Savannah Light

Savannah River, GA
Built: 1922 and 1964
Style: Skeletal Texas tower
No: 31690
Position: 18 20 24 N. 65 05 00 W
Focal plane: 300ft (91m)
Range: 7 miles (11km)

The first Savannah lighthouse was built in 1922 to mark the entrance to the river. This was replaced by an automated steel skeletal Texas tower in 1964.

St. Simons Island Light

St. Simons Island, GA
Built: 1810 and 1872
Style: White conical tower near brick house
No: 520
Position: 31 08 00 N. 81 23 36 W
Focal plane: 104ft (32m)
Range: F 18 miles/29km, Fl 23 miles/37km
Height 104ft (32m)

The present 104-ft St. Simons Island lighthouse was completed in 1872 to replace an earlier 75-ft (23-m) tower dating back to 1810, which was destroyed by retreating Confederate troops in 1862. The white conical tower retains its original third-order Fresnel lens and, according to legend, the ghost of a former keeper, killed in a duel with his assistant, still walks the tower steps at night.

LEFT
St. Simons Island Light, Georgia.

OPPOSITE
Sapelo Island Light, Georgia.

Tybee Island Light
Tybee Island, GA
Built: 1791, 1857 and 1867
Style: Octagonal

The distinctive 154-ft (47-m) black-and-white Tybee Island lighthouse was built in 1867 and still has its original first-order Fresnel lens. It replaced earlier towers that have marked the narrow shallows at Tybee Island in the Savannah River, the first of which was erected in 1791. All succumbed to the ravages of weather, fire and the Civil War. The present tower was restored during the 1990s.

Louisiana

Chandeleur Island Light
Chandeleur Island, LA
Built: 1848, 1856 and 1896
Style: Skeleton tower
No: 350
Position: 30 02 48 N. 88 52 42 W
Focal plane: 65ft (20m)
Range: 9 miles (14.5km)
Height 102ft (31m)

Built in 1848, the original 55-ft (17-m) brick tower at Chandeleur Island was established to help vessels benefit from the anchorage in Chandeleur Sound. The first tower was lost in 1852, when its sand-and-shell sea break failed to protect it from a hurricane. Its 50-ft (15-m) replacement used a fourth-order Fresnel lens to mark the dangerous spreading shoals of Chandeleur Sound. This tower stood for 40 years before succumbing to a storm in 1893. The present tower, built

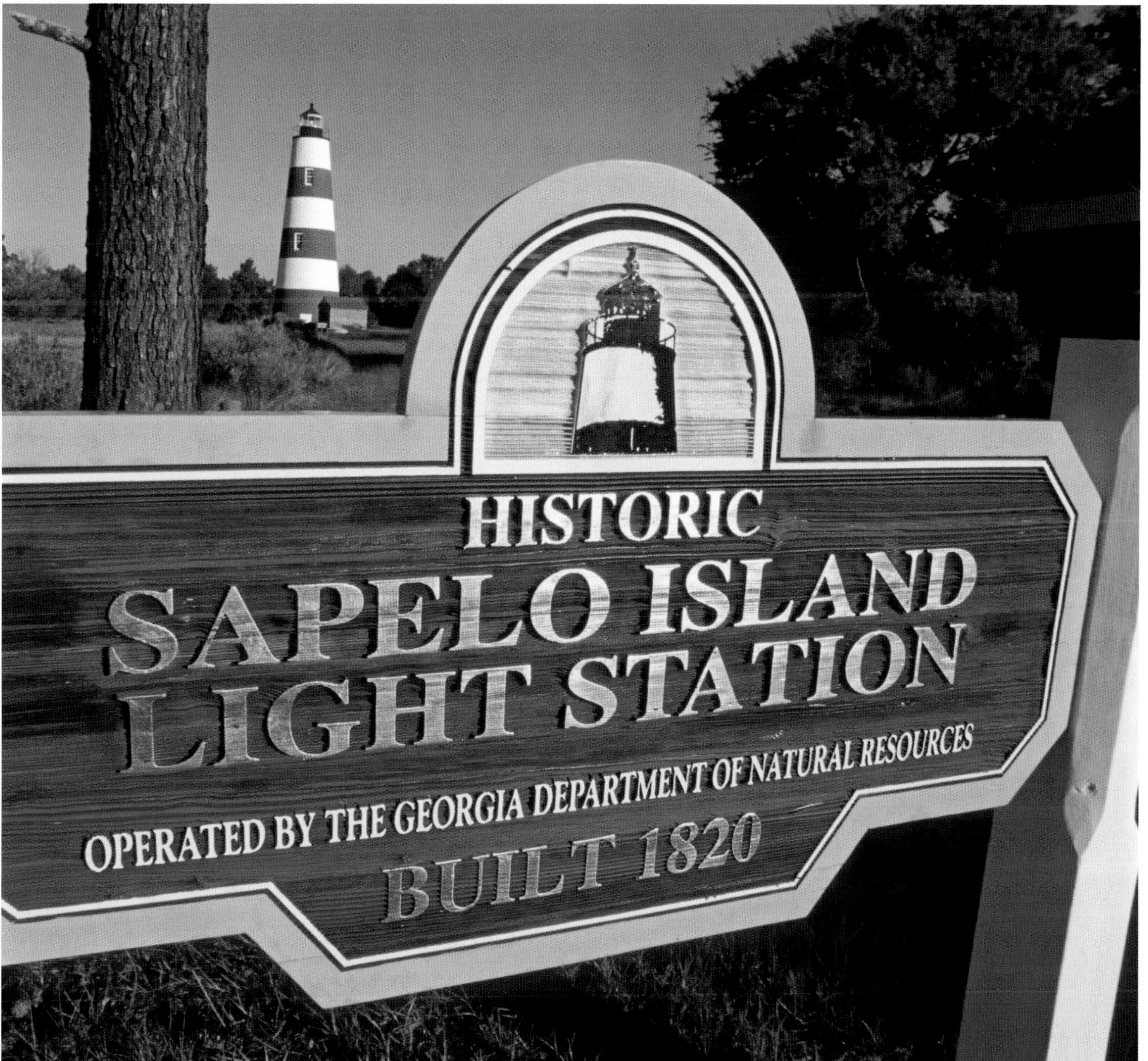
HISTORIC
SAPELO ISLAND
LIGHT STATION
OPERATED BY THE GEORGIA DEPARTMENT OF NATURAL RESOURCES
BUILT 1820

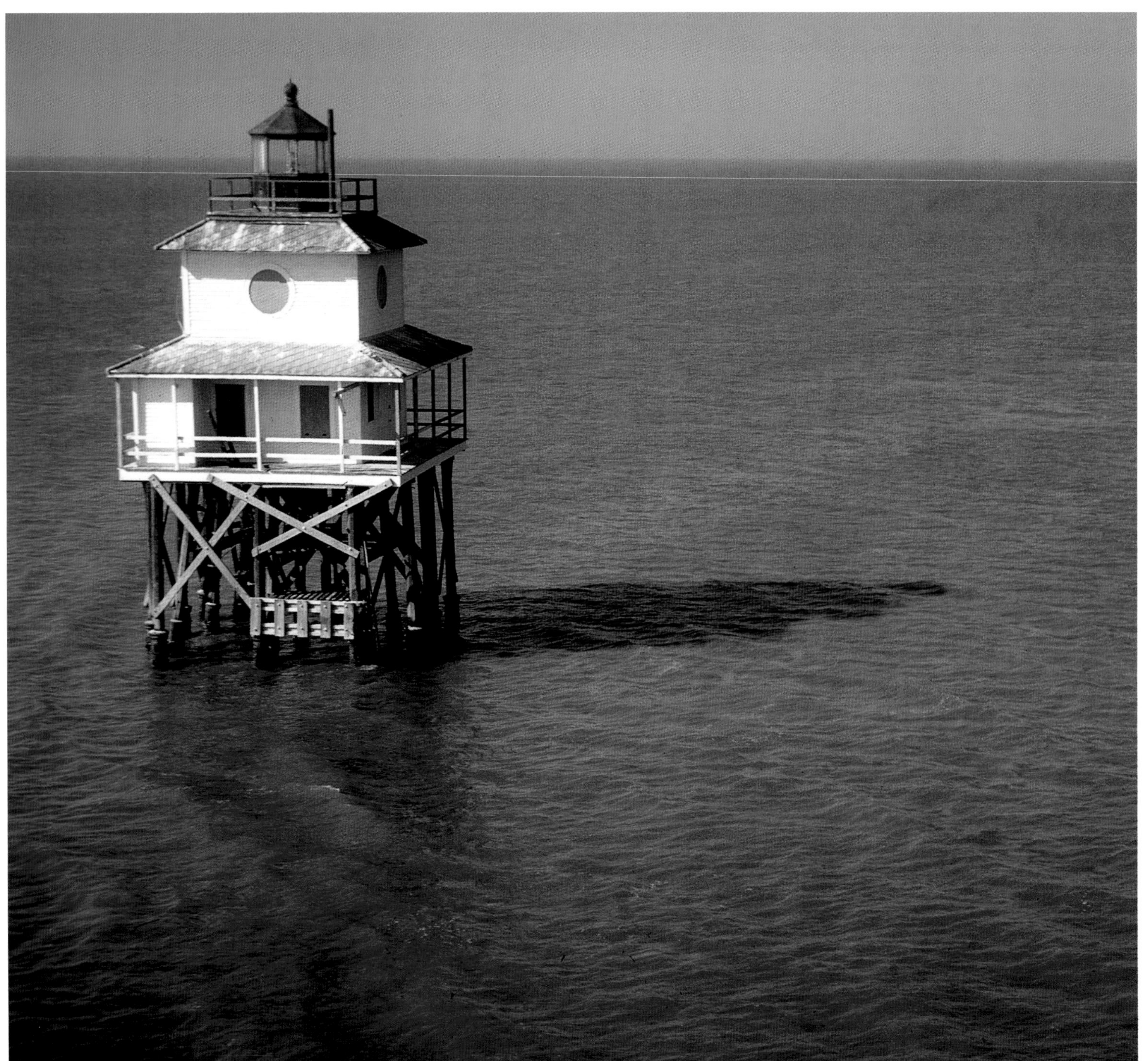

Oyster Bay Light, Louisiana.

in 1896, is a 102-ft skeleton structure which allows the storm-force winds and the waves to pass through it without causing damage. The tower's third-order 'clamshell' Fresnel lens was replaced with a a modern optic when the station was automated.

Franks Island Light

Mississippi River, LA
Built: 1818 and 1820
Style: Conical

The first Franks Island lighthouse was built in 1818 to mark the entrance to the Mississippi River. Designed by Benjamin Latrobe, one of the architects of the Capitol building in Washington, the unusual marble and granite tower proved too heavy, sank into the mud, and collapsed soon after it was built. Its 82-ft (25-m) replacement was built by Winslow Lewis in 1820 but, although the tower still stands, the ever-changing shape of the Mississippi delta meant that by 1856 it was no longer useful for navigation and was therefore decommissioned. Since then the tower has apparently grown shorter, having sunk 20ft (6m) into the Mississippi mud.

New Canal Light

New Orleans, LA
Built: 1838 and 1890
Style: Square tower on square dwelling
No: 9990
Position: 30 01 37 N. 90 06 48 W

Focal plane: 52ft (16m)
Range: 15 miles (24km)

The first New Canal Light was erected in 1838 to guide lake traffic into a never-completed canal that was to connect the Mississippi River wharves in New Orleans with Lake Pontchartrain. The present lighthouse, standing on the roof of its keeper's dwelling, was built in 1890. It used to stand 440yds (400m) offshore, but land reclamation projects have since filled the area. Until recently the station was the local Coast Guard headquarters. It once had a fifth-order Fresnel lens, which was replaced with a modern optic when the light was automated.

Oyster Bay Light

Near Isle au Pitre, LA
Built: 1903
Style: Square

Oyster Bay Light was built in 1903 to mark the waterway, once used by oyster fishermen, connecting the eastern end of the Atchafalaya Bay with the Gulf of Mexico. The station, which consists of a square tower mounted on the roof of the keeper's dwelling, housed a fifth-order Fresnel lens until it was decommissioned in 1975.

Pass à l'Outre Light

Mississippi River Delta, LA
Built: 1854
Style: Conical
The 85-ft (26-m) cast-iron Pass à l'Outre Light first stood at Head of Passes before being dismantled and moved in 1854 to mark the navigable channel in the Louisiana delta. This waterway had silted up within three decades but the light remained in operation until the 1930s. The tower has since sunk 30ft (9m) into the Louisiana mud.

Pass Manchac Light

Ponchatoula, LA
Built: 1839, 1842, 1846, 1859 and 1867
Style: Cylindrical

The Pass Manchac Light was established in 1839 to guide vessels through the narrow passage that connects Lake Pontchartrain with the smaller Lake Maurepas. Since then there have been at least four towers, which have succumbed to storms, erosion, mud and war. The first lasted only three years, which is not surprising as the masons used only mud for mortar. The second tower fell to erosion in the 1840s, the third to mud, and the fourth to Union raiders during the Civil War. The current tower is a 40-ft (12-m) brick construction built on stone foundations, which served for 120 years. It was equipped with a fourth-order Fresnel lens, which was automated in 1952. The lighthouse was finally decommissioned in 1987.

Point au Fer Reef Light

Berwick, LA
Built: 1916
Style: Square
The 54-ft (16.5-m) Point au Fer Reef Light was built in 1916 to mark the entrance to a dredged channel through a treacherous reef near the entrance to the Atchafalaya River. The tower and its keeper's dwelling stand on iron pilings just off Point au Fer Reef. It was equipped with a fourth-order Fresnel lens until it was decommissioned in 1975.

Port Pontchartrain Light

New Orleans, LA
Built: 1832, 1839 and 1855
Style: Conical

The Port Pontchartrain lighthouse, located just north of New Orleans, once guided vessels between Lake Pontchartrain and the narrow passage leading to the Gulf of Mexico. The first tower, built in 1839, was a 28-ft (8.5-m) octagonal wooden structure which was replaced in 1855 by a 40-ft (12-m) masonry tower fitted with a fifth-order Fresnel lens. In 1903, Margaret Norvell, one of several women to have maintained this station, sheltered more than 200 local residents during a hurricane, while still keeping the light burning throughout the storm. It was finally decommissioned in 1929 and, owing to subsequent land reclamation projects, now stands more than a mile inshore.

Sabine Pass Light

Louisiana Point, LA
Built: 1856
Style: Cylindrical with fin supports

The amazing 'finned' lighthouse at Sabine Pass was designed in 1856 by army engineer Danville Leadbetter, who later served as a Confederate general. The idea behind the series of buttresses around the light was to spread its weight and prevent it from settling. The idea worked so well that 140 years later the tower still stands, though its third-order Fresnel lens was decommissioned in 1952 and it is now privately owned.

Ship Shoal Light

South of Grand Isle, LA
Built 1859
Style: Skeletal tower

The 120-ft (36.5-m) screwpile Ship Shoal lighthouse was built in 1859 and was manned for the next 70 years. During that time the tower earned a reputation as a place to avoid, for those who worked there all became inexplicably ill. The trouble was eventually traced to the lead-based paint used in the rainwater tanks. The tower's second-order Fresnel lens was automated in 1929 and the station was finally abandoned in 1972. It is now the subject of a restoration programme.

South Pass Light

Mississippi River Delta, LA
Built: 1832
Style: Skeleton tower
No: 430
Position: 29 00 54 N. 89 10 00 W
Focal plane: 108ft (33m)
Range: 14 miles (22.5km)

The 108-ft skeletal South Pass Light was built in 1832 in an effort to counter the effect of storms and harsh conditions on the existing wooden towers in the region. The

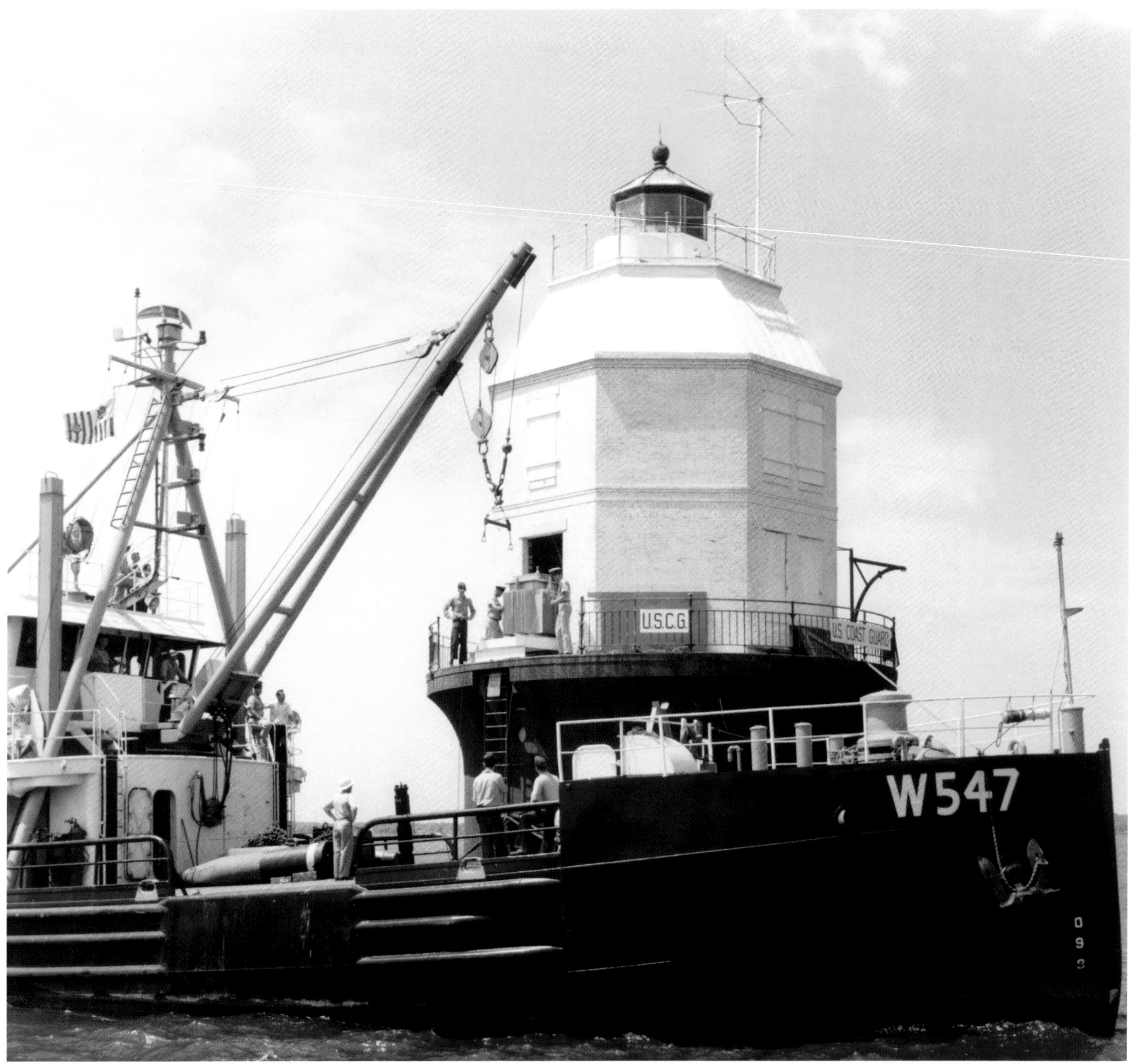

LEFT
Baltimore Light, Maryland.

OPPOSITE
Concord Point Light, Maryland.

light marks a key Mississippi River entrance to South Pass at the south-east end of the delta. The station's first-order Fresnel lens was replaced with a modern optic when the light was automated.

Southwest Pass Light

Mississippi River Delta, LA
Built:1832, 1838, 1873 and 1962
Style: Tower on dwelling on piles
No: 455
Position: 28 54 20 N. 89 25 43 W
Focal plane: 85ft (26m)
Range: 21 miles (34km)

The original Southwest Pass lighthouse was built by Winslow Lewis in 1832 to mark the Mississippi River entrance, but had a short existence. The tower was quickly undercut by erosion, sinking steadily from the moment it was built to a point where the keeper had to wade through chest-deep water to get to the steps. It was accordingly replaced in 1838. The second tower was little better and was replaced in 1873 with a 128-ft (39-m) iron skeletal tower, with a two-storey keeper's dwelling between its iron legs. It had a first-order Fresnel lens and served for 80 years until it was abandoned in 1953. The present lighthouse

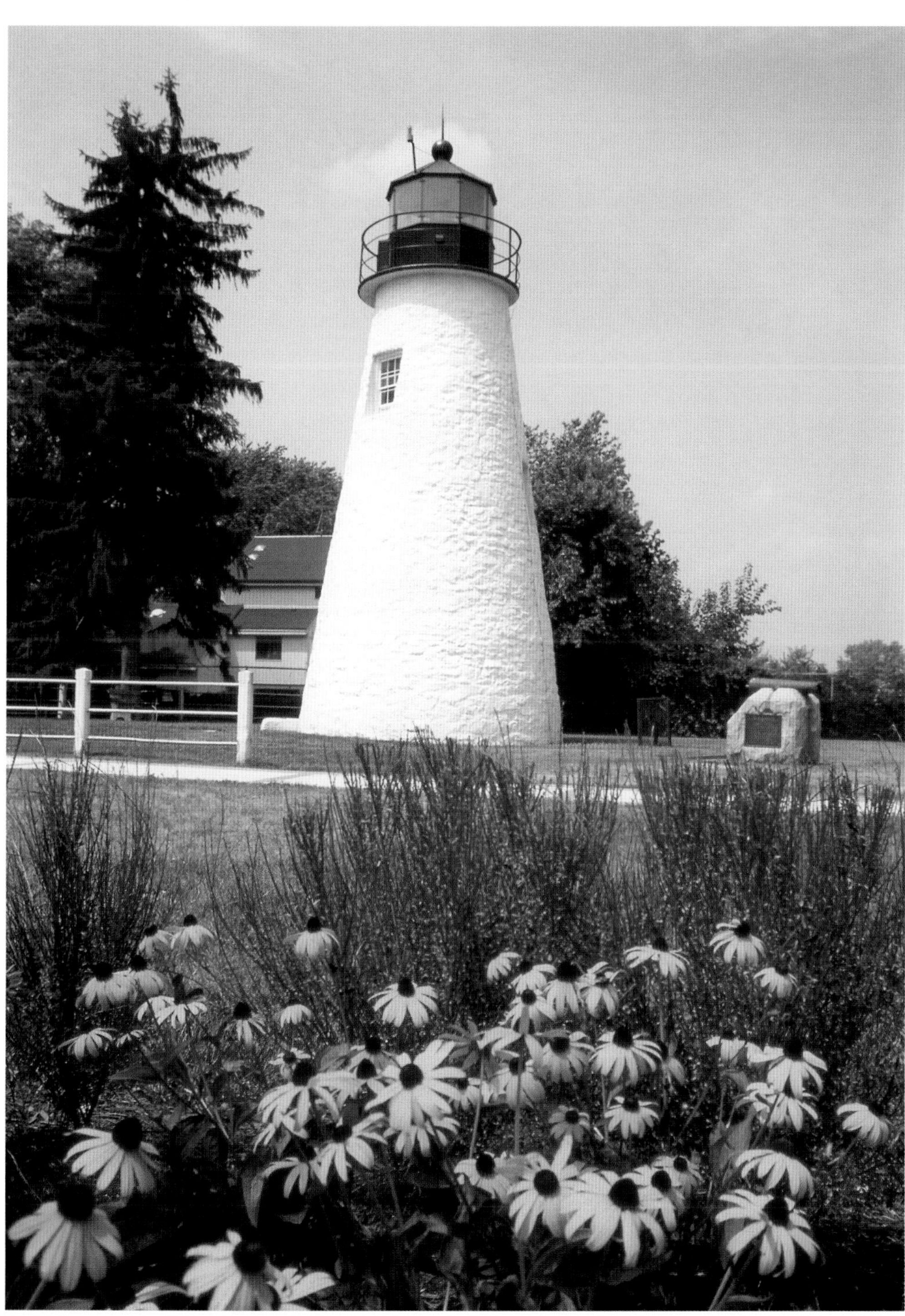

is a hexagonal concrete tower, built in 1962, with a focal plane of 85ft and an automatic beacon.

Tchefuncte River Light

Madisonville, LA
Built: 1837 and 1867
Style: White conical tower
Position: 30 22 43 N. 90 10 10 W
Focal plane: 49ft (15m)

The original Tchefuncte River Light was built in 1837 to guide vessels into the then-prosperous port of Madisonville. The tower was destroyed during the Civil War, and its replacement, built in 1867, acts as a rear range light. The original fifth-order Fresnel lens was replaced by a modern optic when the tower was automated.

West Rigolets Light

West Rigolets, LA
Built: 1855
Style: Cylinder on roof of dwelling

Built in 1855, the West Rigolets lighthouse was of strategic importance in marking a passage linking Louisiana's Lake Pontchartrain with the open waters of the Gulf of Mexico. The lantern sat atop a wooden keeper's dwelling mounted on piles to keep it above the floodtides. The station came under fire during the Civil War and, while the building survived, the keeper became the only employee in lighthouse service to be killed in the hostilities.
The tower was decommissioned after World War II.

Maryland

Baltimore Light

Baltimore, MD
Built:1908
Style: Octagonal on cylindrical base
No: 8035
Position: 39 03 30 N. 76 24 00 W
Focal plane: 52ft (16m)
Range: W 7 miles/11km, R 5 miles/8km
The two-and-a-half-storey brick-built Baltimore Light was completed in 1908 – the last true lighthouse to be erected on Chesapeake Bay – with a small lantern on its roof. For many years it held a fourth-order Fresnel lens, which was replaced with a modern, solar-powered optic when the station was automated.

Bloody Point Bar Light

Claiborne, MD
Built: 1882
Style: Tower on cylindrical foundation
No: 7750
Position: 38 50 02 N. 76 23 30 W
Focal plane: 54ft (16.5m)
Range: W 9 miles/15km, R 7 miles/11km

Bloody Point Bar lighthouse was built in 1882 in Upper Chesapeake Bay. The conical cast-iron structure, which stands on a concrete caisson, was automated in 1960 after a fire gutted the living quarters. Its original fourth-order Fresnel lens was then replaced with a modern solar-powered optic.

FAR LEFT
Craighill Channel Lower Range Front Light, Maryland.

LEFT
Craighill Channel Lower Range Rear Light, Maryland.

OPPOSITE LEFT
Craighill Channel Upper Range Front Light, Maryland.

OPPOSITE RIGHT
Craighill Channel Upper Range Rear Light, Maryland.

Chesapeake Lightship

Built: 1930
Builder: Charleston Dry Dock & Machine Co., SC
No: 116
Length overall: 133ft 3in (41m)
Beam: 30ft (9m)
Draft: 13ft (4m)
Illuminating apparatus: One 375-mm electric lens lantern at each masthead
Design: Diesel-electric-propelled; steel hull; two masts; smokestack amidships

The lightship *Chesapeake* was caught in the path of a hurricane in 1936, but amazingly survived with very little damage. She served in the Chesapeake Bay area for 40 years and, having been decommissioned in 1970, was placed on public display at Hams Point in Washington, D.C., and subsequently in Baltimore's inner harbour.

Station Assignments
1930–33: Fenwick Island Shoal (DE)
1933–42: Chesapeake Bay (VA)
1942–45: Examination vessel (wartime)
1945–65: Chesapeake Bay (VA)
1965–70: Delaware (DE)
1971–80: Displayed at Hams Point, Washington, D.C.
1982: Baltimore Harbor Place, Constellation Dock

Concord Point Light

Havre de Grace, MD
Built: 1827
Style: Conical
The 32-ft (10-m) stone lighthouse at Concord Point was constructed by John Donohoo in 1827 at a cost of $3,500. The tower was originally fitted with an array of

lamps and 16-in (41-cm) reflectors, but now uses a fifth-order Fresnel lens. In 1812 John O'Neil staged a successful one-man stand against a squadron of British warships and, as a reward, was named keeper of the lighthouse. The job passed down the generations until the tower was automated in the 1920s. The light is now maintained as a private aid to navigation.

Cove Point Light

Solomons, MD
Built: 1828
Style: White tower
No: 7630
Position: 38 23 11 N. 76 22 54 W
Focal plane: 45ft (14m)
Range: 12 miles (19km)
Height: 61ft (18.5m)

The brick-built Cove Point Light is one of the oldest on Chesapeake Bay. Erected in 1828 by lighthouse contractor John Donohoo to mark the entrance to the Patuxent River, the tower is considered to be his best work. It was fitted with a 19th-century fourth-order Fresnel lens in 1928, and is now under threat from erosion.

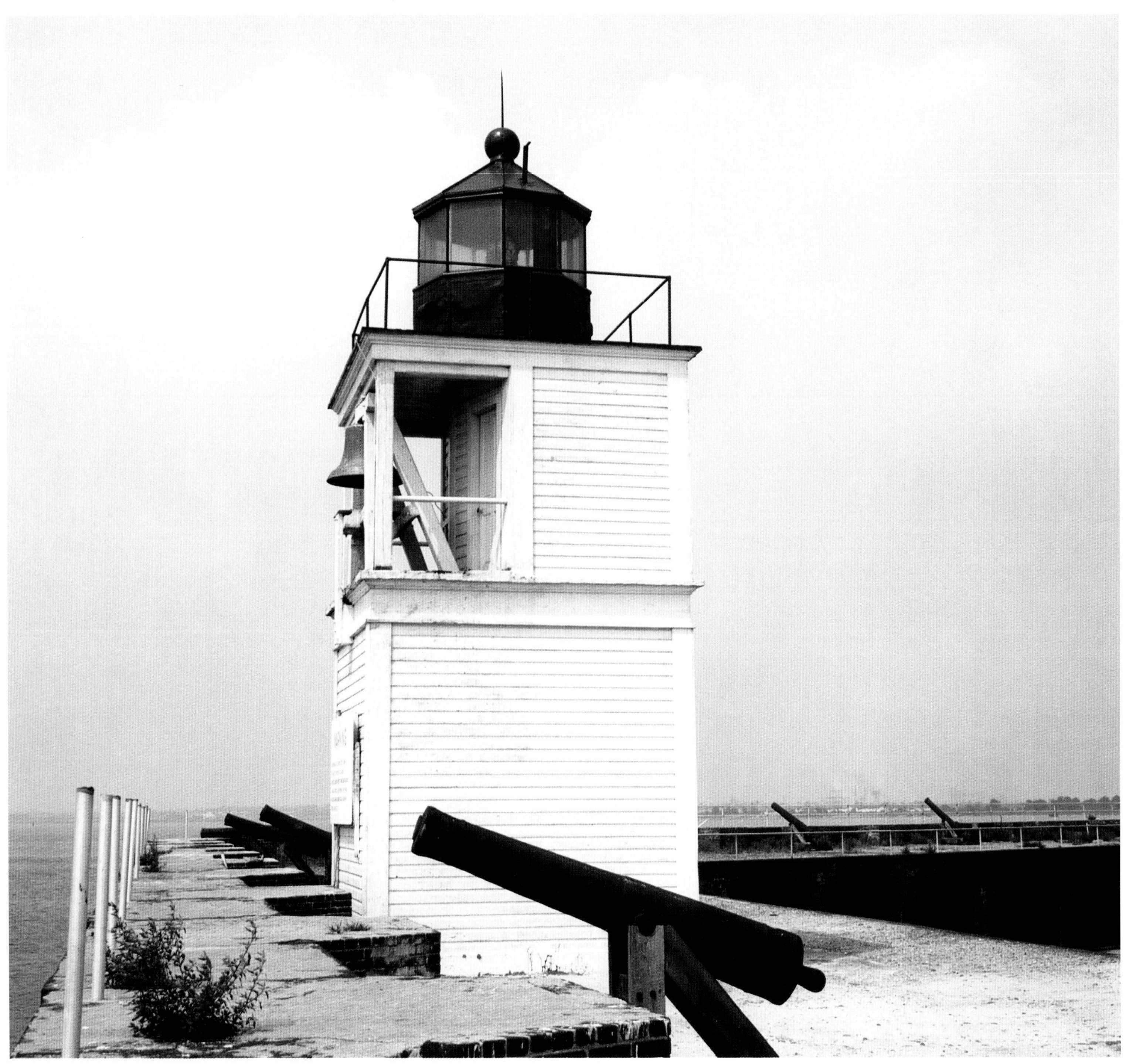

LEFT
Fort Carroll Light, Baltimore, Maryland.

OPPOSITE
Drum Point Light, Maryland.

Craighill Channel Lights

Baltimore, MD
Built: 1873 and 1886
Style: Skeleton, cylindrical and octagonal
No: 7995 (Entrance Range Front Light)
Position: 39 07 41 N. 76 16 08 W
Height: 24ft (7m)

The Craighill Channel Lights comprise two pairs of lights marking the vital channel linking Baltimore harbour with Chesapeake Bay. The Craighill Channel Lower Range Lights were established in 1873 and the Upper Range Lights followed in 1886.

Craighill Channel Lower Range Front Light

The Craighill Channel Lower Range Front Light was built in 1873 to keep vessels in the safe deep-water channel linking Baltimore with the Chesapeake River. The 35-ft (11-m) cast-iron tower stands on a caisson and was equipped with a fourth-order Fresnel lens which has since been replaced with a modern solar-powered optic.

Craighill Channel Lower Range Rear Light

The 105-ft (32-m) Craighill Channel Lower Range Rear Light is the tallest navigational aid on Chesapeake Bay. The original

keeper's quarters, at the base of the tower, were removed when the tower was automated, but it retains its fourth-order Fresnel lens. It works in tandem with the Craighill Channel Lower Range Front Light.

Craighill Channel Upper Range Front Light

The Craighill Channel Upper Range Light was built in 1886 to guide mariners through the channel linking Baltimore with the Chesapeake. The front light in the pair is a cast-iron tower, resembling a pillbox, which stands at only 25ft (8m) tall.

Craighill Channel Upper Range Rear Light

The cast-iron skeletal Craighill Channel Upper Range Rear Light stands 80ft (24m) high and operates in tandem with its front partner to help keep vessels in a safe deep-water channel.

Drum Point Light

Solomons, MD
Built: 1883
Style: Hexagonal screwpile

The lighthouse was built in 1883, at a cost of $5,000, to mark a sandy spit that threatened vessels passing Drum Point on the north side of the entrance to the Patuxent River. A fourth-order Fresnel lens served the lighthouse until it was decommissioned in 1962. When vandalism and neglect threatened its future in 1975, the tower was moved in one piece to the Calvert Marine Museum, where it now stands.

Fishing Battery Light

Havre de Grace, MD
Built: 1853
Style: Lantern on rectangular dwelling

Built in 1853, the two-storey lighthouse once marked the entrance to the Susquehanna River from its position on an island in the north of Chesapeake Bay. Automated in 1921, the tower is still standing, despite an entry in the public records that asserts that it was torn down at that time; however, it is in dire need of restoration.

Fort Carroll Light

Baltimore, MD
Built: 1865 and 1898
Style: Square

The original lighthouse was built in 1865 to alert vessels to the presence of the fort guarding the entrance to Baltimore harbour. The tower remained in place on top of the walls until 1898, when it was torn down to make way for a Spanish-American War gun emplacement. A replacement was then built 100ft (30.5-m) to the north and, fitted with a fifth-order Fresnel lens, continued in service until it was decommissioned in 1946.

Hooper Island Light

Hoopersville, MD
Built: 1902
Style: White conical tower on cylinder
No: 7590
Position: 38 15 24 N. 76 15 00 W
Focal plane: 63ft (19m)
Range: 9 miles (14.5km)

The 35-ft (11-m) cast-iron, spark-plug-style lighthouse stands on a massive cast-iron and concrete caisson. This was one of the last lighthouses built in Chesapeake Bay and, though still in operation, its fourth-order Fresnel lens has been replaced by a modern solar-powered optic.

Hooper Strait Light

St. Michaels, MD
Built: 1867 and 1879
Style: Hexagonal screwpile
The first Hooper Strait lighthouse was a small screwpile structure marking a crooked channel in Chesapeake Bay. Ten years after its completion, a massive ice floe knocked the lighthouse off its piles and swept it several miles down the bay. Although the building was wrecked, the station's Fresnel lens was saved. A larger, hexagonal, replacement tower was built in 1879 and served for three-quarters of a century before being decommissioned in 1954. In 1966, the building was saved from demolition by the Chesapeake Bay Maritime Museum in St. Michaels, where it is now to be seen.

Lazaretto Point Light

Baltimore, MD
Built: 1831
Style: Conical

The light was first established in 1831 to mark the entrance to Baltimore harbour. Built by John Donohoo, the 30-ft (9-m)

Hooper Strait Light, Maryland.

tower was originally equipped with oil lamps and early reflectors, which were replaced by a fourth-order Fresnel lens in 1858. The tower was removed in 1926 and replaced by a steel skeletal tower nearby. The present Lazaretto Point Light is a replica of the original and was erected as a memorial.

Piney Point Light

Piney Point, MD
Built: 1836
Style: Conical

During its 130 years of service the 30-ft (9-m) brick Piney Point Light was visited by four U.S. Presidents – James Monroe, Millard Fillmore, Franklin Pierce and Theodore Roosevelt. The tower's fourth-order beacon served until 1964 when the lighthouse was decommissioned. The tower is now a tourist attraction within the Piney Point Park.

Point Lookout Light

Scotland, MD
Built: 1830 and 1883
Style: Octagonal

The first lighthouse was built in 1830 to mark the entrance to the Potomac River. It was replaced in 1883 by an octagonal iron tower perched on the roof of a two-storey keeper's dwelling and fitted with a fourth-

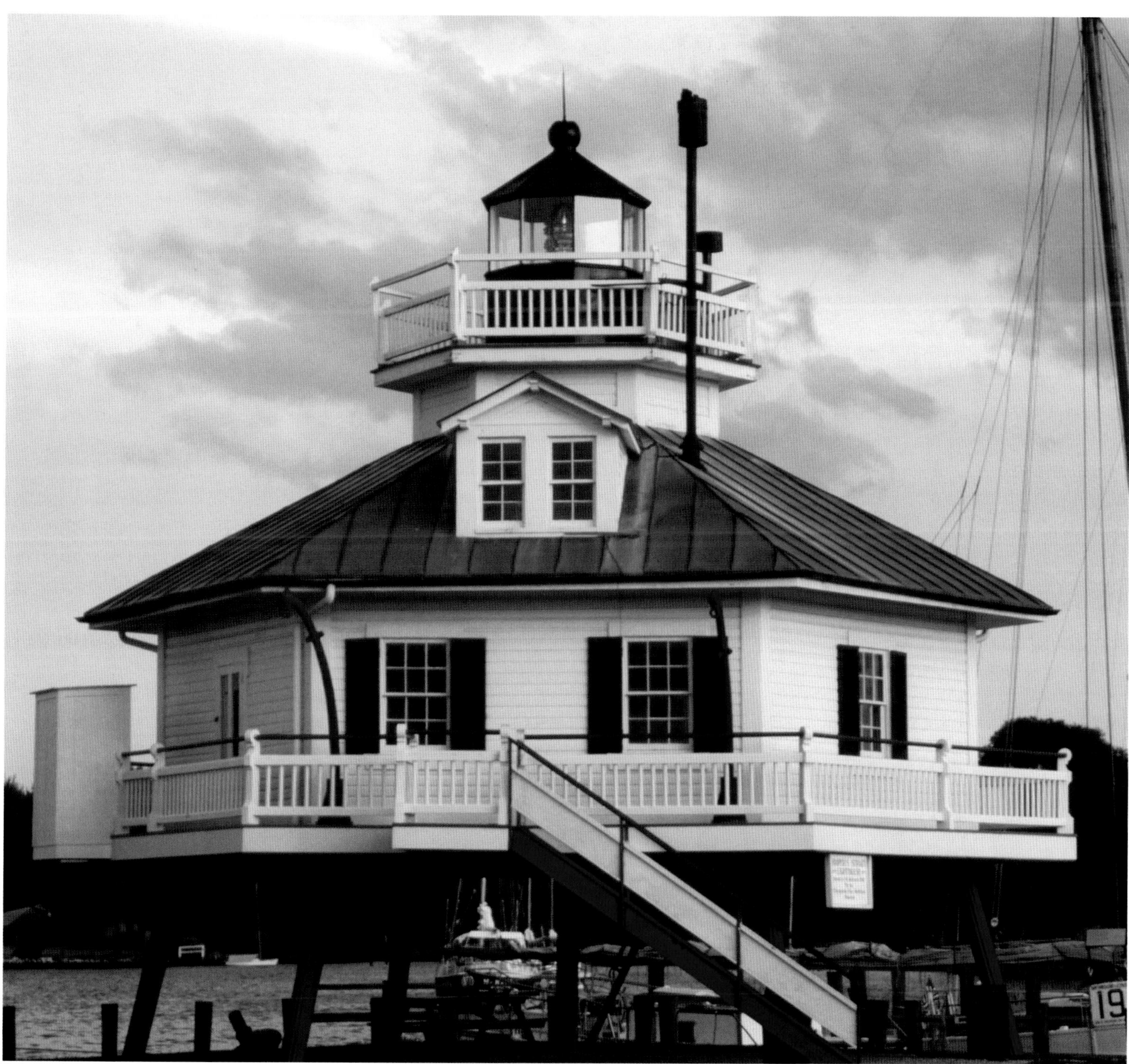

order Fresnel lens. The station was decommissioned in 1965 and replaced by an offshore light buoy. The building is now the subject of a restoration programme.

Point No Point Light

Dameron, MD
Built: 1905
Style: Octagonal
No: 7560
Position: 38 07 42 N. 76 17 24 W
Focal plane: 52ft (16m)
Range: 9 miles (14.5km)

The two-and-a-half-storey brick structure of the curiously named lighthouse (there is another on the West Coast) marks the entrance to the Potomac River, the navigational gateway to Washington, D.C. The lighthouse, which stands on a cast-iron and concrete open-water caisson, was completed in 1905. Its original fourth-order Fresnel lens was replaced with a solar-powered beacon when the station was automated in 1962.

Pooles Island Light

Aberdeen, MD
Built: 1825
Style: Conical

The 40-ft (12-m) lighthouse was built to guide vessels on Chesapeake Bay. The conical tower was fitted with oil lamps, which were replaced later by a fourth-order Fresnel lens. The lighthouse was deactivated in 1939 but remains standing despite being situated in the middle of a bombing range.

Sandy Point Shoal Light

Skidmore, MD
Built: 1853 and 1883
Style: Brick on cylindrical foundation
No: 7990
Position: 39 00 57 N. 76 23 04 W
Focal plane: 51ft (15.5m)
Range: 9 miles (14.5km)

The 50-ft (15-m) lighthouse was built in 1883 and looks remarkably like a 19th-century townhouse stuck on a caisson. The station marks a dangerous shoal near the Chesapeake Bay Bridge and replaced a previous, less effective, onshore tower built in 1853.

Seven Foot Knoll Light

Baltimore, MD
Built: 1855
Style: Cylindrical

The Seven Foot Knoll Light was built in 1855 to warn mariners away from a dangerous shoal near the entrance to Baltimore harbour. Standing on eight iron piles and resembling a large, round, red cheese, the tower was one of the first of its type. The lantern room on the flat roof of the keeper's dwelling housed a fourth-order Fresnel lens. When the station was abandoned after 130 years of service, it was moved to the city of Baltimore, and the 200-ton structure is now a tourist attraction within the Inner Harbor district.

Sharps Island Light

Cambridge, MD

OPPOSITE
Thomas Point Shoal Light, Maryland.

RIGHT
Biloxi Light, Mississippi.

Built: 1838, 1866 and 1882
Style: Conical

The present lighthouse, built in 1882, is nicknamed 'The leaning tower of the Chesapeake' for its 20° tilt, caused by the constant pressure of ice during the winter months. During the 1990s, the Coast Guard had plans to demolish the tower but public protests have saved it so far.

Solomons Lump Light

Near Crisfield, MD
Built: 1875 and 1895
Style: Octagonal on cylindrical base
No: 23475
Position: 38 02 54 N. 76 00 54 W
Focal plane: 47ft (14m)
Range: W 8 miles/13km, R 6 miles/10km

A lighthouse was built in 1895 to replace an earlier screwpile type erected in 1875 to mark a shoal south of Tangier Sound, near Crisfield in Chesapeake Bay. The dwelling was demolished in 1950 when the tower was automated.

Thomas Point Shoal Light

Annapolis, MD
Built: 1825, 1838 and 1875
Style: Hexagonal tower on piles
No: 7760
Position: 38 53 56 N. 76 26 09 W
Focal plane: 43ft (13m)
Range: W 16 miles/26km, R 11 miles/18km

The present screwpile lighthouse was built in 1875 to replace two earlier onshore lighthouses built in 1825 and 1838, which were too far away from the hazardous shoals to be fully effective. The small hexagonal tower is one of the few screwpile structures that remain from that era.

Turkey Point Light

Elk Neck, MD
Built: 1833
Style: Conical

The 38-ft (11.5-m) Turkey Point lighthouse was built in 1833 by John Donohoo. The station's fourth-order Fresnel lens served until the start of the 21st century when the lighthouse, made famous by its female keeper, Fanny Salter, was finally decommissioned. Mrs. Salter was appointed by President Calvin Coolidge in 1925, following the death of her husband, who had been the previous keeper, and became the last female keeper in the old Lighthouse Service.

MISSISSIPPI

Biloxi Light

Biloxi, MS
Built: 1848
Style: Conical tower
No: 7785
Position: 30 23 42 N. 88 54 06 W
Focal plane: 61ft (18.5m)

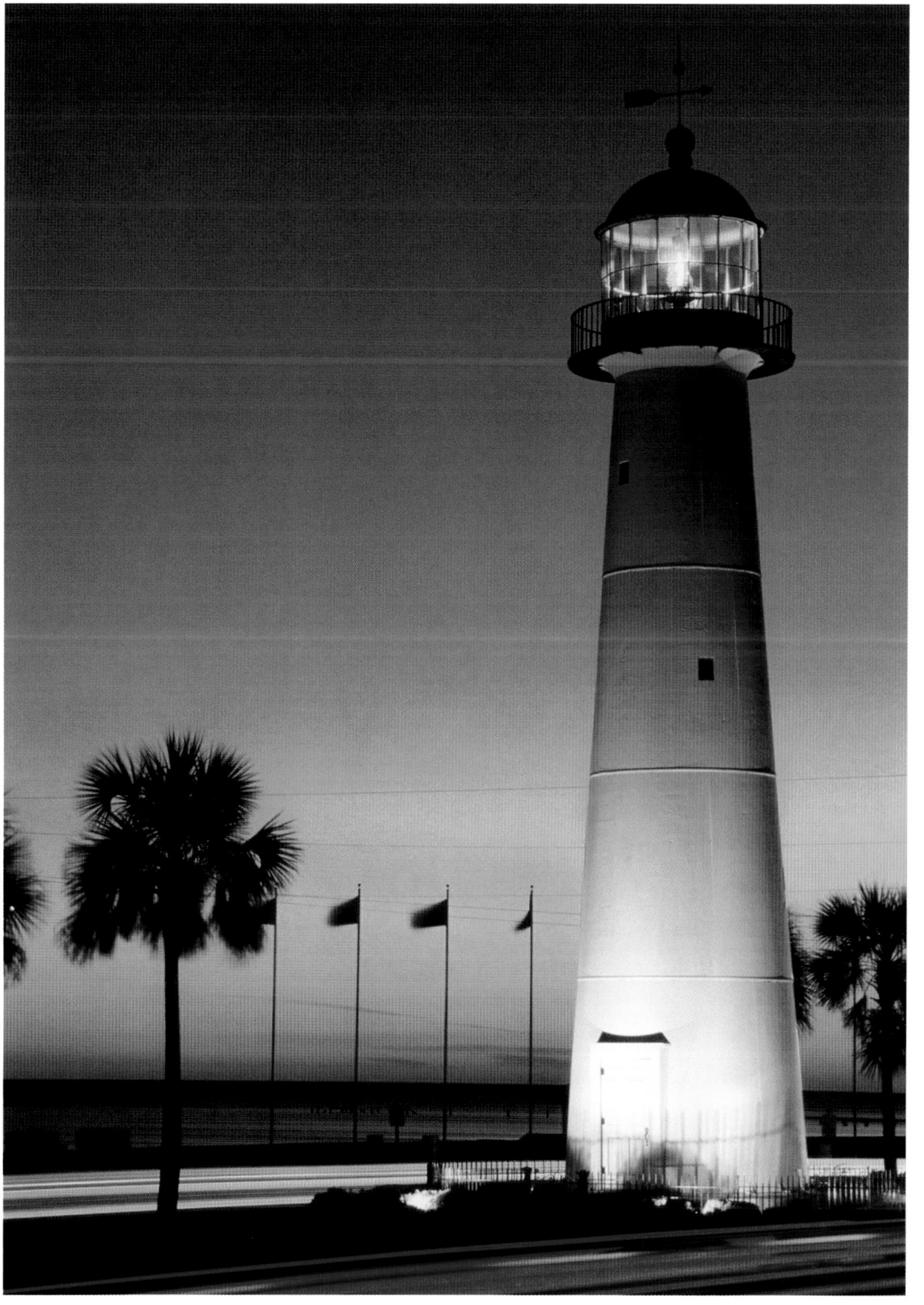

Biloxi Light now stands like a traffic signal on the central reservation of U.S. Highway 90, which bisects the narrow peninsula on which Biloxi is situated. The tower's fifth-order Fresnel lens was buried for protection during the Civil War and the brick-lined, cast-iron structure has withstood many assaults, including Hurricane Camille, which destroyed the keeper's quarters in 1968. The station was manned by female keepers for 81 years of its working life. Maria Younghans, who looked after the light for 51 years, was the first in the history of the service, and her daughter Miranda succeeded her. The lighthouse, which was automated in 1926, is now maintained by the city of Biloxi as a private aid to navigation.

Round Island Light

Pascagoula Harbor, MS
Built: 1833, 1859
Style: Conical

Round Island Light was established in 1833 to guide vessels through Mississippi Sound to the port of Pascagoula. The first 45-ft (14m) lighthouse stood until tidal erosion undercut its foundations in the 1850s. A 50-ft (15-m) replacement, fitted with a fourth-order Fresnel lens, was built on higher ground in 1859. This was extinguished during the Civil War but relit in 1865 and remained in service until 1944, when the station was decommissioned. Round Island was one of several lights kept by a woman. Mrs. Charles Anderson took over as keeper when her husband died in 1871, and remained until 1880. The tower was pulled down in 1998, but the Round Island Preservation Society plans to rebuild it using the original materials.

LEFT
Turkey Point Light, Maryland, with lighthouse keeper Fannie Salter.

OPPOSITE
Bald Head Light, North Carolina.

Ship Island Light

Ship Island, MS
Built: 1853,1886 and 1972
Style: Skeleton tower on concrete block
No: 8390
Position: 30 12 42 N. 88 58 00 W
Focal plane: 84ft (26m)
Range: 10 miles (16km)

The first lighthouse was built in 1853 and was fitted with a state-of-the-art fourth-order Fresnel lens a few years later. The lighthouse was built at the request of Jefferson Davis, then U.S. secretary of war and later president of the Confederacy. During the Civil War the tower was taken over by Union Forces, and by 1886 the building had fallen into disrepair. It was replaced by a pyramidal wooden tower, which survived until accidentally burned down in 1972. The present steel skeleton tower then took its place, but the Friends of the Gulf Islands National Seashore have since built a replica of the 1886 tower.

NORTH CAROLINA.

Bald Head (Cape Fear) Light

Bald Head Island, Southport, NC
Built: 1794 and 1818
Style: Octagonal

The present 100-ft (30.5-m) lighthouse has marked the entrance to the Cape Fear River since 1818. The brick-built tower replaced an earlier lighthouse erected in 1794, which was toppled by a tornado in 1912. Consequently, the existing tower, nicknamed 'Old Baldy', was built with walls 5-ft (1.5-m) thick at the base. The station's light was originally powered by a series of whale-oil lamps, which were later replaced by a fourth-order Fresnel lens. The tower was decommissioned in 1935 and the building is now managed by the Old Baldy Foundation, which is working to restore the station.

Cape Hatteras Light

Cape Hatteras, NC
Built: 1803, 1870 and 1999
Style: Tower with brick base
No: 625
Position: 35 15 08 N. 75 31 44 W
Focal plane: 192ft (58.5m)
Range: 24 miles (39km)

With its lofty, spirally-banded black-and-white tower, the 191-ft (58-m) Cape Hatteras lighthouse is one of the world's best-known maritime sentinels. It is easily spotted not only by ships but also by orbiting spacecraft! It overlooks Cape Hatteras, where the warm waters of the Gulf Stream meet the colder Labrador Current, and warns ships of the dangerous Diamond Shoals offshore. The earlier 95-ft (29-m) sentinel of 1803 was condemned as totally inadequate by naval inspectors, and the present tower replaced it after the Civil War. By the 1990s it was threatened by coastal erosion, and in 1999 the tower was moved on tracks in a $12-million operation to save this American icon from falling into the sea. When the tower was abandoned for a period during the 1930s, souvenir hunters took the prism elements of the first-order Fresnel lens as mementos, and it is now equipped with an aero-marine beacon.

Cape Lookout Light

Beaufort, NC
Built: 1812 and 1859
Style: Black and white tower
No: 670
Position: 34 37 22 N. 76 31 28 W
Focal plane: 156ft (47.5m)
Range: 25 miles (40km)

The present Cape Lookout lighthouse was built in 1859 on Core Banks Island. It replaced an earlier 100-ft (30.5-m) tower that was deemed too small to warn vessels of the shoals that extend south-east from Cape Lookout. The existing tower was fitted with a third-order Fresnel lens, but this was shot at by Confederate troops retreating from Fort Macon during the Civil War. A first-order Fresnel lens replaced it in 1864 when hostilities had ceased. That in turn has since been replaced by an aero-marine beacon, which gives the tower a range of 25 miles.

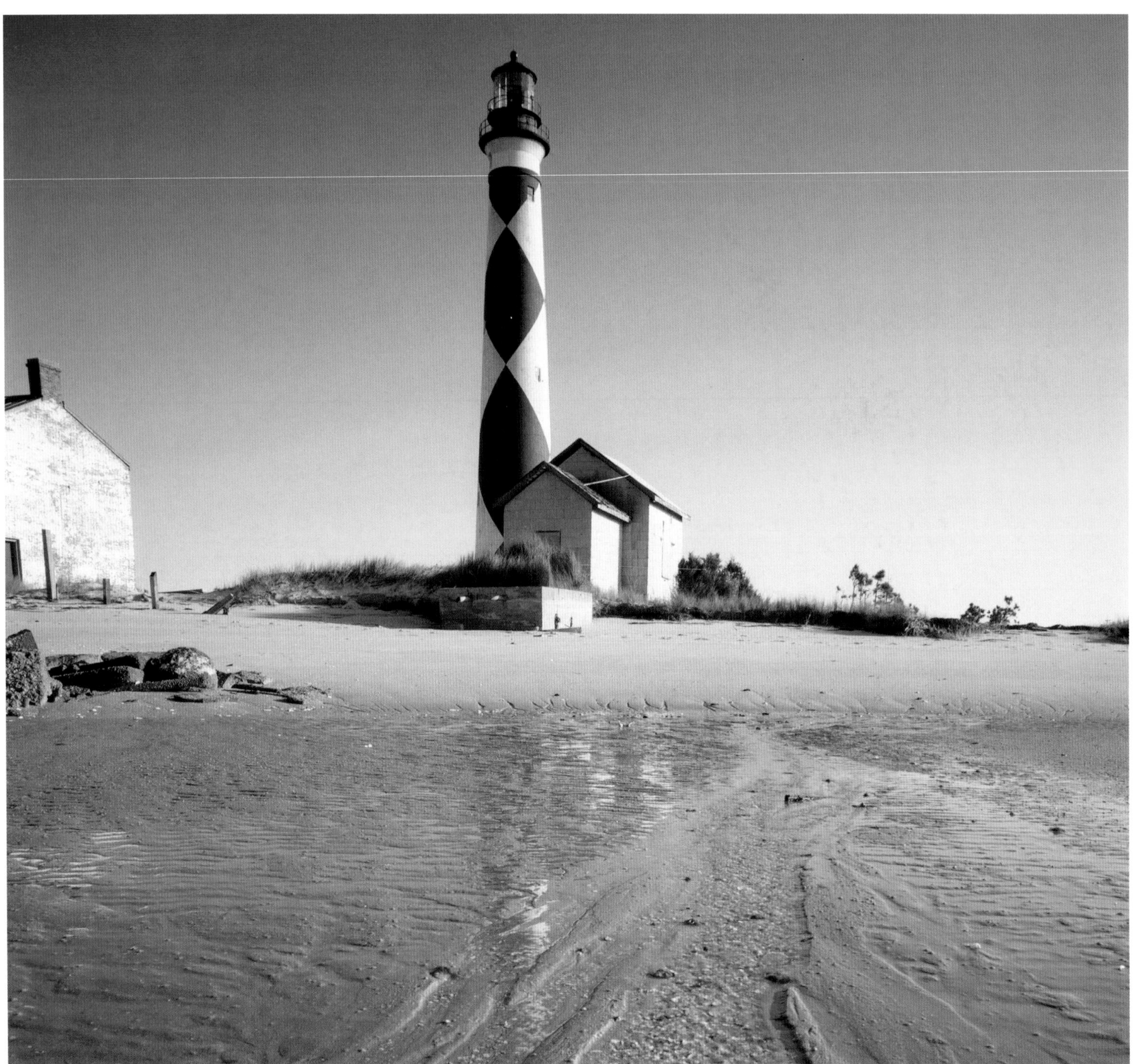

LEFT
Cape Lookout Light, North Carolina.

OPPOSITE
Cape Hatteras Light, North Carolina

Currituck Beach Light

Corolla, NC
Built: 1874
Style: Conical tower
No: 555
Position: 36 22 37 N. 75 49 47 W
Focal plane: 158ft (48m)
Range: 18 miles (29km)
Height: 163ft (50m)

The brick-built lighthouse was erected in 1874 as part of a chain of lights along the Carolina Outer Banks to alert vessels, that elected to take an inshore course to avoid the adverse flow of the Gulf Stream, to the proximity of the shoals and sandbanks that have sunk so many ships in the past. The red tower, which has walls 6-ft (2-m) thick at the base, still has its original 12-ft (4-m) first-order Fresnel bull's-eye lens, giving the beam a range of 18 miles.

Diamond Shoal Light

Cape Hatteras, NC
Built: 1967
Style: Texas tower
Focal plane: 125 ft (38m)
Range: 18 miles (29km)

The present Texas tower-style lighthouse was built 13 miles (21km) off Cape Hatteras

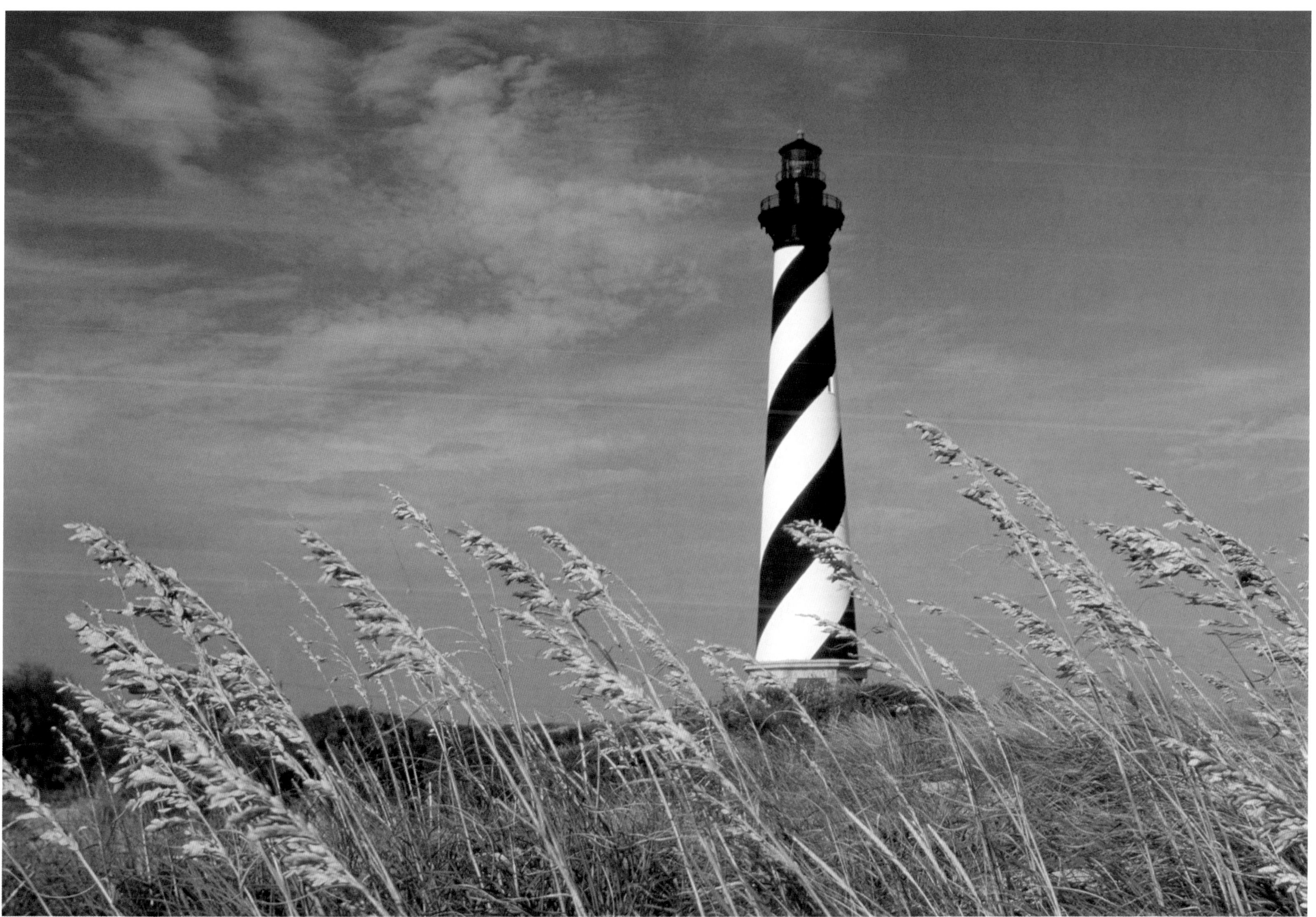

to warn shipping entering what has become known as the 'graveyard of the Atlantic'. The hazard was first marked by a series of lightships, the first of which took up station in 1824 and sank in a gale three years later. The second was sunk by a German U-boat during World War I, and the third, named *Diamond*, served until the present tower was completed in 1967. It was automated ten years later.

Frying Pan Shoal Light

Cape Fear River, Southport, NC
Built: 1966
Style: Texas tower

The 118-ft (36-m) Frying Pan Shoal lighthouse was erected 30 miles (50km) south-east of Cape Fear in 1966. The automated, open-water square tower, painted dark green above a yellow house, remains operational.

Oak Island Light

Caswell Beach, NC
Built: 1958
Style: Cylindrical tower
No: 810
Position: 33 53 36 N. 78 02 06 W
Focal plane: 169ft (51.5m)
Range: 24 miles (39km)
Height: 155ft (47m)

The lighthouse was built in 1958 to mark the entrance to Cape Fear River. The reinforced-concrete tower, painted black, white and grey, has a range of 24 miles and is part of an active Coast Guard station.

LEFT
Currituck Beach Light, North Carolina.

OPPOSITE
Ocracoke Island Light, North Carolina.

Ocracoke Island Light

Shell Island, NC
Built: 1818 and 1823
No: 660
Position: 35 06 32 N. 75 59 10 W

The present 65-ft (20-m) lighthouse was built in 1823 to replace an earlier tower situated on Shell Castle Island, which was struck by lightning in 1818. The tower was equipped with a fourth-order Fresnel lens, which was replaced by a modern optic when the station was automated. The light has a range of 14 miles (22.5km).

South Carolina

Cape Romain Light

McClellanville, SC
Built: 1827 and 1858
Style: Octagonal tower

Cape Romain Wildlife Refuge has two historic lighthouses. When the first, a 60-ft (18-m) tower built in 1827 by Winslow Lewis, proved inadequate, a second tower, 150-ft (46-m) high, was built (using slave labour) in 1858. This larger tower was fitted with a first-order Fresnel lens, and its range of 19 miles (31km) was more than sufficient to warn vessels away from the hazardous shoals 9 miles south-east of the cape. The

OPPOSITE
Harbor Town Light, South Carolina.

RIGHT
Hunting Island Light, South Carolina.

light was extinguished during the Civil War and, though the tower developed a drunken list, it was brought back into commission in 1866. The station was automated in 1937 and decommissioned in 1947, when a series of buoys was laid closer to the shoals.

Charleston Light

Sullivans Island, Charleston, SC
Built: 1962
Style: Triangular tower
No: 195
Position: 32 45 30 N. 79 50 36 W
Focal plane: 163ft (50m)
Range: 26 miles (42km)

The 140-ft (43-m) triangular Charleston Light was built on Sullivans Island in 1962 to replace the Morris Island lighthouse. It remains the only one with an elevator, which has not had much use since the station was automated in 1975.

Georgetown Light

Georgetown, SC
Built: 1801 and 1812
Style: Cylindrical tower
No: 120
Position: 33 13 24 N. 79 11 06 W
Focal plane: 85ft (26m)
Range: 15 miles (24km)

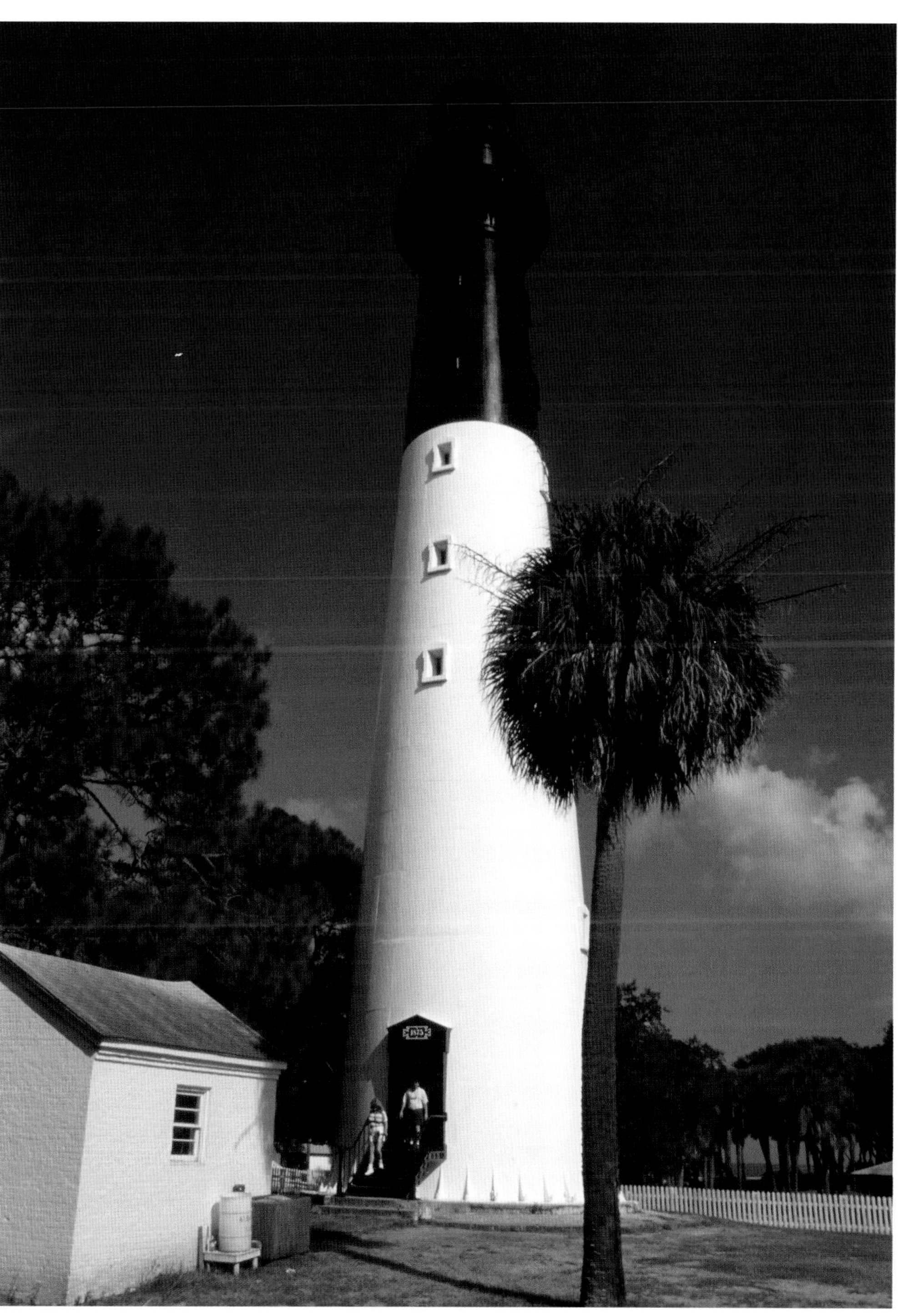

The present 87-ft (26.5-m) Georgetown lighthouse, built in 1812, is the oldest active tower in South Carolina. It replaced an earlier 72-ft (22-m) wooden tower, which was blown down during a cyclone in 1806. The present white brick tower was badly damaged during the Civil War, but was renovated in 1867 and has continued ever since. The light was automated in 1986 when its original Fresnel lens was replaced by a solar-powered optic.

Haig Point Rear Range Light

Daufuskie Island, SC
Built: 1872
Style: White square tower on house
No: 4370
Position: 32 08 42 N. 80 50 12 W
Focal plane: 47ft (14m)

The lighthouse was built in 1872 to partner a lantern attached to a pole set some way out from Daufuskie Island. The wooden lighthouse stands 25ft (8m) above what was the keeper's two-storey dwelling and was equipped with a fifth-order Fresnel lens. The station was decommissioned in 1934 and the building is now an inn within an exclusive estate. The light was relit as a private aid to navigation in 1987.

Harbor Town Light

Harbor Town, Hilton Head Island, SC
Built: 1970
Style: Octagonal

The lighthouse was built in 1970 as a private aid to navigation to guide vessels between

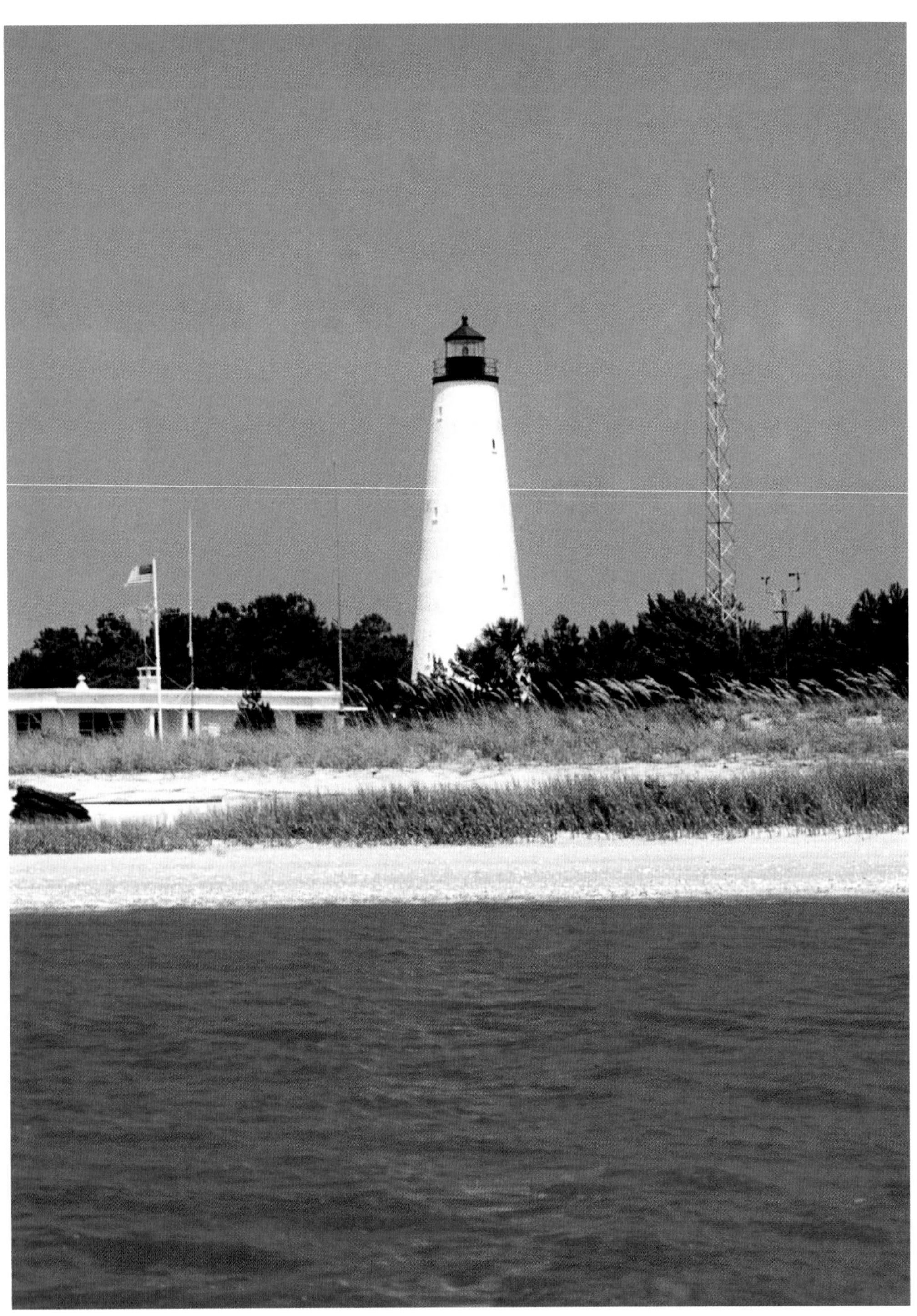

the Inland Waterway and Calibogue Sound. More importantly, perhaps, the tower acts as a point of focus for a marina at Hilton Head and houses a gift shop directly below the lantern room.

Hunting Island Light

Beaufort, SC
Built: 1859, 1875 and 1889
Style: Conical

The first Hunting Island lighthouse, built in 1859, was lost during the Civil War. A 134-ft (41-m) brick-lined cast-iron replacement was built in 1875, but when erosion threatened the structure in 1889, the tower was dismantled and rebuilt a mile from the original site. The station was equipped with a second-order Fresnel lens until it was decommissioned in 1933.

Morris Island Light

Charleston, SC
Built: 1767 and 1876
Style: Conical stone tower

Erosion by the sea has played a significant role in the history and ultimately the demise of Morris Island Light as an active aid to navigation. The first tower, built as long ago as 1767, was sidelined, first by the Civil War and then by the silting-up of the waterways around Charleston harbour. The present 161- ft (49-m) black-and-white-striped tower was built on a concrete foundation 8ft (2.5m) thick, laid on wooden piles driven 50ft (15m) into the mud. Fitted with a first-order Fresnel lens, the tower was automated in 1938 and decommissioned in 1962. It was built well inland, but erosion has left the structure isolated on what is now Morris Island, several hundred feet from the shore. A campaign has been launched to save the brick tower by moving it inland.

TEXAS

Aransas Pass Light (Lydia Ann Light)

Port Aransas, TX
Built: 1857
Style: Brick tower
No: 37710
Position: 27 51 54 N. 97 03 24 W
Focal plane: 65ft (20m)

The Aransas Pass lighthouse was built in 1857 to mark the channel from the Gulf of Mexico to the Texan ports of Matagorda Bay and Port Lavaca. The station, which was designed and built by Danville Leadbetter, a U.S. Army engineer, was equipped with a fourth-order Fresnel lens. The light was extinguished by a Confederate raiding party during the Civil War, but after that remained in use until 1952, when it was sold. The lighthouse has since been restored and is now a private aid to navigation and called the Lydia Ann Light.

Bolivar Point Light

Galveston, TX
Built: 1852 and 1872

The original cast-iron lighthouse built in 1852 was destroyed in 1862, a casualty of the Civil War. Ten years passed before the

OPPOSITE
Georgetown Light, South Carolina.

LEFT
Morris Island (Old Charleston) Light, South Carolina.

present 117-ft (36-m) lighthouse was erected to mark the channel linking Galveston Bay with the Gulf of Mexico. This too is cast-iron and was fitted with a second-order Fresnel lens. In 1900, the tower became a safe refuge for people fleeing the effects of the hurricane that razed Galveston to the ground. The tower was decommissioned in 1933 and is now in private ownership.

Matagorda Island Light

Matagorda Island, TX
Built: 1852 and 1873
Style: Conical tower
No: 1312
Position: 28 20 12 N. 96 25 24 W
Focal plane: 90ft (27m)

The 80-ft (24-m) Matagorda Island lighthouse was built in 1852 as part of a chain of lights along the Texas coast. During the Civil War, Confederate soldiers buried the station's third-order Fresnel lens and tried to topple the cast-iron tower with gunpowder to keep it out of Union hands.

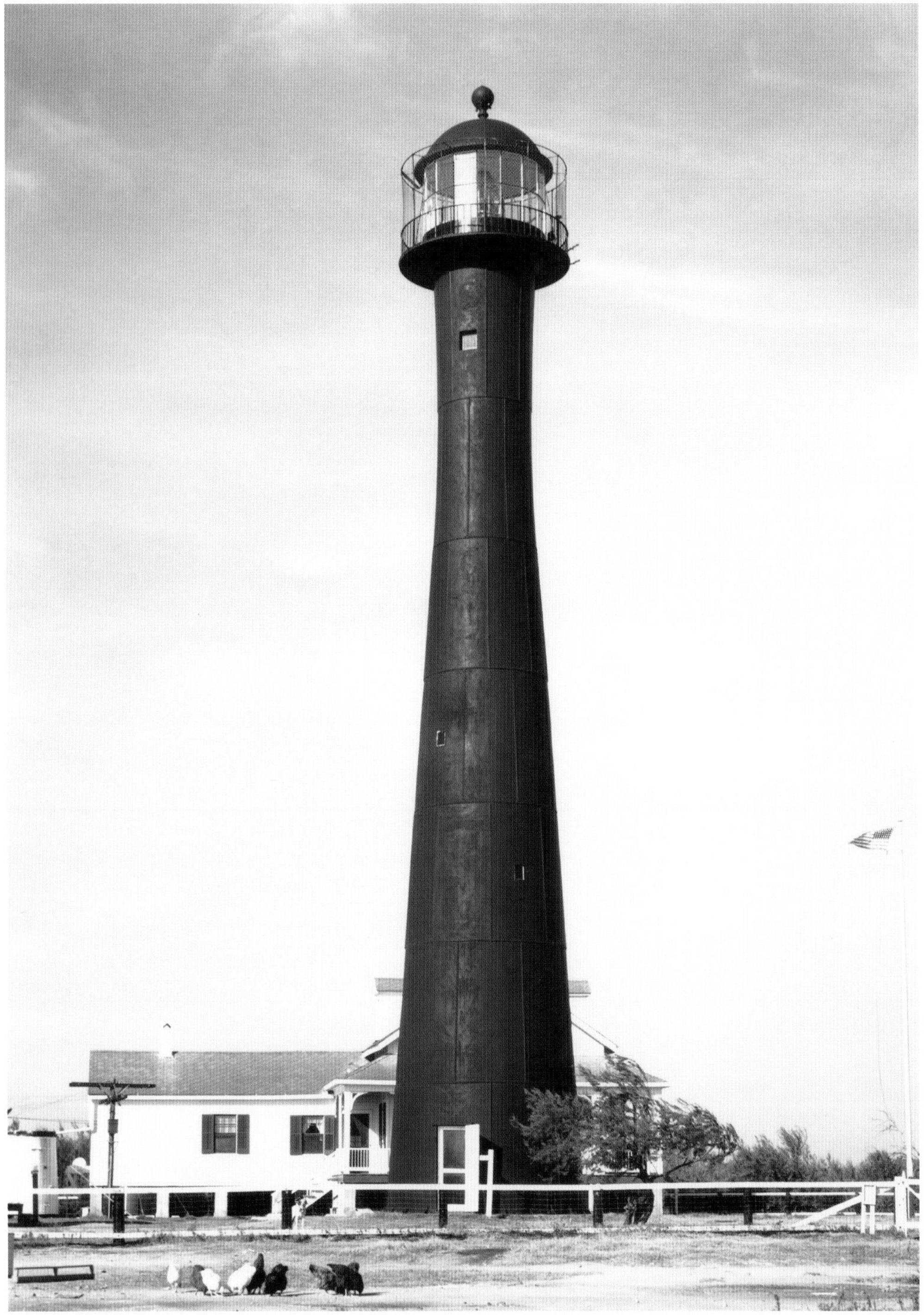

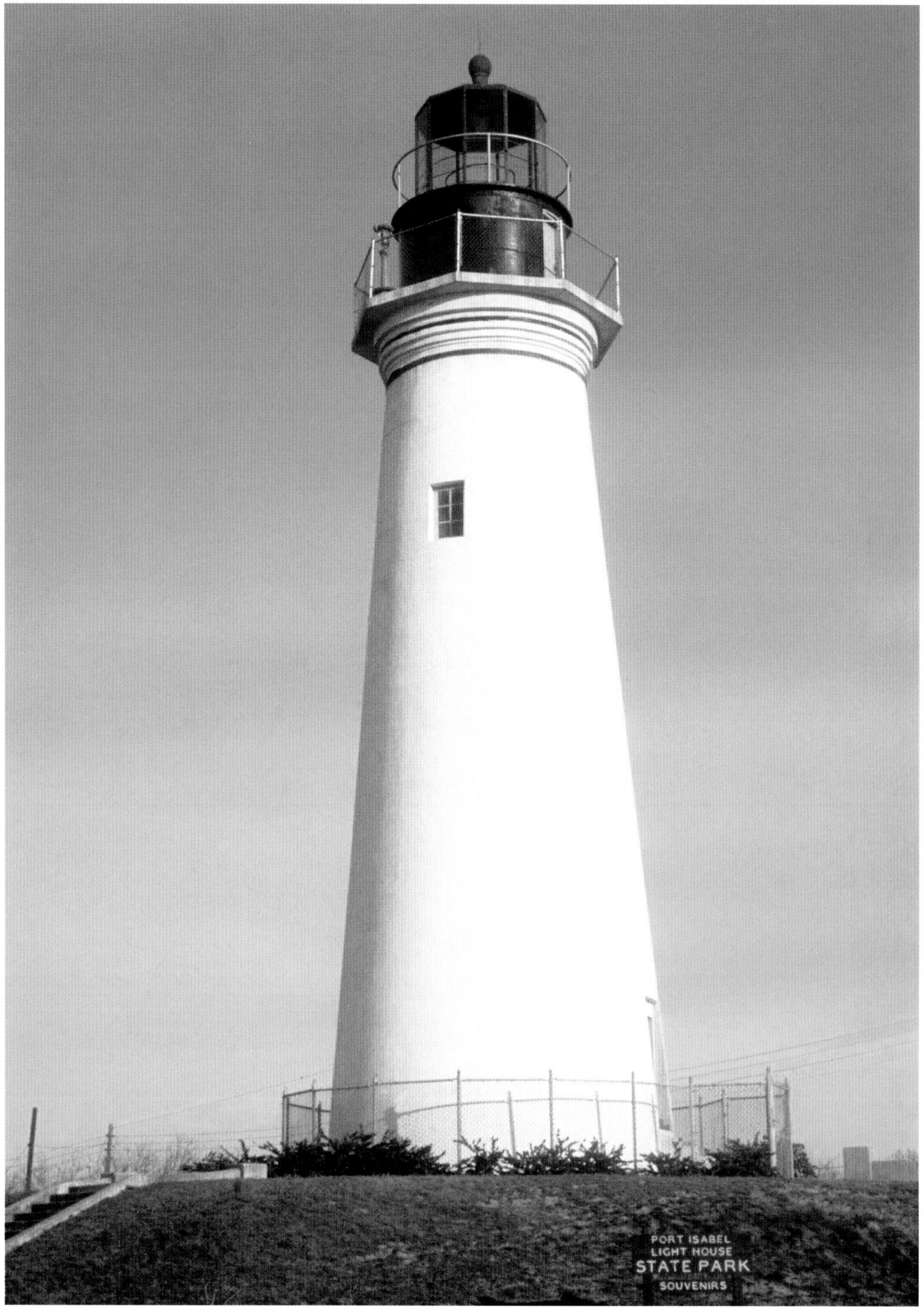
PORT ISABEL
LIGHT HOUSE
STATE PARK
SOUVENIRS

OPPOSITE LEFT
Matagorda Island Light, Texas.

OPPOSITE RIGHT
Port Isabel Light, Texas.

RIGHT
Assateague Island Light, Virginia.

The tower survived the blast but after the war engineers could not repair the building without first dismantling the sections and rebuilding the prefabricated structure. The work was completed in 1873 and the original Fresnel lens continued in operation until 1977, when the station was automated. The tower is now maintained as a private aid to navigation.

Port Isabel Light

South Padre Island, TX
Built: 1852
Style: Conical

The 57-ft (17-m) lighthouse was built to mark the entrance to the harbour. The light was decommissioned in 1905 but the building has since been restored as a tourist attraction.

Sabine Bank Light

Sabine Pass, TX
Built: 1906

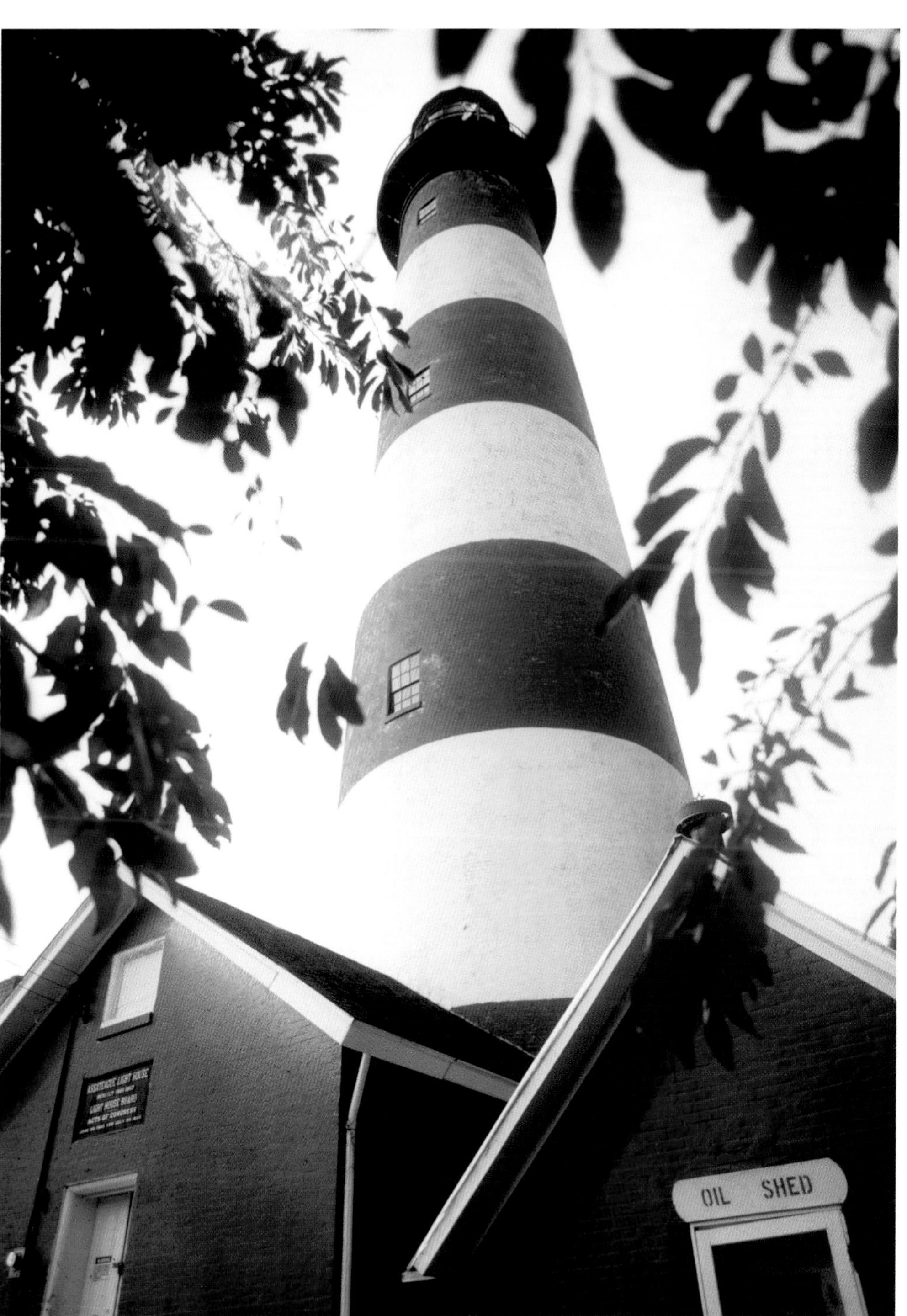

Style: Conical tower on cylindrical caisson
No: 1075
Position: 29 28 18 N. 93 43 24 W
Focal plane: 30ft (9m)
Range: 5 miles (8km)

The caisson-based Sabine Bank lighthouse was erected 15 miles (24km) off the entrance to the Sabine River to provide a reference point for vessels navigating the newly dredged channel from the Gulf of Mexico. The tower was cast in a Detroit foundry and equipped with a third-order Fresnel lens, automated in 1923. It is now in a poor state of repair.

VIRGINIA

Assateague Island Light

Assateague, VA
Built: 1833 and 1867
Style: Conical tower
No: 275
Position: 37 54 40 N. 75 21 22 W
Focal plane: 154ft (47m)
Range: 22 miles (35km)
Height: 145ft (44m)

The first 45-ft (14-m) Assateague Island lighthouse, built in 1833, was neither high enough nor bright enough to stop vessels from running up on the hazardous shoals extending from the island. The light was eventually replaced with the present red-and-white-banded conical brick tower in 1867. It was equipped with a first-order Fresnel lens, but an aero-marine beacon replaced this when the station was automated in 1967.

Cape Charles Light

Smith Island, VA
Built: 1828, 1864 and 1894
Style: Octagonal pyramidal skeleton tower
No: 350
Position: 37 07 23 N. 75 54 23 W
Focal plane: 180ft (55m)
Range: 24 miles (39km)
Height: 191ft (58m)

Standing 191ft high, the Cape Charles lighthouse is one of the tallest navigation towers in North America. Built in 1894, the white, cast-iron skeletal tower was erected a mile inshore to replace a 150-ft (46-m) brick tower built during the Civil War, which was under threat from coastal erosion. This in turn had replaced a 51-ft (15.5-m) stone tower that had proved ineffective. The present tower was fitted with a first-order Fresnel lens, which was replaced with a solar-powered optic when the station was automated.

Chesapeake Light

Chesapeake Bay, VA
Built: 1965
Style: Tower on superstructure on piles
No: 360
Position: 36 54 17 N. 75 42 46 W
Focal plane: 117ft (36m)
Range: 19 miles (30.5km)

The Chesapeake lighthouse, standing 13 miles (21km) out in the bay from Virginia Beach, is one of America's most modern light stations, yet is already deemed obsolete. Built in 1965, the 120-ft (36.5-m)

OPPOSITE
Assateague Island Light, Virginia.

BELOW
Newport News Middle Ground Light, Virginia.

RIGHT
Smith Point Light, Virginia.

caisson-based structure, with its helipad and automated systems, has been outdated by GPS and other navigational tracking systems and is due to be decommissioned in 2004.

Jones Point Light

Alexandria, VA
Built: 1855
Style: Rectangular

The picturesque Jones Point lighthouse, with its small light tower perched on the roof of the keeper's dwelling, was built on the south shore of the Potomac River in 1855 to guide vessels from Chesapeake Bay towards Alexandria and Washington. The station was decommissioned in 1926, but has since been restored and relit as a private aid to navigation.

New Cape Henry Light

Virginia Beach, VA
Built: 1872 and 1881
Style: Octagonal covered with iron plates
Focal plane: 350ft (107m)
Range: W 17 miles/27km, R 15 miles/24km
Height: 163ft (50m)

The lighthouse was built to mark the entrance to Chesapeake Bay, replacing the original lighthouse of 1872. The black-and-white masonry tower, which is protected with iron plates, is still equipped with its original first-order Fresnel lens.

New Point Comfort Light

Mathews, VA
Built: 1804
Style: Octagonal sandstone tower
Focal plane: 63 ft (19m)
Range: 13 miles (21km)
Height: 58ft (18m)

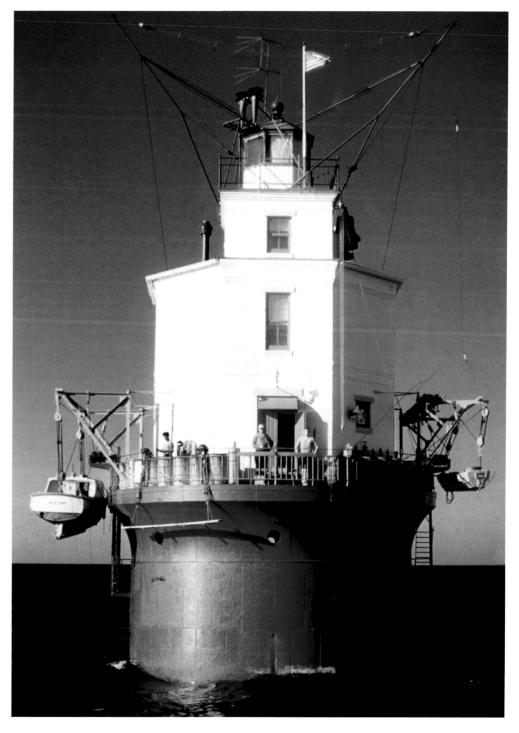

The 58-ft sandstone New Point Comfort lighthouse was one of the first stations to be built on Chesapeake Bay, and is now into its second century of guiding vessels towards Baltimore. Built in 1804, the station's light was deactivated during the 1950s but the tower, which has since been restored by Mathews County, remains as an official day mark.

Newport News Middle Ground Light

Newport News, VA
Built: 1891
Style: Conical tower on cylindrical pier
No: 10815
Position: 36 56 43 N. 76 23 29 W
Focal plane: 52ft (16m)
Range: 12 miles (19km)

The 35-ft (11-m) 'coffeepot'-style lighthouse was built in 1891 to warn vessels entering Hampton Roads of the hazardous, L-shaped Middle Ground shoal. The cast-iron tower, with its concrete caisson base, was equipped with a fourth-order Fresnel lens until it was upgraded with a modern optic when the station was automated.

Old Cape Henry Light

Virginia Beach, VA
Built: 1792
Style: Octagonal

The 90-ft (27-m) Old Cape Henry lighthouse, which dates back to 1792, was one of the first building projects commissioned after the War of Independence. The lighthouse, which marked the entrance to Chesapeake Bay, developed serious cracks in its stonework during the 1870s and was replaced by the New Cape Henry Light in 1881. However, the original tower has defied nature for well over a century since and is now a national monument.

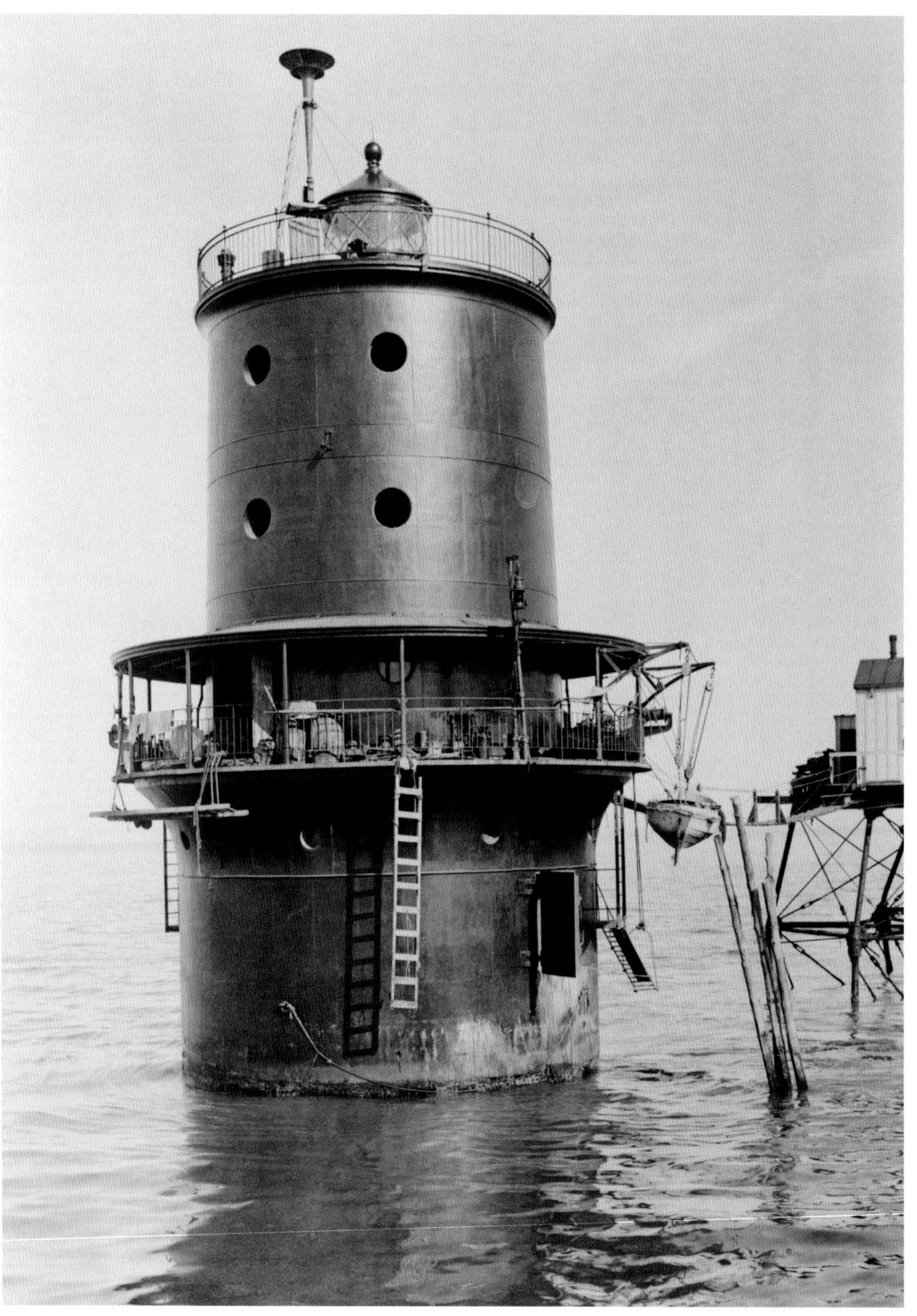

LEFT
Thimble Shoals Light, Virginia.

OPPOSITE
Wolf Trap Light, Virginia.

Portsmouth Lightship

Built: 1916
Builder: Pusey & Jones, Wilmington, DE
No: LV 101
Length Overall: l0lft 10in (31m)
Beam: 25ft (8m)
Draft: 11ft 4in (3.5m)
Displacement: 360 tons
Illuminating Apparatus: 500-mm lens

The *Portsmouth* is now on permanent display in Portsmouth harbour, Virginia. The vessel was launched in 1916 and served at various hazards off the Delaware, Maryland, Massachusetts and Virginia coasts until it was retired in 1964. Like other lightships, she was originally known by a number, not a name, and although she never served off Portsmouth, she was given that name when first opened to the public in dry dock in Portsmouth harbour in 1986.

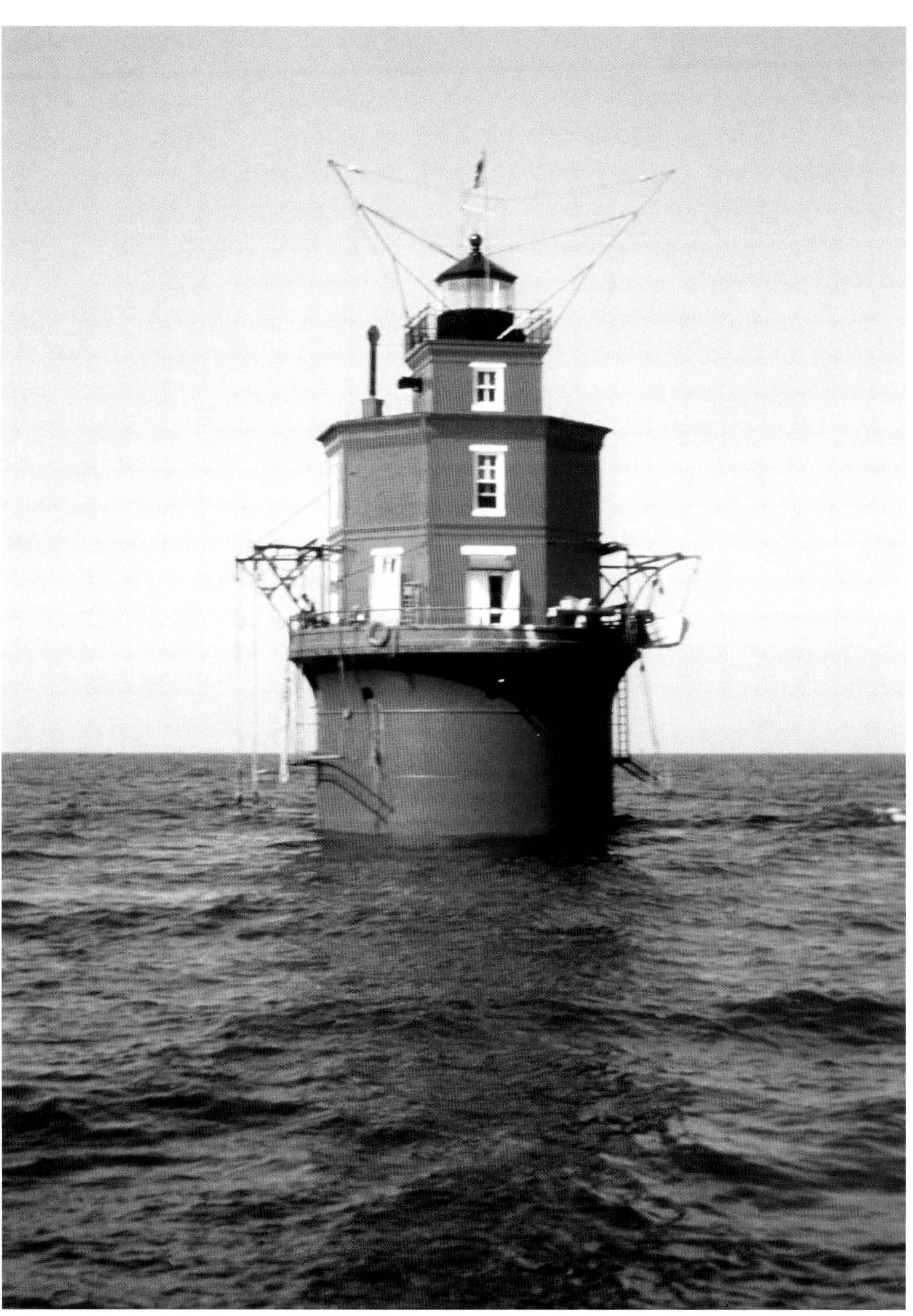

Station Assignments
1916–24: Cape Charles (VA)
1925–26: Relief
1926–51: Overfalls (DE)
1951–63: Stonehorse Shoal (MA)

Smith Point Light

Sunnybank, VA
Built: 1868 and 1897
Style: Hexagonal on caisson

Like other screwpile lighthouses built on Chesapeake Bay during the mid-19th century, the original Smith Point lighthouse of 1868 was finally crushed by ice during the bitter winter of 1897. The station was replaced by the present caisson-based brick tower later that year, and fitted with a fourth-order Fresnel lens. This lens was replaced with a modern optic when the station was automated.

Thimble Shoal Light

Hampton, VA
Built: 1872, 1891 and 1914
Style: Conical cast-iron tower on pier
Focal plane: 40 ft (12m)
Range: 20 miles (32km)
Height: 55ft (17m)

The first two screwpile lighthouses to mark the Thimble Shoal in Hampton Roads succumbed not to ice but fire. The present 55-ft 'sparkplug'-type, caisson-based tower was erected in 1914. It was equipped with a fourth-order Fresnel lens, which was replaced with a solar-powered optic when the station was automated.

Wolf Trap Light

Chesapeake Bay, VA
Built: 1870 and 1893
Style: Octagonal dwelling with square tower
No: 7255
Position: 37 23 24 N. 76 11 24 W
Focal plane: 52ft (16m)
Range: 14 miles (22.5km)

The first Wolf Trap lighthouse highlighted the problems of screwpile structures in standing up to the pressures of drifting ice. The lighthouse was destroyed during the harsh winter of 1893 and was replaced by the present tower on a concrete and iron caisson later that year. It was fitted with a fourth-order Fresnel lens, which was replaced by a modern optic when the station, which marks the Chesapeake shoal where the British warship *Wolf* ran aground in 1691, was automated.

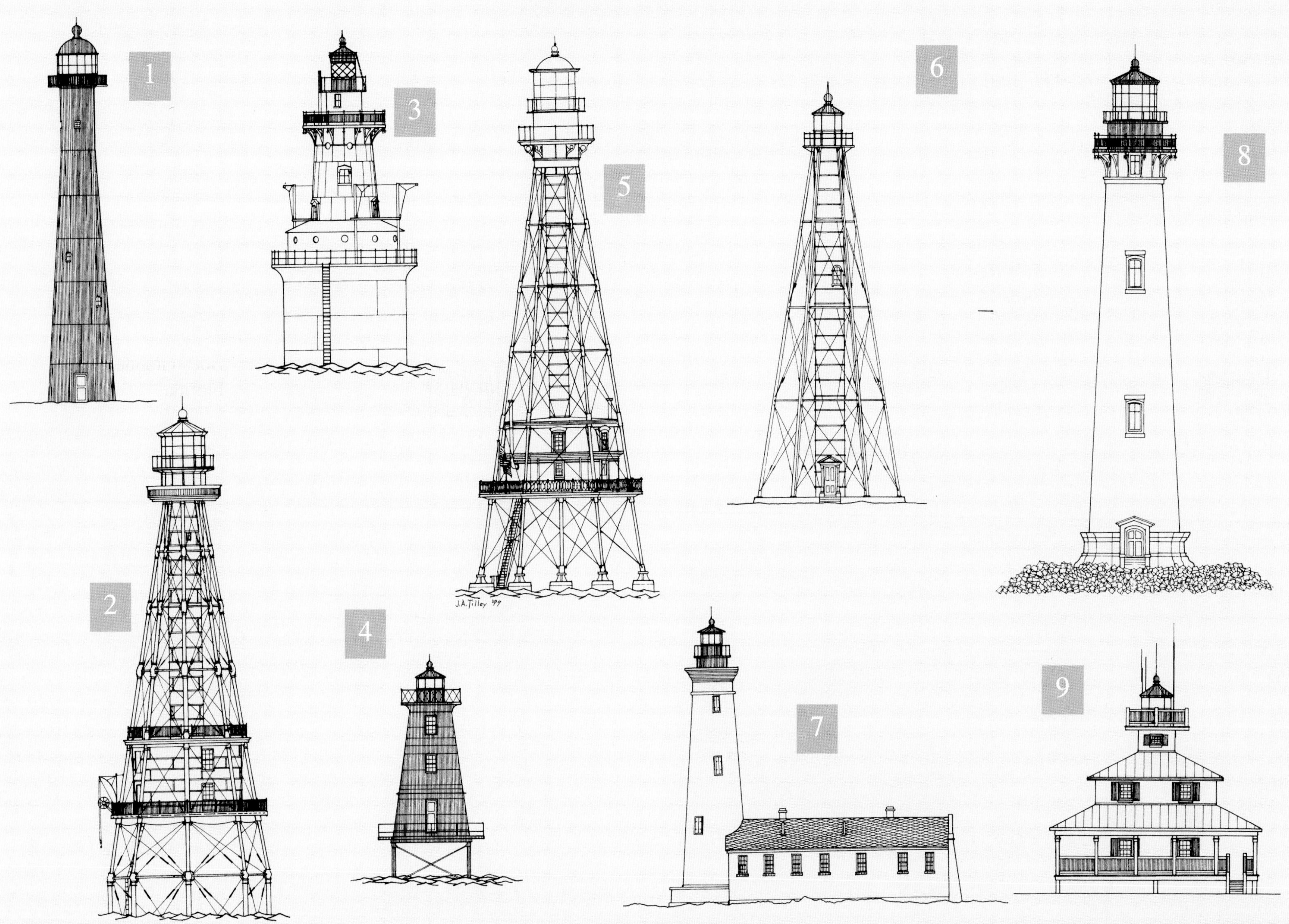
1
3
5
6
8
2
4
7
9
J.A.Tilley '99

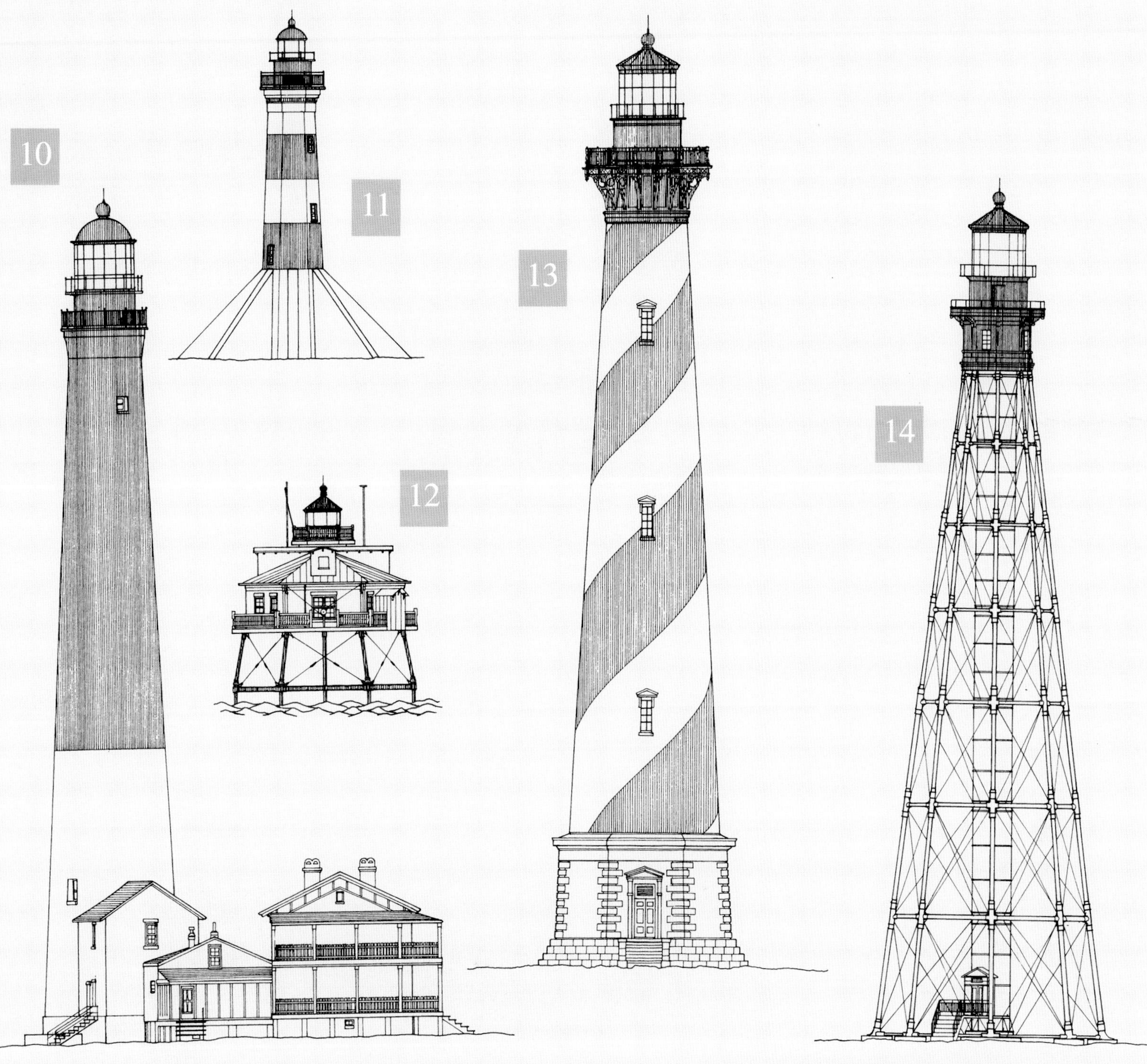

1. Matagorda Island, Texas
2. Ship Shoal, Louisana
3. Sabine Bank, Texas
4. Southwest Reef, Louisana
5. Southwest Pass, Louisana
6. Boca Grande, Florida
7. St. Marks, Florida
8. Sand Island, Alabama
9. New Canal, Louisana
10. Pensacola, Florida
11. Sabine Pass, Louisana
12. Thomas Point Shoal, Maryland
13. Cape Hatteras, North Carolina
14. Cape Charles, Virginia

Chapter Nine
Lighthouses of the West

ALASKA
Cape Decision Light

Cape Decision, AK
Built: 1932
Style: Square tower rising from building
No: 1020
Position: 56 00 05 N.134 08 09 W
Focal plane: 96ft (29m)
Range: 18 miles (29km)

This was the last light to be built in Alaska. The station, which is fitted with a third-order Fresnel lens, stands 96ft up on Cape Decision, the south-eastern point of Kuiu Island. It was automated in 1974.

Cape Hinchinbrook Light

Hinchinbrook Island, AK
Built: 1910 and 1934
Style: Square tower on building
No: 1125
Position: 60 14 15 N. 146 38 48 W
Focal plane: 235ft (72m)
Range: 19 miles (30.5km)

The original lighthouse was a 50-ft (15-m) concrete structure built in 1910 that towered above a fog-signal building also housing four keepers. The station was badly damaged by earthquakes in 1927 and 1928, and the tower was rebuilt five years later on a rock formation. The lighthouse still has its original third-order Fresnel lens and was automated in 1974.

Cape Sarichef Light

Unimak Island, AK
Built: 1904 and 1950
Style: Hexagonal tower

The original lighthouse was built in 1904 to mark the Unimak Passage linking the Pacific with the Bering Sea. Unimak Island is an inhospitable posting at the best of times, and keepers were not allowed to bring their families with them. The 35-ft (11-m) tower was replaced in 1950 by a 'tsunami-proof' concrete tower set higher up the cliff, which retains the original third-order Fresnel lens.

RIGHT
Cape Hinchinbrook Light, Alaska.

OPPOSITE
Cape Spencer Light, Alaska.

The station was automated in 1979 and decommissioned the same year.

Cape Spencer Light

Cape Spencer, AK
Built: 1913 and 1925
Style: Square concrete tower on building
No: 1070
Position: 58 11 56 N. 136 38 26 W
Focal plane: 105ft (32m)
Range: 17 miles (27km)
Height: 25ft (8m)

Cape Spencer lighthouse was built in 1925 to replace an acetylene beacon which had marked the entrance to Cross Sound since 1913. The station's 25-ft tower is equipped with a third-order Fresnel lens, together with the first radio beacon to cover these Alaskan waters. The station used to be supplied by a derrick that lifted equipment and personnel off the decks of Coast Guard ships, but it is now reached by helicopter.

Cape St. Elias Light

Cape St. Elias, AK
Built: 1916
Style: Square tower on building
No: 1100
Position: 59 47 54 N.144 35 56 W
Focal plane: 85ft (26m)
Range: 17 miles (27km)

The Cape St. Elias lighthouse was built in 1916 on the south-west point of Kayak Island in the shadow of 17,000-ft (5180-m) Mount St. Elias. The lonely station was serviced just once a year by supply ship. It received a radio beacon in 1927 and was finally automated in 1974.

LEFT
Cape St. Elias Light, Alaska.

OPPOSITE
Eldred Rock Light, Alaska.

Eldred Rock Light

Haines, AK
Built: 1906
Style: Octagonal tower on building
No: 23880
Position: 58 58 15 N. 135 13 15 W
Focal plane: 91ft (28m)
Range: 8 miles (13m)

The 56-ft (17-m) Eldred Rock lighthouse was built in 1906 to guide vessels into the Lynn Canal following the sinking of the *Clara Nevada* with the loss of 100 lives and $100,000-worth of gold eight years earlier. The station retains it original fourth-order Fresnel lens and was automated in 1973.

Five Fingers Islands Light

Five Fingers Islands, AK
Built: 1903 and 1935
Style: Square tower

The original wooden lighthouse was built in 1903, the first in Alaska, and was destroyed by fire in 1933. A second 40-ft (12-m) tower was constructed of concrete in 1935 on another island within the Five Fingers chain, which remained manned until 1984, when it

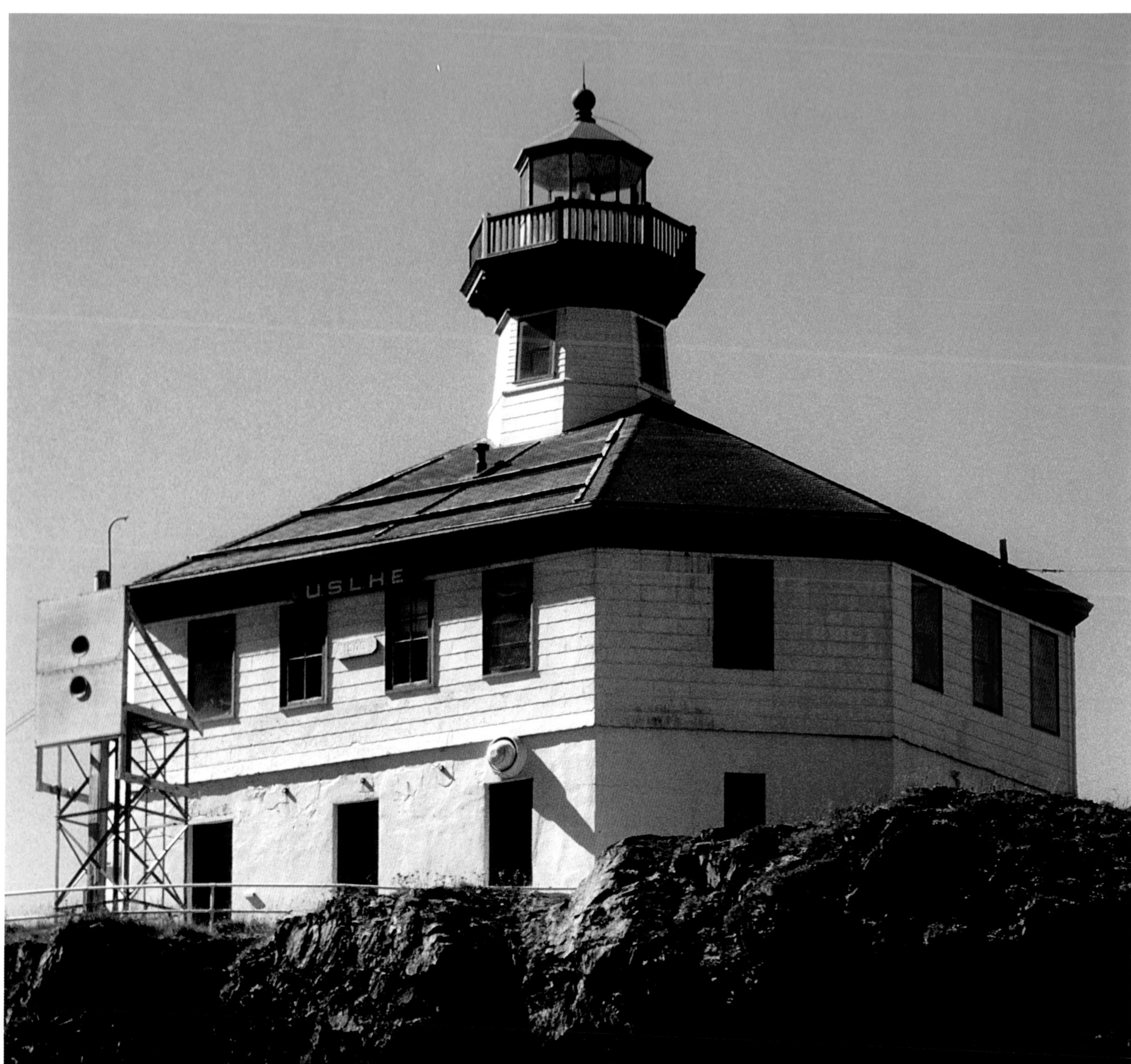

became the last Alaskan station to be automated.

Guard Island Light

Guard Islands, AK
Built: 1904
Style: Square tower on rectangular building
No: 22300
Position: 55 26 45 N. 131 52 52 W
Focal plane: 74ft (22.5m)
Range: 17 miles (27km)

The lighthouse was built a few miles north of Ketchikan to mark the entrance to Tongass Narrows within the Clarence Strait. The wooden tower was fitted originally with a fourth-order Fresnel lens, but now has a solar-powered Vega optic, installed in 1997.

Lincoln Rocks Light

Clarence Strait, AK
Built: 1903
Style: Square tower

Lincoln Rocks lighthouse was built in one of the most desolate areas of Alaska, and if its construction in 1903 did not provide enough headaches, then its maintenance did, and the station was abandoned completely in 1968. It was built to mark Clarence Strait, 50 miles (80km) north-west of Ketchikan. The Lighthouse Board had to fire the first contractor, and the second was forced to cut corners after losing several vessels and a load of lumber during a storm. The lighthouse, which was equipped with a fourth-order Fresnel lens, had to be

LEFT
Five Fingers Islands Light, Alaska.

OPPOSITE
Mary Island Light, Alaska.

abandoned in 1909 following damage caused during a storm, and though an automated acetylene light was installed in 1911, the station proved too costly to maintain and was eventually decommissioned.

Mary Island Light

Mary Island, AK
Built: 1903 and 1937
Style: Square tower on building
No: 21940
Position: 55 05 57 N. 131 10 57 W
Focal plane: 76ft (23m)
Range: 6 miles (10km)

The present reinforced-concrete lighthouse was built in 1937 to replace a round tower that had been guiding vessels along the Revillagigedo Channel on the Inside Passage towards Skagway since 1903. The station was equipped originally with a fourth-order Fresnel lens, but this was replaced with a 250-mm optic when the station was automated in 1969.

Point Retreat Light

Admiralty Island, AK
Built: 1904
Style: Square concrete tower on building
No: 23955
Position: 58 24 41 N. 134 57 18 W

Focal plane: 63ft (19m)
Range: 9 miles (14.5km)

Point Retreat Light, built on Admiralty Island in 1904, was fitted originally with a first-order bivalve Fresnel lens. This was replaced with a 300-mm solar-powered light when the station was automated in 1973.

Scotch Cap Light

Unimak Island, AK
Built: 1903, 1940 and 1950
Style: Skeleton tower
No: 1220
Position: 54 23 42 N. 164 44 42 W
Focal plane: 110ft (33.5m)
Range: 9 miles (14.5km)

Scotch Cap Light marks the southern tip of the Aleutian chain. As related earlier, it has an infamous history. The original 35-ft (11-m) wooden tower and buildings took 30 men a year to complete in 1903, but had to be replaced with a concrete structure in 1940 after it was completely destroyed by a great tsunami that cost five keepers their lives. As a precaution against further tidal waves, the present concrete structure was built in 1950, giving the light a focal plane of 110ft and a range of 9 miles. The station was finally automated in 1971 and operates a rotating aero-marine beacon.

Sentinel Island Light

Sentinel Island, AK
Built: 1902 and 1935
Style: Square tower on fog-signal building
No: 23850
Position: 58 32 46 N. 134 55 22 W

Focal plane: 86ft (26m)
Range: 14 miles (22.5km)

Sentinel Island lighthouse was one of the first stations to be built in Alaska. The original tower was lit on 1 March 1902, the same night as Five Fingers Islands Light, both being built to guide shipping from Frederick Sound through the Lynn Canal towards Skagway. The original structure was replaced in 1935 with a concrete tower fitted with a fourth-order Fresnel lens and was built over a two-storey fog-signal building. The station was automated in 1966 and now relies on solar panels to power the light and fog signals.

Tree Point Light

Revillagigedo Channel, AK
Built: 1904
Style: Square tower

The Tree Point lighthouse was built in 1904 to guide vessels through the Inside Passage towards Skagway. The tower was equipped with a fourth-order Fresnel lens, which was replaced later with a 300-mm optic before the station was decommissioned in 1969.

LEFT
Scotch Cap Light, Alaska, before it was destroyed by a tidal wave.

OPPOSITE
Sentinel Island Light, Alaska.

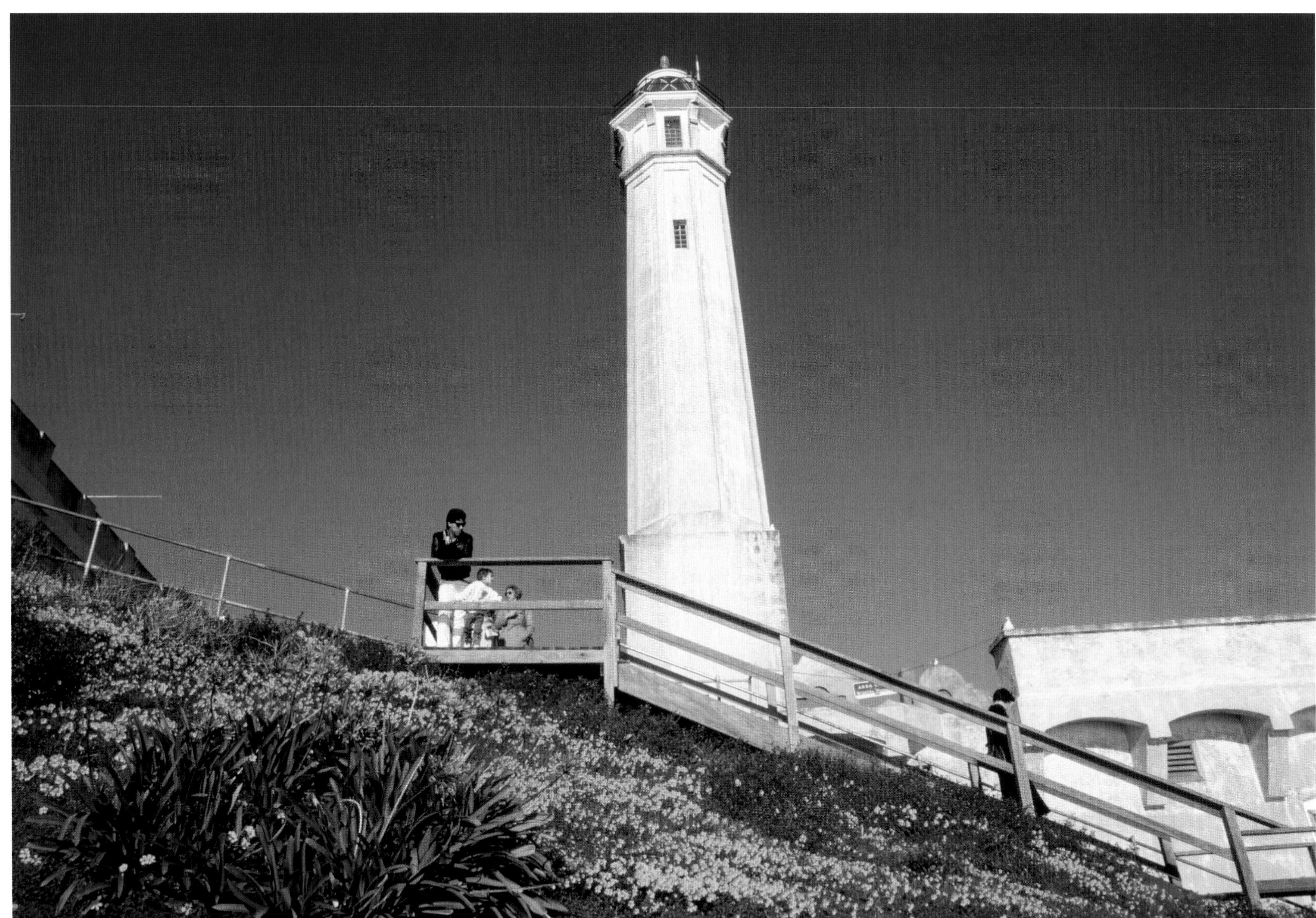

CALIFORNIA
Alcatraz Light

San Francisco, CA
Built: 1854 and 1909
Style: Octagonal tower
No: 4315
Position: 37 49 36 N. 122 25 18 W
Focal plane: 214ft (65m)
Range: 22 miles (35km)

Alcatraz Light was the first U.S. lighthouse on the West Coast. The original tower was built in 1854 in response to a series of shipwrecks in San Francisco Bay during the early days of the Gold Rush. This first lighthouse was a Cape Cod-style tower and dwelling designed by Francis Gibbons and equipped with a third-order Fresnel lens. In 1858, the island was fortified and these buildings were later converted into a prison. The earthquake of 1906 damaged both the light tower and prison, and three years later construction began on a new maximum-security prison and an 84-ft (26-m) octagonal light tower. In 1915 the station's original Fresnel lens was exhibited at that year's Panama-Pacific Exhibition and the new tower built outside the prison walls was re-equipped with a more powerful third-order lens. The light was automated in 1963, six years before the infamous prison

OPPOSITE
Alcatraz Light, California.

RIGHT
Battery Point Light, California.

LEFT
Fort Point Light, California.

OPPOSITE
Cape Mendocino Light, California.

was closed. Shortly after the last prisoner had left, a group of Native Americans occupied the island in a protest and set fire to the keeper's dwelling, which was destroyed. The lighthouse is now preserved as part of the Golden Gate National Recreational Area and, like the old prison, is open to the public.

Anacapa Islands Light

Anacapa Islands, CA
Built: 1912 and 1932
Style: Cylindrical tower
No: 185
Position: 34 01 06 N. 119 21 36 W
Focal plane: 277ft (84m)
Range: 20 miles (32km)
Height: 55ft (17m)

A lighthouse had been planned on the Anacapa Islands to guide vessels safely through the eastern entrance to the Santa Barbara Channel ever since the steamer *Winfred Scott* ran aground here in 1853, leaving 250 of its passengers stranded. Despite this incident, Congress remained reluctant to commit the vast sums required to build the light tower in such a remote area, and it was not until 1912 that the first pyramidal steel structure was built on the east side of the Anacapa Islands. This was

East Brother Light, California.

replaced by the present 55-ft Spanish-style, white cylindrical tower in 1932, which was fitted with a third-order Fresnel lens. The station was automated in 1968 and the Fresnel lens was replaced with a modern optic in 1991.

Battery Point Light

Crescent City, CA
Built: 1856
Style: Two-storey structure
No: 555
Position: 41 44 36 N. 124 12 06 W
Focal plane: 77ft (23.5m)
Range: 14 miles (22.5km)

A restored historic light, Battery Point lighthouse was built in 1856 to guide the logging ships towards Crescent City harbour. The station's white, pyramidal, cast-iron tower is surrounded by a Cape Cod-style keeper's dwelling and is equipped with a fourth-order lens beneath a red lantern. The station was automated in 1951 and is now managed by the Del Norte County Historical Society as a private aid to navigation.

Blunts Reef Lightship

San Francisco, CA
Built: 1950
Builder: Rice Brothers, East Boothbay, ME
Design: Diesel-propelled; steel hull and deckhouses: breakwater on foredeck; two masts; stack amidships
Length overall: 158ft (48m)
Beam: 30ft (9m)
Draft: 11ft (3.5m)
Displacement: 617 tons
Propulsion: Diesel
Speed: 10.7 knots
Illuminating Apparatus: Dunlex 500-mm electric lens lantern on foremast.
Fog Signal: Twin F2T diathones mounted aft of pilot house

Station Assignments:
1951–60: Overfalls (DE)
1960–69: Blunts Reef (CA)
1969–75: Relief (West Coast)

The *Blunts Reef* lightship has marked several danger spots along the West Coast during 25 years in commission, including Blunts Reef (off Eureka), the name carried on her sides since becoming a museum ship in 1989. She is now managed by the U.S. Lighthouse Society and moored on the Oakland waterfront.

Cape Mendocino Light

Capetown, CA
Built: 1868, 1909 and 1951
Style: Conical
No: 480
Position: 40 26 23 N. 124 24 22 W
Focal plane: 515ft (157m)
Range: 19 miles (30.5km)

A lighthouse was first established on the towering cliffs of Cape Mendocino in 1868. This is California's westernmost point and, extending some 1,400ft (427m) above the Pacific surf, is one of the world's most imposing headlands. Building a lighthouse here was no simple task. The first supply ship was wrecked on the rocks below, and when a second vessel finally arrived with a second shipment of prefabricated parts from San Francisco, the items had to be hauled up the cliffs on ropes. The 20-ft (6-m) 16-sided pyramidal iron lighthouse was erected at a point 422ft (129m) above sea level and was fitted with a first-order Fresnel lens. It had a range of 25 miles (40km). In 1951 the light was dismantled and replaced by an automated light set on a pole 515ft above sea level, making this the highest beacon of its type in the world. The original tower is now on display in Mal Coombs Park, Shelter Cove.

East Brother Light

Richmond, CA
Built: 1874
Style: Square tower on dwelling
No: 5865
Positiion: 37 57 48 N. 122 26 00 W
Focal plane: 61ft (18.5m)
Range: 17 miles (27km)

East Brother lighthouse was built to guide vessels between San Francisco and San Pablo Bay. The station was built on East Brother Island only because the Lighthouse Board could not purchase mainland property at a reasonable price. The fifth-order Fresnel lens within the Victorian-style wooden-framed tower and attached keeper's house was automated in 1969 and local preservationists then fought a successful campaign to save the building from being demolished. It has since been fully restored and is now a bed and breakfast inn.

Farallon Island Light

South Farallon Islands, CA
Built: 1856
Style: Conical towe
No: 355
Position: 37 41 54 N. 123 00 06 W
Focal plane: 358ft (109m)
Range: 20 miles (32km)
Height: 41ft (12.5m)

The lighthouse was built at the height of the Gold Rush to warn vessels bound for San Francisco of this jagged island, which was often shrouded in fog. Construction took more than a year to complete, with men scrambling over rocks carrying four or five bricks at a time on their backs until mules could be brought in to transport the materials. The white conical tower, which originally held a first-order Fresnel lens, extends up through the keeper's dwelling. The lighthouse was automated in 1972 when the station was equipped with a radio beacon.

Fort Point Light

San Francisco, CA
Built: 1855 and 1864
Style: Skeletal tower

Fort Point lighthouse has had a troubled existence, having been summarily removed on two occasions by the U.S. Army, then eclipsed by the Golden Gate Bridge. The first lighthouse built in 1855 was never lit. The tower was torn down by the army to make way for stronger fortifications while lighthouse engineers were waiting for the arrival from France of the station's third-order Fresnel lens. Later that year a second tower was built outside the fortress walls and fitted with a fifth-order lens, but this too had to go when the army decided to extend the sea wall during the Civil War. In 1864 a third lighthouse was erected on the north-west corner of the fort, and this 27-ft (8-m) iron skeletal tower enjoyed 70 years of uninterrupted service until completion of the Golden Gate Bridge in 1934 led to it being decommissioned. The tower is now managed by the Fort Point National Historic Site and was restored in 1973.

Lime Point Light

Sausalito, CA
Built: 1883 and 1900
Style: Square
No: 4270
Position: 37 49 30 N. 122 28 42 W
Focal plane: 15ft (4.5m)
Range: 8 miles (13km)

Lime Point Light, situated on the opposite side of the Golden Gate Bridge to Fort Point lighthouse, began life in 1883 as a fog-signal station. The 20-ft (6-m) concrete lighthouse was added in 1900 and the station was automated in 1961, when the keeper's dwelling was pulled down.

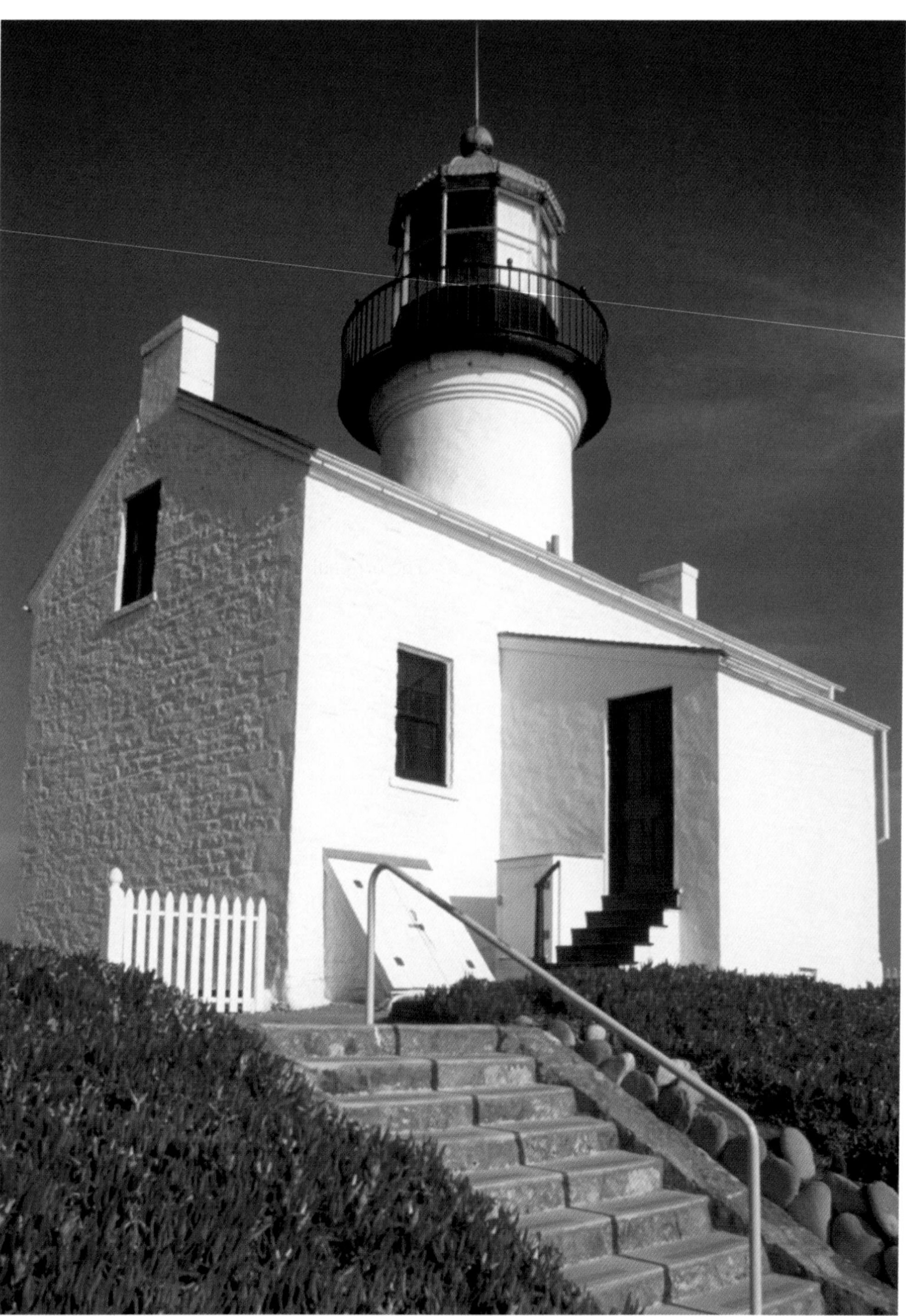

Long Beach Harbor Light

Los Angeles, CA
Built: 1949
Style: Tower on building on columnar base
No: 125
Position: 33 43 24 N. 118 11 12 W
Focal plane: 50ft (15m)
Range: 20 miles (32km)
Height: 42ft (13m)

Long Beach Harbor Light, or 'Robot Light' as it is nicknamed locally, was erected at the end of the San Pedro Middle Breakwater in 1949. The tower, which is designed specifically to withstand earthquakes and is equipped with an aero-beacon, was automated from the outset and is controlled from the Los Angeles Harbor Light.

Los Angeles Harbor Light

Los Angeles, CA
Built: 1913
Style: Cylindrical tower on concrete base
No: 3110
Position: 33 42 30 N. 118 15 06 W
Focal plane: 73ft (22m)
Range: 18 miles (29km)
Height: 69ft (21m)

The lighthouse was built to mark the end of the harbour breakwater. Fitted with a fourth-

LEFT
Old Point Loma Light, California.

OPPOSITE
Pigeon Point Light, California.

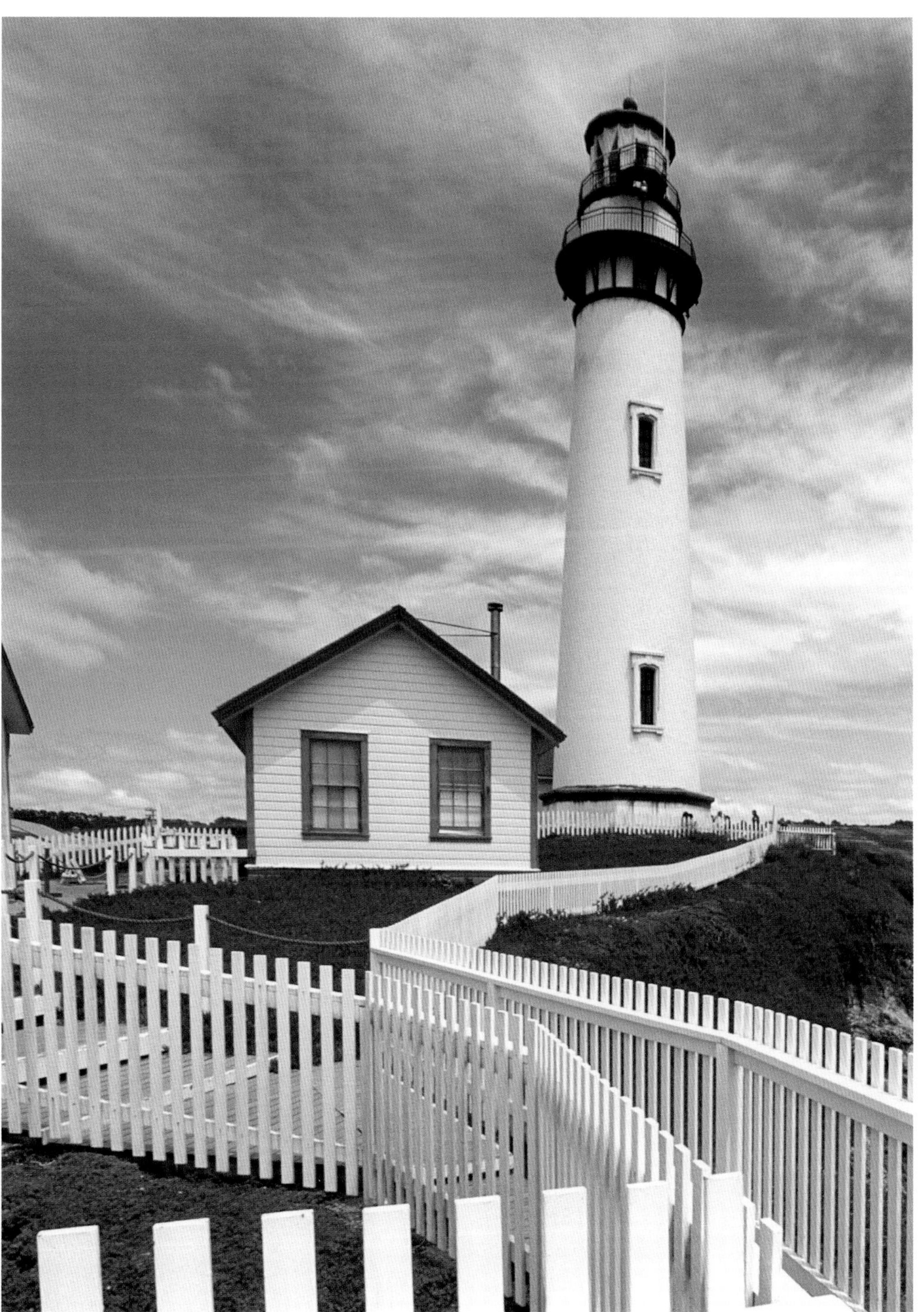

order Fresnel lens, the concrete tower was designed specifically to withstand earthquakes, but it has also stood up to the odd brush with U.S. Navy ships. The station, which remotely controls the Long Beach Harbor Light, was automated in 1971.

Mile Rock Light

San Francisco, CA
Built: 1906 and 1966
Style: Caisson
No: 4245
Position: 37 47 34 N. 122 30 37 W
Focal plane: 49ft (15m)
Range: 15 miles (24km)

The original Mile Rock lighthouse was built in 1906 to mark the outcrop in San Francisco Bay that sank the *Rio de Janeiro* in 1901 with the loss of 128 lives. The steel lighthouse, which was removed in 1966 and replaced with an automated solar-powered beacon, sat on 1,500 tons of concrete set on the top of the rock that measures just 30 x 40ft (9 x 12m) at high water.

Old Carquinez Straits Light

Vallejo, CA
Built: 1908
Style: Square tower

Old Carquinez Straits lighthouse was built in 1908 and relocated from the harbour entrance to mark the western end of San Pablo Bay in 1951. Fitted with a fourth-order Fresnel lens, the wooden tower with its attached keeper's dwelling was automated in 1963, and is now privately owned.

Old Point Loma Light

San Diego, CA
Built: 1855
Style: Skeletal tower

Old Point Loma Light was built in 1855 to mark the entrance to San Diego harbour and was one of the first on the West Coast. The 40-ft (12-m) tower and its Cape Cod-style dwelling stands 460ft (140m) above sea level. Its third-order lens had a range of 40 miles (64km), but only on clear nights! In bad weather or foggy conditions the light shone above the cloud base and proved worse than useless. The station was decommissioned in 1891 and replaced by a skeletal tower situated on the tip of Point Loma. In 1963, the original tower and its buildings were transformed into a museum managed by the National Park Service.

Piedras Blancas Light

Cambria, CA
Built: 1875 and 1949
Style: Flat-topped conical tower
No: 265
Position: 35 39 56 N. 121 17 04 W
Focal plane: 142ft (43m)
Range: 21 miles (34km)

The conical steel Piedras Blancas lighthouse was built in 1875 with an ornate lantern room and first-order bivalve lens. In 1949, the top of the tower was removed completely and an automatic aero-marine beacon was installed instead.

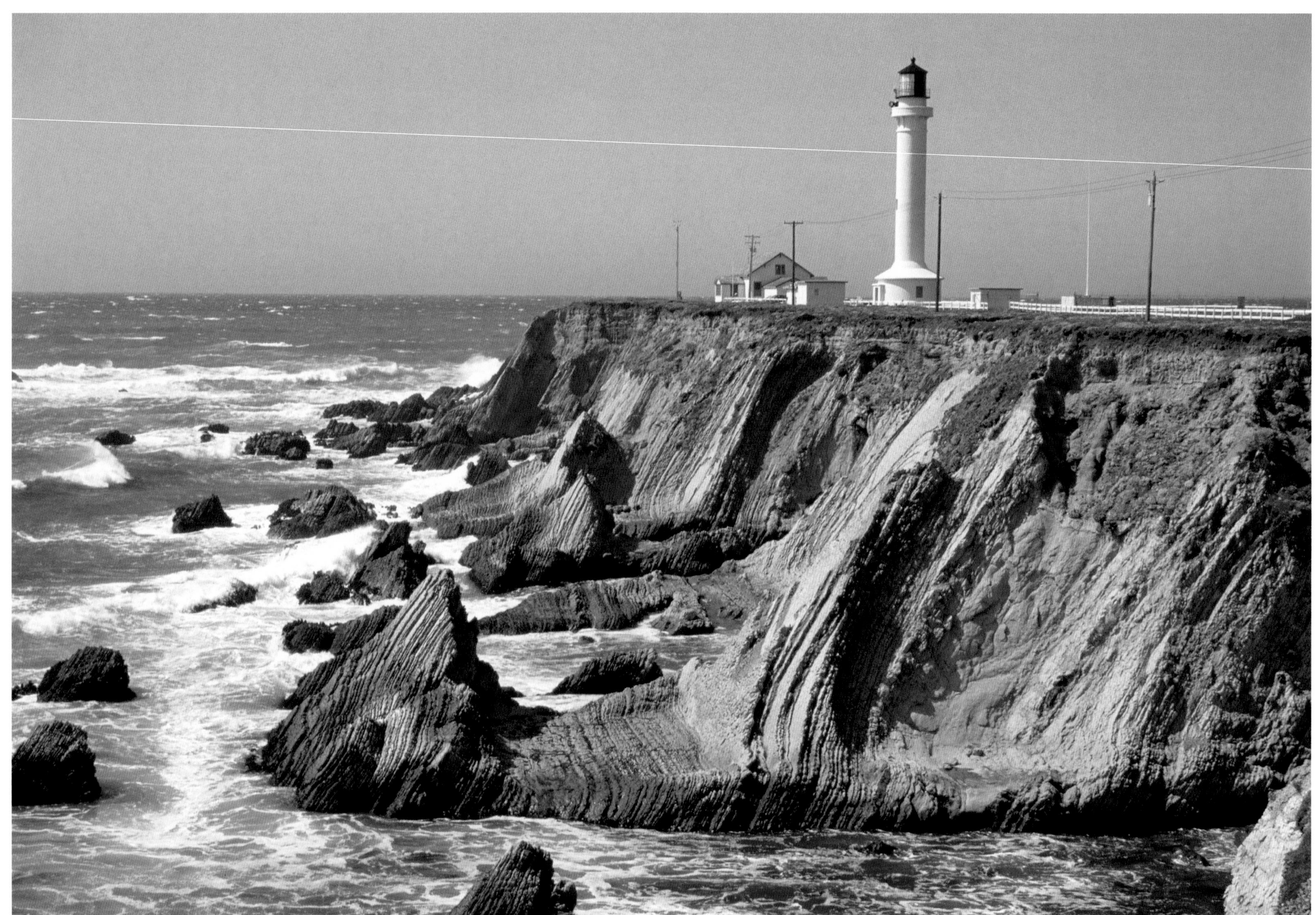

OPPOSITE
Point Arena Light, California.

RIGHT
Point Loma Light, California.

Pigeon Point Light

Pescadero, CA
Built: 1872
Style: Conical tower
No: 320
Position: 37 10 54 N. 122 23 36 W
Focal plane: 148ft (45m)
Range: 24 miles (39km)
Height: 115ft (35m)

The lighthouse was built to guide ships towards San Francisco. It stands on imposing cliffs, 160ft (49m) above the Pacific swell. The point was given its name in memory of the lives lost when the American clipper *Pigeon* foundered on these rocks in 1853. Another to founder here, 12 years later, was the British ship *Sir John Franklin*, which ran onto the rocks directly below the point where the lighthouse now stands; all hands were lost. The lighthouse was automated in 1974 and its light replaced with an aero-beacon. The tower and its buildings now double as a youth hostel.

Point Arena Light

Point Arena, CA
Built: 1870 and 1908
Style: Cylindrical tower
No: 420
Position: 38 57 17 N. 123 44 26 W
Focal plane: 155ft (47m)
Range: 25 miles (40km)
Height: 115ft (35m)

The Point Arena lighthouse stands astride the San Andreas Fault. When the infamous 1906 earthquake levelled much of San Francisco, Point Arena suffered only minor damage apart from its brick-built lighthouse of 1870, which was left with a large crack. This led to the first 'earthquake-proof' concrete lighthouse being built here in 1908; the success of the design of its tower led to others being built in areas prone to seismic activity, including other parts of California, Hawaii and Alaska.

Point Arguello Light

Point Arguello, CA
Built: 1901 and 1934
Style: Skeletal tower on single post
No: 210
Position: 34 34 37 N. 120 38 50 W
Focal plane: 100ft (30.5m)
Range: 9 miles (14.5km)
Height: 20ft (6m)

The original lighthouse was built in 1901 following a series of shipwrecks including that of the *Yankee Blade*, a side-wheel steamer that went down with $153,000 of gold bullion on board in 1854. The 28-ft (8.5-m) tower held a fourth-order Fresnel lens and stood 148ft (45m) above sea level, but it proved inadequate in fog and in 1923 blinked uselessly while one of the biggest peacetime disasters in the history of the U.S.

OPPOSITE
Point Conception Light, California.

RIGHT
Point Vicente Light, California.

Navy unfolded below. On the foggy night of 8 September, Fleet Commander Edward Watson miscalculated his position and turned seven of his destroyers into rocks below the lighthouse, believing that he was heading for the Santa Barbara Channel. He lost 23 men. The lighthouse, which was difficult to supply even in good conditions, was then automated, and was finally replaced with the present skeletal tower fitted with an aero-marine beacon in 1934.

Point Blunt Light

Angel Island, San Francisco, CA
Built: 1956
Style: Square house
No: 4335
Position: 37 51 12 N. 122 25 12 W
Focal plane: 60ft (18m)
Range: 13 miles (21km)

Point Blunt lighthouse was built on Angel Island, 4 miles (6.5km) north-east of the Golden Gate Bridge, and was automated from the start. It remains one of the most modern towers in the United States.

Point Bonita Light

San Francisco, CA
Built: 1855 and 1877
Style: Tower on building
No: 370
Position: 37 48 54 N. 122 31 48 W
Focal plane: 124ft (38m)
Range: 18 miles (29km)
Height: 33ft (10m)

The original lighthouse was built in 1855 to mark a narrow manoeuvring area within what are now called the Golden Gate Straits. Like so many other early lighthouses in this region, the 56-ft (17-m) brick tower was built too high to be effective in the foggy conditions that often affect the area. The U.S. Army attempted to resolve the problem by setting up a cannon on the site, and later a 1,500-lb (680-kg) fog bell was installed. Neither proved effective, so work began in 1872 to construct the present tower lower down the cliff. The project took five years to complete. In 1940 a landslide carried away the bridge linking the station with the mainland and it was replaced by a suspension bridge.

Point Cabrillo Light

Mendocino, CA
Built: 1909
Style: Octagonal frame tower on building
No: 450
Position: 39 20 54 N. 123 49 36 W
Focal plane: 81ft (25m)
Range: 22 miles (35km)
Height: 47ft (14m)

This lighthouse and the Cape Cod-style station became one of the most popular postings within the Coast Guard service. The lighthouse, which stands 50ft (15m) above

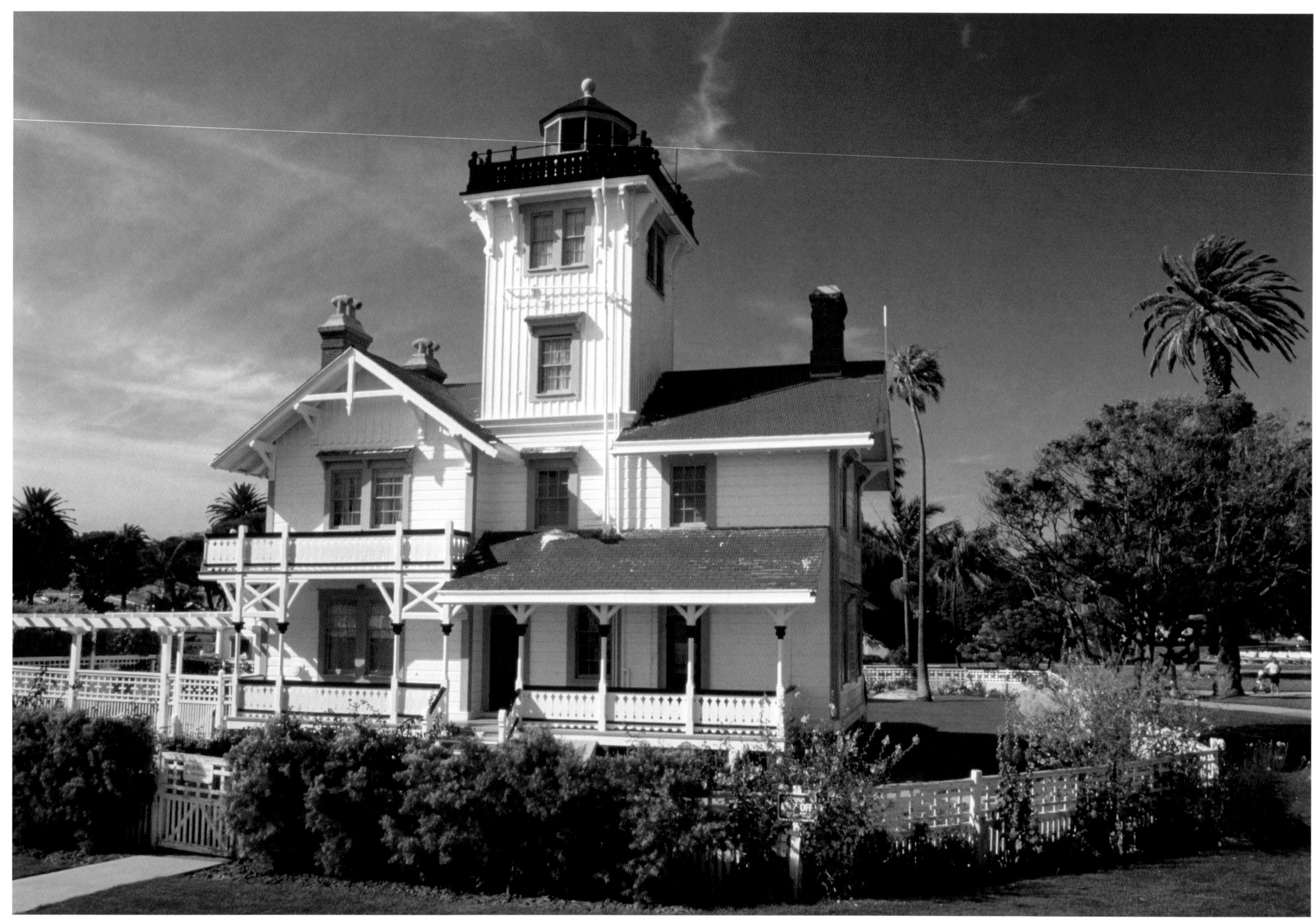

OPPOSITE
Point Fermin Light, California.

RIGHT
Point Montara Light, California.

the Pacific, was equipped with a third-order Fresnel lens, replaced with an aero-beacon when the light was automated. The site is now managed by California Coastal Conservancy.

Point Conception Light

Santa Barbara Channel, CA
Built: 1856 and 1882
Style: Cylindrical tower behind building
No: 200
Position: 34 26 54 N. 120 28 12 W
Focal plane: 133ft (40.5m)
Range: 26 miles (42km)
Height: 52ft (16m)

The lighthouse built in 1856 was one of the first stations established on the West Coast. It suffered not only from a catalogue of construction disasters, including being too small to accept the first-order Fresnel lens allotted to the tower, but also from being built too high up to be effective in foggy conditions. The tower was finally abandoned in 1882 after the present 52-ft cylindrical tower was erected lower down this hazardous stretch of cliffs. The station was automated in 1973.

Point Fermin Light

San Pedro, CA
Built: 1874
Style: Square, skeletal tower

The original Point Fermin Light was built in 1874 on Paseo Del Mar to guide shipping towards San Pedro harbour. The square redwood tower and attached keeper's dwelling is the same Italianate design as its twin at Point Hueneme, farther north. It was equipped with a fourth-order Fresnel lens until World War II, when all lighthouses were subject to security blackout. At Cape Firmin, however, the tower suffered the ignominy of having its lantern room removed and replaced with a watchtower, which transformed it into something locals thought resembled a chicken coop. When peace resumed, the lighthouse was replaced with a skeletal steel tower built on the edge of the cliffs. The original lighthouse has now been fully restored and is a tourist attraction within Point Fermin City Park.

Punta Gorda Light

Petrolia, CA
Built: 1911
Style: Cylindrical

The 27-ft (8-m) Punta Gorda lighthouse was built in 1911 on an inhospitable cape near Petrolia. Prior to this light, the only visitors to Punta Gorda had been the fortunate few washed up after their ships had foundered. Between 1899 and 1907 no less than eight ships were lost, the most notable being the

Santa Barbara Light, California.

Columbia, with a cost of 87 lives. The cast-iron tower was equipped with a fourth-order Fresnel lens which continued to throw its light out over the Pacific until the station was decommissioned in 1951.

Point Hueneme Light

Oxnard, CA
Built: 1874 and 1941
Style: Square tower on building
No: 190
Position: 34 08 43 N. 119 12 36 W
Focal plane: 52ft (16m)
Range: 20 miles (32km)
Height: 48ft (15m)

The lighthouse was built to mark the Santa Barbara Channel in 1874, the same year as its twin tower at Point Fermin. The original tower, which was sold in 1941 and later pulled down, was replaced by an art deco square tower 48ft in height, with an integrated fog-signal building, and was fitted with a fourth-order Fresnel lens. The station was automated in 1972.

Point Loma Light

San Diego, CA
Built: 1891
Style: Square pyramidal skeleton tower
No: 5
Position: 32 39 54 N. 117 14 34 W
Focal plane: 88ft (27m)
Range: 22 miles (35km)
Height: 70ft (21m)

The 70-ft Point Loma Light was erected in 1891 to replace the old light station built 36 years earlier high above the fog banks that sometimes lie around San Diego harbour. The cast-iron skeletal tower, which stands 88ft (27m) above sea level, has a third-order Fresnel lens, which was borrowed for display at the 1893 World Exposition in Chicago.

Point Montara Light

Pacifica, CA
Built: 1900 and 1926
Style: Conical tower
No: 335
Position: 37 32 12 N. 122 31 12 W
Focal plane: 70ft (21m)
Range: 15 miles (24km)
Height: 30ft (9m)

The present 30-ft lighthouse was built in 1926 to replace a beacon sited over an offshore ledge north of Half Moon Bay. This followed the loss of the steamer *Colorado* in 1868 and the freighter *Acuelo* three years later. The station's original fourth-order Fresnel lens had a range of 15 miles, but it was replaced with a modern optic when the tower was automated in 1970. The station now doubles as a youth hostel.

Point Pinos Light

Pacific Grove, CA
Built: 1855
Style: Tower on dwelling
No: 290
Position: 36 38 00 N. 121 56 00 W
Focal plane: 89ft (27m)
Range: 17 miles (27km)
Height: 43ft (13m)

The lighthouse was built in 1855 on the southern tip of Monterey Bay, and is the oldest active lighthouse on the West Coast. Designed by Francis Gibbons, the Cape Cod-style station still has its original third-order Fresnel lens. The granite tower was one of many to be damaged during the 1906 earthquake but was successfully repaired using reinforced concrete. The station was automated in 1975 and is now managed by a local historical society which organizes tours of the lighthouse.

Point Reyes Light

Point Reyes, CA
Built: 1870
Style: Cylindrical structure on building
No: 385
Position: 37 59 42 N. 123 01 24 W
Focal plane: 265ft (81m)
Range: 24 miles (39km)
Height: 37ft (11m)

Point Reyes lighthouse was built in 1870, some 250ft (76m) up the cliffs, to mark one of the most hazardous channels into San Francisco Bay. The rocks below this headland extend a further 15 miles (24km) out to sea and are the graveyard of hundreds of ships that have foundered here since the 18th century. The brick-lined cast-iron tower was set halfway up the cliff, and keepers had to descend 308 steps to maintain the first-order Fresnel light and crawl back up again whenever it was foggy! Much to the relief of those who had to man the tower, perhaps, the station was automated in 1975 and was fitted with a modern optic.

Point Sur Light

Big Sur, CA
Built: 1889
Style: Tower on stone building
No: 280
Position: 36 18 24 N. 121 54 06 W

Point Sur was built on one of the most rugged sections of the West Coast, between Big Sur and Monterey. It took nine years to persuade Congress to agree to site a lighthouse in this remote area and another four years to complete the project, which ended up costing twice the original budget. Engineers first had to build a railway to transport the materials, then cut 395 steps down the steep sandy bluff where the 50-ft (15-m) tower was erected. The lighthouse was equipped with a first-order Fresnel lens with a focal plane of 250ft (76m) above the Pacific. The station had a range of 25 miles (40km). When the tower was automated in 1972, the Fresnel lens was exchanged for an aero-beacon.

Point Vicente Light

Rancho Palos Verdes, CA
Built: 1926
Style: Cylindrical

The 67-ft (20-m) Point Vincente lighthouse was built in 1926 on a 100-ft (30.5-m) cliff

LEFT
Barbers Point Light, Hawaii.

OPPOSITE
Santa Cruz/Mark Abbot Memorial Light, California

overlooking the Pacific at Rancho Palos Verdes. The tower has been the backdrop for a number of Hollywood epics, and because of this film publicity has become one of California's most easily recognized landmarks. The lighthouse still has its original third-order Fresnel lens, which has a range of 20 miles (32km). The tower was automated in 1973.

San Luis Obispo Light

San Luis Obispo, CA
Built: 1890 and 1976
Style: Tower on cylindrical structure
No: 225
Position: 35 09 36 N. 120 45 36 W
Focal plane: 116ft (35m)
Range: 20 miles (32km)

The original 40-ft (12-m) lighthouse was built in 1890 on a remote headland that could only be serviced from the sea. Standing 130ft (40m) above sea level, the square tower was equipped with a fourth-order Fresnel lens. The station was automated in 1975, and was replaced the following year by a cylindrical tower fitted with an aero-marine beacon.

Santa Barbara Light

Santa Barbara, CA
Built: 1856 and 1926
Style: Conical
No: 195
Position: 34 23 48 N. 119 43 24 W
Focal plane: 142ft (43m)
Range: 25 miles (40km)
Height: 24ft (7m)

Santa Barbara was one of the first light stations to be built on the West Coast. Designed and built by George Nagle in 1856, it was first manned by Albert Johnson Williams, who turned his duties over to his wife Julie when he tired of the job nine years later. She continued to maintain the light for the next 40 years until forced to retire in 1905 at the age of 81 after falling and breaking her hip. In 1925 the lighthouse was destroyed in an earthquake and was replaced a year later by the present conical tower.

Santa Cruz Light/Mark Abbott Memorial Light

Santa Cruz, CA
Built: 1870, 1948 and 1967
Style: Square tower attached to building
No: 305
Position: 36 57 06 N. 122 01 36 W
Focal plane: 60ft (18m)
Range: 17 miles (27km)
Height: 39ft (12m)

The original lighthouse was built in 1870 to guide lime and lumber ships in and out of this logging port. The 35-ft (10.5-m) wood and brick lighthouse, equipped with a fifth-order Fresnel lens, was pulled down

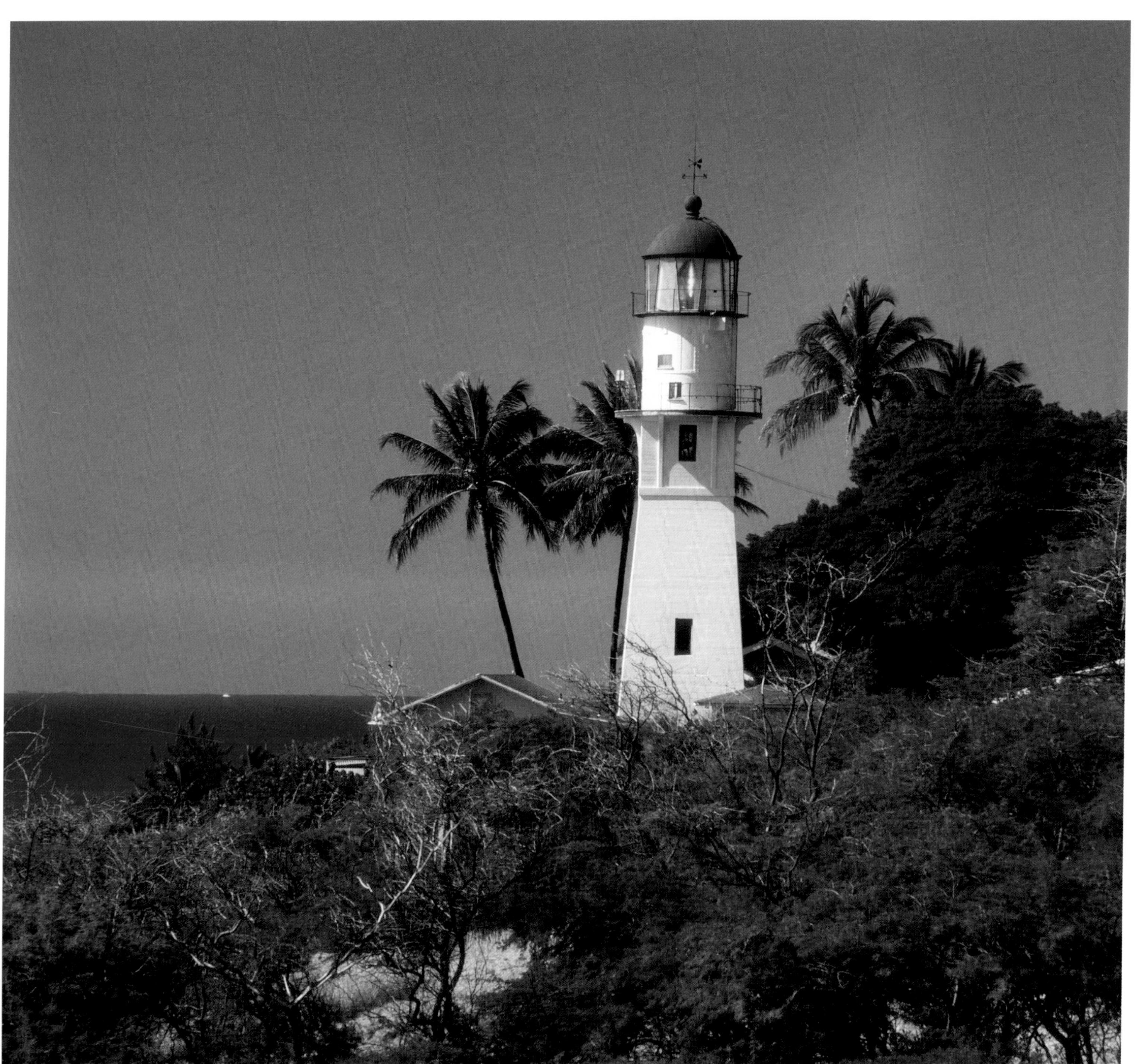

LEFT
Diamond Head Light, Hawaii.

OPPOSITE
Cape Kumukahi Light, Hawaii.

after World War II. The present 39-ft lighthouse was built in 1967 as a memorial to Mark Abbott, a surfer who drowned nearby. The building serves as a surfing museum.

Southampton Shoal Light

Stockton, CA
Built: 1905
Style: Tower with integrated building

The lighthouse began service in San Francisco Harbor and was relocated to mark these rocks off Stockton in 1905. The wooden tower, with its integrated keeper's dwelling, was equipped with a fifth-order Fresnel lens which was automated in 1960, the same year that the station was decommissioned. The building is now home to a yacht club.

St. George's Reef Light

Crescent City, CA
Built: 1892
Style: Square tower
No: 561
Position: 41 50 14 N. 124 22 32 W
Focal plane: 20ft (6m)

The 70-ft (21-m) lighthouse, standing on a wave-swept rock off Crescent City, is the most costly U.S. lighthouse ever

constructed. Building began in 1882, 17 years after a side-paddle steamer, *Brother Jonathan*, ran aground here with the loss of more than 200 lives. The building work took ten years to complete, at a cost of $702,000, and the lighthouse was fitted with an 18-ft (5.5-m) first-order Fresnel lens. In 1923 the tower survived one of the worst storms in history when waves broke over the platform and tore the donkey-engine house from its foundations.

Trinidad Head Light

Trinidad, CA
Built: 1871
Style: Square tower
No: 525
Position: 41 03 06 N. 124 09 06 W
Focal plane: 196ft (60m)
Range: 14 miles (22.5km)
Height: 20ft (6m)

The Trinidad Head Light was built in 1871 on a headland standing more than 170ft (52m) above the Pacific. Despite the height, waves have been known to break right over the station; in 1913 the lighthouse keeper reported that the tower and balcony were awash.

Yerba Buena Light

San Francisco, CA
Built: 1874
Style: Octagonal tower
No: 4595
Position: 37 48 24 N. 122 21 42 W
Focal plane: 95ft (29m)
Range: 14 miles (22.5km)

The lighthouse was built on this 140-acre (56-hectare) island in 1874 to guide the ferries across San Francisco Bay between Oakland and the downtown section of the city. Parts were purloined from across the West Coast, the station's fifth-order Fresnel lens having been taken from the Yaquina Bay lighthouse in Newport, Oregon, and the fog bell from Point Conception. The tower was automated in 1958 and the keeper's dwelling is now the official residence of the commander of the Coast Guard's 12th District.

Hawaii

Barbers Point Light

Kalaelo, Oahu Island, HI
Built: 1888
Style: Cylindrical

Barbers Point was built of reinforced concrete in 1888. The white cylindrical tower was fitted with a fourth-order Fresnel lens which was automated in 1964. The station is now decommissioned.

Cape Kumukahi Light

Big Island, HI
Built: 1934
Style: Pyramidal skeleton tower
No: 28130
Position: 19 30 59 N. 154 48 39 W
Focal plane: 156ft (47.5m)
Range: 22 miles (35km)
Height: 115ft (35m)

The skeletal lighthouse, marking the eastern

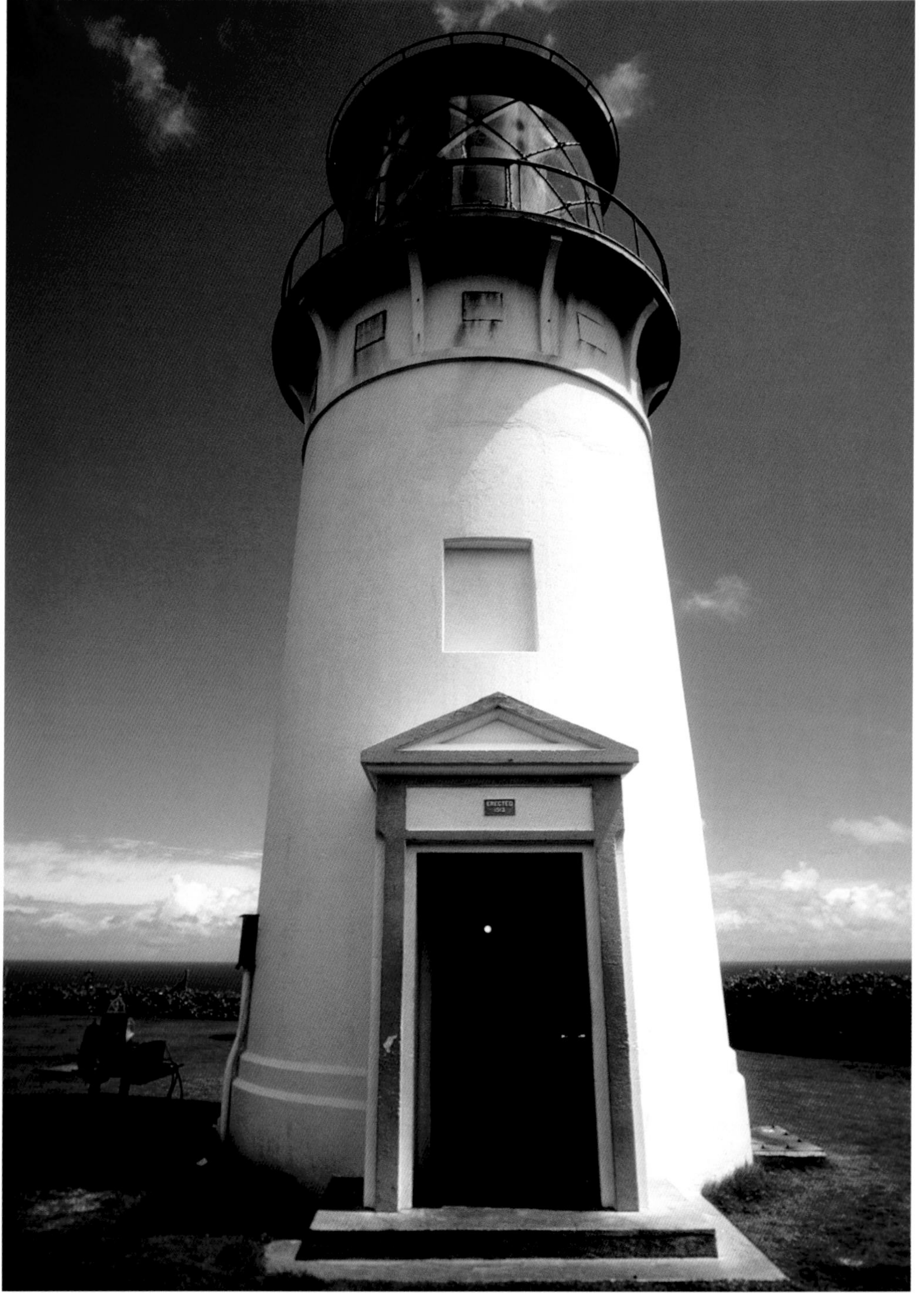

LEFT
Kilauea Point Light, Hawaii.

RIGHT
Makapuu Point Light, Hawaii.

tip of the Hawaiian Islands, was erected in 1934. The tower, which was automated in 1960, retains its original 375-mm lens.

Diamond Head Light

Oahu Island, HI
Built: 1899 and 1917
Style: Concrete tower
No: 29060
Position: 21 15 18 N. 157 48 36 W
Focal plane: 147ft (45m)
Range: W 17 miles/27km, R 14 miles/23km
Height: 55ft (17m)

The present lighthouse at Diamond Head was built in 1917 to replace a similarly-sized square masonry tower that had marked the entrance to Honolulu harbour since 1899. The lighthouse, which contained the third-order Fresnel lens from the earlier tower, was automated in 1924 and the keeper's dwelling is now the official residence of the Commander of the Coast Guard's 14th District.

Kilauea Point Light

Kauai Island, HI
Built: 1913
Style: Conical

The 53-ft (16-m) Kilauea Point Light was built on the north side of Kauai Island in 1913 to mark the northernmost point in the Hawaiian island chain. Standing on the top of high cliffs, the tower's second-order Fresnel lens had a focal plane of 216ft (66m). The lighthouse was manned until the station was decommissioned in 1976. The buildings, which suffered some damage from a hurricane in 1992, are now managed by the Kilauea Point National Wildlife Refuge.

Lahaina Light

Auau Channel, Maui Island, HI
Built: 1840 and 1916
Style: Pyramidal concrete tower
No: 28460
Position: 20 52 20 N. 156 40 43 W
Focal plane: 44ft (13m)
Range: 7 miles (11km)
Height: 39ft (12m)

The present lighthouse marking the Auau Channel to Lahaina, the home of the former Hawaiian monarchs, was built on Maui in 1916. It replaced a series of rudimentary wooden trestle towers that date back to at least 1840, making this station the first in what is now the western United States. Standing 45ft (14m) above sea level, the tower's Vega lens has a focal plane of 44ft.

Makapuu Point Light

Waimanalo, Oahu Island, HI
Built: 1929
Style: Cylindrical concrete tower
No: 28925
Position: 21 18 36 N. 157 38 54 W
Focal plane: 420ft (128m)

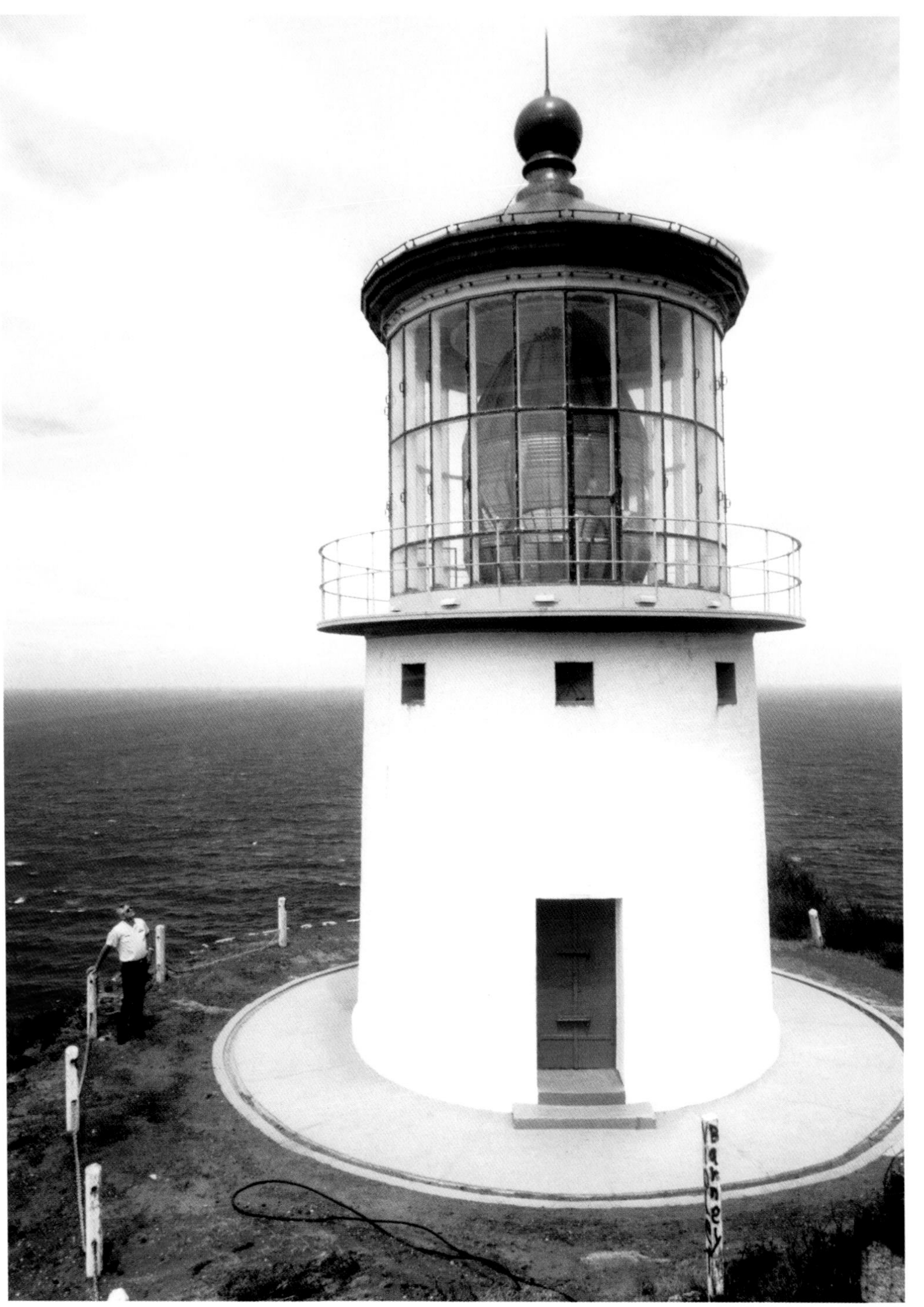

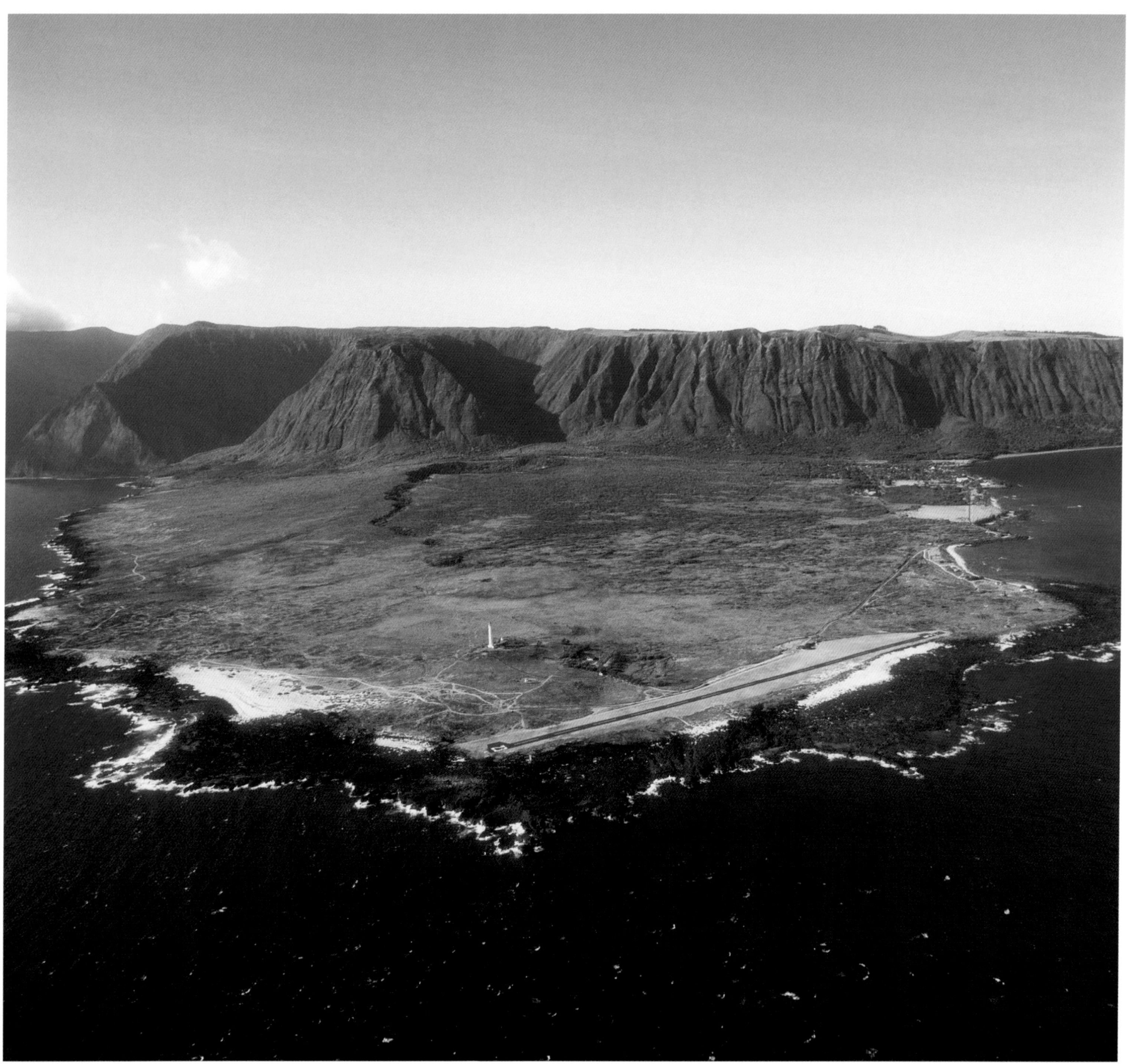

LEFT
Nawiliwili Harbor Light, Hawaii.

OPPOSITE
Cape Blanco Light, Oregon.

Range: 19 miles (30.5km)
Height: 46ft (14m)

The lighthouse was built in 1929 to mark the eastern point of Oahu Island and guide vessels from the United States towards the port of Honolulu. Perched on a lava ledge more than 380ft (116m) above the Pacific, the lighthouse can boast the largest Fresnel lens in North America, having a diameter of 8ft 6in (2.5m). A 12-ft (3.5m) radio beacon was added in 1927 and the station was automated in 1974.

Molokai Light

Kalaupapa, Molokai Island, HI
Built: 1909
Style: Concrete tower
No: 28575
Position: 21 12 36 N. 156 58 06 W
Focal plane: 213ft (65m)
Range: 25 miles (40km)
Height: 138ft (42m)

The lighthouse was built in 1909 to guide vessels around the north of Molokai Island. The station was located close to a leprosy hospital, which caused some concern to the keepers who were stationed here before the light was automated in 1966. The concrete tower was equipped originally with a second-order Fresnel lens but this has since

been replaced by a modern optic. The station and hospital are now part of the Kalaupapa National Historical Park.

Nawiliwili Harbor Light

Kauai Island, HI
Built: 1906
Style: Cylindrical concrete tower
No: 29745
Position: 21 57 18 N. 159 20 12 W
Focal plane: 112ft (34m)
Range: 24 miles (39km)
Height: 80ft (24m)

Nawiliwili Harbor Light was built in 1906, two years after the U.S. Lighthouse Board took over control of the maritime navigation system across the Hawaiian Islands. The concrete tower was equipped with a first-order bivalve Fresnel lens, automated in 1954, to guide vessels into Nawiliwili Bay on Kauai Island.

Oregon

Cape Arago Light

Charleston, OR
Built: 1866, 1908 and 1934
Style: Octagonal tower attached to building
No: 605
Position: 43 20 28 N. 124 22 31 W
Focal plane: 100ft (30.5m)
Range: 17 miles (27km)
Height: 44ft (13m)

A century of sea erosion has forced the lighthouse at Cape Arago to be replaced three times. The first cast-iron tower, built in 1866 as a marker for the Coos River bar,

RIGHT
Cape Meares Light, Oregon

OPPOSITE
Cape Arago Light, Oregon.

was superseded in 1908 by a wooden tower constructed 30ft (9m) farther inland. When the seas began to encroach on this site too, it was decided to build the present 44-ft octagonal concrete tower on the cliffs behind. Completed in 1934, it is still equipped with its fourth-order Fresnel lens and has a range of 17 miles. The lighthouse was automated in 1966.

Cape Blanco Light

Port Orford, OR
Built: 1870
Style: Conical tower
No: 595
Position: 42 50 13 N. 124 33 49 W
Focal plane: 245ft (75m)
Range: 26 miles (42km)
Height: 99ft (30m)

Cape Blanco is Oregon's oldest lighthouse. Built on the 200-ft (61-m) chalk cliffs that gave the cape its name, the 99-ft conical tower, with its attached keeper's cottage, still has its second-order Fresnel lens, giving it a range of 26 miles. The station, which dates back to 1870, was automated in 1980. Twelve years later the building suffered more than $500,000 worth of damage at the hands of vandals.

Coquille River Light, Oregon.

Cape Meares Light

Tillamook, OR
Built: 1890
Style: Octagonal
No: 675
Position: 45 29 11 N. 123 58 42 W
Focal plane: 232ft (71m)
Range: 25 miles (40km)
Height: 38ft (11.5m)

Cape Meares has had a chequered history. For a start, it was built on the wrong headland after a mapmaker erroneously transposed Cape Meares and Cape Lookout on a U.S. Coastguard survey chart. The mistake was not discovered until the cast-iron octagonal tower was almost complete, and rather than bear the cost, not to mention the embarrassment of moving it, the Lighthouse Board decided to leave it at Cape Meares. Standing on cliffs 215ft (65m) above the Atlantic coastline, the light has a range of 25 miles. The station was automated in 1963 but still has its original first-order Fresnel lens despite the work of vandals, who broke into the tower and damaged the light.

Columbia Lightship

Astoria, OR
Built: 1951
Builder: Rice Brothers, East Boothbay, ME
Length overall: 128ft (39m)
Beam: 30ft (9m)
Draft: 11ft (3.5m)
Displacement: 617 tons
Speed: 10.7 knots
Propulsion: Diesel
Illuminating Apparatus: Duplex 500-mm electric lens lantern on foremast.
Fog Signal: Twin F2T diaphones aft of pilot house; hand-operated bell

Station Assignments:
1951–79: Columbia River (OR)

The *Columbia* lightship was launched in 1951 and spent her active life stationed 8 miles (13km) off the Columbia River bar. The ship was decommissioned in 1979 and sold a year later to the Columbia River Maritime Museum in Astoria.

Coquille River Light

Bandon, OR
Built: 1895
Style: Cylindrical

The 40-ft (12-m) white stucco Coquille River Light was built in 1895 to guide vessels into the river. The station was badly damaged by fire in 1939 and the tower lay abandoned until a restoration project was launched by the state. The work was undertaken by the U.S. Corps of Engineers and the brick-built tower is now a tourist attraction within Bullards Beach State Park. The light from its fourth-order Fresnel lens was replaced by a jetty light and series of buoys, but since its restoration, the tower has been relit to shed its light inland.

Heceta Head Light

Florence, OR
Built: 1894
Style: Conical tower
No: 635
Position: 44 08 15 N. 124 07 42 W
Focal plane: 205ft (62m)
Range: 28 miles (45km)
Height: 65ft (20m)

The construction of Heceta Head lighthouse was a logistical nightmare. The site was midway along a 90-mile (145-km) stretch of remote coastline between Cape Foulweather and Cape Arago, and the materials had to be shipped to the Siuslaw River before being hauled overland by wagon to Heceta Head. The project took two years to complete at a cost of $180,000. The 65-ft tower, which stands 205ft (62m) above sea level, was equipped originally with a five-wick oil lamp illuminated by a 640-prism first-order Fresnel lens. The light is now electrically powered but the Fresnel lens was retained when the station was automated in 1963.

Tillamook Rock Light

Seaside, OR
Built: 1881
Style: Square

The 150-ft (46-m) Tillamook Rock Light, which marks the southern approaches to the Columbia River, is one of America's most enduring structures. Built in 1881 on a wind- and wave-swept rock, 'Terrible Tilly', as keepers called the tower, is often dwarfed by the waves of the 'Pineapple Express' – the winter storms blowing up from the South Pacific. One engineer lost his life during the two-year construction, and at times, when conditions were too rough to land a boat, it was necessary to take the keepers in and out by breeches buoy. In 1883 rocks thrown up by the waves smashed through the iron dome in 20 places, and 11 years later the lantern room was breeched by waves, bringing in fish, rocks and seaweed, which shattered 13 glass panels in the station's first-order Fresnel lens. The lighthouse was finally replaced by an automated buoy in 1957 and is now owned by the burial group, Eternity by the Sea, which uses the lighthouse as a final resting place for people's ashes.

Umpqua River Light

Winchester Bay, OR
Built: 1856 and 1894
Style: Conical tower
No: 620
Position: 43 39 42 N. 124 11 54 W
Height: 65ft (20m)

The first lighthouse was completed in 1856 after an odd contretemps with the local people, who appropriated the workers' tools. A flood then undermined the station during the winter of 1862, and the lighthouse collapsed while workmen were removing its first-order Fresnel lens. With the construction nearby of the Cape Arago lighthouse, the site was abandoned until 1894, when the present 65-ft conical tower, equipped with another first-order lens, was built. The light stands 165ft (50m) above sea level and was automated in 1966.

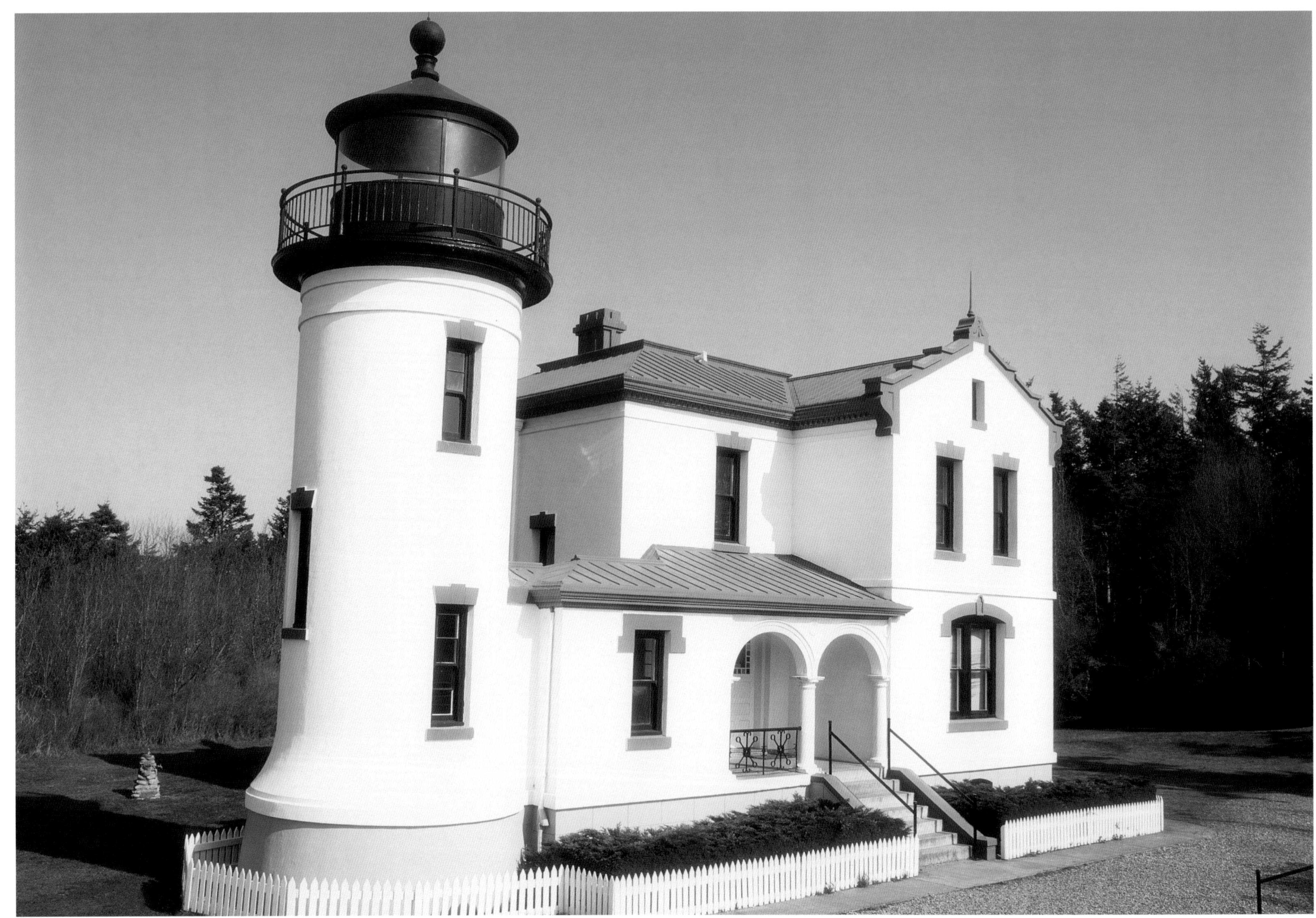

Warrior Rock Light

Sauvie Island, OR
Built: 1858
Style: White pyramidal structure
No: 11060
Position: 45 50 55 N. 122 47 18 W
Focal plane: 28ft (8.5m)
Range: 7 miles (11km)

The Warrior Rock lighthouse was built in 1858 on Sauvie Island to mark a dangerous bend in the Columbia River, which over the years had been responsible for the demise of a number of vessels. They included the lighthouse tender *Manzanita*, the Panamanian tanker *Ypatia Halcoussi*, and a barge which crashed into the lighthouse in 1969. The barge damaged the foundations, and during the repairs workers accidentally dropped the station's fog bell into the water. This was no loss to the keepers, who had nicknamed it 'Black Moria' because its unreliable mechanics meant that it invariably had to be rung by hand. During its recovery, a rope broke, sending the bell crashing down onto the rocks where it cracked. The bell had begun life at Cape Disappointment, where its ring was drowned out by the pounding surf, and is now on display at the Columbia County Historical Society of St. Helens.

OPPOSITE
Admiralty Point Light, Washington.

RIGHT
Burrows Island Light, Washington.

Yaquina Bay Light

Newport, OR
Built: 1871
Style: Square dwelling

The Yaquina Bay lighthouse served its purpose for just three years, from 1871 to 1874. The elegant house was then taken over by the Corps of Engineers and the Life-Saving Service until 1974 when the site was transferred to Oregon State Parks. The building was later saved from demolition and since 1965 has housed a museum managed by the Lincoln County Historical Society.

Yaquina Head Light

Newport, OR
Built: 1873
Style: Conical tower
No: 650
Position: 44 40 36 N. 124 04 48 W
Focal plane: 162ft (49m)
Range: 19 miles (30.5km)
Height: 93ft (28m)

The brick-built Yaquina Head Light is another of Oregon's lighthouses to have been sited, like Cape Meares, in the wrong location. It ended up at Newport instead of Cape Foulweather after a mapmaker erroneously transposed the two points on a U.S. Coast Guard survey chart. One of the most attractive lighthouses in the country, it sits on a bed of heavily magnetized iron which causes wide deviation on a ship's compass. This local phenomenon led to several shipwrecks, including one vessel that

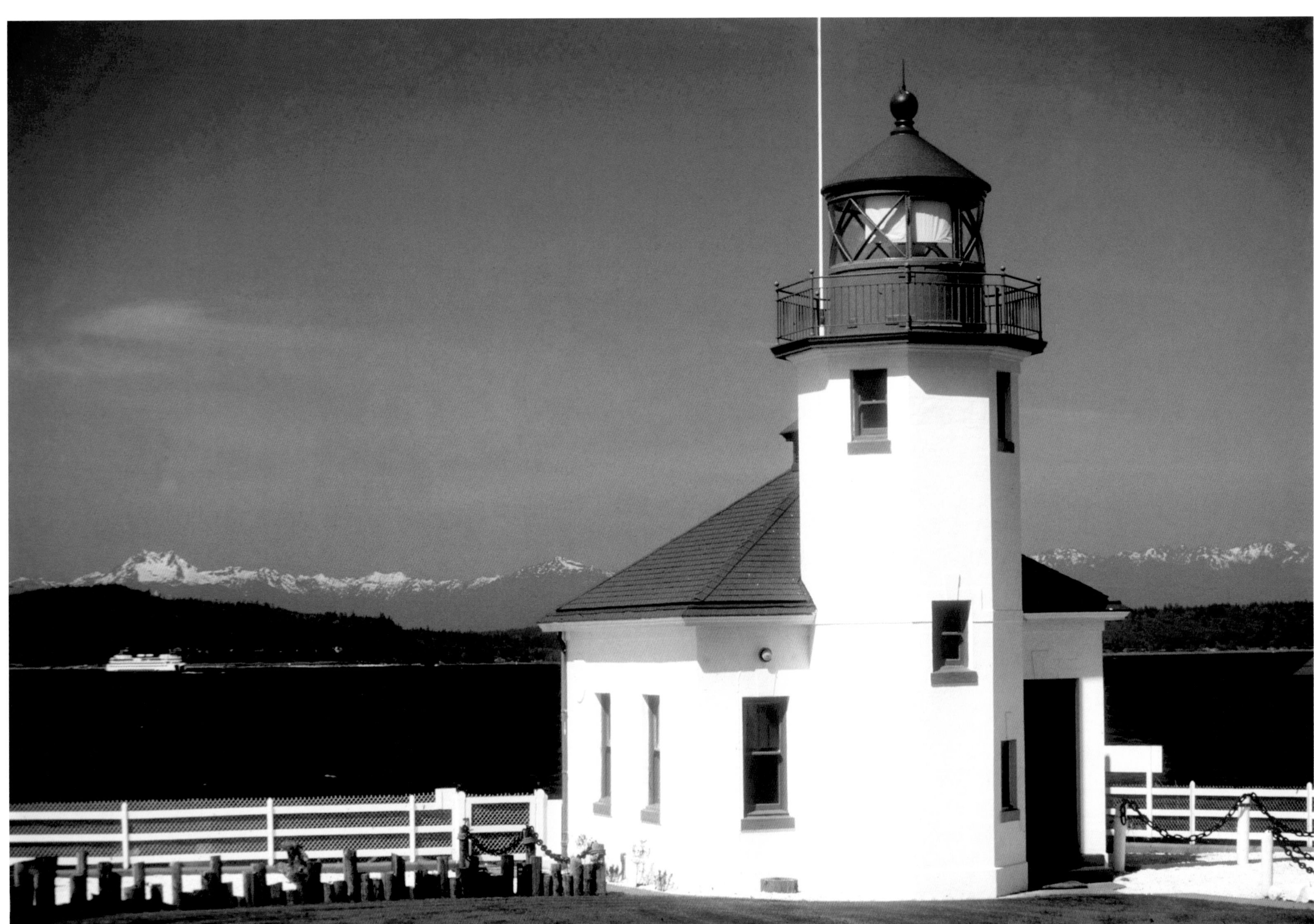

OPPOSITE
Alki Point Light, Washington.

RIGHT
Cattle Point Light, Washington.

was carrying parts intended for the light's original first-order Fresnel lens. The station was automated in 1966 and is now maintained by Oregon State Parks.

WASHINGTON

Admiralty Point Light

Coupeville, Whidbey Island, WA
Built: 1860 and 1903
Style: Cylindrical tower

The lighthouse on Whidbey Island was one of the first stations on the West Coast. The first 41-ft (12.5-m) brick tower was built in 1860 but had to make way for the development of Fort Casey to strengthen defences during the Spanish-American War. In 1903 a second brick lighthouse was built on the high bluff, which gives the light's fourth-order Fresnel lens a focal plane of 120ft (36.5m) and a range of 17 miles (27km). The station was finally decommissioned in 1927 after shipping began to rely more on the beam from Point Wilson lighthouse on the opposite side of Puget Sound. Admiralty Point is now a museum.

Alki Point Light

Seattle, WA
Built: 1887 and 1913
Style: Octagonal tower attached to building

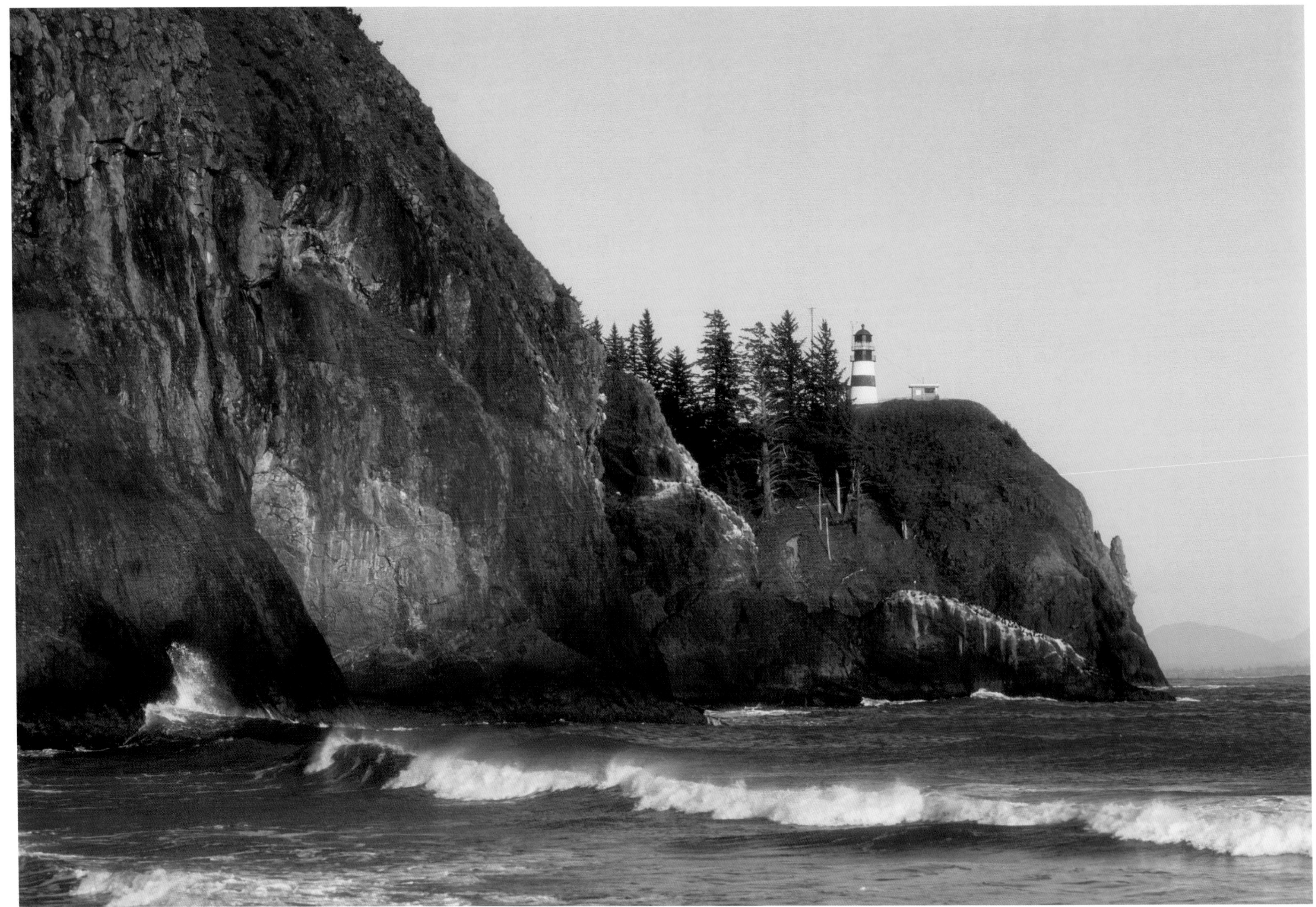

OPPOSITE
Cape Disappointment Light, Washington.

RIGHT
Dofflemyer Point Light, Washington.

No: 16915
Position: 47 34 35 N. 122 25 14 W
Focal plane: 39ft (12m)
Range: 15 miles (24km)
Height: 37ft (11m)

Alki Point Light began life as a lantern hung on a barn by farmer Hans Martin Hanson as an aid to vessels heading up Puget Sound towards Seattle. The steady increase in shipping activity during the late 19th century prompted the U.S. Lighthouse Service to pay $15 a month to maintain a lantern and lens, which it installed in 1887. This arrangement continued for a further 26 years until the Coast Guard decided to establish a station on the site in 1913, and the present 37-ft octagonal stone tower was built. This was equipped with a fourth-order Fresnel lens, which was only replaced when the tower was automated.

Browns Point Light

Tacoma, WA
Built: 1887 and 1933
Style: Square tower
No: 17090
Position: 47 18 22 N. 122 26 35 W
Focal plane: 38ft (11.5m)
Range: 12 miles (19km)
Height: 31ft (9.5m)

The concrete lighthouse at Browns Point was built in 1933 to replace a simple lantern and lens that had served to guide vessels into Port Tacoma since 1887. The station was automated in 1970.

Burrows Island Light

Burrows Island, WA
Built: 1908
Style: Square tower on building
No: 19350
Position: 48 28 41 N. 122 42 49 W
Focal plane: 57ft (17m)
Range: 9 miles (14.5m)
Height: 34ft (10m)

The wood-framed lighthouse has been guiding vessels in and out of Rosario Strait since 1908. It has proved an important reference point because the surrounding cliffs generate a magnetic field that has a considerable pull on a ship's compass.

Cape Disappointment Light

Ilwaco, WA
Built: 1856
Style: Conical tower
No: 695
Position: 46 16 33 N. 124 03 08 W
Focal plane: 220ft (67m)
Range: W 22 miles/35km, R 18 miles/29km
Height: 53ft (16m)

Cape Disappointment is one of the most enduring on the West Coast. It throws its beam over the dangerous Columbia River bar, which is better known as the 'Graveyard of the Pacific'. The 53-ft white stone tower,

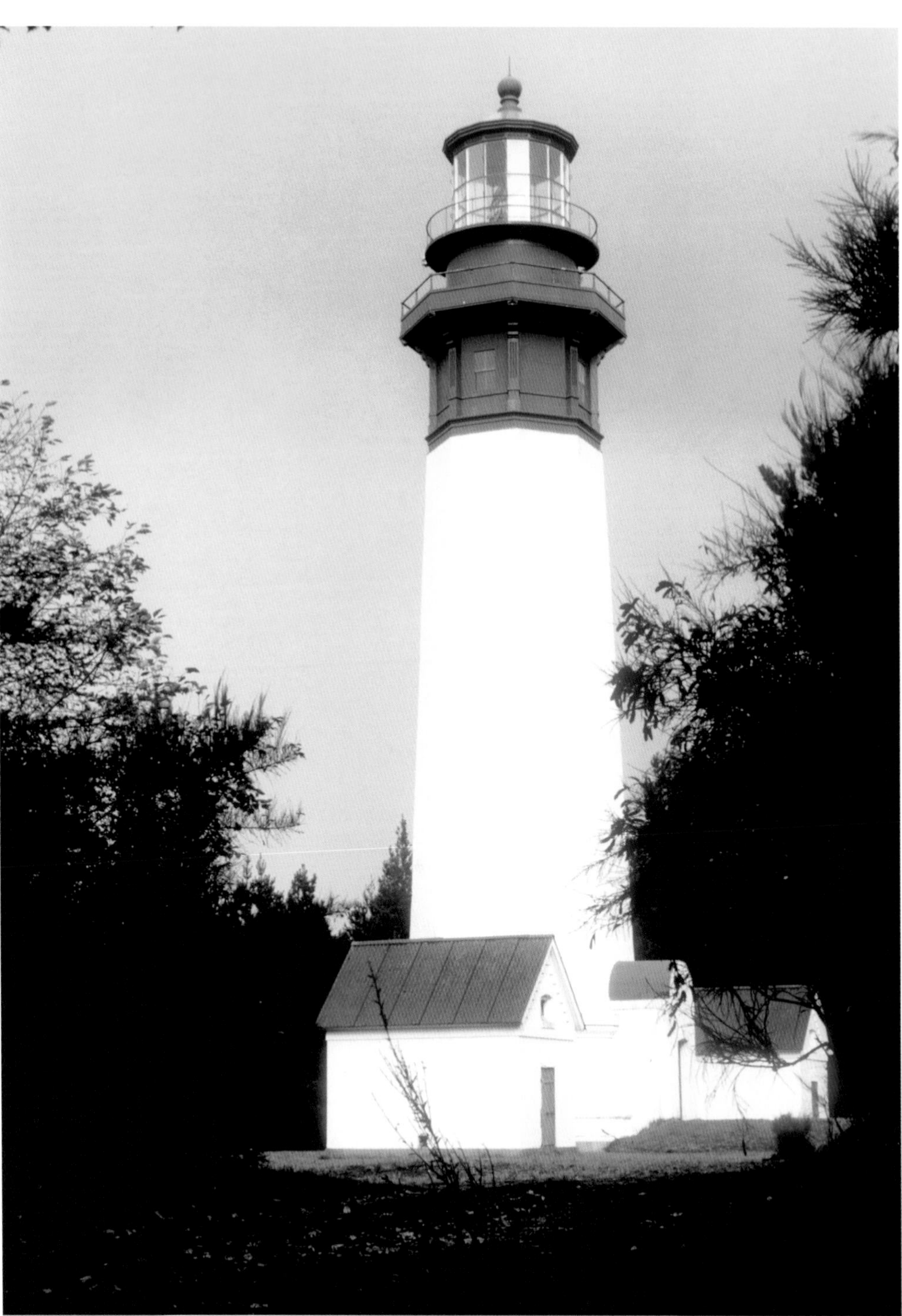

with its central black band, was under construction when the freighter *Oriole*, carrying materials to the site, became a victim of the very hazard that the lighthouse was being built to warn against. This delayed completion until 1856, but the tower, which has walls 5-ft (1.5-m) thick at the base, narrowing to 2ft 6in (0.76m) at the top, has since survived the worst the Pacific can deliver. The tower was originally equipped with a powerful first-order Fresnel lens, but this was later transferred to North Head Light and a fourth-order lens installed in its place.

Cape Flattery Light

Tatoosh Island, WA
Built: 1857
Style: Conical tower on sandstone dwelling
No: 760
Position: 48 23 30 N. 124 44 12 W
Focal plane: 165ft (50m)
Range: W 18 miles (29km)
Height: 57ft (17m)

Cape Flattery lighthouse stands 165ft above sea level to guide vessels towards the Strait of Juan de Fuca. It was always a tough station in which to serve, even for those who constructed the masonry tower in 1857. They were harassed continually by the local people who used the site for fishing and whaling and blamed the workmen for the spread of smallpox in the area. Isolation was another problem. In a fit of despair, one keeper threw himself off the cliffs, but survived and, after a period in hospital, returned to his post. Two more became so irritated with one another that they fought a duel, not knowing that an assistant had loaded their pistols with blanks!

LEFT
Grays Harbor Light, Washington

OPPOSITE
Lime Kiln Light, Washington.

The Cape Cod-style dwelling was attached to the lighthouse to give some protection against the worst of the weather. The tower was fitted with a first-order Fresnel lens with a red sector to warn shipping away from Dugan Rocks. A steam-driven fog signal was added in 1871 and the U.S. Signal Corps established a weather station on the site in 1883. The lighthouse was finally automated in 1977.

Cattle Point Light

San Juan Island, WA
Built: 1888 and 1935
Style: Octagonal tower
No: 19555
Position: 48 27 02 N. 122 57 48 W
Focal plane: 94ft (29m)
Range: 7 miles (11km)

The light dates back to 1888 when the southern end of San Juan Island was a staging post for cattle being shipped to Victoria, British Columbia. The present self-contained octagonal tower was built in 1935 to guide vessels into San Juan Channel.

Destruction Island Light

Olympic Peninsula, WA

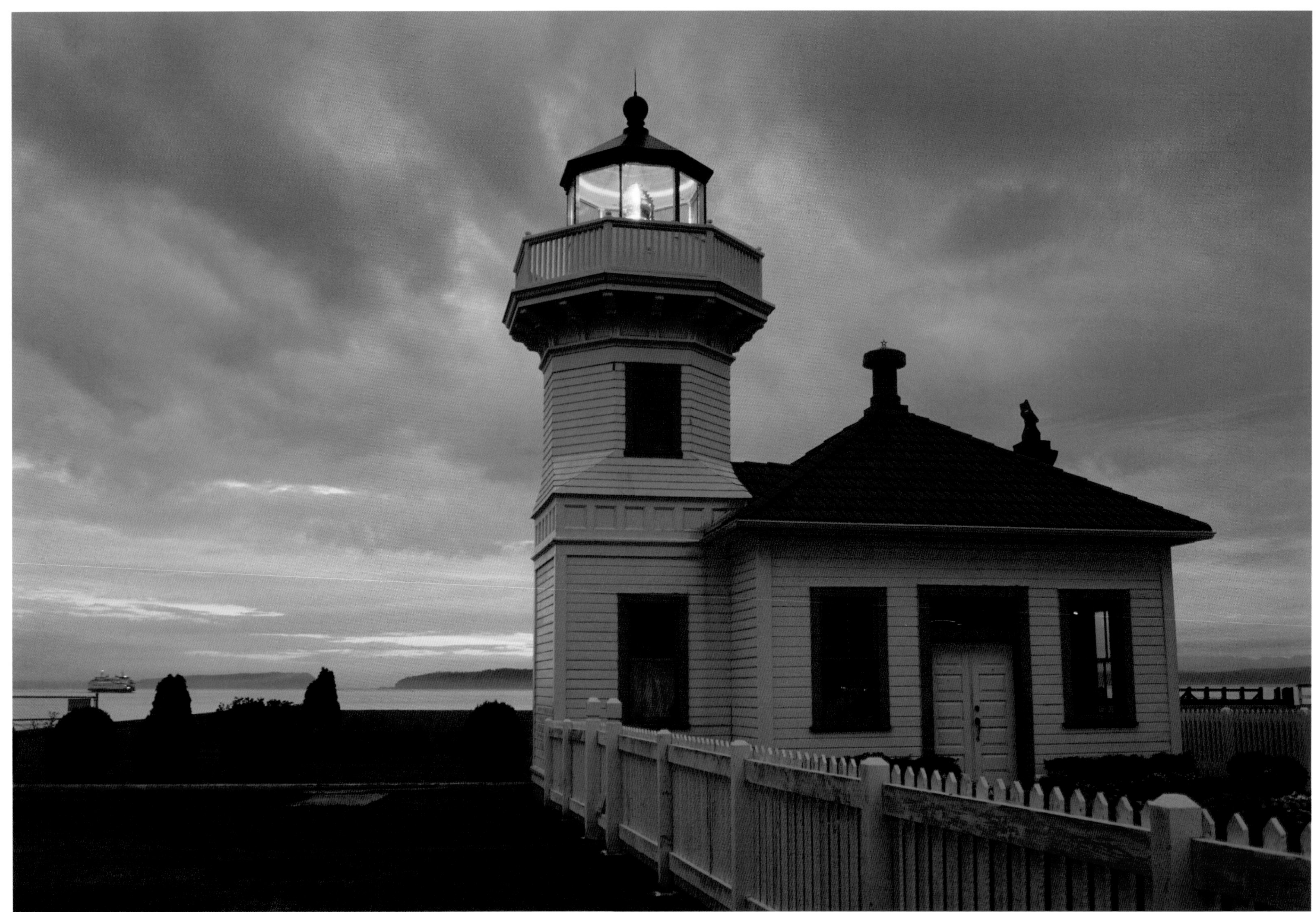

LEFT
Mukilteo Light, Washington.

OPPOSITE
New Dungeness Light, Washington.

Built: 1891
Style: Conical tower with black gallery
No: 735
Position: 47 40 28 N. 124 29 13 W
Focal plane: 147ft (45m)
Range: 18 miles (29km)
Height: 94ft (29m)

Destruction Island Light stands on a desolate islet three miles off the Olympic Peninsula. The masonry tower, which is equipped with a first-order Fresnel lens, took three years to build. It was such an isolated posting that, before automation occurred in 1963, the keepers were encouraged to cultivate their own garden produce and keep livestock on the 30-acre site.

Dofflemyer Point Light

Budd Inlet, Puget Sound, WA
Built: 1887 and 1936
Style: Pyramidal tower
No: 17400
Position: 47 08 30 N. 122 54 30 W
Focal plane: 30ft (9m)
Range: 9 miles (14.5km)

The lighthouse dates back to 1887 when the light guiding vessels into Puget Sound was simply a lantern hung from a post. The present 38-ft (11.5-m) concrete lighthouse was erected in 1936.

Ediz Hook Light

Port Angeles, WA
Built: 1865, 1908 and 1946
Style: Skeleton tower
No: 16280
Position: 48 08 25 N. 123 24 08 W
Focal plane: 63ft (19m)
Range: W 18 miles/29km, G 16 miles/26km

The present Ediz Hook lighthouse is a tower standing on the roof of a hangar at the Port Angeles Coast Guard air station, where it provides guidance for both aircraft and shipping. Its predecessors were a lantern, and later, a 3,200-lb (1450-kg) bell. The first official lighthouse was built in 1865 and was fitted with a fifth-order Fresnel lens. When sea erosion threatened, a second tower was built in 1908, but this too became endangered by the shifting shoreline and the lens was moved to its present location. The original keeper's dwelling is now in private hands.

Grays Harbor Light

Westport, WA
Built: 1898
Style: Truncated octagonal pyramid tower
No: 720
Position: 46 53 18 N. 124 07 01 W
Focal plane: 123ft (37.5m)
Range: W 20 miles/32km, R 18 miles/29km
Height: 107ft (33m)

The Grays Harbor lighthouse was built in 1898 after more than 50 vessels had been

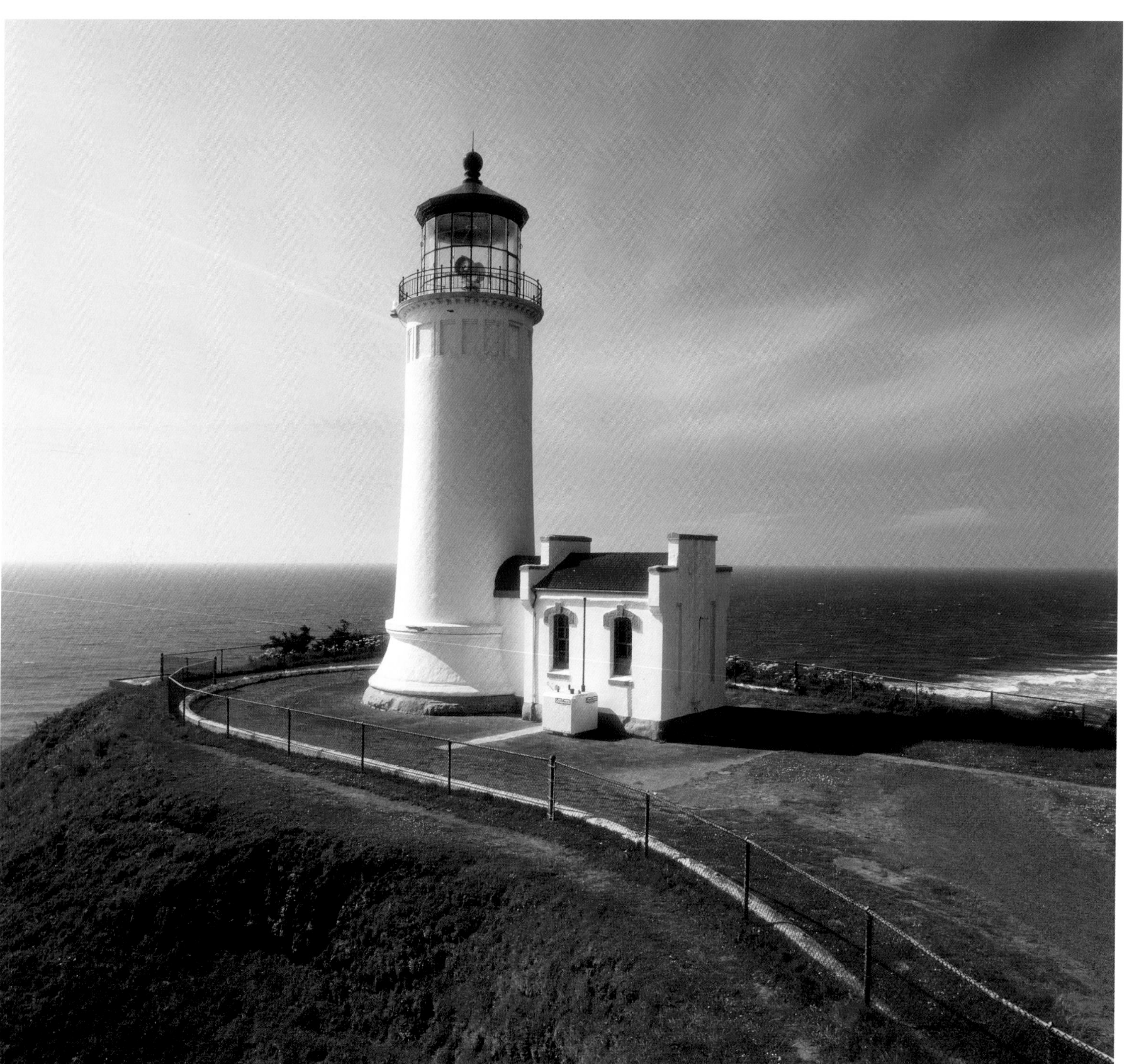

LEFT
North Head Light, Washington.

OPPOSITE
Point No Point Light, Washington.

lost in this treacherous region. The brick tower, which is still equipped with its original third-order Fresnel lens, is one of the tallest lighthouses on the West Coast and has a range of 20 miles.

Lime Kiln Light

San Juan Island, WA
Built: 1914
Style: Octagonal tower attached to building
No: 19695
Position: 48 31 00 N. 123 09 12 W
Focal plane: 55ft (17m)
Range: 17 miles (27km)
Height: 38ft (11.5m)

The Lime Kiln lighthouse was built on San Juan Island in 1914 to serve vessels bound for the Roche Harbor Lime and Cement Company. Appropriately, the tower is of concrete construction and was one of the last major stations to be built in Washington State. It was also the last to be electrified, relying instead on oil-vapour incandescent lamps to illuminate a 375-mm prismatic lens until it was updated during World War II. The light station, which overlooks Haro Strait and Dead Man's Bay, is close to a main migratory route for whales and now houses a whale research centre.

Marrowstone Light

Point Wilson, WA
Built: 1888
Style: Square structure
No: 16500
Position: 48 06 06 N. 122 41 16 W
Focal plane: 28ft (8.5m)
Range: 9 miles (14.5km)
Height: 20ft (6m)

Marrowstone Point lighthouse stands 20ft in height on a fog-bound island south-east of Point Wilson Light. The station's fog signal, which has always been considered more important than its light, is equipped with trumpets on three sides of the tower to minimize dead spots. The station was automated in 1962.

Mukilteo Light

Elliott Point, Mukilteo, WA
Built: 1906
Style: Octagonal tower attached to building
No: 18460
Position: 47 56 55 N. 122 18 22 W
Focal plane: 33ft (10m)
Range: 14 miles (22.5km)
Height: 30ft (9m)

The attractive, wood-framed Mukilteo lighthouse was built in 1906 to guide vessels through Puget Sound towards the port of Everett. The tower still retains its original fourth-order Fresnel lens, thanks in part to protests from locals against plans by the Coast Guard to replace the lamp with an aero-marine beacon in 1990.

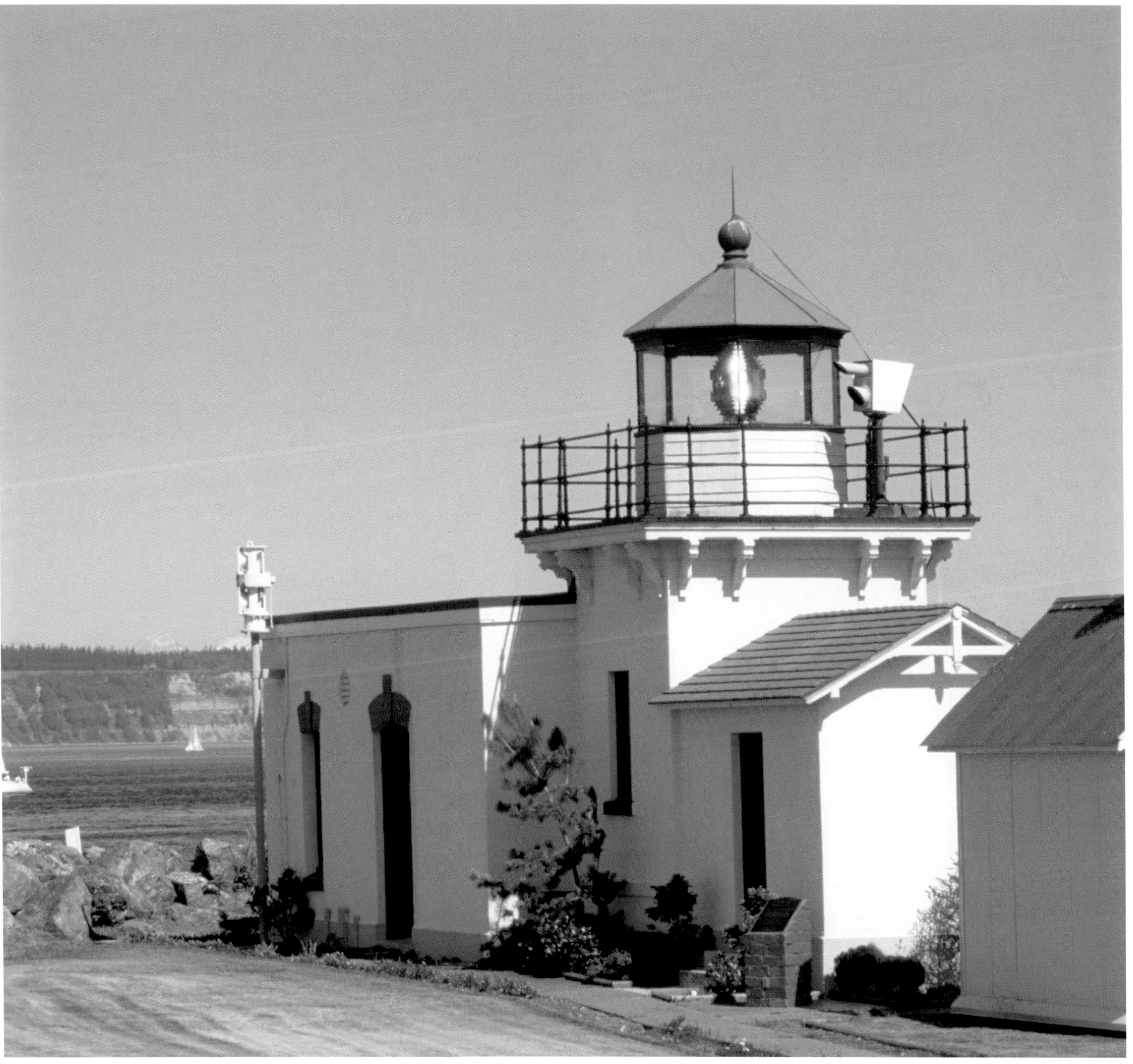

New Dungeness Light

New Dungeness, WA
Built: 1857
Style: Conical tower on dwelling
No: 16335
Position: 48 10 54 N. 123 06 37 W
Focal plane: 67ft (20.5m)
Range: 18 miles (29km)
Height: 63ft (19m)

New Dungeness Light was built in 1857 to guide vessels through the Strait of Juan de Fuca into Puget Sound. It also warns of the dangerous spit of moving sand protruding from New Dungeness, which a storm in 1871 turned into an island for a time. The tower, which was fitted with a third-order Fresnel lens, once stood 89ft (27m) high, but was later lowered to 63ft. The station was automated in 1976 but is still manned by volunteer keepers.

North Head Light

Ilwaco, WA
Built: 1898
Style: Conical tower
No: 700
Position: 46 17 56 N. 124 04 41 W
Focal plane: 194ft (59m)
Range: 26 miles (42km)
Height: 65ft (20m)

The lighthouse stands in one of the windiest regions of the country on cliffs overlooking the entrance to the Columbia River. The sandstone tower was built in 1898 as a result of a series of shipwrecks on Long Beach peninsula. It was originally equipped with a first-order Fresnel lens transferred from the lighthouse on Cape Disappointment, north of what is now Fort Canby State Park. This lens was later replaced by an aero-beacon, which gives the light a range of 26 miles.

Patos Island Light

Puget Sound, Straits of Georgia, WA
Built: 1893 and 1908
Style: Square tower on fog-signal house
No: 19825
Position: 48 47 20 N. 122 58 17 W
Focal plane: 52ft (16m)
Range: W 9 miles/15km, R 6 miles/10km
Height: 38ft (11.5m)

Patos Island lighthouse was established in 1893 as a simple lantern to guide vessels through Puget Sound towards the Straits of Georgia. The present 38-ft wooden tower was built in 1908 on the roof of a fog-signal building and, although automated in 1974, retains its fourth-order Fresnel lens.

Point No Point Light

Hansville, WA
Built: 1880
Style: Octagonal tower on building
No: 16550
Position: 47 54 44 N. 122 31 37 W
Focal plane: 27ft (8m)
Range: 17 miles (27km)
Height: 20ft (6m)

The lighthouse was built in 1880 on the Kitsap peninsula to guide vessels into Admiralty Inlet, and is a sister tower to West Point Light, built a year later on the opposite side of Puget Sound to mark the entrance to Elliott Bay and the port of Seattle. It was equipped with a bull's-eye fourth-order Fresnel lens, giving the 20-ft tower a range of 17 miles, but its presence did not stop the *Admiral Sampson* from colliding with the liner *Princess Victoria* off the point in 1914, a disaster that led to the loss of 12 lives.

Point Robinson Light

Maury Island, WA
Built: 1885 and 1915
Style: Octagonal tower
No: 17070
Position: 42 23 17 N. 122 22 28 W
Focal plane: 40ft (12m)
Range: 13 miles (21km)
Height: 38ft (11.5m)

The Point Robinson station began life in 1885 as a fog-signal station to warn vessels away from a dangerous spit of sand that extends into Puget Sound. By 1915, traffic through this narrow waterway had increased significantly, and the Lighthouse Board built the present masonry tower alongside the fog-signal building. The tower still holds its original fifth-order Fresnel lens.

Point Wilson Light

Port Townsend, WA
Built: 1879 and 1914
Style: Octagonal tower on building
No: 16475
Position: 48 08 39 N. 122 45 17 W
Focal plane: 51ft (15.5m)
Range: W 16 miles/26km, R 15 miles/24km

The present concrete lighthouse at Port Wilson was constructed in 1914 and fitted with a fourth-order Fresnel lens. It replaced an earlier wooden structure of 1897, which first marked the entrance to Admiralty Inlet from the Strait of Juan de Fuca. The station, which is now automated, is equipped with a fog signal and radio beacon.

Point Wilson Light, Washington.

Smith Island Light

Smith Island, WA
Built: 1858 and 1957
Style: Skeletal tower
No: 16375
Position: 48 19 06 N. 122 50 38 W
Focal plane: 97ft (29.5m)
Range: 21 miles (34km)
Height: 45ft (14m)

The 45-ft masonry lighthouse, built in the centre of Smith Island in 1858 to mark the eastern extremity of the Strait of Juan de Fuca, was superseded in 1957 by a modern steel skeletal tower.

Swiftsure Lightship

Northwest Seaport, Seattle, WA
Built: 1904
Builder: New York Shipbuilding Co. Camden, NJ
No. 83
Design: Steam screw; steel hull; two steel masts; stack amidships
Length overall: 129ft (39m)
Beam: 28ft 06in (9m)
Draft: 12ft 06in (4m)

1885

OPPOSITE
Point Robinson Light, Washington.

RIGHT
Smith Island Light, Washington.

Displacement: 668 tons
Propulsion: Steam
Speed: 9 knots
Illuminating Apparatus: Three oil lens lanterns raised to each masthead

The lightship *Swiftsure* was built as a relief vessel and has a number of original features, including her steam engine and sail rig. The vessel is now an attraction at Northwest Seaport, Seattle, where she has been restored.

Turn Point Light
Stuart Island, WA
Built: 1893 and 1936
Style: Concrete tower
No: 19790
Position: 48 41 20 N. 123 14 15 W
Focal plane: 44ft (13m)
Range: 8 miles (13km)
Height: 16ft (5m)

The concrete lighthouse, overlooking Prevost harbour, marks a turning point for vessels negotiating the San Juan island chain. Built in 1936 and fitted with a 300-mm lens, it replaced earlier structures that have stood here since 1893. Four years after the light was first lit, keeper Edward Durgan and his assistant rescued the crew of a tugboat that had run aground close to the station.

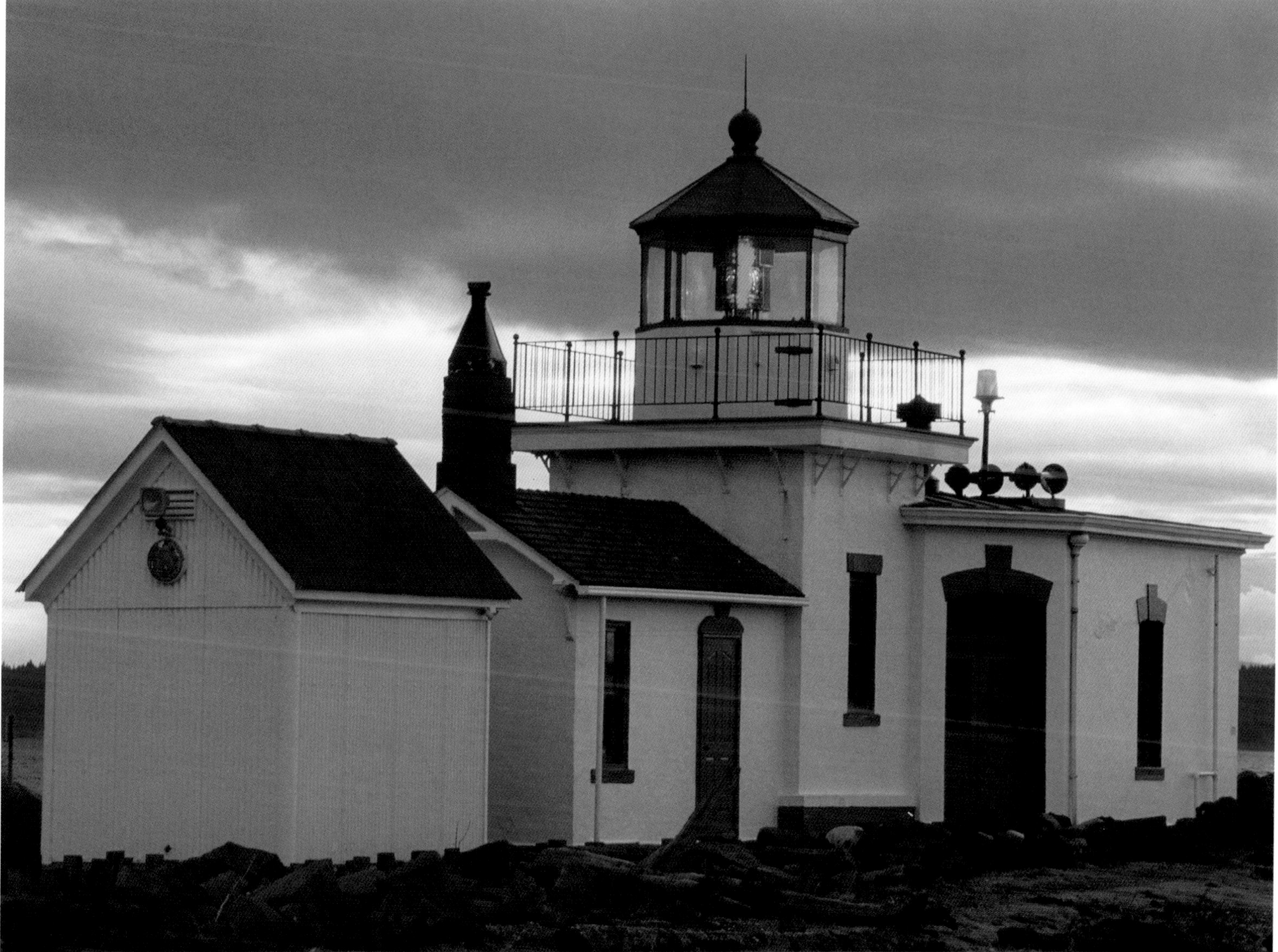

West Point Light
Seattle, WA
Built: 1881
Style: Skeleton tower
No: 26390
Focal plane: 30ft (9m)
Range: 7 miles (11km)

The 23-ft West Point Light, marking the entrance to Elliott Bay and the port of Seattle, is a sister tower to Point No Point lighthouse on the opposite side of the Puget Sound. Built on Magnolia Bluff in 1881, a year after Point No Point, this tower is also equipped with a fourth-order Fresnel lens.

1
5 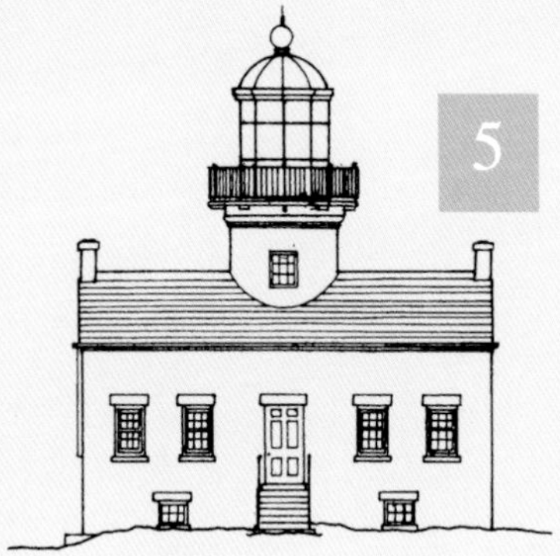
3
6
2 
4
J. A. Tilley '99

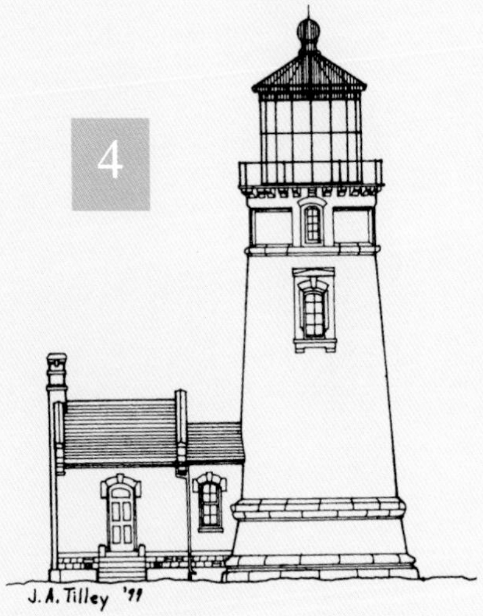

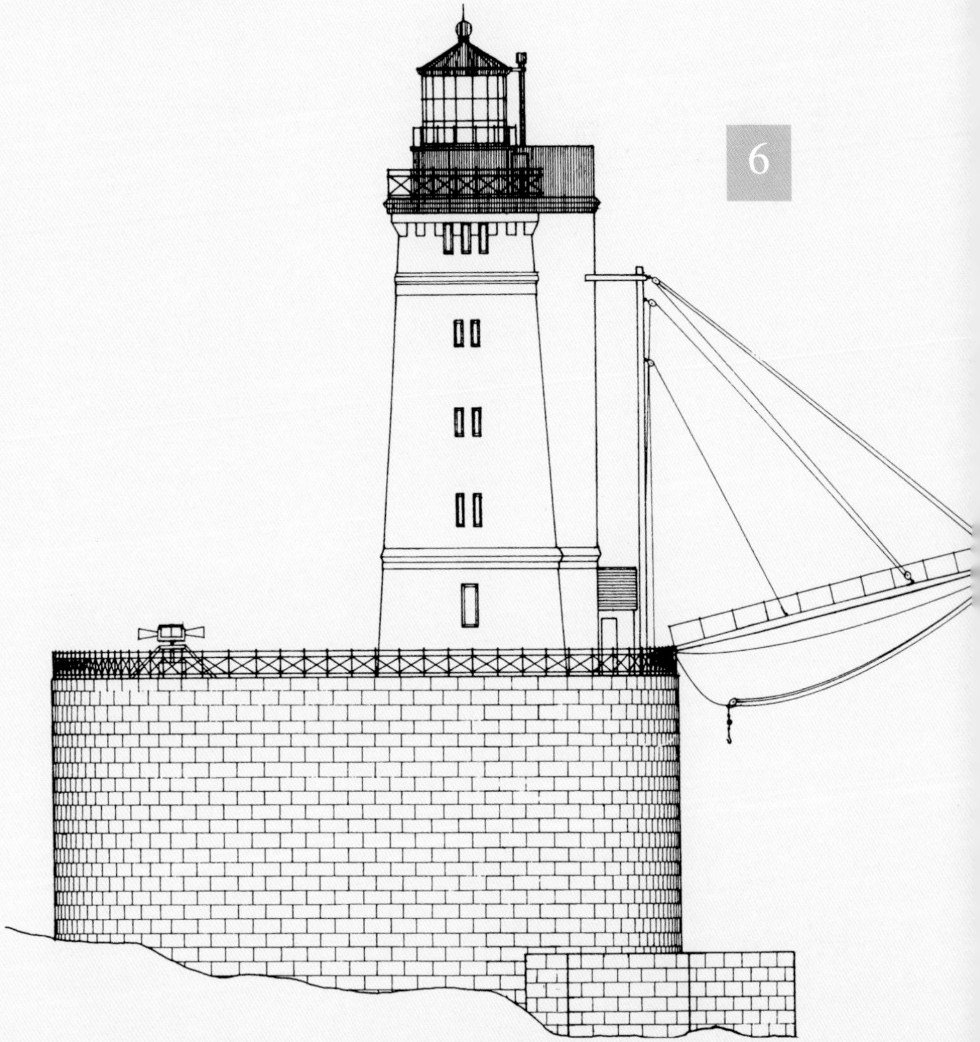

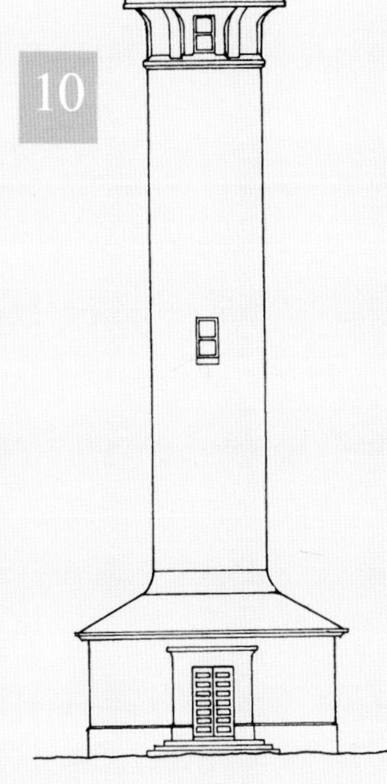

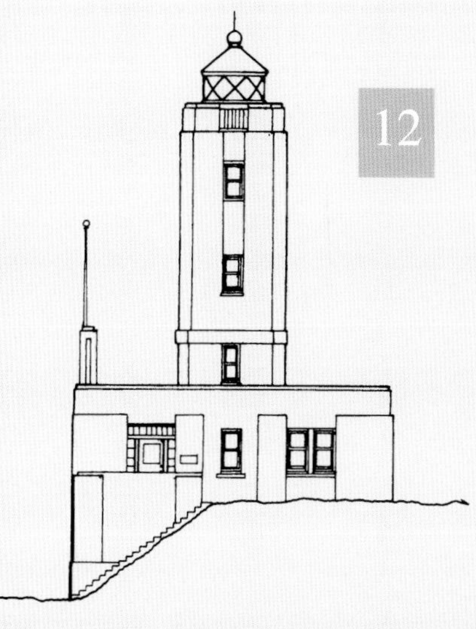

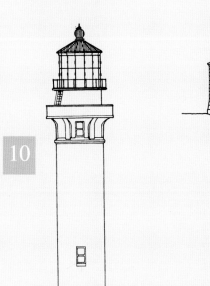

1. Los Angeles Harbor, California
2. Yaquina Head, Oregon
3. Makapuu Point, Hawaii
4. Heceta Head, Oregon
5. Old Point Loma, California
6. St. George's Reef, California
7. Tillamook Rock, Oregon
8. Point Fermin, California
9. Point Wilson, Washington
10. Point Arena, California
11. Point Sur, California
12. Five Fingers Islands, Alaska

Chapter Ten
Lighthouses of Canada

British Columbia
Albert Head Light

Victoria Harbour, Vancouver Island, BC
Built: 1930
Position: 48° 23.1 N. 123° 28.4 W
Style: Square pyramidal tower
Focal plane: 90ft (27m)
Range: 14 miles (22.5km)

Albert Head lighthouse, marking the headland jutting out into Royal Roads, was built in 1930 in response to the near-disastrous grounding of the Canadian Pacific liner *Empress of Canada* in 1929. The station was fitted with a fourth-order dioptric lens.

Boat Bluff Light

Klemtu, BC
Built: 1907
Style: Skeletal tower
Focal plane: 39ft (12m)
Height: 38ft (11.5m)

RIGHT and OPPOSITE
Boat Bluff Light, British Columbia.

OPPOSITE and LEFT
Bonilla Island Light, British Columbia.

BELOW
Brockton Point Light, British Columbia.

Boat Bluff Light is situated at the south end of Sarah Island, inside the passage of the Tolmie Channel. The light is permanently staffed by residential keepers, and can only be accessed by small boat or helicopter.

Bonilla Island Light

Prince Rupert, BC
Built: 1960
Style: Conical fibreglass tower
Height: 30ft (9m)

Bonilla Island is British Columbia's newest lighthouse and is still an active aid to navigation.

Brockton Point Light

Vancouver Harbour, BC
Built: 1890, 1901 and 1914
Style: Square tower, octagonal lantern
No: G5447
Position: 49° 18.1 N. 123° 06.6 W
Focal plane: 40ft (12m)
Range: 11 miles (18km)
Height: 29ft 6in (9m)

Brockton Point Light began life in 1890 as red-and-white lanterns attached to a pole. It marked the sharp turn into Coal Harbour for vessels heading towards Vancouver, and led outward-bound shipping towards First

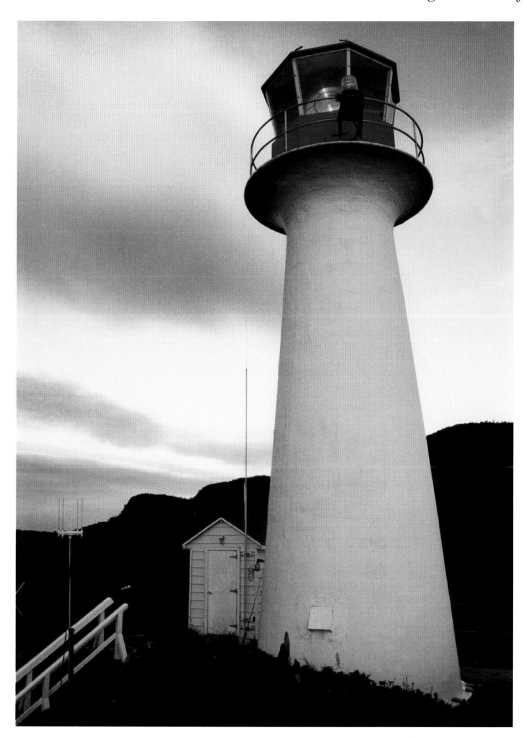

Narrows. There was no house for the keeper, Captain W.D. Jones, who built himself a ramshackle shed from driftwood. The prospect of a royal visit by the Duke of York in 1901 led to a proper house being built, with the light set in the keeper's bedroom window. This was the first Canadian lighthouse with a fitted bath! Captain Jones, who served as keeper until he was 82, saved 16 lives, including eight from the tug *Chebalis*, which sank within seconds of being run down by the steamer *Princess Victoria* off Brockton Point in 1906. The present lighthouse was designed and built in 1914 by Colonel William Anderson, chairman and chief engineer of the Lighthouse Board, as a showcase concrete edifice.

Cape Beale Light

Vancouver Island, BC
Built: 1874 and 1968
Style: Framework tower with octagonal metal lantern.
No: G5256
Position: 48° 47.2 N. 125° 12.8 W
Focal plane: 167ft (51m)
Range: 12 miles (19km)
Height: 32ft (10m)

The 32-ft Cape Beale lighthouse stands on an inaccessible site above formidable cliffs at the entrance to Barkley Sound. The first wooden lighthouse, completed in 1874, took two years to build, and the surveyors experienced the utmost difficulty reaching the site, whether by climbing the rocks or making their way overland. The present lighthouse, built in 1968, is served by a helicopter.

Cape Scott Light

Vancouver Island, Queen Charlotte Sound, BC
Built: 1927 and 1959
Style: Polygonal lantern on square structure
No: G5172
Position: 50° 47.0 N. 128° 25.5 W
Focal plane: 229ft (70m)
Range: 21 miles (34km)
Height: 29ft 6in (9m)

The Cape Scott Light was first established on the north-west tip of Vancouver Island in Queen Charlotte Sound in 1927. The present stubby structure, built in 1959, shares the site with three keepers' dwellings and an impressive-looking radio mast.

Carmanah Point Light

Vancouver Island, West Coast, BC
Built: 1891
Style: White octagonal tower, circular lantern
No: G5288
Position: 48° 36.7 N. 124° 45.0 W
Focal plane: 182ft (55m)
Range: 22 miles (35km)
Height: 29ft (9m)

The first Carmanah Point Light was built in 1891 on an isolated point 10 miles (16km) east of the entrance to the Nitinat River, where vessels bound from China often made their first landfall – or ran up on the fog-shrouded rocks that abound. The present concrete tower and keepers' dwellings, which are now serviced by helicopter, were erected during the 1970s.

Dryad Point

Bella Bella, BC
Built: 1899, 1919
Style: Square concrete pyramidal tower

Dryad Point is also known as Turn Point Light. It is still in active use today.

Estevan Point Light

Vancouver Island, BC
Built: 1910
Style: Octagonal concrete tower
No: G5224
Position: 49° 23.0 N. 126° 32.5 W

LEFT
Cape Beale Light, British Columbia.

BELOW and PAGES 364 and 365
Dryad Point Light, British Columbia.

OPPOSITE
Cape Scott Light, British Columbia.

P&O

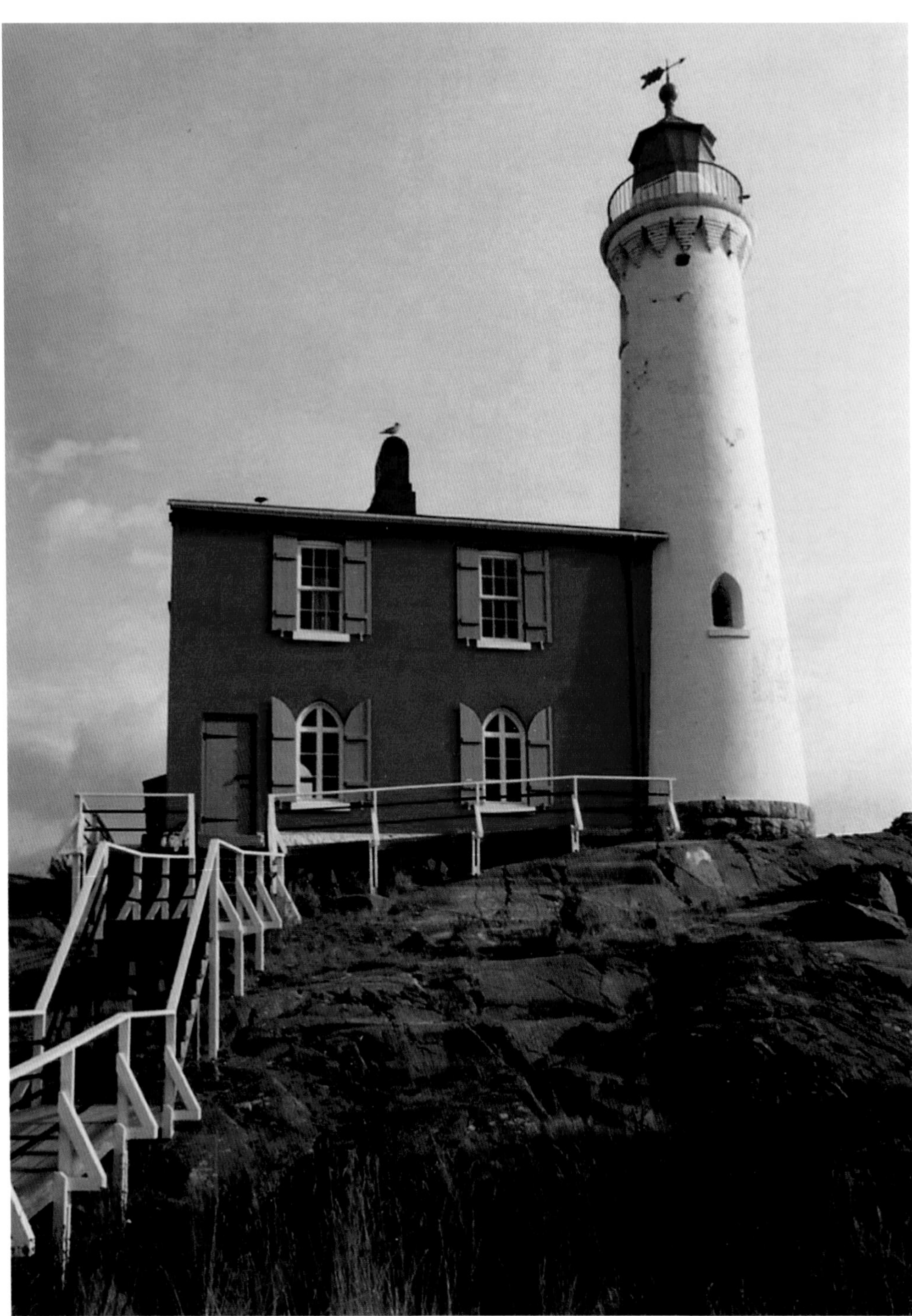

Focal plane: 125ft (38m)
Range: 18 miles (29km)
Height: 100ft (30.5m)

The Estevan Point lighthouse, looking something like a space rocket, is a lasting monument to the Canadian lighthouse builder and administrator, Colonel William Anderson. The reinforced-concrete structure was built in 1910 on the south-west corner of Hesquiat peninsula at a place known as Hole-in-the-Wall. In 1942 the lighthouse came under fire from a Japanese submarine, but no damage was incurred.

Fisgard Light

Victoria Harbour, Vancouver Island, BC
Built: 1860
Style: White conical tower, red lantern.
No: G5306
Position: 48° 25.8 N. 123° 26.8 W
Focal plane: 71ft (22m)
Height: 48ft (15m)

Built in 1860, Fisgurd lighthouse is the oldest in British Columbia. The 48-ft white conical granite tower was designed and built by John Wright and sited on Fisgard Island to mark the entrance to Esquimalt harbour. The station was automated in 1928 and the tower and keeper's dwelling now house a museum within the Fort Rudd National Historic Site and Park.

Ivory Island Light

Queen Charlotte Sound, BC
Built: 1898 and 1953
Style: Steel framework tower

LEFT
Fisgard Light, British Columbia.

OPPOSITE
Langara Point Light, British Columbia.

No: G5713
Position: 52°16.2 N. 128° 24.3 W
Focal plane: 67ft (20.5m)
Range: 15 miles (24km)
Height: 30ft (9m)

The first Ivory Island lighthouse was built in 1898 and rose from the roof of a square wooden dwelling on Robb Point on the south-east side of Milbanke Sound. It was equipped with a seventh-order dioptric lens. The present 30-ft tower was built in 1953 and has a range of 15 miles.

Langara Point Light

Prince Rupert, BC
Built: 1913
Style: White concret tower with red lantern
Focal Plane: 160ft (49m)
Range: 8 miles (13km)
Height 25ft (8m)

Lennard Island Light

Vancouver Island, BC
Built: 1904 and 1968
Style: Circular tower, tapered under gallery
No: G5242

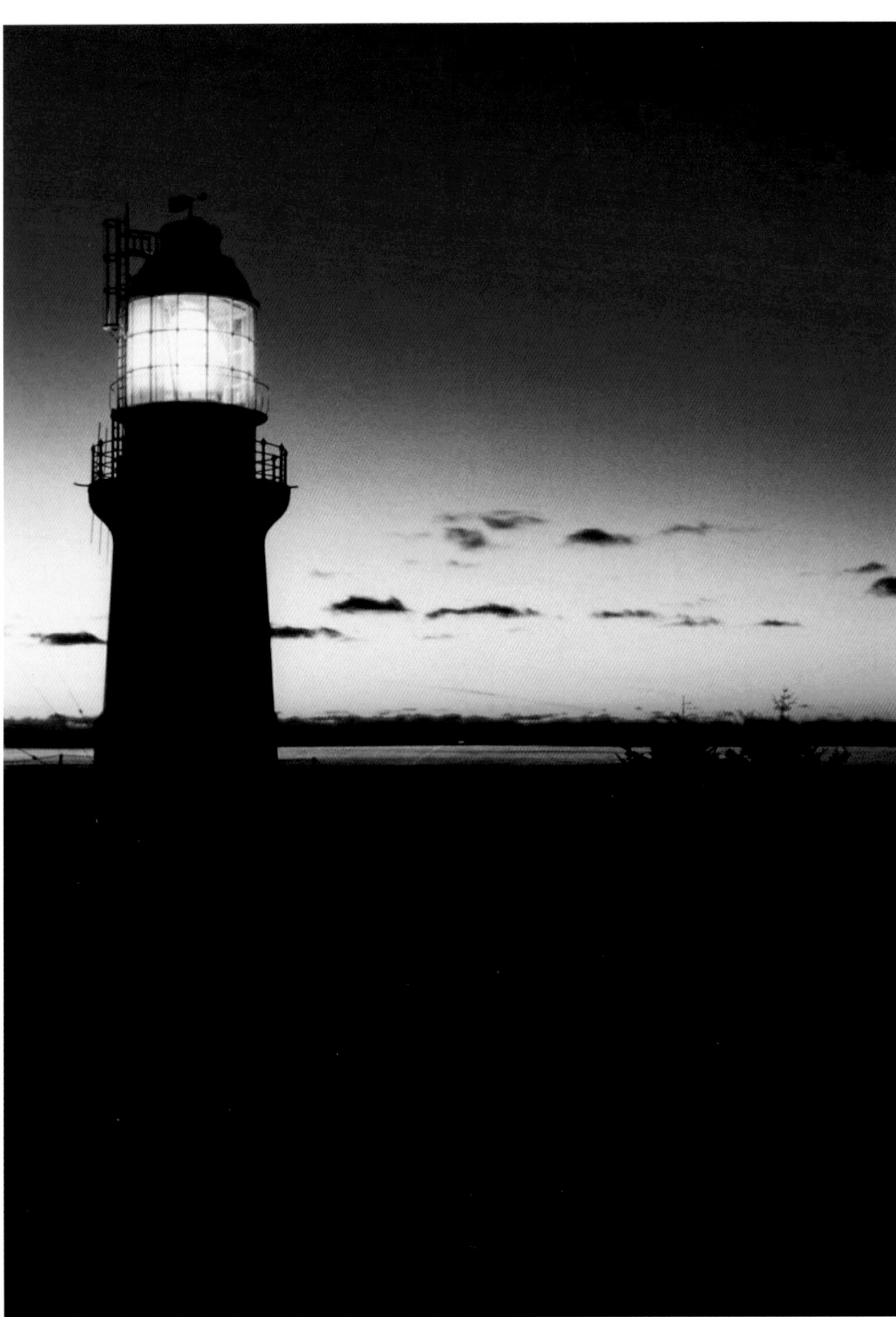

Position: 49° 06.6 N. 125° 55.3 W
Focal plane: 114ft 6in (35m)
Range: 21 miles (34km)
Height: 58ft (18m)

The first lighthouse at Lennard Island was built in 1904 to mark the south entrance to Clayoquot Sound. The wooden tower had a cast-iron lantern room manufactured in Birmingham, England, and was fitted with a first-order Fresnel lens, making it the brightest light along the British Columbian coast.

McInnes Island Light

Queen Charlotte Sound, BC
Built: 1921
Style: Square wooden tower, red lantern
No: G5715
Position: 52° 15.7 N. 128° 43.2 W
Focal plane: 105ft (32m)
Range: 22 miles (35km)
Height: 28ft (8.5m)

The 28-ft wooden McInnes Island lighthouse was built in 1921 on a bluff on the south side of the island to guide vessels towards Milbanke Sound.

Merry Island Light

Strait of Georgia, BC
Built: 1968
Style: Square tower with attached building
No: G5510
Position: 49° 28.1 N. 123° 54.7 W
Focal plane: 105ft (32m)
Range: 16 miles (26km)
Height: 27ft (8m)

LEFT and OPPOSITE
Langara Point Light, British Columbia.

The 27-ft Merry Island lighthouse was built in 1968 on the south-west tip of the island to mark the entrance to Welcome Passage. Its white tower, with attached building, has a red polygonal lantern.

Nootka Light

Vancouver Island, BC
Built: 1911 and 1968
Style: Square steel framework tower
No: G5219
Position: 49° 35.6 N. 126° 36.8 W
Focal plane: 101ft (31m)
Range: 17 miles (27km)
Height: 33ft (10m)

The first Nootka lighthouse was a 37-ft (11-m) wooden tower erected on the summit of San Rafael Island, close to Yuquot Point and Friendly Cove and facing Nootka Sound. The present 33-ft tower was built in 1968. It has a white, square, enclosed stairwell in the centre and a red lantern.

Pachena Point Light

Vancouver Island, BC
Built: 1908
Style: Octagonal wooden tower
No: G5180
Position: 48° 43.3 N. 125° 05.8 W
Focal plane: 185ft (56m)
Range: 17 miles (27km)
Height: 40ft (12m)

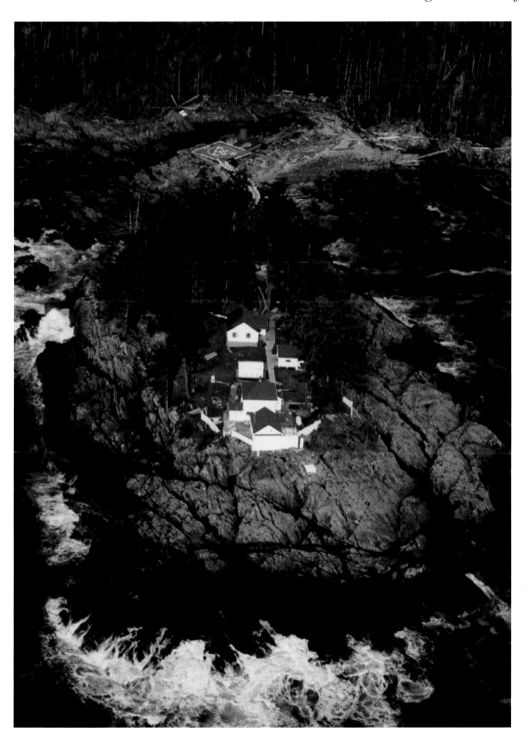

OPPOSITE, LEFT and BELOW
Ivory Island Light, British Columbia.

PAGES 372 and 373
Lennard Island Light, British Columbia.

Pachena Point lighthouse was built in 1908 in response to the verdict of a court of enquiry into the sinking of the steamer *Valencia* with the loss of 117 lives. Her captain had mistaken this fog-ridden point for Cape Beale, 6 miles (10km) to the north-west. The wooden tower has a cast-iron lantern room equipped with a large first-order lens, giving a range of 17 miles.

Pine Island Light

Queen Charlotte Strait, BC
Built: 1907
Style: Square framework tower
No: G5649
Position: 50° 58.6 N. 127° 43.6 W
Focal plane: 86ft (26m)
Range: 13 miles (21km)
Height: 32ft (10m)

The first Pine Island lighthouse was a 43-ft (13m) wooden tower erected on the south-western tip of the island in 1907 to mark the northern entrance to Queen Charlotte Strait. The present steel framework tower stands 32ft high and is fitted with a first-order dioptric lens, providing a range of 13 miles.

Point Atkinson Light

Vancouver Harbour, BC
Built: 1875 and 1910
Style: Hexagonal concrete tower
No: G5426
Position: 49° 19.8 N. 123° 15.8 W
Focal plane: 108ft (33m)
Range: 20 miles (32km)
Height: 41ft (12.5m)

The original Point Atkinson lighthouse, marking the entrance to English Bay and Burrard Inlet, would have been lit in 1874 but for an administrative error in England which led to the wrong light being shipped from Birmingham. As a result, the tower stood idle for a further winter until the correct optic arrived. The present 41-ft concrete tower was built in 1910. In 1942, the station was armed with an 18-lb (8-kg) cannon, and Ken 'Gunfire' Brown, who served at the tower during World War II, gained some notoriety for firing warning shots at the slightest provocation. One shell, aimed across the bows of a fishing boat, skipped across the sound and went straight through the 9,600-ton freighter *Fort Rae*, which had just been launched and was undergoing her first speed trials. Her captain saved his ship from sinking only by running her aground!

Race Rock Light

Victoria Harbour, Vancouver Island, BC
Built: 1860
Style: Conical tower, red polygonal lantern.
No: G5300
Position: 48° 17.9 N. 123° 31.8 W
Focal plane: 118ft (36m)
Range: 15 miles (24km)
Height: 80ft (24m)

The Race Rock lighthouse was built in 1860 to mark a notorious race that ebbs and floods at 7 knots around the aptly named Great Race Rock, close to the entrance to Victoria Harbour. The tidal rip is so strong that the *Nanette*, the ship that had carried the granite blocks for the tower from Scotland, was wrecked on the very rock that the lighthouse was designed to guard. More wrecks followed. On Christmas Day, 1865, the lighthouse keeper's wife, brother-in-law and two friends were lost when their skiff capsized within a few feet of the rock. The following year, the keeper, George Davies, died after his wife had tried in vain to summon help by flying the Union Jack at half-mast and waving frantically at every

OPPOSITE
Pine Island Light, British Columbia.

RIGHT
Triple Island Light, British Columbia.

BELOW
Point Atkinson Light, British Columbia.

passing ship. This led to the introduction of a flag-signalling system that allowed keepers to alert the outside world to an emergency. The *Nanette* was the last ship to hit the rock in clear conditions, but others continued to run aground here in fog. After six ships had been lost, their crews all complaining that they had not heard the tower's fog bell, the Lighthouse Department installed a steam

plant and compressed-air horns in 1892. That too proved insufficient. Within the next few years, the SS *Tees* was wrecked, so was the *Prince Victor*, and the ferry *Sechet* capsized and sank with the loss of 50 lives. Four more vessels ran aground in the early 1920s because, it transpired, the tower and surrounding rocks deflected the sound signal to create a 'silent zone'. The problem was not solved until Race Rocks became one of the first light stations to be equipped with a radio beacon.

Sand Heads Light

Vancouver Harbour, BC
Built: 1960
Style: Tower on building on steel pile
Built: 1960
No: G5401
Position: 49° 06.4 N. 123° 18.1 W
Focal plane: 52ft (16m)
Range: 12 miles (19km)

The present Sand Heads screwpile lighthouse, marking the entrance to the Fraser River, was built in 1960 to replace a series of lightships that had marked this ever-shifting channel since 1859. The last of these, *Sand Heads* No. 16, had broken from her mooring during a storm in 1957 and was driven up on Point Roberts. A stone jetty built out to the light tower now holds the main channel in place.

Triple Island Light

Hecate Strait, BC
Built: 1913, 1915 and 1921
Style: Octagonal concrete tower

No: G5812
Position: 54° 17.7 N. 130° 52.8 W
Focal plane: 92ft (28m)
Range: 16 miles (26km)
Height: 72ft (22m)

The building of the Triple Island Light, to mark Brown Passage on the most north-westerly rock of this islet chain, was a considerable feat. The swirling tides around the rock made it difficult to land materials from the sea, and the first beacon, established in 1913, was an unmanned lantern set on a steel frame anchored to the rock. In 1915, a keeper was installed on the rock and in 1921 the present 72-ft tower and its three-storey attached house were erected. The light has a range of 16 miles and is now serviced by helicopter.

New Brunswick

Cap des Caissie Light

Shediac Bay, Northumberland Strait, NB
Built: 1872
Style: Square pyramidal wooden tower
No: H1350
Position: 46° 19.2 N. 64° 30.7 W
Focal plane: 47ft (14m)
Height: 39ft (12m)

The 39-ft Cap des Caissie lighthouse was built on the point just north of Shediac Bay in 1872 and named after a prominent local family. The classic 'pepper-pot'-style tower

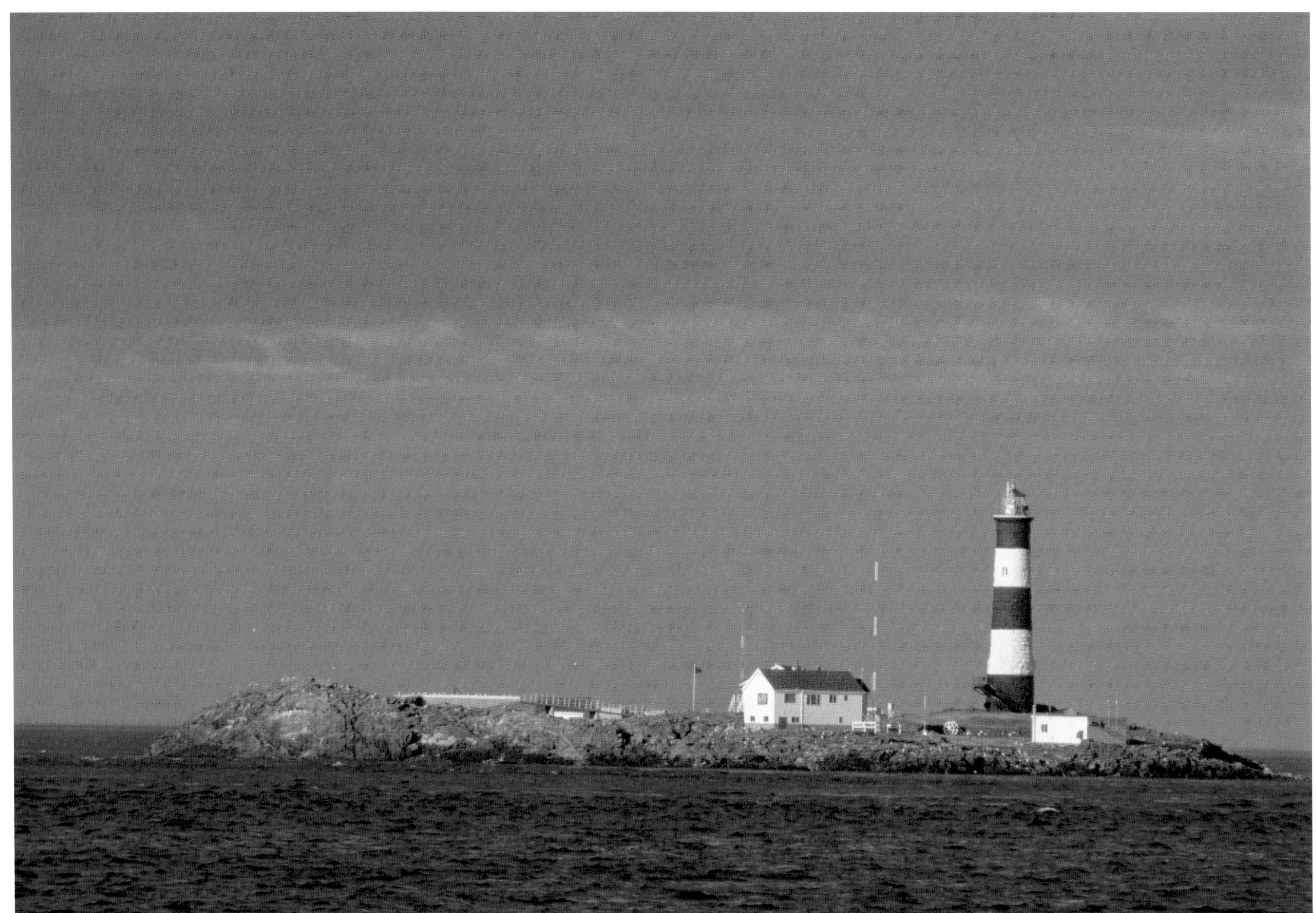

OPPOSITE
Race Rock Light, British Columbia.

RIGHT
Gannet Rock Light, New Brunswick.

was originally attached to the keeper's dwelling, but the two were separated in 1980 when the tower was automated.

Gannet Rock Light

Grand Manan Island, NB
Built: 1831
Style: Octagonal wooden tower
No: H4188
Position: 44° 30.6 N. 66° 46.9 W
Focal plane: 92ft (28m)
Range: 19 miles (30.5km)
Height: 72ft (22m)

The 72-ft Gannet Rock lighthouse is the second-oldest working lighthouse in Canada as well as one of the most lonely. Built in 1831, the tower stands on an isolated rock 8 miles (13km) south of Grand Manan Island. In 1837, keeper E.G. Miller and his assistant drowned while rowing across to Kent Island to collect fresh water. Walter McLaughlin started work as a keeper at this station in 1845 at the age of 16 and spent the next 35 years here, keeping a meticulous diary. During the 1930s the tower was believed to have one of the most powerful lights in the world, second only to the Eddystone lighthouse in England. Currently it has a range of 19 miles.

Head Harbour Light

Passamaquoddy Bay, NB
Built: 1831 and 1887
Style: Octagonal wooden tower with dwelling attached.
No: H4154
Position: 44° 57.5 N. 66° 54 W
Focal plane: 58ft (18m)
Range: 13 miles (21km)
Height: 51ft (15.5m)

The Head Harbour Light was first established on East Quoddy Head at the north-east end of Campobello Island in 1831. It is Canada's oldest working lighthouse. The shingle-clad, white-painted tower has a distinctive red cross on two sides, and is equipped with a fourth-order dioptric lens. A red polygonal cast-iron top section replaced the original wooden lantern room in 1887. The station was automated in 1986.

Machias Seal Island East Light

Fundy West, NB
Built: 1832 and 1915
Style: Octagonal tower, flared under gallery
No: H4192
Position: 44° 30.1 N. 67° 06.1 W
Focal plane: 82ft (25m)
Range: 17 miles (27km)
Height: 60ft (18m)

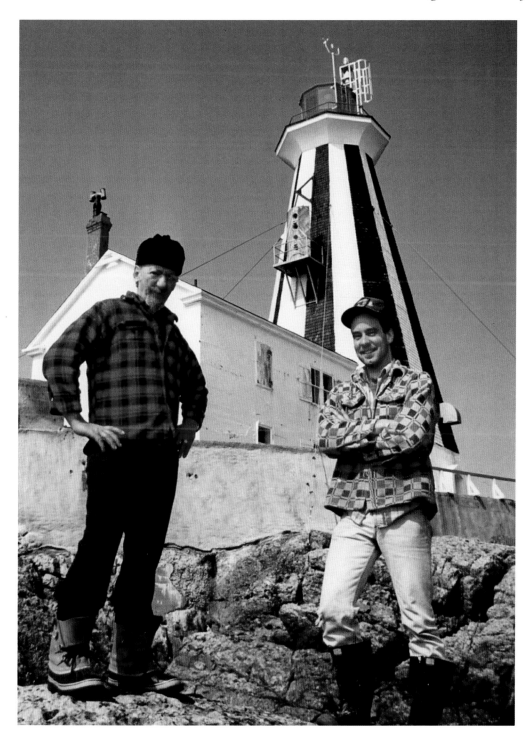

OPPOSITE and RIGHT
Views of Gannet Rock Light, New Brunswick.

LEFT
The keepers of Gannet Rock Light.

PAGES 380 and 381
Head Harbour Light, New Brunswick.

Machias Seal Island East lighthouse stands on the island's summit, giving the light a range of 17 miles. The station has been fully manned since 1832 to maintain Canada's territorial claim over the island, which has long been disputed by the United States. The lighthouse is managed by the Canadian Coast Guard, while the island is maintained by the Canadian Wildlife Service as a bird sanctuary. The present 60-ft lighthouse was built in 1915.

Mulholland Point Light

Campobello Island, NB
Built: 1885
Style Octagonal tower with red lantern
Focal plane: 60ft (18m)
Range: 4 nautical miles
Height: 44ft (13m)

Mulholland Point Light is situated on the east side of the Lubec Channel in Passamaquoddy Bay. It now forms the central attraction in the grounds of a public park. The lighthouse is no longer operational.

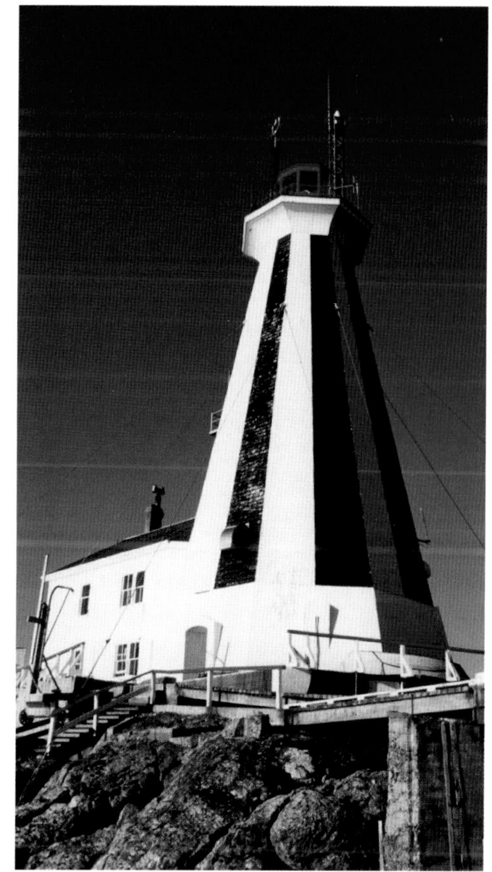

Point Escuminac Light

Gulf of St. Lawrence, NB
Built: 1841 and 1971
Style: Hexagonal concrete tower
No: H1424
Position: 47° 04.4 N. 64° 47.9 W
Focal plane: 68ft (21m)
Range: 18 miles (29km)

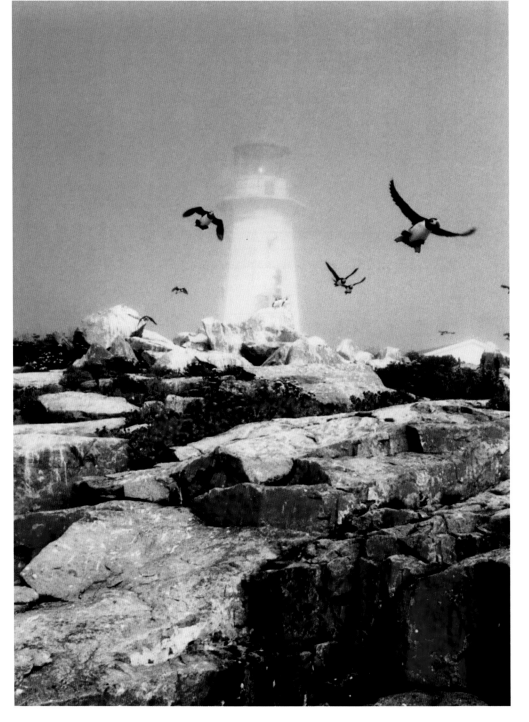

ABOVE, RIGHT and OPPOSITE Machias Seal Island East Light, New Brunswick.

The first Point Escuminac lighthouse was a 58-ft (18-m) wooden tower built to mark the southern entrance to Miramichi Bay. In 1971 it was replaced by the present reinforced-concrete tower, tapered under the gallery, and with a red polygonal steel lantern which is of similar design to those at Cape Fourchu in Nova Scotia and the Brighton Beach Rear Range Light on Prince Edward Island.

Swallowtail Light

Grand Manan Island, NB
Built: 1860
Style: Octagonal tower with a red lantern.
Focal Plane: 122ft (37m)
Range: 12 nautical miles
Height: 53ft (16m)

The Swallowtail lighthouse was automated in 1986. It is still active as a navigational aid as well as serving as a bed and breakfast inn.

RIGHT
Swallowtail Light, New Brunswick.

OPPOSITE
Mulholland Point Light, New Brunswick.

PAGES 386 and 387
Cape Anguille Light, Newfoundland.

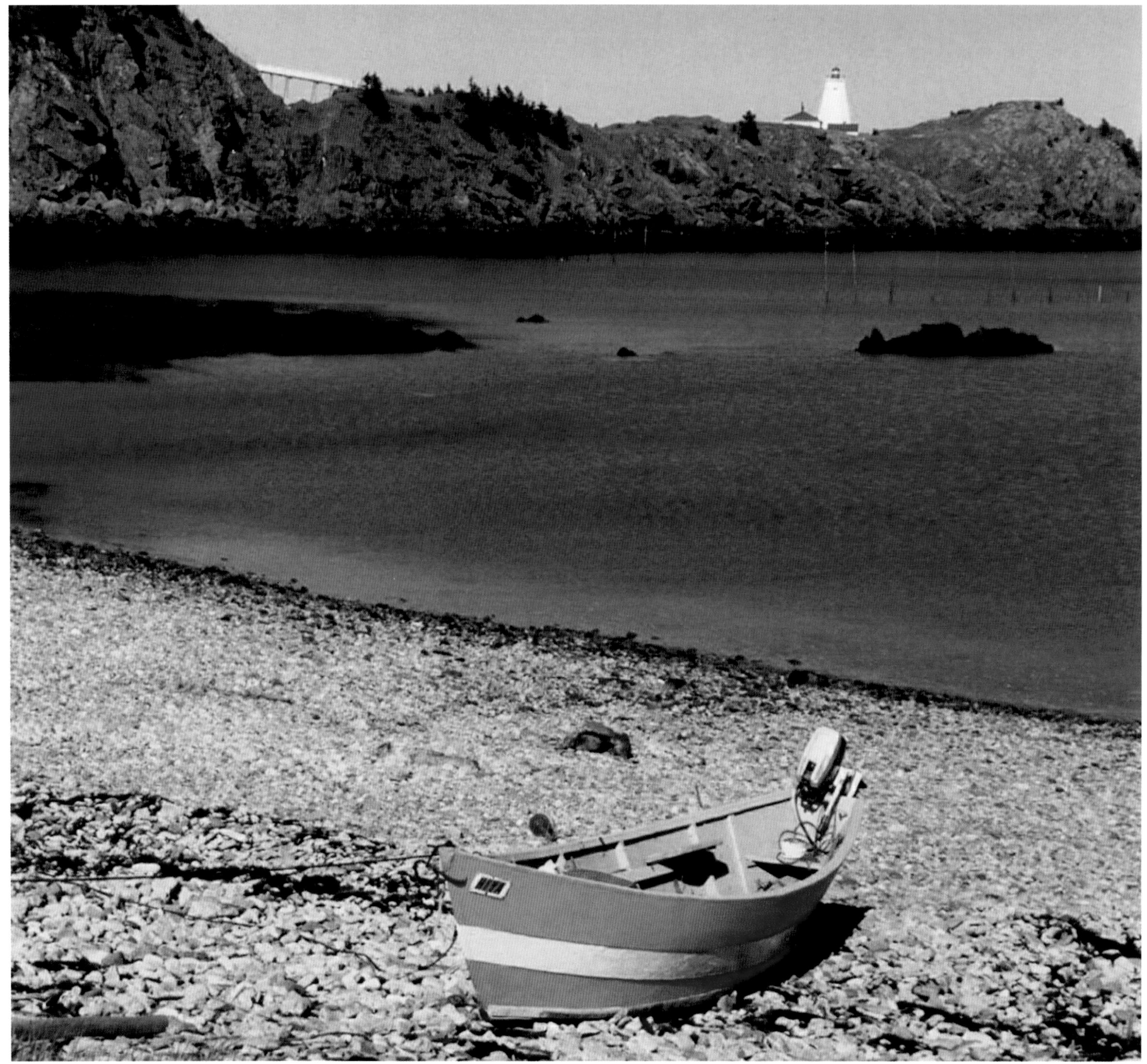

NEWFOUNDLAND & LABRADOR

Belle Isle South Lights

Strait of Belle Isle, NF
High Light
Built: 1858 and 1880
Style:White, conical brick tower covered with shingles; dwelling attached; circular red-roofed lantern
No: H0102
Position: 51° 52.8 N. 55° 23 W
Focal plane: 470ft (143m)
Range: 18 miles (29km)

Low Light
Built: 1880
Style: White circular metal lantern on a masonry foundation
No: H0104
Position: 1,200ft (365m) below main light
Focal plane: 124ft (38m)
Range: 17 miles (27km)
Height: 23ft (7m)

The two Belle Isle lighthouses stand directly above one another on the south point of this

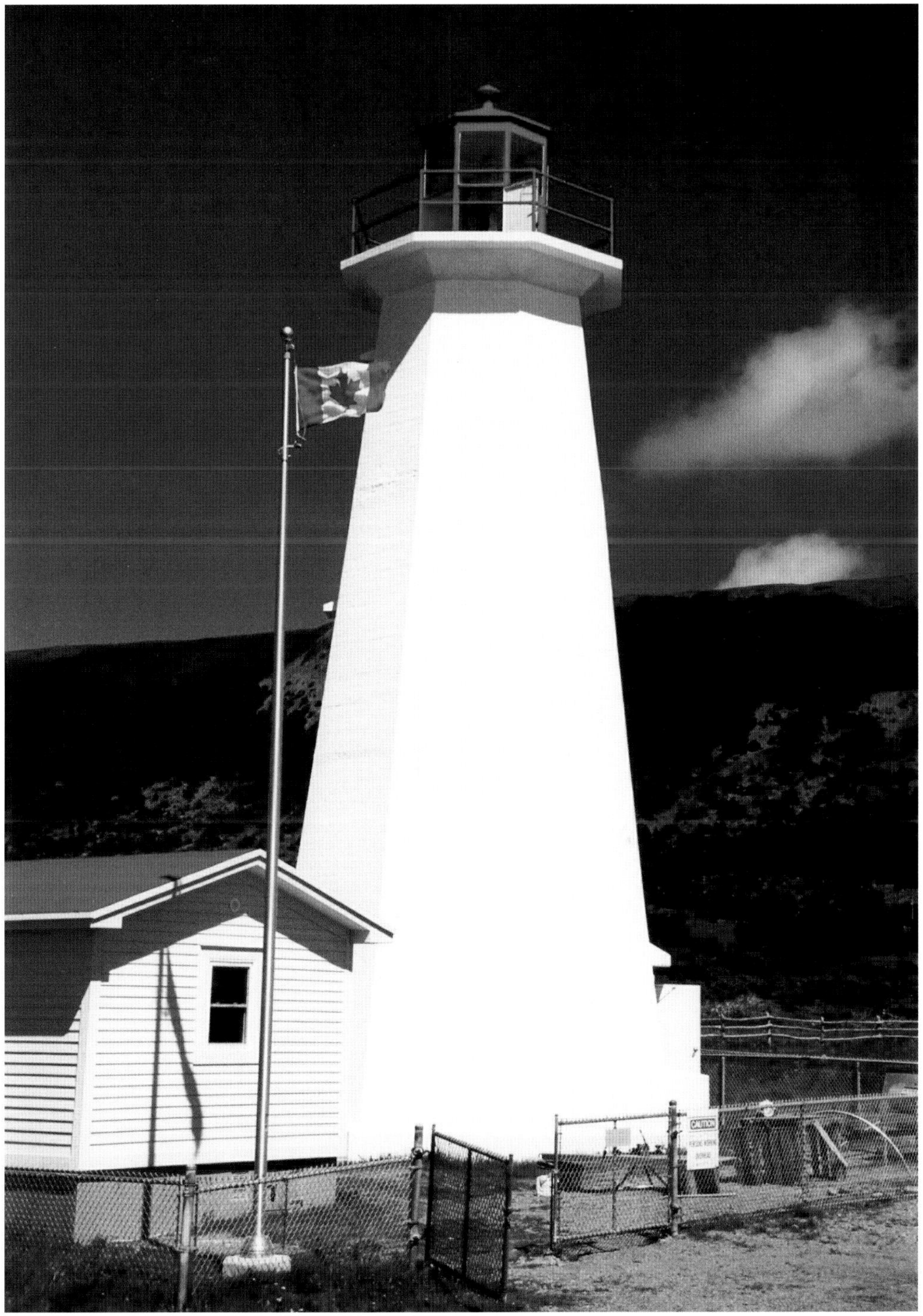

barren 10-mile (16-km) long island. The High lighthouse was built in 1858 to mark what is described as one of the most treacherous passages in the world, but was often obscured by fog, which led to several shipwrecks and the consequent siting of a second lighthouse in 1880, 1,200ft lower than the first, together with a fog-signal tower halfway between the two. A marine telegraph and ice-report offices were added in 1908.

Brigus Light

Conception Bay, NF
Built: 1885
Style: Circular iron tower
No: H0478
Position: 47° 32.9 N. 53° 10.9 W
Focal plane: 113ft (34m)
Range: 8 miles (13km)
Height: 20ft (6m)

The cast-iron red-and-white-striped Brigus lighthouse, standing 20ft high, was built on North Head in 1885 to mark the entrance to Brigus Bay. The tower was equipped with a sixth-order Fresnel lens, but this was replaced with a modern optic when the station was automated and now has a range of 8 miles. The keeper's dwelling was demolished in the 1930s.

Cape Anguille Light

Codroy, NF
Built: 1908, 1960
Style: White octagonal tower
Focal plane: 115ft (35m)
Height: 59ft (18m)

Cape Anguille Light is situated south-west of Newfoundland. It was automated in 1990 but still has a keeper on site. The keeper's house on Cape Anguille is also an inn and offers accommodation to visitors.

Cape Bauld Light

Strait of Belle Isle, NF
Built: 1884 and 1908
Style: Octagonal tower
No: H0132
Position: 51° 38.4 N. 55° 25.7 W
Focal plane: 177ft (54m)
Range: 23 miles (37km)
Height: 83ft (25m)

The red-and-white cast-iron Cape Bauld lighthouse was erected on Quirpon Island at the northern end of Newfoundland in 1908. The tower, which is encased in concrete, is fitted with a second-order dioptric lens and marks the entrance to the Strait of Belle Isle. It replaced an earlier wooden tower built on this barren headland in 1884.

Cape Bonavista Light

Bonavista Bay, NF
Built: 1843 and 1966
Style: Circular stone tower on dwelling
No: H0536
Position: 48° 42.1 N. 53° 05.2 W
Focal plane: 165ft (50m)
Range: 16 miles (26km)

The Cape Bonavista lighthouse was built on the northern tip of the peninsula that was probably the first land sighted by John Cabot, discoverer of North America, on the *Matthew* in 1497. In 1966 the light was

LEFT
Memorial to John Cabot, discoverer of North America.

OPPOSITE
Cape Bonavista Light, Newfoundland and Labrador.

moved to a framework tower nearby, and the original lighthouse was converted to a museum.

Cape Race Light

Cape Race, Avalon, NF
Built: 1851, 1856 and 1907
Style: White cylindrical tower
No: H0444
Position: 46° 39.5 N. 53° 04.5 W
Focal plane: 170ft (52km)
Range: 28 miles (45km)
Height: 68ft (21m)

Cape Race was the first Canadian headland seen by immigrants arriving from Europe in the 19th century – providing it was not fogbound. A wooden beacon was erected in 1851, but two shipwrecks in 1854 prompted the decision to erect a 46-ft (14-m) cast-iron tower here two years later. Ships continued to run up on the rocks, which are often shrouded in fog, and in 1866 the light was replaced with a stronger, revolving apparatus. In 1872, a steam-powered fog whistle was also installed. None of these precautions ended the shipwrecks, and about 2,000 people lost their lives off Cape Race in 94 shipwrecks during the next 40 years. Finally, in 1907, the present 68-ft tower was built and fitted with a hyper-radial lens that gives the light an optimum range of 28 miles. The old tower was dismantled and shipped first to Cape North in Nova Scotia, then to Ottawa, where it now stands in the grounds of the Museum of Science and Technology.

Cape Ray Light

St. John's, Avalon, NF
Built: 1871, 1885 and 1959
Style: Octagonal pyramidal concrete tower
No: H0220
position: 47° 37.3 N. 59° 18.3 W
Focal plane: 118ft (36m)
Range: 23 miles (37km)
Height: 44ft (13m)

The Cape Ray Light, situated in the extreme south-west of Newfoundland, guides vessels towards the little Port-aux-

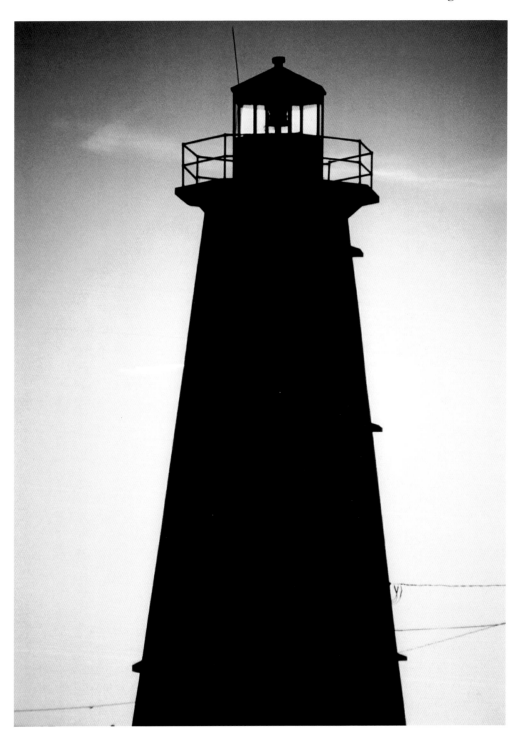

Basques. The first 41-ft (12.5-m) wooden tower of 1871 burned down in 1885. A 75-ft (23-m) tower took its place but it too was consumed by fire in 1959. This led to the construction of the present 44-ft tower in less vulnerable concrete. The light has a range of 23 miles.

Cape Spear Light

St. John's, Avalon, NF
Built: 1835 and 1955
Style: Octagonal pyramidal concrete tower
No: H0454
Position: 47° 31.3 N. 52° 37.3 W
Focal plane: 233ft (71m)
Range: 20 miles (32km)
Height: 35ft (10.5m)

FAR LEFT
Cape Ray Light, Newfoundland.

BELOW LEFT
Cape Spear Light, Newfoundland.

Cape Spear is the most easterly point of North America. The first lighthouse was built here in 1835 to mark the approach to St. John's harbour and, though decommissioned in 1955, the 38-ft (11.5-m) circular stone tower, that rose from the centre of the square keeper's house, was Newfoundland's oldest standing light; the building is now a museum. The present 35-ft concrete tower is fitted with a fourth-order dioptric lens and has a range of 20 miles.

East End Long Island Light

Notre Dame Bay, NF
Built: 1904
Style: Cylindrical iron tower
No: H0675
Position: 49° 36 N. 55° 34.4 W
Focal plane: 103ft (31m)
Range: 15 miles (24km)
Height: 30ft (9m)

East End Long Island lighthouse was built on Southern Head in 1904. The 30-ft cast-iron tower, which is known locally as South End Light, is fitted with a fourth-order dioptric lens giving it a range of 15 miles.

Fort Amherst Light

St. John's Harbour, Avalon, NF
Built: 1813, 1852 and 1952
Style: Square, pyramidal wooden tower.
No: H0458
Position: 47° 33.8 N. 52° 40.8 W
Focal plane: 131ft 7in (40m)
Range: 13 miles (21m)
Height: 17ft (5m)

A lighthouse has stood on South Head, marking the entrance to St. John's harbour, since 1813. The original stone tower was built within the protected confines of Fort Amherst, and the garrison maintained the three whale-oil lamps with voluntary dues paid by those entering the harbour. St. John's was one of the first European settlements in America and the site was possibly visited – on St. John the Baptist's Day, 1497 – by John Cabot in the *Matthew*. By 1835, when responsibility for the light was transferred to the newly established Commissioners of Lighthouses, St. John's had become a thriving port. The light, however, was accurately described as 'quite a flimsy concern', and a second 39-ft (12-m) tower with an attached keeper's dwelling was built within the fort in 1852. This was fitted with a fourth-order dioptric lens to give the light a range of 16 miles. Part of the fort was demolished in 1952 to make way for the present 17-ft wooden tower.

Green Island Light

Trinity Bay, NF
Built: 1908 and 1957
Style: Octagonal tower with dwellings
No: H0526
Position: 48° 30.2 N. 53° 02.6 W
Focal plane: 92ft (28m)
Range: 18 miles (29km)
Height: 24ft (7m)

The first Green Island lighthouse to guide vessels towards Catalina harbour was erected in 1908. It was a circular lantern extending from the roof of the keeper's house, which stood on the south side of the island, but it was replaced with the present 24-ft tower in 1957. This is fitted with a fourth-order Fresnel lens and has a range of 18 miles.

Gull Island Light

Notre Dame Bay, NF
Built: 1884
Style: Circular iron tower
No: H0686
Position: 49° 59.9 N. 55° 21.5 W
Focal plane: 492ft (150m)
Range: 16 miles (26km)
Height: 23ft (7m)

Gull Island is the highest lighthouse on the North Atlantic coast. Standing 525ft (160m) above sea level on the summit of a barren granite island off Cape St. John on the north-east corner of the Baie Verte peninsula, the 23-ft cast-iron tower was built in 1884. It followed two notorious strandings, the first in 1867 when the brigantine *Queen* crashed into the rocks during a snowstorm. The crew managed to scramble ashore, but the ship was picked up by a wave and vanished in the blizzard. Wthout food or shelter, the sailors died of hypothermia. A diary written by a doctor from the *Queen,* and found later, described their fate. On 24 December 1867, he wrote, 'We are still alive. We have not tasted a bite of food since we were stranded here ... my clothes are completely saturated ... who would ever have imagined this would be my ending.' In a second incident soon afterwards two Newfoundlanders landed on Gull Island to hunt birds, but a storm blew up and their boat was swept away. They had a small wooden shelter which they dismantled and made a boat of sorts in which they returned to St. John's long after they had been given up for dead. The cast-iron tower subsequently erected on the island was fitted with a fourth-order dioptric lens with a range of 16 miles.

Point Amour Light

Forteau Bay, NF
Built: 1855
Style: Conical stone tower with dwelling
No: H0114
Position: 51° 27.4 N. 56° 51 6 W
Focal plane: 152ft (46m)
Range: 24 miles (39km)
Height: 90ft (27m)

Point Amour lighthouse was built in 1855 on the south side of Forteau Bay to guide vessels along the Strait of Belle Isle. The 90-ft masonry tower has a strapped and shingled exterior and was fitted with a second-order dioptric lens. In 1957, the tower and buildings were extensively renovated.

Point Riche Light

Port au Choix, NF
Built: 1870 and 1892
Style: Octagonal wooden tower
No: H0154
Position: 50° 41.9 N. 57° 24.7 W
Focal plane: 96ft (29m)
Range: 15 miles (24km)
Height: 45ft (14m)

The first Point Riche lighthouse was a 40-ft (12-m) wooden tower built in 1870 to guide vessels towards Port au Choix. It stood for 22 years until it was replaced by the present 45-ft octagonal structure fitted with a cast-iron lantern room. Both towers were equipped with a catoptric (employing mirrors) apparatus. The keeper's dwelling burned down during the late 1970s but, since the light is automated, the building was not replaced.

Puffin Island Light

Bonavista Bay, NF
Built: 1878
Style: Square pyramidal tower
No: H0556
Position: 49° 03.7 N. 53° 33.1 W
Focal plane: 70ft (21m)
Range: 14 miles (22.5km)
Height: 25ft (8m)

The first Puffin Island lighthouse was a tower set on the end of a stone keeper's cottage built in 1878 to mark the entrance to Greenspond harbour. The tower was fitted with a fourth-order dioptric lens and had a range of 12 miles (19km), although the

PAGES 392, 393, OPPOSITE and RIGHT
Green Island Light, Newfoundland.

BELOW
Point Riche Light, Newfoundland.

LEFT and OPPOSITE
Rose Blanche Light, Newfoundland.

beam was obscured between Big Pools Island in the north and Fox Island. The present 25-ft red-banded pyramidal tower provides a more powerful light with a range of 14 miles.

Rose Blanche Light
Rose Blanche Harbour, NF
Built: 1873 and 1940
Style: Granite building, light tower at one corner
No: H0244
Position: 47° 36 N. 58° 42.2 W
Focal plane: 50ft (15m)
Range: 8 miles (13km)

The original Rose Blanche lighthouse was built in 1873 to mark the entrance to the harbour, and is known locally as Cains Island lighthouse. The light was transferred to a framework tower in 1940, and the old lighthouse became increasingly dilapidated. It has since been restored by a local historical group.

Nova Scotia

Abbot's Harbour Light
West Pubnico, NS
Built: 1884, 1922
Style: Pyramidal wooden tower
Focal Plane: 38ft (11.5m)
Height: 31ft (9.5m)

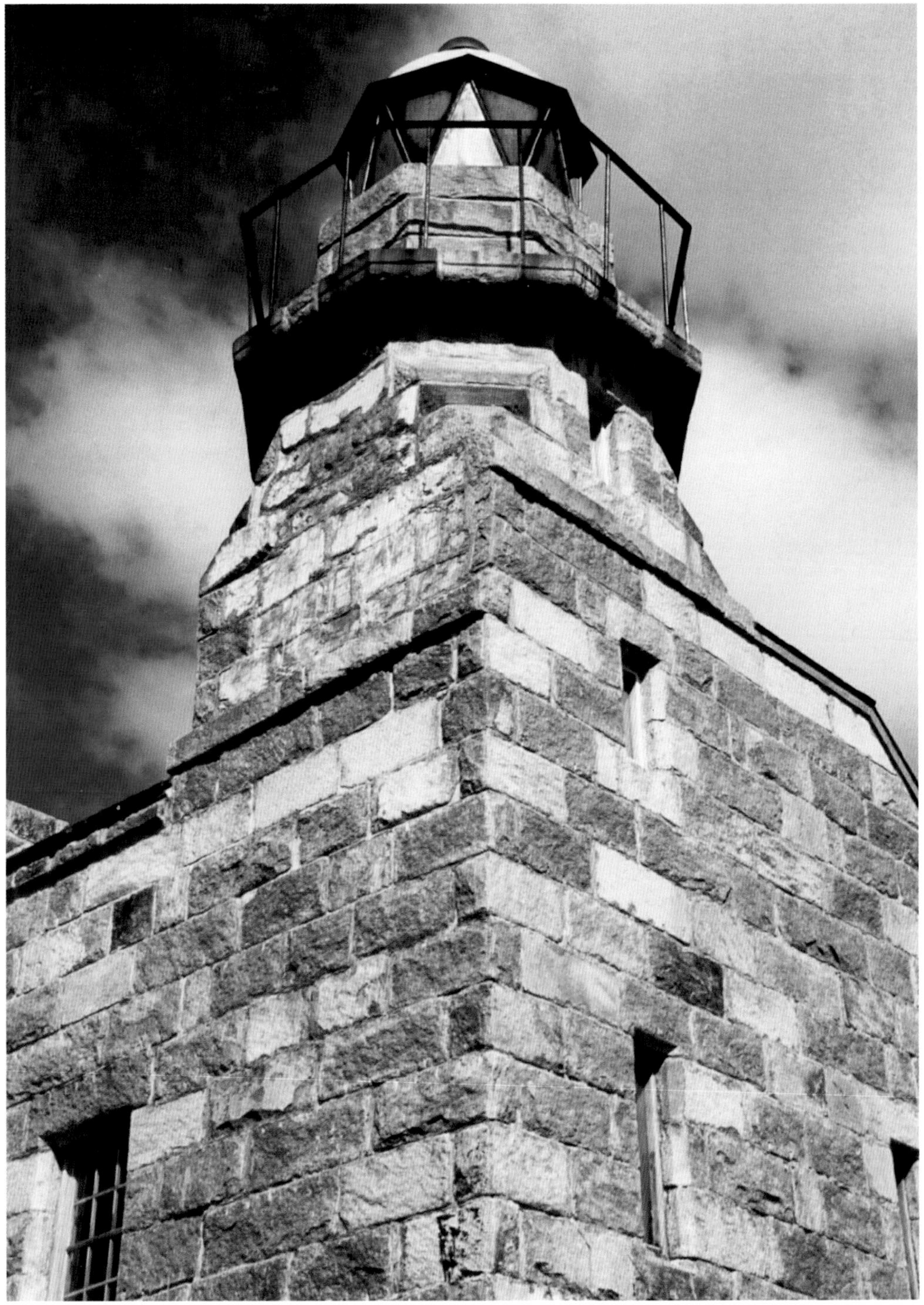

OPPOSITE and LEFT
Rose Blanche Light, Newfoundland.

PAGES 400 and 401
Annapolis Light, Nova Scotia.

The original navigation aid for Abbot's Island was a simple lantern mounted on a mast which was erected in 1884. Today's more substantial structure was built in 1922. The lighthouse is situated on the east side of Abbot's Harbour and stands in a municipal park. It is still in service and was automated in 1966.

Annapolis Light

Annapolis River, NS
Built: 1889
Style: Square, pyramidal wooden tower
No: H3908
Position: 44° 44.7 N. 65° 31.2 W
Focal plane: 30ft (9m)
Range: 8 miles (13km)
Height: 28ft (8.5m)

The small but ornate Annapolis lighthouse, set on the Annapolis River north-east of the pier to mark the town of Annapolis Royal, was built in 1889. The 28-ft classic 'pepper-pot' tower has a range of 8 miles.

Baddeck Light

Cape Breton Island, NS
Built: 1875
Style: Square pyramidal wooden tower

Baddeck Light is one of three lighthouses on Cape Breton Island and is part of the Cabot Trial which also includes the lighthouses at Chéticamp and Peggy's Point.

Baccaro Point Light

Barrington Bay, NS
Built 1850 and 1934
Style: Square pyramidal wooden tower
No: H3782
Position:43° 27 N. 65° 28.3 W
Focal plane: 52ft (16m)
Range: 16 miles (26km)
Height: 45ft (14m)

The first Baccaro Point lighthouse was a three-storey structure with the lantern extending from the roof. It was built in 1850 to guide vessels towards Port La Tour in Barrington Bay. Seal oil was used to fuel the light until 1865, when the station was upgraded to kerosene burners. In 1934, the building burned down and was replaced by the present 45-ft tower with its red octagonal iron lantern. The old keeper's dwelling was pulled down when the station was automated in 1984.

Beaver Island Light

Beaver Island, NS
Built: 1846, 1954 and 1985
Style: Conical tower with a red lantern.
No: H3534
Position: 44° 49.5 N. 62° 20.3 W
Focal plane: 65ft (20m)
Range: 14 miles (22.5km)
Height: 28ft (8.5m)

The first Beaver Island lighthouse was a 35-ft (10.5-m) wooden tower erected on the

CAUTION
TRAVEL BEYOND
THIS POINT
MAY BE DANGEROUS
TO YOUR HEARING
FOG HORN MAY SOUND
AT ANY MOMENT

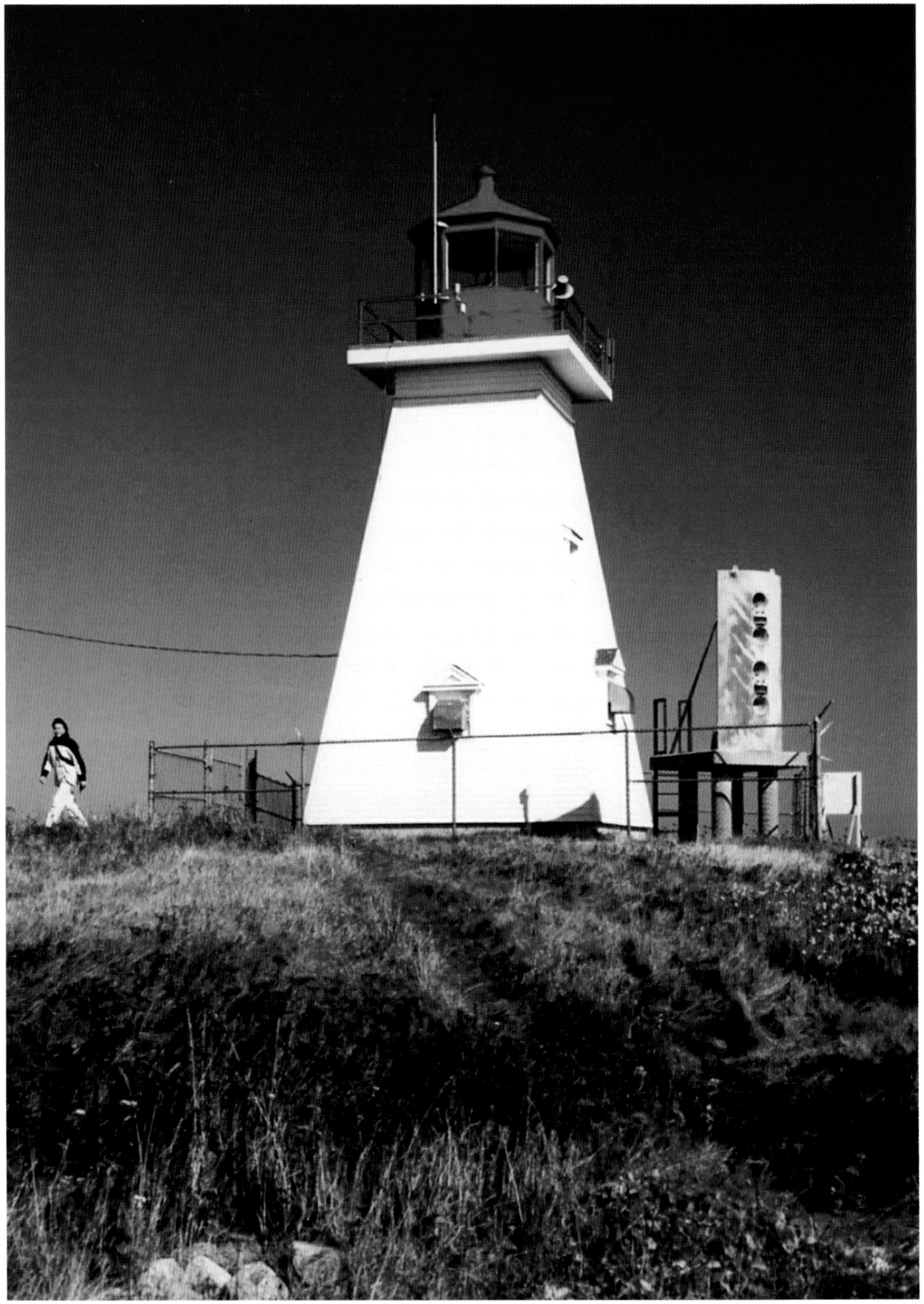

PAGE 402
Abbot's Harbour Light, Nova Scotia.

PAGE 403
Baddeck Light, Nova Scotia.

OPPOSITE and RIGHT
Baccaro Point Light, Nova Scotia.

eastern end of the island in 1846 to guide vessels towards Port Dufferin. In February 1860 Simon Fraser, the keeper, was caught up in ice floes while attempting to row between Beaver Island and Port Dufferin. Attempts to reach him by boat failed and Fraser was left stranded overnight. A comprehensive search the following day failed to find any trace of him, and it was concluded that he must have been carried out to sea with the ice. Fraser's son, Robert, succeeded him as keeper. The old lighthouse was rebuilt in 1954 before being replaced by the present 28-ft conical tower in 1985.

Bon Portage Island Light

Shag Harbour, NS
Built: 1874 and 1964
Style: Square tower on square building.
No: H3790
Position: 43° 27.4 N. 65° 44.6 W
Focal plane: 46ft (14m)
Range: 14 miles (22.5km)

OPPOSITE PAGE and FAR RIGHT
Bon Portage Island Light, Nova Scotia.

RIGHT
Cape d'Or Light, Nova Scotia.

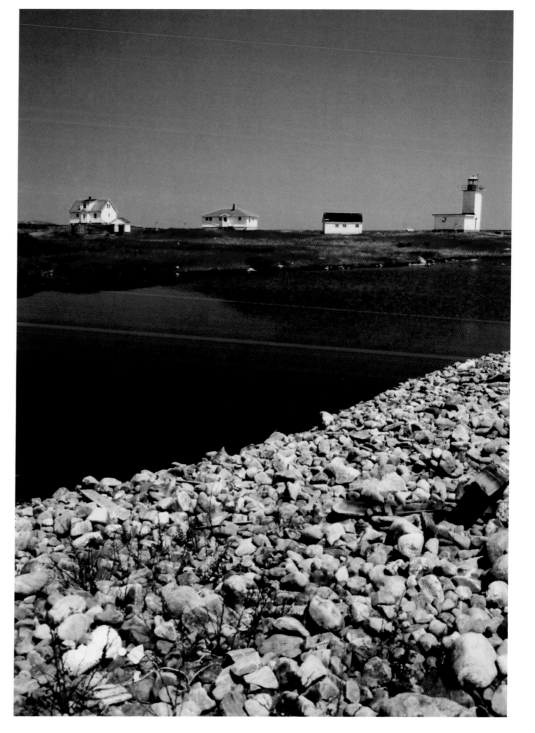

The first Bon Portage Island lighthouse was a 46-ft (14-m) wooden tower on the roof of the keeper's dwelling, built in 1874 on the south point of the island to guide vessels towards Shag Harbour. On some charts it is referred to as the Outer Island Light. For 110 years, the light on this small barren island was maintained by 16 light keepers and their families. The longest serving were Morrill Richardson and his wife Evelyn, who bought the island in 1929 and lived there for the next 35 years. Evelyn Richardson wrote a classic lighthouse book, *We Keep a Light*, published in 1945, describing the joys and deprivations of living on an isolated island. In 1964 the Richardsons retired and the old lighthouse was replaced by the present concrete tower. The island is now owned by Acadia University, which uses the buildings as a biology field station.

Brier Island Light

Digby Neck, NS
Built: 1809, 1832 and 1944
Style: Octagonal concrete tower
No: H3872
Position: 44° 14.9 N. 66° 23.5 W
Focal plane: 95ft (29m)
Range: 17 miles (27km)
Height: 60ft (18m)

Brier Island lighthouse was one of the first to be built in Canada. A light was recorded on what locals call West Point as early as 1809 to guide vessels into St. Mary's Bay. A 55-ft (17-m) wooden lighthouse was erected in 1832 and burned down in 1944, when it was replaced by the present 60-ft concrete tower with its three red bands.

Bunker Island Light

Yarmouth, NS
Built: 1874, 1960
Style: Square tower, octagonal red lantern.
Focal plane: 32ft (10m)

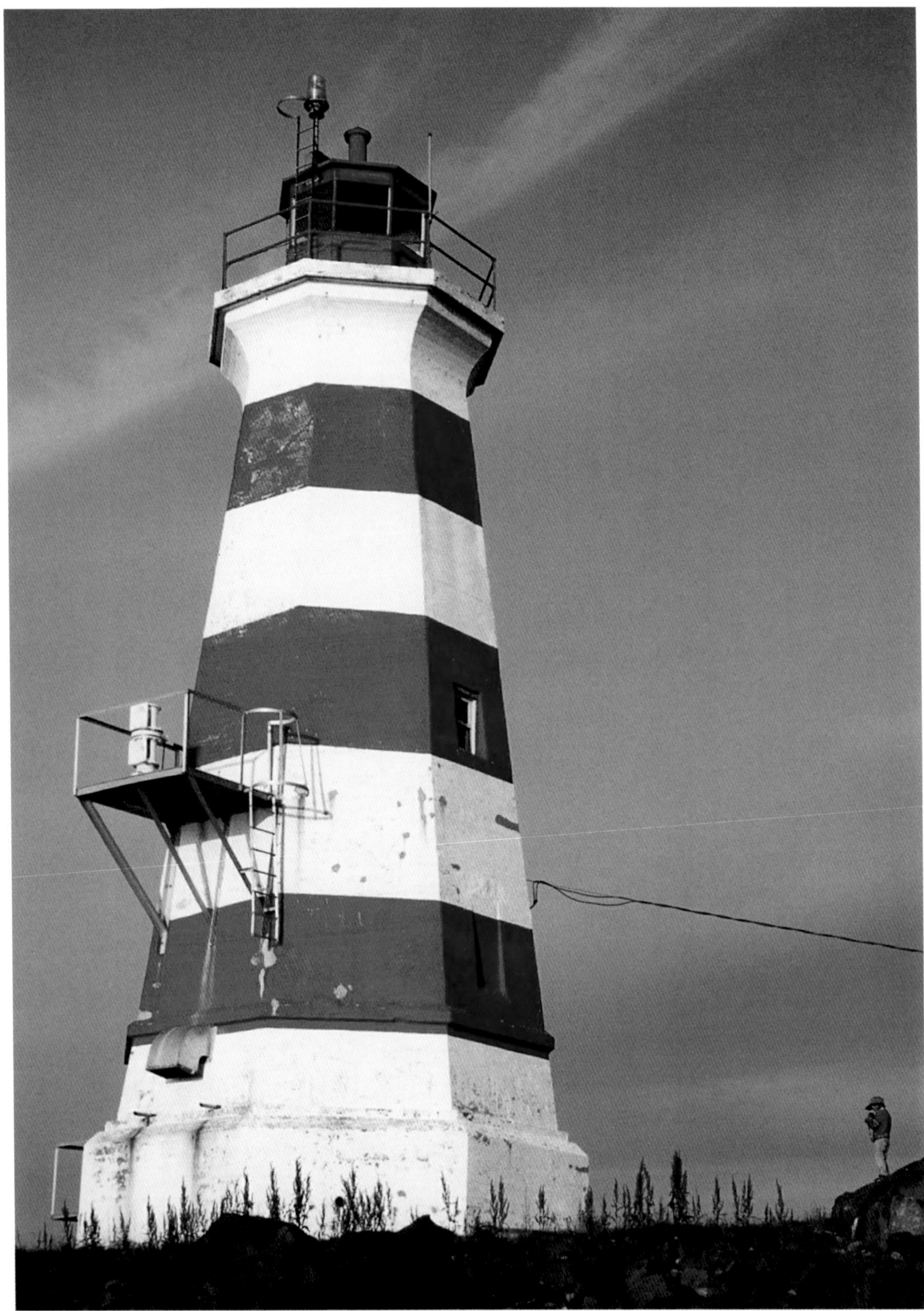

Range: 6 nautical miles
Height: 30ft (9m)

Bunker Island Light was buit in 1966 and replaced an earlier wooden structure from 1874. It is situated just off the coast and is in current use. The light was automated in 1981.

Cape d'Or Light

Minas Channel, NS
Built: 1875, 1922 and 1965
Style: Square concrete tower
No: H3938
Position: 47° 17.5 N. 64° 46.5 W
Focal plane: 79ft (24m)
Range: 13 miles (21km)

Cape d'Or was first marked with a fog whistle in 1875 to warn vessels of the hazardous rip tides in the Minas Channel. The first lighthouse was erected on the banks of the Apple River in 1922 and was moved to the cape by boat, along with a new steam-powered fog signal. The present concrete tower, built on the corner of a white square building and with a red octagonal iron lantern, was built in 1965 and automated in 1980. The two keepers' dwellings are now used as an inn.

Cape Fourchu Light

Evangeline, NS
Built: 1839 and 1962
Style: Octagonal concrete tower
No: H3820
Position: 43° 47.6 N. 66° 09.3 W
Focal plane: 113ft 6in (34.5m)
Range: 13 miles (21km)

The first Cape Fourchu lighthouse was an attractive octagonal wooden tower built in 1839. The station is often the first sight ferry passengers travelling from Bar Harbour and Portland, Maine, have as they enter Canada. The much-photographed tower was replaced in 1962 with what locals were led to believe would be an outward replica. What they got was a modern concrete edifice 77ft (23.5m) high, with red stripes tapered below the red polygonal metal lantern. This they disdainfully nicknamed 'the Apple Core'. In 1980 Cape Fourchu became the monitoring station for other automated lighthouses in the area, but in 1993 the tower was automated itself, and the monitoring transferred to Letete, New Brunswick. Originally, the new tower had a range of 22 miles (35km)), but it was reduced to 13 miles in 1998, the same time that the foghorn was removed. The site is now managed by the Friends of the Yarmouth Light Society, which has opened the 1912 keeper's house to visitors.

Cape Roseway Light

McNutt's Island, NS
Built: 1788, 1865, 1879 and 1960
Style: Octagonal concrete tower
No: H3762
Position: 43° 37.4 N. 65° 15.8 W
Focal plane: 109ft (33m)
Range: 14 miles (22.5km)
Height: 48ft (15m)

Cape Roseway is the site of one of Canada's earliest light stations. The first tower was raised in 1788, the earliest bar two,

OPPOSITE
Brier Island Light, Nova Scotia.

RIGHT
Cape Fourchu Light, Nova Scotia.

Louisbourg (1734) and Sambro Island (1759). The first 92-ft (28-m) octagonal Cape Roseway lighthouse was built of locally quarried stone to guide vessels into Shelburne harbour, which once rivalled Halifax as a commercial port and shipbuilding centre. In 1865 the tower had two lights set 38ft (11.5m) apart vertically, increased to 55ft (17m) apart in 1879. In 1959 the tower was struck by lightning and caught fire, whch caused so much damage it had to be demolished. The building was replaced by the present 48-ft octagonal concrete tower with its red lantern, which was automated in 1986. The station's foghorn was decommissioned in 1989.

Cape Sable Light

Cape Sable Island, NS
Built: 1861 and 1924
Style: Octagonal concrete tower.
No: H3784
Position: 43° 23.4 N. 65° 37.3 W
Focal plane: 97ft (29.5m)
Range: 22 miles (35km)

The first Cape Sable lighthouse was built in 1861 following the sinking the previous year of the SS *Hungarian* with the loss of 205 lives, after she struck the hazardous rocks that extend 5 miles (8km) south and west of this low-lying island. The 65-ft (20-m) octagonal tower was equipped with 19 oil lamps but had a range of only 8 miles (13km) because of the red glazing of the lantern. In an effort to improve visibility, the glazing was changed to clear glass eight years later, while ruby chimneys were fitted on the lamps to maintain the station's red signal. In 1870, a clockwork mechanism was installed and the light was changed to flashing white, and in 1876 the station was equipped with a fog-alarm steam whistle. A third-order Fresnel lens was fitted in the lantern room in 1902 but because of its low focal plane the light was still not sufficiently visible. In 1923 the decision was taken to replace the old tower with a taller lighthouse to extend the light range to 22 miles. The tower was automated in 1986 and two years later the Coast Guard demolished all the other buildings on the site. The Cape Sable lighthouse is now a classified building and thus protected from a similar fate.

Carter Island Light

Lockeport Harbour, Carter Island, NS
Built: 1872, 1932 and 1982
Style: Conical tower with two red bands.
No: H3753
Position: 43° 42.3 N. 65° 06.1 W
Focal plane: 54ft (16.5m)
Range: 8 miles (13km)
Height: 31ft (9.5m)

OPPOSITE and LEFT
Cape Fourchu Light, Nova Scotia.

The first Carter Island lighthouse, to guide vessels into Lockeport inner harbour, was a 29-ft (9-m) square wooden tower with a seventh-order dioptric lens. A second tower replaced it in 1932 and stood for 50 years until it was superseded by the present 31-ft automated conical tower.

Chebucto Head Light

Ketch Harbour, Halifax, NS
Built: 1872, 1940 and 1967
Style: Octagonal concrete tower
No: H3600
Position: 44° 30.4 N. 63° 31.4 W
Focal plane: 162ft (49m)
Range: 14 miles (22.5km)
Height: 45ft (14m)

A lighthouse at Chebucto Head was first established in 1872 to guide vessels towards Ketch Harbour and Halifax, one of the finest natural harbours in the world. The lighthouse was replaced by a second tower in 1940, which is still standing although it was superseded by the present 45-ft concrete tower in 1967.

Coffin Island Light

Liverpool Bay, NS
Built: 1812 and 1914
Style: Octagonal concrete tower
No: H3728
Position: 44° 02.0 N. 64° 37.5 W
Focal plane: 60ft (18m)
Range: 13 miles (21km)
Height: 54ft (16.5m)

The original Coffin Island lighthouse dated back to 1812 and was the fifth to be built in Nova Scotia. The 50-ft (15-m) black-and-white-ringed wooden tower was built on land originally named Bear Island to mark the entrance to the Mersey River and Liverpool harbour. The island was renamed five years after the tower was built in memory of Pelg Coffin, an early landowner. The lighthouse was replaced with the present 54-ft octagonal concrete tower with its red octagonal lantern and white rectangular wooden dwelling in 1914. It was automated in 1962 and the keepers' dwellings were pulled down two years later. The tower is now managed by the Coffin Island Lighthouse Heritage Society, but is under threat from sea erosion.

Eddy Point Light

Strait of Canso, NS
Built: 1851, 1895 and 1988
Style: Conical fibreglass tower
No: H3420
Position: 45° 31.3 N. 61° 15 W
Focal plane: 38ft 9in (12m)
Range: 16 miles (26km)
Height: 28ft (8.5m)

Eddy Point Light station was established in 1851 to mark the eastern entrance to the Strait of Canso, which separates Cape Breton Island from mainland Nova Scotia. This first lighthouse was a 25-ft (8-m) square dwelling with a black diamond painted on it. It was fitted with two lights, 25ft apart, set in windows at each end of the building. It was replaced by a 44-ft (13-m) square wooden tower in 1895. The structure was twice rebuilt in 1929 and 1938 and was finally pulled down in 1988, when it was replaced by the present 28-ft fibreglass tower with automated lantern.

Five Islands Light

Sand Point, Minas Basin, NS
Built: 1914
Style: Square, pyramidal wooden tower
No: H4028
Position: 45° 23.3 N. 64° 04.1 W
Focal plane: 43ft (13m)
Range: 11 miles (18km)
Height: 33ft (10m)

The 33-ft Five Islands lighthouse was built at Sand Point on the west side of the entrance to the East River in 1914 to guide vessels towards the Minas Basin, where the rise and fall of the tides are among the highest in the world. These fast-flowing waters cause considerable erosion and the lighthouse had to be moved in 1952, 1957 and finally in 1996, three years after it was decommissioned. The 'pepper-pot' tower was purchased by Colchester County, moved 180ft (55m) inland and leased to the Five Islands Lighthouse Preservation Society, which has restored the tower and opened it to the public.

LEFT and OPPOSITE
Chebucto Head Light, Nova Scotia.

Fort Point Light

Liverpool, NS
Built: 1855
Style: Square wooden tower on dwelling

Fort Point Light is situated in the southern entrance to Liverpool harbour. It is the third oldest lighthouse in Nova Scotia. The lantern, which is situated on a tower built on top of the keeper's house, has three lamps and 12 reflectors and is fitted with a 1951 Fresnel lens. The lighhouse was deactivated in 1969 and is now a tourist attraction.

George's Island Light

Halifax Harbour, NS
Built: 1876, 1916 and 1919
Style: Octagonal concrete tower
No: H3618
Position: 44° 38.4 N. 63° 33.6 W
Focal plane: 59ft (18m)
Height: 54ft (16.5m)

A lighthouse on George's Island – named after King George II of England – was first erected in 1876 to lead vessels into Halifax harbour. The station has a unique history, for its original keeper, Robert Ross, served here from its first day until 1920, overseeing the building and operation of three successive

OPPOSITE
Chebucto Head Light, Nova Scotia.

RIGHT
Louisbourg Light, Nova Scotia.'

PAGE 416
Coffin Island Light, Nova Scotia.

PAGE 417
Eddy Point Light, Nova Scotia.

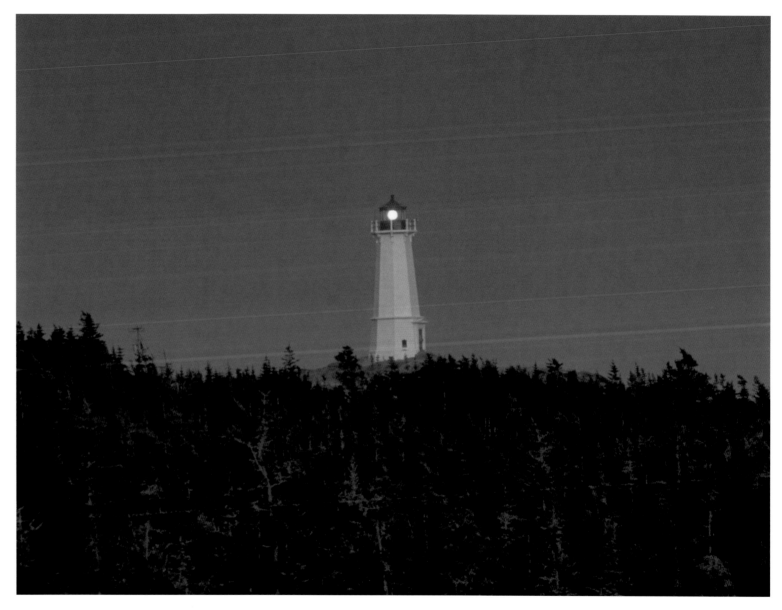

lighthouses on the site. The first wooden tower burned down in 1916 and a temporary light replaced it until the present 54-ft concrete tower was built in 1919. This tower, with a red stripe on the south side and a red aluminium lantern, was upgraded with a fourth-order dioptric lens in 1922, but a further 70 years passed before an electric lantern was installed. The station was automated in 1972 and is now the front light of the Halifax Harbour Inner Range.

Henry Island Light

St. George's Bay, NS
Built: 1902
Style: Octagonal wooden tower
No: H1222
Position: 45° 58.6 N. 61° 36 W
Focal plane: 200ft (61m)
Range: 6 miles (10km)
Height: 38ft (11.5m)

The 38-ft wooden Henry Island lighthouse, with its red-and-white stripes on alternating sides and red polygonal iron lantern, was built on the west side of the island in 1902 by the Canadian lighthouse engineer Joseph MacDonald. Originally, the tower was equipped with a catoptric lens, which was changed to a fourth-order dioptric lens in 1966. The light was not electrified until 1985 and has since been automated. The island is now owned by the Henry Island Preservation Society, which has restored the buildings.

Louisbourg Light

Cape Breton East, NS
Built: 1734, 1842, 1924
Style: Octagonal pyramidal concrete tower
No: H3344
Position: 45° 54.4 N. 59° 57.5 W

Focal plane: 105ft (32m)
Range: 21 miles (34km)
Height: 55ft (17m)

The original Louisbourg lighthouse was built on Lighthouse Point, on the north side of the harbour, by the French in 1734. It was the first in Canada and second in North America after the Boston Light (1716). Louisbourg was built as a fortress port from which the French intended to hold New France against the English. The 68-ft (21-m) rubblestone tower, which was equipped with a circle of wicks burning cod-liver oil and set in a copper ring mounted on cork floats, was first lit on 1 April 1734. The heat from the flames was intense, and on the night of 11 September 1736 the wooden supports within the lantern room caught fire. The tower survived and the light was replaced temporarily with a coal burner until a new 32-wick oil lamp was installed in 1738. The tower was destroyed by cannon fire during the British siege of Louisbourg in 1758 and was not replaced until 1842. This second lighthouse was erected on the roof of a two-storey, wooden keeper's dwelling which was destroyed by fire in 1922. The present concrete lighthouse was completed in 1924 across the harbour from the old fortress, and has since been automated.

Margaretsville Light

Bay of Fundy, NS
Built: 1859
Style: Square pyramidal tower
No: H3926
Position: 45° 03.3 N. 65° 04 W

LEFT
Fort Point Light, Nova Scotia.

BELOW
Medway Head Light, Nova Scotia.

OPPOSITE and PAGES 420 and 421
Peggy's Point Light (Peggy's Cove Light), Nova Scotia.

70 YEAR OLD
LIGHTHOUSE

Salmon River Light, Nova Scotia.

Focal plane: 30ft (9m)
Range: 12 miles (19km)
Height: 21ft (6m)

The black-and-white 21-ft Margaretsville lighthouse, with its broad black band and white square lantern, may be small in stature, but it figures prominently in the history of Canadian navigation lights. Until the mid-1850s the Nova Scotia shoreline around the Bay of Fundy was largely unlit. The residents of Margaretsville decided that a lighthouse would attract more vessels to their harbour, and in 1859 Sir Brenton Haliburton agreed to allow the building of a public lighthouse on his land. Construction was supervised by William Earley, the first keeper, who had been steward to Sir Brenton. Earley was succeeded by his son John, who converted the second floor of the lighthouse into living quarters for use in bad weather. After John Earley's death, his widow Ruth continued the family profession and oversaw the replacement of the old lantern room with a cast-iron top in 1911. The light was originally powered by eight red kerosene lamps with brass reflectors. The reflectors had to be cleaned each day and the reservoir refuelled with oil carried up from below until the tower was automated in 1963.

Maugher Beach Light

McNab's Island, Halifax, NS
Built: 1828 and 1941
Style: Octagonal concrete tower
No: H3607
Position: 44° 36.1 N. 63° 32 W
Focal plane: 57ft (17m)
Range: 14 miles (22.5km)
Height: 58ft (18m)

The first lighthouse at Maugher Beach at the end of a spit on McNab's Island, was a Martello-tower structure completed in 1828, though some accounts suggest that a light had been shown from this point whenever vessels were expected into Halifax harbour as early as 1815. The height of the tower was raised to 60ft (18m) three years later, when a fog signal was also installed. The keeper's dwelling, demolished in 1987, dated from 1913. The present concrete tower, with its red octagonal metal lantern, was built in 1941 and was automated in 1983.

Medway Head Light

Port Medway, NS
Built: 1851, 1927, 1963 and 1983
Style: Square pyramidal wooden tower
No: H3722
Position: 44° 06.2 N. 64° 32.4 W
Focal plane: 79ft (24m)
Range: 13 miles (21km)
Height: 28ft 6in (9m)

The original Medway Head lighthouse was a 23-ft (7-m) wooden tower built in 1851 to guide vessels towards Port Medway. The tower was rebuilt in 1927, then replaced with a conical fibreglass tower in 1963. The present 28ft 6-in concrete tower, with its white, square, red-roofed lantern, was erected in 1983 and was automated four years later.

Peggy's Point Light

St. Margaret's Bay, NS
Built: 1868, 1915
Style: Octagonal concrete tower
No: H3660
Position: 44° 29.5 N. 63° 55 W
Focal plane: 67ft (20.5m)
Range: 11 miles (18km)
Height: 50ft (15m)

The 50-ft concrete Peggy's Point lighthouse, marking the eastern entrance to St. Margaret's Bay, is one of Canada's best-known icons. The present tower, known locally as Peggy's Cove lighthouse, was built in 1915 to replace a wooden tower built above the keeper's dwelling that dated back to 1868. This had displayed a red light through a catoptric reflector, but the new tower had a white light, at first, which was changed to green in 1979.

Port Greville Light

Minas Channel, NS
Built: 1908
Style: Square pyramidal wooden tower
No: H3948
Position: 45° 24.3 N. 64° 33 W
Focal plane: 59ft (18m)
Range: 6 miles (10km)
Height: 25ft (8m)

The stocky 25-ft Port Greville lighthouse, with its square white lantern, is typical of the short-range towers built around the Nova Scotia coast in the late 19th and early 20th centuries. Built on cliffs overlooking Port Greville when it was a bustling shipyard and fishing port, the wooden tower held a sixth-order dioptric lens and acted as the front light of a range to guide vessels into the harbour. The tower was decommissioned in 1981, cut in half, and transported to the Canadian Coast Guard College campus in Sydney, Cape Breton Island, where it stood on display until 1998. It has now been returned to Port Greville and has been resited as a tourist attraction at the Age of Sail Heritage Centre, a few miles from its original position.

Salmon River Light

West Pubnico, NS
Built: 1924
Style: Square pyramidal tower

Salmon River Light was originally situated on a breakwater at Salmon River near Yarmouth. In the 1980s it was moved to West Pubnico, where it became part of a craft shop.

Salvages Light

Green Point, NS
Built: 1915 and 1965
Style: Red lantern on rectangular building
No: H3778
Position: 43° 28.1 N. 65° 22.7 W
Focal plane: 55ft (17m)
Range: 15 miles (24km)
Height: 49ft (15m)

The 49-ft Salvages lighthouse was built above the keeper's dwelling to mark a group of hazardous rocks extending 2 miles (3km) east of Green Point. The lighthouse is situated on the south-eastern tip of the highest rock in the chain, about 6 miles (10km) from Port La Tour.

Sambro Island Light

Halifax Harbour, NS
Built: 1759
Style: Octagonal stone and concrete tower
No: H3632
Position: 44° 26.2 N. 63° 33.8 W
Focal plane: 140ft (43m)
Range: 24 miles (39km)
Height: 82ft (25m)

Sambro Island is the oldest standing lighthouse in North America, and was the second light tower to be built in Canada. The 82-ft stone tower, with its three red bands and red circular iron lantern, is sited at the centre of Sambro Island, 2 miles (3km) from the entrance to Halifax, one of the largest ice-free harbours in the world at this latitude. It was built, at a time when Halifax was a major British naval port, to warn vessels of the 30 or more shoals at the entrance to the inlet. Initially the light, which was equipped with lamps burning fish oil, was neither efficient nor run with any kind of discipline. The first keepers were government appointees who collected the harbour dues for themselves and neglected the lamps. Fish oil is notorious for its blackening smoke and the reflectors and glass were not always cleaned; moreover, much to the chagrin of crews attempting to reach Halifax harbour at night, the light was not always relit if the flame went out. The loss of the Boston sloop *Granby* with all hands at the entrance to the harbour in 1771 brought matters to a head. A report on the tragedy accepted that '...the fatal accident happened for want of a light being properly kept in the lighthouse'. It also noted that naval ships had, on occasion, to fire at the lighthouse in order to make the keepers show a light. Glass flues were then installed over the lamps to carry off much of the smoke, but it was not until 1864 that a new lantern room was installed. In 1906 the height of the tower was increased by 20ft (6m) and it was equipped with a first-order Fresnel lens. Two years later the white-painted sentinel was given three red stripes to make it more easily visible in snow. In 1968, the lantern room was upgraded once more, this time with an aero-beacon, giving the light a range of 24 miles. The tower was automated in 1988 and has since undergone complete renovation, including extensive underpinning.

Seal Island Light

NS
Built: 1831
Style: Octagonal wooden tower
No: H3812
Position: 43° 23.7 N. 66° 00.8 W
Focal plane: 102ft (31m)
Range: 21 miles (34km)
Height: 68ft (21m)

Seal Island, 18 miles (29km) west of Cape Sable Island, lies off the south-west tip of Nova Scotia where the Bay of Fundy meets the Atlantic. Fog, storms and powerful tides have conspired to wreck more than 160 vessels on the three-mile-long island over the past three centuries, making it one of the most notorious maritime graveyards on the Atlantic coast. Those who managed to make it ashore on this remote and barren island invariably died from exposure during the winter months. Ministers made a pilgrimage to the island during the first weeks of spring to bury their remains. The 68-ft Seal Island lighthouse was built in 1831 as part of a sea-rescue base set up to reduce the number of maritime disasters, while a steam-powered fog whistle was established nearby in 1870, replaced by a diaphone in about 1900. The original light was powered by seal oil until replaced by a kerosene lamp in 1892. A second-order revolving Fresnel lens was installed in 1902, and the station was finally electrified in 1959. In 1978 the Fresnel lens was replaced with an aero-marine beacon and the station became semi-automatic. In 1986 the keepers' families were moved off the island and the station changed to rotational status, with teams of two keepers working alternate 28-day shifts. The light was automated in 1990 and is now monitored by the light keepers at the Machias Seal Island East Light (page 377).

LEFT
Seal Island Light, Nova Scotia.

OPPOSITE
Sambro Island Light, Nova Scotia.

Spencers Island Light

Minas Channel, NS
Built: 1904
Style: Square wooden tower
No: H3940
Position: 45° 20.3 N. 64° 42.5 W
Focal plane: 34ft (10m)
Range: 7 miles (11km)
Height: 33ft (10m)

The 33-ft Spencer's Island lighthouse, with its square white lantern, was built in 1904 when this was a major shipbuilding community. It also provided a good anchorage for sailing vessels waiting for favourable winds in the Bay of Fundy. At the time that the lighthouse was built, the port was busy converting old sailing ships into barges to carry gypsum from Windsor, Nova Scotia, to New York. The lighthouse,

LEFT
Yarmouth Light, Nova Scotia.

OPPOSITE
Christian Island Light, Ontario.

which was equipped with a seventh-order dioptric lens, was decommissioned during the 1980s and the historic tower now houses a museum managed by the Spencer's Island Community Association.

Western Head Light

Liverpool, NS
Built: 1962
Style: Octagonal tower with red lantern
Focal plane: 55ft (17km)
Range: 14 nautical miles

Western Head Light, built in 1962, is situated on the west side of the entrance to Liverpool Bay. It is still an active aid to navigation and was automated in 1988.

Yarmouth Light

Yarmouth, NS
Built: 1840, 1962
Style: Concrete tower
Focal plane: 114ft (35m)
Range 13 nautical miles
Height: 77ft (23.5m)

The original Yarmouth Light was built in 1840 and its second-order Fresnel lens can be seen at Yarmouth County Museum. The

present light was built in 1962 and has a modern plastic lens. It is an active navigational aid and was automated in 1993. There is a museum on the site and the light is open to the public.

ONTARIO

Chantry Island Light

Port Elgin, Bruce Peninsula, Lake Huron, ON
Built: 1859
Style: Conical stone tower with dwelling
Position: 44° 29.2 N. 81° 24.1 W
Focal plane: 103ft (31m)
Range: 6 miles (10km)
Height: 86ft (26m)

The 86-ft stone-built Chantry Island lighthouse was designed to guide vessels towards Port Elgin. Fitted with a second-order dioptric lens, the historic tower is one of six 'Imperial Lights' (built by the British Imperial Lighthouse Service in 1859) on the Great Lakes. The others are at Christian Island, Cove Island, Griffith Island, Nottawasaga Island and Point Clark. The Chantry Island station was automated in 1954.

Christian Island Light

Georgian Bay, Nottawasaga Bay, ON
Built: 1859
Style: Conical limestone tower
Focal plane: 64ft (19.5m)
Range: 15 miles (24km)
Height: 51ft (15.5m)

The 51-ft Christian Island Light is one of six

imperial towers built around the Great Lakes during the mid 1800s. The others are situated at Chantry Island, Cove Island, Griffith Island, Nottawasaga Island and Point Clark. The limestone tower stands on Bar Point, at the south-east end of Christian Island. The beacon was decommissioned in 1922 and the lantern was removed during tWorld War II, since when the station has been re-activated.

Cove Island Light

Gig Point, Bruce Peninsula, Lake Huron, ON
Built: 1859
Style: Conical limestone tower
Position: 45° 19.4 N. 81° 44.1 W
Focal plane: 101ft (31m)
Range: 16 miles (26km)
Height: 85ft (26m)

The 85-ft stone-built Cove Island lighthouse, with its red, circular iron lantern and dwelling attached, was built on Gig Point in 1859 to mark the southern entrance to Georgian Bay. Fitted with a second-order dioptric lens, this is one of the six 'Imperial Lights' erected on the Great Lakes. The tower was automated in 1991.

Gibraltar Point Light

Toronto Harbour, Lake Ontario, ON
Built: 1808
Style: Octagonal brick tower
Position: 43° 37.0 N. 79° 22.6 W
Focal plane: 66ft (20m)
Range: 14 miles (22.5km)

LEFT
Chantry Island Light, Ontario.

BELOW LEFT
Cove Island Light, Ontario.

OPPOSITE
Gibraltar Point Light, Ontario.

The 62-ft (19-m) brown, brick-built Gibraltar Point lighthouse, with its red polygonal lantern, standing on the south-west side of the point on Centre Island within Toronto harbour, is the oldest standing lighthouse on the Great Lakes. The tower was decommissioned in 1959.

Griffith Island Light

Georgian Bay, Owen Sound, ON
Built: 1859
Style: Conical limestone tower
Position: 44° 51.0 N. 80° 53.3 W
Focal plane: 103ft (31m)
Range: 5 miles (8km)
Height: 64ft (19.5m)

The 64-ft Griffith Island lighthouse, with its red, polygonal iron lantern, was built in 1859 on the north-east side of the island to guide vessels into Colpoy's Bay. The tower is equipped with a third-order dioptric lens and is one of the six 'Imperial Lights' on the Great Lakes.

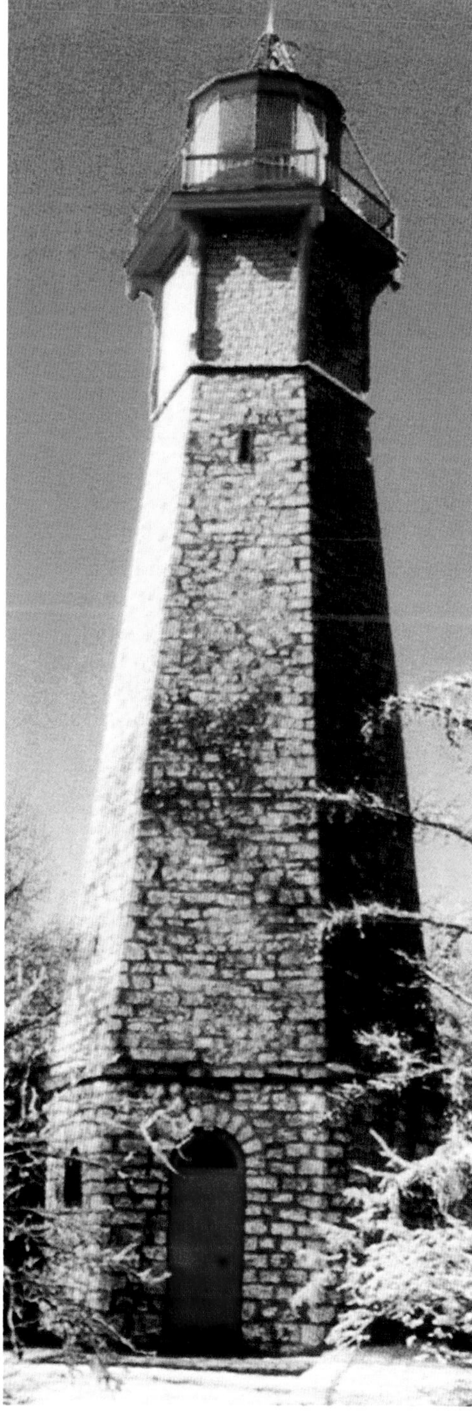

Oakville Light

Lake Ontario, ON
Built: 1836, 1888 and 1963
Style: Cylindrical tower
Position: 43° 26.2 N. 79° 39.6 W
Focal plane: 27ft (8m)
Range: 6 miles (10km)
Height: 19ft (6m)

The original 42-ft (13-m) Oakville lighthouse built in 1836 was deemed by some to provide such a poor light that it was scarcely visible six or seven miles out in the lake, about half the distance claimed for it by official records. Built on Oakville's east pier, it was perhaps fortuitous that the tower was blown down in a storm in April 1886. A second 31-ft (9.5-m) wooden tower, equipped with a fourth-order dioptric lens, was built to replace it in 1888. This tower now takes pride of place at a private marina, having been replaced in 1963 by a modern 19-ft white cylindrical tower with a red band at the top.

Nottawasaga Island Light

Nottawasaga Bay, ON
Built: 1859
Style: Conical limestone tower
Position: 44° 32.2 N. 80° 15.3 W
Focal plane: 97ft (29.5m)
Range: 5 miles (8km)
Height: 94ft (29m)

The 94-ft stone Nottawasaga Island lighthouse, with its red-roofed polygonal lantern, was built in 1859 on the northern tip of the island to guide vessels towards Collingwood harbour. Fitted with a second-order dioptric lens, it is one of the six 'Imperial Lights' on the Great Lakes.

Point Clark Light

Eastern Shore, Lake Huron, ON
Built: 1859
Style: Conical stone tower
Position: 44° 04.2 N. 81° 45.3 W
Focal plane: 93ft (28m)
Range: 14 miles (22.5km)
Height: 69ft (21m)

The 69-ft Point Clark lighthouse was built in 1859 10 miles (16km) south-west of Kincardine Point, and was equipped with a second-order dioptric lens. The tower is one of the six 'Imperial Lights' built on the Great Lakes in 1859, and the only one on the mainland. It was electrified in 1953 and automated during the 1960s. The keeper's dwelling now houses a museum.

Presqu'ile Point Light

Lake Ontario, ON
Built: 1840
Style: Octagonal stone tower
Position: 43° 59.5 N. 77° 40.3 W
Focal plane: 76ft (23m)
Range: 8 miles (13km)
Height: 60ft (18m)

The 60-ft stone-built Presqu'ile Point lighthouse was erected in 1840 on the eastern point of this peninsula, 6 miles (10km) south of Brighton. The station's fourth-order dioptric lens was electrified in 1935 and the tower was automated in 1952. The original lens was replaced with an aero-beacon in 1965.

Western Islands Light

Georgian Bay, ON
Built 1895.
Style: Octagonal wooden tower
Position: 45° 02.0 N. 80° 21.3 W
Focal plane: 74ft (22.5m)
Range: 15 miles (24km)
Height: 50ft (15m)

The 50-ft classic wooden Western Islands lighthouse, with its red polygonal iron lantern, was built on Double Top Rock, 27 miles (43km) south-west of Parry Sound in 1895. The tower was equipped with a fourth-order dioptric lens which was automated in 1967. The keeper's dwelling was demolished soon afterwards.

Prince Edward Island

Annandale Range Rear Light

Juniper Point, PE
Built: 1898
Style: Square pyramidal wooden tower
No: H0928.1
Position: 46° 16.0 N. 62° 26.3 W
Focal plane: 76ft (23m)
Height: 66ft (20m)

Annandale Range Rear lighthouse, with its red stripe and red square lantern, was built in 1898 on the east coast of the island and, with its front range partner, led vessels into Boughton River. Records show that this 66-ft wooden tower, one of the tallest on Prince Edward Island, was moved in 1901,

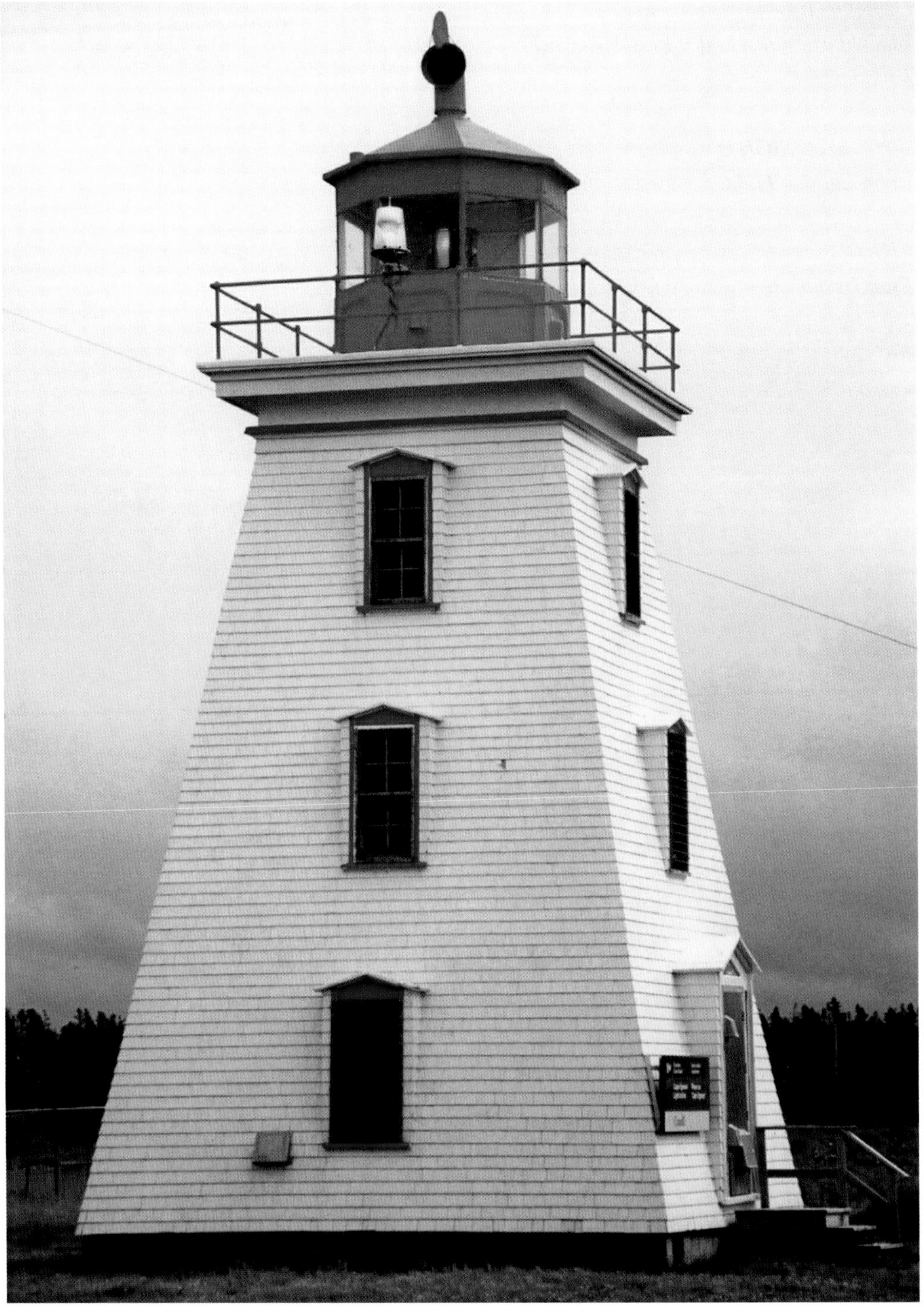

OPPOSITE LEFT
Blockhouse Point Light, Prince Edward Island.

OPPOSITE RIGHT
Cape Egmont Light, Prince Edward Island.

RIGHT
Cape Tryon Light, Prince Edward Island.

BELOW
Presqu'ile Point Light, Ontario.

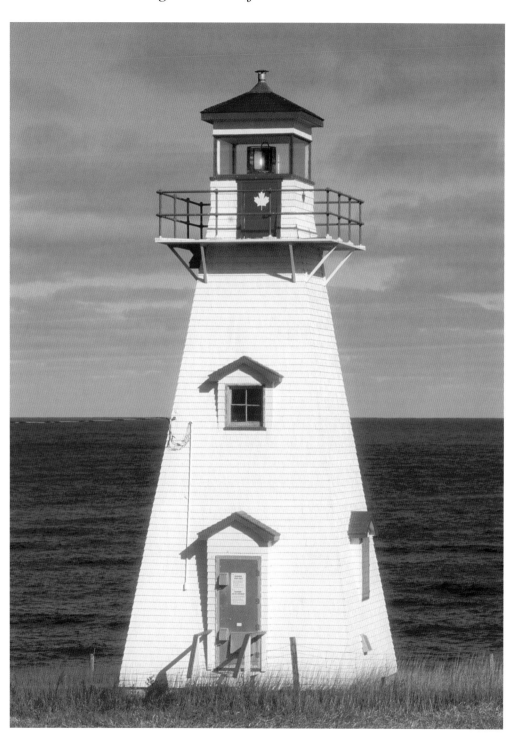

possibly the year when it was fully enclosed. Its light has emitted a quick flash since it was automated in 1964.

Blockhouse Point Light

Northumberland Strait, PE
Built: 1851 and 1876
Style: Square pyramidal wooden tower
No: H1008
Position: 46° 11.3 N. 63° 07.5 W
Focal plane: 56ft (17m)
Range: 18 miles (29km)
Height: 40ft (12m)

The present 40-ft Blockhouse Point lighthouse, with its red lantern and two-storey dwelling attached, was built in 1876 on the site of Fort Amherst, on Northumberland Strait. The wooden tower replaced a pair of leading lights dating back to 1851 to guide vessels on the approach to Charlottetown.

Cape Bear Light

Murray Harbour, PE
Built: 1881
Style: Square pyramidal wooden tower
No: H0950
Position: 46° 00.2 N. 62° 27.6 W
Focal plane: 74ft (22.5m)
Range: 15 miles (24km)
Height: 40ft (12m)

The classic Cape Bear lighthouse, with its red lantern, was built by John Whalen in 1881 and bears a marked similarity to other Canadian light towers at Blockhouse Point,

FAR LEFT and LEFT
Cape Tryon Light, Prince Edward Island. The old lighthouse (far left) and the lighthouse rebuilt in 1969 (left).

BELOW
Cape Bear Light, Prince Edward Island.

OPPOSITE
New London Light, Prince Edward Island.

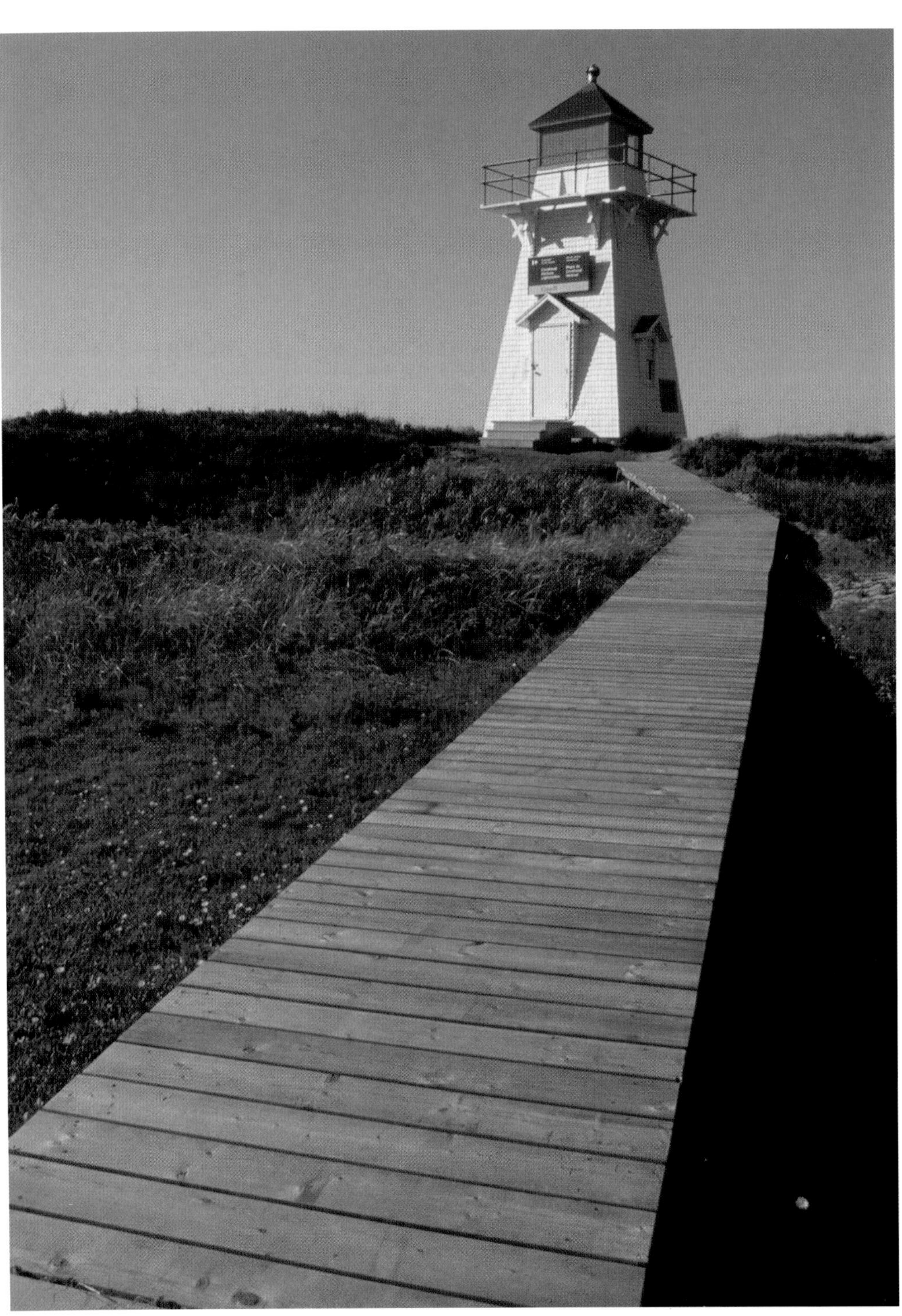

Cape Egmont and Wood Islands. Built on a headland that marks the south-eastern tip of Prince Edward Island to guide vessels into Murray Harbour, the 40-ft tower had to be moved back from the eroding cliff face in 1947. The tower was the base for a Marconi wireless station between 1905 and 1922, but all evidence of this and the keeper's attached dwelling was removed when the lighthouse was automated in 1960.

Cape Egmont Light

Cape Egmont, PE
Built: 1884
Style: Square pyramidal wooden tower
Focal Plane: 72ft (22m)
Range: 12 nautical miles
Height: 42ft (13m)

Cape Egmont Light, with its red trim and red lantern, was originally much closer to the sea, but by 1998 was in severe danger of falling in, so it was moved to its present position. There was another building attached which was removed at this time. The lighthouse is still active.

Cape Tryon Light

French River, PE
Built: 1905 and 1969
Style: Square pyramidal wooden tower
No: H1129
Position: 46° 32.0 N. 63° 30.4 W
Focal plane: 115ft (35m)
Range: 18 miles (29km)
Height: 39ft (12m)

The 39-ft wooden Cape Tryon lighthouse, with its red lantern, was built in 1969, replacing an earlier tower that had marked the entrance to the fishing port of French River on the northern shore of Prince Edward Island since 1905. This classic Canadian 'pepper-pot' design is in danger of being eroded by the sea and, like Cape Bear lighthouse, will need to be moved back if it is to be prevented from falling down the cliff face.

LEFT
North Rustico Harbour Light, Prince Edward Island.

OPPOSITE
Panmure Head Light, Prince Edward Island.

East Point Light

PE
Built: 1867
Style: Octagonal tower; red lantern and trim
No: H0920
Position: 46° 27.1 N. 61° 58.3 W
Focal plane: 100ft (30.5m)
Range: 20 miles (32km)
Height: 64ft (19.5m)

The East Point lighthouse was built by William MacDonald in 1867 and, with its imposing white structure and red trimmings, remains a prime example of the standard Canadian octagonal design. Initially, the lighthouse was positioned some distance inland and not, as Admiralty charts suggested, right on this easternmost point of Prince Edward Island. This confusion led to at least two shipwrecks, that of the Dominion line steamer *Québec* in 1879, and the British HMS *Phoenix* in 1882. Three years after the latter drama, the lighthouse was moved to within 200ft (60m) of the point, only to be moved back again in 1908 when erosion threatened.

New London Range Rear Light

New London, PE
Built: 1876
Style: Square pyramidal tower with red trim and dwelling attached
Focal plane: 44ft (13m)
Range: 7 nautical miles
Height: 34ft (10m)

North Cape Light

Northumberland Strait, PE
Built: 1865
Style: Octagonal wooden tower
No: H1076
Position: 47° 03 N. 63° 59 W
Focal plane: 78ft (24m)
Range: 18 miles (29km)
Height: 62ft (19m)

The 62-ft North Cape lighthouse, with its red trim and red lantern, was built in 1865 on the north-western tip of Prince Edward Island to replace a portable lantern warning vessels away from what is the longest reef in North America. The tower's original fourth-order dioptric light was replaced with a long-focus catoptric lens in 1875 and the station was finally electrified in 1975. Like other lighthouses on Prince Edward Island, the North Cape tower has had to be relocated to avoid the threat of eroding cliffs. The keeper's dwelling was pulled down in 1950.

North Rustico Harbour Light

Rustico, PE
Built: 1876
Style: Square pyramidal wooden tower
No: H1141
Position: 46° 27 N. 63° 17 W
Focal plane: 40ft 9in (12.5m)
Range: 8 miles (13km)
Height: 34ft (10m)

The 34-ft North Rustico Harbour lighthouse, with its red trim, red lantern and small keeper's dwelling attached, was built in 1876 on the north-eastern shore of Prince Edward Island to mark the entrance to Rustico Bay and the Hunter River. Sea erosion led to the tower being moved in 1884, and in 1899 the building was blown down during a storm and moved to better ground. It was moved again in 1914 when erosion threatened its position once more. In 1973 the old lighthouse was decommissioned and the light was placed on a new framework tower, but local protests led to the older tower being recommissioned in 1976.

Panmure Head Light

Panmure Island, PE
Built: 1853
Style: Octagonal tower

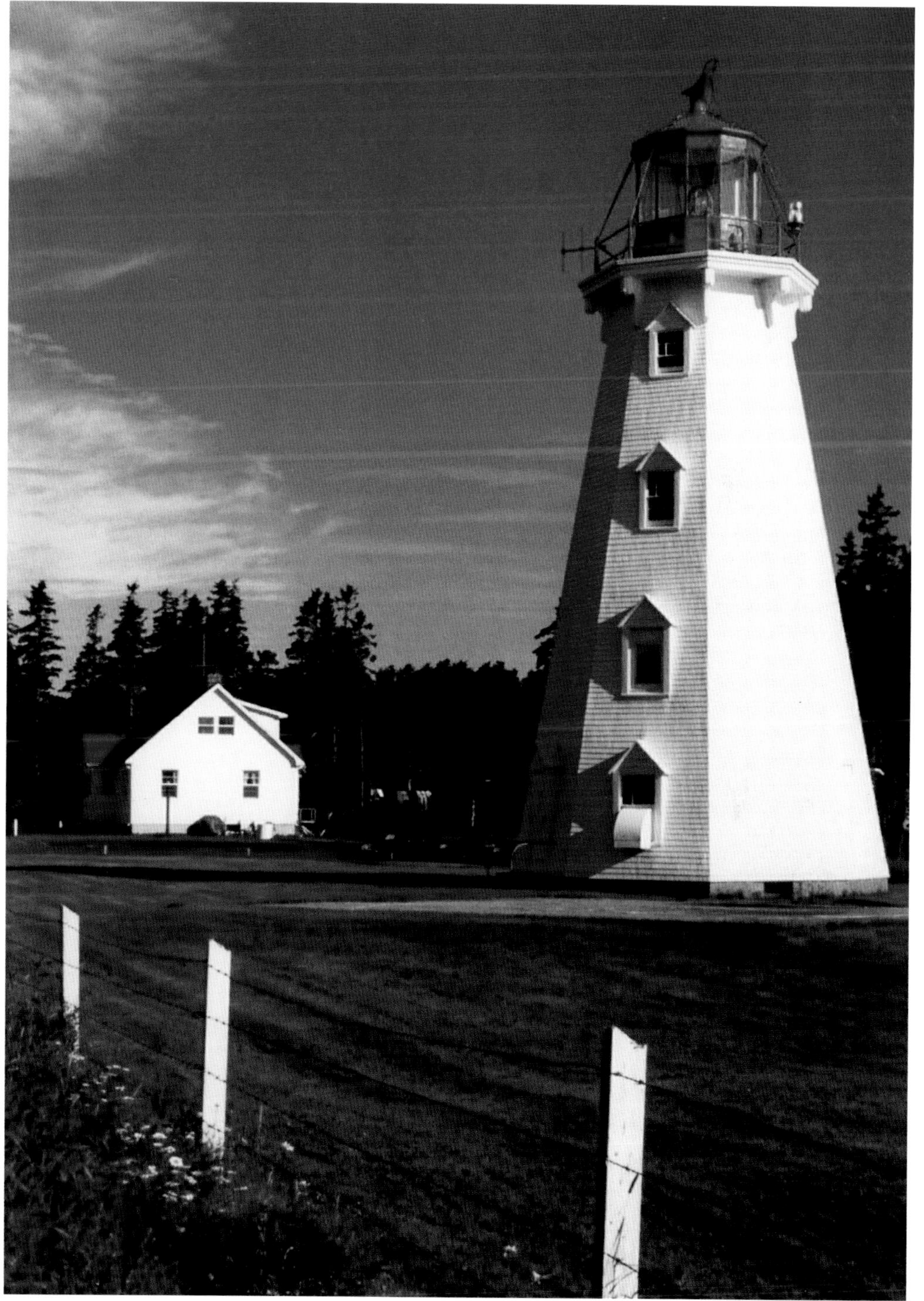

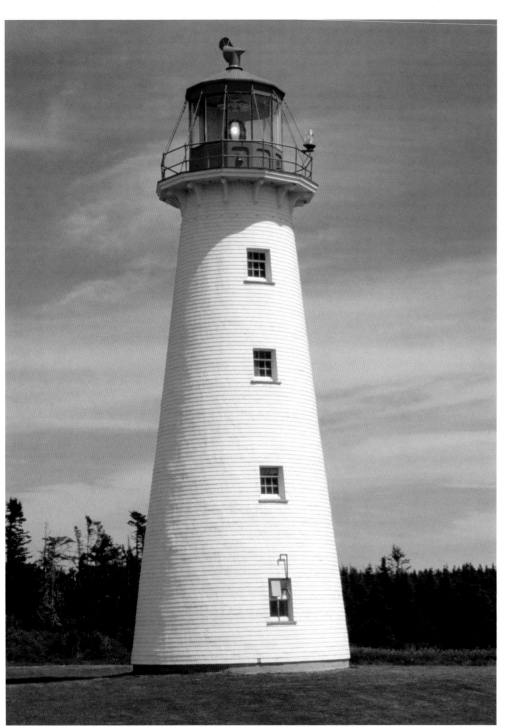

Focal plane: 82ft (25m)
Range: 17 nautical miles

Panmure Head Light is situated by the entrance to Georgetown Harbour on the east coast of Prince Edward Island on Cardigan Bay. The light is still active and was automated in 1986.

Prim Point Light

Northumberland Strait, PE
Built: 1846
Style: Conical brick tower, red lantern
No: H0982
Position: 46° 03 N. 63° 02 W
Focal plane: 68ft (21m)
Range: 20 miles (32km)
Height: 60ft (18m)

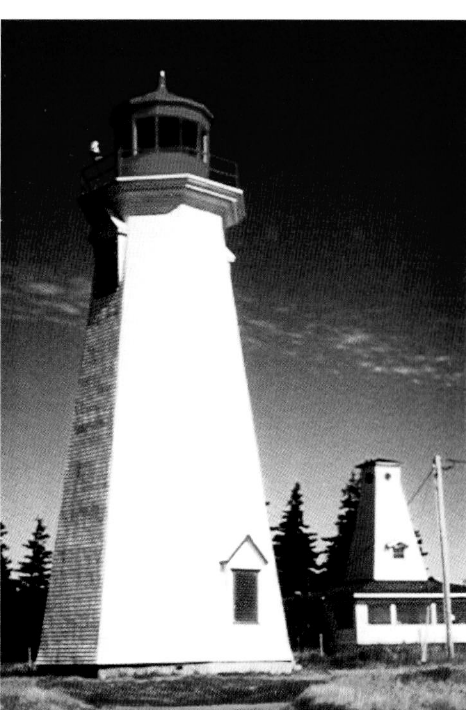

FAR LEFT
Prim Point Light, Prince Edward Island.

BELOW LEFT
Seacow Head Light, Prince Edward Island.

OPPOSITE LEFT and RIGHT
Souris East Light, Prince Edward Island.

The 60-ft Prim Point lighthouse, built by Richard Walsh in 1846 at the eastern entrance to Hillsborough Bay to guide vessels towards Charlottetown, is one of the few brick-built lighthouses in Canada. The tower was designed by Isaac Smith, Prince Edward Island's most prominent 19th-century architect. It was originally named Hillsborough Bay Light and was equipped with a fourth-order Fresnel lens. The original keeper's dwelling was demolished when the tower was automated in 1969.

Seacow Head Light

Bedeque Bay, Northumberland Strait, PE
Built: 1863
Style: Octagonal wooden tower
No: H1046
Position: 46° 19.0 N. 63° 48.4 W
Focal plane: 94ft (29m)
Range: 15 miles (24km)
Height: 60ft (18m)

Seacow Head lighthouse, with its red polygonal lantern, was built in 1863 at the eastern entrance to Bedeque Bay to guide vessels towards Summerside harbour. The 60-ft wooden, octagonal tower was moved in 1884 when erosion threatened its position.

The tower once had a sixth-order Fresnel lens exhibiting a fixed red light, but this was changed in 1915 to a fourth-order lens which extended the light's range from 10 miles (16km) to 14 miles (22.5km). Between 1915 and 1935 the keeper was also responsible for firing a fog explosive every five minutes during the winter months whenever the ice-breaking supply steamer was due. The tower was automated in 1947 and the lantern was changed once more to a sixth-order lens in 1958.

Souris East Light

Knight Point, PE
Built: 1880
Style: Square pyramidal tower
No: H0922
Position: 46° 20 N. 62° 14 W
Focal plane: 89ft (27m)
Range: 15 miles (24km)
Height: 47ft (14m)

The 47-ft Souris East lighthouse, with its red trim and red circular metal lantern, was built by Peter Aylward on Prince Edward Island's eastern shore to mark the entrance to Colville Bay and the Souris River, and to guide the ferries to and from the Magdalen Islands. The tower is equipped with a fourth-order Fresnel lens which was automated in 1991. The original keeper's dwelling was demolished in 1959, two years before the station was electrified.

St. Peters Light

St. Peters Harbour, PE
Built: 1865
Style: Square pyramidal wooden tower
No: H1164
Position: 46° 26 N. 62° 44 W
Focal plane: 33ft 6in (10m)
Range: 18 miles (29km)

St. Peters Light was built in 1865 on the sand dunes of Prince Edward Island's north-east shore to guide vessels towards St. Peters Harbour. The classic square pyramidal wooden tower, with its red trim and black lantern, began life as a rear range light 1,350ft (410m) from a front light that was moved on occasions to match the shifting patterns of the main channel.

Warren Cove Front and Rear Range Lights

Northumberland Strait, PE
Built: 1907
Style: Square pyramidal wooden towers
No: H1016 (Front Light)
Position: 46° 11.0 N. 63° 08.0 W
Focal plane: 56ft (17m)
Height: 30ft (9m)

No: H1016.1 (Rear Light)
Position: 991ft (302m) from front range light
Focal plane: 76ft (23m)

The two classic 'pepper-pot'-style lighthouses that make up Warren Cove Range Lights were built in 1907 north of Blockhouse Point to guide vessels into Charlottetown harbour. They were originally equipped with seventh-order Fresnel lenses to display red lights, but were later changed to yellow beams. These pepper-pot lighthouses were a popular design for range lights in Canada because it was relatively easy to relocate the front light if or when the course of the main channel changed.

West Point Light

Egmont Bay, Northumberland Strait, PE
Built: 1876
Style: Square pyramidal wooden tower
No: H1062
Position: 46° 37.2 N. 64° 23.3 W
Focal plane: 68ft (21m)
Range: 12 miles (19km)
Height: 49ft (15m)

Originally painted red and white, the banding was changed to black and white in 1915 because black fades less quickly and is more easily visible from a distance. During the 87 years before automation, the lighthouse had only two keepers, William MacDonald, from 1875 to 1925, and Benny MacIsaac, from 1925 to 1963. Automation ended the need for a keeper, and the keeper's house disappeared along with the job. However, in 1984 local efforts raised the money for a second building alongside the tower, and the two now serve as an inn and a museum.

Wood Islands Main Light

Northumberland Strait, PE
Built: 1876
Style: Square pyramidal wooden tower
No: H0962
Position: 45° 57 N. 62° 44 W
Focal plane: 71ft 6in (22m)

West Point Light, Prince Edward Island.

Range: 12 miles (19km)
Height: 52ft 6in (16m)

The Wood Islands Main Light, which rises from a red-roofed dwelling and has a red lantern, was built in 1876 to guide the ferries crossing Northumberland Strait to Pictou, Nova Scotia. This 'pepper-pot'-style tower was equipped with a fourth-order Fresnel lens and a range of 15 miles (24km), downgraded when the lighthouse was electrified in 1958 to 12 miles. The station was automated in 1991.

Wood Islands Range Lights

Northumberland Strait, PE
Built: 1902
Style: Front Range: white square tower and lantern, rising from a small white building with sloping walls, red trim
No: H0964 (Front Light)
Focal plane: 24ft (7m)
Range: 6 miles (10km)
Height: 19ft (6m)

No: H0964.1 (Rear Light)
Style: White, square, pyramidal wooden tower with red stripe and white square lantern
Focal plane: 37ft (11m)

Range: 7 miles (11km)
Height: 32ft (10m)

The pair of lighthouses that make up Wood Islands Range Lights were built in 1902 on the east training pier to guide vessels into Wood Islands harbour. Originally, both range lights were red and visible over a 6-mile range. When they were moved in 1940, their beams were changed to white, then in 1963 to green; they assumed their present flashing mode in 1967.

QUÉBEC

Cap au Saumon Light

Lower St. Lawrence, Charlevoix, QC
Built: 1894 and 1920
Style: White, octagonal tower, red lantern.
No: H2182
Position: 47° 46.2 N. 69° 54.4 W
Focal plane: 82ft (25m)
Range: 20 miles (32km)
Height: 46ft (14m)

The original Cap au Saumon lighthouse was a 46-ft wooden tower with attached keeper's dwelling built in 1894 on Pointe des Rochers, above Saint-Siméon on the northern shore of the St. Lawrence River. The present lighthouse is a standard Canadian octagonal concrete tower of the same height as and similar in design to the 50-ft (15-m) Peggy's Point (or Peggy's Cove) lighthouse guarding the entrance to St. Margaret's Bay in Nova Scotia, which was built in 1915. The Cap au Saumon Light is also known locally as the Pointe des Rochers and Cape Salmon lighthouse. The light has a range of 20 miles.

Cap Chat Light

Gaspé, QC
Built: 1875 and 1909
Style: Square concrete tower; red circular metal lantern
No: H1860
Position: 49° 05.3 N. 66° 44.5 W
Focal plane: 120ft (36.5m)
Range: 17 miles (27km)
Height: 33ft (10m)

The original Cap Chat lighthouse was a

OPPOSITE LEFT and RIGHT
Wood Islands Main Light, Prince Edward Island.

square wooden tower 32ft (10m) high, built on the north-east point of Cape Chat in 1875. The station's third-order dioptric lens was carried over to the 33-ft concrete tower that replaced it in 1909.

Cap d'Éspoir Light

Gaspé, QC
Built: 1874 and 1939
Style: Octagonal concrete tower
No: H1718
Position: 48° 25.2 N. 64° 19.1 W
Focal plane: 84ft (26m)
Range: 17 miles (27km)
Height: 49ft (15m)

The first Cap d'Espoir lighthouse was a 43-ft (13-m) square wooden tower dating back to 1874 set on the tip of the cape south-west of Percé. The present 49-ft standard concrete tower that replaced it was built in 1939.

Cap de la Tête au Chien Light

Lower St. Lawrence, QC
Built: 1909
Style: Octagonal concrete tower
No: H2166
Position: 47° 54.7 N. 69° 48.4 W
Focal plane: 206ft 9in (63m)
Range: 13 miles (21km)
Height: 36ft (11m)

The 36-ft Cap de la Tête au Chien lighthouse is another standard Canadian concrete lighthouse with a red-roofed wooden dwelling, built on the steeply forested cape below Saint-Siméon on the northern shore of the St. Lawrence River. The tower, also called Cape Dogs, has a third-order dioptric lens with a range of 13 miles. It is a great place from which to spot whales.

Cap des Rosiers Light

Gaspé, QC
Built: 1858
Style: Circular stone tower
No: H1768
Position: 48° 51.4 N. 64° 12.1 W
Focal plane: 134ft 6in (41m)
Range: 24 miles (39km)
Height: 88ft (27m)

At 88ft, the stone-built Cap des Rosiers lighthouse, with its boarded, circular red-roofed lantern, is the highest in Canada. Built in 1858, the tower was one of four lighthouses ordered by the Commissioners for Public Works. The others in the programme were Anticosti West Point, Belle Isle and Point Amour. John Page, chief engineer, supervised their construction, while François Baby managed the work. Because Cap des Rosiers is so remote, the materials were delivered by sea, which was difficult during the winter months and slowed progress considerably. The tower was originally fitted with a first-order catadioptric lens powered by an Argand lamp that burned porpoise oil until coal oil became readily available in 1868.

Cap Gaspé Light

Baie de Gaspé, QC
Built 1873, 1892 and 1950
Style: Octagonal concrete tower
No: H1762
Position: 48° 45.1 N. 64° 09.8 W
Focal plane: 351ft (107m)
Range: 10 miles (16km)
Height: 30ft (9m)

The first Cap Gaspé lighthouse was a 30-ft wooden tower standing high on the cliffs to guide the Grand Banks fishing boats in and out of the Bay of Gaspé. The 1873 tower was replaced in 1892 with a 29-ft combined tower and keeper's dwelling, which stood until 1950 when the Coast Guard replaced it with a standard concrete lighthouse.

Île Verte Light

Lower St. Lawrence, QC
Built: 1809
Style: Circular stone tower
No: H2146
Position: 48° 03.0 N. 69° 25.4 W
Focal plane: 54ft (16.5m)
Range: 19 miles (30.5km)
Height: 49ft (15m)

The 49-ft stone-built Île Verte lighthouse, with its boarded wooden dwellings, was constructed on the north-west tip of Green Island on the Lower St. Lawrence in 1809. This is Canada's third-oldest surviving lighthouse, and the only one dating from British rule. The tower, which is boarded on the outside to protect the mortar from cracking in the winter months, was built by Scotsman Charles Hambleton, who became its first keeper, and was fitted with a fourth-order dioptric lens. The station was automated in 1988.

Îles aux Perroquets Light

Mingan, QC
Built: 1888
Style: Octagonal tower
No: H1958
Position: 50° 13.2 N. 64° 12.5 W
Focal plane: 78ft 9in (24m)
Range: 15 miles (24km)
Height: 34ft 9in (10.5m)

The first Îles aux Perroquets lighthouse was a 55-ft (17-m) square wooden tower and attached dwelling on the farthest north-westerly island within the chain along Québec's northern shore, near the village of Mingan. The present 35-ft octagonal lighthouse, with its red lantern and attached dwelling, protrudes from the roof of the main dwelling and has a range of 15 miles.

Îlet Rouge Light

Lower St. Lawrence, QC
Built: 1848
Style: Round stone tower with three horizontal ribs
No: H2104
Position: 48° 4.2 N. 69° 33.3 W
Focal plane: 65ft (20m)
Range: 16 miles (26km)

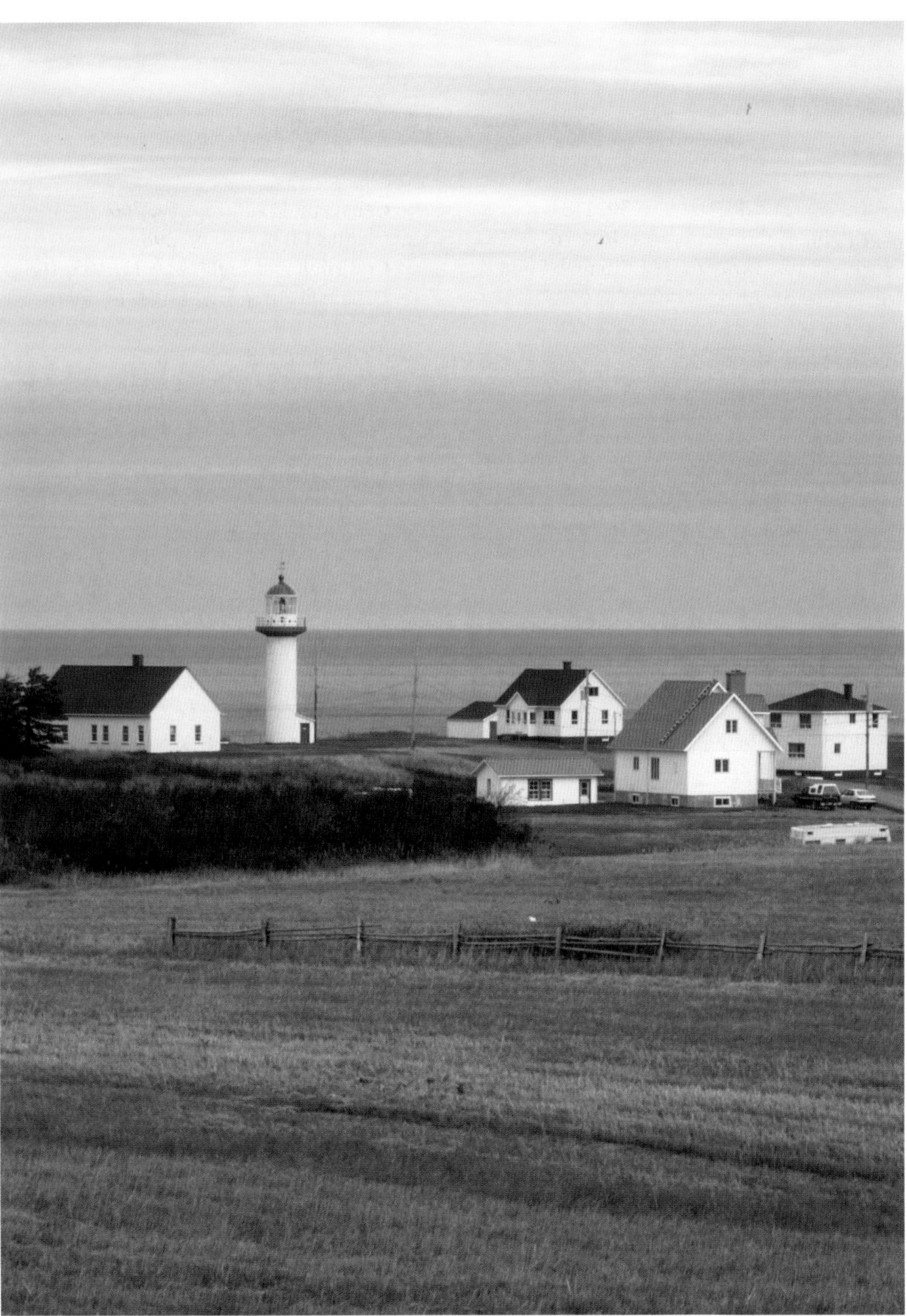

Cap Gaspé Light, Québec.

The 62-ft (19-m) stone-built Îlet Rouge lighthouse, with its red circular metal lantern and white dwelling attached, was built in 1848 on Red Islet in the middle of the St. Lawrence River at the request of local mariners, to guide vessels into the Saguenay River. The unusual tower has a large lantern room that originally housed 24 oil lamps. The station was one of the last lighthouses in Quebéc to be automated, in 1988.

Rochers aux Oiseaux Light

Magdalen Islands, QC
Built: 1870, 1887, 1915
Style: Hexagonal pyramidal tower.
No: H0822
Position: 47° 50.3 N. 61° 08.7 W
Focal plane: 161ft (49m)
Range: 20 miles (32km)
Height: 31ft (9.5m)

Records confirm that there have been three lighthouses on Great Bird Rock in the Magdalen Island chain since the first one was built on this barren rock in 1870. Its construction was a formidable task. The builders first had to climb steep cliffs 100ft (30.5m) high, then construct rope hoists to lift all the materials before building any shelter for themselves. This first 50-ft (15-m) lighthouse was equipped with a second-order Fresnel lens, which was transferred to the second 39-ft (12-m) wooden tower built in 1887. In 1915 the station still had its Fresnel lens, but the wooden tower had risen to 51ft (15.5m). The present tower stands 31ft high and has a range of 20 miles.

Stone Pillar Light

Lower St. Lawrence, QC
Built: 1843
Style: Circular stone tower
No: H2228
Position: 47° 12.3 N. 70° 21.6 W
Focal plane: 83ft (25m)
Range: 12 miles (19km)
Height: 42ft (13m)

The 42-ft Stone Pillar lighthouse is one of a number of towers built during the 19th century to warn of the many rocky outcrops in the lower St. Lawrence River. This drab-looking, grey circular stone tower, which is also known as Pilier de Pierre, was built in 1843 and its red lantern was equipped with a catoptric apparatus.

Index

Page numbers in italics refer to illustrations

A

Abbot's Harbour, NS *28,* 396, *402*
Absecon Light, NJ 193, *194*
Admiralty Point Light, WA *340*, 343
Albert Head Light, BC 358
Alcatraz Light, CA 13, *312*, 313
Algoma Pierhead Light, WI 92
Alki Point Light, WA *342*, 343
Alligator Reef Light, FL 257, *257*
Alpena Light, MI 51
Ambrose Light, NJ *39*, 40, 48, 193
Ambrose lightship 33, 47, 201
Amelia Island Light, FL 258, *259*
American Shoal Light, FL 258, *258*
Anacapa Islands Light, CA 314
Anclote Key Light, FL 258
Annandale Range Rear Light, PE 429
Annapolis Light, NS 399, *400, 401*
Annisquam Harbor Light, MA 161, *162, 163*
Aransas Pass Light (Lydia Ann Light), TX 294
Arecibo Light, Puerto Rico 250
Ashland Breakwater Light, WI 93, *93*
Ashtabula Light, OH 87, *87*
Assateague Island Light, VA 297, *297, 298*
Avery Point Light, CT 108

B

Baccaro Point Light, NS 399, *404, 405*
Baddeck Light, NS 399, *403*
Bailey's Harbor & Range Lights, WI 93
Baker Island Light, ME 120
Bakers Island, MA 11, 161, *161*
Bald Head (Cape Fear) Light, NC 11, 287, *287*
Baltimore Light, MD *276*, 277
Barbers Point Light, HI *329*, 332
Barbers Point Light, NY 201
Barcelona Light, NY 201
Barnegat Light, NJ 193, *195*
Bass Harbor Head Light, ME *121*, 123
Bass River Light, MA 161, *164*
Battery Point Light, CA *313*, 317
Bear Island Light, ME *122*, 123
Beaver Island Harbor Light (St. James), MI 51, 53, *53*
Beaver Island Light, NS 399
Beavertail Light, RI 11, *12*, 229, *229*
Belle Isle South Lights, NF 384
Bellevue Rear Range Light, DE 113
Big Bay Point Light, MI 53, *55*
Big Sable Point Light, MI 53, *54*, 67
Biloxi Light, MS 285, *285*
Bird Island Light, MA 161, *165*
Black Rock Harbor Light, CT 108, *108*
Block Island North Light, RI 229
Block Island Southeast Light, RI 230, *230*
Blockhouse Point Light, PE *430*, 431
Bloody Point Bar Light, MD 277
Blue Hill Bay Light, ME 123
Bluff Point Light, NY 201
Blunts Reef lightship 317
Boat Bluff Light, BC 358, *358, 359*
Boca Grande Rear Range Light, FL 259
Bois Blanc Island Light, MI 53, *56*
Bolivar Point Light, TX 13, 29, 294
Bon Portage Island Light, NS 405, *406, 407*
Bonilla Island Light, BC *360*, 361, *361*
Boon Island Light, ME 123
Borden Flats Light, MA 161
Boston Light, MA 11, 22, 161
Braddock Point Light, NY 201, *203*
Brandywine Shoal Light, DE 30, 113
Brant Point Light, MA 11, 28, 163, *166*
Bridgeport Breakwater Light (Tongue Point Light), CT 108, *109*
Brier Island Light, NS 407, *408*
Brigus Light, NF 388
Bristol Ferry Light, RI 231, *231*
Brockton Point Light, BC 361, *361*
Browns Head Light, ME 123, *124*
Browns Point Light, WA 345
Buffalo Main Light, NY 201
Buffington Breakwater Light, IN 50
Bunker Island Light, NS 407
Burkhaven Light, NH 189
Burnt Coat Harbor Light, ME 123
Burnt Island Light, ME 123
Burrows Island Light, WA *341*, 345
Butler Flats Light, MA 163
Buzzards Bay, MA 32, 164

C

Cana Island Light, WI 93, *94*
Cap au Saumon Light, QC 440
Cap Chat Light, QC 440
Cap d'Espoir Light, QC 441
Cap de la Tête au Chien Light, QC 441
Cap des Caissie Light, NB 375
Cap des Rosiers Light, QC 441
Cap Gaspé Light, QC 441, *442*
Cape Anguille Light, NF *386, 387*, 388
Cape Ann, MA 11, 164
Cape Arago Light, OR 335, *337*
Cape Bauld Light, NF 388
Cape Beale Light, BC 362, *362*
Cape Bear Light, PE 431, *432*
Cape Blanco Light, OR *335*, 336
Cape Bonavista Light, NF 388, *389*
Cape Canaveral Light, FL 259, *260*
Cape Charles Light, VA 30, 298
Cape Cod Highland Light, MA 11, 165, *168*
Cape Disappointment Light, WA 13, *344*, 345
Cape d'Or Light, NS *407*, 408
Cape Egmont Light, PE *430*, 434
Cape Elizabeth Light, ME 19, 23, 24, 123, *125*
Cape Flattery Light, WA 13, 346
Cape Florida Light, FL 259, *260*
Cape Fourchu Light, NS 408, *409, 410, 411*
Cape Hatteras Light, NC 11, 29, 287, *289*
Cape Hinchinbrook Light, AK 24, 304, *304*
Cape Kumukahi Light, HI *331*, 332
Cape Lookout Light, NC 287, *288*
Cape May Light, NJ 42, 193, *194*
Cape Meares Light, OR *336*, 339
Cape Mendocino Light, CA *315*, 317
Cape Neddick Light, ME 125, *126*
Cape Poge Light, MA 165, *170*
Cape Race Light, NF 388
Cape Ray Light, NF 388, *390*
Cape Romain Light, SC 290
Cape Roseway Light, NS 408
Cape Sable Light, NS 409
Cape St. Elias Light, AK 306, *306*
Cape St. George Light, FLA 262, *262*
Cape San Blas Light, FL 259, *261*
Cape San Juan Light, Puerto Rico *250*, 252
Cape Sarichef Light, AK 13, 304
Cape Scott Light, BC 362, *363*
Cape Spear Light, NF 390, *390*
Cape Spencer Light, AK *305*, 306
Cape Tryon Light, PE *431, 432*, 434
Cape Vincent Breakwater Light, NY 201, *202*

Index

Cardona Island Light, Puerto Rico 252, *253*
Carmanah Point Light, BC 362
Carter Island Light, NS 409
Carysfort Reef Light, FL 262
Castle Hill, RI 29, 231, *232–233*
Cattle Point Light, WA *343*, 346
Cedar Island Light, NY 202
Cedar Key Light, FL 263
Cedar Point Light, OH 88
Chamber's Island Light, WI 93, *95*
Chandeleur Island Light, LA 273
Chantry Island Light, ON 428, *428*
Chapel Hill Light, NJ 194, *196*
Charleston Light, SC 11, 293
Charlevoix South Pierhead Light, MI 54
Charlotte-Genessee Light, NY 202
Chatham Light, MA 165, *167*
Cheboygan Crib Light, MI 54, *57*
Cheboygan River Range Light, MI 56, *58*
Chebucto Head Light, NS 411, *412, 413, 414*
Chequamegon Point Light, WI 93, *96*, 102
Chesapeake Light, VA 298
Chesapeake lightship 278
Chicago Harbor Guide Wall Lights, IL 50
Chicago Harbor Light, IL 50
Christian Island Light, ON *427*, 428
Clark's Point Light, MA 167
Cleveland East Ledge Light, MA 168, *172*
Cleveland East Pierhead Light, OH 88
Cleveland West Breakwater Light, OH 89
Cockspur Island Light, GA 271
Coffin Island Light, NS 411, *416*
Columbia lightship 339
Conanicut Island Light, RI 232
Concord Point Light, MD *277*, 278
Coney Island Light, NY 203, *204*
Conimicut Light, RI 232
Conneaut West Breakwater Light, OH *88*, 89
Conover Beach Light, NJ 194
Copper Harbor Light, MI 56
Copper Harbor Rear Range Light, MI 57
Coquille River Light, OR *338*, 339
Cove Island Light, ON 428, *428*
Cove Point Light, MD 279
Craighill Channel Lights, MD *278, 279*, 280–282
Crescent City Light, WA 13
Crisp Point Light, MI 57
Crossover Island Light, NY 203
Crown Point Light, NY 205
Cuckolds Light, ME 125, *128*
Culebrita Island Light, Puerto Rico 252, *252*
Cumberland Head Light, NY 205
Currituck Beach Light, NC 288, *290*
Curtis Island Light, ME 127, *127*

D
Deer Island Light, MA 168
Deer Island Thoroughfare Light, ME 127, *129*
Delaware Breakwater East Light, DE *114*, 115
Derby Wharf Light, MA 169, *169, 173*
Destruction Island Light, WA 346
De Tour Reef Light, MI 58, *59*
Detroit River Light, MI 58, *59*
Devil's Island Light, WI 94, *96*, 97, 102
Diamond Head Light, HI 45, *46*, 47, *330*, 333
Dice Head Light, ME 127, *130*
Dofflemyer Point Light, WA *345*, 349
Doubling Point Range Lights, ME 129, *131*
Drum Point Light, MD *281*, 282
Dry Tortugas Light, FL 264
Dryad Point Light, BC 362, *362, 364, 365*
Dunkirk Light, NY *205*, 206
Dutch Island Light, RI 232
Duxbury Pier Light, MA 169, *173*

E
Eagle Bluff Light, WI 94, *97*
Eagle Harbor Light, MI 59, *60*
Eagle Island Light, ME 130
Eagle River Light, MI 60
East Brother Light, CA *316*, 317
East Charity Shoal Light, NY 207
East Chop Light, MA 169, *171*
East End Long Island Light, NF 390
East Point Light, NJ 194
East Point Light, PE 434
Eastern Point Light, MA 170, *175*
Eatons Neck, NY 11, 207
Eddy Point Light, NS 411, *417*
Edgartown Harbor Light, MA 170, *174*
Ediz Hook Light, WA 349
Egg Rock Light, ME 130, *132*
Egmont Key Light, FL *263*, 264
Elbow of Cross Ledge Light, NJ 196
Eldred Rock Light, AK 306, *307*
Erie Land Light, PA 226
Erie Pierhead Light, PA 226, *228*
Escanaba Harbor Light, MI 60
Esopus Meadows Light, NY *206*, 207
Estevan Point Light, BC 362
Estevan Point Light, VI 32
Execution Rocks Light, NY 207

F
Fairport Harbor Light, OH 89
Fairport Harbor West Breakwater Light, OH 89
Farallon Island Light, CA 13, 317
Faulkner's Island Light, CT 109
Fenwick Island Light, DE 115, *115*
Finns Point Rear Range Light, NJ 196
Fire Island Light, NY 207, *207*
Fisgard Light, BC 29, 366, *366*
Fishing Battery Light, MD 282
Five Fingers Islands Light, AK 306, *308*
Five Islands Light, NS 412
Five Mile Point Light, CT 109
Fort Amherst Light, NF 391
Fort Bonita Light, CA 13
Fort Carroll Light, MD *280*, 282
Fort Gratiot Light, MI 60, *61*
Fort Mifflin Light, NJ 196
Fort Niagara Light, NY 208, *208*
Fort Pickering Light, MA 172
Fort Point Light, CA 13, *314*, 317
Fort Point Light, ME 132, *133*
Fort Point Light, NS 412, *418*
Fort Wadsworth Light, NY 208
Forty Mile Point Light, MI 61
Fourteen Foot Bank Light, DE 32, 115
Fourteen Foot Shoal Light, MI 61
Fourteen Mile Point Light, MI 61
Fowey Rocks Light, FL 264, *264*
Frankfort North Breakwater Light, MI 61, *62*
Franklin Island Light, ME 132, *135*
Franks Island Light, LA 274
Frying Pan Shoal Light, NC 290

G
Galloo Island Light, NY 208, *209*
Gannet Rock Light, NB 377, *377, 378, 379*

Garden Key Light, FL 264
Gary Breakwater Light, IN 50
Gasparilla Rear Range Light, FL 265
Gay Head Light, MA 11, 172, *176*
George's Island Light, NS 412
Georgetown Light, SC 293, *294*
Gibb's Hill Light, Bermuda *32*, 248, *249*
Gibraltar Point Light, ON 428, *429*
Gloucester Breakwater Light, MA 172
Goat Island Light, ME 133, *134*
Goat Island Light, RI 25
Goose Rock Light, ME 133
Grand Haven Pier Lights, MI 62,*64*, *65*
Grand Marais Harbor Range Lights, MI 62
Grand Traverse Light, MI 63,
Granite Island Light, MI 63
Gravelly Shoal Light, MI 63
Graves Light, MA 22, 172, *177*
Grays Harbor Light, WA *346*, 349
Grays Reef Light, MI 63
Great Beds Light, NJ 196, *197*
Great Beds Light, NY 209
Great Captain Island Light, CT 109, *110*
Great Duck Island Light, ME 135, *136*
Green Bay Harbor Entrance Light, WI 95, *98*
Green Island Light, NF 391, *392, 393, 394, 395*
Greens Ledge Light, CT 109, 112
Griffith Island Light, ON 428
Grindle Point Light, ME 137, *137*
Grosse Île Channel Light, MI 63
Grosse Point Light, IL 50, *51*
Guard Island Light, AK 307
Gull Island Light, NF 391
Gull Rock Light, MI 63
Gurnet Point Light, MA 17

H
Haig Point Rear Range Light, SC 293
Halfway Rock Light, ME 23, 137, *138*
Harbor Beach Light, MI 63
Harbor of Refuge Light, DE 115. *116, 117*
Harbor Town Light, SC *292*, 293
Head Harbour Light, NB 377, *380, 381*
Heceta Head Light, OR 339
Hendricks Head Light, ME 20, 138, *139*
Henry Island Light, NS 415
Hereford Inlet Light, NJ 199
Heron Neck Light, ME 138
Herrick Cove Light, NH 189
Hillsboro Inlet Light, FL 265
Hog Island Shoal Light, RI 232
Holland Harbor Light, MI 63, *66*
Hooper Island Light, MD 282
Hooper Strait Light, MD 282, *283*
Horn Island Light, MS 25
Horse Island Light, NY 209
Horton Point Light, NY 209, *210*
Hospital Point Range Lights, MA 175, *178*
Hudson-Athens Light, NY 209, *211*
Humboldt Harbor Light, WA 13
Hunting Island Light, SC *293*, 294
Huron Harbor Light, OH 89, *90*
Huron Lightship 65
Hyannis Harbor Light, MA 176

I
Ida Lewis Rock Light (Lime Rock Light), RI *18*, 232, *234*
Île Verte Light, QC 441
Îles aux Perroquets Light, QC 441
Îlet Rouge Light, QC 441
Indian Island Light, ME 138
Indiana East Breakwater Light, IN 50
Isle au Haut Light, ME 138, *140*
Isle La Motte Light, VT 238
Isle of Shoals Light, NH *192*, 193
Isle Royale Light, MI 65
Ivory Island Light, BC 366, *370, 371*

J
Jeffrey's Hook Light, NY 209, *212*
Jones Point Light, VA 299
Juniper Island Light, VT 238
Jupiter Inlet Light, FL 265, *266*

K
Kauai Light, HI 13
Kenosha Pierhead Light, WI 97, *98*, 100
Keweenaw Pierhead Light, MI 66, *67*
Keweenaw Waterway Lower Entrance Light, MI 65
Key West Light, FL 265
Kilauea Point Light, HI *332*, 333
Klein Curaçao Light, Netherlands Antilles *256*, 257

L
Lady's Delight Light, ME 138
Lake St. Clair Light, MI 66
Langara Point Light, BC *15*, 366, *367, 368, 369*
Lansing Shoal Light, MI 66
La Pointe Light, WI 97, 102
Latimer Reef Light, NY 210, *213*
Lazaretto Point Light, MD 282
Lennard Island Light, BC 366, *372, 373*
Libby Island, ME *29*, 141, *142*
Lime Kiln Light, WA *347*, 350
Lime Point Light, CA 318
Lime Rock Light, RI (see also Ida Lewis Light) *17*, 18, 19, 20
Lincoln Rocks Light, AK 307
Liston Front and Rear Range Lights, DE 116, *120*
Little Cumberland Island Light, GA 272
Little Gull Island Light, NY 210, *214*
Little River Light, ME 141
Little Sable Point Light, MI 67
Little Traverse Light, MI 67
Lloyd Harbor Light, NY 210
Long Beach Bar Light, NY 210
Long Beach Harbor Light, CA 318
Long Island Head Light, MA 177, *179*
Long Point Light, MA 177, *180*
Loon Island Light, NH 193
Lorain Light, OH *28*, 89, *91*
Los Angeles Harbor Light, CA 318
Louisbourg Light, NS 11, 415, *415*
Lubec Channel Light, ME *141*, 143
Ludington North Breakwater Light, MI 67
Lynde Point Light, CT 109

M
Machias Seal Islands Light, ME 143
Machias Seal Island East Light, NB 377, *382, 383*
Mackinac (Old) Point Light, MI 67, *68*
Makapuu Point Light, HI 13, *14*, 333, *333*
Manhattan Range Lights, OH 89
Manistee North Pierhead Light, MI 67
Manistique Light, MI 69
Manitou Island Light, MI 69, *69*
Manitowoc Light, WI 97, *99*
Marblehead Light, MA 177
Marblehead Light, OH 89, *92*
Marcus Hook Range Lights, DE 118, *118*
Margaretsville Light, NS 418

Index

Marquette Harbor Light, MI 70, *70*
Marrowstone Light, WA 351
Marshall Point Light, ME 143, *144*
Martin Reef Light, MI 70
Mary Island Light, AK 308, *309*
Matagorda Island Light, TX 295, *296*
Matinicus Rock Light, ME 22, *143*, 145
Maugher Beach Light, NS 423
Mayport/St. Johns Light, FL 265
McInnes Island Light, BC 368
Medway Head Light, NS *418*, 423
Mendota Light, MI 70
Menominee Pierhead Light, MI 71, *71*
Merry Island Light, BC 368
Miah Maull Shoal Light, NJ *197*, 199
Michigan City East Pier Light, IN 51
Michigan City Light, IN 50, *52*
Michigan Island Light, WI 98, 102
Michigan Reef Lights, MI 71
Middle Bay Light, AL 248
Middle Island Light, MI 71, *72*
Mile Rock Light, CA 319
Milwaukee Breakwater Light, WI 99, *100*
Milwaukee Pierhead Light, WI 99, *100*
Minneapolis Shoal Light, MI 71, *73*
Minots Ledge Light, MA 13, *23*, 25, 27, 177, *181*
Mispillion Creek Light, DE 118
Mohegan Island Light & Manana Island Fog Signal Station, ME 145, *146*
Molokai Light, HI 334
Mona Island Light, Puerto Rico 13, 252, *255*
Monomoy Point Light, MA 181
Montauk Point Light, NY 11, 210, *215*
Moose Peak Light, ME 145, *147*
Morgan Point Light, CT 111
Morris Island Light, SC 294, *295*
Mount Desert Light, ME 145
Mukilteo Light, WA *348*, 351
Mulholland Point Light, NB 379, *385*
Munising Range Lights, MI 72
Muskegon South Pier Light, MI 73
Mystic Seaport Light, CT 111, *111*

N

Nantucket lightship 25, 33
Nantucket Great Point Light, MA 181, *182*
Narraguagus Light, ME 145
Nash Island Light, ME 145, *149*
Nauset Beach Light, MA 181, *183*
Navsink Twin Lights, NJ *198*, 199, *199*
Nawiliwili Harbor Light, HI *334*, 335
Ned Point Light, MA 183, *184*
Newburyport Harbor Lights, MA 11,183, 185, *185*
New Canal Light, LA 274
New Cape Henry Light, VA 299
New Dorp Light, NY 211, *216*
New Dungeness Light, WA 13, *349*, 352
New London Harbor Light, CT *110*, 112
New London Ledge Light, CT 112, *113*
New London Range Rear Light, PE *433*, 435
New Point Comfort Light, VA 299
Newport Harbor Light, RI 235, *236*
Newport News Middle Ground Light, VA *299*, 300
New Presque Isle Light, MI 73
Nobska Point Light, MA 185, *186*
Nootka Light, BC 368
North Cape Light, PE 435
North Dumpling Light, NY 211, *218*
North Head Light, WA *350*, 352
North Manitou Shoal Light, MI 73, *73*
North Point Light, WI 100
North Rustico Harbour Light, PE *434*, 435
Nottawasaga Island Light, ON 429
Nyatt Point Light, RI 235

O

Oak Island Light, NC 290
Oakville Light, ON 429
Ocracoke Island Light, NC 11, 290, *291*
Ogdensburg Harbor Light, NY 212, *217*
Old Cape Henry Light, VA 11, 300
Old Carquinez Straits Light, CA 319
Old Field Point Light, NY 212, *217*
Old Front Range Light, NY 214
Old Michigan City Light, IN 51
Old Mission Point Light, MI 75
Old Orchard Shoal Light, NY 214, *221*
Old Point Loma Light, CA *318*, 319
Old Port Clinton Light, OH 90
Old Presque Isle Light, MI 73, *74*, 75, 78
Old Southport (Kenosha) Light, WI 100
Ontonagon Light, MI 77
Orient Point Light, NY 216, *219*
Oswego West Pierhead Light, NY 216, *220*
Outer Island Light, WI *101*, 102
Oyster Bay Light, LA *274*, 275

P

Pachena Point Light, BC 368
Pacific Reef Light, FL 265
Palmers Island Light, MA 185
Panmure Head Light, PE 435, *435*
Pass à l'Outre Light, LA 275
Pass Manchac Light, LA 275
Passage Island Light, MI 77
Patos Island Light, WA 352
Peck Ledge Light, CT 112
Peggy's Point Light, NS *419, 420, 421*, 423
Pemaquid Point Light, ME *148*, 149
Penfield Reef, CT 22
Pensacola Light, FL 265, *267*
Perkins Island Light, ME 149
Perry Memorial Light, OH 90
Peshtigo Reef Light, WI 102
Petit Manan Light, ME 149, *150*
Piedras Blancas Light, CA 319
Pigeon Point Light, CA *319*, 321
Pilot Island Light, WI 102
Pine Island Light, BC 371, *374*
Piney Point Light, MD 282
Pipe Island Light, MI 77
Plum Beach Light, RI 235
Plum Island Light, NY 218
Plum Island Range Lights, WI 102
Plymouth Light, MA 11, 185, *187*
Poe Reef Light, MI 61, *75*, 77
Point Amour Light, NF 29, 391
Point Arena Light, CA 32, *320*, 321
Point Arguello Light, CA 321
Point Atkinson Light, BC 32, 374, *375*
Point au Fer Reef Light, LA 275
Point au Roche Light, NY 218
Point Betsie Light, MI 77
Point Blunt Light, CA 323
Point Cabrillo Light, CA 323
Point Clark Light, ON 429
Point Conception Light, CA *322*, 325
Point Escuminac Light, NB 379
Point Fermin Light, CA 45, *324*, 325
Point Gammon Light, MA 187
Point Hueneme Light, CA 327
Point Iroquois Light, MI *76*, 77
Point Judith Light, RI 235

Point Loma Light, CA *29*, *321*, 327
Point Lookout Light, MD 282
Point Montara Light, CA *325*, 327
Point No Point Light, MD 283
Point No Point Light, WA *351*, 352
Point Pinos Light, CA 327
Point Retreat Light, AK 308
Point Reyes Light, CA 327
Point Riche Light, NF 391, *395*
Point Robinson Light, WA 352, *354*
Point Sur Light, CA 327
Point Tuna Light, Puerto Rico 252, *254*
Point Vicente Light, CA *323*, 327
Point Wilson Light, WA 352, *353*
Pointe aux Barques Light, MI 77
Pomham Rocks Light, RI 235
Ponce de Leon Inlet Light, FL 266, *268*
Pond Island Light, ME 150, *151*
Pooles Island Light, MD 283
Poplar Point Light, RI 235
Port Austin Reef Light, MI 78
Port Boca Grande Light, FL 267
Port Greville Light, NS 423
Port Isabel Light, TX *296*, 297
Port Pontchartrain Light, LA 275
Port San Juan Light, Puerto Rico 255, *255*
Port Sanilac Light, MI 78
Port Washington Light, WI 102
Portage River Light, MI 77
Portland Breakwater Light/Petroleum Docks Light, ME 150
Portland Head Light, ME 11, 150, *152*
Portsmouth Harbor (New Castle) Light, NH 193
Portsmouth lightship 300
Pottawatamie Light, WI 102
Presque Isle Harbor Range Lights, MI 78
Presque Isle Harbor West Breakwater Light, MI 78
Presque Isle Light, PA 226
Presqu'ile Point Light, ON 429, *431*
Prim Point Light, PE 436, *436*
Prince's Bay Light, NY 218
Prospect Harbor Point Light, ME 151, *155*
Prudence Island Light, RI 25, 235
Puffin Island Light, NF 391
Pulaski Shoal Light, FL 267
Pumpkin Island Light, ME 151
Punta Gorda Light, CA 325

R

Race Point Light, MA 187, *188*
Race Rock Light, BC 374, *376*
Race Rock Light, NY 13, 220, *222*
Racine North Breakwater Light, WI 102
Ram Island Ledge Light, ME 151, *153*
Ram Island Light, ME 153
Raspberry Island Light, WI 102, *103*
Rawley Point Light, WI 104
Reedy Island Rear Range Light, DE 118
Robbins Reef Light, NY 221, *223*
Rochers aux Oiseaux Light, QC 442
Rochester Harbor Light, NY 221
Rock Harbor Light, MI 78
Rock Island Light, NY 221
Rock of Ages Light, MI 20, 78, *79*
Rockland Breakwater Light, ME 153, *154*
Romer Shoal Light, NY 221, *224*
Rondout Creek Light, NY 222
Round Island Light, MS 286
Roosevelt Island Light, NY 222
Rose Blanche Light, NF 396, *396, 397, 398, 399*
Rose Island Light, RI 235, *237*
Round Island Light, MI 78

S

Sabine Bank Light, TX 297
Sabine Pass Light, LA 275
Sable Island, NS 23
Saddleback Ledge Light, ME 153, *156*
Saginaw River Rear Range Lights, MI 78
St. Augustine Light, FL 270, *270*
St. Clair Flats Old Canal Range Lights, MI 83
St. David's Light, Bermuda 29, *31*, 44, 45, 250, *251*
St. George's Reef Light, CA 330
St. Helena Light, MI 83
St. Johns River Light, FL 270
St. Joseph North Pier Lights, MI 83
St. Marks Light, FL 270
St. Martin Island Light, MI 83
St. Peters Light, PE 438
St. Simons Island Light, GA 272, *272*
Sakonnet Point Light, RI 236
Salmon River Light, NS *422*, 423
Sambro Island Light, NS 11, 424, *425*
San Luis Obispo Light, CA 329
Sand Heads Light, BC 375
Sand Hills Light, MI 80
Sand Island Light, AL 25, 248, *248*
Sand Island Light, WI 102, 104, *104*
Sand Key Light, FL 25, 267, *269*
Sand Point, MI 25
Sand's Point Light, NY 222
Sandy Hook Island Light, NJ 11, 199, *200*
Sandy Neck Light, MA 187
Sandy Point Shoal Light, MD 284
Sanibel Island Light, FL 268
Sankaty Head Light, MA 187, *189*
Santa Barbara Light, CA 20, 24, *326*, 329
Santa Cruz Light/Mark Abbott Memorial Light, CA *328*, 329
Sapelo Island Light, GA 272, *273*
Saugerties Light, NY 223
Savannah Light, GA 272
Saybrook Breakwater Light, CT 112
Scituate Light, MA 187
Scotch Cap, AK 13, *20, 21, 22*, 24, 309, *310*
Seacow Head Light, PE 436, *436*
Sea Girt Light, NJ 199
Seal Island Light, NS 424, *424*
Seguin Island Light, ME 11,153, *157*
Selkirk Light, NY 223
Sentinel Island Light, AK 309, *311*
Seul Choix Point Light, MI 80
Seven Foot Knoll Light, MD 284
Sharps Island Light, MD 284
Sheffield Island Light, CT 112
Ship Island Light, MS 286

Ship John Shoal Light, DE 118, *119*
Ship John Shoal Light, NJ 199
Ship Shoal Light, LA 275
Sisters Island Light, NY 223
Skillagalee Light (Île aux Galets), MI 80
Smith Island Light, WA 13, 352, *355*
Smith Point Light, VA *299*, 301
Sodus Point (Sodus Outer) Light, NY 223
Solomons Lump Light, MD 285
Sombrero Key Light, FL 269, *271*
Souris East Light, PE *437*, 438
South Bass Island Light, OH 91
South Buffalo South Side Light, NY 224
South Fox Island Light, MI 80, *80*
Southampton Shoal Light, CA 330
South Haven South Pierhead Light, MI 80
South Manitou Island Light, 81, *81*
South Pass Light, LA 275
Southwest Ledge Light, CT 112
Southwest Pass Light, LA 276
Spectacle Reef Light, MI 32, 81, *82*
Spencers Island Light, NS 424
Split Rock Light, NY 225
Spring Point Ledge Light, ME 155, *158*
Squaw Island Light, MI 81
Squirrel Point Light, ME 156
Stage Harbor Light, MA 188, *190*
Stamford Harbor Light, CT 112
Stannard Rock Light, MI 83
Staten Island Rear Range Light, NY 225
Statue of Liberty, NY 13, 225, *226*
Stepping Stones Light, NY 225, *227*
Stone Pillar Light, QC 442
Stonington Harbor Light, CT 112
Stony Point Light, NY 225
Straitsmouth Light, MA 188
Stratford Point Light, CT 113
Stratford Shoal Middle Ground Light, CT 113
Sturgeon Bay Canal Light, WI 105
Sturgeon Point Light, MI 83
Sunken Rock Light, NY 225
Superior South Breakwater Light, WI 105
Swallowtail Light, NB 382, *384*
Swiftsure lightship 352

T
Tarpaulin Cove Light, MA 188
Tarrytown Light, NY 225
Tawas Point Light, MI 83, *84*
Tchefuncte River Light, LA 277
Ten Pound Island Light, MA 188
Tenants Harbor Light, ME 156
Tennessee Reef Light, FL 271
Thimble Shoal Light, VA *300*, 301
Thirty Mile Point Light, NY 225
Thomas Point Shoal Light, MD *30*, *284*, 285
Thunder Bay Island Light, MI 84
Tibbetts Point Light, NY 225, *228*
Tinicum Range Lights, NJ 201
Toledo Harbor Light, OH 91
Tree Point Light, AK 310
Trinidad Head Light, CA 332
Triple Island Light, BC 375, *375*
Turkey Point Light, MD *16*, 17, 285, *286*
Turn Point Light, WA 355
Turtle Rock Light, PA 229
Two Bush Island Light, ME 156
Tybee Island Light, GA 11, 273

U
Umpqua River Light, OR 339

V
Vermilion Light, OH 92

W
Warren Cove Front and Rear Range Lights, PE 438
Warrior Rock Light, OR 341
Warwick Light, RI 236, *239*
Watch Hill Light, RI 236
Waugoshance Light, MI 84
West Bank Front Range Light, NY 226
West Chop Light, MA 189
West Point Light, PE 438, *439*
West Point Light, WA 355
West Quoddy Head Light, ME 156, *160*
West Rigolets Light, LA 277
West Sister Island Light, OH 92
Western Head Light, NS 426
Western Islands Light, ON 429
Whale Rock Light, RI 25, 238
Whaleback Light, NH 193
White River Light, MI *86*, 87
White Shoal Light, MI 86, 87
Whitefish Point Light, MI 22, *85*, 86
Whitehead Light, ME 159
Whitlock's Mill Light, ME 159, *159*
Wickford Harbor Light, RI 238
William Livingston Memorial Light, MI 87
Windmill Point Light, MI 87
Windmill Point Light, VT 238
Wind Point Light, WI 105
Wing's Neck Light, MA 189
Winter Harbor Light, ME 159
Wolf Trap Light, VA 301, *301*
Wood End Light, MA 189, *191*
Wood Island Light, ME 159
Wood Islands Main Light, PE 438, *440*
Wood Islands Range Lights, PE 438

Y
Yaquina Bay Light, OR 341
Yaquina Head Light, OR 341
Yarmouth Light, NS 426, *426*
Yerba Buena Light, CA 332